Cyclopedia

of

LITERARY

PLACES

Cyclopedia

of

LITERARY

PLACES

Volume One

Abraham and Isaac–The Glass Menagerie

Consulting Editor
R. Baird Shuman
University of Illinois at Urbana-Champaign

Editor
R. Kent Rasmussen

Introduction by
Brian Stableford
King Alfred's College

SALEM PRESS, INC.
Pasadena, California   Hackensack, New Jersey

Editor in Chief: Dawn P. Dawson

Editor: R. Kent Rasmussen *Acquisitions Editor:* Mark Rehn

Manuscript Editors: Melanie Watkins *Research Supervisor:* Jeffry Jensen

Christine Steele *Production Editor:* Joyce I. Buchea

Assistant Editor: Andrea E. Miller *Layout:* William Zimmerman

Library of Congress Cataloging-in-Publication Data

Cyclopedia of literary places / editor, R. Kent Rasmussen.
    p.   cm.
Includes bibliographical references and index.
    ISBN 1-58765-094-0 (set : alk. paper) — ISBN 1-58765-095-9 (vol. 1 : alk. paper) —
ISBN 1-58765-096-7 (vol. 2 : alk. paper) — ISBN 1-58765-097-5 (vol. 3 : alk. paper)
    1. Setting (Literature) 2. Literary landmarks. 3. Literature—Encyclopedias
I. Rasmussen, R. Kent.
    PN56.S48C97 2003
    809′.922—dc21

2002156159

First Printing

CONTENTS

CONTENTS

CONTENTS

COMPLETE LIST OF CONTENTS

Volume 1

Volume 2

Volume 3

PUBLISHER'S NOTE

Cyclopedia of Literary Places is built around a new concept: the use of place in individual literary works. It is doubtful that anything similar to this title-driven reference work has ever been published before. However, while the content of *Cyclopedia of Literary Places* is entirely original, its organization and form of presentation will be familiar to users of other publications in Salem Press's family of literary reference works, which include *Masterplots, Revised Second Edition*, *Cyclopedia of Literary Characters*, and *Cyclopedia of World Authors*. What *Cyclopedia of Literary Places* adds to these now-standard reference works is extensive and intensive coverage of *place* in literature. This is a subject that has hitherto received little treatment in library reference materials but has long been a part of literary scholarship and is now receiving increasing attention, as Brian Stableford discusses in his Introduction to this set.

Cyclopedia of Literary Places contains articles on 1,304 literary works selected from the titles covered in *Masterplots, Revised Second Edition* (1996). The selected titles are those that best lend themselves to meaningful discussion of place as a literary device. These include virtually all the novels, most of the plays, and a selection of the volumes of poetry covered in *Masterplots*. Nonfiction titles are not included here, though it may be argued that some included titles have elements of nonfiction. While *Cyclopedia of Literary Places* does not cover every title in *Masterplots*, every title it does cover is also covered in both *Masterplots* and *Cyclopedia of Literary Characters*. Users of this set can therefore be confident that for every article they consult in these pages, they can also find parallel articles providing detailed synopses and plot analyses in *Masterplots* and detailed character analyses in *Cyclopedia of Literary Characters*. For this reason, articles in this set focus closely on matters of place, leaving most plot and character details to the other reference sets.

Cyclopedia of Literary Places articles range in length from half-page articles of about 300 words, for short stories and most plays and works of poetry, to full-page articles and longer of between 700 and 1,000 words,

mostly for novels, with most articles around 700 words in length. Articles are arranged in alphabetical order by title. The Title Index in volume 3 includes variant titles.

Like articles in *Cyclopedia of Literary Characters*, articles in *Cyclopedia of Literary Places* provide standard top-matter information on individual literary works: full titles, authors' names and vital dates, types of work, types of plot, times of plot, and dates of original publication. Brief introductory paragraphs explain where the works are set and comment on broad themes and patterns in the use of place. Then follow individual entries discussing important real and imaginary places that figure into the work.

Boldfaced subheads that begin paragraphs identify the nearly 6,000 places that are subjects of individual entries. Some entries also contain additional boldfaced names within paragraphs; these are places that merit attention but do not have entries of their own. Boldfacing of additional names is limited to fictional places about which substantive remarks are made and which readers might possibly seek to find in the Place Index, which is discussed below. For example, "King Arthur's Court," discussed within the entry on "Camelot" in the article on Mark Twain's *A Connecticut Yankee in King Arthur's Court*, is boldfaced because the entry on Camelot says something substantive about it; it is also a term that readers may reasonably expect to find in the Place Index. Place-names mentioned only in passing are neither bolded nor indexed.

Help with pronunciation of possibly unfamiliar foreign place-names is provided in many entries, in which phonetic spellings appear within parentheses following boldface subheads. These guides are provided only for names in subheads; an explanation of the pronunciation guides and a key to the symbols used in them appear at the beginning of each volume.

The Editors asked contributors of the articles to focus on the literary dimensions of place, and not on plot details and mere physical descriptions of places, in stories, novels, plays, and poems in which they appear. The essential question that each article attempts to answer is how place matters within the literary work and then how it functions as a literary device. In addition to establishing where the places are and how they relate to one another, the entries address such issues as how places help to establish mood, how they reflect the actions and characters of the story, how they appear to change as the story develops, and what their overall contribution to the work is. In some literary works, place plays such an integral role that individual places seem to take on the attributes of characters.

Although this set does not cover strictly nonfiction works, its articles do cover real places that figure into fictional, dramatic, and poetical works. This fact, incidentally, sets *Cyclopedia of Literary Places* apart from other reference books on places in literature—a subject discussed at length in the Introduction to this set. As the entries here focus on how the literary works themselves use the places within which they are set, distinctions between real and imaginary places often become of little consequence. For example, while the London of C. P. Snow's *The Conscience of the Rich* is clearly a real place, the London of George Orwell's *Nineteen Eighty-Four* is largely imaginary. Nevertheless, to assist readers to differentiate among the places, entries on real places are asterisked (*).

The question of what constitutes "place" for the purposes of this set does not lend itself to simple answers, and it will be seen that the scholars who have contributed to these volumes have different views on the subject. However, in order to set manageable parameters to this project, the Editors asked the contributors to construe "place" as *physical* locations, both real and imaginary— not metaphysical states of mind, dreams, or the inner consciousness of characters. Even with this limitation, the variety of places covered in these articles is so extraordinary that it will alert many readers to literary techniques they may previously have overlooked or underestimated. Types of places discussed in these articles range from articles of furniture to rooms to buildings to neighborhoods to cities to countries to planets, and the range of ways in which all these places are used is even greater.

Articles in this set are arranged alphabetically, by the titles of the works they discuss. A complete list of the titles, including cross-references from variant titles, can be found at the back of volume 3. There, readers will also find a list of all the authors whose works are covered here. By contrast, the Place Index is selective. Consideration was given to listing *every* boldfaced place-name in a subhead or text, but this idea was abandoned after it became clear that such an approach would overload the index with names that no reader would ever seek in an index—names such as "Alexias's house" or "Bessie Burgess's room." Anyone interested in such places should already know in what works they appear and have no trouble finding the appropriate articles. What readers will find in the Place Index are the names of virtually all the *real* places that are the subjects of entries, as well as fictional towns, cities, countries, and substantial geographical features.

Many places, both real and unreal, are listed more than once in the Place Index: under their own names and as subentries under the names of the cities, states, and countries in which they are located. For example, the Brazilian city "Bahia" appears under its own name and as a subentry under "Brazil" and "Westminster Palace" appears under its own name and as a subentry under "London." Cities and towns constitute the plurality of entries; most are entered under the names of the states or countries in which they are located. Major cities that are covered in scores of articles—such as New York and London—are listed only by themselves but are given cross-references in the entries on the countries and states in which they are located.

The Editors wish to thank the 300 scholars who have contributed articles to *Cyclopedia of Literary Places*; they have brought to the project a wealth of expertise and imagination that make these volumes a rich trove of original insights. The Editors wish especially to thank R. Baird Shuman, for his advice and assistance in assembling the title list, and Brian Stableford, the author of *The Dictionary of Science Fiction Places* (1999), for his thoughtful introduction and many other contributions to this set.

CONTRIBUTORS

Patrick Adcock
Independent Scholar

R. Allen Alexander, Jr.
Nicholls State University

Emily Alward
Henderson, Nevada, District Libraries

Corinne Andersen
University of Illinois at Urbana-Champaign

Phillip B. Anderson
University of Central Arkansas

Debra D. Andrist
University of St. Thomas

Philip Bader
Independent Scholar

L. Michelle Baker
Catholic University of America

Jane L. Ball
Independent Scholar

Carl L. Bankston III
Tulane University

Jack V. Barbera
University of Mississippi

Henry J. Baron
Calvin College

David Barratt
Independent Scholar

Thomas F. Barry
Himeji Dokkyo University

Melissa E. Barth
Appalachian State University

Kathleen M. Bartlett
RSK Assessments

Greg Beatty
University of Phoenix Online

Cynthia S. Becerra
Humphreys College

Alan T. Belsches
Troy State University, Dothan

Carol F. Bender
Alma College

Alvin K. Benson
Brigham Young University

Kathryn N. Benzel
University of Nebraska—Kearney

Michael A. Benzel
University of Nebraska—Kearney

James J. Berg
Minnesota State Colleges and Universities

Milton Berman
University of Rochester

Anthony J. Bernardo, Jr.
Cecil Community College

Dorothy M. Betz
Georgetown University

Cynthia A. Bily
Adrian College

Margaret Boe Birns
New York University

Nicholas Birns
New School University

Shalom E. Black
Catholic University of America

Pegge Bochynski
Salem State College

Bernadette Lynn Bosky
Independent Scholar

Tammy J. Bowles
Portland State University

Jay Boyer
Arizona State University

Harold Branam
Savannah State University

Douglas Branch
Southwest Tennessee Community College

Marie J. K. Brenner
Bethel College

Peter Brigg
University of Guelph

William Brooks
University of Bath

David D. Buck
University of Wisconsin—Milwaukee

Susan Butterworth
Salem State College

Joseph P. Byrne
Belmont University

Clare Callaghan
Catholic University of America

Ann M. Cameron
Indiana University, Kokomo

Edmund J. Campion
University of Tennessee

Byron D. Cannon
University of Utah

Glenn Canyon
Independent Scholar

Paula L. Cardinal
Independent Scholar

Joseph R. Carroll
Rhode Island College

Sharon Carson
University of North Dakota

Warren J. Carson
University of South Carolina at Spartanburg

Erskine Carter
Black Hawk College

Caroline Carvill
Rose-Hulman Institute of Technology

Cherie Castillo
University of Wisconsin—Fox Valley

Laurie Champion
San Diego State University

Diane L. Chapman
William Carey College

Edgar L. Chapman
Bradley University

C. L. Chua
California State University, Fresno

David W. Cole
University of Wisconsin Colleges

Julian W. Connolly
University of Virginia

Holly Dworken Cooley
Independent Scholar

Richard Hauer Costa
Texas A&M University

Martha J. Craig
Bradley University

Marsha Daigle-Williamson
Spring Arbor University

Richard Damashek
Calumet College of St. Joseph

Anita Price Davis
Converse College

Delmer Davis
Andrews University

Molly M. Dean
Independent Scholar

Bill Delaney
Independent Scholar

James I. Deutsch
George Washington University

M. Casey Diana
University of Illinois at Urbana-Champaign

Carolyn Dickinson
Columbia College

Margaret A. Dodson
Independent Scholar

Stefan Dziemianowicz
Independent Scholar

Robert Eddy
Fayetteville State University

K. Edgington
Towson University

Margaret V. Ekstrom
St. John Fisher College

Robert P. Ellis
Independent Scholar

Thomas L. Erskine
Salisbury University

Jo N. Farrar
San Jacinto College

Thomas R. Feller
Independent Scholar

Elizabeth A. Fisher
George Washington University

Robert J. Forman
St. John's University

Ronald Foust
Loyola University, New Orleans

Joseph Francavilla
Columbus State University

Tom Frazier
Cumberland College

C. George Fry
University of Findlay

Robert L. Gale
University of Pittsburgh

Jo K. Galle
University of Louisiana at Monroe

Ann D. Garbett
Averett University

Keith Garebian
Independent Scholar

Marie M. Garrett
Patrick Henry Community College

Eleanor Parks Gaunder
University of North Alabama

Sheldon Goldfarb
University of British Columbia

Margaret Bozenna Goscilo
University of Pittsburgh

Charles A. Gramlich
Xavier University of Louisiana

Sharon L. Gravett
Valdosta State University

John L. Grigsby
Appalachian Research and Defense Fund of Kentucky

Daniel L. Guillory
Millikin University

Kenneth Hada
East Central University

H. George Hahn
Towson University

Elizabeth A. Hait
McNeese State University

Irwin Halfond
McKendree College

Gavin R. G. Hambly
University of Texas—Dallas

Hayes Hampton
University of South Carolina at Sumter

Betsy P. Harfst
Kishwaukee College

Susan Tetlow Harrington
University of South Florida

Emma Sue Harris
Lincoln Memorial University

Stephen M. Hart
University College, London

Donald M. Hassler
Kent State University

Robert W. Haynes
Texas A&M International University

Barbara A. Heavilin
Taylor University

Peter B. Heller
Manhattan College

Terry Heller
Coe College

Michael Hennessy
Southwest Texas State University

Diane Andrews Henningfeld
Adrian College

Joyce E. Henry
Ursinus College

Anna Dunlap Higgins
Gordon College

Paula R. Hilton
University of New Orleans

William Hoffman
Independent Scholar

W. Kenneth Holditch
University of New Orleans

Daryl Holmes
Nicholls State University

John R. Holmes
*Franciscan University of
    Steubenville*

Joan Hope
Independent Scholar

Gregory D. Horn
*Southwest Virginia Community
    College*

Pierre L. Horn
Wright State University

Anna Hollingsworth Hovater
Freed-Hardeman University

Eric Howard
Independent Scholar

Mary Hurd
East Tennessee State University

William Hutchings
University of Alabama—Birmingham

Mary Anne Hutchinson
Utica College

Mabel Illidge
Nicholls State University

Miglena I. Ivanova
*University of Illinois at Urbana-
    Champaign*

Kimberly Jackson
*State University of New York
    at Buffalo*

An Lan Jang
Independent Scholar

Doris O'Donnell Jellig
Tidewater Community College

Jeffry Jensen
Independent Scholar

Christopher D. Johnson
Francis Marion University

Sheila Golburgh Johnson
Independent Scholar

Susan Johnston
University of Regina

Ginger Jones
Lincoln University

Rhona Justice-Malloy
Central Michigan University

Daven M. Kari
Vanguard University

Linda L. Keesey
Eastern Michigan University

Steven G. Kellman
University of Texas—San Antonio

Christopher E. Kent
Independent Scholar

Claire Keyes
Salem State College

Mabel Khawaja
Hampton University

Kimberley H. Kidd
King College

Leigh Husband Kimmel
Independent Scholar

Paul Kincaid
Independent Scholar

Wm. Laird Kleine-Ahlbrandt
Purdue University

Elaine Laura Kleiner
Indiana State University

Grove Koger
Boise Public Library

Kathryn Kulpa
Independent Scholar

Andrew J. Kunka
University of South Carolina at Sumter

J. Roger Kurtz
*State University of New York
    College at Brockport*

Esther K. Labovitz
Pace University

David Larmour
Texas Tech University

William Laskowski
Jamestown College

William T. Lawlor
University of Wisconsin—Stevens Point

Henry A. Lea
University of Massachusetts, Amherst

Beverly Haskell Lee
Independent Scholar

L. L. Lee
Independent Scholar

Leon Lewis
Appalachian State University

Barbara Lounsberry
University of Northern Iowa

Bernadette Flynn Low
*Community College of
    Baltimore County*

R. C. Lutz
University of the Pacific

Clyde S. McConnell
University of Calgary

Andrew Macdonald
Loyola University, New Orleans

Gina Macdonald
Nicholls State University

Grace McEntee
Appalachian State University

John L. McLean
Missouri Valley College

Magdalena Mączyñska
Catholic University of America

David W. Madden
*California State University,
Sacramento*

Rachel P. Maines
Cornell University Libraries

Nancy Farm Mannikko
Independent Scholar

Lois A. Marchino
University of Texas—El Paso

Kathryn D. Marocchino
*California State University Maritime
Academy*

Mira N. Mataric
Butler Community College

Laurence W. Mazzeno
Alvernia College

Michael R. Meyers
Independent Scholar

Vasa D. Mihailovich
University of North Carolina

P. Andrew Miller
Northern Kentucky University

Craig A. Milliman
Fort Valley State University

William Mingin
Independent Scholar

Christian H. Moe
*Southern Illinois University at
Carbondale*

Elise Moore
University of Regina

Chris Morgan
Independent Scholar

Pauline Morgan
Independent Scholar

Bernard E. Morris
Independent Scholar

Toni J. Morris
University of Indianapolis

Sherry Morton-Mollo
*California State University,
Fullerton*

Roark Mulligan
Christopher Newport University

Stephen V. Myslinski
Salve Regina University

Wayne Narey
Arkansas State University

William Nelles
*University of Massachusetts,
Dartmouth*

Hanh N. Nguyen
University of California, Riverside

Terry Nienhuis
Western Carolina University

Gisela Norat
Agnes Scott College

Joe Nordgren
Lamar University

Bruce Olsen
Alabama State University

Robert J. Paradowski
Rochester Institute of Technology

David B. Parsell
Furman University

David Partenheimer
Truman State University

Glenn Patterson
Independent Scholar

David Peck
*California State University,
Long Beach*

Connie Pedoto
Miles College

Joe Pellegrino
Eastern Kentucky University

Marion Boyle Petrillo
Bloomsburg University

Allene Phy-Olsen
Austin Peay State University

H. Alan Pickrell
Emory & Henry College

Charles S. Pierce, Jr.
Tidewater Community College

Bonnie C. Plummer
Eastern Kentucky University

Marguerite R. Plummer
Louisiana State University, Shreveport

Stanley Poss
California State University, Fresno

Luke A. Powers
Tennessee State University

Julie D. Prandi
Illinois Wesleyan University

Andrew B. Preslar
Lamar State College, Orange

Verbie Lovorn Prevost
*University of Tennessee,
Chattanooga*

Charles Pullen
Queen's University

Nicolas Pullin
Loyola University, Chicago

Edna B. Quinn
Salisbury University

Ronald L. Raber
Grace College and Seminary

R. Kent Rasmussen
Independent Scholar

Rosemary M. Canfield Reisman
Charleston Southern University

Michael S. Reynolds
Independent Scholar

Martha E. Rhynes
Independent Scholar

Velma Bourgeois Richmond
Holy Names College

Peter S. Rogers
Loyola University, New Orleans

Carl Rollyson
Baruch College of the City University of New York

Robert L. Ross
Independent Scholar

Kelly Rothenberg
Independent Scholar

Robert A. Rushing
University of Illinois at Urbana-Champaign

Scott Samuelson
Brigham Young University, Idaho

Richard Sax
Madonna University

William Sayers
Cornell University

Roy Scheele
Doane College

Wilma J. Schmeller
Independent Scholar

Paul John Schmitt
U.S. Military Academy at West Point

Beverly Schneller
Millersville University

Kathleen Schongar
The May School

Lucy M. Schwartz
State University of New York at Buffalo

Nan C. L. Scott
University of Kansas

James Scruton
Bethel College

R. Baird Shuman
University of Illinois at Urbana-Champaign

Thomas J. Sienkewicz
Monmouth College

Charles L. P. Silet
Iowa State University

Carl Singleton
Fort Hays State University

Amy Sisson
Independent Scholar

John Slocum
Independent Scholar

Robert W. Small
Massasoit Community College

Jane Marie Smith
Slippery Rock University

Linda E. Smith
Fort Hays State University

Newton Smith
Western Carolina University

Roger Smith
Independent Scholar

Jean M. Snook
Memorial University of Newfoundland

George Soule
Carleton College

Maureen Speller
Independent Scholar

Brian Stableford
King Alfred's College

Isabel Bonnyman Stanley
East Tennessee State Uuniversity

August W. Staub
University of Georgia

Paul Stuewe
St. Jerome's University

Michael Stuprich
Ithaca College

Roy Arthur Swanson
University of Wisconsin— Milwaukee

Patricia E. Sweeney
Independent Scholar

Glenn L. Swygart
Tennessee Temple University

Sue Tarjan
Independent Scholar

Charlotte Templin
University of Indianapolis

Nancy Conn Terjesen
Kent State University

Michele Theriot
Nicholls State University

Jonathan L. Thorndike
Belmont University

Shelley A. Thrasher
Lamar State College, Orange

Adriana C. Tomasino
City University of New York Graduate Center

Anne Trotter
Rosemont College

Richard Tuerk
Texas A&M University, Commerce

Robert D. Ubriaco, Jr.
Illinois Wesleyan University

Scott D. Vander Ploeg
Madisonville Community College

Paul Varner
Oklahoma Christian University

Martha Modena Vertreace-Doody
Kennedy-King College

Constance Vidor
The Cathedral School

Albert Wachtel
Pitzer College

Mark Walling
East Central University

Gordon Walters
Independent Scholar

Kathryn A. Walterscheid
University of Missouri, St. Louis

Shawncey Webb
Independent Scholar

Lynn Wells
University of Regina

Douglas W. Werden
West Texas A&M University

James Whitlark
Texas Tech University

Anne F. Widmayer
*University of Wisconsin—
Washington County*

Barbara Wiedemann
Auburn University at Montgomery

Thomas Willard
University of Arizona

Judith Barton Williamson
Sauk Valley Community College

Jennifer Preston Wilson
Appalachian State University

Michael T. Wilson
Appalachian State University

Sharon K. Wilson
Fort Hays State University

Michael Witkoski
University of South Carolina

Scott Wright
University of St. Thomas

Robert L. Wyatt III
East Central University

Gary Zacharias
Palomar College

AN INTRODUCTION TO PLACE IN LITERATURE

Cyclopedia of Literary Places completes Salem Press's trilogy of title-driven reference literary books, whose other components are *Masterplots* and *Cyclopedia of Literary Characters*. The series as a whole now provides comprehensive analyses of classic texts in terms of their stories, their characters, and their settings. Given that story, character, and setting are familiar instruments of textual analysis, one might expect to find many more reference books akin to *Cyclopedia of Literary Places* on the library shelves; however, this set of volumes is, in actuality, unique. Although there are a great many literary surveys cataloging and analyzing stories and a considerable number cataloging and analyzing literary characters, there are only a few that attempt to tackle the third element of the natural triumvirate—place—and those few adopt an approach and a system of organization quite different from the one employed here.

It would be unlikely to occur to a literary historian to begin a study of plots by cataloging and categorizing events in the real world with which various authors might have had some acquaintance, then examining literary works as modified representations of those events. Nor would a student of literary characterization commence the project by compiling the biographies of real individuals known to various authors, then proceeding to an analysis, the means by which those biographies had been adapted to produce fictional individuals. Why, then, do the majority of reference books that deal with settings in literature model themselves on gazetteers, listing the real places with which writers were familiar, and then pointing out—sometimes in a rather desultory manner—which of their published works were set in approximately similar locations?

Literary Geography

Whatever the reason, the fact is that the fugitive field of "literary geography" has always been primarily concerned with analyzing the relationships between writers and the places in which they write, and only secondarily with the processes of filtration that the authors apply in moving those actual places into naturalistic fictions. The dealings of writers with wholly invented settings has al-

ways taken third place, with the result that even reference books that deal exclusively with places that do not exist—of which *The Dictionary of Imaginary Places* (1980; rev. ed. 1999), by Alberto Manguel and Gianni Guadalupi, is the most prominent example—tend to follow the pattern of a tourist guide rather than the kind of text-by-text analysis presented in *Cyclopedia of Literary Places*.

The book that first laid down the conventional pattern of the literary tourist-guide was *Literary Geography* (1904), by William Sharp, which collected a series of essays from *The Pall Mall Magazine*. Sharp apologized in his introduction for the limitations of his patchwork, noting that its omissions would not be made good until someone took the trouble to compile a *Cyclopedia of Literary Geography*. No one was in any hurry to attempt anything so comprehensive, and it is arguable that no one has ever done a thorough job of it; however, Sharp would surely have been glad to recognize *The Oxford Literary Guide to the British Isles* (1977), by Dorothy Eagle and Hilary Carnell, as the kind of thing he had in mind.

Sharp's essays deal with the literary works of seven individual writers and one close-knit family, and four geographical locales of varying magnitude. The perennial focus of his attention is the manner in which real landscapes are translated into fictional ones by a process of careful selection and metaphorical illumination. His analyses examine both the methods of literary reference by which the naming of landmarks and a few carefully culled details combine to create the impression of a whole landscape, and the closely related methods by which key aspects of the areas thus put in place are "highlighted" with particular narrative significance. This metamorphic process fascinated Sharp, as it had fascinated others before him. Although the pleasures of wordplay enabled Sharp to deal particularly extravagantly with the relationship between the "Scott-Land" of Sir Walter Scott and the Scotland of history and geography, his most penetrating analysis was that of "Dickens-Land."

The unique imaginative authority of Charles Dickens's representations of English life—which licensed the widespread use of the adjective "Dickensian"—was celebrated twenty years before the publication of Sharp's book by Joris-Karl Huysmans in *Against the Grain* (1884; English translation, 1922), whose hero, Jean des Esseintes, is seized by a fervent desire to visit Dickensian London but realizes after a brief visit to what would now be called a "theme pub" that it is an artifact of the imagination that had better remain unclouded by comparisons with actual streets and buildings. Des Esseintes was right, of course, but he was not *entirely* right, as Sharp took care to point out in another of his essays, "The Brontë Country." In that essay, Sharp observed that there is a part of northern England that really had become "Brontë Country" by the end of the nineteenth century—thanks to the sheer mass of American tourists flocking to it. The actual focal point of this literary pilgrimage was, of course, the parsonage where Charlotte, Emily, and Anne Brontë lived and wrote; however, there was a sense in which the entire surrounding landscape was, for the tourists, both informed and transformed by the representations of it in the Brontës' novels, *Jane Eyre*, *Wuthering Heights*, and *The Tenant of Wildfell Hall*. Brontë Country is, for this reason, rather different from England's other major location of nineteenth-century literary tourism, Stratford-upon-Avon, which was merely the birthplace of William Shakespeare, never a setting in any of his plays. The real landscape of the moors surrounding Haworth is nowadays seen through the lenses of the Brontë sisters' literary imagination—a visionary process that automatically edits out such modern embellishments as the vanes and pylons of the nearby wind farm.

The important lesson to be learned from Sharp's pioneering textbook—and especially from its observations on Brontë country—is that literary geography involves a curious admixture of conservation and transformation. Literary geography, even as practiced in America, is uniquely preoccupied with the British Isles because the isles have generated a great deal of both history and literature. The lenses provided by British literature transform British landscapes, but they transform them in order to preserve them as they once were—or, to be strictly accurate, as they once *seemed*. It is the literary geography of England—not the actual landscape—which makes England seem forever quaint, especially to American eyes—an illusion to which the actual landscape panders, merchandising its quaintness in the names as well as the stock of shops, parks, and public houses.

The process of transformation that began in Great Britain has spread to other European countries, the volume of coverage roughly equating to the volume of tourism attracted by the various nations. It is for this reason that the most important predecessor acknowledged by the compilers of *The Oxford Literary Guide to the British Isles* is Margaret Crosland's *A Traveller's Guide to Literary Europe* (1965), which devotes one volume to the British Isles and one to the rest of Europe. It was the strength of this publishing tradition that persuaded Manguel and Guadalupi to compile their satirical *Dictionary of Imaginary Places* for armchair tourists, although their survey might have produced more interesting revelations had they undertaken it in a slightly less frivolous spirit. Many "guide-books" of this kind have been devoted to the work of individual writers, sometimes to individual books. Some of these guides are very earnest indeed, even when they deal with imaginary settings. Robert Foster's *The Complete Guide to Middle-Earth* (1978; rev. ed. 2001) is a good example—but the lack of any general and comparative dimension sets a severe limit to the potential achievements of such texts. *Cyclopedia of Literary Places* is therefore a vital contribution to the repair of this deficit.

It is a mistake to see the transfiguration of real settings by the literary imagination as a trivial matter. As Oscar Wilde pointed out, life imitates art more assiduously than art imitates life, and it is arguable that we cannot see landscapes as "landscapes" or settings as "settings" until we look at them with eyes informed by art. Moreover, once we have seen them in that way, it is difficult indeed to see them in any other way. Theme parks are the most obvious large-scale manifestations of our ongoing attempts to remake actual environments in the image of fictions, but they are the ostentatious tip of a much more extensive iceberg. There are very few real places named after novels, although the Devon, England, resort of Westward Ho! even retained Charles Kingsley's exclamation mark, but there are a great many places whose existing names have been modified in significance by famous literary works set therein. For example, few visitors to Paris can look at Notre Dame Cathedral for the first time without thinking about a hunchbacked bell-ringer, even if they have never read Victor Hugo.

Maps and Spatial Relationships

It is easy to forget how recently maps of the world became objective to any real degree, and how much fiction is still contained in two-dimensional representations. We have all become used to the global representation of the world, which accurately represents the outlines of the continents even if their multicolored divisions are products of the political imagination. However, it was not so long ago that the majority of people thought that the earth was as flat as most of its maps. Mercator projections, which stretch actual geography into rectangular frames with the equator as their central baselines, also split the world in two so that west becomes left and east becomes right. The selection of the Greenwich meridian as a center was a hard-fought political contest that is by no means conclusively won even in Europe.

The first maps of the world—as opposed to navigational charts, which were primarily diagrams of the sea in which coastlines were walls with "port-holes" and islands were either oases or hazards—were Medieval "mappemondes" like the famous *mappa mundi*. They were usually circular, often centered on Jerusalem or Rome (for religious reasons), and sometimes featured land masses subtly distorted by artists to suggest recognizable shapes—faces, perhaps, or symbolic apples. Their example reminds us that "the world" is itself an imaginative construct, whose meaning and connotations are remarkably elastic. The negotiations regarding that meaning and its implications have always been partly conducted in and considerably influenced by literary works, and even the simplest terms generated by the logic of map-construction have acquired additional meanings reflected in and modified by literary consciousness.

The most elementary theoretization of living-space is the establishment of coordinates. East and west are given to us by the rising and setting of the sun (with appropriate latitudinal adjustments), north and south by a logical derivation that was marvelously endorsed by the magnetic compass. In every location, however, these four terms take on additional meanings. The history and geography of the United States of America are partly defined by the special meanings attached to the West and the South—notions so powerful that they have reduced their opposites to almost entirely negative connotations (East is usually "back East," and North is rarely cited outside the context of the Civil War, in which it designates that region against which the South rebelled).

West and South are so fully loaded with meaning in America that they have spawned such subcategories as "Midwest" and "Deep South." They also crop up in descriptive phrases such as "Wild West" and "Southern Gothic." The spirit of America's own West is also carried over into the much grander version of the "West" that distinguishes the primary political products of the Industrial Revolution from the "East" and the "Third World." Britain, by contrast, is socially organized mainly along a north-south axis, the north of England being industrialized, provincial, and relatively poor, with Scotland lying even farther to the north. Although Wales is in the west, and Ireland even farther west, the notion of "westernness" in Britain has been almost completely taken over by the lands that lie beyond the Atlantic horizon. Throughout Europe the "East" is usually "mysterious," and the Orient has a particular resonance in the literature of France, many of whose most famous writers undertook actual journeys there in search of fuel for their imagination.

The implications of these meanings—and their equivalents in Eastern Europe, Asia, South America and so on—can be found in hundreds of the analyses presented in *Cyclopedia of Literary Places* and are sketchily present even in the contents page. For instance, two different books discussed in these pages that are called *North and South* embody very different notions of the symbolism of those descriptions. There is also an *Eastward Ho!*, as well as a *Westward Ho!*, an epic *The Journey to the West*, as well as a symbolic one that leads *East of Eden*. There is also a war novel set on a "Western Front," where all is ironically quiet, as well as a "Western World" ironically inhabited by a playboy.

The metaphorical imagery of up and down also features elaborately in the geography of literary texts, where the ocean is often a surface overlaying abyssal depths, and the peaks of mountains point, in Olympian fashion, to the heavens. Subterranean caves and lofty towers reproduce a similar symbolism on a more limited scale, while attics and cellars are often deployed in such a way as to make the architecture of houses echo the anatomy of the human body or the imagined topography of a psyche in which high-minded reason struggles ceaselessly to suppress "baser" instincts and impulses. Within the world of literary geography, rising and falling are never simple matters, as *The Rise of Silas Lapham* and *The Fall of the House of Usher* readily illustrate.

Place in Novels

To some extent, the dearth of literary reference books that look at settings in the manner of *Cyclopedia of Literary Places* reflects the fact that novelists—unlike poets—are far less inclined to use entirely imaginary settings than they are to use entirely imaginary characters and entirely imaginary stories. Most "realistic" fictions are set in imaginary houses, but those imaginary houses are often placed along real streets, in real districts of real cities, or at least in real nations. That, after all, is how much of the "realism" of "realistic" fiction is derived. By contrast, wholly imaginary cities, nations, and worlds are, almost by definition, the provinces of Romance—it is not a coincidence that the contemporary reference book whose subject-matter and format are most closely akin to this one is the *Dictionary of Literary Utopias* compiled in 2000 by Vita Fortunati and Raymond Trousson.

It would be a mistake to judge that the reliance of literary realists on "real" settings makes their use of those settings any less artificial. Indeed, the construction of the environment of a story lies much closer to the heart of the creative enterprise than casual readers may suppose. The realism of character is only partly a matter of "literary psychology"; it is achieved on the page largely by demonstrating how characters reflect and embody those elements of their environment that have shaping influences upon them, and how they determine and decorate those aspects of the environment that they control. The realism of plot has little to do with matters of rational plausibility—the improbable is normal even in the most realistic fiction—and much to do with the efficient manipulation of settings and objects.

It is natural enough that "literary geography" should be so preoccupied by the relationships between the real and the imaginary—but the fact that so many of its productions should be restricted to the form of real and imaginary tourist guides does scant justice to the actual significance of setting within literary works, or to the subtleties of its manipulation.

Readers are by no means alone in taking settings too much for granted. Six fundamental questions of literary composition separate into three natural pairs: Where and when is the story happening? Who is it happening to and why do they care? What is the problem, and how are the characters going to tackle it? The first two questions are usually passed over in a cursory manner as mere matters of happenstance. Although writers are more evenly divided in their inclinations than readers—most of whom are interested in the story first, and after that, the characters—far fewer modern writers find their initial inspiration in place than in plot or character, although places played a far more significant inspirational role while poetry retained its dominance in the hierarchy of literary fashion.

Place in Dramatic Works

It is rare for novelists to organize their stories around particular places rather than networks of characters. Thornton Wilder's *The Bridge of San Luis Rey* (1927), which examines the lives of the people coincidentally present on the eponymous edifice at the moment of its collapse, seemed very unusual and quite original at the time of its publication. Although the necessities of stagecraft require playwrights—and theatrical directors—to pay close attention to settings, the same necessities require that the main priority of that consideration should be economy. A play that moves through many scenes must represent each scene sketchily, because the scenery has to be shifted at every change. A play set against a single background must use that background to maximum effect, in that every object to be employed in the action must be present on the set, and—ideally, at least—every object that is present must have some significance to the story.

The principles of theatrical economy were carried over into the cinema and television, although the gradual sophistication of technology and methods has resulted in a conspicuous liberation, particularly in terms of the license granted to the movie camera to range far and wide across increasingly expansive landscapes. Although *Cyclopedia of Literary Places* is solely concerned with literary texts, this evolution of media is by no means irrelevant to its contents. In much the same way that our experience of real landscapes can be, and routinely is, informed by literary representations, so our experience of novels and plays can be, and routinely is, informed by film and television adaptations. Although many film adaptations attempt to re-create the settings of the original stories as faithfully as possible, a great deal of improvisation is required—and some film directors set out unrepentantly to reconfigure the settings of their raw material.

The value of a carefully designed standing set is very obvious in the television medium because of the domination of that medium by the series format. However, even in the world of series television there are relatively few shows in which settings are as important as generators of stories as relationships among regular cast members; the exceptions, significantly, usually feature "magical places" that have their own power to move events along. The same is true of those novels and short stories which, for one reason or another, closely confine their characters. The texts described in *Cyclopedia of Literary Places* in which places are more important than the characters who move within them, tend to use magical places, pregnant with mysterious forces. They are *haunted*, if not literally, then metaphorically.

Realism in Settings

This effect combines with the fundamental reliance of "realistic" texts on "real" settings to draw texts whose primary emphasis is on place, rather than plot or characters, away from the center of modern critical concern, often taking them across the boundary into the oft-despised genres of supernatural fiction. The more "realistic" settings are, the more settings tend to "fade into the background." That "fading" process should not, however, be construed as a diminution of importance; it is precisely because backgrounds may be unobtrusive that they can do vital narrative labor in a subtle and ingenious manner.

Although it was natural for the series of literary reference works of which *Cyclopedia of Literary Places* is a part to produce analyses of plots first and then analyses of characters, there was still a great deal of useful work to be done—and useful insight to be gained—when those analyses had been completed. These volumes are particularly useful because this third-stage labor is so rarely attempted in other literary reference books.

In order to illustrate the results of this kind of literary dissection, it is necessary only to consider the book that is likely more familiar to readers than any other: the Bible. The Bible is easily representable as a set of stories which—like many other plots, but on a grander scale—begins with a Creation and ends, after much complication, with a final Revelation. Seen in terms of its characters, it begins with Adam and Eve and descends through Moses, Solomon, Job, Jesus, Saint Paul, and a host of others, to the Four Horsemen of the Apocalypse. Viewed from the perspective of geography, the Bible makes its way from Eden to Armageddon via such settings as Noah's Ark, Babylon, Sodom and Gomorrah, the Promised Land, the Walls of Jericho, a stable in Bethlehem, Golgotha, and the Road to Damascus. There is nothing "mere" about the decor of the Bible; every one of the mentioned locations is so fully laden with significance, thanks to its appearance in the Bible, that most of us carry them around with us constantly, as key reference points for the organization of our own experience. They retain such immense power as metaphors that references to them crop up, by necessity, in a large portion of the literary texts examined within *Cyclopedia of Literary Places*.

Journeys

The most elementary form of story is the journey—necessarily so, given that we can hardly help conceiving of human life as a journey from the cradle to the grave, in whose course we accumulate experiences and, we hope, *make progress*. One of the cornerstones of modern prose fiction is John Bunyan's account of life in Christendom as *The Pilgrim's Progress* (1678), in which every believer must make a way from the City of Destruction to the Celestial City, traversing a symbolic landscape strewn with such traps as the Slough of Despond, the Valley of Humiliation, Vanity Fair, and Doubting Castle. Like the Bible, Bunyan's book provided a stock of symbols on which later writers could draw, but—more important—it also provided a methodological example. Although allegory went out of fashion as a form in its own right, it remains fundamental to all literary endeavor, dissolved within the rich solution of narrative design.

The words "journey" and "pilgrimage" recur continually in the contents pages of *Cyclopedia of Literary Places*. Alongside such direct quotations as *Vanity Fair*, Bunyan's terminological method resounds in many other titles featured in these volumes, including *Bleak House*, *Castle Rackrent*, *Heartbreak House* and *Night-*

mare Abbey; fainter echoes, each with its own wry twist, are discernible in *Cold Comfort Farm*, *New Grub Street*, and *The Well of Loneliness*.

This notion of life as a journey often supposes, as Bunyan did, that "the world" in which we find ourselves is only the first stage. The most elaborate description of the greater world, of which "the world" is but an element, was provided by Dante in *The Divine Comedy*, whose settings recur continually in modern literature, both literally and metaphorically. *Cyclopedia of Literary Places* covers John Milton's *Paradise Lost* and *Paradise Regained* as well as another *Purgatory* and a record of *A Season in Hell*. The conception of life's journey as a prelude inevitably transforms its representations, allowing the world to be reinterpreted as a *Ship of Fools*. The contrary assumption, that life's journey has no alternative but to find a terminus in this world, and that we had better be careful where we decide to go, is equally well represented herein, in such texts as *Heart of Darkness*, *Green Mansions*, *As I Lay Dying*, and *Journey to the End of the Night*.

Place in Literary Titles

The irresistible growth of literary naturalism has not weakened the metaphorical force of imagery derived from the Bible or from the analogy between life and a journey. No matter how mundane a description of setting might be, it takes on a peculiar gravity when a literary text devotes time and space to it; this is especially true when a seemingly modest description is deployed as a title. Such restrained appellations as *The Bridge*, *Bus Stop*, *The Dining Room*, *Main Street*, *Middlemarch*, and *The Village* do not imply limitation but typicality. They refer to microcosms in which, despite their humility, all human life is contained. Paradoxical as it may seem, minute explorations of confinement generally aspire to a greater comprehensiveness than works whose titles refer to such broader and more disordered spans, such as *Earth*, *Tropic of Cancer*, *U.S.A.*, and *The Waste Land*.

It is significant, in view of these observations, that the most frequent term of location to be found in the contents pages of *Cyclopedia of Literary Places* is "House" (and also that the second most frequent is "Castle") even though we have the assurance of Thomas Wolfe and Jack Kerouac that once life's journey is seriously commenced *You Can't Go Home Again*, because we are, or

ought to be, forever *On the Road*. What all people need in order to find their way is an atlas, not of the world as it is or any particular fictitious world, but of that vast collective realm of the imagination, whose entirety contains and extrapolates our homes and our horizons alike.

The hypothetical atlas of the world that is the sum of all the worlds within literary texts differs from atlases of the actual world in several significant respects, of which the least important is its sheer size. As literary geographers have demonstrated—albeit within relatively narrow fields of concern—even an atlas of scrupulously naturalistic fictions exhibits some striking differences in detail. The careful study of literary works should enable us to construct a series of highly detailed maps showing the evolution of Paris or London during the last three centuries, but any comparison with actual street maps would immediately expose considerable gaps. Any town or village featured in a mere handful of literary works, no matter how evocative their descriptions might be, would be composed of a handful of disconnected landmarks and a huge bank of fog.

On the other hand, we would not need to expand our consideration very far beyond scrupulous naturalism to find an elaborate record of a whole series of parallel worlds, in which the villages, towns, cities, counties, and even nations of our world were replaced by mysterious clones like Thomas Hardy's Wessex, Arnold Bennett's Five Towns, or Anthony Trollope's Barchester, or supplemented with considerable tracts of land for which real maps have no available space, like Sinclair Lewis's Zenith, William Faulkner's Yoknapatawpha County, and Anthony Hope's Ruritania. Real and imaginary settings, and some that overlap the boundary, can be equally convincing stages for the dramas of human life, as demonstrated by *Bartholomew Fair*, *Berlin Alexanderplatz*, *Bullet Park*, *The Charterhouse of Parma*, *Howards End*, *Hyde Park*, *Mansfield Park*, *Raintree County*, *Riceyman Steps*, *Tobacco Road*, *Tortilla Flat*, *Washington Square*, and *Winesburg, Ohio*.

Hinterlands of the Imagination

As we move away from naturalistic fictions into the hinterlands of the imagination, the literary atlas becomes much more elaborate. Its reconfigurations of the actual world become cluttered with all manner of addenda—especially islands—and its parallel worlds, vastly multiplied, become much more elaborate and fanciful. Travel broadens the mind, and a lifetime's reading broadens it in ways that no other kind of experience can. We can only understand the places we know by comparing them to other places. "Home" means nothing until we have been out of it; "here" is unmeasurable unless we have a notion of "there"; "the world" is impossible to evaluate accurately until we can explore other worlds in which things work differently. We could not fully appreciate the limits of practicality had we not made imaginative forays into worlds where magic works; that is why the tales that were told and retold—and still are told and retold—before we had reading and writing to improve our resources, are mostly tales of an imaginary world in which the wishes reflected in daydreams really can have consequences. That world is revived, revised, and revisited time and time again in countless literary fairylands, and in such kindred constructs as Aristophanes' Cloudcuckooland, the Never Land of *Peter Pan*, and the worlds that Alice finds in *Alice's Adventures in Wonderland* and in *Through the Looking-Glass*.

It is because we can only really find ourselves by going away that literature is full of havens designed for exactly that purpose—and why the only part of *Robinson Crusoe* that anyone takes the trouble to remember is the castaway's sojourn on the island. Utopia, in the literal meaning of "no place" rather than the acquired meaning of an "ideal state," is one of the most vital locations on any literary map, just as the most important journeys, from *The Odyssey* onward, have taken travelers into *terra incognita* where, as old maps used to put it, "Here be Dragons." That description is, of course, intended to serve as a lure as well as a warning; dragons traditionally guard treasures, and the conventional literary reward for facing the hazards of extraordinary voyages is the gold of El Dorado, frequently mingled with gemstones, although even such innocent fantasies of enrichment as *King Solomon's Mines* and *Treasure Island* have significant metaphorical dimensions. Enlightenment is the ultimate treasure, even when its acquisition is costly and its taste less than sweet, as it is for such conventional travelers as Strether in *The Ambassadors*, Charles Ryder in *Brideshead Revisited*, and Johann Wolfgang van Goethe's Wilhelm Meister, as well as such explorers of exotica as the heroes of *Out of the Silent Planet*, *The Sirens of Titan*, and *The Time Machine*.

Imaginary places can be refined and purified in ways that real ones cannot, as Plato demonstrated in the *Republic*. Their refinement can sometimes instill a remarkable yearning for their realization, as Plato demonstrated when he suggested, playfully, that his ideal republic had once existed in Atlantis. Such processes of refinement, no matter what kind of perfection for which they aim, always tend to be tinged with irony and regret precisely because they do take us away from the practical. It is no coincidence that utopian fantasy is intricately entwined with satirical fantasy, even in its nostalgic Arcadian or Cockaynean mode.

The compendium of satirical locations featured in *Gulliver's Travels* prompted a sequence of echoes comparable to those of *The Pilgrim's Progress*. *Cyclopedia of Literary Places* offers cautionary accounts of such exemplary locations as *Animal Farm*, *The City of the Sun*, *Erewhon*, *Herland*, *Penguin Island*, and *Solaris*, as well as Thomas More's archetypal *Utopia*. However, ideals of a more self-indulgent kind are represented too, in images of *Arcadia*, *The Earthly Paradise*, the Middle-Earth of *The Lord of the Rings*, the Shangri-La of *Lost Horizon*, the Nepenthe of *South Wind*, and James Branch Cabell's Poictesme. Such realms fully deserve their pages in the atlas of the imagination—but they also deserve more careful comparison and more penetrating analysis than an atlas or a series of gazetteers can provide; this is one of the tasks *Cyclopedia of Literary Places* undertakes.

Literature and the Real World

There are two principal respects in which the worlds within texts differ from the world in which we actually live. One is that worlds within texts have inescapable moral orders. If principles of poetic justice are violated within them, it is because the authors violate them, calculatedly and brutally. Because readers are conscious of that fact, they are able to experience the bittersweet sensation of tragedy. The other difference is that worlds within texts are packed with meaning; if an element of the text has no aesthetic purpose, it ought not to be there. For this reason, the objects present in the environment of a well-wrought story to which the reader's attention is specifically directed are always more than "mere" decor.

Even an object that has a utilitarian purpose within a story usually carries a symbolic burden as well—timepieces are particularly prone to this kind of dual role—and those that are primarily ornamental, especially works of art and cut flowers, are dutiful servants of symbolism. The description of actual landscapes and quotidian weather in emotional terms may constitute a "pathetic fallacy." However, in literary works, changes of scenery and the weather always tend to reflect the emotional states of the characters and the uneven flow of their stories.

In literary works, a mountain is never *merely* a mountain, a mere—or any other body of water—is never merely a mere, and mist or fog is invariably symptomatic of deeper confusions. Because these meanings tend to be embedded in the "background" of the story, however, they often go unapprehended by readers whose attention is firmly fixed on the events of the story, vicariously experienced by identification with one or more of the char-

acters. This is not to say that these meanings do not ordinarily have an effect on the reader, but their situation in the background ensures that the effect is more likely to be subliminal than the effects of story and character.

There is, therefore, a sense in which *Cyclopedia of Literary Places* comes after its two companions because it goes a little deeper, and a little further, in its analysis of texts. It is itself a new phase of a journey, a further enrichment of experience, and an extra measure of progress. For that reason, it is likely to be uniquely valuable, whether considered as an accessory to its predecessors or as an endeavor in its own right. The analyses presented herein have their own revelations to offer, which are all the more interesting because they are fresh; they mark the beginning of a brand-new era in the strange science of literary geography.

— *Brian Stableford*

KEY TO PRONUNCIATION

As an aid to users of *Cyclopedia of Literary Places*, guides to English pronunciations of foreign place-names are provided for particularly difficult words. These guides are rendered with easy-to-understand phonetic symbols enclosed in parentheses after boldfaced subheads and use the symbols listed in the table below. Stressed syllables are indicated by capital letters, as in "**Yoknapatawpha County** (YOK-nuh-puh-TAW-fuh)." It should be understood that some of the phonetic pronunciations are merely approximations, as both English and foreign pronunciations of many place-names vary.

Symbols	*Pronounced as in*	*Phonetic spellings*
Vowel sounds		
a	answer, laugh, sample, that	AN-sihr, laf, SAM-pul, that
ah	father, hospital	FAH-thur, HAHS-pih-tul
aw	awful, caught	AW-ful, kawt
ay	blaze, fade, waiter, weigh	blayz, fayd, WAYT-ur, way
eh	bed, head, said	behd, hehd, sehd
ee	believe, cedar, leader, liter	bee-LEEV, SEE-dur, LEED-ur, LEE-tur
ew	boot, lose	bewt, lews
i	buy, height, lie, surprise	bi, hit, li, sur-PRIZ
ih	bitter, pill	BIH-tur, pihl
o	cotton, hot	CO-tuhn, hot
oh	below, coat, note, wholesome	bee-LOH, coht, noht, HOHL-suhm
oo	good, look	good, look
ow	couch, how	kowch, how
oy	boy, coin	boy, koyn
uh	about, butter, enough, other	uh-BOWT, BUH-tur, ee-NUHF, UH-thur
Consonant sounds		
ch	beach, chimp	beech, chihmp
g	beg, disguise, get	behg, dihs-GIZ, geht
j	digit, edge, jet	DIH-jiht, ehj, jeht
k	cat, kitten, hex	kat, KIH-tehn, hehks
s	cellar, save, scent	SEL-ur, sayv, sehnt
sh	champagne, issue, shop	sham-PAYN, IH-shew, shop
ur	birth, disturb, earth, letter	burth, dihs-TURB, urth, LEH-tur
y	useful, young	YEWS-ful, yuhng
z	business, zest	BIHZ-ness, zest
zh	vision	VIH-zhuhn

Cyclopedia
of
LITERARY
PLACES

ABRAHAM AND ISAAC

Author: Unknown
Type of work: Drama
Type of plot: Mystery play

Time of plot: Biblical antiquity
First performed: Fifteenth century

The dramatic structure of this miracle play centers on the movement of the biblical Abraham from his home to a climactic event atop a mountain, followed by his return home. The play's structure follows the basic thematic elements of a divine command, the testing of Abraham's faith, and the subsequent blessing announced to Abraham for faithfully passing his test.

Abraham's home. This miracle play does not specify where Abraham lives, apart from his early statement that he understands his home to be a gift from God. According to biblical accounts, however, Abraham lived in Beersheba, a town in southern Palestine where Abraham entered into an oath with Abimelech that guaranteed him both water and grazing rights. In the play, the residents of Abraham's land practice human sacrifice; when he is called upon to take his son on a journey, he expects it will end in his son's sacrifice. After being tested on the mountain, Abraham returns home and receives further blessing.

Mountain. Crest of an unnamed mountain on which the play reaches its climax three days after Abraham leaves his home. Biblical texts identify this place as Moriah. Abraham's three-day journey to the mountain advances the plot and informs the audience that Abraham's son Isaac is unaware that he is to be sacrificed, although Abraham is fully aware of what he is expected to do. A raised elevation on the stage suggests the proximity to divinity of the participants. It also removes the act from the normal realm of life, thus reinforcing the sacred obligation involved. The place of devotion to God and human elevation, in this play, ironically, becomes a temporary place of despair since Abraham fully intends to slay his son.

Dramatic tension is relieved when an angel interrupts Abraham's sacrifice and a ram is substituted for his son. The mountain thereafter symbolizes complete devotion to the deity and marks a milestone in Abraham's evolving theology. The mountain is the place of epiphany on which Abraham realizes that human sacrifice is not required of him, thus separating him from his social context. It also comes to be recognized as a place of divine provision. The play's fifteenth century audiences associated Isaac symbolically with Jesus Christ and saw the play as a prefiguring of Christ's Crucifixion; they therefore associated its mountain with the place of the Crucifixion.

— *Kenneth Hada*

ABSALOM, ABSALOM!

Author: William Faulkner (1897-1962)
Type of work: Novel
Type of plot: Psychological realism

Time of plot: 1807-1910
First published: 1936

As in most of William Faulkner's fiction, Yoknapatawpha County functions in this novel both as a narrowly defined microcosm of a pre- and post-Civil War South whose racial prejudice contributes to spiritual depravity and physical devastation and as a universal setting in which Faulkner examines the struggles of what he termed the "human heart in conflict with itself."

Yoknapatawpha County (YOK-nuh-puh-TAW-fuh). Fictional county in northwestern Mississippi that Faulkner called his "little postage stamp of native soil." By the time Faulkner wrote *Absalom, Absalom!* he had used this setting in five novels. For this novel, however, he drew a map of the county on which he identified places used in both this and the earlier novels. Faulkner gave the county an area of 2,400 square miles and a population of 6,298 white residents and 9,313 black residents.

With the Tallahatchie River serving as the northern boundary, the Yoknapatawpha River—an old name for the actual Yocona River—as the southern boundary, Yoknapatawpha bears a remarkable resemblance to, but is not identical with, Mississippi's real Lafayette County. **Jefferson**, Yoknapatawpha's fictional county seat, is likewise patterned after Oxford; however, Faulkner also includes a town called "Oxford" in the novel. A rural, agricultural county with a large number of plantations, including Sutpen's Hundred, Yoknapatawpha is a miniature of the South during the nineteenth century. Amid a society permeated with racial prejudice and class consciousness, the character Thomas Sutpen is both spurred toward his goal and denied the opportunity for success. Despite his efforts to achieve respectability, most members of Jefferson's aristocracy regard him as an outsider and fail to recognize that he mirrors the flaws of their society.

Sutpen's Hundred (SUHT-penz). Plantation built by Thomas Sutpen on a "hundred square miles of some of the best virgin bottom land in the country." Having failed in an earlier attempt in the West Indies to achieve his "design," Sutpen purchases land from a local Chickasaw chief. With the help of a French architect and slave labor, he ruthlessly sets out to establish a dynasty in Yoknapatawpha County. He spends two years building his mansion, leaves it unfinished and unfurnished for three years, and finally completes it in time for his marriage to Ellen Coldfield. It serves as the setting for the major actions of the story. Although the house is unquestionably grand in its early days, the various narrators of the novel focus on its later rotting, decaying, desolate stage with "its sagging portico and scaling walls, its sagging blinds and blank-shuttered windows." The house clearly symbolizes Sutpen's failed dream and the fallen South. When it finally goes up in flames, years after Sutpen's death, Sutpen's only living descendant, the idiot Jim Bond, "howls" about the place.

*West Virginia.** Originally part of Virginia, West Virginia became a state in 1863. Sutpen is born in a primitive farm society of the region's mountains in 1807. During his first ten years he lives there with no real awareness of racial prejudice and class distinctions. His earliest years contrast sharply with his later experiences.

*Virginia.** When Sutpen's family moves from the mountains into Virginia's tidewater region, the ten-year-old Sutpen encounters the aristocratic southern social code in a humiliating experience that changes his life. Sent as a messenger to the home of a wealthy plantation owner, he is told by the black servant to go around to the back of the house. From his experience in this society, Sutpen formulates his "design"—his plan to gain, through whatever means necessary, the possessions and position in society to prevent ever being similarly humiliated again.

*Harvard University.** Prestigious institution of higher learning in Cambridge, Massachusetts. Although Mississippi is the setting for most of Sutpen's story, the last half of the novel is narrated by Jefferson native Quentin Compson and Shreve McCannon, his Canadian roommate at Harvard. In a cold dormitory room far from his Jefferson home, Quentin tries to come to terms with his feelings about the South as he and Shreve piece together Sutpen's story. His confusion and intense feelings about his place of birth are reflected in his response to Shreve's asking him why he hates the South. He quickly responds that he does not hate it; however, his subsequent reiterated thoughts clearly reflect his anguished ambivalence: "I dont. I dont! I dont hate it! I dont hate it!"

*Haiti.** West Indian island nation ruled by descendants of African slaves and the site of Sutpen's first failure to achieve his design. As a young man Sutpen emigrates to Haiti. Amid a slave insurrection, he heroically helps a landowner save his plantation and subsequently wins the hand of the man's daughter, who then bears him a son. Soon thereafter Sutpen discovers that his wife has African blood and renounces her and all the possessions he has gained through his marriage. The romanticized

land of promise has left him bereft, and his only hope is to start anew elsewhere.

*Oxford. Site of the University of Mississippi, where Sutpen's two sons, Henry Sutpen and Charles Bon, meet. The university atmosphere enables them to become close friends despite Charles's being ten years older.

— *Verbie Lovorn Prevost*

ABSALOM AND ACHITOPHEL

Author: John Dryden (1631-1700)
Type of work: Poetry
Type of plot: Satire

Time of plot: Biblical antiquity
First published: 1681

John Dryden's choice of ancient Jerusalem as the setting for his poem is mandated by the story he tells in this heroic-couplet satire. The poem recounts the rebellion of Absalom and Achitophel against King David recorded in the Old Testament, but is actually about contemporary English politics, with Jerusalem representing late seventeenth century London.

*Jerusalem. Capital city of the ancient Israelites (also called Sion), beginning with King David's reign. Within the poem itself, Jerusalem is never described; its presence is merely assumed as the backdrop for the action, as dictated by history. What interests Dryden is not so much the location of the story, but the psychology of the characters involved in the rebellion. Insofar as he uses a biblical story to reflect political events in England, Jerusalem represents London. Dryden uses biblical events and characters in the poem to mirror the political situation in late seventeenth century London—which can be equated with Jerusalem—when Lord Shaftesbury (equated with the biblical Achitophel) opposed Charles II (King David) in the choice of his brother, James, as heir to the throne. Shaftesbury conspires with the Duke of Monmouth (Absalom), the king's illegitimate son, to become king.

Dryden's narration utilizes biblical history as a model for other historical events, with its characters incarnating great archetypes that recur through history. Since Absalom's rebellion may be seen as an archetype for political uprising by a family member against a legitimate ruler, Jerusalem may also be seen as an archetype—a symbol of any major capital city in which legitimate government is threatened by insurgency from within.

Although Dryden's contemporaries understood his poem as a veiled statement about events in London, the poem's narrative widens the potential interpretations of the story, its characters and its setting. Thus, Dryden's Jerusalem transcends time and space, becoming not only London but a city anywhere at any time whose government is threatened by internal rebellion.

— *Marsha Daigle-Williamson*

THE ABSENTEE

Author: Maria Edgeworth (1767-1849)
Type of work: Novel
Type of plot: Social realism

Time of plot: Early nineteenth century
First published: 1812

Maria Edgeworth's novel chronicles the near dissolution of the Clonbrony family, whose members are caught up in the Anglo-Irish social class system that the family represents and who live lavishly in London. Ultimately, the family finds salvation by returning to Ireland. Intent on realism, Maria Edgeworth spares nothing in describing the corruption inherent in the Anglo-Irish social system and calls for the abandonment of absenteeism and the return to duty of residential landlords.

*London. Capital of Great Britain and leading city of the British Isles, in which the Anglo-Irish absentee landlord Lord Clonbrony and his ruthless, social-climbing wife maintain an extravagant lifestyle. *The Absentee* is set in a historical period when the Irish social order was split over the question of union with Britain. Although the class of people known as "Anglo-Irish"— wealthy Protestant landowners—had dominated Ireland for generations, many of them, like Edgeworth's fictional Clonbronys, spend their lives in England and on the European continent, living in luxury, while reaping profits from their Irish agricultural properties. Many of them never even set foot in Ireland, leaving management of their lands in the hands of exploitative overseers.

Ireland's absentee landlord system, coupled with the emerging greedy Irish middle-class, oppressed the disenfranchised, indigent Irish peasants. In London, the Clonbrony family, especially Lady Clonbrony, attempts to buy its way into high society. Going to great lengths to deny her Irish roots, Lady Clonbrony denigrates her former country and attempts to marry off her son, Lord Colambre, to a local heiress. London here represents decay, and because of the absentee landlord system, the Clonbrony family sinks into decline.

*Ireland. Roman Catholic country ruled by Britain. The hero of Edgeworth's novel, Lord Colambre, finds hope and salvation for the Clonbrony family in Ireland. Young and intelligent, he travels incognito to Ireland to investigate his family's Irish estates and learn whether his mother's negative ideas about Ireland are justified. Traveling anonymously to each of his father's estates, he comes to know the truth. Known as Evans, on the first of his father's estates, he finds that his father has just fired the likable and honest estate agent Burke for not extorting sufficient income from the estate's tenants. The Brothers Garraghty manage the second estate, which Lord Colambre finds in complete disorder: Its church is falling down, its roads are almost impassable, and its tenants are terribly abused. Although the brothers almost openly embezzle estate funds, Lord Clonbrony fails to take action against them because they still send him enough money to support his sumptuous lifestyle in London. Again, Edgeworth emphasizes the decay of the Anglo-Irish social order.

Lord Colambre also finds a more peaceful existence in Ireland, where he comes to realize the true quality of the people his mother so severely criticizes. Eventually, he begins to view Ireland as a haven. Upon his return to London, he promises to pay off the family debts himself on the conditions that the Garraghty brothers are let go and his family ceases being absentee landowners. They must, he declares, return to Ireland and take up their ancestral responsibility of caring for their estates. Eventually, his family finds salvation by returning to Ireland—precisely what Edgeworth urges as the political solution to the decaying Anglo-Irish social order.

— *M. Casey Diana*

THE ACHARNIANS

Author: Aristophanes (c. 450-c. 385 B.C.E.)
Type of work: Drama
Type of plot: Satire

Time of plot: 431-404 B.C.E.
First performed: Acharnēs, 425 B.C.E. (English translation, 1812)

Numerous topical references to public figures of Aristophanes' time and a vivid depiction of locales fix the political and social criticism organic to this play firmly in its original Greek audiences' own time and place— Athens in 425 B.C.E.

***Athens.** Greek democratic city-state at the height of its power when Aristophanes wrote in the late fifth century B.C.E. and the setting for most of his plays. The play's action begins at the Pnyx, an open hillside overlooking the city center where the Assembly of Citizens meets to vote on state business. Its focus then shifts to a street in front of three houses that belong to the hero, the historical early fifth century B.C.E. tragedian Euripides, and the warrior Lamachos in a fictional juxtaposition of actual Athenian places convenient for the drama. At the hero's insistence, Euripides' house opens to reveal him in his cluttered study. The realities of peace and war contrast when weaponry is brought from Lamachos's house and festival gear from the hero's. The hero's wife observes festival preparations from the roof of the house; outside it, the hero establishes a free-trade zone, in which he negotiates illicit exchanges under his private peace treaty.

Clownish caricatures of nearby peoples at war with Athens visit the illegal market, for example, a starving bumpkin from Megara to the west and an aristocratic fop from Boiotian Thebes to the north. Athenian officials who attempt to enforce the realities of real-life war restrictions upon the hero's private market space are repelled. Other characters represent contending regional interests in the war. For example, these include a chorus of belligerent charcoal burners from the rural Athenian township of Acharnai seven miles north of Athens; the outlandish envoy from the wealthy Persian Empire, cultivated by the government in the hope of financial support; and the boorish and gluttonous Odomanian allies from Thrace to the north. An enigmatic choral reference implies that Aristophanes, himself an Athenian citizen, has family connections to Aegina, a real island subjugated by Athens and visible from her harbor.

— *Elizabeth A. Fisher*

ADAM BEDE

Author: George Eliot (Mary Ann Evans, 1819-1880)
Type of work: Novel
Type of plot: Domestic realism

Time of plot: 1799
First published: 1859

This novel of guilt, alienation, and retribution is set in the rural Midlands of England, where contrasting prosperity and bleakness provide a strong sense of place. That earlier, turn-of-century place presents the moral coherence of the old feudal economic system and the interdependence of all those rooted within it, including tenant farmers, laborers, artisans, servants, and landowners. Squire Arthur Donnithorne's self-deluding and irresponsible seduction of Hetty Sorrel, a pretty but penniless dairy maid, violates that mutual trust, disrupts the community, and almost causes its breakup. The sense of place is further strengthened by chapter titles that name each place of action.

Hayslope. Midlands village in the fictional county of **Loamshire** where Adam Bede, a skilled carpenter, works for Jonathan Burge. Scenes alternate between the indoors (the workshop, the Bede home, the rectory, the Hall farm) and the outdoors (the green, the woods, the churchyard, the orchard and garden) picturing the full range of a community. The novel opens in the village carpentry workshop, where Adam praises industrious creativity, which, he argues, God favors as much as the religious singing, praying, and preaching of the Methodists, a group to which his "dreamy" brother Seth belongs. The workplace emphasizes Adam's strong integrity and reliability, as well as his tendency to be unsympathetic toward others' weaknesses.

Bede cottage. Cottage that Adam shares with his brother and parents. His work ethic dominates this place; he has been doing his father's work for several years and is disgusted because his father too often visits the nearby pub. Eventually, however, Adam relents from his hard stance toward weakness, when he and Seth discover their drunken father has drowned.

Hall farm. Managed by Martin and Rachel Poyser, this is the best-kept tenant farm on the estate of Squire Donnithorne. Here the reader meets the fantasy-driven Hetty, niece of Martin, and sees the visiting squire flirting with her. Mr. Irwine, the rector, accompanies the squire and cautions him against turning Hetty's head. After Hetty's disgrace, the Poysers and Adam feel they must relocate; their move over a distance of only twenty miles is presented as a complete uprooting from their former sense of permanence. George Eliot is contrasting a lost agrarian world, Old England, with mid-century industrialized England.

Snowfield, Stoniton, and **Stonyshire.** Bleak areas, unlike the fertile Hayslope of Loamshire, that are associated not with agricultural productivity, but with the cotton mill where Dinah Morris works and with Hetty's imprisonment and trial. They are also associated with the religion of the poor—outdoor Methodism—and Stoniton is the place of the upper room in which Bartle Massey looks after Adam, giving him bread and wine. Dinah says that the harsh conditions make the inhabitants responsive to religion.

— *Carolyn Dickinson*

THE ADMIRABLE CRICHTON

Author: Sir James M. Barrie (1860-1937)
Type of work: Drama
Type of plot: Satire

Time of plot: Early twentieth century
First performed: 1902; first published, 1914

The two locations in which the play is set contrast the highly artificial aristocratic society with a "state of nature," from which the elements of subsistence—food, water, and shelter—must be directly derived. In these very different contexts the worth of an individual is determined by entirely different criteria.

Loam House. Home of the earl of Loam in London's Mayfair district—one of the most expensive districts of London, where the cream of the English aristocracy maintained their town houses in the days before World War I. Loam House, like its eponymous owner, is apparently not of the highest rank. It contains several reception rooms of varying quality, some of which are to be "lent for charitable purposes," while those reserved for private use are lavishly furnished. Act 1 takes place in the most luxurious of the rooms, which is lavishly equipped with a carpet, couches, and cushions. Its walls are decorated with paintings by well-known artists. A thousand roses are distributed in basins, while shelves and tables contain library novels, illustrated newspapers and, as the play opens, all the paraphernalia required for the serving and consumption of that hallowed English tradition, high tea.

By the time this room reappears in act 4, its decor has changed considerably. Various animal skins, stuffed birds, and the weapons used to kill them have replaced the paintings, and other items have been replaced by mementos of Crichton's castaway experience. The tale tacitly told by these exhibits is, however, transparently false. Labels attached to the trophies on the walls emphasize the fact that all Crichton's achievements have been rudely appropriated by the aristocrats, who are his social betters. However, the true story behind the sham can be perceived now, much more easily than in act 1.

Island. Desert island on which various members of the Loam household are shipwrecked, somewhere in the Pacific Ocean. Its shore is fringed by a thicket of bamboo. Trees, including coconut palms, are abundant, and its fauna includes monkeys, snakes, and wildcats. In act 2 the only edifice that the castaways have erected is a half-finished hut, and the only person working constructively on it is Crichton. When act 3 opens two years later, the castaways have moved to a larger log cabin, set on higher ground close to a stream. A mill wheel erected on the stream provides the cabin with electric light.

The furniture of the cabin's main room stands in careful contrast to that of the reception room in Loam House. Improvised spades, saws, and fishing rods are placed on the joists supporting the roof. Cured hams are suspended from hooks, while barrels and sacks of other foodstuffs are lodged in recesses. The floor is bare save for a few animal skins. Although various pieces of wreckage have been put to new uses—the ship's steering wheel is now a chandelier, and a life buoy provides a back for one of the chairs—most of the furniture is the result of "rough but efficient carpentering." Its main door consists of four swinging panels, and its unglazed window is equipped with a shutter. There are several sleeping rooms and a work room.

At the first appearance of this miracle of improvisation, its architect, the butler, is conspicuously absent, while other cast members drift in and out, emphasizing by their conduct that they are now entirely subservient to his mastery. The meal that is eaten when he does appear is an extreme contrast, in terms of its constituents, its apparatus, and the roles of its participants, to the tea served in the reception room of Loam House. The spontaneity of the after-dinner dancing, to the tune of a makeshift concertina, contrasts sharply with the stiff formality of social intercourse at Loam House. What kind of social progress is it, the play meekly wonders, that has transformed one setting into another, and how can such perverse artificiality possibly survive?

— *Brian Stableford*

ADOLPHE

Author: Benjamin Constant (1767-1830)
Type of work: Novel
Type of plot: Psychological realism

Time of plot: Late eighteenth and early nineteenth centuries
First published: 1816 (English translation, 1816)

In this semiautobiographical and psychological study of an ill-fated passion, the protagonist's movements among various European sites mark his vacillations between his mistress and his father's way of life. The novel shows a classical disregard for physical description of locations, concentrating instead on the human interactions that they frame.

*Cerenza. Village on the River Neto, near the larger town of Cosenza, in southern Italy. Although the novel situates Cerenza in the region of Calabria, at the tip of Italy's "boot," Cerenza actually belongs to the region of Basilicata, north of Calabria. There, the flooding of the Neto briefly brings together the hero and the fictional publisher of Adolphe's journal, whose comments on it open and close the novel. Adolphe's other travels—and especially his indifference to his enforced stay in Cerenza—suggest a restless, even wasted life. The publisher comments on this in the final lines of the novel, noting the inability of people to make themselves "any better by a change of scene." This and similar reflections make Adolphe's various moves in the story a symptom more of his conflicts and aimlessness than of the kind of cosmopolitan ease evidenced in Benjamin Constant's own sojourns throughout Europe.

*Göttingen. City in central Germany on the Leine River, where Adolphe's first-person narrative opens at the time of his graduation from the University of Göttingen—the only specific German location mentioned in the novel. It is unclear where Adolphe lived earlier, since he identifies his father only as minister to a German prince. Constant himself attended the university at Erlangen in southeastern Germany; he may have chosen to use Göttingen in his novel because he lived there with his wife from 1811 to 1813.

D——. Small, unnamed German town near Göttingen in which Adolphe takes up residence after leaving Göttingen, instead of accepting his father's offer to send him on the traditional young man's tour of Europe. D—— is ruled by an enlightened prince and is possibly based on the real town of Duderstadt, southeast of Göttingen. In keeping with the vagueness of D——'s identity, the publisher mentions meeting "some people in a German town" from Adolphe and Ellenore's past. Without naming or identifying the town or court, Constant nevertheless has it embody what Adolphe disdains as the "artificial and highly-wrought thing called society." In Constant's own life, the corresponding place that developed his youthful distaste for tedious court life was Brunswick (Braunschweig), in north-central Germany.

*Germany. Native country of Adolphe, who in chapter 7 frets over being unable to "resume [his] rightful place in [his] own country" because of a clinging mistress, while a friend of his father reprimands him for "vegetating" in Poland when he could be building a brilliant career back home.

Although Adolphe's hometown in Germany, where he once inhabited an ancient castle with his father, obviously symbolizes conventional success as opposed to the irregular life he leads with Ellenore, Constant never identifies the location. When Ellenore follows Adolphe here from D——, Adolphe already feels constrained by their relationship. Then, accompanying her after his father has her officially ordered from this unspecified "big city," he crosses the border as a reluctant exile. Perhaps Constant, himself Swiss by birth and a native of Lausanne, intended an indirect portrait of sober, conservative Switzerland in the paternal site of bourgeois propriety and prosperity.

Caden. Little Bohemian town, in what is now the Czech Republic, where Adolphe and Ellenore take refuge for a year after crossing the border from Germany, then depart for Poland. While living in this apparent backwater, Adolphe chafes at Ellenore's dependence on him, while Ellenore sacrifices a fortune from Monsieur de P—— by refusing to leave Adolphe.

*Poland. Ellenore's homeland, from which her father was exiled to Russia while her mother, accompanied by the three-year-old Ellenore, sought refuge in France. By the time Adolphe accompanies Ellenore to Poland, where she is to inherit her father's estate near Warsaw, their affair is doomed. In the chapters set in Poland, Constant includes more description of place than in the rest of the novel. These details function symbolically, as, for example, when Adolphe restlessly wanders all night in the "greyish countryside" surrounding the estate or when Ellenore resigns herself to his departure, and subsequently dies, in a frozen winter landscape.

— *Margaret Bozenna Goscilo*

THE ADVENTURES OF AUGIE MARCH

Author: Saul Bellow (1915-   )
Type of work: Novel
Type of plot: Picaresque

Time of plot: 1920-1950
First published: 1953

This picaresque novel takes its hero as far as Mexico and France, but the city of Chicago is the central place throughout; Chicago is intricately connected to both its main character and its major themes. The city sprawls across the pages in a manner that reflects Saul Bellow's fresh, urbane, rollicking, erudite, streetwise style. The book explores every corner of the city, from the upscale Lakefront to the depths of Hell's Kitchen, the sections teeming with opulence, despondency, boredom, duplicity, and violence, united by the common quest of the human heart, embodied most dramatically in Augie March, a desire for place and purpose.

*Chicago. Growing midwestern metropolis whose diversity and harshness in the post-Depression era create opportunities and conflicts at every corner. The novel alludes to the city's ethnic diversity but pays greater attention to its economic diversity and variety of locales. Augie's coming-of-age is shaped by place as he brims with hope and imagined possibilities yet struggles against economic realities, competing ideas and desires, the manipulations of friends and strangers, and freedom of choice in an economic downturn. Chicago offers Augie philosophers, hucksters, con men, shrewd businessmen, thieves, fallen aristocrats, and new-monied didacts who influence his understanding and direction.

The novel offers a smorgasbord, more than a melting pot, of human habitation and business: the free eyeglass dispensary on Harrison Street, a greasy spoon restaurant on Belmont Avenue frequented by truckers, conductors, and scrubwomen, Dearborn's unemployed musicians, South Side slums, the stockyards, the coal yards, leather-goods shops on Lincoln Street, Crane College, the penthouses and lavish hotels of Benton Harbor, and the millionaire suburbs of Highland Park, Kenilworth, and Winnetka.

Bellow's Chicago renders the harsh, unfair disparity of wealth in twentieth century America, the unpredictable opportunity and promiscuity of a struggling free market economy, the temptations of criminal behavior in a discriminating yet widely unregulated society. Augie's adventures reveal the variety of possibilities in metropolitan America as he bounces from job to job, while simultaneously depicting the existential angst of living in such freedom where boredom is pervasive and, according to this novel, the source of modern evil. Augie's period as a petty thief is motivated by both his family's lack of money and his own lack of professional direction. Yet when he meets the affluent Renlings, who seek informally to adopt and support him, his desire for experience and understanding is not satiated, even though his basic necessities are met, and he leaves the city. Through both Augie and Chicago, Bellow shows that the glory, misery, and disparity of place are products of the restlessness of vibrant, sympathetic, yet unresolved people.

The Irish author James Joyce once observed that one could rebuild the city of Dublin from the pages of his novel *Ulysses* (1922). One could say the same about Chicago and *The Adventures of Augie March.*

March home. Impoverished Chicago home in which Augie grows up in a family that relies on benefits from "charities." The family also draws support from Grandma Lausch, a boarder who is the widow of a Russian busi-nessman and not Augie's true grandmother. Here, Bellow reveals the struggle to survive and maintain dignity in difficult economic conditions. The necessity of human relationships and, at the same time, the development of individual initiative are demonstrated in Augie's childhood home, a place poor in material comforts but resonant with survival instincts, an appreciation for intellectual life, and a sense of a lost aristocratic past conveyed through the presence of Grandma Lausch.

Einhorn's poolroom. Public tavern in which Augie works as an assistant and encounters a wide variety of Chicago characters, including the owner, William Einhorn, a paraplegic who is a successful and diverse entrepreneur, a streetwise trader, and a lay philosopher. Serving as a crossroads of human traffic, the poolroom brings Augie into contact with the wide range of possibilities that exist for him, and the type of American Renaissance man he will aspire to be in the figure of Einhorn.

*Buffalo. Upstate New York city to which Augie flees after having to leave Chicago when a scheme in which he participates with Joe Gorman to smuggle immigrants in from Canada fails. Buffalo is Augie's first venture out of Chicago.

*Acatla. Mexican town about one hundred miles southeast of Mexico City to which Augie goes with his occasional mistress, Thea Fenchel, who wants to divorce her husband in order to be with Augie. Thea wants Augie to train an eagle to capture giant iguanas at her home in Acatla. The town and the eagle symbolize the exotic freedom of the world outside Chicago, but the eagle's inability to defend itself against the iguanas it attacks and to live freely demonstrates the difficulty of survival even in a place of beauty. Despite the romance of living in a house with beautiful red tiles, patios, fountains, and oxhide chairs, Augie severs his relationship with Thea in order to assist Stella Chesney to escape from an abusive man. Beauty, struggle, and survival are intrinsically connected in Acatla, a place where Augie's adventure transforms him from a wishful young man to an experienced man of insight.

Lifeboat. Boat on which Augie is adrift at sea after a German submarine sinks the merchant marine ship *Sam McManus* on which he is serving during World War II. His only companion is a man named Bateshaw, who wants to go to the Canary Islands, where he can be interned and do research for the rest of the war. Bateshaw is a mad genius who articulates Augie's developing understanding of the pervasive nature of boredom as a cause of modern illness. As a castaway at sea, unsure of his location, Augie exemplifies the nature of the human predicament.

*Paris.** City in which Augie's restlessness finally abates. There, married to Stella, he finds a sense of internal peace selling army surplus goods after recognizing that other restless thinkers, such as the French philosopher Jean Jacques Rousseau, discovered their true na-

tures and deepest wisdom only when they developed a sense of home. While admitting that he and Stella may continue to roam, Augie is no longer searching for a single answer to his desire, finding peace in marriage and work that allows him to survive, living in a city that is both historic and contemporary. The elements of the new, burgeoning America and the old culture of Europe present in his childhood home are unified finally in Paris, where Augie, first and always a Chicagoan and an American, finds a home.

— *Mark Walling*

ADVENTURES OF HUCKLEBERRY FINN

Author: Mark Twain (Samuel Langhorne Clemens; 1835-1910)
Type of work: Novel

Type of plot: Social satire
Time of plot: Early to mid-nineteenth century
First published: 1884 (1885; United States)

Like The Adventures of Tom Sawyer *(1876), to which it is a sequel, this novel opens in the fictional Mississippi River village of St. Petersburg. However, its action soon shifts to Huck and Jim's long raft trip down the river— one of the most notable in a long line of literary voyages. Along their way, they repeatedly encounter symbols distinguishing the free North from the slave South and the movement and purity of the river from the stagnation and decadence of the shore. Although the novel's broad geographical setting is real, every place—apart from the river itself—in which action takes place is fictional, typically a composite of real places that Mark Twain personally knew.*

*Mississippi River.** The novel's primary backdrop, the Lower Mississippi is the motive force that drives both the raft and the narrative. Most of the novel's action actually takes place ashore, but no character ever strays far inland, and the river's presence always looms. Rich in symbolism, the river washes away sin (such as bawdy houses and murderers), bestows wealth (including bountiful fish and valuable flotsam), and wreaks destruction (destroying both steamboats and towns), all the while inexorably carrying everything upon it ever deeper into the South and its harsh plantation slavery— exactly where Huck and Jim do not want to go. They allow the river to carry them south because they lack the means to navigate *up*river and because forces beyond their control repeatedly prevent them from obtaining such means.

Twain was intimately acquainted with the river. He spent his childhood on its banks and as a young man piloted steamboats between St. Louis and New Orleans. *Adventures of Huckleberry Finn* does a masterful job of conveying the river's beauty and terrible majesty through the eyes of its ingenuous narrator, Huck.

St. Petersburg. Sleepy riverfront Missouri village in which Huck lives with the Widow Douglas and her sister when the novel opens. It is modeled on Twain's boyhood home of Hannibal, Missouri. The village and the widow's proper home represent decency and the forces of civilization, against which Huck rebels. After his alcoholic father kidnaps him and takes him upstream to a crude hut on the Illinois shore, Huck initially feels liberated. However, after his father repeatedly abuses him, Huck runs off on his own. He never expresses an interest in returning to St. Petersburg. Indeed, the novel ends with him expressing a wish "to light out for the Territory"—presumably an allusion to the untamed West.

Jackson's Island. Mississippi River island below St. Petersburg to which Huck flees on a canoe after faking his own murder. There he finds Jim, a slave running away from St. Petersburg because he fears he is about to be sold "down the river"—every Missouri slave's worst nightmare. The island is easy swimming distance from the free state of Illinois, but that state offers no refuge to Jim because fugitive slave laws make its western shores the dangerous hunting ground of slave catchers. Huck and Jim remain on the island until the prospect of imminent discovery spurs them to load their things on a raft and flee downriver.

Raft. Flat craft on which Huck and Jim float down the river. After a brief idyll on the island, Jim and Huck learn that slave catchers are coming and flee together on a lumber raft with a pine-plank deck about fifteen feet long and twelve feet wide that they have salvaged from flotsam delivered by the rising river. Their primary home through most of the remaining narrative, the raft represents their most reliable sanctuary from the evils of the shore and thus symbolizes the freedom they both seek. Huck's descriptions of life on the raft contain several idyllic masterpieces.

****Cairo** (kay-ROH). Town at Illinois's southern tip where Huck and Jim intend to land, sell their raft, and buy steamboat passage up the Ohio River into free territory. In a critical juncture in the narrative, however, they drift past Cairo in the fog. The Mississippi continues carrying them ever deeper into slave territory and thwarts every plan they make to return upstream.

****Ohio River.** Major tributary of the Mississippi River, which it joins below Cairo. As the major physical barrier separating northern "free" states from southern "slave" states, the Ohio represented a threshold of freedom to African Americans and was thus an appropriate choice as Huck and Jim's primary destination. Although Huck and Jim never actually see the river, the distinct clear-water channel that its water creates in the muddy Mississippi alerts Huck to the fact that he and Jim have drifted past Cairo. A detailed and colorful explanation of the differences between the waters of the Ohio and the Mississippi Rivers is a crucial part of the novel's so-called "raft chapter," which has been omitted from most editions of *Adventures of Huckleberry Finn* because Mark Twain used it earlier in *Life on the Mississippi* (1883).

Grangerford home. Prosperous plantation apparently located on the Kentucky side of the river. After their raft is smashed by a steamboat, Huck is separated from Jim and taken in by the prosperous Grangerford family, whose home represents the thin veneer of southern civilization. It offers everything Huck wants in life, but after all the Grangerford men are killed in a senseless feud that unmasks southern degeneracy, he returns to the river with Jim, who has repaired the raft while hiding nearby.

****Pike County.** Real Missouri county, about fifteen miles south of Hannibal, from which Huck claims to come when he meets the King and Duke, scoundrels who board the raft and take control, again making it impossible for Huck and Jim to return upriver. The county was notorious as the birthplace of worthless frontier characters before the Civil War and is thus another symbol of the South's decadence.

Bricksville. Arkansas town in which Huck witnesses still more depravity: a shooting, a would-be lynch mob, and the King and Duke's lurid stage show, the Royal Nonesuch. "Bricksville" is ironically named, as its streets are all mud, and its houses are rotting wood-frame structures gradually sliding into the river.

Pikesville. Shabby Arkansas village that is the raft's last stop. Jim becomes a prisoner on the nearby farm of Tom Sawyer's Uncle Silas and Aunt Sally Phelps. In a wholesale departure from the tone and movement of the narrative, Huck and Tom spend the novel's last chapters in a farcical plot to free Jim. Afterward, Huck rebels against Aunt Sally's plan to adopt and "sivilize" him and proposes "to light out for the Territory"—presumably the vast Indian territory west of Arkansas and Missouri.

— *R. Kent Rasmussen*

THE ADVENTURES OF PEREGRINE PICKLE

Author: Tobias Smollett (1721-1771)
Type of work: Novel
Type of plot: Picaresque
Time of plot: Early eighteenth century

First published: The Adventures of Peregrine Pickle, in Which Are Included Memories of a Lady of Quality, 1751

Although Tobias Smollett's title character visits many places and sees many things, Smollett uses the traditional picaresque framework primarily to satirize the manners and conventions of his day, not to examine the places his rogue hero, Peregrine, passes through. Peregrine is an impetuous, but kindhearted, youth who blusters his way through adventures, always taking life on his own terms. Hence, his changing environments do not reflect or inform him; they are but something for him to conquer.

*England. Peregrine's home and the scene of many of his adventures. Most members of the genteel society in which Peregrine prefers to move, spend the great majority of their time in London and at various country estates, entertaining and visiting friends. Smollett's setting is England before the Industrial Revolution. For Peregrine, the great metropolis of London does not significantly differ from the rural counties, with lovers and scoundrels to be found in both places, and ruination or advancement equally likely to happen in either.

Very much a writer of his time, Smollett is unlike the Romantics of a later generation in that he does not use location as an organic or emotional backdrop for his characters and their actions. The landscape is a knowable quantity, as it had been for centuries. Thus when Peregrine visits London the first time, he is not overwhelmed by new sensations. New places merely represent new opportunities—usually for mischief.

*Continental Europe. The grand tour of Europe was requisite for all gentlemen of fashion. Peregrine is sent on a journey through France and the Low Countries (future Belgium and Holland) with the idea of improving his education and exposing himself to the niceties of French society. Being a spirited young man, however, he tends to devote his energy to wooing women, getting in fights, playing pranks on his companions, and avoiding the law. He dutifully sees the various tourist sights of the day, usually at the instigation of his tutor or a local person, but he is far more interested in the people he meets, as Smollett's aim is to critique society's follies, not to write a travelogue. Though some peculiarities of nationality are observed, the people Peregrine encounters in Europe do not differ greatly from those he meets in England.

Commodore's Garrison. Home of Peregrine's salty old sea-captain uncle, Commodore Hawser Trunnion, who adopts Peregrine after the latter's parents disown him. The commodore has outfitted his home like a ship. He and his mates, Lieutenant Hatch and Tom Pipes, sleep in hammocks, fire cannons from the roof, and generally carry on as though they are aboard a ship at sea. Built like a fortress, the garrison becomes a loving home for Peregrine and, in the commodore's parlance, a "safe harbor" to which he can always return.

When Peregrine and his entourage arrive back from the Continent, they are welcomed at the garrison like conquering heroes. Guns are fired, torches are lit, and a giant keg of beer is tapped. It is a warm, festive atmosphere indicative of the love the commodore has for the young man. After the cruelty Peregrine has been shown by his own parents and a sometimes hostile world, the garrison is a sorely needed refuge.

*Bath. Fashionable English resort and spa town. Bath was one of the favorite "in" spots of the *beau monde* (upper class) in Georgian England. Peregrine and his friend Godfrey conquer the town soon after their arrival. They outwit a band of con men at billiards, humiliate a notorious bully, and win the hearts (and favors) of many women. Although Peregrine emerges a local gentleman of some fame, it is a dubious distinction, as Bath society itself is exposed for all its chicanery, vanity, and hypocrisy. It is a world in which Peregrine's showy brilliance can triumph but ultimately not a place in which substantiality and human goodness are prized.

*Fleet Street Prison.** Large citylike jail in London. A victim of bad judgment and duplicitous schemers, Peregrine at last finds himself behind bars. The Fleet is really more like a small village with gates. Prisoners can go to a coffeehouse, receive visitors, and buy their own necessities. It is actually a microcosm of the world outside. But here, Peregrine is made acquainted with some truly noble human beings who have been reduced to their present condition by the wicked ways of the supposedly virtuous society outside the walls. He finally realizes that the *beau monde* is fickle and deceitful and chooses to snub them when his fortune and good name are finally returned.

— *John Slocum*

THE ADVENTURES OF RODERICK RANDOM

Author: Tobias Smollett (1721-1771)
Type of work: Novel
Type of plot: Picaresque

Time of plot: Eighteenth century
First published: 1748

Roderick Random's travels cover Scotland, England, the Caribbean, France, Germany, the coast of Africa, South America, and Scotland again. There is usually little physical description of place, except when it is necessary to be explicit, such as with the British attack on Cartagena. Nevertheless, the places Roderick visits, if only briefly, are called to the mind of the reader by the people and the events that occur there.

*Scotland.** Roderick's Scottish home is sketchily described, but, as his grandfather is a landowner, the house and estate must be somewhat grand and extensive. After Roderick is driven out by the malice of his relatives, that home becomes a kind of lost and found Eden, for, as an adult, he will return to it, rich, happily married, and reunited with his lost father.

*London.** Capital of Great Britain and leading city of England where Roderick's first visit becomes a descent into a kind of slapstick hell. For though the novel's tone is comic, Tobias Smollett nevertheless emphasizes the poverty, degradation, physical dirtiness, and viciousness of the city. It is a dark place, physically as well as morally unlit, with narrow, dangerous streets. It is no surprise that many of Roderick's mishaps take place at night. Smollett, perhaps unintentionally, makes a savage indictment of the abuses of the class structure. However, Roderick, although a critic, is not a revolutionary. London's lower classes are usually presented not merely as victims but also as violent and evil in themselves; they are quite willing to steal from, cheat, and physically attack other poor people. Roderick, resentful of being treated like a member of the lower class, insists upon his status as a gentleman, while he has no shame in using and mistreating his schoolmate Hugh Strap.

Roderick's later adventures in London introduce him to yet other examples of social degradation and discrimination: For instance, Marshalsea prison, where Roderick is imprisoned for debt, is also not well described. Once more, however, there is a sense of darkness, and the lives of its inmates, especially the poor, are concretely conjured. At the same time, if a prisoner has access to money, he can have a private room and his own food. Roderick does visit coffeehouses, where he meets men of the middle class but no women, for women are excluded. Here London seems more cheerful but no less cruel.

*Bath.** Resort city in western England. This is the Bath of ballrooms and gamerooms, where rich nobles and pretenders come. Almost all the action takes place in the ballrooms, crowded, noisy, implicitly sweaty, where people come to see and to be seen. The emphasis is on the sheer vulgarity of the place.

Ships. Vessels on which a good deal of the novel's action occurs. Their divisions; the exalted place and power of the officers; the dark, crowded, filthy, and stinking quarters of the crew; the bad food and water are all images of the general society. However, the slaving voyage, from which Roderick gains a good deal of money, is barely sketched, with no description of the enslaved Africans nor of their treatment. Perhaps Smollett really knew little of such voyages, and the voyage is a mere plot device. However, the moral implications are hidden by the thinness of the narrative.

Cartagena. Caribbean port city of the South American nation of Colombia whose defenses are sufficiently well described to enable readers to follow the attacks, victories, and defeats. There are forts, redoubts, trenches, cannon, and the English commanders know absolutely nothing of what to do.

— *L. L. Lee*

THE ADVENTURES OF TOM SAWYER

Author: Mark Twain (Samuel Langhorne Clemens; 1835-1910)
Type of work: Novel

Type of plot: Adventure
Time of plot: Early to mid-nineteenth century
First published: 1876

More than perhaps any other work by Mark Twain, this novel is suffused with a sense of place. It so vividly depicts a fictional Mississippi Valley village as a microcosm of mid-nineteenth century life at the edge of the Western frontier that Tom Sawyer's village has become an icon of small-town American life, just as Tom himself has become an icon of carefree boyhood.

St. Petersburg. Fictional Missouri village on the west bank of the Mississippi River in and around which the entire novel is set. The village is modeled on the real, and somewhat larger, Hannibal, Missouri, in which Twain himself lived as a boy. Like Hannibal, it has a wooded promontory on its north side and a huge limestone cave to its south. Tom Sawyer lives near its center in a two-story house that closely resembles Twain's own home of the 1840's. However, the fictional St. Petersburg also has elements of the tiny inland village of Florida, Missouri, where Twain was born and spent most of his summers while growing up, and thus evokes an even more rustic flavor than a real riverfront village might have had.

Seen through Tom's eyes, St. Petersburg is a world in itself, an epitome of positive nineteenth century small-town American values that offers almost everything that a boy coming of age could want: rugged sports, Fourth of July picnics, itinerant entertainers, romance, imaginary adventures, and even genuine life-and-death adventures. A mostly sunny place, St. Petersburg reflects Twain's cheerful nostalgia for his childhood haunts, which he regarded as a "paradise" for boys—hence the name "St. Petersburg," after the gatekeeper to Heaven. Although it appears generally safer and more comfortable than its historical counterpart, it also has an ominous dark side, symbolized by the lurking presence of the murderous Injun Joe, a haunted house, the danger of drowning in the river, and recurrent epidemics. A striking false note in the St. Petersburg of *Tom Sawyer*, however, is the near invisibility of African American slavery, which was a brutal fact of everyday life in both Twain's Hannibal and the St. Petersburg of *Adventures of Huckleberry Finn* (1884), *Tom Sawyer*'s sequel.

Missouri. State in which St. Petersburg appears to be located. A frontier state at the time of Twain's youth, Missouri represents a remote western outpost of American civilization in *Tom Sawyer*. Tom reads enough to be aware of the outside world, but the Missouri in which he lives is so remote from the rest of the United States that a senator who visits his village is looked upon as something akin to a god.

Mississippi River. North America's mightiest river, the Mississippi plays a less important role in *Tom Sawyer* than it does in *Huckleberry Finn*, but its presence is nonetheless felt throughout. It represents a possible avenue of escape to the outside world—as when Tom and his friends take a raft to the river's **Jackson's Island** to become pirates—and a force that swallows up drowning victims.

Cardiff Hill. Promontory on the north side of St. Petersburg modeled closely on Hannibal's real Holliday's Hill (now usually called "Cardiff" itself), which rises three hundred feet above the river. Described as a faraway and "Delectable Land, dreamy, reposeful and inviting," it is the place to which Tom usually flees to evade responsibility by playing make-believe games. However, it is also the site of the haunted house and is a place menaced by Injun Joe—both reminders that perhaps no place in St. Petersburg is completely safe.

McDougal's Cave. Limestone cavern several miles south of St. Petersburg modeled on a huge cave that Twain explored as a youth. The fictional cave is even larger and provides an apt setting for the novel's dramatic climax, in which Tom and Becky Thatcher get lost in the pitch-black cave. After a terrifying near-encounter with Injun Joe—who uses the cave as a hideout—Tom faces an apparently hopeless situation. However, he performs his greatest act of heroism by leading Becky to safety, and his emergence from the cave symbolizes his final coming of age.

— *R. Kent Rasmussen*

AENEID

Author: Vergil (Publius Vergilius Maro, 70-19 B.C.E.)
Type of work: Poetry
Type of plot: Epic

Time of plot: After the Trojan War
First transcribed: c. 29-19 B.C.E. (English translation, 1553)

As Imperial Rome's national epic, this poem links the origins of Augustus's city to a glorious mythic past characterized by the rise and fall of city-states, many of which had been incorporated into the early empire.

*Troy. Site of the Trojan War, located in Turkey, in northwestern Asia Minor. Homer sets the *Iliad* (c. 800 B.C.E.; English translation, 1616), the Greek epic that directly influenced the *Aeneid*, in the last days before the city's defeat at the hands of the Greek forces. Vergil chooses to have Aeneas describe Troy's destruction through the ruse of the Trojan horse. This element establishes an ethnic connection between the Trojans, who fled the dying city to establish what Vergil calls a "New Troy" in Italy, and the Romans. Southern Italy was called *Magna Graecia* by the Romans because of its extensive Greek colonization, and Vergil establishes the Roman race as comprising other groups, including Greeks, Anatolians, Etruscans, and native Latin peoples. Connecting Augustus's Rome to Troy thus establishes what the emperor most desired for his city: a noble antiquity that could account for Imperial Rome's preeminence.

*Carthage. Ancient North African city in what is now Tunisia. The same storm that sends Homer's Odysseus and his crew to Circe's island also strikes Aeneas and the Trojans, who successfully escape from burning Troy. The storm, recorded in the *Aeneid*, brings the Trojans to Carthage, a city particularly noteworthy in Roman history. Located in Tunisia, Carthage was, in Vergil's time, in the Roman province known as Numidia Proconsularis. Vergil emphasizes the longstanding connections between Rome and Carthage. For Aeneas, Carthage is where he is granted the chance to rest and recuperate by two goddesses, themselves enemies: Juno, who wishes to delay the founding of a new Troy, and Venus, Aeneas's mother, who wants some respite for her hero son. The casualty of this episode is Dido, Carthage's brave, widowed queen, who has founded Carthage after the overthrow of Tyre, in Phoenicia, and the murder of her husband Sychaeus. The divinely contrived love affair between Dido and Aeneas results in the queen's suicide and her curse, which results in the three Punic Wars between Rome and Carthage. Vergil has Jupiter specifically refer to Hannibal's invasion of Italy in the *Aeneid*. By doing so, he continues to provide plausible mythic links to Roman history through indisputably real sites, which would have been known to readers of his time.

Cumae. Ancient site of Apollo's temple and of the Sybil, its priestess. The town is located near Pozzuoli just north of Naples. The soft tufaceous rock and its seismically active topography made this site appear to be a point of access to the realm of the dead. Indeed, in the *Aeneid* it is Apollo's Sybil who guides Aeneas to the underworld to consult the shade of his mortal father Anchises on what fate holds in store for the Trojan people. Anchises warns his son that he will have to fight what is in effect a second Trojan War, this one in Italy, to marry the princess Lavinia and establish Lavinium.

The temple of Apollo described by Vergil would have been familiar to Imperial Roman visitors to Cumae. Here again he ties Roman prehistory to a place that would have been familiar to Romans of his time. By the time of Augustus, Cumae was more a resort than a place of pilgrimage, another of the sulfur-bath towns frequented by wealthy Romans. However, the shrine and the sibylline priesthood continued to be maintained until the early Christian church decreed destruction of the Sibylline Books. Augustus used many of the caves that dotted the Bay of Naples as storage facilities for his legions.

Latium. Roughly equivalent to the region of Lazio, the region of Italy that includes the city of Rome. Latium in the *Aeneid* also incorporates Lavinium, the city of King Latinus, father of Lavinia, the future bride of Aeneas. Lavinium thus becomes the site of a second Trojan War for a second contested bride. In 1975 archaeologists determined that the modern Prattica di Mare, a small farming community south of Rome, contains the citadel of Lavinium. They have unearthed thirteen ancient altars used for farm offerings as well as several late Mycenaean grave sites, one given the appellation "Grave of Aeneas" based on a problematic inscription.

Pallanteum. Vergil's name for the Etruscan settlement on the Palatine Hill at the future site of Rome. Aeneas tours this site with King Evander, his new ally in the battle to overcome the native Latin tribes living near Rome. All the details of topography that would have been familiar to Imperial Romans are present in Vergil's description. There was, in fact, an Etruscan settlement on the site of Rome.

— *Robert J. Forman*

AESOP'S FABLES

Author: Aesop (c. 620-c. 560 B.C.E.)
Type of work: Short fiction
Type of plot: Fable

Time of plot: Antiquity
First collected: Aesopea, fourth century B.C.E. (English translation, 1484)

Although these stories were originally composed by the ancient Greek fabulist Aesop, they contain few clear evidences of the time and place in which they originated. Instead, they have a universal and timeless appeal that makes their moral lessons equally relevant in almost any time or place.

Earthly settings. Tales in *Aesop's Fables* rely on diverse settings to frame the ethical conflicts that lead to the point of each fable—a moral lesson illustrated by the actions and comments of both humans and animals with humanlike qualities. Specific geographical references are sparse, but some tales contain allusions to places, such as a tale concerning an Arab and a camel, a tale set in the fields near Rome, a tale about a man in the East, and one involving a vat of blue dye that could only be made in the East. Allusions such as these were familiar to audiences of antiquity, as well as to those of the era when the tales were first translated into English. Setting the fables among images evoking predictable responses made them more likely to achieve their goal of moral instruction.

Reflecting and reinforcing the moral consequences of good and evil actions, dualities frame more than one fable and can be found both in place and title, including town and country, sky and moon, and wind and sun. Familiar and timeless, these elements too, and the animals and human characters who speak from them, are comfortable constructs for the preservation and communication of social values. The pairing of dichotomies echoes the moral choices faced by characters in the fables and simplifies most life choices to an either/or dilemma, a comfortable logic for children's tales. Important too, as is reflected in these settings, is the suspension of disbelief that fables, by their nature, require. Rooted in superstition and early pagan and mythical belief systems, speech among animals and elements of the sky is presented as a naturally occurring event in the times and places where the tales are set.

Celestial and exotic settings. At least one fable betrays its Greek classical origins because it is set in Olympus, the mythical land of the gods. Some of the other more exotic settings involve encounters with lions, leopards, apes, and monkeys. While these are not the most common scenes, these atypical frameworks provide a vivid contrast to the scenes of domestic drudgery and serve to reinforce the notion that lessons may be learned from animals of all sorts. In addition, although these junglelike settings may not have been part of the everyday life of ordinary people during the time of the English translation, in that period, as well as in the period of antiquity from which these tales originate, lions and leopards and the like would have inspired awe among the stories' largely untravelled listeners.

Domestic settings. To appeal to audiences of largely uneducated children and adults, most of the fables take place in simple domestic settings drawn from the everyday lives of ancient agrarian people. Such settings include the tiled roof of a house, a butcher's shop, a well, a rim of a pot of jam, a jar containing nuts and figs, a manger, a farmyard, a straw yard, a heath, a cornfield, a meadow, and the outskirts of a village. This use of common, familiar images creates homelike settings that would appeal to peasant farmer families, who for centuries constituted the bulk of the fables' audiences. The domestic world is, after all, where people make many of their ethical choices. Thus, it is a practical matter to set most of the lessons in that timeless environment.

References to time appear in several fables, but they are as general as most of the settings, expressed in phrases such as "many years ago," "before your great-great grandparents were born," and "in days of old." Such phrasings resemble those of oral tradition in conveying a sense of universality of experience that includes and involves the audience in the tales and permits a broad identification of the setting in time. The individual fables are brief; to suit their audiences and to stress their moral points, they tended to compress time.

Hazardous settings. Perils of travel in ancient and medieval times are typically reflected in settings such as forests, thick woods, and high roads. Harsh weather also occasionally provides a challenging element to both domestic and travel tales. One fable, for example, is set amid a severe winter, another is set on a farm in a cold part of the world, while still another tale occurs on a hot day in June. Realistic and frightening natural events, such as powerful winds or rain, snowstorms, and particularly dark nights, represent the sort of conditions that might have created tension and suspense in the lives of early peoples, and which served, no doubt, to add excitement to the tales.

— *Kathleen M. Bartlett*

THE AFFECTED YOUNG LADIES

Author: Molière (Jean-Baptiste Poquelin, 1622-1673)
Type of work: Drama
Type of plot: Comedy of manners

Time of plot: Seventeenth century
First performed: 1659; first published, 1660 as *Les Précieuses ridicules* (English translation, 1732)

Molière set this one-act farce in Paris, which under the reign of Louis XIV was the center of fashion for the whole of Europe and was continually spawning bizarre innovations in clothing, speech, and manners. "Preciosity" was at it its height in Paris when the play was first produced in 1659. It was almost inevitable that the action should take place within the home of a wealthy bourgeois family—Molière's favorite target of ridicule. The two "country girls" had to be newcomers to Paris in order to be duped by a couple of servants disguised as noblemen.

***Paris.** Capital of France and fashion capital of Western Europe. To pinpoint the place represented in his play, Molière deliberately wrote the name of Paris into his dialogue many times. For example, when Mascarille asks several young ladies what they think of Paris, one of them replies that Paris is the "great bureau of marvels, the center of good taste, wit, and gallantry." It is the sophisticated manners of the great city at the zenith of France's *ancien régime* that are satirized as much as the naïve young women who are victims of a practical joke.

Stage settings in Molière's plays were always minimalistic, partly because he never knew where his plays would be performed. Often the plays were taken from town to town over muddy roads and performed in tennis courts, in private homes, or even outdoors. The primitive travel conditions made it impossible to transport elaborate scenery and furniture. In *The Affected Young Ladies* the stage is so barren that characters must call for chairs to be brought for their visitors. However, the elaborate gowns worn by the young ladies and the extravagant costumes worn by the Marquis de Mascarille and Viscount Jodelet would establish that the scene represented was a mansion in the capital city.

It was important to Molière to make it clear to audiences that his comedy was taking place in a specific location, a city where fantastic fashions appeared and disappeared with remarkable swiftness. His provincial young ladies are made ridiculous because their affectations have been superseded by new affectations which can only be learned at court.

— *Bill Delaney*

AGAINST THE GRAIN

Author: Joris-Karl Huysmans (1848-1907)
Type of work: Novel
Type of plot: Character study

Time of plot: Late nineteenth century
First published: À rebours, 1884 (English translation, 1922)

When Jean Des Esseintes begins his attempt to create the perfect lifestyle, he selects a house that will avoid the extremes he has already experienced: the quiet setting of his family's country house and the metropolitan turmoil of Paris. Physically, the house embodies the irreconcilable paradox of his contrasting desires—to live in splendid isolation while maintaining the best possible connection to human society.

Fontenay-aux-Roses (fahn-teh-NAY-oh-rohz). French town in which Des Esseintes takes up residence. The suburban house he selects seems at first to be a sensible compromise between the Château de Lourps in the Seine Valley and the clamorous crowds of central Paris. The stifling ennui generated by the provinciality of his family estate encourages him to the opposite extreme in Paris, where he takes great delight in furnishing his apartments in the most bizarre fashion imaginable. His desire is to create a retreat that will be both calm and curious.

Surrendering the second floor of the house to his servants, Des Esseintes decorates the walls and ceiling of the study in imitation of the bindings of his books, using coarse-grained morocco leather instead of wallpaper. Orange is the principal color, with blue-tinted windows curtained in dark red-gold. His dining room, separated by a padded corridor, becomes a smaller enclosure contained within the one designed by the house's architect. It is timbered so as to resemble a ship's cabin, with a window like a porthole looking out toward an aquarium stocked with mechanical fish.

In order to provide a suitable contrast to the violet and yellow tints of an Oriental rug, Des Esseintes adds to the decor of his study a large tortoise, the shell of which is glazed in gold and embellished with gems. The paintings he acquires for his study include Gustave Moreau's two famous depictions of Salome, while his bedroom houses an El Greco, and his dressing room is decorated with ebony-framed engravings by Jan Luyken and works by Francisco de Goya and Odilon Redon. When the time comes to liven up his abode with flowers he selects carnivorous plants. As a backdrop for his hallucinatory nightmares, he purchases a black marble sphinx and a multicolored earthenware chimera.

The purpose of this environment—an archetypal expression of decadence—is not so much to reflect Des Esseintes's flagrantly contradictory personality as to facilitate his research into the possibility of escape into a world of imagination. In violating all the customary norms of decorative taste and deploying the work of the most extreme artistic outsiders, Des Esseintes contrives to make the house into a kind of porthole through which the possibility of a gloriously perverse and wholly artificial existence is briefly glimpsed.

Bodega. London pub that Des Esseintes imagines visiting when he is seized by a desire to experience the England of Charles Dickens's novels. He takes a train into Paris on a rainy day and imagines that the Seine River is the Thames. After buying a travel guide to London, he descends into a drinking establishment where English patrons are known to gather and transports himself, by the power of fantasy, into a world that is reminiscent of Dickens and Edgar Allan Poe. However, the relief his fantasy provides is brief, and he is glad to return to his books. Even more than the house, this establishment is symbolic of the borderline between fact and fantasy, where actual locations become magic casements overlooking the enticing but unreachable landscapes of the imagination.

— *Brian Stableford*

THE AGE OF INNOCENCE

Author: Edith Wharton (1862-1937)
Type of work: Novel
Type of plot: Social realism

Time of plot: Late nineteenth century
First published: 1920

The setting of this novel is the city of New York as it was when ruled by members of the wealthy upper class. Comprising the prosperous descendants of the original English and Dutch settlers, this society governed New York from the American Revolution through World War I. This was the world in which Edith Wharton herself was raised, and her great subject in almost all her work was this once-powerful society whose rigid rules concerning food, dress, manners, and morals both shaped and thwarted Wharton's own life.

***New York City.** The novel's city is the "Old New York" of the second half of the nineteenth century, comprising affluent old families who descended from earlier settlers and revolutionaries. Presided over by well-off bankers, lawyers, businessman, and their fashionable wives, this community was situated in lower Manhattan, in areas such as Lafayette Street or Washington Square, rarely venturing north of Thirty-fourth Street. The social lives of these Old New Yorkers was governed by church-going, dinner parties and balls in individual homes, and ritual attendance at the Academy of Music, a luxurious opera house on Fourteenth Street. Children were reared to a strict standard of manners and morals, which allowed for little independence or originality. Although narrow-minded and exclusive, this society lived well, with the women attired in impeccable dresses, jewels, and elaborate hairstyles, and the men exuding an aura of affluence and entitlement. Fearful of innovation or change, this dignified society was engaged in forestalling the future and secured their power by encouraging conservative views and marriages only within their established social set. This "Old New York" background is a deep subject in this novel; the power of this particular place is overwhelming, and individuals are often defeated in their efforts to overcome its influence on their personal lives and choices. At the end of the novel, however, after World War I, it is clear that Old New York has lost its power and prestige. What had seemed inalterable before the war is now subject to tremendous change. Even before the war, individual characters in Wharton's novel undergo an awakening in which they realize they have allowed their lives to be shaped by outdated and arbitrary conventions.

Newland Archer's home. Much of the story in this novel takes place in a number of different private residences, but it is at the home of Newland Archer and his new bride May that the power of Old New York exerts itself most triumphantly. Newland's house is the site of the farewell party for May's rival, the expatriate Old New Yorker now known as the Countess Ellen Olenksa. The lavish dinner May has arranged is one in which all the glittering movers and shakers of Old New York seem to surround Newland like guardians to ensure he will not defy convention for the sake of the woman who is the great love of his life.

Mrs. Manson Mingott's house. While most of the homes in Old New York replicate Archer's, one exception is the house of the obese Mrs. Manson Mingott, who lives quite unfashionably in the open fields of Central Park. This house is a little enclave of free-spiritedness that acts as a bracing antidote to the otherwise stifling respectability of Old New York.

Ellen Olenska's house in New York. Home of the Countess Ellen Olenska on an unfashionable part of West Twenty-third Street and is another outpost that resists the rigid decorum of Old New York.

*Newport. Affluent Rhode Island port town in which vacationing Old New Yorkers maintain well-appointed summer homes. It is here that Archer is once again frustrated in his attempt to establish a close relationship with Ellen.

Ellen Olenska's home in Paris. Situated on an avenue near Invalides, this apartment is where Archer comes at the end of the novel, when he is a widower past middle age. Although the passage of time and the fact that he is in Paris have freed him from the rules and restrictions of Old New York, Newland still struggles with a variety of inner restraints and fails to call on Ellen, instead gazing up at her window from a bench below until night falls.

— *Margaret Boe Birns*

AGNES GREY

Author: Anne Brontë (1820-1849)
Type of work: Novel
Type of plot: Domestic realism

Time of plot: Mid-nineteenth century
First published: 1847

Places in this novel serve simply as locations for the various stages in the plot and in Agnes's life. Although each house is more opulent than the one before, this does not indicate any rise in Agnes's social position or fortune. Only the final house, which is more modest, symbolizes some degree of financial independence. Places in the novel are rural, and all except the last are deep in the countryside of northern England.

Parsonage. Family home in an unnamed village in the north of England, that is provided to Agnes's father because he is the parish priest. It is portrayed as modest but well-furnished and comfortable. The landscape is moorland, with narrow valleys, streams, and woods. Though neither the landscape nor her father's labors as priest in the community are described in any detail, the parallels to Anne Brontë's own parsonage home in Haworth in the Yorkshire Dales are very strong, although Haworth was somewhat less rural than Agnes's home. Agnes and her mother are forced to leave the parsonage after her father's death, as the house is owned by the church.

Wellwood. Newly built house of Mr. Bloomfield, the nouveau riche purse-proud manufacturer, whose wife first employs Agnes as governess to her two older children. Situated some twenty miles from the parsonage, it has well laid out grounds and woods with a large garden.

It is Agnes's home for a year until she is dismissed for incompetence. Brontë's first post as governess at Blake Hall, Mirfield, seems to have served as material for the portrayal of Wellwood.

Horton Lodge. Home of Mr. Murray, Agnes's second employer, located near O——, seventy miles away from the parsonage. O—— itself is a large town, but not in an industrial area. Horton Lodge is older and larger than Wellwood, with a deer park. The grounds are much more established, with fine old trees. It stands in fertile country, with green lanes and hedgerows, as opposed to the stone walls more typical of Yorkshire. Agnes finds its flatness boring after the moors of her hometown. Here she tutors the two girls of the family, Rosalie and Matilda, and, until they are sent away to school, the two younger boys. In the estate lie a number of cottages and farmhouses, at times visited by Agnes and the Murray girls to aid the sick and destitute. Horton Lodge is almost certainly modeled on Brontë's second post as governess to the Robinson family at Thorp Green, and O—— is almost certainly York itself.

Horton. Village briefly described in the novel, whose main focal point is the parish church, lying two miles from the lodge. The Murrays attend regularly, sometimes by coach, sometimes on foot. It is here that Mr. Weston is appointed curate, assistant to the vicar, Mr. Hatfield. By contrast to Hatfield, Weston preaches evangelically and visits the poor with real compassion. In the cottage of the poor Nancy Brown, Agnes first has the opportunity to make his acquaintance.

Ashby Park. Stately home of Sir Thomas Ashby and his mother, situated ten miles from Horton Lodge. Sir Thomas is an eligible bachelor, even though he has lived a somewhat dissolute life. It has been generally supposed he would propose to Rosalie Murray, which he dutifully does at a society ball held there. Thus Rosalie becomes Lady Ashby. When Agnes visits her, she describes it as commodious and elegant, standing in beautiful parkland, with herds of deer and ancient woodland. Rosalie means Agnes to be impressed by its magnificence; in fact, she is not. Underneath her pride in its grandeur, Rosalie regards it as bleak and isolated. She would much rather be in London, enjoying high society life. Her description of her husband's behavior is not dissimilar to the account of Mr. Huntingdon in Brontë's other novel, *The Tenant of Wildfell Hall* (1848). Brontë's sojourn with the wealthy Robinsons had given her much material for her descriptions of country gentry.

A——. Seaside town in which Agnes and her mother decide to set up a small girls' school after the death of Mr. Grey. The school itself is situated in a rented house on the edge of town. The house lies some way from the beach, where Agnes loves to walk either with her students or with her mother. It is on one such early morning walk along the beach that she again meets Mr. Weston, who has recently become vicar of F——, a village only two miles away. The town is certainly modeled on Scarborough, a fashionable seaside resort on the Yorkshire coast. Brontë frequently vacationed there, especially with the Robinson family. She also died there. Agnes's description of its promontory, cliffs surrounding the bay and the hills behind match the description of Scarborough exactly. The latter town is also mentioned in *The Tenant of Wildfell Hall*.

— *David Barratt*

AJAX

Author: Sophocles (c. 496-406 B.C.E.)
Type of work: Drama
Type of plot: Tragedy

Time of plot: Trojan War
First performed: Aias, early 440's B.C.E. (English translation, 1729)

Sophocles' play is set at the conclusion of the long Greek siege of Troy, when the hero Ajax disgraces himself and loses his status as the greatest living Greek warrior. The locations in which the unfolding events are set provide subtle but important statements on the meaning of the events themselves.

Greek camp. Encampment of the Greek army outside the walled city of Troy where the play opens in front of the Greek hero Ajax's hut. His position is dangerously exposed; the location reflects both his reputation for reliability as a warrior and his political marginality. To appreciate this setting, one must understand the disposition of troops in ancient Greek war camps. Inferior in strength only to the dead Greek hero Achilles, Ajax guarded the second most vulnerable area, providing protection for the Greek ships. Since Achilles is dead when the play opens, the location of Ajax's hut suggests that Ajax now is the preeminent warrior.

However, there are more ways than geography to judge merit. Athena, goddess of wisdom, as well as the Greek commanders Agamemnon and Menelaus, believe that clever Odysseus is more deserving than Ajax of being awarded the fallen Achilles' armor. Feeling affronted, Ajax sets out to kill those who have slighted him, and his hut becomes both the location of his mad acts and a visual reminder of his disastrous intent. Col-ored by what can be learned through dialogue about Ajax's actions there, the site becomes an encapsulation of the plot: Ajax's physical preeminence, the affront to him, and his madness in mistaking cattle for humans and dragging them into the hut to torture and kill them.

Wooded area. The second setting is the area to which Ajax, sane again and shamed by his mad assault upon animals instead of enemies, withdraws to commit suicide. The remoteness of the site reflects Ajax's isolation from his former comrades and his desolation. Other characters enter the area only after he dies, and his corpse then functions as part of the setting, silently testifying to the issue that confronts survivors: Should the former hero be honored with burial, or should he be abandoned in this desolate terrain to become carrion for wild dogs and vultures? In the end, the traditional belief in honoring the dead triumphs, promoted by the noble Odysseus. Under the direction of Teucer, the dead man's brother, Ajax receives a hero's burial at the site.

— *Albert Wachtel*

ALCESTIS

Author: Euripides (c. 485-406 B.C.E.)
Type of work: Drama
Type of plot: Tragicomedy

Time of plot: Antiquity
First performed: Alkēstis, 438 B.C.E. (English translation, 1781)

The setting of Euripides' earliest known play is Thessaly, where King Admetus hosts the god Apollo, where his wife dies for him, and where his old friend Hercules travels to complete the labor of capturing the horses of Diomedes. On the way, Hercules visits Admetus and rescues his wife.

Admetus's palace. Pherae, Thessaly, Greece. All of the action of the play takes place in front of this palace. The house itself connects Admetus with the other characters in the play. For his wife Alcestis, this palace, and especially her marriage bed, provide the motivation for her decision to die for Admetus. While Admetus's father Pheres has given the palace and its authority over to his son, Pheres is not prepared also to die on his son's behalf.

The palace also creates a bond of guest-friendship between Admetus and Apollo. Because Admetus has earlier hosted Apollo during the latter's earthly servitude, Apollo grants him a means of avoiding his fated early death. The palace also unites Admetus with Hercules. According to the Greek custom of *xenia* or guest-friendship, a guest-friend deserves particular honor in the house. For this reason Admetus does not tell his friend about his wife's death and Hercules only hears of the event from servants upset by his inappropriate behavior in a house of mourning. Hercules responds by bringing to the house of his grieving friend a woman he claims to have wrested from the hands of death. Hercules relies upon his rights as a guest in Admetus's house to persuade his friend to marry this woman.

— *Thomas J. Sienkewicz*

ALECK MAURY, SPORTSMAN

Author: Caroline Gordon (1895-1981)
Type of work: Novel
Type of plot: Social realism

Time of plot: Late nineteenth and early twentieth centuries
First published: 1934

The classically educated protagonist of this novel's title is truly at peace only when he is fishing or hunting. While viewing himself as a creature in harmony with the rhythms of nature, he is in fact becoming an anachronism. His hunter's code becomes an obsession, rendering his teaching profession secondary, and he distances himself from both his family and other human beings. He seeks out remote areas of the American South that meet his need to be constantly in the fields. As a modern rustic, an embodiment of the ancient hero of folklore and epic, he must prove himself over and over through the ordeal of the ritual hunt, for a time staving off old age and death, until he too is overcome by failing eyesight and other infirmities which bring even the hunt to an end.

*Virginia. Southern state in which Aleck spends his early years. His first memories are of the woods and pastures he sees from his doorway. Always the dark woodland calls him, with the "hallooing" of its hunters, the baying of their hounds, mingling risk with the scent of rain-soaked forest. Dogs and men share these adventures, both sniffing the air and communicating in sounds and gestures. As he reaches adulthood, Aleck attends the University of Virginia in Charlottesville—the institution founded by Thomas Jefferson for young gentlemen. Aleck is not a rogue, but he begrudges the time he spends cooped up in lecture rooms, from which he can hear the hounds in the distance. He receives the education befitting a gentleman, learns his classics, and scans blank verse, and eventually graduates honorably, but without a dollar in his pocket or any idea of how to make one.

Oakland. Mississippi town just south of Memphis, Tennessee, in which Aleck accepts a position as president of a small seminary. Oakland is in a swampy lowland with patches of cotton fields. Aleck's quest for income to feed a growing family and, more importantly, to find satisfactory hunting grounds takes him to several states during the course of his life, but it is finally in Mississippi that he is offered his opportunity for strongest professional growth. Pleased to discover that the seminary is already competently managed by an underling, he concentrates on acquiring and training new hunting dogs. However, the signs in Mississippi are not auspicious, as his favorite hunting dog dies during his trip to Oakland. Later, a swimming accident takes the son he has never been able to transform into a hunter.

*Poplar Bluff. Small town by the Black River in Missouri's Ozark region where Aleck accepts a position in the fictional Rodman College. Missouri is another good hunting state where Aleck again manages to arrange his work schedule so he is free to fish every afternoon. For seven years his life follows a pleasant routine, until his wife, who has functioned largely as an impediment to his sporting plans, dies suddenly. Although his marriage is generally agreeable, his wife is never his soul mate; that role has been more fully filled by his favorite hunting dog.

*Florida. Aleck's sojourn in the lake region of Florida is brief. The region's celebrated fishing turns out to be a disappointment because the lakes' heavy eelgrass prevents fish from putting up the kind of fight that pleases true sportsmen.

*Tennessee. State that Aleck comes to regard as a sportsman's paradise, to which he repeatedly returns. Here he resumes his teaching career in Gloversville, lives with his wife, and gains the affection of Gypes, his beloved thoroughbred bird dog. Most importantly to him, however, Tennessee offers endless opportunities for fishing and hunting, and he moves through different regions of the state in this pursuit. Everywhere, he finds congenial folk with whom to discuss shooting squirrels, hunting quail, and stalking deer. To his delight, he has access to thirty thousand acres of land in which to roam and shoot. Aleck's daughter is able to ensure his Tennes-

see retirement, even in his old age, with the promise of good hunting grounds.

Caroline Gordon knew Tennessee well. She was born on a farm in Todd County, Kentucky, close to the Tennessee border. This region was known as Black Patch after the local tobacco, which provided the livelihood for most of the farmers.

— *Allene Phy-Olsen*

THE ALEXANDRIA QUARTET

Author: Lawrence Durrell (1912-1990)
Type of work: Novel
Type of plot: Psychological realism
Time of plot: Before and during World War II

First published: The Alexandria Quartet, 1962: *Justine*, 1957; *Balthazar*, 1958; *Mountolive*, 1958; *Clea*, 1960

Lawrence Durrell called a later selection of his writing "Spirit of Place," but none of his works reflects that title so well as these four novels, whose various characters and differing plot perspectives are presented as reflections of the multifarious atmosphere of the great Egyptian city Alexandria.

*Alexandria. Egyptian port city whose position, on the Nile Delta, has made it one of the most important trading cities in the Mediterranean and a magnet for an extraordinary mix of peoples and travelers. If one theme unites the complex web of political and sexual liaisons and betrayals layered throughout Durrell's intricate sequence of novels, it is memory. Durrell calls Alexandria the "capital of Memory" and a place where "the wind blew out one's footsteps like candle-flames," making it the perfect setting for the rememberings and forgettings that are explored in his books.

A press attaché at the British embassy in Alexandria during World War II, Durrell describes with colorful vigor the city's crumbling buildings, stultifying heat, and especially the mix of peoples—Jews, Copts, Greeks, English, and French as well as native Egyptians—who make up the city. It is this racial stew that provides the main impetus for Durrell's story, as various English visitors—the teacher L. C. Darley, the author Percy Pursewarden, and the diplomat Sir David Mountolive—are seduced by Alexandria's exotic atmosphere and sexual freedom. The theme of an inhibited Englishman becoming free in the warm, easy-going Mediterranean atmosphere was popular in postwar British fiction; it was a theme that Durrell would explore again and again.

Around his three Englishmen, Durrell assembles a cast of characters who represent every aspect of Alexandria: the Coptic financier Nessim Hosnani who, with his Jewish wife Justine, is revealed to be involved in political plots; the doctor S. Balthazar, whose cabalistic studies stand in for the extraordinary belief systems that are rife in the city; the exotic dancer Melissa who, as Darley's lover, provides his entry into this society; the French sensualist George Gaston Pombal; the artist Clea Montis; and the garrulous old transvestite spy chief Joshua Scobie, who, in one of the novel's more bizarre twists, evolves into a local saint. Between them, these characters represent not only the various races making up Alexandria's population, but also the entire social mix from the very wealthy to the very poor. Moreover, the large cast of characters are not merely players in the drama but also aspects of the city itself. The characters move freely from high-society balls to the dark and threatening lairs of child prostitutes; from the cool, detached air of the British embassy to the fervid gossip-mongering of cafés and barber shops. Each fresh location casts a fresh light upon them, and each of the four *Alexandria Quartet* novels is named after one of them.

The overwhelming impression of the city projected through Durrell's four novels is of a disturbing, almost threatening place in which betrayal at every level is a matter of course. Although the narrator, Darley, repeatedly feels guilty about betraying Melissa Artemis through his affair with Justine Hosnani, it is a relationship that is almost forced upon him by the city itself, that is inescapable precisely because of the hot-house atmosphere of Alexandria. Likewise, Nessim and Justine's plots are presented not so much as power plays but rather as part of a way of life imposed by the history and multiracial character of the city. Nevertheless, despite the fact that the characters are drawn again and again to the more unsavory parts of the city, and the multifarious betrayals of the plot result in one suicide and several murders, it is clear that Durrell considers this beady mix of beliefs and sexual infidelities to be life-affirming.

Island. Unnamed Greek island in the Cyclades group, where Durrell's narrator, Darley, writes and then amends his memoirs of the city in *Justine* and *Balthazar*, and where he retreats at the end of *Clea*. The unnamed island may be related to the Greek island of Rhodes, where Durrell lived after his wartime experiences in Alexandria. Within *The Alexandria Quartet*, the Greek island serves to provide a clear emotional and spiritual contrast to the Egyptian city. Where Alexandria is full of named streets, buildings, and neighborhoods, the only detail revealed about the island is that it has no antiquities. Where Alexandria is described in a sensual language that is almost overly rich, the island receives virtually no description. Where Alexandria is crowded with characters, Darley is alone on the island, except for Justine's daughter. The island, therefore, is a place of deliberate emptiness and silence to contrast with the only significant character in the book who is never described: life and excess of Alexandria.

Karm Abu Girg. Nessim Hosnani's family estate outside Alexandria, vaguely located on the fringe of the desert, near Lake Mareotis. The most significant thing revealed about the estate is that visitors must abandon their cars and travel by ferry and horse to reach it. Like the Greek island, it contrasts sharply with Alexandria: It is a world of ancient, timeless rituals, quite unlike the twentieth century city. It is also a harsher, crueler world, in which Narouz Hosnani, Nessim's brother, deals on equal terms with the desert Bedouin and crazed religious fanatics, and where he demonstrates his ability with the whip by using it casually to kill wild animals. Here the old lecher Paul Capodistria is apparently murdered after the set-piece shoot on Lake Mareotis that is the climax to *Justine*, and here Narouz is brutally killed in *Mountolive*. By the time the estate is revisited in *Clea*, it is decaying, nearly deserted, and fallen on hard times as a result of Nessim's plotting and being left behind by the twentieth century.

— *Paul Kincaid*

ALICE'S ADVENTURES IN WONDERLAND

Author: Lewis Carroll (Charles Lutwidge Dodgson, 1832-1898)
Type of work: Short fiction

Type of plot: Fantasy
Time of plot: Victorian era
First published: 1865

Wonderland is a wholly imaginary world of transmutation, in which one loses one's physical size and identity and searches for new ones—a telescoped version of the process of growing up, translated into a dream's incongruities and shifting landscapes. Many of its settings consequently contain images symbolic of birth or entering a new life. Wonderland's bizarre creatures are a child's-eye view of grownups, arbitrary, incomprehensible, and dictatorial.

River bank. The story opens on the bank of a river. The location is not specified, but it is presumably near Oxford, England. In a prefatory poem, Lewis Carroll recalls a boat trip he made in that region in 1862 with Alice Liddell (his model for the fictional Alice), two of Alice's sisters, and a friend. At the village of Godstow, about three miles up a branch of the River Thames called the Isis, he first imagined and told the story that became *Alice in Wonderland*. The book begins and ends on the river bank, whose quiet and order are bookends surrounding a noisy and disordered dream world.

Rabbit hole. Passage through which Alice enters Wonderland. Just as Wonderland is a realm of transformation, the tunnel through which she reaches that realm is a classic symbol of birth. Much of the book unfolds against a background of symbols of gestation and birth, such as a too-small passage to a bright new world through which she can see but not pass; the pool of salt water produced by Alice's own tears, in which she swims; the too-tight room in the rabbit's house, where she kicks out; and her many changes in size.

Wonderland. Despite Alice's fall down the rabbit hole and her references to being "down here," there is no definite indication that Wonderland itself is underground. It is a parody of Victorian England from a child's point of view: rule-bound, moralistic, and didactic, and of the Oxford town and university that Carroll knew. Often, Carroll describes no more of the setting than is minimally necessary for the action. There are no scenic descriptions of the surrounding territory, which is of no interest to either dreamers or children. In dreamlike fashion, scenes fade from one into one another in ways impossible to observe closely; the sizes of things and creatures are variable and inconsistent with one another.

Hall. Room in which Alice finds herself after falling through the rabbit hole. It is a "long, low hall," with locked doors all around it, from which Alice peers through a fifteen-inch-high door and sees the "loveliest garden you ever saw." In psychological terms, the desire to reach the garden can be interpreted as a longing to return to paradisal childhood innocence (or more crudely, to the womb). Conversely, it can also be interpreted as reflecting a desire to attain womanhood. Alice's frustration at being unable at various moments to get the key, open the door, or fit through the door, is true both to the frustrations that arise in dreams and to those of children, who must often perform tasks they do not understand, tasks at which they are awkward, and tasks for which they are the wrong physical size.

White Rabbit's house. Place in which Alice fetches the White Rabbit's gloves and fan. Resenting his high-handed command, she grows so large that the room she is in becomes like a womb, a place in which there is insufficient space in which to grow up. She is thus symbol-

ically trapped in the constricting limits of childhood—stuck in a world in which one is ordered about and has no say in one's own affairs.

Caterpillar's woods. With a dream's lack of consistency, the size perfect for the White Rabbit's house (three inches, which makes no sense for a rabbit) makes Alice as small as an insect in the surrounding forest (and the exact size of the caterpillar). Alice's normal height—regaining which was one of her goals—seems to fit the forest, but she keeps it only briefly.

Duchess's house. Alice must again shrink to enter the Duchess's house, which is only four feet high. Inside she finds the perfect reversal of an orderly Victorian household and of the proper rearing of a child: pepper reigns in the cooking and the temper, children are spoken to roughly, beaten, and shaken, and cooks indulge in casual assault by saucepan. The Duchess's baby does the opposite of what a well-reared child like Alice is trying to do: instead of growing up (becoming more civilized, socialized), it transforms into a pig.

March Hare's house. This house, with chimneys shaped like ears and a roof thatched with fur, is larger than the Duchess's; Alice grows to two feet in order to approach it. A table is set out in front of the house for a never-ending tea party, as Time, insulted by the Mad Hatter, will not advance past 6 o'clock. It has been speculated that the tea party is Carroll's satire on his college dining table at Oxford, where the same people gathered every evening for the same—it may have seemed to him—inane conversation.

Queen of Heart's garden. This can be viewed as the lovely garden of childhood, haunted by the bullying of adults. Since reaching it is Alice's goal throughout most of the book, the garden may also represent womanhood, which can appear glorious from a child's view, but when reached, may prove difficult and confusing. Such an interpretation may reflect Carroll's own views on being a grown-up; he was intensely shy around other adults and preferred the company of young girls.

Mock Turtle's shore. Small rock ledge by an otherwise undefined shore. There, nearly all that the Mock Turtle and Gryphon tell Alice has to do with fish and the sea, including their many puns and the poem/dance, "The Lobster Quadrille."

Court. Room in which the King and Queen of Hearts try the Knave for stealing tarts. The trial over which they preside is a parody of an English courtroom, a symbol of adult, autocratic authority. Characters from throughout the book, of all sizes, come together for the finale. During the trial, Alice gradually grows larger than everyone about her, as she stands up against the kind of bullying and illogic that have pursued her throughout the book. At this point, the dream of childhood ends.

— *William Mingin*

ALL FALL DOWN

Author: James Leo Herlihy (1927-1993)
Type of work: Novel
Type of plot: Bildungsroman

Time of plot: Late 1950's
First published: 1960

Viewed through the experiences of one midwestern family, this novel is a penetrating portrait of America on the cusp of a social transformation that would forever alter the nation's spiritual and physical structure. The novel echoes the themes of many Beat novels in which roads crisscrossing the landscape and vehicles carrying characters on their odysseys are emblems of escape, freedom, and tragedy. The Williams family home provides a permanent locus of chaos and brief stability, and the recorded meditations of Clinton Williams, the young hero, explore the spiritual realm of his awakening consciousness.

Williams family home. Located in Cleveland, Ohio, the family home, in its moods and changing states of cohesion, reflects the periods of alienation, dislocation, and close community experienced by its occupants and, in a larger sense, by the American family. The first two sentences of the novel read, "It is well known that in every neighborhood in the United States there is at least one house that is special. Special because it is haunted, or because of an act of violence that took place there." The levels of the house and those who dominate them are Freudian in nature.

Casual in his relations with others, Ralph Williams, the father—an intellectual, anarchist, atheist, and entrepreneur—occupies the basement, as he does his drinking, doing jigsaw puzzles, and avoiding the world within and without the house. The mother, Annabel, remains on the main floor, a kind of mitigating super ego; she is domestic, worried about her children, cut off from love and her favorite son, Berry-berry, who wanders from home and remains a mythic presence that shadows everyone in the house. Clinton, a younger son, cut off from the comfort of the Old Neighborhood, ventures into the streets of the New Neighborhood, absorbing life, visiting drugstores, a magazine store, a chili place, working at the White Tower restaurant, surrounded and alone, a rebel without a cause, retreating to his bedroom, a realm of consciousness, to contemplate and write down conversations and phone calls, undertaking furtive forays through the house to poke through correspondences or eavesdrop outside or through air vents.

*****Cleveland.** Ohio's largest city is depicted as dull, unresponsive, and smothering. The promise of magic exists beyond its bounds where Berry-berry has flown. Only with the arrival of the lovely Echo O'Brien do the Williamses come alive, and both their house and Cleveland transform into sparkling representations of the joy and love she offers so freely.

Key Bonita. Fictional Florida port town to which Clinton travels by bus in order to team up with Berry-berry, in trouble for stabbing a woman. The journey takes on mythic proportions, an acceptance of the call and the descent into the underworld. Berry-berry is long gone, but in the midst of this seamy town, Clinton loses his virginity to a prostitute in a moment of precious innocence that emblemizes the kindness and compassion he will give to and receive from others. Even in the midst of (indeed, in spite of) depravity, dishonesty, and disillusion, innocence can survive and spread beauty, Herlihy suggests, even to the point where the police, the hookers, and the toughs respond to the boy in ways that compel them to connect with their own humanity.

*Toledo. Ohio city, which like Cleveland to the east, stands on Lake Erie. As the home of Echo O'Brien and her ailing mother in this novel, it is a setting of sickness and, ultimately, death. Toledo blooms forth Echo, a short-lived rose who dies on the road, returning there after being forsaken by Berry-berry. Beneath its deceptively benign exterior, Toledo, like Cleveland and all other "respectable" cities, harbors the beast of betrayal and tragedy.

*Apple Mountain farm. Ohio location in which Berry-berry establishes a brothel; however, but his ensuing apparent conversion to stability is mirrored in the change of the farm from a house of prostitution to a respectable plumbing business. However, there remains a foulness there, symbolized by the cash and gun hidden in a hollowed-out phone directory and Berry-berry's violent sexual liaisons with his partner's girlfriend. Clinton goes to Apple Mountain to kill Berry-berry for what he has done to Echo, and in this place where innocent Nature and corrupt society have been fused, he finally realizes that he is not like Berry-berry, that he is on this earth to love, not to use.

— *Erskine Carter*

ALL FOR LOVE: Or, The World Well Lost

Author: John Dryden (1631-1700)
Type of work: Drama
Type of plot: Tragedy

Time of plot: First century B.C.E.
First performed: 1677; first published, 1678

John Dryden's version of the popular Antony and Cleopatra plot, which William Shakespeare's earlier drama had fixed in the British consciousness, follows the neoclassic rule of the unity of place. The abstract and eloquent ideas in his version of the tragedy evoke his own Restoration London, linking past and present.

*Alexandria. Egyptian port city in whose Temple of Isis all the play's action is set. The temple is more like a palace or government building than a religious temple, in the capital city of Cleopatra's Egypt. Actually, Egypt is a satellite state of Rome assigned to Mark Antony. In the Shakespeare play, based on the internecine warfare between Octavius, the future Augustus Caesar, and Antony, battle scenes and other grand events are depicted on stage; Dryden expresses all the conflict in one location and over a short period of time. This practice exhibits the power of the neoclassical rules of dramatic unity of place and time. The focus in setting also emphasizes the theme of the exotic and mysterious East in conflict with the aggressive and modern empire building of Rome.

*London. Continually present to the perceptions of the audience due to the balanced verse and the elegant, courtly setting is the London court of Charles II, which is modeled on the French court of Louis XIV. The courtly culture also supports the neoclassical dramatic rules of unity by which generalized analogies from history can be used to explain current events. Dryden does not leave such analogies merely implicit, however, and includes several pieces of valuable prose along with the play, which make the connections to his own London clearly explicit.

— *Donald M. Hassler*

ALL HALLOWS' EVE

Author: Charles Williams (1886-1945)
Type of work: Novel
Type of plot: Allegory

Time of plot: October, 1945
First published: 1945

This novel is set primarily in London as Great Britain's capital city is adjusting to peace after the conclusion of World War II. However, the city is both a real place and an eternal city, in which all times and places are available to ghosts and the preternaturally acute.

*Westminster Bridge. Bridge over the River Thames near London's Westminster Abbey and Houses of Parliament, where the novel opens with Lester Furnival standing by the bridge and coming to the realization that she is dead. She also realizes that she, along with her friend Evelyn Mercer, was killed on this spot by a warplane dropping out of the sky. From there she and Evelyn begin to wander around London.

*London. From the moment when Lester finds herself alone on Westminster Bridge to the climax of her disappearance from Simon's house, there is always a strong sense of London as the background to the action. At first, Lester can see only the city, but as her spirit develops, she hears all the familiar noises of people and traffic, feels the pavement under her feet, and smells the river and the October rain. The literalness of London sights, sounds, and locations is not merely a device to root the supernatural story in the natural world. For Charles Williams, London is an image of the City of God, the Holy City, the community of the saints.

When the city is first mentioned, the term indicates the ancient borough of London, site of St. Paul's Cathedral, as distinguished from Holborn, where Simon's headquarters are. Through Lester's developing spiritual perception, however, the spiritual reality of the eternal city is revealed. Its identity is hinted to mortal eyes on the fateful afternoon when Lady Wallingford and Betty call to look at Jonathan's portrait of Simon. Lady Wallingford is equally antagonized by another painting that Jonathan and Richard consider the best that Jonathan has done, a painting of a part of London after a raid, a scene of desolation bathed in living light.

Three domiciles in London are key: the top-floor apartment of artist Jonathan Drayton, near St. Paul's Cathedral; the house of the magician, Simon the Clerk, in Holborn; and the house of Lady Wallingford, Simon's mistress and acolyte, in Highgate. The characters, including the newly dead spirits of Lester and Evelyn, move among these places. Williams builds a sense of reality by mentioning locations in the exact but familiar way of a longtime resident; characters describe Simon's residence as between Holborn and Red Lion Square, and

behind Holborn, close to Great James Street. Williams also mentions streets that characters traverse to get from one place to another, again giving a sense of textured reality: Blackfriars, Victoria Street, Millbank, Euston Road.

However, the city that Lester wanders is really the eternal city; she sees it as London because that is where she was when she was killed, and that is what she expects. The sky goes through quick cycles of night and day, but no sun appears and the moon gives no light. Lester's City is also silent and devoid of people, until she finds Evelyn. Moreover, at times her perception of London is broken by, or fades into, other times and places. She thinks of an incident from her past, concerning a date with a man and the taxi-ride home, and she sees a taxi race past her. Later Lester thinks of her school days with Evelyn and Betty, and she finds herself actually in the schoolyard. One scene hints that the City is open to all times and places, including prehistory, depending on the person involved and how he or she encounters it.

When Lester and Evelyn visit real places in London, they can be seen by people living in those places now, as Lester is seen by her husband Richard near Westminster Bridge, and Evelyn is seen and called by Simon outside his house in Holborn. Betty is magically sent into the future by a week, reading the newspapers at King's Cross Station to report back.

*Underground. Also known as the "Tube," London's great subway system also exists both materially and spiritually. After Lester and Evelyn are placed in a magically constructed body, they borrow money to use a pay phone at the Charing Cross Underground station. Within this city, however, the Tube is a kind of Hell—the lair of newly dead spirits who will not accept death and redemption, and so fail to go into true eternity.

*England. No physical action is set outside London, but readers learn that Lady Wallingford owns property up north in Yorkshire. Flashbacks show that when Betty and her mother go there, Betty is treated as a servant; Betty remembers with dread the train porter calling off stations closer and closer to York. Betty's father, Sir Bartholomew, owns property in Hampshire. The distance between York and Hampshire may be symbolic of the lack of communication—or much of anything in common—between husband and wife.

Lester briefly recalls a honeymoon with Richard in the Berkshire Woods, and later, when Simon leads Richard and others into a magical trance, Richard imagines he is once more surrounded by those woods. Again, magic or any supernatural experience overcomes boundaries of time and space, and a character's mind calls forth the setting.

— *Bernadette Lynn Bosky*

ALL MEN ARE BROTHERS

Author: Shi Nai'an (c. 1290-1365)
Type of work: Novel
Type of plot: Adventure
Time of plot: Thirteenth century or earlier

First published: Shui-hu chuan, possibly the fourteenth century (English translation, 1933; also translated as *Water Margin*)

This lengthy work blends fiction and Chinese mythology, collecting one hundred stories as they had been told by various authors (primarily Shi Nai'an and Lo Kuan-chung) over a period of some two hundred years. More than one hundred characters carry out Robin Hood-type robberies and adventures as they roam through what are today China's Shantung, Hopei, Anhuei, and Hunan Provinces. The main setting is thus the mountain hideout of the benign bandits.

Mountain lair. Hideout in the most remote mountains of Shantung Province that provides the central, unifying setting for the collected stories. Here the bandits form a society for themselves, one in which they assure a system of justice and patriotism. They make outcasts of themselves on a particularly large mountain near an idyllic lake that is surrounded by boundless reeds forming a marsh. The ever-present mists create a heavenly backdrop as the skies verge into the habitats of the gods themselves. Long, moving, and invisible waterways and passages provide the bandit group with easy places to hide and help them carry out ambushes and surprise attacks. This idyllic setting is all in contrast to Chinese society at lower altitudes, where the wealthy ruling class maintains a corrupt government.

Battlefields. The largest section of the book (chapters 20 through 41) covers the adventures of Wu Sung and the battle of Chiangchow, in which Sung Chiang joins the band and becomes its leader. These eleven adventures include the story of Wu Sung's killing of the great tiger of Ching Yang Ridge. Repeated battles occur in and near the village of Chu (Chuchiachuang) as the further adventures of Sung Chiang are recorded in later chapters. The Ridge of the Lonely Dragon is the scene of the fighting of some ten thousand men from three different families in tribal warfare. At Tamingfu and Tsengtoushih, all the bandits fight and defeat the government troops, at least for the time being.

China. Innumerable descriptions of China occur throughout the narrative, which was set in the twelfth century and put into its final form in the fourteenth. Large cities, villages, inns, homes (bedrooms for adultery, even), shops, forests, temples, farms, and so on all recur repeatedly. At times they are the main backdrop for the adventures of a particular bandit. Instances literally number in the hundreds. Examples include the story of a tattooed priest in the Wood of the Wild Boar, bandits gathering at the Temple to the White Dragon, and a great turmoil on the Great Hua Mountain in the west. This final, assembled version of these legends collected into stories reveals much about China and Chinese life in these centuries.

Heaven. Because the mountain lair opens directly into the mists of the skies (heavens), there is often direct contact with Taoist gods who occupy it. As early as chapter 8, guests from both heaven and everywhere under heaven are admitted to the Hall of Justice and Patriotism. More than one dozen different temples appear in the work, and in each instance references to heaven as setting consistently occur. The most significant of these is at the end of the stories when the Taoist gods come directly from heaven with messages, poems, and directions for the bandits. Hell, too, is mentioned, and the work concludes with the men having an evil dream in which their afterlife is painful because of their many murders in their sundry adventures.

— *Carl Singleton*

ALL MY SONS

Author: Arthur Miller (1915-   )
Type of work: Drama
Type of plot: Psychological realism

Time of plot: Mid-twentieth century
First performed: 1947; first published, 1947

The dramatic demise of Joe Keller and the unraveling of his family occur in a backyard setting of an upper-middle-class suburban home somewhere in the eastern United States. Keller's backyard is transformed from a symbol of luxury and moral justification to a place of self-recognition in which the truth about his family is realized.

Keller's backyard. This setting represents a family having achieved the American Dream, but the dream is realized by unethical profiteering during the context of the recently completed World War II. Keller's backyard is a place where members of the family socialize, recall pleasant memories of younger innocent days, and interact with neighbors. However, it is also a place where secrets are revealed, such as Larry's suicide, Annie's desire to marry Chris, and Joe Keller's guilt about manufacturing faulty airplane parts. A broken tree in the backyard symbolizes the breaking of the family.

This setting underscores the typical upper-middle-class home in which American affluence presumes American moral superiority. However, in this place the truths that are revealed transform it from a haven of moralization to the place of Keller's demise. Thus it fulfills playwright Arthur Miller's intention of suggesting that all Americans who put business above personal integrity demonstrate a lack of moral integrity.

Keller's house. Throughout the play, characters enter the house to avoid the intensity of the discussions and potential revelations occurring in the backyard. The interior of the house thereby becomes a place in which secrets are nourished, while the backyard is a place of revelation.

Prison. Offstage location. Annie's father, a former business associate of Joe Keller, is in prison for his role in making faulty airplane parts. Though offstage, the prison exists prominently in the minds of the characters, prompting justification on the part of Joe Keller and denial on the part of his wife. It also represents the place to which Joe Keller will go, once the truth about his own complicity is discovered and he is expelled from his comfortable house and yard.

*****New York City.** The American city suggesting wealth and business, it is seven hundred miles from the setting of the play. Its distance and prominence as a great center of American business contrast with the suburban life of the Kellers. It is also the place in which Annie and her brother choose to live after their father goes to prison, so it serves as a temporary escape from the scrutiny of the neighbors in their former neighborhood.

— *Kenneth Hada*

ALL QUIET ON THE WESTERN FRONT

Author: Erich Maria Remarque (Erich Paul Remark, 1898-1970)
Type of work: Novel
Type of plot: Political

Time of plot: World War I
First published: Im Westen nichts Neues: serial, 1928; book, 1929 (English translation, 1929)

Considered one of the greatest of modern antiwar novels, this story depicts the disillusioning experiences and tragic death of an innocent young foot soldier impressed into the German army during World War I. His experience is based on that of the author, who was himself conscripted into service in the war. As a consequence, the narrative provides a realistic sense of place and authority in depicting the conditions in which soldiers fought.

*Western front. Theater of World War I in which German forces faced the Western Allies along an extensive series of battlefields that ran from the Belgian coast south into northern France. (The eastern front was the line along which Germany confronted Russia.) Much of the western front was made up of intricate systems of trenches from which troops sallied forth across treacherous "no-man's-lands" in mostly futile attacks on enemy positions. Through most of the war, the battlefronts moved very little, and many troops stationed in the trenches endured continuous bombardment and suffered from appalling health conditions as formerly peaceful farmlands and pleasant countryside were converted into bloody battlefields.

It was along the western front that the French and British armies and those of their allies aligned themselves against the armies of Germany and its allies, using such modern weapons and implements as poison gas, tanks, powerful explosives, flame throwers, hand grenades, machine guns, long-range artillery, aircraft, and barbed wire. Thanks to modern technology, the scale of death and injury was catastrophic. Individual soldiers were considered expendable in outmoded military strategies governed by policies of attrition dictating the winners would be the last side to have soldiers still standing. This was especially true on the western front, where battles continued for months while corpses and casualties mounted.

The novel neither locates its protagonist, Paul Baumer, in any specific battlefield nor focuses on the larger strategies or battles of the war. Instead, it reveals the war only as it is experienced through the limited and subjective perspective of Paul, who knows little about the larger purposes of the war. Paul represents all the nameless soldiers who fought on the western front. To him, the battles seem both meaningless and frightening; ordinary days with his comrades are interrupted by unreal but frenetic periods of battle. Ironically, it is during one uneventful day on the front that the young, poetic Paul is unexpectedly shot by desultory enemy fire shortly before the Armistice is declared and the fighting stops. The impersonality and randomness of his death brings home the entire character of war on the western front as depicted in this novel—the inconsequential value of the millions of individual soldiers who died.

Home front. While most of the narrative takes place on the battlefront lines, one section of the novel takes Paul back to his hometown in Germany, allowing readers to contrast that world with his experiences on the front lines. During his leave, Paul returns home to a typical German small town of the time that is accustomed to the comforts and securities of peaceful middle-class life. The unnamed town represents all small German towns of the time.

Remarque uses Paul's visit to his home to indicate the vast gulf between his perspective of the war and that of those who remain on the home front. The people at home, while suffering some deprivations, have no idea of the dimensions and depth of the suffering on the battlefields of the western front. Paul's trip back home consolidates his feelings of a generational shift in which he and his peers represent a dramatic break with the past.

— Margaret Boe Birns

ALL THAT FALL

Author: Samuel Beckett (1906-1989)
Type of work: Drama
Type of plot: Absurdist

Time of plot: Twentieth century
First performed: 1957

Originally conceived as a script for a radio program, this play portrays life as an endless struggle punctuated by moments of mirth, tenderness, and melancholy that moves at a shuffling pace toward the grave. Mrs. Rooney's journey along the country road takes her past decaying homes and decaying people, whose conversation focuses primarily on the degrees to which they and their loved ones are suffering. The sounds of rural animals, bicycle bells, and automobiles create a sense of motion, of vitality. In the end, however, they reinforce the themes of decay and death. An animal is run over on the road, a bicycle gets a flat tire, a car has trouble starting, and the strains of Richard Schubert's Death and the Maiden, *coming from a house along the road, correspond to Mrs. Rooney's own preoccupation with death.*

Village. Unnamed rural community in Ireland that serves as the peripheral setting of the play and establishes the foundation of its humor and tragedy. While Samuel Beckett's dramatic themes are universal in scope, they are also rooted in his native Ireland.

Country road. Road to the village that is a dangerous and toilsome place—one on which a person might be run over by a passing motor van at any moment and whose dust and filth cling to people. In a broader sense, the country road mirrors the human condition as Beckett presents it—a place where every action is merely a hesitation before death. Parents rear children only to be struck down by disease or by the wheels of a train. Mrs. Rooney shuffles along the country road, suffering under the weight of her own body and the memory of her dead daughter, toward a meeting at the train station with her blind and embittered husband.

Boghill train station. The station is initially a source of hope. Mrs. Rooney plans to surprise her husband on his birthday by meeting him there. It becomes, however, another source of death when she discovers that a child has fallen beneath a train's wheels and has died—a tragedy that might have been caused by Mr. Rooney. Mrs. Rooney's trip to the station also compels her to leave home, where she would prefer to stay, waiting for death to come, as she describes it, by a "drifting gently down in the higher life, and remembering, remembering . . . all the silly unhappiness . . . as though . . . it had never happened. . . ."

— *Philip Bader*

ALL THE KING'S MEN

Author: Robert Penn Warren (1905-1989)
Type of work: Novel
Type of plot: Social realism

Time of plot: Late 1920's and early 1930's
First published: 1946

Robert Penn Warren sets this novel in a fictional state in the Deep South that resembles Louisiana. Most of its action takes place in the small towns of Mason City and Burden's Landing and in the state's unnamed capital city. Places within the novel are symbolic of the human fall from innocence and of the corruption in human actions. Although Warren's geography cannot be reduced to allegory, all the major place-names he uses symbolize his theme of the struggle with imperfection and sinfulness.

Southern state. Unnamed state in the Deep South that appears to be modeled on Louisiana, whose governor Huey P. Long had a political career during the 1930's closely resembling that of Warren's fictional governor, Willie Stark. Warren always denied that Willie Stark, the corrupted politician at the center of the novel, was a fictional version of Huey P. Long. However, there are many parallels between his fictional state and Louisiana, and there can be little doubt that Louisiana's famous populist governor was the inspiration for the fictional Stark.

Mason City. Stark's hometown, where he begins his climb to political power, is the seat of Mason County. Lying northeast of the unnamed capital of the fictional state, on Highway 58, Mason City represents Stark's "hick" background, his original innocence and his lack of sophistication at the beginning of his career. It is aptly named because it is also the place where Stark begins his efforts to build a better world by campaigning against the shoddy masonry in a local school building.

Upton. Town in the western part of the state that is a center of the state's rural vote. Immediately north of Upton are coal mines, whose workers constitute an important source of votes for political candidates appealing to socially disadvantaged voters. Upton is a pivotal location, because it is there that Stark turns from the purity of intent of Mason City to the cynical, rabble-rousing appeals to the resentments of the common people that will put him in power in the capital city. The name "Upton" symbolizes the upward political movement that Stark begins in the town by compromising his original purity.

Burden's Landing. Town lying 130 miles southwest of Mason City that is the ancestral home of the novel's narrator, Jack Burden. Burden's Landing complicates Warren's story of a political fall from grace, represented by Stark's movement from Mason City to the capital. The name of the narrator's home appears to be symbolic; the site is where the *burden* of earthly imperfection is found. If Mason City represents the desire to build, Burden's Landing suggests original sin and inherited guilt. All those from Burden's Landing turn out to be tainted. After the apparently upright local judge Irwin declares his political opposition to Stark, for example, Burden uncovers evidence that Irwin once took a bribe and drove a man to suicide. This revelation drives Irwin himself to suicide. Afterward, Burden learns that the Judge was actually his biological father. Burden's Landing, then, is the place where the narrator uncovers the inherited corruption that infects the striving for achievement.

State capital. Unnamed city in which much of the novel's action is set—particularly in the state capitol building and in the governor's mansion. Dr. Adam Stanton shoots Stark in the halls of the capitol, as, in reality Dr. Carl Weiss apparently shot Louisiana governor Huey Long in the halls of Louisiana's capitol in 1936. The real capital of Louisiana is Baton Rouge, but Warren's fictional capital city more closely resembles nearby New Orleans.

While the capital city is a place of power and of corruption, it is also a place where Stark makes efforts at virtuous action, once again through the act of building. However, in his attempt to return to the purity of Mason City by building a hospital untainted by graft and without using inferior building materials, Stark alienates his former cronies, and his noble efforts lead to his assassination.

— *Carl L. Bankston III*

ALL'S WELL THAT ENDS WELL

Author: William Shakespeare (1564-1616)
Type of work: Drama
Type of plot: Comedy

Time of plot: Sixteenth century
First performed: c. 1602-1603; first published, 1623

As a literary device, place accents the problematic nature of this play, which is constructed on a foundation of deceits and truths that attempt to cancel out each other, so that ultimately "all is well ended." The truth for Helena is that she loves Bertram, a selfish cad; her quest to win him takes her from Rousillon to Paris to Florence and back, and each locale is a metaphor for the health or illness at the core of the play. Place, therefore, also functions as a mechanism for revelation and exposure: depending on the location, the true self of each character is revealed.

***Rousillon** (rew-see-YOHN). Region in southern France in which the play opens. The palace of Bertram, the count of Rousillon, is a scene of mourning and shadows, shot through with beams of love and goodwill, ruled by a man in complete self-absorption, ignorant of the kindness of his mother and the healing qualities of Helena. The problem is presented in this atmosphere of dark ambivalence, and here it will be resolved in the end. However, the mood of uncertainty that opens the play is not completely dissipated, for audiences remain wondering if Helena's unconditional love and powers of healing will be sufficient to remedy Bertram's overriding sense of self.

***Florence.** Cultural center of Italy. Like Paris, Florence is sick in its soul with war and conspiracy. Bertram attempts to seduce Diana there, but Helena puts herself in the bed (an unhealthy one, like the French king's sick bed in Paris), and he makes love to her, unwittingly helping to fulfill his impossible conditions: "When thou canst . . . show me a child begotten of thy body that I am father to, then call me husband." Florence embodies the theme of means justifying an end: Bertram achieves the military glory he covets, Parolles is exposed as a liar and a coward, and Helena uses trickery to fulfill the contract promised by the king.

***Paris.** France's capital is a somber and spiritually ill city, in which the king is stricken by fistula, and men are leaving for the Italian wars. Helena's potion cures the king, who rewards her with Bertram's hand, a fairy-tale resolution set in a palace, but Bertram is insulted, and their unconsummated marriage speaks to the intrigue, sickness, and sterility that plagues the royal court.

— *Erskine Carter*

ALMAYER'S FOLLY: A Story of an Eastern River

Author: Joseph Conrad (Jósef Teodor Konrad Nałęcz Korzeniowski, 1857-1924)
Type of work: Novel

Type of plot: Social realism
Time of plot: Late nineteenth century
First published: 1895

Like much of Joseph Conrad's fiction, this novel situates a European protagonist in a colonial world and focuses on the ensuing clashes of culture and personality. Here, Borneo's eastern coast is the setting for a tale of thwarted ambition and mutual misunderstanding. The forbidding natural environment of treacherous waterways and dense jungle functions throughout as a symbol of the barriers that separate cultures and individuals from one another.

Pantai River (pan-TI). Fictional river in the Dutch East Indies to which the novel's subtitle alludes ("A Story of an Eastern River"). Conrad modeled the Pantai on the real Berau River in Borneo. The subtitle accurately reflects the importance that the river plays in the narrative. All the major events take place either on or next to the Pantai, and its ceaseless motion and dangerous turbulence serve as both menacing background and active foreground to the development of the plot.

Conrad often uses the literary technique of personification, which attributes human qualities to inanimate objects, to portray the river as having strong emotional reactions to the uses to which people put it. As a result, the Pantai becomes a character in its own right, and there is a sense in which its actions are as significant as those of the novel's human cast of performers.

The river also represents the flow of life passing by Almayer. The novel's opening scene finds him envying the fate of a log tossed about in the stream's violent currents, because its temporary suffering will be rewarded by a journey to freedom when the river eventually carries it to the sea. This moment foreshadows an episode at the conclusion of the novel when Almayer's daughter, the only person he still loves, leaves him by sailing down the Pantai to the sea.

Conrad's career as a merchant seaman included several visits to Borneo's eastern coast during the late 1880's, when he encountered a Dutch trader upon whom he based Almayer. The novel closely follows the actual topographical and sociological character of the region.

Almayer's house. Combination residence and business premise located on the banks of the Pantai. The novel stresses the decrepit, rundown condition of what is both literally and figuratively Almayer's "folly." The living area of the house is a shambles uncared for by Almayer's estranged wife and lax servants. On the rare occasions when visitors call, not even a full set of glasses can be assembled. The warehouse portion of the house is equally pathetic and contains only a few rotting specimens of unsalable merchandise. Particular stress is placed on the ramshackle condition of the jetty that runs down to the river from the house, which symbolizes the decayed relationship between Almayer's commercial ambitions and his actual capacity to conduct business.

In architectural terminology, a "folly" is an excessively ornamental tower or mock ruin with only decorative value, which makes it an apt term for the literal ruin of Almayer's home. His house is also a figurative representation of the folly that has accumulated as the result of his unsuccessful business, unhappy marriage and failed relationship with his daughter. The novel concludes with the final destruction of both follies: Almayer burns his home to the ground and then wills his own death as an escape from earthly failure.

Abdulla's godown. Business premises, or "godown," of Almayer's main competitor, the Arab merchant Abdulla. The atmosphere of bustling activity at Abdulla's place contrasts strongly with the desolate air of Almayer's house and implies that the latter's lack of success is due to personal inability rather than poor business conditions in the region.

Rajah of Sambir's house. Residence of the ruler of the fictional state of **Sambir**, a province of what was then the Dutch East Indies. Its prosperity and liveliness again suggest that Almayer's misery is due to his individual failings rather than a daunting environment.

*Macassar (mah-kah-SIHR). City in Indonesia's Celebes Islands (later renamed Ujung Pandang). Briefly portrayed as the location of Almayer's first employment as a businessman, its frenetic and profitable commercial life serves as an image of the paradise lost that he is unable to re-create on the Pantai.

— *Paul Stuewe*

ALTON LOCKE: Tailor and Poet

Author: Charles Kingsley (1819-1875)
Type of work: Novel
Type of plot: Social realism

Time of plot: 1840's
First published: 1850

Under the guise of an autobiography of its eponymous narrator, this novel is as much about ideas as about the history of Great Britain's Chartist movement. Charles Kingsley is not greatly interested in place for itself, only in centers of power, exploitation, and powerlessness. His novel provides no overall sense of cities as complete geographical organisms. The novel deals with isolated specifics—sweatshops, a starving farm—that form the scenarios out of which it constructs political dialogue. In the end, movement almost stops and the clergyman novelist takes over the protagonist's autobiography to complete his "tract for the times."

*London. The novel's London is a place of two nations: the powerful and the dispossessed, signed by the terms "West End" and "East End" respectively. The West End comprises the fashionable parts of London, such as Piccadilly or the Dulwich Art Gallery, in which the Dean Winnstay's family lives and moves. The East End, the "cockney" side of London is the area of grinding poverty, slums, insanitary conditions and disease. Places are not named here, as they are in Dickens's novels, apart from a brief excursion to Bermondsey, on the south bank of the River Thames, where, symbolically, houses of the poor are being demolished to make way for more fashionable homes.

As Dickens would do several years later in *Bleak House* (1852-1853), the reformer Kingsley shows particular interest in disease caused by lack of sanitation. However, unlike Dickens, he makes little symbolic use of the condition. On the other hand, the poor tailor Alton Locke's boyhood London is invested with the literary features of the City of Destruction of John Bunyan's *Pilgrim's Progress* (1678, 1684). Its suburbs spread like tentacles deep into the countryside, devouring its natural beauty and life.

Sweatshops. Alton's first place of work is ostensibly a respectable tailor's shop, situated in London's Piccadilly district. Downstairs it seems to promise high life. However, each higher floor of the building represents some disease caused by the dreadful work conditions. Similarly, as the novel progresses, each workplace seems worse than the one before, as the tailors' working conditions deteriorate in the laissez-faire economics of the day, finally becoming an appalling prison whose workers have become bonded slaves.

Kingsley wrote at a time when Britain had emancipated its slaves, but the United States had not. The scheme at the end of the novel for dispossessed British workers to emigrate to the southern states of the United States is thus deeply ironic: Britain has established a system of slavery far worse than anything in America. Only Sandy Mackay's bookshop and Eleanor's co-operative stand against the loss of hope and the despair of the tailors in the failure of Chartism.

*Cambridge University. One of England's two great centers of higher learning, the university here only superficially represents a center of learning. It is shown to be an institution taken over by the powerful for their sole benefit. Historically, the powerless had entry, but Alton Locke, representative of the nineteenth century's talented powerless, finds none. He remains an outsider, forced to admire from afar the beauty of Cambridge's architecture and its privileged denizens, including the dean's daughter, Lillian Winnstay. While Locke is able to see through his cousin's hypocrisy in advancing himself through his studies, he is unable to see through Lillian's siren voice, and so compromises his poetry. Cambridge is thus another corrupting and debilitating place.

D——. Unidentified English town that represents anywhere else in the novel. While the town appears to be a cathedral city near Cambridge, it suggests Ely in the Fenlands, a flat marshy area of East Anglia. However, later agricultural scenes suggest a quite contradictory landscape, more akin to the Dorset of southwest England, where the Tolpuddle Martyrs became the first workers to attempt to form a trade union. For Alton, D—— represents both his greatest success, in having his poetic powers recognized by the dean, and his greatest failure, being imprisoned for three years for "inciting" the farm laborers' food riot. It is altogether a place of false values and ideologies, much more so than Cambridge, where Kingsley was, after all, professor of modern history for some years. Kingsley's own membership in the Church of England does, however, give rise to some sentimental inconsistencies over the dean of the cathedral.

— David Barratt

AMADÍS OF GAUL

Author: Attributed to Vasco de Lobeira (c. 1360-c. 1403)

Type of work: Novel

Type of plot: Chivalric romance

Time of plot: Dark Ages, before the time of King Arthur

First published: Amadís de Gaula, 1508 (English translation, 1619)

The far-ranging geography of Amadís of Gaul *is confused and uncertain, being too liberally scattered with so-called islands; however, this is deliberate, symbolizing the divided state of Dark Age Christendom. The Firm Island is firm because it constitutes a foundation on which Christian factions driven to conflict by the mischief of antichrists, such as Arcalaus the Enchanter, can be reconciled—and on which its knightly defenders can attain their just and duly certified reward.*

*Great Britain. Island comprising England, Scotland, and Wales, where the knight Amadís spends his early years after being rescued from the sea by Gandales, and where the greater part of *Amadís of Gaul* is set. The vast majority of the towns, castles, and geographical features casually named in the text are invented, the principal exceptions being the cities of London, Bristol, and Windsor. However, Windsor—the site where Lisuarte establishes his quasi-Arthurian court—is one of many locations falsely described as an "island"; the actual Windsor, about fifteen miles west of London, is the site of an important royal palace.

In addition to those listed below, invented locations include **Leonis**, the offshore island to which the giant Gandalac carries away the young Galaor; the rock **Galtares**, where Galaor fights the giant Albadan; **Angaduza**, the forest where Amadís and Galaor are reunited; the castle **Miraflores**, two leagues from London, where Oriana awaits the return of Amadís; **Tagades**, the coastal city where Lisuarte establishes a court in book 4; and **Lubayna**, the monastery where Lisuarte assembles all his chiefs and knights to proclaim his reconciliation with Amadís.

Firm Island. Imaginary peninsula seven leagues long, connected to Britain by a thin neck of land, which provides the major location of the action of book 4. Amadís establishes himself and his knights there after his brief career as the Greek Knight. He is subsequently forced to defend the peninsula against the forces of Lisuarte and the emperor of Rome (the fictitious Sidon). The introduction of book 2 explains how the peninsula was colonized by Apolidon, the son of a Greek king and the sister of the emperor of Constantinople, after he sailed from Rome. Firm Island is the site of the enchanted **Arch of True Lovers**, under which no one may go who has been unfaithful to his or her first love, and through which Amadís and Oriana triumphantly pass in the conclusion.

Sobradisa (soh-brah-dee-SAH). Imaginary kingdom that provides the site for the rescue mission mounted by Amadís, Galaor, and their associates. The episode brings book 1 to a close.

Poor Rock. Also called the **Rock of the Hermitage**, the abode of the hermit Andalod—with whom Amadís lives as Beltenebros—to which Corisanda comes in search of Florestan and on which Oriana takes shelter from a storm while returning to Lisuarte's court from Scotland.

Mongaza (mahn-GAH-zah). Island also known as the island of the **Boiling Lake**, on which King Arban of North Wales and Angriote of Estravaus are briefly imprisoned, and to which an important expedition is mounted by Lisuarte.

Devil's Island. Abode of the monster Endriago, where the Green Sword Knight is shipwrecked en route to Constantinople; when Endriago has been killed it is renamed the **Island of St Mary.**

*Lesser Britain. Region of continental Europe—later known as Brittany, in western France—ruled from his court at Alima by Garinter, the father of Amadís's mother, Elisena.

*Constantinople. Capital of Eastern Christendom, visited by Amadís in his guise as the Green Sword Knight. Amadís's fortunes are revived there, and he is able to summon help therefrom, as well as from Gaul and Bohemia, for his defense of Firm Island in book 4.

*Romania. Region of Eastern Europe, here encompassing much more than the modern state of Romania, which—like other divided lands—is described by the text as a set of "islands." It is where the Green Sword Knight encounters Grasinda, niece of King Tafinor of Bohemia.

— *Brian Stableford*

THE AMBASSADORS

Author: Henry James (1843-1916)
Type of work: Novel
Type of plot: Psychological realism

Time of plot: c. 1900
First published: 1903

Henry James's novel is a tale of two cities in the foreground of which stands Paris, sophisticated center of Old World culture. In the background is the fictional Woollett, Massachusetts—a provincial New England industrial city where the Newsomes have accumulated a fortune, the source of which James does not disclose. Lambert Strether, a middle-aged bachelor and her intended, is dispatched from Woollett by a wealthy widow, Mrs. Abel Newsome, to rescue her son Chad from his immoral life in Paris.

*England. The book opens at Chester, England, where Strether—Mrs. Newsome's "ambassador"— arriving from Liverpool to meet his friend Waymarsh, has a first encounter with Maria Gostrey, who will become his confidant. This brief English scene constitutes a prologue that strikes the theme of Europe—the Europe of old houses and crooked streets which was being stamped upon American imaginations by Henry James's fellow expatriate, painter James Whistler. London launches Strether's eager growth through first impressions, but Paris will complete it.

*Paris. France's capital, the centerpiece of the novel, is a jewel-like city. The initiation of Strether into a Parisian mode of life so different from that of his native Woollett leads him to symbolic gambols through winding passages of darkness and light to a realization, as James put it in his preface, of "more things than had been dreamed of in the philosophy of Woollett." Metaphorically, then, Paris rules Strether's discriminations and attitudes, the only ones to which the reader is privy. At no time does Strether take on his mission with fervor. As the "ambassador" partakes of Paris's enchantments—its natives, streets, and especially its gardens— he becomes subtly aware of how much the city's eternal spring has broadened Chad Newhouse, his charge, and now he himself. For a time, Strether forgets Woollett and all he has left behind, as his eyes scan the picture of Paris, the stir and shimmer of life in the rue de Rivoli and the gardens of the Tuileries. It is to these scenic frames, and the ways in which they envelope Parisians like tableaux, that he succumbs. In fact, Paris defines Strether's perceptions of character.

Behind Paris, interpreting it for Chad, is the adorable and exalted figure of Madame Marie de Vionnet.

Strether's gradual awareness that the French countess and Chad are lovers—hence by all rights she should be the archenemy of all Woollett stands for—is tempered by the powerful sense that she has been largely responsible for the finer person Chad has become. James is careful to situate Strether's major encounters with her at places that convey a special ambience. He first meets Madame de Vionnet among distinguished company in the sculptor Gloriani's old garden. He sees her next in the stillness of her house among old possessions that bespeak for him "her rare unlikeness" to any woman he has met in America. Finally, he has a sudden—and accidental—revelation of her intimate link to Chad in the French countryside, "a land of fancy for him—background of fiction, the medium of art."

Thus does Henry James emphasize Strether's response to place—the pictorial and associational that are so lacking in Woollett. He comes to accept as a matter of course that he is "mixed up with the typical tale of Paris." This final—this Paris-induced reading of his dilemma—amounts to an identification of himself with the Parisians.

Woollett. Massachusetts town from which Strether comes. No scenes are set in Woollett, but its presence even in absence looms like a shadow. In the end it will win its battle with Paris. In a sense, the roles of Paris and Madame de Vionnet are identical. James created her as inseparable from the old city. Every touchstone in her demeanor is related to Strether's impression of her house, where each chair and cabinet is suggestive of the history of the city and of France. With the arrival from Woollett of a second batch of "ambassadors," including Mamie, the girl Chad will marry, both the city and its stunning embodiment falter. The New—Woollett and the Newsomes—will triumph over the old—Paris, Marie de Vionnet, and the convert from the new to the old, Lambert Strether. She bows to Chad's Parisian infatuation; he bows to his own rectitude in denying for himself both Woollett and Paris. He cannot marry Mrs. Newsome and he will not pursue his love for the Frenchwoman.

— *Richard Hauer Costa*

AMELIA

Author: Henry Fielding (1707-1754)
Type of work: Novel
Type of plot: Domestic realism

Time of plot: c. 1733
First published: 1751

Almost the whole of this novel is set in easily recognized, real places within London, with the exception of the beginning and the end of the narrative, which are set in Wiltshire. The relationship between the city and the country is vexed; whereas the city is where country folk go to escape scandals, the country is where Amelia and William Booth happily retire from their many troubles in the city. The Booths manage to return to the security of the country only after William repents of straying from the paths of virtue.

***Newgate Prison.** Notorious London prison in which the narrative begins after Captain William Booth is arrested for beating a watchman when he is, in fact, saving a stranger from ruffians. The prison then becomes the place in which the seeds of both his ruin and final deliverance are sown; there William commits adultery but also makes the acquaintance of the man whose testimony in court at the end of the novel saves Booth's wife from being defrauded of her fortune. Fielding's detailed characterization of the prison exposes the inhuman treatment the poor receive there, while the rich appear to thrive. Newgate is a microcosm of London's corruption.

***Verge of the court.** Area immediately surrounding London's Whitehall and St. James Palaces, within which criminals are safe from arrest because civil law officers have no authority within its precincts. Debtors, such as William Booth, often lived years within the verge, ranging outside its boundaries on Sundays, when civil officers could not make arrests or serve processes of law on debtors. The first time William is held on bail occurs when he is lured to Mrs. Chenevix's fashionable toy shop located just outside the verge of the court, by a tale that Amelia is ill. The verge is a place of relative safety within London precisely because the Booths are insulated from the city's most vicious entertainments.

Sponging house. House of a bailiff, an officer of justice, used as a place of preliminary confinement for debtors. Booth is twice imprisoned for debt at the same sponging house; both times he is delivered by Dr. Harrison. The sponging house serves an important symbolic role in the narrative, for it is here that William embraces religion after reading a book of sermons. It is also where Dr. Harrison realizes that Mr. Murphy has defrauded Amelia. As a place where extraordinary good fortune follows repentance, the sponging house resembles purgatory to William Booth.

***Wiltshire.** County in southwestern England from which several major characters come. Amelia and William become farmers in this county after their marriage but become bankrupt within four years, after William purchases a coach and horses. The other farmers think the Booths are acting too much above their station and force William to buy at the highest prices and sell at the lowest to lessen their pride. After Amelia regains her fortune, the Booths live in Wiltshire for ten happy years.

***Gibraltar.** Peninsula on the south-central coast of Spain dominated by a massive rock formation, around which Great Britain owns a colony and military base. William Booth serves in the British army as a lieutenant and is twice wounded during a Spanish siege of Gibraltar in early 1727. Afterward, the Booths go to Montpellier, a popular medical resort in the south of France, and then to Paris to allow Amelia to recover from the nervous illness she contracts while nursing William's wounds. Although William's service is alluded to throughout the novel as heroic, the swiftness with which he is wounded makes his service appear a little ridiculous.

***London.** Capital and greatest city of Great Britain and place where country folk go to repair their fortunes. Miss Matthews follows her lover there, and Mrs. Bennet/ Atkinson goes there to find her first husband a better living as a clergyman and to flee her aunt's slanders. Typically, however, country people who go to London end up in worse condition than they are in when they arrive because they incur more debts or are debauched by rich lords. Fielding characterizes London's theaters, opera houses, and pleasure gardens as places where affairs are carried on because a woman's virtue is not security enough against strange men's attentions.

***City of London.** District about one mile square within London enclosed by ancient stone walls, within which the Booths escape their creditors. The verge of the court was not part of the City, but was instead part of Westminster, an adjacent town, although colloquially, both the City and Westminster are called "London."

***Haymarket Opera House.** Fashionable London place of entertainment, near the verge of the court, where public masquerades are frequently held. Masquerades were denounced by social reformers because social classes mixed and the disguises were thought to invite sexual license. Colonel James gives the Booths tickets to a masquerade with the view of debauching Amelia, while Mrs. James hopes to snare William there. However, Amelia does not attend the masquerade, having earlier been warned by Mrs. Bennet/Atkinson that such events are often dangerous places for women's virtue, as demonstrated by her own unhappy experience.

— *Anne F. Widmayer*

THE AMERICAN

Author: Henry James (1843-1916)
Type of work: Novel
Type of plot: Psychological realism

Time of plot: Mid-nineteenth century
First published: 1877

Place is almost always important in the fiction of Henry James, an American writer who lived most of his adult life in Europe. In this novel, James uses symbolic and metaphorical descriptions of place primarily to illustrate his novel's central character.

***Europe.** Europe represents culture and sophistication, but also mystery and corruption. Christopher Newman (the "American" of the title), a self-made American millionaire educated in the school of hard knocks, comes to Europe to complete his cultural education and perhaps to find a wife. He visits hundreds of notable churches and a host of museums and palaces. Though he seldom fully understands the great works of art and architecture that he sees, he is willing to concede their worth. Likewise, he never fully understands the members of the aristocratic Bellegarde family or their French Catholic society; in the end, they defeat him.

***Louvre.** Famous Parisian art museum that occupies a former royal palace. Henry James uses the museum to display the lack of cultural sophistication of Newman and his American acquaintance, Tom Tristram. Newman prefers badly painted copies of a pretty aspiring artist to the priceless originals, and Tom Tristram, visiting the Louvre for the first time though he has lived for six years in Paris, wonders aloud if the paintings on the walls are originals or copies.

Tristram home. House in a quarter of Paris that is relatively new during the 1860's—the period in which the novel is set. Like the French aristocrats' gray stone mansions in the Faubourg St. Germain, the newer houses in the Tristrams' neighborhood have pompous white facades, though as yet unweathered. Inside, the modernity and hospitality of the Tristrams' house contrast sharply with the Bellegardes' two-hundred-year-old mansion. The Tristrams' house has gaslights and central heating, as well as an open invitation to Newman, who visits often. There Newman also finds the friendship of Mrs. Tristram, who tries to educate him in the ways of French society. The Tristrams' home radiates warmth and hospitality.

*Rue de l'Université. Street in the Faubourg St. Germain, the aristocratic quarter of Paris, where the Bellegardes' mansion is located. James no doubt chose this name because it is here that the Bellegardes teach Newman the most painful lesson of his life. The houses in this quarter, with their massive facades of gray stone, represent for Newman the secrecy and privacy of the closed world of the European aristocracy. The houses contrast sharply with his own egalitarian ideal of wealthy homes ablaze with the light of hospitality. Three steps—one each to suggest Valentin de Bellegarde, his elder brother Urbain, and their mother, the three obstacles Newman must surmount—lead from the courtyard into the house. Inside, the vestibule is cold, and the house is dimly lit, suggesting not only the cold hearts and the mystique of the Bellegardes, but also how far the family's fortunes have fallen.

Fleurières. Late sixteenth century country home of Claire de Cintré's Bellegarde family. The timeworn château, with its stained bricks, deep-set windows, and cracked causeway, symbolizes the antiquity, mystery, and fallen fortunes of the Bellegarde family. Like the Bellegardes themselves, the house is ugly but still impressive. Its grand central portion is flanked by two low wings, suggesting the beautiful Claire guarded by her mean and low keepers, Urbain de Bellegarde and his mother. The two arches of the bridge also suggest Urbain and his mother, who bar Newman's path to Claire. Inside, the main drawing room is grand and imposing but nearly empty, as the aristocratic Bellegardes are morally bankrupt. The château also gives Newman the feeling of a museum, suggesting that members of the European aristocracy, typified by the Bellegardes, are themselves museum pieces.

Newman's apartment. Residence that Newman rents in Paris. Huge and gilded, the apartment symbolizes Newman's nouveau riche understanding of culture. The sophisticated Valentin de Bellegarde nearly laughs aloud at the apartment's enormous and gaudy parlor. Parlors should be small and intimate, but this one, as Valentin notes, is large enough to be a ballroom or a church. The apartment shows that while Newman is wealthy, he is not yet cultured.

— *Craig A. Milliman*

AN AMERICAN TRAGEDY

Author: Theodore Dreiser (1871-1945)
Type of work: Novel
Type of plot: Naturalism

Time of plot: 1897-1908
First published: 1925

The principal places of this novel are based on the real-life drama of the Chester Gillette-Grace Brown murder case of 1905-1906, which began in New York's Cortland County and ended with Brown's death at Big Moose Lake. Theodore Dreiser, who visited these places, calls the ill-fated couple Clyde Griffiths and Roberta Alden in his novel and makes corresponding changes in place-names.

*Kansas City. Northwestern Missouri city in which the novel opens when the fictional Clyde Griffiths at the age of twelve years is living an uneasy life there with his urban-missionary parents. The dingy neighborhood of his parents' Bickel Street mission contrasts sharply with the life of luxury and excitement that Clyde craves and eventually seeks, first in employment as a bellhop in an upscale hotel, where a "fast" crowd gets him into serious trouble, and later in the small eastern city where most of the novel's action takes place.

Lycurgus. New York town between Utica and Albany, near the actual location of Troy, where Clyde Griffiths arrives at the age of twenty, goes to work in his uncle's collar-manufacturing factory, and takes a room in a rooming house. Nearly all of the descriptions of the fictional town match the real town of Cortland, where Chester Gillette worked at a skirt factory owned by a relative. Moreover, like the historical Grace Brown, Clyde's lover Roberta Alden works in the same factory and lives in another rooming house nearby, occasionally returning home to the rural community of Biltz.

Biltz. New York town fifty miles from Lycurgus where Roberta grew up on a poverty-stricken farm to which she returns after working in Lycurgus. Biltz's bleak landscape contrasts depressingly with the pleasures Roberta remembers from her time in Lycurgus, and she sends Clyde distraught letters, begging him to come and take her away. These letters, later produced at Clyde's murder trial, form part of the narrative in the third part of the novel.

The fictional Biltz corresponds with South Otselic, in New York's Chenango County, which was Grace Brown's hometown.

Twelfth Lake. Adirondack summer home of the young socialite Sondra Finchley's friends that Clyde

visits just before taking Roberta to Big Bittern Lake in the summer of 1906. The leisurely life of swimming, tennis, boating, and golf reinforces his decision to remove the penniless Roberta from his life. He returns to Twelfth Lake and Sondra after Roberta's death and is arrested at nearby Bear Lake while camping with Sondra's friends.

*Utica. New York town that is the first stop on Clyde and Roberta's journey north into the Adirondacks, where Roberta hopes Clyde will propose marriage to her. Their historical counterparts also stopped in Utica, leaving behind evidence that would later help convict Chester Gillette of Grace Brown's murder.

Big Bittern Lake. Lake in the Adirondacks in which Roberta drowns when the rented boat on which she and Clyde are riding overturns and Clyde abandons her. The eerie loneliness of the bay in which the drowning occurs is emphasized both in the novel and in historical accounts of Grace Brown's drowning in the real Big Moose Lake.

— *Rachel P. Maines*

AND QUIET FLOWS THE DON

Author: Mikhail Sholokhov (1905-1984)
Type of work: Novel
Type of plot: Historical realism
Time of plot: 1913-1918

First published: Tikhii Don, 1928-1940 (*And Quiet Flows the Don*, 1934; *The Don Flows Home to the Sea*, 1940)

This epic novel covers the turbulent years in Russian history shortly before and during World War I and the Bolshevik Revolution. The wreckage of Russia is epitomized by the efforts of individuals, mostly Cossacks and peasants, to comprehend the nature of the conflict and to survive.

*Don. River flowing north to south through the most fertile region of Russia and emptying into the Black Sea. It is the central character of the novel, figuratively speaking. Providing the inhabitants living on its shores with ample basic provisions and fertilizing the land on which they depend, the Don is present in their every activity. Called by the peasants "the Mother Don," it seems to initiate and conclude every historical event, especially during World War I and the revolution. The author uses its very name as a stark contrast to the turbulent happen-

ings around it during this period. At the same time, it exerts a calming influence on the peasants as a bastion of permanence, something they can always depend on no matter how unstable their life may be. It also gives its name to the entire region.

Mikhal Sholokhov is eminently qualified to describe the Don region. He was born there. Though not of Cossack ancestry, he spent practically all his life there, wrote almost exclusively about life on the Don and, most importantly, was able to paint a remarkably objective picture of the civil war around the Don.

Tatarsk. Fictional village in the northern part of the Don's course, the home of the Melekhov family, and the place where the novel begins and ends. It is a typical Russian peasant village of modest huts and little else except for fertile fields and river banks. Life is hard but gratifying. The biggest drawback is its relative isolation from the rest of the world, so that news reaches Tatarsk slowly and, when it does, the peasants usually do not know what to make of it. However, what they lack in education, they make up for in their natural intelligence and hard work. Though Tatarsk itself is not always described in precise detail, the reader gets the impression of a vibrant life expressed in joy and sorrow, love and hate, work and play, and the everyday inspiration villagers derive from the majestic Don. The name itself hints at a Melekhov ancestor, a Turkish (Tatar) beauty brought to the village and married to Gregor's grandfather.

Vieshenska (VYE-shen-ska). Town near Tatarsk, a district center, where the Tatarsk villagers go to buy provisions they cannot produce themselves and to take care of official business. When the revolution enveloped the region, Vieshenska played a significant role for both the Red revolutionaries and their opponents, the Whites.

Yagodnoe (YA-gohd-no-ee). Country estate near Tatarsk, home of important characters in the novel, where Gregor and his lover Aksinia find refuge as workers, after falling out with their families.

*Petrograd. Russian city formerly (and now again) known as St. Petersburg that plays a short but important role in the novel. When the first signs of the revolution manifested themselves in Petrograd, some Tatarsk inhabitants happened to be there. This gives the author a chance to bring the peasants closer to understanding this historical event.

*Rostov. Large Russian port at the confluence of the Don and the sea, the final destination of many participants in the struggle between the Whites and the Reds.

Battle front. Several battles between the warring sides are located on both sides of the Don. These scenes are not described geographically in great detail. Instead, the author dwells on the combatants' behavior, especially their bravery and ferocity. Most of the battles occur in or near Tatarsk. None of them was in itself crucial for the outcome of the struggle, but they each had a fateful impact on Tatarsk villagers, often resulting in death and property destruction.

— *Vasa D. Mihailovich*

ANDROMACHE

Author: Euripides (c. 485-406 B.C.E.)
Type of work: Drama
Type of plot: Tragedy

Time of plot: Shortly after the Trojan War
First performed: Andromachē, 426 B.C.E. (English translation, 1782)

The setting of Euripides' play before the altar of a Greek temple, shortly after the Trojan War, derives part of its significance from Andromache's presence there as a captive Trojan princess seeking protection. However, it also functions as a standard for judging the integrity of the characters.

Temple of Thetis. Temple in Thessaly, the central region of ancient Greece, near Phthia, the home of Neoptolemus, the goddess Thetis's grandson and son of Achilles, and Pharsala, the home of Peleus, Thetis's mortal husband. The ancient Greeks considered temples, and particularly temple altars, sanctuaries—places of asylum for both good and evil people. In Euripides'

play, the Trojan hero Hector's widow, Andromache, is seeking refuge at the Temple of Thetis from the threat of Neoptolemus's Spartan wife, Hermione, and her father, Menelaus. She trusts that whoever respects the gods will honor the tradition of sanctuary. However, the Greek king Menelaus does not respect that tradition and lures Andromache away from the altar and lies to her by telling her that her son will be spared if she forfeits her own life. His disrespect for the temple reflects both his untrustworthiness and his barbarism.

Euripides' symbolic use of temples also occurs when the report comes that Neoptolemus is killed by Spartans while praying in the temple of Apollo in another gross example of Spartan treachery, arrogance, and brutality. Unlike the Spartans, Peleus—who could despise Andromache because his son was killed by her brother-in-law—honors Andromache's request from the altar for protection, rescuing her from Menelaus.

Euripides thus uses temples as sacred places of refuge, and, by extension, as measuring rods of civilized decency. Characters such as Menelaus who dishonor the sanctity of sanctuaries, demonstrate their vileness, while those who show respect for the sanctuary demonstrate their nobility and righteousness.

— *Marsha Daigle-Williamson*

ANDROMACHE

Author: Jean Baptiste Racine (1639-1699)
Type of work: Drama
Type of plot: Tragedy

Time of plot: Shortly after the ancient Trojan War
First performed: 1667

This tragedy unfolds in the palace of Pyrrhus, king of Epirus, where Andromache and her young son Astyanax are prisoners after the defeat of the Trojans and Andromache's late husband, Hector, by the Greeks. Jean Baptiste Racine portrays Pyrrhus's palace as a threatening place in which a despot abuses his authority and treats his prisoners arrogantly and arbitrarily.

*Epirus (ih-PAR-rahs). Region along the northwestern Greece coast and what is now southern Albania. In ancient times Epirus was a Greek kingdom whose most famous ruler was Pyrrhus.

Pyrrhus's palace. In the preface to *Andromache*, Racine quotes a passage from Vergil's *Aeneid* that identifies the place, action, and major characters in his own tragedy. After the defeat of the Trojans, Hector's widow Andromache becomes Pyrrhus's prisoner, but other Greek leaders grow concerned by his behavior. His rejection of his fiancé, Hermione, and announced intention to wed Andromache convince them that he is unreliable. In Racine's tragedy, Pyrrhus's palace becomes the center of gross violations of basic human rights in which he tells Andromache that he will execute her son if she does not marry him. Pyrrhus's palace also contains separate cells for Andromache and Astyanax and execution chambers. Pyrrhus seems to conform to no accepted codes of conduct, and this makes his palace an unreasonably dangerous place not only to his prisoners but also to his subjects and to other Greek city states as well. His irrational and violent behavior makes it clear to everyone but himself that he will be killed, either by his own subjects or by other Greek leaders, so that chaos can be ended and moral order restored to Epirus.

— *Edmund J. Campion*

ANGELS IN AMERICA: A Gay Fantasia on National Themes

Author: Tony Kushner (1956-   )
Type of work: Drama
Type of plot: Political
Time of plot: Mid-1985 to 1990

First performed: Part 1, *Millennium Approaches*, 1991, first published, 1992; part 2, *Perestroika*, 1992, first published, 1994

This play follows a number of disparate people trying to make sense of the new world that is taking shape in the light of the fall of the Soviet Union, the rise of American conservatism, and the AIDS crisis. The largely gay, liberal circle of a youthful Prior Walter, who is afflicted with AIDS, is juxtaposed with the right-wing world of Roy Cohn, a fictional version of the powerful lawyer of the same name who died of AIDS in 1986. In addition, there are a number of other characters—both natural and supernatural—who cross the paths of Prior and Cohn, creating a complex mosaic of different times and places, and more than one level of reality.

***New York City.** This play uses many real locations in and around New York City, such as the East Village, the Lower East Side, the South Bronx, and Brooklyn Heights. However, the most important of these exterior settings is Bethesda Fountain in Central Park, a large fountain with a statue called the Bethesda Angel. It is a place around which New Yorkers like to relax, talk, and play music. This final setting of the play suggests that spiritual forces have aligned themselves to produce a new lease on life for him.

The other important New York venue is one that is interior, namely the hospital or sickrooms of two men suffering from AIDS. One room is that of Prior Walter, the other is Roy Cohn's. Both rooms are often transformed, however, into spaces for hallucinations and visions, especially the appearance of an august, opalescent, winged angel who crashes into Prior's room to declare him a prophet and charge him with a great mission.

Other worlds. These include an imaginary Antarctica, supernatural levels of reality, and various versions of the **Afterworld**, ranging from a bleak hell to a gathering place for worried angels heavily invested in the outcome of life on earth.

***Salt Lake City.** Capital of Utah and headquarters of the Mormon church, this venue and the characters in the play who come from there suggest a mainstream midwestern conservative perspective.

— *Margaret Boe Birns*

ANGLE OF REPOSE

Author: Wallace Stegner (1909-1993)
Type of work: Novel
Type of plot: Historical realism

Time of plot: 1860-1970
First published: 1971

This novel explores a marriage that founders on the principal characters' differing reactions to the economic and cultural opportunities of the American West. Susan Burling, a talented young artist and writer, marries a mining engineer, Oliver Ward, and joins him as he follows an unexpectedly difficult career in remote, though often beautiful, places. She increasingly regards her life in the West as an exile from the familiar places of her youth in the East, and from beloved friends whose lives are linked to the pleasures and advantages of urban life.

Zodiac Cottage. Last home of Oliver Ward, the grandfather of Lyman Ward, a retired history professor who is constructing a narrative of his grandparents' lives from documents and personal reminiscences. Located in Grass Valley, California, the cottage takes its name from the Zodiac Mine, which Oliver superintended in his later career. The cottage and its gardens resonate with the lives of Lyman's grandparents and also serve as the stage for his painful recuperation from the amputation of a leg. Throughout the novel, which is threaded with Lyman's first-person narration, the self-sufficiency of his virtual but self-imposed confinement to Zodiac Cottage is used as a counterpoint to Susan and Oliver Ward's shifting domestic circumstances half a century earlier.

*New Almaden.** California community built near the New Almaden Mine, located about twelve miles by stage road from San Jose. Some weeks following their marriage, Susan Ward joins her husband at the New Almaden Mine, where he is employed as chief engineer. Susan expects her new home to be merely a cottage on a bare hill amid ugly mine buildings but instead finds a handsome, though modest, new house with a veranda. At the moment of her arrival she feels sensations about space and size that are emblematic of pioneers in the American West. Wallace Stegner knew the New Almaden region intimately, as he lived for many years not far from it, in Los Altos Hills.

A brief interlude set in the nearby coastal town of Santa Cruz provides Lyman Ward with one of several opportunities in the novel to remark upon the contemporary face of the landscape. As one who writes books and monographs about the frontier, Ward is well suited to contrast the physical and social environment of the present with that of the nineteenth century.

*Leadville.** Colorado mining town located high in the Rocky Mountains, about eighty miles from Denver, near the headwaters of the Arkansas River. A note of adventure, even physical peril, is introduced to the novel by a vivid passage describing Susan Ward's two-day journey to Leadville from Denver, first by train and stage, and then by wagon over Mosquito Pass. The stark contrast between the civilized East and the near-barbaric West is moderated by an account of the Wards' dwelling. Though the cottage is a modest cabin by a stream on the edge of town, it becomes a cozy, even gracious, home through ceaseless work and especially through Susan Ward's capacity for hospitality and for sophisticated conversation with the notable men and women who pass through Leadville. In Stegner's treatment of the Ward cabin, the significance for Susan of a secure home emerges as a foremost theme. If she is able to create such a home, Susan believes that even in the absence of material wealth she can resist the transience and social crudity of the frontier West, and also provide an opportunity for her children to experience a home they can love.

*Boise River Canyon** (BOY-zee). Valley located about ten miles upstream from Boise, Idaho—a city that was a territorial capital and then a state capital during the long period during which the novel unfolds. Oliver Ward spends a decade trying to bring a regional irrigation project to completion.

The Wards' struggle to rise from rude beginnings to gentility is embodied in two houses in which they live in the valley. Susan narrates the building of the first house in a letter to her successful Eastern friends and offers them a worthy destination for the visit she longs for but which never occurs. Oliver builds the second house— which has a lane of Lombardy poplars and a rose garden—as a surprise for Susan, while she is visiting friends in the East with the children. This house represents a last burst of optimism about the Wards' prospects, which are soon to be extinguished simultaneously with the accidental drowning of their youngest child in one of the project's irrigation canals.

*Michoacán** (mee-choh-ah-KAHN). State in northwestern Mexico in which Oliver Ward is commissioned to evaluate a mine located several days' journey from Morelia, the state capital. Susan accompanies him and is enraptured by the style and ambience of Mexican culture. Prevented by her transient and economically insecure existence from traveling in Europe as her well-off Eastern friends have done, she eagerly accepts Mexico as her only glimpse of the Old World civilizations that she yearns to know first-hand.

*Milton.** Rural New York town on the Hudson River, about three miles below Poughkeepsie, in which Susan Burling is reared. Her upbringing in a Quaker household in Milton is contrasted, though not emphatically, with the material and social comforts of the life she later enjoys in New York City, where she encounters urban culture and society. After graduating from an excellent Manhattan art college, Susan applies her talents as a writer and illustrator equally well to city and country life. This circumstance suggests that Stegner, despite his particular devotion to western places in virtually all his writings, considers the artist, or writer, capable of a range of geographic sympathies greater than that of most of his own fictional characters.

— *Clyde S. McConnell*

ANIMAL FARM

Author: George Orwell (Eric Arthur Blair, 1903-1950)
Type of work: Novel
Type of plot: Satire

Time of plot: Mid-twentieth century
First published: 1945

Like George Orwell's other famous novel, Nineteen Eighty-Four *(1949),* Animal Farm *is an exposé of the threat of totalitarianism. While* Nineteen Eighty-Four *is set in a fictionalized future England,* Animal Farm *is written like a children's fable, set on a farm. Tired by being exploited by humans, the animals of Manor Farm decide to rebel and run the farm themselves. At first an egalitarian paradise, the farm eventually devolves into a totalitarian hell.*

Manor Farm. English farm at which the entire novel is set. When the novel opens, it is called Manor Farm and is run by a farmer named Jones. These names indicate that this farm stands for any farm, or any place, and that the entire novel should be read as an allegory. However, since Orwell wrote in the introduction to the Ukrainian edition that he wanted to expose the Soviet myth, *Animal Farm* also stands for the Soviet Union in particular. When the animals take over the farm, they rename it Animal Farm; when the pigs revert to the name Manor Farm in the final pages of the book, the complete failure of the animals' revolution is indicated. No animal leaves the farm unless it is a traitor (Molly), declared an enemy of the state (Snowball), or sold to the enemy to be killed (Boxer). When they do leave, the animals rewrite history. Animal Farm is like the Soviet Union in having its own official history that serves the purposes of its rulers.

Orwell's love of animals and his practice of raising his own vegetables and animals are clear in his loving description of the farm; his socialist politics come through in his sympathies with the animals as real workers and in his descriptions of the barn.

Farmhouse. House in which Jones originally lived. Like the farm, the farmhouse is perfectly ordinary, until the animals drive the humans from what the humans see as their rightful place. The farmhouse symbolizes the seat of government; no real work is done there. When the pigs move into the farmhouse, it is a sign that the revolution will fail. The novel closes with the other animals, the workers, watching through the windows of the farmhouse as the pigs meet with Mr. Pilkington to toast the renaming of Animal Farm as Manor Farm. This symbolizes the tendency of rulers to ignore the abuses suffered by the common people in all countries, British socialism's betrayal of the worker in particular, and how the animals/workers are always excluded from gatherings of their leaders.

Barn. Originally an ordinary barn used for work, shelter, and storage. Under the rule of the animals, the barn becomes a meeting place, a place to resolve disputes, and the place where all legitimate political decisions are made. The barn is where all the real work is done, and it is where the revolution is born. The laws of Animal Farm are painted on the side of the barn.

Foxwood. One of farms bordering Manor Farm. Foxwood is described as large and neglected, with run-down hedges. It represents England, with its substandard military and ill-kept borders. Its clumsy but easygoing owner Mr. Pilkington symbolizes British politicians.

Pinchfield. Another of the neighboring farms. Pinchfield is described as smaller and better kept than Foxwood. It symbolizes Germany; its owner, Mr. Frederick, stands for Hitler. Pinchfield and Foxwood put pressure on the animals' revolution, are threatened by it, and threaten it in turn. Jones asks for help after the animals' rebellion, and the farmers reject his plea, as the nations of Europe rejected the pleas from the displaced czars. The business deals between farms symbolize the political deals in which the Soviet Communists sold out their own people.

Sugarcandy Mountain. Imaginary utopia in the preachings of Moses, the raven. Sugarcandy Mountain is animal heaven. Moses is useful to Jones because he preaches a dream beyond this life and keeps the animals pacified, but Moses leaves when the animals actually try to establish a utopia on earth. At the end of the book, he is not only back, but actively supported by the pigs. This indicates that the idea of heaven is threatening to real revolutionaries, but that tyrants find it useful for their subjects to have another realm about which to dream.

— Greg Beatty

ANNA CHRISTIE

Author: Eugene O'Neill (1888-1953)
Type of work: Drama
Type of plot: Social realism

Time of plot: Early twentieth century
First performed: 1921; first published, 1923

This story of a young, embittered prostitute who leaves a degrading and frustrating life inland to seek a new life near the sea is highly dependent on the locale, namely the waterways between New York and Massachusetts. The barge on which most of the action takes place represents the nexus between land and sea. The sea, which is indicated by the presence of fog, beckons as a symbol of life itself, with all its possibilities for magical fulfillment or deep disappointment.

North Atlantic seacoast. Eugene O'Neill's depiction of the seacoast is based on his own youthful experience as a seaman during a time when he had dropped out of college. The barge on which most of the action takes place stops in New York City, Provincetown, and Boston, moving from the Long Island Sound to the Nantucket Sound, around Cape Cod, and ending in Boston Harbor. While the barge hugs the coast, the greater sea intrudes in the person of Matt Burke, a virile sailor rescued from an open boat after the wreck of his steamer. For Anna, the sea and her seaman are rejuvenating and spiritually transformative. For Chris, however, the sea is an "old devil" which will destroy all who venture onto it.

Simeon Winthrop. Commercial barge that is the home and livelihood of Christopher Christopherson, a Swedish immigrant of fifty. The play's stage directions describe the barge in some detail. For Chris, the barge is a retreat, but the barge inspires Anna with new possibilities.

Johnny-the-Priest's Saloon. Rough waterfront bar on New York City's South Street, where Anna first reunites with her father. This location is based on O'Neill's own memories of a bar known as Jimmy-the-Priest's. Stage directions indicate double swinging doors and half barrels of cheap whiskey drawn by spigots, characteristic of saloons of its time and place.

— *Margaret Boe Birns*

ANNA KARÉNINA

Author: Leo Tolstoy (1828-1910)
Type of work: Novel
Type of plot: Social realism

Time of plot: Nineteenth century
First published: 1875-1877 (English translation, 1886)

The sociogeographic location of this novel is the family life of the Russian nobility in the late nineteenth century, at the time of great social and political reforms and disintegration of the old patriarchal values preserved in the rural areas under the influence of the moral corruption of the big cities. The novel is a double-plotted spiritual autobiography, offering two alternatives: faith-salvation or destruction-suicide.

*Moscow. Traditional capital and largest city of Russia, in which the novel opens in the prosperous, comfortable home of Stepan Arkadievich Oblonsky, Anna's brother. The whole household, including five children and a complex structure of servants, suffer from the turmoil caused by Oblonsky's secret indiscretion with his children's governess. Gradually Tolstoy portrays other families and their households, showing their beliefs, life styles, and consequently the level of harmony and happiness or the lack of it.

*St. Petersburg. Capital of Imperial Russia and rival of Moscow as Russia's chief social and cultural center. While Moscow is the more traditional, more religious, and more Russian, St. Petersburg is more European and more avant-garde. The novel's protagonists spend considerable time in both cities. When the novel opens, Anna and Karénin's household is in St. Petersburg; later, Anna moves to Count Vronsky's home in Moscow.

Leo Tolstoy depicts the easy, idle lives of Russia elite society in Moscow and St. Petersburg. Members of the elite are "infected" by modern ideas coming from the West and corroding natural and healthy family life. They spend most of their time in parlors, ballrooms, clubs and restaurants, horse tracks, ice skating rinks, and other pleasure centers that the book portrays as the Sodom and Gomorrah of their time. In these places, people gossip, flirt with one another, drink, gamble, and engage in debauchery and kill one another in duels—all to combat the emptiness and boredom of their lives. Meanwhile, governesses, nurses, valets, cooks, coachmen, and other servants are responsible for raising their children and tending their households.

To Tolstoy, cities, as sites of civilization and corruption, deviate from the natural, healthy lives of the working class, whose members are truly religious. The educated, the nihilists, the atheists, and the agnostics often choose lives of "worldly" pleasures, often based on vanity, greed, lust, gluttony, sloth, bigotry, and prejudice.

Levin estate. Country home of Konstantin Levin, who—in contrast to Anna and Vronsky—dislikes cities. Although from a Moscow family, he lives on his estate, away from the city, actively working his farm. The beauty of nature and his search for the meaning of life lead him to God and a feeling of complete happiness with life. His choice of the right mate, unlike Anna's and Vronsky's, is not based on physical passion. Levin and Kitty have much in common: their upbringing, value systems, and life philosophies. Through marriage and parenthood their love deepens and matures.

Railway station. Moscow station in which Anna and Vronsky meet amid the confusion of a bloody accident. The same station is later the site of Anna's suicide under the wheels of a monstrous freight train, which symbolizes the impersonal blindness and unnaturalness of Anna and Vronsky's obsessive lust.

— *Mira N. Mataric*

ANNA OF THE FIVE TOWNS

Author: Arnold Bennett (1867-1931)
Type of work: Novel
Type of plot: Domestic realism

Time of plot: Late nineteenth century
First published: 1902

As this novel's title indicates, the story is set in the "Five Towns"—Arnold Bennett's own name for the Potteries, the district in central England's Staffordshire known for the manufacture of china and pottery. Bennett portrays the Five Towns as a bleak industrial environment that powerfully shapes the life of his central character, Anna Tellwright, a young woman who comes of age in the house of a miserly, tyrannical father.

Five Towns. Chief setting of the novel, modeled closely on the Potteries, the pottery-manufacturing area of central England where Bennett grew up. Much of Bennett's fiction is set here. The Five Towns—Turnhill, Bursley, Hanbridge, Knype, and Longshaw—are based on the actual Midlands towns of Turnstall, Burslem, Hanley, Stoke-upon-Trent, and Longton, which were administratively merged in 1910 to form the present-day city of Stoke-on-Trent.

Bennett portrays the Five Towns as a dark, dreary place, devoted unabashedly to the business of getting and spending. The towns are mean, somber, hard-featured, and uncouth, and the poison vapors emitted by their ovens and chimneys have shrivelled the surrounding country. In Bursley, where Anna Tellwright lives with her father and sister, residents have created a park, but even it is "unlovely"; it is a sign, says the narrator, of the first faint longings for beauty in a district resigned to unredeemed ugliness. With their ever-present factories and cramped red-brown streets, the Five Towns provide a broad context for the lives of Bennett's characters. While other settings offer residents respite, even beauty, the bleak industrial setting is never far away, a reminder of the narrow, oppressive quality of life in the Five Towns.

Manor Terrace. Home of the miser Ephraim Tell-wright's family in Bursley. Many of the domestic scenes in the novel take place in this unimpressive yellow brick house with a long narrow garden behind it. Although Anna Tellwright's father is one of the wealthiest men in the Five Towns, he insists on living an austere existence, devoid of even the smallest luxuries. His house and its daily routines mirror his tyrannical, miserly nature. The house's rooms are stark and gloomy, the family's plain meals—eaten mostly in silence—are served with dreary precision and sameness. For Anna and her sister Agnes, the house is a cheerless place where they live in constant fear of their father's seething anger.

Anna's kitchen. Room in Manor Terrace that stands out from the rest of the house as *Anna's* place—the only satisfactory space in the house. Bennett describes this room in loving detail, making it a key location in the novel, the place where Henry Mynors first expresses his admiration for Anna. Everything in the room is bright and spotless and in perfect order, giving it the air of human use and occupation. Mynors tells Anna that it is nicest room he knows. For both Henry and Bennett, the kitchen—clean, simple, and dignified—is the highest possible proof of Anna's fine character.

Landsdowne House. Home of the Sutton family, which Anna visits for a sewing party. Here, as elsewhere in the novel, Bennett develops Anna's character by describing her reaction to a particular place. The house is everything that the Tellwright house is not—rich, luxurious, overstuffed—its rooms filled with expensive furnishings, its walls adorned with beautiful pictures. Anna's friend Beatrice Sutton shows Anna the upstairs art studio that her father has furnished for her. Later, Mrs. Sutton serves an ample tea of fancy breads and cakes, jams, sandwiches, and pork pies. Anna, who has

had almost no social life, is amazed by the opulence of the Sutton household, a stark contrast to her own meager life.

Price's pottery works. Factory Anna inherited from her mother, who died when Anna was five. After her twenty-first birthday, her father forces her to go to the factory personally to collect the overdue rent that Titus Price owes. Anna finds the condition of the run-down factory shocking—its "yard" is a small square paved with black, greasy mud—and she is humiliated by having to collect money from a man she has long regarded as a pillar of the Five Towns. The incident illustrates Anna's deep emotional sensitivity and her helplessness before the demands of her overbearing father.

Mynors's pottery works. Factory that Anna tours as Henry Mynors's guest. In sharp contrast to Titus Price's pottery works, Mynors's factory is one of the best of its size in the district. Just as Anna's kitchen is a testament to her character, so Mynors's factory is a testament to his. His factory is clean and orderly, its workers skilled and efficient. Anna's visit to the facility heightens her admiration for Mynors and strengthens the growing bond between them. The scene at the factory also gives Bennett an opportunity to write a set piece—a detailed, affectionate description of the operation of a model manufacturing plant. One of few scenes in the novel that shows the Five Towns in a positive light, it suggests a certain nostalgia on Bennett's part for the place of his youth.

*****Isle of Man.** Island in the Irish Sea, off the west coast of England, that the Suttons, Anna Tellwright, and Henry Mynors visit for a summer holiday. The Isle of Man is an important location in the novel—a place away from, and in dramatic contrast to, the gritty, industrial atmosphere of the Five Towns. Bennett describes the island's scenery in considerable detail—its steep mountains and beautiful bays, its quaint fishing village of Port Erin, and the cottage in which Anna and Mynors stay as guests of the Suttons. The island holiday is a pastoral interlude—a time for Anna of unprecedented freedom and contentment, and a time for Mynors to complete his courtship of Anna. Near the end of the island holiday, after Anna has competently nursed the seriously ill Beatrice Sutton back to health, Mynors proposes, and he and Anna leave the island engaged to be married.

Priory. Home of Titus Price, which Henry Mynors

purchases for himself and Anna after Price commits suicide. For Anna, though she does not say so to Mynors, the Priory is a grim, dreary place, a reminder of her unpleasant dealings with Price and of her sense of responsibility for his death after his business failed. Toward the end of the novel, Anna realizes that her true passion—a sort of powerful maternal love—is for Titus's orphaned son, Willie. Although she does not love Mynors, she marries him out of duty. The Priory, the home that she will occupy as a married woman, thus becomes a place of sorrow rather than joy.

— *Michael Hennessy*

ANOTHER COUNTRY

Author: James Baldwin (1924-1987)
Type of work: Novel
Type of plot: Social realism

Time of plot: Mid-twentieth century
First published: 1962

In this novel, New York City provides Harlem-born James Baldwin with settings in which to explore the ambiguities, tensions, and corrupting influences that beset interracial relationships, especially sexual ones, even among people with considerable personal freedom, liberal social views, and relatively little racial bias.

*New York City. Great northern city in whose borough of Manhattan most of the novel's action unfolds. New York plays a determining role in the lives of the book's eight principal characters. To the two southerners, it is a magnet that has drawn them from native surroundings that they regard as limiting and unsatisfactory in their search for a more stimulating life. Manhattan has also formed the novel's two African American characters, Rufus Scott and his younger sister Ida, culturally and socially. The lone married couple of the novel, Richard and Cass Silenski, have most likely chosen to live in Manhattan because Richard is a writer who wishes to work amid the world of publishers and editors. Daniel Vivaldo Moore, another, but unsuccessful, writer, has a "stony affection" for New York, a city that offers him a chance to exercise his talent for friendship with its varied racial and ethnic types.

A young Frenchman named Yves persuades his male lover to return to Manhattan after a sojourn abroad, but because the former arrives, confident and hopeful, only at the end of the story, it is left to readers to imagine what the city will come to represent for him. For the others New York has proved a difficult place to live. One of the southerners leaves New York disenchanted after three years, while the other returns home, her mental health destroyed by her stormy relationship with Rufus, who thereafter commits suicide.

James Baldwin's New York is a place where disparate and socially nonconforming people can develop intense relationships and discover exciting, if precarious, career opportunities, but it is also a place of brutalizing influences. It brims with people, many of them ironically seeking a respite from desperate loneliness. Much of the socializing takes place in bars and cheap apartments where the principals frequently obey the urge to overdrink and vent their hostilities on even their friends. The liberal social attitudes of most of the white principals allow them to develop strong affection for the two black characters, but despite their best efforts the white characters cannot totally empathize with Rufus and Ida, and racial tension crackles among them. Life in the city has made Ida perhaps the strongest character in the novel; she is hard and cynical, though only barely out of her adolescence.

*Greenwich Village (GREH-nich). Neighborhood in the lower west side of Manhattan that had—in the time in which the novel is set—a longstanding reputation as a cosmopolitan neighborhood attractive to artists and writers. Baldwin himself spent much time in Greenwich Village in the 1940's. Among his novel's characters, Rufus a musician, and his sister, an aspiring singer, both perform there, and the would-be writer Vivaldo lives there. The Village's live-and-let-live atmosphere enables the Harlem-bred Rufus to feel reasonably comfortable visiting his friend Vivaldo there. Later Vivaldo and Ida are able to live together in his apartment without arousing the curiosity and hostility that an interracial couple might face elsewhere.

Harlem. Northern section of Manhattan, centering on 125th Street, that had become a predominantly African American community by the middle of the twentieth century. Harlem is the home of Rufus and Ida, as well as vast numbers of other African Americans. The novel never describes their home directly, however, and restricts its Harlem scenes mainly to bars and night clubs. While racial tension lurks close to the surface in the night spots, they offer opportunities for black and white people to mingle and share the African American musical heritage often on display.

France. European country in which the lovers Eric Jones and young Yves spend time, living in Paris and vacationing on the Mediterranean coast. As an American who lived in Europe himself, Baldwin could understand why southerners would want to come to New York, but New Yorkers, he thought, could escape their surroundings only by going to France. In this novel Eric does both, but later returns to New York because Yves sees no future for himself in France.

— *Robert P. Ellis*

ANTIGONE

Author: Jean Anouilh (1910-1987)
Type of work: Drama
Type of plot: Tragedy

Time of plot: Antiquity
First performed: 1944; first published, 1946 (English translation, 1946)

This play is nominally set in ancient Thebes, a place so remote in time and geography from France in the 1940's when Jean Anouilh wrote that it enabled Anouilh to situate the crucible of action in the minds of his principal characters while simultaneously inviting his contemporary French audiences to reflect on the play's parallels with their own lives in German-occupied France.

Thebes (theebz). Ancient Greek city northwest of Athens that provides the nominal setting of this play. The play mentions Thebes a dozen times but provides no other historical or mythical references to strengthen its deliberately weak sense of place. On the contrary, other places mentioned in the text are resolutely unspecific.

Anouilh is determined not to provide local or historical color that could delay his audiences' growing awareness that Thebes is merely a convenient label and the Greek princess Antigone an opportunistic topic, as his primary intention was to blur the distinction between reality and dramatic illusion and to confront the opposing themes of youth and age, resistance and collaboration, irresponsibility and the burdens of power, especially within the exceptional context of occupation by a foreign enemy. Thus, although the visible action never shifts from the royal Theban palace, there are references to the countryside just outside the city, where Antigone attempts to bury her brother, the drinking houses discussed enthusiastically by the guards as they gossip and ignore her distress, the garden and the beach, mention of which reveals the childlike side of her character, and the sinister Caves of Hades, where she is to be buried alive as a punishment for her crime.

Palace. Center of the royal Theban government and the principal stage setting for the play. Anouilh specified a neutral décor for the palace. On one level, ornate splendor would not befit this court, mourning the recent loss of so many members of the royal family. On another, it would delay the audiences' realization that the action is also appropriate to contemporary France and, moreover, is often self-consciously theatrical. The creation of tension between the audience's natural desire to suspend disbelief and its sophisticated awareness of these other levels is one of Anouilh's major achievements.

— *William Brooks*

ANTIGONE

Author: Sophocles (c. 496-406 B.C.E.)
Type of work: Drama
Type of plot: Tragedy

Time of plot: Antiquity
First performed: Antigonē, 441 B.C.E. (English translation, 1581)

This classic treatment of the clash between individual conscience and civic authority is set in the ancient Greek city of Thebes, outside the Theban royal palace, home of both Antigone and her uncle Creon, who is now king.

*Thebes (theebz). Ancient Greek city located in Boeotia, a district northwest of Athens, Thebes was famous in the ancient world for its tragic royal family and the seven-gated wall surrounding the city. The long-standing enemy of Athens, Thebes was the setting of several Greek tragedies. Despotic Thebes seems to have served Athenian playwrights of the fifth century B.C.E. as a kind of inverted mirror image of democratic Athens, providing them with a context within which to discuss social and political issues that might prove too disturbing if dramatized within a contemporary Athenian setting. By setting *Antigone* in Thebes, in the remote, mythical past, Sophocles freed himself to explore the tensions between personal freedom and legal restraint, household and city, male and female—all tensions of keen interest to contemporary Athenians, whose radically democratic system of government involved a constant program of public discussion and debate.

Royal palace. Represented, probably with no attempt at physical "realism," by a two-story wooden building at the rear of the stage. Athenian audiences would have been well versed in the tragic history of the royal house of Thebes, a history of internecine conflict, incest, and treachery, and may well have recognized the palace as a place where the two meanings of the word "house" mingle in interesting and problematic ways. The palace, as the royal residence, is Antigone's home.

Cave. Place in which Creon entombs Antigone. It is an axiom of the Greek tragic theater that particularly unpleasant events, especially those involving violence and death, occur offstage but are described on stage, after the fact, by various characters. In *Antigone*, the most interesting offstage place is the cave in which Creon entombs Antigone. This "bridal-cave of Hades," where Antigone hangs herself, is one of the play's more important symbols, representing death but also, in its symbol of the womb and thus the female, ironically commenting on Creon's stridently masculine rhetoric and political stance.

— *Michael Stuprich*

THE ANTIQUARY

Author: Sir Walter Scott (1771-1832)
Type of work: Novel
Type of plot: Fiction of manners

Time of plot: Late eighteenth century
First published: 1816

This is a novel about how the past lives on to shape, influence, and sometimes threaten the present, in which the present is represented mainly by the mercantile Scottish town of Fairport. The past is mostly embodied in the ruins of St. Ruth's Priory. Most of the main characters are haunted by, or even trapped in, the past, and their various relationships to the past are represented in Walter Scott's treatments of dwellings.

Fairport. Fictional town on the eastern coast of Scotland that forms the novel's central setting. Fairport is based on the real Scottish coastal town of Arbroath. Like its original, Fairport is a lively provincial mercantile town. Throughout *The Antiquary*, it functions not only as a setting, but also as a symbol for the energetic, if sometimes vulgar, present. In contrast to most of the novel's main characters, the people of Fairport have little interest in the past. Their modern focus is on making money, gossip, and the threat of invasion at a time when Great Britain was locked in war with France.

St. Ruth's Priory. Beautiful gothic ruin near Fairport and the scene of many of the novel's most important episodes. It is here that Lovel and the Highlander Hector duel, that Dousterswivel practices his necromancy, that Sir Arthur Wardour seeks the treasure of Misticot, that the old Countess Glenallen is buried at night, and that Oldbuck explains antiquities to his friends. Although the priory is a peaceful and serene ruin, it functions as the novel's main symbol for the past and its power. As such, it reveals and represents the antiquated Scottish Highland pride of Hector, the exploitation of the past by Dousterswivel, the aristocratic credulity toward the past of Sir Arthur, the guilty and arrogant past of Countess Glenallen, and the pedantic obsession with the trivialities of the past in Oldbuck.

Monkbarns. Home of Jonathan Oldbuck, the antiquary who gives the novel its title. Oldbuck is a kindly and generous man whose good qualities are often obscured by his crusty manner and his devotion to old books, artifacts, and antiquities in general. Oldbuck is often referred to as "Monkbarns," and indeed his house reflects his character and qualities. Monkbarns is an old monastic structure. Its many rooms are oddly joined together, and those rooms are filled with a huge collection of dusty and often useless fragments of the past. Monkbarns even has a "Green Room" which seems literally haunted by the past. Despite all this, Monkbarns is in the end a place of humanity, vitality, and hospitality. Like its owner, Monkbarns is an odd combination of the antiquated and the warmly human.

Glenallen House. Grand mansion of the Glenallen family. This great house is dark, gloomy, and melancholy. Its rooms are draped in black, and the subjects of its paintings are martyrdoms and torments. The earl of Glenallen lives here in bleak and broken solitude, haunted by guilt and grief. The house is a perfect reflection of the lofty pride of an ancient family and of a family history overshadowed by insane arrogance, intrigue, suicide, and supposed incest.

Knockwinnock Castle. Family home of Sir Arthur and Isabella Wardour. Like Sir Arthur himself, Knockwinnock is a combination of the aristocratic and the vulnerable. The splendor of the house reflects Sir Arthur's aristocratic pride and his mad dreams of grand estates and limitless wealth. Sir Arthur at Knockwinnock is essentially Scott's symbol of an outmoded aristocracy that can no longer deal adequately with the world of reality. Sir Arthur's folly and credulity about the past, his family history, and money nearly bring ruin to Knockwinnock, which is under a modern siege from creditors and lawyers.

Mucklebacket cottage. Humble home of the Mucklebackets, a family of fishermen. Scott vividly describes the cottage as a center of vigorous, if somewhat chaotic, peasant life. The human dignity of the Mucklebackets is reflected in their sense of the sanctity of their dwelling. When grief comes to Mucklebacket cottage, the genuineness of feeling seen here is a marked contrast to the icy inhumanity of life at Glenallen House. Old Elspeth Mucklebacket's broken tales of the dark Glenallen past form a strange contrast to the cottage in which they are told, and show how long and dark the shadows of the past are in *The Antiquary*.

Sands. Coastal path between Monkbarns and Knockwinnock. Here, early in the novel, a great storm nearly kills Sir Arthur and Isabella as they are caught between a raging sea and rocky cliffs. Scott's unforgettable account of their peril and rescue by Edie Ochiltree and Lovel is a brilliant foreshadowing of how the Wardours are later rescued by Edie and Lovel from financial ruin.

— *Phillip B. Anderson*

ANTONY AND CLEOPATRA

Author: William Shakespeare (1564-1616)
Type of work: Drama
Type of plot: Tragedy

Time of plot: c. 30 B.C.E.
First performed: c. 1606-1607; first published, 1623

Among William Shakespeare's dramatic works, this play is noted for its many rapidly shifting scenes. It is also remarkable for the great distances over which its scenes shift. The many locales include Rome, southern Italy, Sicily, Syria, Greece, and Egypt. However, all the scenes coalesce around the very different cultures of Rome and Egypt, which represent established empire and civilization on the one hand and untamed provincial wildness on the other. Rome reflects the character of Octavius Caesar, Egypt the character of Cleopatra, and Mark Antony is caught between the two worlds.

*Egypt. Located on the outskirts of the vast Roman Empire, the Egypt of 30 B.C.E. is portrayed as an exotic land of mystery, fecundity, extravagance, and unconventional behavior, where the Nile River rises and falls to signal the crudely designed planting and harvest seasons, and open sexual experimentation includes transvestism. Cleopatra embodies Egypt in her wildly extravagant behavior and passion. As one of Rome's three rulers after the death of Julius Caesar, Mark Antony has been sent in a period of political instability to govern Egypt but soon wavers in his commitment to Roman values and falls in love with Cleopatra. As the scenes shift rapidly between Cleopatra's palace in Alexandria and various locations in Rome, Italy, and Greece, the shifting of place symbolizes the conflict of values in Antony's mind. In act 1, Antony feels guilty about his un-Roman behavior and temporarily returns to Rome, where he marries Octavia to strengthen his political power, but he soon quarrels with Octavius, his fellow triumvir, and returns to Egypt in act 3. As Antony battles Octavius for political power, the scenes shift rapidly between Cleopatra's palace and various battle scenes in the eastern part of the empire until Antony finally loses the political struggle with Octavius.

*Rome. Rome is seen in the play as the center of a highly ordered and established civilization with stately political and social values. In the first words of the play, set in Cleopatra's palace, Antony is being judged harshly by his followers for ignoring his Roman duties in order to satisfy sensual pleasures. When a messenger from Rome arrives with news from Octavius, Antony dismisses the him, symbolizing his break with Rome. From the very first moments of the play, then, Shakespeare is juxtaposing the two cultures and forcing the audience into a complex assessment of their competing values. This conflict has been described in various ways, for example as a conflict between culture and barbarity, reason and passion, duty and desire, or decorum and hedonism. Plutarch, the source for Shakespeare's story, clearly chooses sides in this conflict and sees Antony as a foolish old man, but Shakespeare remains uncommitted, suggesting value and limitations in both cultures. This leaves the thematic conflict richly open-ended and the rapidly shifting places that embody this thematic conflict serve as another reflection of the play's great tension.

Cleopatra's monument. The play ends in this mausoleum near Cleopatra's Alexandria palace as she takes her own life after learning of Antony's suicide at the end of act 4. The scope of the play's action shrinks after act 3, scene 6, in which Rome is last used as a setting. Thereafter, the action begins moving eastward, contracting toward the more intimate setting of the tragic conclusion. The intimacy of Cleopatra's monument is contrasted with the epic scope at the beginning of the play, but even here, with Antony close by in Cleopatra's palace, Shakespeare emphasizes how distant the lovers are from each other. Cleopatra's sequestration and initially false report of suicide leads to Antony's real suicide. Then the two struggle, almost comically, to be near each other, as Antony's body is hoisted up the monument walls for a final kiss. After he dies, Roman soldiers invade Cleopatra's space and Rome and Egypt are finally merged, with Cleopatra a prisoner and in danger of being carried to Rome to be put on humiliating display as a trophy of war. In her own suicide, Cleopatra thwarts this plan and "marries" herself to Antony at last.

— *Terry Nienhuis*

THE APOSTLE

Author: Sholem Asch (1880-1957)　　　　　*Time of plot:* First century C.E.
Type of work: Novel　　　　　*First published:* 1943
Type of plot: Historical

This novel is the final volume of a trilogy that fictionally retells the New Testament story. While the first two books are set in Palestine, recalling the life of Christ, this book—which is based on the Acts of the Apostles—has as its setting the entire Roman Empire, through which the apostles Peter and Paul spread the "good news" of Christianity.

*Roman Empire. Caesar's dominion, stretching from the River Thames in Britain to the Tiber in Italy to the Tigris in the Middle East, is the essential setting for Sholem Asch's story of the expansion of Christ's kingdom. A sense of place is as essential to the novel as it is to the New Testament, nine of whose books take their names from Roman cities.

*Jerusalem. With roots going back a millennium earlier than the novel's period, Palestine's City of David has just been acclaimed the "City of Christ" by Jesus' followers. A three-way clash among the city's Jews, Christians, and Romans ensues. Their three ways of life sharing one city are illustrated in Jewish synagogues, Christian congregations, and the Roman temple, as well as the homes of the disciples, schools, gardens, prisons, the stoning pit. The novel accurately reflects all these places, which are central to the Acts. Asch not only shows "three cities"—Jewish, Roman, and Christian— but he also ably indicates the unity of all persons of goodwill that transcends creed.

*Road to Damascus. On the road to Damascus in Syria, Paul, the hero of *The Apostle*, is dramatically converted. The road is doubly symbolic: Christianity is the "religion of the way" and Paul's life will be that of a pilgrim for Christ. The way takes him from his boyhood home of Tarsus, the third city of learning in the Roman Empire after Athens and Alexandria, then to Antioch, on the River Orontes. From Tarsus Paul takes Roman citizenship, Greek culture, and Jewish scholarship, adding, in Damascus, Christian faith.

*Antioch. Cosmopolitan city on the road to Damascus where Paul finds his identity as an apostle to the Gentiles. Antioch becomes his base. From there he goes to the island of Cyprus in the eastern Mediterranean, and then to Anatolia (now eastern Turkey). On both the island and the peninsula he founds Christian congregations—some Jewish, some Gentile, many mixed in background. These are transitional zones, in the novel and in Acts, from the Jewish Christianity of Jerusalem to the predominantly Gentile Christianity of Rome.

*Greece. Biblical scholars have described the apostle Paul's life as "a gazetteer of cities." From Asia he goes to Greece, founding predominantly Gentile churches in such places as Philippi, Corinth, and Athens, where Christ's philosophy was presented on Mars Hill to the cultured Greeks.

*Rome. A city with at least a million inhabitants in Paul's time, Rome is the political hub of Paul's world, just as Athens is its cultural center and Jerusalem its religious heart. Three important structures sharply contrast these three worlds: the Temple in Jerusalem, a place of sacrifice and study; the Acropolis in Athens, a center of lecture and debate; and Nero's palace in Rome, the seat of an empire that dominates the Mediterranean world. Paul works in all three places. For him, Rome has a double function: It is a destination that serves as the apex of his life and faith, and it is a termination, the site of his martyrdom, at what will become St. Paul's-Outside-the Walls.

— C. George Fry

APPOINTMENT IN SAMARRA

Author: John O'Hara (1905-1970) *Time of plot:* 1930

Type of work: Novel *First published:* 1934

Type of plot: Naturalism

This novel's swift, relentless unravelling of protagonist Julian English's life is meant to have universal implications, but the claustrophobic atmosphere of the Pennsylvania town in which he lives contributes in no small measure to his suicide. The socially privileged Julian lives in an insular world, and while he is possessed of many of the sophisticated, outer trappings of his class, his inner resources and imagination are limited, at least partially owing to his community's provinciality, to the point that he finds himself unable to cope when the fragile props on which he has constructed his identity are threatened.

Gibbsville. Pennsylvania town that John O'Hara invented for this novel and to which he repeatedly returned in his later books. Here, the central character is hard-drinking car dealer Julian English. O'Hara always valued getting his details precisely correct, so he tells readers that Gibbsville's population in 1930 is 24,032. A minor character in the novel has occasion to think that Gibbsville is exactly 94.5 miles from Philadelphia. O'Hara knows these details well because his fictional Gibbsville, in his fictional **Lantenengo County** corresponds closely with the real town of Pottsville in Pennsylvania's Schuylkill County—the heart of the eastern part of the state's Pennsylvania Dutch and anthracite coal regions. The son of a respected Irish doctor, O'Hara grew up in Pottsville, and although he moved away as a young man, his imagination continually drew back to the region. Like his contemporary, William Faulkner, who also wrote with a great deal of historical, topographical, and sociological accuracy about his hometown of Oxford, Mississippi, scarcely veiling the town's identity by giving it a fictional name, O'Hara makes no attempt to obscure the real identity of Gibbsville.

Although O'Hara's own life in Pottsville was reasonably secure and happy, he does not sentimentalize Gibbsville, especially in the rather dark *Appointment in Samarra*. At one point, Julian English thinks of Gibbsville as a small room. He has a point. Living in the shadow of New York, Philadelphia, and even Reading, Pennsylvania, Gibbsville's residents, especially members of its social elite, like Julian, have deep insecurities that often cause them to become small-minded and narrow. Both magnanimous and petty characters inhabit all social levels in O'Hara's world, but strains begin to show among Gibbsville's wealthy because of their dependence on the waning anthracite coal industry and their times, on the verge of a Great Depression. The pressures Julian faces, brought on by financial uncertainly, a shifting social order, and changing sexual mores, eventually lead him to suicide. The tragedy, however, is not only Julian's, but is meant in part to symbolize the coming breakdown of his entire social class.

Gibbsville is a place unto itself, but it also represents small-town America. Yet even though O'Hara understands that small-town American life has its stultifying aspects, he does not wholly condemn or satirize it. Gibbsville's attractions are strong and real. The residents' sense of shared history, their occasional flashes of moral decency, and the town and countryside's physical beauty are genuinely appealing. Many Gibbsvillers—Julian's employee Lute Fliegler and his wife Irma are examples—live fulfilling lives, even if these lives are marred by prejudice and shortsightedness.

Lantenengo Country Club. Social club named after the county, to which Julian and his wife belong. The elaborate caste structure of Gibbsville can be seen in microcosm at this club, to which only members of Gibbsville's upper class belong. Subtle hierarchies within that class mirror those of society at large. For example, everybody understands that there are differences between the club dinner-party hostesses who opt for the dollar-fifty roast chicken dinner, the two-dollar roast turkey dinner, or the two-fifty filet mignon dinner. The notion of admitting African Americans to the club has not even been considered, and although Jews have recently moved to Gibbsville's prestigious Lantenengo

Street, they are an unwelcome presence and are still not admitted to the club.

An incident that ultimately leads to Julian's unraveling takes place at the club, late in the evening of December 24, 1930, when he throws a drink into the face of a fellow club member, Harry Reilly. A powerful businessman who has lent money to Julian's Cadillac dealership, Reilly is a reasonably well-liked locker-room tenor and joke-teller. He is also Irish and nouveau riche, in contrast to Julian, whose Anglo-Saxon ancestors were among Gibbsville's early settlers and whose family has been wealthy for generations. The extent to which Julian consciously realizes that the principal reason he hates Harry so deeply is that Harry represents the dissolution of the old Anglo-Saxon hierarchy, including its manners and morals, that is so much a part of his own identity is debatable. What is certain, however, is that Julian's inability to understand the changing social order leaves him vulnerable to his tragic fate.

*Samarra. Iraqi city, located about sixty miles from Baghdad. Samarra appears only in the novel's title and foreword, not in the story itself. O'Hara borrows the phrase "appointment in Samarra" from a play, *Sheppy* (1933), by W. Somerset Maugham, whose allusion is to an ancient Arabic fable in which a merchant's servant desperately attempts to avoid death by traveling to Samarra. The point of the fable is that the servant's fate, death, is inescapable; the relevance to Julian English is clear. Julian, like the servant in the fable, dies without ever understanding that his own fate is controlled by forces beyond his control or understanding.

— *Douglas Branch*

ARCADIA

Author: Sir Philip Sidney (1554-1586)
Type of work: Novel
Type of plot: Pastoral

Time of plot: Antiquity
First published: 1590; revised, 1593 as *The Countess of Pembroke's Arcadia*; revised, 1598

Building on the tradition of the pastoral romance, Philip Sidney creates a flawed world full of uncontrollable passions that threaten to bring chaos to the peaceful Arcadia of literary convention. Setting his novel in the distant past enables Sidney to satirize and explore in depth his own Elizabethan world.

Arcadia. Arcadia is a real place in southern Greece's mountainous Peloponnese region; however, its name has been used conventionally for idyllic pastoral settings since Heliodorus's *Aethiopica* (third century C.E.). Sidney depicts Arcadia both as the ideal realm of eternal youth and joy and as a real kingdom that has fallen into chaos because its ruler, Basilius, has allowed his passion for Zelmane to overcome the reasonable rule of his family and his subjects. The peaceful Arcadia of literary tradition serves both as an example of what the real Arcadia could be and as a basis for satire, showing how far the real world has fallen from the ideal.

*River Ladon. Clear stream near Basilius's Arcadian retreat, where Philoclea and Zelmane (Pyrocles) are finally able to be alone together. It is also the stream in which Philoclea and Pamela are bathing when Zelmane discovers the love-stricken Amphialus spying on them. The river symbolizes Philoclea's natural, swiftly flowing feelings (Philoclea is described as "environed with sweet rivers of clear virtue"), in contrast to Pamela's more solid use of reason to temper her own feelings.

Cecropia's castle. Located on a high rock in the middle of a large lake, this castle, in which the princesses are held captive by Amphialus and his ambitious mother, is the emblem of Pamela, whose "determination was built upon so brave a rock that no shot of hers [Cecropia's] could reach unto it. . . ." Pamela resists not only Cecropia's attempts to persuade her to marry Amphialus, but also the courtship of Prince Musidorus, disguised as the shepherd Dorus. Only after he rescues her from the castle does she confess her love and agree to elope with him.

Zelmane's cave. Found near Basilius's lodge, this

cave is used by Zelmane as a sanctuary for the expression of her unrequited feelings for Philoclea, just as Gynecia uses it to weep over her inability to win the disguised Pyrocles. Driven to extremes by Gynecia's threats of exposure, Zelmane tricks both Gynecia and Basilius into a rendezvous in the cave, where Basilius mistakenly believes he has finally slept with Zelmane. In the cave Basilius drinks the magic potion intended for Zelmane and is presumed dead, precipitating the final trial scene. The cave is a symbol both of death and of the eventual rebirth from passion into reason.

*Laconia.** Barren country troubled by civil war, in which the opening scenes of *Arcadia* are set. There two shepherds lament the departure of their beloved Urania, symbol of virtue and reason. Laconia foreshadows the anarchy with which its hitherto peaceful neighbor to the north, Arcadia, will be threatened because of Basilius's irresponsibility and Cecropia's malice. Laconia's desolate environment also mirrors the desperate straits of Pyrocles and Musidorus when they are shipwrecked on its shores.

Kalander's house. Home of an Arcadian nobleman who befriends the shipwrecked Musidorus. His house, built of durable yet beautiful stone, indicates its owner's upright character. The home's decoration, depicting such myths as those of Aeneas, virtuous son of Venus;

Actaeon, destroyed because he spied on the bathing Diana; Atalanta, swift enough to outrun her suitors; and Omphale, who inspired Hercules to dress as a woman, foreshadows some of *Arcadia*'s major characters and events. Also, in Kalander's house, Pyrocles first sees Philoclea's portrait and falls in love with her.

*Thessalia** and *Macedon.** Homes of Musidorus and Pyrocles, respectively. Euarchus of Macedon, Pyrocles' father and Musidorus's uncle, is the major figure of reason in the *Arcadia*, reminiscent of Alexander the Great. His severe judgment of his passion-ridden son and nephew restores order to the political chaos that threatens the country and the private intemperance that threatens the major characters.

*Asia Minor.** Region—which is now the eastern part of Turkey—in which Musidorus and Pyrocles prove their prowess and virtue through chivalrous deeds. Sidney uses the geography of the ancient Greek world to comment on England's contemporary, close-knit royals and their intrigues. For example, his tale of Leonatus and his bastard brother Plexirtus, sons of the king of Paphlagonia and the inspiration for the Gloucester plot of Shakespeare's *King Lear* (pr. c. 1605-1606), illustrates how these brothers fall far short of the ideal friendship between cousins Pyrocles and Musidorus.

— *Shelley A. Thrasher*

THE ARMIES OF THE NIGHT: History as a Novel, the Novel as History

Author: Norman Mailer (1923-   )
Type of work: Novel
Type of plot: New journalism

Time of plot: October, 1967
First published: 1968

This quasi-fictional book chronicles Norman Mailer's adventures, as both a historian and a novelist, over the four days of a great anti-Vietnam War march on the Pentagon in 1967, drawing heavily on traditional battlefield strategy and imagery to construct the Washington, D.C., landscapes upon which opposing forces collide.

*Pentagon.** Mammoth government building located across the Potomac River from Washington, D.C., that houses the headquarters of the U.S. Department of Defense. Norman Mailer refers to the structure as the "true and high church" of the military-industrial complex, "the blind five-sided eye of a subtle oppression which had come to America out of the very air of the century."

It is portrayed as a geometrical anomaly, an aberration rising from the Virginia fields, a misfit to its natural surroundings, and a creature deserving of its isolation. Nonetheless, the building's overwhelming size appears to dwarf not only the capital's monuments but also the demonstrators themselves. On Mailer's landscape, the structure sits as a mighty fortress. He notes in the beginning that it is not the demonstrators' intent to capture it, but to symbolically wound it. Tellingly, it appears to have no need for visible guards, since the extensions of the edifice serve as its own defense. Every feature of the building is described as "anonymous, monstrous, massive, interchangeable." Even the parking lot, utilized by the demonstrators as a staging point for their final approach, is of massive proportions. According to the author, however, it is the size of the crowd that in the end is more significant than the participants, the speeches, or the government structures.

***Lincoln Memorial.** Washington, D.C., monument honoring the sixteenth president of the United States, which serves as the starting point for the march on the Pentagon. The sound of a trumpet signaling the start of the march evokes in Mailer images of other trumpets announcing a legacy of battles leading back to the Civil War. Clusters of demonstrators dressed in Confederate gray and Union blue contribute to the Civil War imagery. Mailer's constant references to America's greatest internal conflict demonstrates the magnitude with which he views the level of civil strife taking place in the capital and the disdain he holds for the Vietnam War, a conflict he believes was close to precipitating a second American Civil War.

***Washington Monument.** Memorial located in Washington, D.C., honoring the first president of the United States, George Washington. The proximity of the Washington Monument to the demonstrators' line of march underscores the author's description of the participants as true revolutionaries, reminiscent of those citizen soldiers who joined in the American Revolution or those who stormed the Bastille in the French Revolution.

Streets. The network of roads leading from the Lincoln Memorial in Washington, D.C., to the Pentagon in Alexandria, Virginia. The federal monuments and institutions dotting the landscape along the route represent all together the nation's center of authority and democratic rule of law, yet stand in stark contrast to the disorder occurring on the streets. Mailer views the conflicting images and ideas as essentially street theater without a script.

Post office. Alexandria, Virginia, government building that serves as a makeshift prison for marchers arrested during the demonstrations, including Mailer. He thus spends a weekend in jail within the confines of a far less imposing structure than the Pentagon, largely because some government official believes a man of his literary reputation is deserving of more punishment. A redbrick building, the prison's interior architecture appears "more agreeable than the average of spanking new junior colleges." No longer preoccupied with the havoc being played out on the streets, Mailer takes advantage of his prison time to replay in his mind the arguments for and against the war.

***Vietnam.** Southeast Asian country that was divided at the time of the war into northern and southern zones. Hovering over all of the activities in the march against the Pentagon are images of the battlefields in Vietnam. Mailer's frequent allusions to the American Civil War are a reminder of the generally accepted notion among the war protesters that the conflict being waged halfway across the world was itself a civil war.

— *William Hoffman*

ARMS AND THE MAN: An Anti-Romantic Comedy

Author: George Bernard Shaw (1856-1950)
Type of work: Drama
Type of plot: Comedy

Time of plot: 1885-1886
First performed: 1894; first published, 1898

George Bernard Shaw believed that every play should present a conflict. The conflict in this play arises from the appearance of an enemy army officer in the bedroom of a young Bulgarian woman's home. While developing the humorous ramifications of this situation, Shaw attacks the snobbery of the woman's family by unmasking their pretensions about their home.

Bedroom. Bedroom of twenty-three-year-old Raina Petkoff, a member of an upper-class Bulgarian family, in which the play opens with Raina's mother rushing in to tell her that her fiancé, Sergius Saranoff, has led a victory in battle in the Russian-Austrian War. George Bernard Shaw's stage directions describe the bedroom as "half rich Bulgarian, half cheap Viennese," with "oriental and gorgeous" drapes, bedclothes, and carpet, along with "occidental and paltry" wallpaper and a dressing table made of common pine. Thus, while the Petkoffs have money, they do not know how to decorate their home. Raina reveals her family's snobbery when she brags to the Swiss army captain Bluntschli that her family has the only Bulgarian home with "two rows of windows . . . [and] a flight of stairs." The final proof of her family's being "civilized people" is they actually have a library in their home.

Library. Room symbolizing the Petkoffs' mistaken belief in their own superiority that is the setting for act 3 of the play. In the first act, Raina brags about the family library to the enemy soldier; in the second act her father brags to his wife that he has made sure that every officer he has encountered while fighting in the war knows that he has a library. In the third act, the audience finally sees for itself this prized place: The library contains a single bookshelf lined with torn paper-covered novels. The play's stage directions do, however, indicate that the room's chairs and tables make it "a most comfortable sitting room."

Garden. Part of the Petkoff home that is the setting for act 2. While the garden attests to the material wealth of the Petkoffs, the fact that Mother Catherine hangs wet laundry on garden shrubs to dry is another indication that the family is not as superior as its members think. When Catherine's husband tells her that "civilized people don't hang out their washing to dry where visitors can see it," she merely responds, "Oh, that's absurd."

— *Marie M. Garrett*

ARROWSMITH

Author: Sinclair Lewis (1885-1951)
Type of work: Novel
Type of plot: Social realism

Time of plot: Early twentieth century
First published: 1925

Martin Arrowsmith's odyssey across the landscape of the United States first takes him outward, by stages, from the imaginary geography of Sinclair Lewis's imaginary archetypal midwestern state of Winnemac to the actual capital of New York. Then it returns him, via a subtropical Inferno, to a Waldenesque cabin beside a pool, where he can pursue his idealistic researches for the world's ultimate benefit without the world's distraction.

Winnemac. Imaginary midwestern state—bordered by Michigan, Ohio, Illinois, and Indiana—in which many of Lewis's novels are set. Martin spends his boyhood in the small Winnemac town of Elk Mills, where he is introduced to medical science and treatment by Doc Vickerson, whose practice is above his father's New York Clothing Bazaar. He attends the University of Winnemac at Mohalia on the Chaloosa River, fifteen miles from the state capital **Zenith**; it is a progressive institution, the first in America to offer extension courses via radio, which Lewis likens to a Ford Motor factory of the intellect. There Martin finds a spiritual home in Max Gottlieb's bacteriology laboratory, imagining a future life spent amid labyrinths of glass tubing and Bunsen burners. His first visit to Zenith General Hospital brings him into contact with Leora; after his graduation Martin becomes an intern there. An excursion to the Dodsworth Theatre and Martin's brief meeting with George F. Babbitt, the real estate king, embed the novel firmly within the Lewis canon.

Wheatsylvania. Leora's North Dakota hometown, located in Crynssen County in the Pony River valley, twenty-four miles from Leopolis. Martin marries Leora there after traveling across the country on a whim to see her; after his internship they return so that he may set up his medical practice, for which he initially rents a one-story shack a half block from Main Street. Martin never fits in there, however, as he is always regarded with suspicion in spite and because of his efforts to improve local standards of hygiene and medical treatment.

Nautilus. Iowa city with a population of 70,000, where Martin goes to work for the Department of Public Health on the rebound from Wheatsylvania. He finds this town more progressive, although the agricultural technology whose manufacture drives its economy is a trifle hidebound, as indicated by the prominence of the Steel Windmill Company and the fact that Nautilus is the headquarters of Cornbelt Co-operative Insurance. Martin thrives there, becoming director of public health when Almus Pickerbaugh becomes the first scientist ever elected to the U.S. Congress; however, he makes enemies when he demolishes a block of tenements as a health hazard.

New York City. Location of the McGurk Institute, where Martin goes to work after spending a year in the Rouncefield Clinic in Chicago. The institute allows him freedom to do the fundamental research he has always craved, alongside his old teacher Max Gottlieb, who came there after an unsatisfying stint with the pharmaceutical company Dawson T. Hunziker & Company of Pittsburgh. Martin and Leora rent a three-room apartment overlooking Gramercy Park and are gradually absorbed into the society of the institute via McGurk Scientific Dinners. After the institute takes up military research in World War I, Martin becomes increasingly disaffected in the face of pressure to direct his work to more immediately practical ends. Although his experiments with bacteriophages get positive results, he is not the same man when he returns to New York—without Leora—after testing the efficacy of his methods in the field. Although his second marriage to Joyce Lanyon anchors him in New York for a while, his new work on pneumococcus is subject to so many tribulations that his departure becomes as inevitable as his abandonment of Wheatsylvania and Nautilus.

St. Hubert. Fictional island south of Barbados in the West Indies, with a population of about 100,000; an outpost of the British Empire. When the *Pendown Castle* imports plague to Point Carib and the capital, Blackwater, the colonial governor and the feud-riven house of assembly are slow to react, thus turning the crisis into a disaster and providing a perfect natural laboratory for Martin to test the efficacy of his bacteriophages.

Birdies' Rest. Mean residence beside a Vermont lake where Martin and Terry Wickett eke out the latter stages of their careers.

— *Brian Stableford*

THE ARTAMONOV BUSINESS

Author: Maxim Gorky (Aleksey Maksimovich Peshkov, 1868-1936)
Type of work: Novel
Type of plot: Family

Time of plot: c. 1863-1917
First published: Delo Artamonovykh, 1925 (English translation, 1927)

In this, Maxim Gorky's next-to-last novel, Gorky creates a vivid portrayal of the rise and fall of a family that pulled itself up from its peasant origins to become capitalists, only to have all their successes swept away by Russia's Bolshevik Revolution. Throughout the novel, Gorky keeps the focus of the narration tightly upon the town in which the Artamonov family has built its business, and upon the relationships between the family's members and the various people with whom they interact. Outside events such as Russia's 1905 Revolution, World War I, and the Bolshevik Revolution are mentioned, but only described as they have an impact on the main characters.

Dromov (droh-MOV). Russian town in which the Artamonov family establishes its business. Located on the Oka River in central Russia, not far from Nizhny Novgorod, it is based heavily upon many of the towns Gorky himself knew in his difficult youth, when he was working various menial jobs to survive while honing his literary powers. The novel begins not long after 1862, when Czar Alexander II abolished the institution of serfdom—the time when the Artamonov patriarch Ilya brings his family to Dromov, whose name means "sleepytown" in Russian.

A large, brusque man full of raw animal energy, the elder Ilya Artamonov makes his first appearance by barging in on a church service. Not long afterward, he barges in on the mayor just as presumptuously and announces his intention to marry his eldest son to the mayor's daughter. Artamonov's forwardness alienates many of the established figures of the town, and he runs roughshod over their various objections to build his factory. However, he is soon removed from the action, killed in an industrial accident at his factory, and the business is taken over by his son Peter. Yet Peter lacks his father's essential characteristics, and from that point the success of the factory wavers and declines. Several times Peter comments upon the steady coarsening of the residents of Dromov, and ponders what relationship that has to the presence of his family's business.

*Oka. River on which Dromov is located. One of the major rivers of central Russia, it is upon its banks that the elder Ilya Artamonov builds his linen factory, upon which the family fortune rests. Thus the factory is on the edge of the town of Dromov, but is never truly integrated with it, and in fact is often regarded with hostility by the more respectable citizens of the town.

Monastery. Russian Orthodox religious community in which Nikita becomes a monk. After the elder Artamonov's hunchback son, Nikita, attempts to kill himself in a fit of despair, it is decided that he is more suited to the religious life and sent to the monastery on the outskirts of Dromov. There he finds a place, and is actually spoken well of by the abbot. However, when Nikita is old, he returns to his family, against the rule of his order, and attempts to evade the necessity of being taken back to the monastery to die and be buried.

Vorgorod (vorh-goh-rod). Nearby town from which police and other authorities come to Dromov. Several of the major characters visit it, but it is never actually seen in the narrative.

*Moscow. Traditional capital of Russia until 1712. Although it would not be Russia's political capital again until 1918, when the Bolsheviks restored the seat of government to Moscow's Kremlin, Moscow remained in many ways a cultural capital. Several of Gorky's major characters visit the city repeatedly. Yakov complains after one such visit that middle-class Muscovites care nothing but to ape the manners of the nobility and are buying their betters' cast-offs to further their ambitions.

*St. Petersburg. Political capital of Imperial Russia at the time in which the novel is set. In this northern city, built by orders of Czar Peter the Great to be his "window on the West," the czar and his government rule. Although some of the characters of the novel write letters of protest to various government officials in St. Petersburg, or discuss political events going on there, it remains a distant city, never seen in the narrative.

— *Leigh Husband Kimmel*

AS I LAY DYING

Author: William Faulkner (1897-1962)
Type of work: Novel
Type of plot: Psychological realism

Time of plot: Early twentieth century
First published: 1930

As in most of William Faulkner's novels, the setting in this novel is Yoknapatawpha, his fictional Mississippi county that reflects his own corner of the re-created American South. As such, it is meant to be archetype, prototype, and mythotype combined into one. Herein, geography abets theme in order to reveal the social corruption and moral decay of the unreconstructed post-Civil War Old South of the pre-Depression 1920's in America.

Bundren house. Home of Addie and Anse Bundren, located in **Yoknapatawpha County** on a ridge far removed from a secondary gravel road and nearly inacces- sible. The house is a fortress of "white-trash" values, tension, and ignorance. There, Anse and Addie have reared five children, all of whom characterize some aspect of the

Old South in its demise. The family members occupy the house in disharmony, at odds not only with one another but with the universe itself. Nevertheless, they are representative members and products of their society, who manifest the stench of the South's decay. Addie dies in the house in the opening chapter, and the family's struggle to dispose of her body drives the rest of the narrative.

Road. Unnamed and little-traveled road leading to New Hope Baptist Church and Varner's Store that provides the main backdrop of the novel's setting during the Bundrens' six-day journey conveying Addie's body forty miles to Jefferson. Taking the form of a mock epic, the funeral journey occurs mostly on a backwoods route that is beset by a dangerous flood and a fire. Though remote and isolated, the road contains much to mimic and intimates the cosmic setup of the universe as the Bundren family attempts to get Addie's decomposing body to town so they can bury her in the cemetery she chose before she died.

Barns. Like most barns in totally agrarian societies, the barns in the novel indicate the livelihood and sustenance of the society itself. Symbolic of continued perseverance and orderliness and more important even than homes to these farmers and share croppers, barns provide settings for two pivotal scenes in the novel. In the barn of the Bundrens' neighbors, the Tulls, buzzards discover Addie's body and begin to follow the wagon and funeral procession ominously. Later when the body is being stored in a barn belonging to a helpful stranger named Gillespie, who lives outside Jefferson, Darl Bundren tries to perform an act of sanity by burning down the barn to cleanse his mother's body with fire. Instead, he fails and is sent to an asylum for the insane.

River. Unnamed stream that is more a creek than a river and that impedes the Bundrens' progress when it becomes too swollen to cross. The river's waters universally represent the water of cleansing, purification, birth, and baptism that a flood can provide through total destruction. Although the river is the most formidable obstacle that the Bundrens confront on their journey, it is the one that can, perhaps, provide the greatest chance of redemption: Nature itself rebels against the continued attempt of the family to outrage God by not burying the body at once. The family escapes the river just as it escapes the flames of the burning barn.

Drugstore. Pharmacy where Dewey Dell Bundren tries to buy an abortion "medicine" from a corrupt employee, who later seduces her as part of his treatment. Representative of the ability of science to correct moral faults, this pharmacy fails to provide any relief and serves only to worsen the predicaments of the members of the family.

Jefferson. Seat of Mississippi's Yoknapatawpha County, in whose cemetery Addie is finally buried, after Anse borrows a shovel to dig her grave. This small southern town gives shelter and approval to the Bundren family for their actions by hypocritically ignoring the violation against nature that the delayed burial manifests. Thus, the town itself participates in the further corruption of the entire society.

— *Carl Singleton*

AS YOU LIKE IT

Author: William Shakespeare (1564-1616)
Type of work: Drama
Type of plot: Comedy

Time of plot: Middle Ages
First performed: c. 1599-1600; first published, 1623

Devoted to romance, this festive comedy is particularly memorable for its major setting in the Forest of Arden. Here is the harmonious and relaxed world of nature, a green world which underscores the play's themes concerning human nature and coexistence.

*Arden Orest. Arden, William Shakespeare's mother's maiden name, is also an actual forest north of Stratford. Shakespeare's forest owes more to associations with Arcadia, the legendary home of pastoral poetry, and with the Garden of Eden than to reality. In this setting the banished Duke Senior and his band of followers find a world free from envy and flattery, where a man can weep for a wounded deer and there are "books in the running brooks" and "sermons in stones." Separated from society, it is a region of freedom where the banished Rosalind can costume herself as a man and "teach" Orlando how to woo her, and the company of courtiers, exiles, shepherds, and even country bumpkins can mingle and interact with little regard for society's strictures. It is a haven of song and laughter, of wit and wooing, of acceptance and forgiveness, seasoned only by half-hearted criticism, which vanishes with the multiple weddings in the last act.

Orchard of Oliver's house. Customarily a fruitful setting, the first scene of the play serves as an ironic background for the hatred of Oliver toward his younger brother Orlando.

Duke's palace. Although not delineated physically by Shakespeare, the scenes in the palace show a dangerous court ruled by the tyrant Duke Frederick, who arbitrarily banishes his niece Rosalind and threatens both Orlando and Oliver. In this setting the palace paranoia contrasts pointedly with the relaxed harmony of the forest.

— *Joyce E. Henry*

ASHES

Author: Stefan Żeromski (1864-1925)
Type of work: Novel
Type of plot: Historical

Time of plot: 1796-1812
First published: Popioły, 1904 (English translation, 1928)

As expansive as the Napoleonic Wars it depicts, this novel spans vast territories of Europe and beyond. Most of its action takes place in late eighteenth and early nineteenth century Poland, then under triple occupation by Russia, Germany, and Austria. Placing their hopes for liberation in Napoleon Bonaparte, increasing numbers of Poles joined his far-reaching military campaigns and, in an act of historical irony, came to oppress other freedom-loving nations. Contrasted with the horrors and ironies of war are the hospitable country houses of the Polish gentry and the sublimity of nature.

*Holy Cross Mountains. Mountain range in the east of Poland in whose Lysica vicinity (the Bald Mountain), the young protagonist Raphael Olbromski first appears, hunting with his uncle Nardzewski. Raphael inherits Nardzewski's land at the end of the novel and returns to rebuild the war-destroyed house and tend the farm before his final engagement in the Napoleonic Wars in 1812.

Tarniny (tahr-NEE-nih). House of Raphael's father, situated on the Sandomierian Plateau, to which Raphael returns repeatedly, following his many disgraces. Due to his father's sternness, Tarniny is a place of punishment and labor. The house acquires a playful aspect only once, on the night of a sleigh party, at which Raphael meets Helena.

*Sandomierz (sahn-DO-myehzh). City in eastern Poland where Raphael attends school until he is expelled, following a risky nocturnal boating expedition

on the Vistula River. His daring in face of the raging river provides an early glimpse of his recklessly courageous nature. Later, the adult Raphael returns as a soldier to help defend Sandomierz from an Austrian siege. When the defenders are forced to destroy the chapel of St. Jacob, which is being held by the Austrians, Raphael aids the quixotic Prince Gintult in his attempt to prevent the destruction of the holy site. Wartime and peacetime values are painfully juxtaposed as, in spite of the intervention, the chapel holding sacred ashes is destroyed.

Derslavice (dehr-swah-VEE-tzeh). Home of Raphael's beloved Helena. Raphael's secret nighttime escapade through snow-covered woods to steal a brief encounter with Helena in her garden ends tragically with his horse being torn apart by wolves, his own severe injuries, and his consequent expulsion from his father's home.

Vygnanka (vihg-NAHN-kah). Home of Raphael's brother Peter, another exile from Tarniny. Peter's liberal government granted a degree of freedom to his peasants. After Peter's death, the new owner reverts to the custom of ruthless exploitation.

Grudno (GREWD-noh). Seat of Prince Gintult where Raphael resides after Peter's death and where he first experiences the powerful attraction of Princess Elisabeth Gintult. For the provincial youth, Grudno provides the first glimpse of aristocratic life.

***Italy.** Prince Gintult's Italian journeys include Venice, where he is appalled by the sight of Polish soldiers being used for pulling down the sculpted horses of Alexander, and Verona, where he complains about the pillage to General Dombrovski. From Italy, Gintult goes on to Paris, and becomes further disillusioned with the Napoleonic ideal.

***Cracow** (KRAH-kow). Former capital city of Poland, where Raphael continues his interrupted education thanks to Prince Gintult's patronage. Under the dubious influence of his schoolmate Yarymski, Raphael comes to value fashion, cards, and drinking.

***Warsaw** (war-sah). Capital city of Poland, where Raphael is summoned by Gintult to become his secretary. After an encounter with the fun-loving Yarymski, Raphael briefly becomes involved with the city's gambling and drinking crowd. He also becomes a member of a Masonic lodge, where he once again meets his beloved Helena, who is now married.

Cottage. House in the wilderness along the Hungarian border, where Raphael flees with his beloved Helena. There they live in a state of paradisal harmony and happiness, which is eventually brutally interrupted by rape and suicide. The author's neo-Romantic fascination with the sublimity of nature dominates the entire novel. It is exemplified most poignantly by the descriptions of the mountains, forests, streams and lakes surrounding the cottage.

Stoklosy (sto-KWO-sih). Home of Raphael's friend Christopher Cedro. Raphael stays there cultivating the land, until he and Christopher are stirred by a veteran's tale and decide to join the war effort. Stoklosy represents the rural ideal of life, which the novel constantly juxtaposes with the powerful but morally ambiguous military ideal.

***Antilles** (an-TEEL-eez). Island chain in the West Indies to which the veteran whose tale Christopher and Raphael hear at Stoklosy was sent to fight, to defend Napoleon's interests. There he and fellow Polish soldiers take part in a ruthless suppression of the rebellion of the enslaved black population after fighting in Bohemia, Austria, Germany, Lombardy, the Italian Alps, and France.

***Saragossa** (sar-ah-GOZ-ah). Spanish city in whose siege Christopher takes part, while Raphael remains in Poland. The novel conveys both the energy and ecstasy of war, and the horrors it holds for civilians, particularly women. As in the case of the French campaign in the Antilles, the participation of Polish soldiers in the conquest of Saragossa reveals the bitter irony of their struggle for freedom under Napoleon's command.

— *Magdalena Mączyñska*

THE ASPERN PAPERS

Author: Henry James (1843-1916)
Type of work: Novella
Type of plot: Psychological realism

Time of plot: Late nineteenth century
First published: 1888

An apartment in the rambling old Venetian palazzo of Juliana Bordereau, rented by the narrator, an unnamed American literary scholar searching for papers of a poet named Aspern, serves as the backdrop for the events of the novel.

Juliana's palace. Venetian home of the American expatriate Juliana Bordereau. Arriving at this home by gondola via one of Venice's hundreds of canals, the unnamed narrator observes not only his expensive quarters and the stairway from them down to Juliana's receiving room but also her hallway, her doors, the location of her and Tina's private rooms, and their tattered garden. A main feature of Juliana's bedroom is her old secretary desk, in which the narrator concludes the Aspern papers are secreted. His late-night advance toward the desk is imaged as a combination of the military and the sexual. His being seen and thwarted by Juliana amounts to an ignominious retreat and an embarrassing rebuff.

Tina's garden. Garden of Juliana's niece, or grand-niece, Tina Bordereau (called Tita in the original edition of the novel). The narrator courts Juliana's favor by planting flowers and bombarding her "citadel" with bouquets. The garden becomes edenic when Juliana, with devilish intent, encourages the narrator to tryst there with innocent Tina, who promises to help him. Juliana's death causes trouble, because Tina, at best a twisted Eve, will surrender the papers only upon condition of marriage. Ultimately the narrator suffers expulsion.

*****Venice.** Northeastern Italian city famous for its avenues of canals. In lacking streets and vehicles and having sociable pedestrians, Venice strikes the narrator as communal, even apartment-like—ironically, because the Bordereaus become no family for him. He delights in the Piazza of San Marco but never prays in its beckoning church. He takes Tina to Florian's, a restaurant famous for its ices. He goes to the Lido, Venice's famous beach, but never bathes. At sunset he stands before the equestrian statue of Bartolomeo Colleoni, the cruel Venetian mercenary, again, ironically, because though also cruel and greedy the narrator is both dwarfed by the lofty statue and unsuccessful in his mission.

The sinuous waterways of Venice, along which the narrator often moves between the palazzo and the main parts of town, both alone, sometimes aimlessly, and once with Tina, symbolize by means of alternate sunshine and darkness his mental maze, combining ambition, hopes, doubts, worries, and gloom.

— Robert L. Gale

THE ASSISTANT

Author: Bernard Malamud (1914-1986)
Type of work: Novel
Type of plot: Social realism

Time of plot: 1930's
First published: 1957

Most of this novel's action occurs in Morris Bober's pathetic grocery store, the constant symbol of his immigrant Jewish family's will to endure terrible hardship. Paradoxically, the story is also the scene of regeneration for Frank Alpine, the drifter and thief who becomes Morris's son-in-law and heir, and who also "becomes a Jew" in the last sentence of the novel.

Grocery store. Morris Bober's family store in Manhattan. As an economic and social barrier, the store resembles a bit of European ghetto transported to New York, though it could be located in any large city in which European refugees gather. Having escaped Adolf Hitler's rise to power in Germany, Morris has nevertheless contrived a prison of his own making, one which threatens to kill the spirit of his wife, Ida, and his daughter, Helen. Poverty ceaselessly grinds them down. Every morning at 5:30 A.M. Morris crawls out of bed to give the "Polish woman" her three-cent roll, even though she threatens to spit out anti-Semitic insults at him. For hours thereafter, no customer is likely to come into the store. Most of his customers have deserted him for "the German," who has opened a fancy delicatessen around the corner. When the German becomes ill, his business is bought and refurbished by Norwegians—more Nordic types—and Morris's misery continues. At the end of the day, the cash register seldom holds enough money to pay the day's expenses. Only Helen's paycheck as a secretary keeps the family going.

In this scene of suffering, the street person Frank Alpine makes his appearance. In an apparent example of gross black comedy, Morris's store is the one that Frank and a companion choose to rob. After being bumped on the head, Morris fails to recognize Frank in the holdup. However, something about the store and Morris's dignified suffering fascinates Frank, something beyond his immediate needs. He later breaks his way into the store's cellar and takes up residence there, stealing from the milk and rolls left in the morning. During Morris's illness, he insinuates himself into the store as an unpaid "assistant." Even though he continues to steal from the cash register, the store's income rises slightly because of his energy and new ideas. However, the honesty, patience, and kindness that Morris embodies in his store work upon Frank, who determines to stop his pilfering of the cash register and confess his part in the holdup in order to make himself worthy of the love of Helen. When Morris finally succumbs to his final illness, Frank is there to sell the business and to claim Helen's hand. Throughout, the image of the grocery is closely tied to the moral action of the story.

*Manhattan. New York City borough in which the story is set; a place notable for its distinct neighborhoods and famous landmarks. However, given the specificity with which the grocery store is described, it is odd that readers are not told exactly where the store is. Is it uptown or downtown, East Side or West Side? Readers are told that the grocery is in a "mixed neighborhood" and that only three Jewish families live on its block; otherwise, readers must drift in a strange placelessness. This mood seems appropriate to the obsessions of the characters, who recognize little beyond their immediate circumstances.

Library and park. In the sense of abstract placelessness in which the grocery exists, two locations are especially important and can be accurately called symbols. The library, where Frank and Helen escape to meet each other, represents the desire of both to reach out and to make something of themselves. The park as well is a place where they can temporarily experience the freedom they cherish, and their love can flourish.

— *Bruce Olsen*

ATALA

Author: François-René de Chateaubriand (1768-1848)
Type of work: Novel
Type of plot: Philosophical realism

Time of plot: Early eighteenth century
First published: 1801 (English translation, 1802)

Enormously popular in its time, this novel is set vaguely in the vast North American wilderness region between the Appalachian Mountains and the Mississippi River. Its author's sketchy knowledge of American geography and Native American cultures did not prevent him from creating highly imaginative and somewhat believable settings for the numerous scenes in this novel.

New York State. When François-René de Chateaubriand visited the United States in 1791, he saw only parts of New York and the New England states. Nevertheless, he impressed his readers with an imaginative description of the Niagara Falls, although the nearest he ever got to them was New York City. Accuracy was never important to him.

American wilderness. Chateaubriand's novel, which he later combined with *René* (1802) in a work he titled *Le Génie du Christianisme* (1802; *The Genius of Christianity*), develops the theory of the French philosopher Jean-Jacques Rousseau that "noble savages"—such as Native North Americans—who are uncorrupted by European influences are purer and more religious than their European counterparts. Rousseau himself admitted that the "noble savage" was a myth and never claimed that it corresponded to reality; however, Chateaubriand made effective use of this myth by transforming North America's "noble savages" into committed converts to Roman Catholicism.

The Indian characters in *Atala* live in a never-never land that has some resemblance to the Louisiana bayous, the Florida Everglades, the Mississippi Delta, and the mountains of eastern Tennessee and North Carolina. However, it is not possible to determine exactly *where* events in the book occur because of the book's vagueness and a number of geographical impossibilities, such as the assertion that the narrator, Chactas, can see the Mississippi River from the Appalachian Mountains.

Chateaubriand describes the incredible geographical diversity of the American wilderness in prose that is so exquisitely beautiful that it almost seems wrong to wonder whether what he describes corresponds to reality at all. He evokes Native Americans traditions such as the "festival of the dead" and presents them as amazingly similar to Catholic religious holidays such as All Souls Day. The title character, Atala, is converted to Catholicism by European missionaries and assures her people that their traditions are perfectly compatible with Christian practices. A small crucifix hangs on her necklace at all times and she is a proper Catholic woman who simply dresses somewhat differently from European Catholic women.

Chateaubriand made no serious effort to understand Native American cultures, and readers do not even know to which tribes the various characters are supposed to belong. His novel seems to suggest that all tribes are essentially the same.

Exotic locales and strange customs would not have threatened Chateaubriand's contemporary readers because his fictional characters are uniformly virtuous. Atala, for example, though strongly attracted to Chactas, regards premarital sex as a mortal sin and refrains from yielding to temptation lest she lose her immortal soul.

Although Chateaubriand's locales are strange and exotic, his book suggests that even people from the most remote parts of the world are receptive to Christianity. Unlike real missionaries, Chateaubriand's missionaries need not struggle to find converts because his Native American characters accept Christianity eagerly. His Catholic priests need merely point out to potential converts that nature is so exquisitely beautiful that God must exist, and conversions follow rapidly. Moreover, these converts remain committed to their new faith.

— *Edmund J. Campion*

ATALANTA IN CALYDON

Author: Algernon Charles Swinburne (1837-1909)
Type of work: Poetry
Type of plot: Tragedy

Time of plot: Antiquity
First published: 1865

In this poem, Algernon Charles Swinburne's version of a Greek tragedy, the ancient Greece of myth and pagan gods serves as a backdrop for a lyrically rich re-creation of the havoc the ancient gods can impose on both place and people when their wishes are not heeded.

*Greece. Ancient Mediterranean land in which the poem is set. Greece is famous for its gods, myths, and philosophy that individual destinies are controlled by fate. By employing the setting of an ancient and pagan Greece, Swinburne is able to express an anti-Victorian point of view.

*Calydon. Ancient Greek city that is at the center of *Atalanta in Calydon*. When Oneus, the king of Calydon, mistakenly forgets to pay homage to Artemis, the goddess of the hunt, Artemis sends a wild boar to ravage Calydon. In addition to killing all who get in its path, the great boar destroys the farmlands, vineyards, and olive groves of Calydon. It then becomes incumbent for Greek heroes to come from far and wide to hunt down the boar and kill it. From a swamp, the boar attacks the hunters, and only after a fierce fight is it killed by Meleager.

*Arcadia. Mountainous region of ancient Greece from which come some of the warriors—including the beautiful athletic, virginal Atalanta—who hunt the boar destroying Calydon. Atalanta has grown up in the Arcadian wilderness, where she was reared by a female bear.

Because of her rugged childhood, Atalanta is a fierce hunter and wounds the mighty boar with an arrow. Prince Meleager is so taken with her that he decides that she should be awarded the head and hide of the boar. This angers Meleager's uncles, who believe that a woman from Arcadia should not be given the spoils of the hunt.

— *Jeffry Jensen*

AUCASSIN AND NICOLETTE

Author: Unknown
Type of work: Fiction
Type of plot: Romance

Time of plot: Twelfth century
First published: Aucassin et Nicolette, early thirteenth century (English translation, 1880)

European and North African lands are the locales of this medieval romance. Because other regions were largely unknown, people readily believed that strange and mythical places existed beyond their familiar shores. The wandering minstrels, or jongleurs, who sang of those exotic settings also incorporated the everyday conditions of battles, ruling nobles, subservient subjects, love, and devotion to add reality to this tale of unfailing love.

*Provence. Region of southeastern France composed of fiefdoms controlled by various noblemen. At the time of this tale, Provence was part of the Kingdom of Naples. The nobles of the territory wage ongoing battles for land and power.

Beaucaire (boh-kayr). Fiefdom of Count Garin, father of the lovelorn Aucassin, located near France's Mediterranean coast. Most of the story's action takes place here: the beginning and development of Aucassin's and Nicolette's love, their imprisonments, their eventual escapes, and their ultimate return and marriage. The count's castle, located in the walled town, has a dungeon that becomes Aucassin's prison when his father locks him up for misdeeds. At Beaucaire, Aucassin first infuriates his father and then makes him proud. The youth, his father's only heir, sees the fiefdom as a hindrance to his pursuit of Nicolette. However, he has a bond with it and returns to it after several years of exile to take his rightful place as ruler.

Beaucaire's castle. Home of Nicolette who, though a "slave-girl," has been reared as the viscount's godchild. The viscount secretly confines her in a vaulted chamber in the high tower after Count Garin insists that she be exiled. The chamber is marvelously painted and has a window that gives Nicolette a view of a garden. Though locked in, she can listen to the birds sing and watch the roses bloom. Her life within the castle keep is much as her life outside has been: outwardly charming and even comfortable but restricting her every move. Determined to escape, she uses the window to get away, swims across a moat to elude pursuit, and even manages to get word to Aucassin that she will wait for him.

Forest. Region surrounding the town where Nicolette hides in wait for Aucassin. She believes there might be wolves, wild boars, lions, and snakes in the forest, but it is also a place where shepherds congregate to watch their herds. A highway runs through it, and seven roads meet at one point, providing a significant landmark for giving directions. It is both an obstacle to the young lovers and a safe haven for them as they search for each other and seek sanctuary from their pursuers.

Torelore. Kingdom in which Aucassin and Nicolette live for three years after escaping from Beaucaire. It is an odd land, in which the queen commands the army and fights the wars, while the king lies abed pregnant with their child. Battles are fought with apples, eggs, mushrooms, and cheeses, and custom dictates that opponents are not to be killed. Torelore is a sanctuary for the young lovers; they spend three years there in uneventful tranquillity.

*Carthage. North African city in which Nicolette was born and to which she is returned by Saracen marauders. The king of Carthage is, it is learned, Nicolette's father, so she is royalty. Her return to Carthage allows her to reclaim her identity as a princess and paves the way for her at last to become Aucassin's lawful bride. When her father decides to marry her to a prince of his own choice, she flees Carthage to find Aucassin. A house near Carthage belonging to a poor woman is her place of refuge when she sets out to find Aucassin again. Here she darkens her skin with herbs, disguises herself as a minstrel, and sails away for Beaucaire and Aucassin.

— Jane L. Ball

AUGUST 1914

Author: Aleksandr Solzhenitsyn (1918-   )
Type of work: Novel
Type of plot: Historical realism
Time of plot: Early twentieth century

First published: Avgust chetyrnadtsatogo, 1971; expanded version, 1983 (English translation, 1972; expanded English translation, 1989, as *The Red Wheel*)

The first in Aleksandr Solzhenitsyn's planned series of novels correcting the falsifications of Russian history, this novel examines a broad cross section of Russian society during the days surrounding Russia's massive defeat at the Battle of Tannenberg during its disastrous invasion of East Prussia at the beginning of World War I. Viewing the war primarily from the Russian perspective, the novel also examines the growing revolutionary ferment in Russia.

*Tannenberg. Village in East Prussia that gave its name to the great battle that led to Russia's overwhelming defeat in late August, 1914. Although the battle was actually fought over a large area, encompassing many towns, the Germans named the battle after Tannenberg because Teutonic knights had suffered a historic defeat in this village at the hands of Polish-Lithuanian forces in 1410. The Russian army clashed with German forces at Tannenberg while marching on Berlin. (In 1945 Tannenberg was transferred to Poland and renamed Stebark.)

*Gumbinnen. German name for the Russian industrial city Gusev, where the Russians defeated a German army in the Battle of Gumbinnen about a week and a half before the Battle of Tannenberg. The novel points up how the Russian failure to capitalize on this initial victory led to their defeat in the later battle.

*Willenberg. East Prussian town that was the pivotal point of a Russian movement to encircle German forces. However, the main column of Russian relief troops was recalled, and the town became a pivot for German encirclement of Samsanov's forces, which began running in panic.

*Neidenberg. Small town in East Prussia (now Nidzica, Poland) that became headquarters for Russian General Samsanov. Neidenberg was isolated from the major battles taking place and lacked the capacity to handle the Russian wounded. Communications to and from headquarters were slow, and messages were carried mostly on horseback. The town became a refuge for Russian wounded and deserters.

*Soldau. Town on Russia's border with East Prussia that Russian forces held after heavy fighting. However, with each passing day, Russia's uncoordinated operations disintegrated into separate actions by individual corps commanders, while the German army acted as a cohesive whole. The Germans eventually took Soldau and then occupied Neidenberg without a fight. In frustration, the Russian general committed suicide.

*Lvov. City in East Prussia (now part of Poland) evacuated by Austrian forces. Russian General Ruzsky celebrated the taking of this nearly empty city as a great Russian victory. The novel ends with Ruzsky's telegram announcing victory. Instead he incompetently let the Austrian army escape.

*Masurian Lakes. Region in East Prussia in which Russian forces attempted another invasion in mid-September, only to experience another disastrous defeat by the Germans.

*St. Petersburg.** Capital of Russia, in which the novel traces the growth of the revolutionary movement, going back to the days of the earlier disastrous war with Japan in 1904-1906. The novel depicts the czar's palaces in and around St. Petersburg as islands completely cut off from the real world.

*Kiev.** Western Russian city (now part of Ukraine) that is home to Dmitri Bogrov, a Jewish revolutionary who assassinates the government minister Peter Stolypin, whom the novel depicts as a person who might have saved Russia from the disasters of World War I and the Revolution.

— *Irwin Halfond*

AURORA LEIGH

Author: Elizabeth Barrett Browning (1806-1861)
Type of work: Poetry and novel (verse novel)
Type of plot: Künstlerroman

Time of plot: Mid-nineteenth century
First published: 1856

This verse novel uses philosophical speculation, often in the form of letters and dialogue, to challenge society's view of women in the arts. Although the protagonist, Aurora Leigh, marries, the novel suggests that her marriage is a blend, the result of her questing for artistic truth and the love that sustains her. The book proceeds chronologically, from Aurora's childhood in Italy to her triumph as a mature artist in France and contains many references to places that Elizabeth Barrett Browning herself visited and lived in.

*Italy.** Country in which Aurora Leigh begins her life. She is born in Florence—a major Italian cultural center—to a Florentine mother and an English father. Barrett Browning portrays Aurora's first years in Florence as edenic, although her mother dies when she is only four years old. Afterward, Aurora and her father moved to Pelago, a mountainous village, where she is sheltered and raised with the assistance of Assunta, a servant. Her father provides her with books and treats her as an intellectual equal; his last words to her—advice to seek love—shape the context of the evolving verse novel. After her father dies when she is thirteen, she is whisked away to "frosty" England, in contrast to the "green reconciling earth" of Italy, the latter country being, in all senses, her "motherland." Italy remains ever afterward the place to which Aurora always returns, even in her imagination, for comfort and safety.

*England.** While Aurora lives with her father's sister in England, her life takes a different turn. Her aunt's country home has a wild beauty that differs from the warm Pelago. Nevertheless, Aurora learns to love it and continues to pursue the life of the mind. She tests her fa-

ther's advice, to find love, when her cousin Romney falls in love with her and she refuses to marry him.

*London.** Capital city of Great Britain, in which Aurora struggles to support herself as a writer after her aunt's death. Now alone, she must face many trials in a strange city in order to prove herself. London stands in direct contrast to the wild innocence of Italy, even to her aunt's country house. She visits St. Margaret's Court, an area known for prostitution, to meet the seamstress Marian, whom her cousin now intends to marry, and Barrett Browning provides readers with a glimpse of the wretched conditions in which London's poor live—the desolation of the area, the sickness of its children, and the hopelessness of its people.

*Paris.** France's capital city presents the occasion for the renewal of Aurora's artistic dreams. Having lost confidence in her abilities, she is refreshed by the similarities of geography. Finding art all around her, she is greatly moved by the beauty of nature, very much like that of Italy.

— *Martha Modena Vertreace-Doody*

THE AUTOBIOGRAPHY OF ALICE B. TOKLAS

Author: Gertrude Stein (1874-1946)

Type of work: Novel

Type of plot: Historical realism

Time of plot: 1903-1932

First published: 1933

This work of literature is as much about Paris in the early twentieth century as it is about the characters and events that the plot comprises. Gertrude Stein evokes the excitement of the place and time in which many great works of art and literature were created. Stein's friendship with the artists and writers who made Paris the center of the art world at the time is the main topic of this work.

***Paris.** France's capital city, in which Gertrude Stein spent much of her adult life, including years of it lived with her companion Alice B. Toklas. Her book describes Paris at a time when many of the most important artists and writers of the era congregated in the city. Indeed, in the early twentieth century, Paris was the center of the art world. There, Stein and Toklas were friends with, among others, Pablo Picasso, Henri Matisse, Juan Gris, Ernest Hemingway, Tristan Tzara, and Man Ray. They witnessed the rise of such art movements as cubism and Dadaism. Stein's own writing style was influenced by the developments in visual art that she witnessed, making this setting important not only to this autobiographical work but also to her works not set in Paris.

***Rue de Fleurus** (rew duh fluhr). Parisian street on which Stein and Toklas live. In the home's large atelier, Stein displayed her collection of artworks and entertained on Saturday evenings. Because it provided a meeting place for the artists and writers of the time, this place, as well as the art collection which it housed, helped to shape and define the artistic movements of the time. At one particularly successful dinner party, Stein seated her artist friends facing their own works. Everyone enjoyed themselves, and no one noticed the seating arrangement until the end of the party.

***Montmartre** (mon MAR-treh). Parisian neighborhood in which many artists lived and had their studios. Picasso lived there during his first marriage, to Fernande, before his work was widely recognized. Stein and Toklas frequently visited their friends in Montmartre.

***United States.** The native country of Gertrude Stein and of Alice B. Toklas figures in the book largely as background—a place that formed them both but which does not offer the same possibilities for art as Europe—and particularly Paris—does. Two chapters about Toklas and Stein before they go Paris briefly describe their childhoods in America, beginning with their births in San Francisco and Allegheny, Pennsylvania, respectively. Significant events of their adult lives such as Stein's training at Johns Hopkins Medical School in Baltimore also receive mention. However, in general, their lives in America are depicted merely as preparation for their lives in Paris.

***England.** Stein and Toklas visited friends in English country houses, an experience which Toklas enjoyed but which Stein tired of quickly. She disliked the constant conversation in English. Toklas found these homes especially relaxing, enjoying the slow pace and friendly atmosphere. The two were in England when World War I broke out, and spent several weeks with friends in the country until they could return to Paris.

***Nîmes** (neem). City in southern France in which Stein and Toklas spent time during World War I, when they served as volunteers for the American Fund for French Wounded. Stein learned to drive so that she could participate in the war effort and ran errands for hospitals in the area. The two women met many American soldiers who were stationed there, and even "adopted" a few with whom they corresponded later.

— *Joan Hope*

THE AUTOBIOGRAPHY OF AN EX-COLOURED MAN

Author: James Weldon Johnson (1871-1938)
Type of work: Novel
Type of plot: Psychological realism

Time of plot: Early twentieth century
First published: 1912

This novel infuses sociological insights into its story about a character of mixed race who cannot find a place for himself in either black or white culture. To dramatize the contradictions and inconsistencies of American racial thinking, the novel places the protagonist in different parts of the eastern United States and Europe to present a panoramic overview of race relations and of the economic and cultural conditions of African American life in early twentieth century America.

*****Connecticut.** New England state to which the unnamed Georgia-born narrator moves as a small child. There he is reared by his mulatto mother with the financial support of his father, a prominent white southerner. Johnson had considered titling the novel *The Chameleon*, and he shows his protagonist, who is kept unaware of his racial ancestry, adapting his own protective cultural "coloring" as he adopts the mores of the white culture that match his skin color. He identifies with the white students at the integrated school he attends and joins them in tormenting the black students. When his own African American ancestry is unexpectedly revealed, he, too, is ridiculed and ostracized by his white classmates. However, by then he has already internalized their prejudices to a degree that will prove inescapable.

*****Atlanta.** Georgia city to which the narrator goes to attend college when his mother dies, shortly after he graduates from high school. In Atlanta he encounters lower-class black people in large numbers for the first time and is appalled and repelled by their dialect, manners, and appearance. Johnson's viewpoint is different from that of his unreliable narrator; his purpose is to demonstrate the dwarfing and distorting influence of racial discrimination on his protagonist and, by implication, on all Americans. Johnson also takes advantage of the narrative opportunity of his narrator's train ride to Atlanta to document the work of Pullman railroad car porters—an occupation that offered cultural as well as geographical mobility to several generations of young black men.

*****Jacksonville.** Northeastern Florida city in which the narrator works in a cigar factory—a trade in which no color-line is drawn. Johnson extends his analysis of mi-

nority cultures in America to the Cuban American community that the narrator encounters in Florida. There the narrator also begins giving music lessons to the children of the emergent African American bourgeois class, "the best class of colored people," giving Johnson the opportunity to analyze their mores and the social and economic threat they pose to the middle-class whites who attempt to undermine their success.

*****New York City.** City in which the narrator associates with black entertainers, athletes, and gamblers and experiences another completely different range of black culture. Johnson continues the narrator's ascent up the social scale indirectly, not by showing large numbers of upper-class black characters—a virtual impossibility in a realistic novel of the time—but by depicting the upper-class white patrons—primarily women—who make up the primary audience for the black artists and musicians.

*****Europe.** Continent to which the narrator travels as the companion of a white American millionaire. In Europe he himself is accepted as white, and his experiences there allow Johnson to contrast the more liberal and enlightened racial views of Europeans with the generally narrower views of white Americans.

Ocean liner. Ship on which the narrator returns home from Europe. Aboard the ship, he meets an educated and well-to-do black doctor, who introduces him to other highly cultivated black men. As elsewhere in the book, Johnson's protagonist shows himself to be as bigoted as many white Americans in his acceptance of only those upper-class African Americans who are the most thoroughly acculturated to white standards of behavior. His experiences among white Americans have caused him to become white himself in many ways, particularly in accepting and internalizing white stereotypes about race.

*Deep South. After returning to America from Europe, the narrator tours the Deep South to study African American spirituals and ragtime music with a view toward commercializing them for a large white audience. The traumatic experience of witnessing a lynch mob burn a black man alive prompts him to return to New York City to spend the rest of his life "passing" as a white man.

— *William Nelles*

THE AUTOBIOGRAPHY OF MISS JANE PITTMAN

Author: Ernest J. Gaines (1933-   )
Type of work: Novel
Type of plot: Historical realism

Time of plot: Mid-1860's to early 1960's
First published: 1971

This fictional narrative tells the life story of a former slave who is nearly 110 years old when she is interviewed during the early 1960's. Her story is a panorama of southern social history, from her childhood on a Louisiana plantation at the outbreak of the Civil War to the Civil Rights movement of the mid-twentieth century.

Bryant plantation. Louisiana farm on which Jane Pittman is born into slavery with the name Ticey. There she spends the first ten years of her life. Things begin to change when the Civil War reaches the plantation—first when a Confederate army occupies it, then when a Union army arrives. Rejecting her slave identity by insisting that her name is Miss Jane Brown, Ticey is whipped and returned to field work.

After hearing about President Abraham Lincoln's Emancipation Proclamation, the idealistic Jane expects to find freedom in the North and tries to make her way to Ohio with a younger boy, Ned. She and Ned struggle through swamps and farms burned and devastated by war. After thinking she has reached Ohio, she discovers the bitter truth that she is still in Louisiana.

Bone plantation. Prosperous Louisiana plantation much like Bryant's, where Jane lives in a sparsely furnished cabin for about ten or twelve years after she gives up on reaching Ohio. After she enjoys life in an environment safe from post-Civil War Reconstruciton violence and receives some education from an excellent schoolteacher, violence eventually reaches the plantation and her situation reverts to a condition resembling slavery.

Clyde farm. Place on the Louisiana-Texas border that becomes Jane's happiest home. There she lives for ten years with her common-law husband Joe Pittman and his two daughters. Joe's job of breaking wild horses and their meager cash income give Joe a sense of manhood and independence, but Jane still feels like a slave working as Mr. Clyde's cook.

*Bayonne. Louisiana town near where Jane has a home on the St. Charles River—a site based upon Gaines's own birthplace near New Roads, Louisiana. There Jane lives with another man for three years and then is rejoined by Ned. The peaceful fishing she enjoys on the river with the sinister Albert Cluveau contrasts ironically with Cluveau's cold-blooded killing of Ned, whose spots of blood the rain cannot wash away. A threat to the social order in the South, Ned teaches African Americans that their "people's bones and their dust make this place yours more than anything else."

Samson plantation. Louisiana sugar cane and cotton farm on which Jane lives from around 1911 until the 1960's, when she is interviewed by the novel's fictional author. The Samson family tries to exert traditional white social control over its black employees, who become increasingly outspoken and assertive as the years go by, and the story concludes with Jane becoming an active participant in the Civil Rights demonstrations of the 1960's.

— *Eleanor Parks Gaunder*

THE AWAKENING

Author: Kate Chopin (1851-1904)
Type of work: Novel
Type of plot: Psychological realism

Time of plot: Late nineteenth century
First published: 1899

Characters in this novel define themselves by their geography, but Edna Pontellier feels comfortable nowhere and finds her final home in suicide in the sea. Setting is thus one of the major determinants of a character's future in this naturalistic novel: People define themselves by place in this novel, and Edna is a stranger out of place.

*Grand Isle. Island resort in the Gulf of Mexico about fifty miles south of New Orleans, Louisiana, where Léonce Pontellier's family stays in a summer cottage. Léonce goes to his office in Carondelet Street in the financial quarter of New Orleans during the week, returning to the island on weekends.

The Pontelliers do not have a happy marriage. Like most characters in the novel, Léonce is a Creole descendant of New Orleans's original French and Spanish settlers, and he is quite content with his life. His wife, Edna, however, was raised in a Presbyterian home in Kentucky, and is restless under the restrictions of Louisiana's patriarchal Roman Catholic society. At Grand Isle, she displays the first signs of independence and begins to become her own person—to "awaken." She befriends Mademoiselle Reisz, whose creativity she admires, and carries on a summer flirtation with Robert Lebrun, a son of the property owner. She also spends time at the beach with Robert and her children, learns to swim, and even swims out far from the shore alone. Her resistance to Léonce has begun; she is, Kate Chopin writes, "like one who awakens gradually out of a dream." Grand Isle thus represents her first feelings of freedom.

At the end of the novel, Edna returns to Grand Isle in the off season and, feeling no further possibilities in her life, removes all her clothes, swims far out into the sea, and drowns.

*Chenière Caminada. Island between Grand Isle and the Louisiana coast to which Edna, Robert, and others go by boat to attend mass on Sunday. After falling asleep during the service, Edna awakens and asks how many years she has slept. Chenière Caminada is one of many islands in this area that represent choices in life. Edna talks of going with Robert to look for pirate gold at Grand Terre, for example, an island adjacent to Grand Isle.

*New Orleans. Colorful and culturally diverse Gulf port city, at the mouth of the great Mississippi River, where the Pontelliers own a charming home on Esplanade Street in the city's most fashionable neighborhood. Pontellier is proud of his house, for he values all his possessions highly—including his wife, Edna. However, their life on Esplanade Street feels increasingly restrictive to Edna after the family's summer on Grand Isle. Regarding her home as a prison, she starts to break free, first by failing to be "at home" when other women call, and then by beginning an affair with the experienced playboy Alcée Arobin. New Orleans is thus the hub of the repressive Creole society Edna seeks to flee.

Pigeon House. Smaller house into which Edna moves after failing to find freedom in her own home, even when her husband and children are away. Edna is happy in her new surroundings: "Every step which she took toward relieving herself from obligations added to her strength and expansion as an individual." The house thus represents her physical removal from conventional and repressive Creole society.

Garden restaurant. Suburban restaurant in which Edna runs into Robert, and their affair seems about to begin. However, Robert is a product of the same Catholic and patriarchal Creole society that produced Léonce and would not think of taking another man's property—unless to make her his own property. Edna feels trapped by every relationship; only when she is away from the city—as when she is on Grand Isle or in this garden restaurant—does she begin to feel her true nature.

Edna's childhood home. House in Kentucky bluegrass country in which Edna grew up and about which she often thinks. Her last thoughts in her life return there, to the site of her early romances and happiness. It is not her childhood family that matters to her, for she later argues with her father and refuses to go to her sister's wedding. Rather, the Kentucky home and her Presbyterian upbringing signify Edna's differences from both her husband and most of the other Creoles in New Orleans.

"She is not one of us; she is not like us," the Creole woman Madame Lebrun warns her son—meaning, she is not from New Orleans Creole society.

— David Peck

THE AWKWARD AGE

Author: Henry James (1843-1916)
Type of work: Novel
Type of plot: Social realism

Time of plot: 1890's
First published: 1899

This novel offers a scathing portrayal of the hypocrisy and self-interest of British society, in which women at the "awkward age" between girlhood and adulthood are vulnerable to the machinations of older women and men. The drawing room of Nanda Brookenham's mother is the symbolic center of the novel, which turns on the question of whether Nanda—who has come of age—should be allowed to join guests who gather in the room to listen to racy talk. The drawing room is the focus of not only the plot but also James's criticism of the modern era, which, like Nanda, is caught in an awkward transition between past and present, between knowledge and innocence.

Mrs. Brookenham's drawing room. Central meeting place in the home of the Brookenhams' home at Buckingham Crescent in London. It is not the room itself but what happens in it that provides its great symbolic importance for Henry James and his characters. What happens in the room is mainly talk—talk that is described by the characters who engage in it as free and outrageous. However, talk leads to knowledge, and knowledge can violate the innocence of the young Victorian woman Nanda Brookenham and thereby ruin her chances in the marriage market.

James places an almost salacious symbolic importance on the fact that Nanda must "come down" if she is to become a regular visitor to the drawing room, instead of remaining safely upstairs in her bedroom. He and his characters view Nanda's passage from innocence to knowledge as a mini-fall, both in the modern sense and in the popular Victorian image of the "fallen woman." Only in one of his novels could a fall be accomplished by talk alone; however, from the beginning of his writing career James set a much higher store in the workings of consciousness than in those of action.

Mertle. Country house let to Mitchy, a friend of Nanda's mother and one of Nanda's suitors, in which most of the novel's characters gather for a getaway. Despite the house's beauty, it becomes the subject of a debate between Nanda and Mr. Longdon, who cannot understand the modern carelessness that allows a family casually to rent its own home to unknown guests, who heedlessly tramp through it without even knowing to whom it belongs. To Longdon, a country estate signifies order and tradition. Nanda, on the other hand, is excited by the confusion and breakneck pace of modern life, which inspires Longdon to invite her to give his home and his own kind of life a try.

Longdon's country house. Suffolk home of Mr. Longdon. A beautiful museum surrounded by an edenic garden located far from the corrupting influences of the city and modern life, this country house becomes Nanda's retreat from her fate of becoming more and more soiled with knowledge. Nanda herself is already too tainted to be the Victorian ideal of womanhood; however, unlike her unapologetically modern mother, she has a great appreciation for the more mannerly past represented by Longdon and his house, with its "old windows and doors, the tone of old red surfaces, the style of old white facings, the age of old high creepers, the long confirmation of time." Longdon's house is also full of precious old things, through which Nanda is permitted to rummage. In one sense, she becomes a rightful and spiritual inheritor of the treasures of the past by taking up residence in Longdon's home; in another sense, she joins Longdon in a willful retreat from reality—and particularly from sex, as the frequently repeated word "old" also painfully reminds readers.

Tishy Grendon's house. Hill Street, London, home of Nanda's racy best friend, Tishy Grendon, who represents the kinds of risqué influences to which Nanda is exposed in London. As everything in Longdon's home is old, and therefore harmless, so everything in Tishy Grendon's home is French, which is to say, improper. The walls of her house are "covered with delicate French mouldings . . . so fair that they seemed vaguely silvered; the low French chimney had a French fire. There was a lemon-colored stuff on the sofa and chairs, a wonderful polish on the floor that was largely exposed, and a copy of a French novel in blue paper on one of the spindle-legged tables."

— Elise Moore

B

BABBITT

Author: Sinclair Lewis (1885-1951)
Type of work: Novel
Type of plot: Social satire

Time of plot: 1920's
First published: 1922

Sinclair Lewis treats his fictional city of Zenith as an archetypical midwestern urban center. He satirizes the middle-class businessmen who run it, contrasting the technological marvels of the city with the banality of its inhabitants' everyday behavior and social institutions.

Zenith. Midwestern city that Lewis made a principal setting in this novel, as well as in *Elmer Gantry* (1927) and *Dodsworth* (1929). The opening sentences of *Babbitt* celebrate the material majesty of the twentieth century city: "The towers of Zenith aspired above the morning mist; austere towers of steel and cement and limestone, sturdy as cliffs and delicate as silver rods. They were neither citadels nor churches, but frankly and beautifully office-buildings." The physical beauty of "a city built—it seemed—for giants" dwarfs Zenith's inhabitants and the institutions they build—their homes, offices, clubs, and churches.

While preparing to write his novel, Lewis visited cities in Ohio, Illinois, Wisconsin, and Michigan absorbing the sights and sounds of midwestern American urban life. He filled a large loose-leaf notebook with observations on the language of middle-class businessmen, on how they lived, and on what their working lives were like, and constructed detailed "biographies" for even minor characters. Above all, he compiled elaborate maps of downtown Zenith and its suburbs, and even drew floor plans of Babbitt's house and office, indicating doors, stairways, and furniture. He plotted the location of the city's stores, factories, and hotels, and also specified the businesses that occupied the ground floor of each office building.

The novel effectively contrasts the majestic view of the city Babbitt sees as he awakens, with the bickering of his family over breakfast and the corrupt deals of his business day. Babbitt is proud of Zenith and admires the houses and stores he passes on his way to his office. He has a precise knowledge of urban real estate prices, but little understanding of how his city really works—how the police, the fire department, and the schools are organized and managed.

Lavish descriptions of buildings provide effective backgrounds for devastating portraits of Babbitt and his friends at work and play. The Zenith Athletic Club—the largest social club in the city—occupies an impressive nine-story building with a vaulted lobby resembling a cathedral crypt. Despite the club's name, its activities are not particularly athletic, although the club sponsors youth teams, and a few members use the gymnasium when they try to reduce their weight. The major function of the building is to provide a lunch-time meeting place for businessmen who cannot qualify for the snobbish Union Club. In their own territory, Babbitt and his buddies joke ponderously with each other, entertain out-of-town visitors, and remain alert for profitable business opportunities.

The city's churches glorify the values of their parishioners. Babbitt's own Presbyterian church meets in a magnificent Gothic-style brick building, housing a large auditorium with indirect lighting from ornate electric globes. Its minister, famous for publishing an article on "The Dollars and Sense Value of Christianity," boasts that he has made the church a true community center with its nursery, gymnasium, and library—Lewis interjects that "it contained everything but a bar." The great cultural triumph of Babbitt's life is his reorganization of the church's Sunday school on businesslike lines, complete with a marketing program that greatly increases attendance. His church efforts lead to useful business opportunities. Zenith's unchurched citizens are offered the tent revival services of evangelist Mike Monday, celebrated as the world's greatest salesman of salvation, who has converted over two hundred thousand souls at an average cost of less than ten dollars a head.

*New York City. During a short layover in the great American metropolis, while Babbitt takes a vacation trip to Maine, the sight that most impresses Babbitt is the newly opened **Pennsylvania Hotel.** He marvels at this architectural wonder of twenty-two hundred rooms, each with its own bath, and he is awed when he estimates the hotel's gross receipts as between eight and fifteen thousand dollars a day.

Lake Sunasquam. Babbitt goes to a Maine vacation resort, seeking a restful escape from the hectic pace of city life. However, his shiny new khaki clothing appears out of place against the worn flannel shirts of the natives. Babbitt finds it romantic hiking through the woods to a fishing place, overruling his guide's preference for motorboat travel, and is surprised to discover that his guide's life ambition is to open a shoe store in the nearby town. Lewis uses the bucolic rural setting to intensify his satiric portrait of the American businessman.

— *Milton Berman*

THE BACCHAE

Author: Euripides (c. 485-406 B.C.E.)
Type of work: Drama
Type of plot: Tragedy

Time of plot: Antiquity
First performed: *Bakchai*, c. 405 B.C.E. (English translation, 1781)

The plot of this play centers around the relationship between Dionysus, the Greek god of wine, and his Greek birthplace. Dionysus's parents were the god Zeus and the Theban princess Semele, the daughter of Cadmus. Since Dionysus grew up in the East, not in his mother's homeland, the people of Thebes not only question his divinity but also view him as a barbarian rather than a Greek.

Pentheus's palace. Home of the Theban ruler Pentheus, Dionysus's cousin, in front of which the action of Euripides' play takes place. The palace represents the social structure of Thebes and the power of its king. For this reason the god drives the women of Thebes, who had refused to accept Pentheus willingly, away from the palace. The women worship him in the countryside, that is, beyond the boundary of Thebes. This place provides a way for Aeschylus's Greek audiences to connect with the plot of this exotic play. When Dionysus is captured and brought before the palace, Pentheus questions his divinity and imprisons him in the palace as a fraud. In re-taliation, Dionysus demonstrates his power and divinity by destroying the palace and driving Pentheus insane. The destruction of the palace illustrates the ability of the god to dominate human civilization in general and Theban society in particular. The tension between the worlds of Pentheus and Dionysus is further emphasized by the place of Pentheus's death, which occurs offstage. Savagely torn apart by the women of Thebes, including his own mother, the king dies not in his city but in Dionysus's realm, the countryside.

— *Thomas J. Sienkewicz*

THE BACHELORS

Author: Muriel Spark (1918-   )
Type of work: Novel
Type of plot: Social satire

Time of plot: Mid-twentieth century
First published: 1960

Places in this social satire are well suited to its large cast of strange characters, most of whom are isolated or confined—literally or figuratively. Some want to escape from what holds them; others want to be closely tied to someone else or remain protected by walls they have erected. The action of the novel is itself limited to London, and specifically, to such areas as Kensington, Hampstead Heath, Chelsea, and the City of London. Most of the action, conversation, and conspiracy takes place in close quarters—often in small seedy flats.

***London.** Great Britain's capital city and largest metropolis. Muriel Spark's characters do not inhabit the showplace London of St. Paul's Cathedral and Buckingham Palace. Instead, she sets her story in London's grubby, everyday, lower-middle-class and middle-class residential corners. Events unfold in coffeehouses, grocery shops, quirky private clubs such as the Pandaemonium, and old houses subdivided into apartments.

None of the characters in *The Bachelors* appears to be married (except, perhaps, Patrick Seton). Some have been married, some want to be married, others avoid marriage—but all are alone. Patrick, for example, avoids any close connection. He notes that it is easier to escape a pursuing woman in the provinces than in London—where, as he sees it, a woman knows everyone her man knows and can track a fleeing fellow down. The pervasive claustrophobia that Spark creates derives fundamentally from the restricted areas in which the characters move. There is only occasional talk of the world outside London. Patrick, the sinister spiritualist medium/confidence man and forger, imagines escaping to Austria—where he plans to murder Alice, the waitress whom he has impregnated. However, his plans never materialize.

Spark thus cleverly represents in physical terms the themes on which she focuses—tension between the material and the spiritual, contrasts between people who long for love and commitment and those who work to free themselves from entangling alliances. Ronald Bridges, the novel's main character, ends a relationship because his lover is *too* devoted to him; Alice wants to marry Patrick, who wants only to be rid of her and the baby she is carrying.

Spark's motifs of physical, material, and spiritual constraint reflect one of her major artistic themes—the relationship between individuals and God. Characters such as Alice, Matthew, and Ronald think and talk about God, religion, and moral obligations—and ways in which the soul is imprisoned in the body. Ronald suffers from epilepsy but nevertheless worships the God who, he realizes, is ultimately responsible for his disabling condition. Matthew is burdened by a fear of sin—caused by his preoccupation with sex—and knowledge of his own weakness, and Alice renounces any belief in God at the novel's end.

Homes. The apartments, flats, and rooms of the novel's characters define their personalities, circumstances, fears, and desires. For example, Tim Raymond is a young petty functionary who can afford nothing better than a single furnished room, in which he sleeps on a fold-out sofa and cooks and brushes his teeth in an adjacent alcove. Dr. Lyte, whom Patrick is blackmailing, tries to wall himself off from the threatening outside world by carefully decorating his office and matching accessories, hoping to deny the chaos beyond his doors. However, his facade of respectability is easily pierced by Patrick and Alice.

Among the most important rooms depicted are those in Marlene's flat in an old house divided into apartments. It is here that seances are conducted by a group known as the Circle, or the Interior Spiral—terms conveying closing-in and confinement. Moreover, the seances are illusion—theatrical experiences in which Patrick is a star who confuses performance and reality.

Courtroom. Court of criminal justice in which Patrick is tried. The trial is also theater of a sort, as Patrick is the center of attraction on the witness stand, while Alice and others watch from a gallery reserved for the public. Unfortunately for Patrick, his sentence—handed down by the jury-spectators—distinguishes the reality of imprisonment from cheap self-stimulation and fakery after all.

— *Gordon Walters*

BACK TO METHUSELAH: A Metabiological Pentateuch

Author: George Bernard Shaw (1856-1950)
Type of work: Drama
Type of plot: Fantasy

Time of plot: From the beginning of time to 31,920 C.E.
First published: 1921; first performed, 1922

This play's "metabiological Pentateuch" provides a speculative account of the entire history of humankind, from the beginning imagined in the Christian creation myth to the attainment of a kind of collective apotheosis. Its locations appear to be arbitrary but include playwright George Bernard Shaw's birthplace and place of residence. The recurrence therein of a classical temple is significant.

Garden of Eden. Playground of the biblical Adam and Eve, whose petty quarrels are interrupted by a gigantic and gloriously colored serpent.

Oasis. Location in Mesopotamia where, a few centuries after leaving Eden, Adam and Eve are confronted by their son Cain's adolescent rebellion.

*London. Capital city of Great Britain, where, after the end of the Great War, in a house overlooking Hampstead Heath, the Brothers Barnabas conceive a scheme of Creative Evolution to recover the longevity of Adam and Eve. They attempt, unsuccessfully, to interest various politicians.

Board. Parlor of the president of the British Islands in the year 2170. The room's end wall is a massive television screen. The *Gospel of the Brothers Barnabas* has been rediscovered, and its principles found to be in action; however, the president cannot convince the representatives of various religions of this fact.

*Galway Bay. Atlantic Ocean inlet in western Ireland where, in the year 3000, a confrontation occurs among a diplomat from the capital of the British Commonwealth (located in Baghdad), the emperor of Turania, and representatives of a long-lived, culturally superior race. The revelations of an oracle voiced in a temple near Burrin pier fail to convince the visitors that their folkways are obsolete.

Temple on the hill. Edifice on a wooded slope, perhaps on the same site as the temple previously featured. A ritual performed before its altar ends with the oviparous birth of a Newly Born individual, whose curiosity requires a prompt education in the mysterious ways of the Life Force. The ghosts of Adam, Eve, and Cain subsequently reappear outside the temple, so that Lilith can explain to them that their ultimate descendants have given up on vulgar matter to become purified souls.

— *Brian Stableford*

BADENHEIM 1939

Author: Aharon Appelfeld (1932-   )
Type of work: Novel
Type of plot: Parable

Time of plot: 1939
First published: Badenheim, 'ir nofesh, 1975 (English translation, 1980)

Jewish perceptions of specific government actions leading to the Holocaust are the focus of this novel, in which the Austrian resort town Badenheim and its inhabitants symbolize the Jews' tenure in Austria—outsiders enjoying a deceptively gay vacation in a death row that masquerades as a music festival. The Jews' freedoms are steadily removed until they become prisoners—naïve victims who accept what the government does with only minor grumblings and some anger at one another for causing their own problems.

Badenheim (BAH-dehn-him). Fictitious Austrian resort town based on real Austrian resorts that Aharon Appelfeld and his family visited during the late 1930's. The entire novel is set in and around Badenheim. The main attraction at this beautiful vacation resort is its music festival.

The original Hebrew title of the novel, which translates as "Badenheim, resort town," emphasizes place even more than the book's English title. By adding a date, the English title clearly sets the story in the context of the Holocaust.

Hotel. Huge Badenheim building adjoined by the spacious, beautiful Luxembourg Gardens. The clientele of the hotel are entirely Jewish, and most of its workers are Jews from Austria and Poland.

The novel starts at the beginning of the resort season, early spring. As the novel progresses, the Sanitation Department erects fences, puts out rolls of barbed wire, and erects cement pillars enclosing the hotel and its gardens and thus enclosing the Jews. Although to the reader, the nature of the changes the Sanitation Department makes clearly relate the setting of the story to the Holocaust, the visitors and workers in the hotel blissfully misinterpret what is happening; they see the changes as a sign of the Sanitation Department's efficiency. They eat, drink, listen to music, and enjoy themselves.

As the seasons progress, the abundance of the spring season gives way to the scarcity of fall. People begin to pack. Dogs and sentries patrol outside the barriers erected around the hotel. The post office closes. There is less and less food and drink for the visitors and workers. People loot the pharmacy, stealing drugs, and begin to take them in private.

Sanitation Department. Government department that quickly becomes the center of the town's activity. All Jews, both visitors and workers, must go there to register. Even Christians who have Jewish parents or grandparents must register there. To both visitors and workers at Badenheim, the Sanitation Department itself begins to look like a travel agency decorated with posters about the value of labor and the wonders of Poland. However, it is the government agency that is overseeing the destruction of the town's Jews. Aside from a few people who do not consider themselves Jews, but whom the Sanitation Department considers Jews, no one confronts the department or even tries to leave, despite the ominous warnings.

Railway station. Badenheim train depot through which virtually all visitors pass. Visitors to Badenheim get there by various means, but most come by train, arrive at the railroad station, and take carriages to the hotel. All of them leave by train. At the end of the novel, policemen and dogs accompany the Jews as they walk through the town and the fields to the railroad station. When they arrive, they are excited about their trip. The sun comes out, and they get a beautiful view of the area around the station. Even when an engine followed by four dirty freight cars enters the station and the people are forced into the freight cars, they do not lose their enthusiasm. One passenger even optimistically suggests that the fact that the coaches are dirty must mean they have not far to go.

***Poland.** Apparent final destination of all the Jews at Badenheim. Austrian Jews at Badenheim blame the Polish Jews for all their problems; they consider themselves more cultured than the Polish Jews and thus less Jewish. The Polish Jews reply that they are all Jews. It is apparent from the circumstances of the novel that Nazi death camps in Poland are the final destination of all the Badenheim Jews.

— *Richard Tuerk*
— *The Editors*

THE BALD SOPRANO

Author: Eugène Ionesco (1912-1994)
Type of work: Drama
Type of plot: Absurdist

Time of plot: Mid-twentieth century
First performed: 1950; first published, 1954 as *La Cantatrice chauve* (English translation, 1956)

Ionesco intended the opening moments of this play to amuse but not to startle. The play's English setting reflects this intention, as the French regard the English as eccentric. In translation, the play's more outlandish references are normalized to suit English cultural expectations: for example, boiled potatoes flavored with salt bacon, and cooking oil, typically French but unthinkable in 1950's England, are transformed. Despite this dilution of Ionesco's humor, enough incongruities remain for English-speaking audiences to be suitably shocked.

***London.** Great Britain's capital city, in a suburb of which Mrs. Smith and her husband live. Numerous references to things English are enhanced by stage directions that continually stress Englishness. Almost all these references occur, however, in the first quarter of the play, because as it progresses, its geographical location decreases in importance.

Smiths' sitting room. Living room of the London suburban flat in which the Smiths live. The reassuring dullness of a humdrum middle-class English home in 1950 conflicts with the illogical events and incongruous conversations that occur within it. The sitting room remains an essential context even when geographical location ceases to matter. The numerous discrepancies between setting and action emphasize Ionesco's challenge to social conventions, warn against placing trust in language (even when it obeys the rules of grammar and syntax), and exemplify its potential meaninglessness.

***Australia.** Subject of a subtle joke, when Mrs. Smith regrets not drinking some Australian burgundy—a wine that was not obtainable in England during the 1950's. After such wine later became available in England, Ionesco's joke became unnoticeable.

***Andrinopolis** (an-dree-NAP-oh-lihs). Also known as Adrianople and later Edirne, a Turkish city near the Greek frontier, where Mrs. Parker's Balkan grocer obtained his yogurt-maker's diploma before emigrating to England. Balkan yogurt, later popular in England, was unheard of when the play was first produced and would have puzzled the play's 1950's audiences. The grocer originated in Romania, likewise in Eastern Europe. With this group of references, Ionesco, himself Romanian, shares a joke with spectators in the know.

— *William Brooks*

BAMBI: A Life in the Woods

Author: Felix Salten (Siegmund Salzmann, 1869-1945)
Type of work: Novel
Type of plot: Fable
Time of plot: Indeterminate

First published: Bambi: Eine Lebensgeschichte aus dem Walde, serial, 1922; book, 1923 (English translation, 1928)

This children's novel depicts the life cycle of a deer from birth to adulthood. Unlike the famous Disney animated film adaptation of this story, Felix Salten's book is an unsentimental portrayal of the stark realities of the natural world. Its animal characters speak and have names, but their behaviors remain relatively faithful to their real animal natures as predators and prey—forest creatures united solely by their fear and awe of humans, the only hunters with guns.

Forest. The location of this story is not specified but appears to have been inspired by woods that Salten saw during a vacation in Europe's Alps. Bambi's woodland home may thus be envisioned as an alpine forest in the heart of Europe, remote enough from human settlements to offer a haven for wild creatures—but only some of the time. This setting is crucial to the story, for the animals' security is always conditional. They are never completely free of the fear of "Him," the possessor of a "third arm" (that wields a gun or an ax), who invades the natural world to kill and destroy unnaturally.

Many children's books portray the natural world as a benign Garden of Eden, but the forest in *Bambi* is no such place. There death, even violent death, is accepted as part of the natural scheme of things. However, humans are depicted as apart from, and alien to, Bambi and his fellow forest dwellers. Humans are superpredators who wreak havoc on the entire forest, not just on individual prey. That Salten wrote such a negative view of humankind's relationship to the natural world in the aftermath of World War I is not surprising, as he was one of many Europeans of his time who turned from what they believed to be the false promise of human civilization toward the imagined solace of a natural world devoid of the demonstrated inhumanity of humankind.

Little glade. Hidden center of a thicket that serves as Bambi's mother's home and Bambi's birthplace. Surrounded by dense foliage on all sides and overhead, the area resembles a nest or womb, safe and secure in the middle of the forest.

Deer trails. Deer tracks through the forest, on one of which Bambi first encounters death when he sees a ferret kill a mouse. There he also first witnesses anger when he overhears an argument between two blue jays. Later, Bambi's father tells him that he no longer uses the trails because humans have found them and made them dangerous. To serve as a warning, he takes Bambi along while he rescues Friend Hare from a snare set in the middle of a track. From that day on, Bambi avoids the trails and survives to inherit his father's mantle as the great prince of the forest.

Meadow. Center stage in the forest, the most alluring and most dangerous destination for the deer, the place where deer emerge from the shadows of the trees to graze and play under the open sky, though never in broad daylight. The meadow is teeming with life. On Bambi's first visit there, he encounters butterflies, ants, and a grasshopper, whose fear of Bambi foreshadows the presence of danger that can often be found lurking in the meadow. There he meets Friend Hare, his aunt, Ena, and his cousins, Gobo and Faline, with whom he discusses the frightening new concept of "danger." The meadow is also where Bambi first sees his father, the old stag, where he first sees a hunter shooting a deer, and where he himself is shot by a hunter.

Great oak. Old tree growing on the edge of the meadow that is the squirrels' home and shelter for many animals, including the deer. The oak serves as a landmark for both the deer and the reader until humans chop it down, leaving its residents homeless.

Little clearing. Place where Bambi first sees a man, first hears a gun being fired, and first speaks to his father. Like the meadow, the clearing presages both good and evil.

Hollow under the beech log. Bambi's father's home, the refuge where Bambi recovers after being shot. Like Bambi's mother's home in the thicket, it is a secure womb where humans do not intrude.

— *Sue Tarjan*

BARABBAS

Author: Pär Lagerkvist (1891-1974)
Type of work: Novel
Type of plot: Moral

Time of plot: First century C.E.
First published: 1950 (English translation, 1951)

The three settings of this novel, Jerusalem, Cyprus, and Rome, produce a geographical movement from east to west, corresponding to the movement of Christianity itself, with Barabbas, who completes this movement, constituting the negative alter ego of the Christian Messiah.

*Jerusalem. Leading city of Judaea and its environs, during the tenure of Pontius Pilate as prefect of Judaea in the first century C.E., that is the scene of the crucifixion of Jesus of Nazareth and the activities of Barabbas, in whose stead Jesus was crucified. Jesus is introduced in a brilliance of light, Barabbas in darkness; and darkness follows the crucifixion of Jesus. The contrast of light and darkness is extended as a contrast of positive and negative, with the Mount of Olives, for example, opposed to the valley of Ge-hinnom (Hinnom), the wretched repository of the corpses of vanquished enemies. The Gate of David exists in contrast to the Dung Gate. The topographical polarities are consistent with the moral polarities of Jesus and Barabbas—and with the spiritual polarities of the two: Jesus is the Son of the Father, who causes him to die on the cross; Barabbas (the name means "son of the father") is shown to have killed his father, Eliahu (Elihu). The site of the crucifixion, the hill of Golgotha, stands in ugly contrast to the pleasant Vale of Kedron (Kidron). The contrast is furthered by the persons of the Fat Woman, Barabbas's immoral consort, and the Woman with the Harelip (a Mary Magdalene figure). Barabbas rejoins his outlaw companions in the hills outside Jerusalem. Estranged from his cohorts, he leaves Palestine altogether.

*Cyprus. Large island off the coast of Asia Minor in the eastern Mediterranean Sea. The account of Barabbas, after a lacuna of uncertainty about his post-Palestine activities, resumes with the elderly Barabbas chained to a fellow prisoner, the Christian Sahak, in the copper mines of Cyprus. Prisoners remain permanently underground in these mines and are not released until death. After Barabbas's indication that he wants to believe in Christ, he and Sahak are, almost miraculously, released from the mines to serve as farmworkers. With the mines as a virtual world of the dead, Barabbas is, as it were, resur-rected therefrom, only to be subsequently crucified in Rome. His Cyprian resurrection followed by his cruci-fixion near Rome reverses the sequence of Christ's crucifixion followed by resurrection. Sahak and Barabbas had become, when released from the copper mines, the slaves of the Roman governor of Cyprus. By Roman decree, Sahak, who would not recant his Christian faith, was crucified. Barabbas, who recanted the faith he did not have, witnessed the crucifixion of Sahak as he had witnessed that of Jesus. When the governor returns to Rome, he takes Barabbas with him.

*Rome. Capital and leading city of the ancient Roman Empire, which was to become the focal city of Christianity, is the scene of Barabbas's last days as a would-be Christian who cannot believe in Christ. Here he mingles with Christians in the catacombs, finding himself once again in the subterranean darkness of a world of the dead. Later, under the misapprehension that Christians are setting fire to Rome, Barabbas joins in the arson, is arrested, and is crucified, commending his spirit, as he dies, either to the darkness that he seems to be addressing or to the Messiah in whom he has been unable to believe. Rome, in completing the east-to-west sequence, completes also the movement from light (the radiance in which Barabbas first glimpses Jesus) to darkness, as from dawn to night. The geographical movement is enhanced by its own consonance with the human movement of life to death. Jesus remains in the region to the east (life), where his death by crucifixion is succeeded by a return to life. Barabbas moves to the western region, where his various returns to life (his own crucifixion in Jerusalem having been assigned to Jesus; his death in the Cyprian mines having been averted by his attachment to the Christian Sahak) are now concluded by his death through crucifixion.

— *Roy Arthur Swanson*

THE BARBER OF SEVILLE: Or, The Useless Precaution

Author: Pierre-Augustin Caron de Beaumarchais (1732-1799)
Type of work: Drama
Type of plot: Comedy

Time of plot: Eighteenth century
First performed: 1775; first published, 1775 as *Le Barbier de Séville: Ou, La Précaution inutile*, 1775 (English translation, 1776)

Although this play is ostensibly set in Spain, its biting satire of France is readily identifiable. Through this ironic setting of the action, a veneer of innocence is given to the criticism of the social inequalities distinguishing the lower and middle classes and the nobility.

*Seville. Though a real Spanish city, Seville is never portrayed as a real place. However, it provides a pretext for Pierre-Augustin Caron de Beaumarchais to mention stereotypical Spanish customs, such as singing to the accompaniment of a guitar, an instrument regarded as exotic in France in the 1770's, and to include spurious supporting color by naming other real places in Spain, such as Madrid, the provinces of Extremadura and Andalucía, and the mountains of Sierra Morena.

Bartholo's house. Street scene set outside Bartholo's house enables Beaumarchais to have the count and Figaro meet by chance and to have the count's hat pulled down low because of the rain, so that he is not immediately recognized. The street decor emphasizes Rosina's window, later to be seen from inside, through which a note is thrown and through which the conspirators, having stolen the key, will enter.

Rosina's apartment. With its locked window, this is where Bartholo keeps his ward away from outside contacts, athough Figaro and the count gain access to the apartment. Bartholo's removal of the ladder from outside the window constitutes the useless precaution which, by preventing the count's escape, ironically ensures his triumph by trapping him in the apartment with Rosina, the notary, and enough witnesses to have their marriage legally registered.

*Madrid. Spain's capital city is mentioned several times, partly to emphasize that the action is not taking place in France and partly because it is here that the count first glimpses Rosina. Seville is far from Madrid, and the count's determination to pursue her so far emphasizes the strength of his passion.

*France. France merits a single ironic mention, when Bartholo contrasts French courtesy toward women, unfavorably as he sees it, with less liberal social attitudes in Spain.

— *William Brooks*

BARCHESTER TOWERS

Author: Anthony Trollope (1815-1882)
Type of work: Novel
Type of plot: Social satire

Time of plot: Mid-nineteenth century
First published: 1857

This novel is the second in a series of novels set in the fictional county of Barsetshire that are collectively known as The Chronicles of Barsetshire. *Anthony Trollope's settings are integral to the personalities, social positions, and aspirations of his characters and help create the sense of reality that readers encounter in his books. Homes in particular reflect their inhabitants' personalities and moral worth. Places, particularly individual rooms, are also vital to the enactment of the social rivalries around which much of the plot revolves. Throughout* Barchester Towers *characters gather in a room and vie to establish superiority by forcing another character out of the room. The room provides a concrete, defined arena in which the right to stay represents an enormous social and psychological victory.*

Barsetshire. Fictional English county based, according to Trollope, on Somerset. A peaceful rural environment where families have lived for generations, Barsetshire is emblematic of traditional English values: respect for class differences, propriety, time-honored religious observance, and honest agricultural labor.

Barchester. Principal city in Barsetshire and the cathedral city for the Diocese of Barchester, a governance area established by the Church of England. Barchester attracts a wide variety of people whose lives are tied to the church and whose social and economic ambitions focus on its preferments and opportunities. As a center of religious and economic activity, Barchester is a place where newcomers and outsiders challenge the privileges and power of the establishment.

Bishop's palace. Official residence of the bishop of the Diocese of Barchester. The grandiose appellation of "palace" is a traditional term for a bishop's residence and is more suggestive of the religious and social prominence of its residents than of their personal wealth. When two longtime parish clerics pay their first call on the new bishop, his wife, Mrs. Proudie, harangues the visitors with niggling complaints about the palace's dilapidated condition. This scene throws light on Mrs. Proudie's personality, revealing her to be a vulgar, social newcomer with little sense of propriety or grace. A further comment on Mrs. Proudie's character may be adduced from the fact that she has converted a bedroom, a study, and the bishop's sitting room into a suite of drawing rooms and a boudoir for her own particular use. As a result of this renovation, the bishop must work in a back parlor and conduct his clerical meetings in the dining room.

The palace is also the site of Mrs. Proudie's first big party. It is a notable example of one character's driving another from the room. In this scene, the beautiful, seductive, and disreputable Signora Neroni places herself on a sofa in a prominent position in a drawing room. As gentlemen jockey for position around the sofa, Mrs. Proudie's dress is ripped, and she is forced to quit the room in mortified rage. Significant also is Trollope's description of the drawing rooms as "really very magnificent." The palace rooms are, like Mrs. Proudie: specious, flashy, and cheap. The treatment of the bishop's palace typifies Trollope's approach to setting as an integral element in the portrayal of character and conflict.

Ullathorne Court. Ancestral home of Wilfred Thorne and his sister Miss Thorne. Ullathorne Court exemplifies the traditions of the English country gentry. Uncharacteristically, Trollope devotes a great deal of attention to his description of this home and its gardens. Neither large nor elegant, its chief qualities are its Tudor architecture and its "beautiful rich tawny yellow color, the effect of that stonecrop of minute growth, which it had taken three centuries to produce." Like its inhabitants, Ullathorne Court is solid, comfortable, and homey. Its windows do more than merely let in light, they impart happiness. The home's quiet comfort and dignified age, like its owners, represent the highest values in Trollope's world: sincerity, respect for tradition, enjoyment of nature, steadiness, and kindness. It forms a marked contrast to the bishop's palace.

Hiram's Hospital. Church-run almshouse where twelve indigent old men are housed and fed. The hospital has a pleasant garden and a comfortable house, where its warden lives. The hospital first appears in Trollope's *The Warden* (1855), where it is the subject of heated public debate about the church's use of charitable resources. In *Barchester Towers*, the hospital figures as a further source of contention as various characters (Mrs. Proudie, Archdeacon Grantly, and Mr. Slope) compete for power by trying to influence the bishop's choice of a new warden.

*Italy. Country in which the Stanhope family has been living for many years prior to their return to Barchester. Mr. Stanhope, a prebendary of the cathedral and a priest of several parishes in the vicinity, has been living in Italy for twelve years, collecting his income while curates perform his priestly work. Ordered to return to Barchester by the new bishop, Mr. Stanhope and his family are a "giddy, thoughtless, extravagant set of people," who appear to have been corrupted by their Italian sojourn. Through their behavior and manners, Italy is evoked as a seductive place where the idle English acquire loose morals and suspicious financial habits.

St. Ewold's Parsonage. Small but pleasant home of the vicar of St. Ewold, a parish in the Diocese of Barchester, located near Plumstead Episcopi, the residence of Archdeacon Grantly and his family. Mr. Arabin, an old friend of Grantly, is installed as the new vicar of St. Ewold through his friend's influence. Like Mr. Arabin himself, St. Ewold's parsonage is a modest but respectable house. Trollope tends to give lovely gardens to the homes of characters of whom he approves, and St. Ewold's is no exception in this regard. Its spacious grounds are dotted with trees and give a beautiful view of the cathedral and of Hiram's Hospital.

Puddingdale. Home of a desperately poor clergyman, Mr. Quiverful. Father of fourteen children, Mr. Quiverful desires the wardenship of Hiram's Hospital. Trollope says nothing in particular of his house, but its poignantly comical name underscores Mr. Quiverful's lowly social status and contrasts with the dignity of Ullathorne Hall and Plumstead Episcopi.

— *Constance Vidor*

BARNABY RUDGE: A Tale of the Riots of 'Eighty

Author: Charles Dickens (1812-1870)
Type of work: Novel
Type of plot: Historical

Time of plot: 1775-1780
First published: 1841

Set primarily in eighteenth century London and the surrounding areas, this novel presents ambivalent portrayals of its locations, reflecting thematic ambivalence about the opposition between country and city, Nature and civilization, past and present, and order and disorder.

Maypole Inn. Old building near the real English village of Chigwell, twelve miles northeast of London. It is believed to be based on an actual Chigwell inn, the King's Head, that Charles Dickens liked to visit. However, Dickens gave it the name of another inn found in the neighboring village of Chigwell Row. The inn is the site of a homelike little community in which the innkeeper, John Willett, enjoys the company of his regular customers. Its bar is a snug, cozy place, and fragrant odors emanating from its kitchen, along with the pleasant hum of voices and warm glow of the fireplace in its common room, make it a tempting refuge from stormy weather for Gabriel Varden, the traveling locksmith. When participants in the Gordon Riots attack the inn, the damage they cause seems to be a desecration of an almost sacred place.

However, the inn also has gloomy stables and grotesque carvings. Its timbers are decaying, and its bricks have become yellow and discolored. Homelike though it may seem at times, the Maypole is actually no longer a home but a commercial establishment, and its convivial community is repeatedly disrupted by antagonism between John Willett and his son Joe. The complex world of the Maypole reflects the larger world of England in being both flawed and enticing. Its attempted destruction, however, is clearly portrayed as a horrifying crime.

*London. Like his portrayal of Maypole Inn, Dickens's portrayal of London is contradictory. His first description of it comes after a scene in which the Maypole's appealing aspects are emphasized. In contrast, London is described as a dark shadow and a labyrinth, lit by its own lights rather than Heaven's. It is as if this urban world is less wholesome and blessed than the rural world of the Maypole.

Praise of the rural world and Nature, in contrast to the city, continues a few pages later, but this time the picture is complicated by another contrast: between the London of 1775 and the London of Dickens's own time. The earlier London is much more rural than the London of 1841. Fields, trees, and gardens are nearby; Nature is not far off; merry hay-making goes on. This London, says the narrator, is purer and fresher than its modern, squalid descendant. However, in a later chapter the presence of fields in the London of 1775 suddenly shows a bad side because it is easy for thieves to escape into the fields. Moreover, the London of 1775 is so poorly lighted at night that crime is rife, making the streets unsafe at night. Eighteenth century London is also the place of such vices as gambling.

It is not entirely clear whether Dickens wants his readers to prefer the old London to the new, or even if he wants them to prefer Nature to the town. What is clear, though, is that however flawed London is, the riots that nearly destroy it are worse: the London the rioters create is a hellish, horrifying one of a city set ablaze.

Warren. Decaying, melancholy mansion near the Maypole Inn whose owner was murdered years earlier.

Unlike the Maypole, which is restored after the riots, the Warren is reduced to ruins, perhaps reflecting its sad past, perhaps reflecting Dickens's unhappy personal memories of working as a child in Warren's Blacking Warehouse, whose name he borrowed for the mansion.

Golden Key. Combined home and workshop of the locksmith, Gabriel Varden, in Clerkenwell, a suburb of London. Another site of contradiction: at times a jovial place of honest labor, at other times a place of antagonism between Gabriel and his wife, his wife's maid, and his apprentice. There is also some contradiction in the fact that Gabriel's honest labor is in the service of creating locks for such unsavory uses as prison doors.

Newgate Prison. Notorious London prison. A harsh example of the social order: it holds prisoners condemned to death for trivial crimes and is a major target of the Gordon rioters in the novel.

Apprentices' meeting place. Underground rooms in the Barbican district of London where Simon Tappertit, Gabriel Varden's apprentice, chairs meetings of apprentices devoted to overthrowing society. The rooms are nastily unpleasant, suiting the nastiness of the apprentices' plans.

Paper Buildings. Actual buildings in the Temple district of London. They have a lazy air to them, appropriate to Sir John Chester, an idle, hypocritical gentleman who lives there.

Rudges' later home. Poor cottage in a small unnamed country town where Barnaby Rudge and his mother live after fleeing London in 1775. Barnaby wanders happily in the neighboring fields; Nature here seems idyllic—except the sunlit clouds make Barnaby think of gold and lead to his involvement in the riots.

— *Sheldon Goldfarb*

BARON MÜNCHAUSEN'S NARRATIVE OF HIS MARVELLOUS TRAVELS AND CAMPAIGNS IN RUSSIA

Author: Rudolf Eric Raspe (1737-1794)
Type of work: Novel
Type of plot: Picaresque

Time of plot: Eighteenth century
First published: 1785

This is a light-hearted series of tall tales narrated by the baron, of his amazing—and often impossible—exploits in many parts of Earth and the Moon.

Moon. The baron twice visits the Moon. In chapter 6 he tries to recover a silver hatchet from the Moon, which he reaches by climbing up quick-growing turkey-beans that he plants. On the Moon, everything is silvery bright, but the baron finds the hatchet in a heap of hay and straw, which he plaits into a rope for his return to Earth. His second trip, in chapter 18, is aboard a sailing-ship, lifted into the sky by a hurricane. The Moon now is like Earth, with cities, trees, mountains, rivers, and seas, where all creatures are extraordinarily large. The Moon's people, the Lunarians, stand more than thirty-six feet tall; they carry their heads under their right arms and have only a single finger on each hand. They eat only once a month, by opening doors into their stomachs and placing whole meals inside themselves at one time. Their eyes are removable and interchangeable.

Africa. Traveling north from the Cape of Good Hope, the baron discovers an unknown land. It is green and fertile, full of trees and wildlife. The inhabitants are white-skinned pygmies. As described in chapter 26, the only barbarity of these otherwise charming and civilized people is that they eat the raw and still-living flesh of cattle (a practice attributed to Ethiopians by European travelers in the late eighteenth century). By a ruse, the baron persuades the pygmies to eat fudge instead. He causes a great bridge to be built, linking the center of Africa with Great Britain. It is soon completed, dwarfing the Tower of Babylon and the Great Wall of China. When the baron uses the bridge he admires the view from its high point. Africa seems "in general of a tawny brownish color, burned up by the sun."

***Egypt.** The baron's first tale about Egypt (chapter 9) begins with a diplomatic mission. Afterward, he hires a barge to travel down the River Nile, from Cairo to Alexandria. A great flood covers the land, and the barge becomes entangled with an almond tree. For more than forty days the travelers are stuck sixty feet from the original ground level, living on almonds; then the waters recede rapidly.

On another occasion the baron is traveling in a great chariot pulled by bulls. His chariot gets mixed up with the Needle of Cleopatra and leaves a deep track across the swampy ground of the isthmus of Suez. This gives the baron the idea for a canal that will link the Mediterranean and Red Seas. (The real Suez Canal was completed more than seventy years after Rudolf Eric Raspe wrote this book.) The baron digs the channel with his chariot (rediscovering the long-lost great library of Alexandria in the process) but requires two million laborers from Russia and Turkey to finish the job.

Strange islands. While sailing home from Australia, the baron's ship is caught in a storm and conveyed to an island from which is flowing a river of milk, fresh and delicious. On landing, he discovers that the island is made of cheese. Upon it grow vines, with grapes full of milk, and corn, "the ears of which produce loaves of bread, ready made." The island, larger than Europe, contains many rivers of milk and wine, fruit trees of all kinds, and large birds.

On a later voyage the baron encounters an island of ice, off the Guinea coast of West Africa. His ship is wrecked upon it, but he manages to secure the ship to the ice and to tow it back to England. En route he has seeds planted and succeeds in growing crops of fruit and vegetables on the ice, one of which is a tree that bears plum-puddings.

While sailing across the Atlantic to North America, the baron's ship discovers a floating island inhabited by both white- and dark-skinned peoples. Although he describes the island as delightful, sugarcane fails to grow properly there due to the great mixture of climates to which the island is subject. The baron then finds a huge iron stake, which he thrusts through the center of the island and fastens to the bottom of the sea.

***North America.** While the baron is exploring the "frightful deserts and gloomy woods" of North America (chapter 32), he and three companions become separated from the rest of their party and are set upon by hundreds of savage Indians. All four men are scalped and tied to stakes to be burned, but they escape when their captors become drunk. They recover their scalps and fasten them back in place with the sap of a tree.

***Poland.** In chapter 2, while the baron is in Poland, he spends a winter night in the open. It is an apparently deserted area, covered by snow. He ties his horse to a stump sticking out of the ground. Overnight there is a thaw, and he wakes to find himself in the middle of a village, actually lying in the churchyard. His horse is hanging by its bridle from the weather-cock on the steeple of the village church, but a well-aimed shot from his pistol releases the horse, which seems none the worse for its ordeal. In chapter 6 the baron mentions a European winter so severe that the postilion on a horse-drawn coach could not get a sound out of his horn until, later at an inn, the notes and tunes inside the horn had thawed out.

***London.** Although England's capital is mentioned several times, the book contains little description of the city. In chapter 12, when the baron constructs a balloon in London (the Montgolfier brothers demonstrated hot-air balloon ascents in Paris only two years before the book's publication), he must buy silk from all the mercers and weavers in London in order to get enough for the canopy. Later, he goes to sleep inside a cannon at the Tower of London and is inadvertently fired across the River Thames, landing in a haystack between Bermondsey and Deptford.

— *Chris Morgan*

BARREN GROUND

Author: Ellen Glasgow (1873-1945)
Type of work: Novel
Type of plot: Social realism

Time of plot: Late nineteenth and early twentieth centuries
First published: 1925

As this novel's title and sections titled "Broomsedge," "Pine," and "Life-Everlasting" suggest, the soil and plant life of its Virginia settings play a significant role, not only in lending substance to the novel's realistic depictions of the landscape, but also in underscoring major themes. Dorinda Oakley, the novel's protagonist, initially pulls her roots out of the barren ground of her upbringing and, with romantic whimsy, seeks a more fulfilling life. Experience eventually teaches her the value of both the solitary pine and the human need for connection, rootedness, and life-everlasting.

Pedlar's Mill. Fictional Virginia community located in fictional **Queen Elizabeth County**. Pedlar's Mill is a rural, farming community whose inhabitants are embattled by their long and arduous struggles with poor soil that seems better suited for broomsedge and scrub pine than for cash crops. Pedlar's Mill was around a century before the time in which the novel is set. It is a poor community, comprising primarily descendants of Scotch-Irish families who migrated from Virginia's Shenandoah highlands to Virginia's low country. Most come from families that have seen better times, both economically and socially.

The lives of Pedlar's Mill residents are quite different from the romantic ideals popularly associated with the Old South in Ellen Glasgow's time. They are not landed gentry living off the fat of the land and the labor of slaves; they survive by tilling their soil, planting seeds, tending crops, milking cows, and reaping meager harvests. Instead of ordering their lives around a chivalric code of manners, they grapple with the laws of nature, finding in them both a sense of continuity, as in the cycle of the seasons, and an unconquerable coarseness, represented by their inability to make headway against the ever-expanding and almost-impossible-to-eradicate broomsedge or their impoverished condition.

Old Farm. Farm owned by the Oakley family in which much of the novel's first section, "Broomsedge," is set. There, Dorinda's parents, Joshua and Eudora, labor tirelessly to sustain their family and the estate left to them by Eudora's grandfather. Joshua's ineptness as a farmer and Eudora's bleak, Calvinistic religious instincts push Dorinda to look beyond her immediate situation to find fulfillment elsewhere, first in a romantic dalliance with Jason Greylock and later in her travels to New York City. Eventually she returns to Old Farm, however, and after the deaths of her father and mother turns it into a profitable business, one made even more lucrative after she marries Nathan Pedlar and combines her estate with his.

Five Oaks. Farm initially owned by the Greylocks and later purchased by Dorinda and Nathan after their marriage. Dr. Greylock had been a man of high social standing and considerable economic means before labor shortages and his addiction to alcohol led him to neglect his estate. As he sinks further into social degradation, which is made even greater in the minds of local white residents by the presence on the farm of several mulatto children rumored to be his offspring, Greylock comes to represent the opposite of the industry, frugality, and pragmatism that become the driving forces behind Dorinda's success. Greylock's son, Jason, likewise begins a downward spiral, leading Dorinda to wonder why she ever fell in love with him. Her subsequent marriage to Nathan Pedlar, based on practical economic concerns and not romantic love, and their joint purchase and revival of Five Oaks, demonstrate Dorinda's ultimate triumph over the romantic follies of her youth.

*****New York City.** Where Dorinda flees after learning of her jilting by Jason Greylock. The city's stony pavement and the cold, impersonal nature of its buildings and inhabitants lead Dorinda to withdraw further into herself. Feeling depressed, she wanders through the urban landscape without direction, sickened unto dizziness by her self-pity. The full reality of the city finally crashes into her when she steps in front of a taxicab and is slammed to the pavement. A doctor named Faraday oversees her long recovery and in turn offers her a job as his office assistant and part-time attendant to his children. For the next two years she works steadily in New York and re-evaluates her life, determining in part from her vibrant urban environment that human experience is much more complex than her earlier romantic inclinations suggested. Armed with a more mature perspective, she returns to Old Farm after hearing of her father's illness.

— *R. Allen Alexander, Jr.*

BARRIO BOY: The Story of a Boy's Acculturation

Author: Ernesto Galarza (1905-1984)
Type of work: Autobiography
Type of plot: Historical

Time of plot: 1910-1920
First published: 1971

This autobiographical novel begins in a small mountain village in western Mexico and soon shifts from one town to another and finally to another country, as a young boy and his family flee from the developing Mexican Revolution. Ernesto's physical journey symbolizes the process of acculturation he goes through as he struggles to establish and maintain his identity. Each place he visits represents a stage in his maturation.

Jalcocotán (hal-ko-ko-TAN). Small mountain village in central Mexico. Referred to as Jalco, this isolated and seemingly inaccessible pueblo provides the idyllic, almost edenic, setting for young Ernesto. In this small village, the only street with no name is a place that belongs to everybody. Although the living conditions are primitive—with extremes in weather, torrential downpours that cause flooding, and back-breaking labor—Ernesto's innocence flourishes here. In the village he lives a safe, secure life and learns a set of values by which to measure his life; these values he metaphorically later carries with him throughout his journey.

Before the *rurales*—special national police who maintain order in the countryside through violence and terror—enter and threaten the village's idyllic existence, the greatest danger Ernesto faces is getting his ear pulled for being disrespectful to adults. However, after the *rurales* invade his sanctuary, his family flees the village to find safety and work. Uprooted, they are forced to leave many belongings behind, but they take their two most valuable items: an Ajax sewing machine and a cedar chest. Throughout their arduous travels, these tangible possessions symbolize the intangibles of their village life that give their life meaning and promise.

Tepic (TAY-pik). Large city south of Jalco that provides Ernesto's family with temporary security and a safe haven from the violence of the Revolution. Here, Ernesto and his family confront a series of challenges, one of the most important being the rigid social barrier separating those who have money from those who do not. However, the Ajax sewing machine provides them with some measure of economic security. They also struggle to cope with the rush of big-city activity. Since they know no one in Tepic, Ernesto goes everywhere with his mother. After a brief respite in

Acaponeta, a city north of Tepic, the family moves on.

Mazatlán (mah-zaht-LAHN). Western coastal city on the Vigia Peninsula where Ernesto's family lives in a barrio. Although they are refugees in a new city, Mazatlán is the first place in which the family feels as if they belong, as friends belong to one another. Ernesto joins a gang that provides him with a sense of social importance and a new family. He also attends his first formal school and finds his first job. This city begins to provide Ernesto with the same constancy and feelings of safety and economic security that Jalco provided. When the Revolution reaches their front door, however, they are again forced to become refugees. This time they leave their valuable sewing machine behind, and they go north to the United States.

Sacramento. Northern California city that is the final destination of Ernesto's family, after a brief stay in Tucson, Arizona. While the family is free from the violence of the Mexican Revolution, they are now foreigners who face more complex challenges. Not yet economically stable, they live in a ghetto-like area of "leftover houses," where their rooms are "dank and cheerless." They stay in this awful place because their objective is not to make money but to "make a living." In Sacramento's barrio, they find no plazas or parks in which people gather and visit; even the houses are fenced off from one another.

Ernesto, too, finds new barriers to defining his own cultural identity. He attends a school in which only English is spoken, is immersed into a new culture, and has physical confrontations with boys who make fun of him. Despite these difficulties, he is sustained by his family values and the shared experiences of those who live in his barrio. As a result, he maintains his sense of self in this new, alien culture. His journey is complete.

— *Sharon K. Wilson*

BARRY LYNDON

Author: William Makepeace Thackeray (1811-1863)
Type of work: Novel
Type of plot: Picaresque

Time of plot: Mid- to late eighteenth century
First published: serial, 1844; book, 1852

This picaresque novel traces the far-flung travels of an Irish rogue waging a private war against British oppression, while trying to attain a higher station in life for himself. During his travels, he becomes a soldier, a spy, a gambler, and a violent mad man. Each region through which he moves represents a stage in his continuing moral and social decline.

Barryville. Irish town that is the birthplace and early home of the braggart and bully Redmond Barry—later to become Barry Lyndon. The novel opens with Barry Lyndon, at age forty, looking back over his life in an attempt to give it shape. He begins his memoir with a description of the tiny house in Barryville where he was born and expresses his bitter regret over the loss of his family's vast ancestral lands to a British aristocrat named Lyndon.

In Barryville, Barry falls from grace. After watching British soldiers parading in the Irish fields, he fights a duel with a British officer named Quin over a woman. This familial model parallels the history of Ireland's subjugation by the British and, in a manner, justifies Barry's frustration with his life and his subsequent career as a scoundrel and rogue. It may be argued that Barry is merely attempting to recover what he believes to be his birthright, his family lands, and, though perhaps inadvertently, his family honor. In the middle nineteenth century, Ireland was an exploited and deeply impoverished land that many people were anxious to leave.

Deluded into believing that he has killed the British officer in the duel, Barry predictably leaves for Dublin. Along the way he is robbed, finds he has nowhere to turn and so he enlists in the British army to fight in the Seven Years' War. The only two people Barry ever finds any modicum of comfort with, and love for, are his uncle and fellow con man, Cornelius Barry (Chevalier de Baliban) with whom he travels as a professional gambler, and his devoted mother—both from his home in Ireland.

*The Continent. European continent on which a large part of the novel develops, as Barry travels almost constantly from country to country. In this regard, Thackeray details the European courts' dissipated lifestyle, rife with gambling and illicit romantic interludes.

As a soldier in the battlefields of France, Barry sees that the British soldiers are simply mowed down as they march straight into enemy fire, so he deserts in the hope of reaching neutral Belgium. When his chance comes, he returns to a life of traveling, this time in the disguise of a British officer, after which the devious soldier of fortune is forced to enlist in the Prussian army. This army, he finds, is even worse than the British army, and he winds up in Germany. Given his Irish ancestry, it is not difficult to understand Barry's lack of patriotic feeling of any kind for the British crown. He has no more love for the Prussian army than he did the British and, indeed, looks upon them as the dregs of Europe.

Disheartened, Barry feels he will never achieve his dreams of glory. However, his sojourn with the Prussians soon ends when an officer engages him to spy on a French gambler. When Barry discovers that the gambler is his own uncle, he instead joins up with him. Both rascals travel through Europe as swaggering gentleman cardsharps at the continental courts every night, scheming, gaming, and womanizing. Rubbing shoulders with the rich helps make Barry wealthy, but only by cheating.

In the decadent European court environment Barry meets the married Lady Lyndon, an arrogant and wealthy woman and mother of Lord Bullingdon. Barry indirectly causes Lady Lyndon's apoplectic husband—who is of the same Lyndon family responsible for the demise of Barry's noble ancestral Irish family—to suffer a fatal stroke. Thus, continental Europe, in contrast to the more sober Britain, represents a covert, profligate lifestyle, rife with all sorts of vices: gambling, drunkenness and violence.

*London. Capital of Britain, in which Barry settles after marrying Lady Lyndon and usurping her dead husband's title by taking his name. As an uncouth Irishman, Barry is doomed in England, like his father before him who died in London in a duel shortly after renouncing his Catholic faith in an attempt to recover his family fortunes. Although Barry has the wit to gain a fortune, he is incapable of keeping it. In due course, London sober society becomes his undoing, and he soon begins to fall from social respectability.

Under constant pressure to behave himself under the social constraints of his wife's position, Barry cannot abide the drawing-room manners of the English ruling classes. He brutalizes his wife and imprisons her. His marriage becomes miserable, and his stepson despises him. His only saving grace is the loving way he treats his devoted old mother and his young son. However, he eventually loses everything and is forced to live abroad on a pension. He dies penniless, drunk, and mad in Fleet prison, cared for by his aging mother.

— *M. Casey Diana*

BARTHOLOMEW FAIR

Author: Ben Jonson (1573-1637)

Type of work: Drama

Type of plot: Satire

Time of plot: Early seventeenth century

First performed: 1614; first published, 1631

The entire action of the play takes place in seventeenth century London, primarily at the annual Bartholomew Fair. The fair and its lower-class denizens come into conflict with the officers of justice and the religious zealots who object to it, ultimately transforming or humiliating those characters.

*Bartholomew Fair (BART-le-mee). London's raucous Bartholomew Fair, held at Smithfields from 1120 onward. The original site was the area where animals were slaughtered and sold. During the reign of Queen Mary, the fair was suspended, and Smithfields became the site where heretics were burned at the stake. The fair was reestablished in the 1560's after the accession of Elizabeth I. Symbolically, the fair represents the world, with all its liveliness, riot, and sinfulness. Representatives of the law, such as Justice Overdone, and the rigid Puritan sect, such as Zeal-of-the-Land Busy, invade the fair to ferret out its evils and ultimately shut it down. Their encounters with the cutpurses, pimps, horse thieves, pig women, and gingerbread sellers, who ply their wares at the fair, leave these self-righteous individuals humiliated and chastened. The vitality of the fair exerts its influence and defeats the intentions of those who would condemn it.

*Ursula's pig booth. Booth at which "Bartholomew Pig" is sold—where the fair's ultimate excesses are centered. The Littlewits go to the booth hoping that indulgence in greasy roast pork will help Win to conceive. Mrs. Overdone and Dame Purecraft, representatives of middle-class morality, become drunk and are mistaken for whores.

*Leatherhead's puppet booth. Country bumpkin Bartholomew Cokes, who thinks the fair is his fair since they share the same name, is drawn into the world of the puppet show featuring Hero and Leander, though he understands not a word of it, just as he is lost in the world of the fair.

*Hope Theatre. Bankside theater in which Jonson's play was first produced in 1631. It becomes the site of a scene in the play itself. The introduction sees the book holder, the stage manager, and the scrivener make a compact with the audience not to condemn the excesses of either the stage production or Bartholomew Fair.

— *Mary Anne Hutchinson*

BATOUALA

Author: René Maran (1887-1960)
Type of work: Novel
Type of plot: Social realism
Time of plot: 1917

First published: Batouala, véritable roman nègre,
    1921; definitive edition, 1938 (English translation,
    1922; definitive edition, 1972)

The central African landscape of this novel is described in attentive detail that shows how different a place it is from the homelands of the book's original, mainly European and American, readers. To many non-Africans, Central Africa itself appeared almost as strange, mysterious, and alien as the novel's African characters. The natural majesty and wilderness of the African setting is shown as influencing all aspects of the lives of its original inhabitants. The French colonizers are seen as unwelcome outsiders and oppressors who bring nothing good to Africa and its people.

*Grimari (gree-MAH-ree). Village in the southern part of French Equatorial Africa's Ubangi-Shari colony (which is now the Central African Republic) that is the novel's principal setting. Grimari lies in a hilly terrain with many small rivers running through the grasslands, forests, and jungles in its immediate vicinity. During the rainy season, its rivers swell and make travel and communications difficult. At the time in which the story is set, game and beasts such as lions and panthers are still abundant in the bush outside the village limits. The village's people grow rubber for the country's French colonizers, while growing millet and hunting wild game for their food and raising livestock.

The novel's action is contained within a radius of no more than thirty miles around Grimari, which houses a colonial outpost governed by one French commandant and a few local militiamen. Every time the militia's commandant is away, the atmosphere and mood of the place changes, and the village's African residents become happier. However, while the people are depicted as clearly being better off without their French masters, they still resign themselves to foreign occupation of their homeland. Every time the commandant returns, he brings a more oppressive mood to the town by enforcing harsher aspects of French rule and terminating frowned-upon tribal rituals and festivals, such as the Ga'nza, during which male and female genitalia of teenagers are mutilated in an ancient initiation rite.

By restricting the action of his novel to a relatively small space, René Maran draws a powerful and detailed picture of the environment and its people where he himself, an Afro-Caribbean man, served in the French colonial administration. His first-hand experience gives his description of Grimari and its environs an eye-witness clarity, and his criticism of the abuses of French rule appear as trustworthy as his depiction of the place where the French govern.

Batouala's hut. Home of the paramount chief Batouala in which the novel opens and closes. A traditional house near Grimari, the hut has an open entrance so close to the edge of the forest and jungle that Batouala always keeps fires burning through the night to keep out predatory animals and to repel mosquitoes with its smoke. Batouala and his first wife, Yassigui'ndja, sleep on mats on the hut's earth floor, along with some of their small livestock. Nearby are huts Batouala has built for his other eight wives and children.

After Batouala receives a mortal chest wound from a panther, he is carried into his hut, which his people believe is the best place for exorcising evil spirits that threaten his life. The exorcisms fail, and Batouala dies a slow, painful death. Before dying, he rises a last time to chase out Yassigui'ndja and his young rival Bissibi'ngui, after they engage in sexual intercourse beside his death bed, thereby desecrating his home.

*Bangui (bahn-GWEE). Capital city of Ubangi-Shari to which Yassigui'ndja dreams of fleeing with her young lover. The capital represents her hope of escaping from her husband Batouala's oppressive power over the villages he rules around Grimari.

Land of Koliko'mbo. Land of the dead where spirits go in the system of belief of Batouala's Banda people. Free of worldly cares, it represents a paradise.

M'Poutou (mm-PEW-tew). Banda name for France, the colony's ruling country. To the Banda, France is an almost mythic place, the home of their colonial masters, who despite their arrogance are quite ridiculous to the Africans. With World War I engulfing France at the time in which the novel is set, France also represents a detested place to which Africans dread going, out of fear of being inducted into the French army.

— *R. C. Lutz*

THE BAY OF SILENCE

Author: Eduardo Mallea (1903-1982)
Type of work: Novel
Type of plot: Existentialism

Time of plot: 1926-1939
First published: La bahía de silencio, 1940 (English translation, 1944)

This novel of an Argentine youth's coming of age is characterized by a profound sense of the interrelation between places and persons as well as extended philosophical discussions among its dramatis personae. *Martín Tregua is a young intellectual painfully conscious of the gap between his ideals and the reality in which he lives, whose quest for a satisfactory mode of life takes him on metaphysical as well as geographical journeys through the heritage of Western civilization. Since the novel's locations are treated as an integral part of the lives of those who inhabit them, they play a correspondingly prominent part in the protagonist's story.*

Buenos Aires. Capital of Argentina and the primary setting of the novel. Argentina's only major urban center, Buenos Aires is represented as an essentially heterogeneous metropolis, populated by immigrants from all over the world who maintain many of their cultural traditions and have not yet succeeded in synthesizing them into a homogeneous, organic community. This view is often expressed in terms of the unplanned jumbling together of various foreign styles of architecture, which effectively symbolizes the diverse and often incompatible influences that characterize the city's intellectual as well as social life.

The manner in which Tregua presents an objective account of his subjective impressions of Buenos Aires is central to the narrative's thematic and stylistic concerns. Although often critical of the banality and immaturity of his fellow citizens, Martín is so alert to the subtle nuances of Buenos Aires that even his harshest comments display an affecting sensitivity. His extraordinarily active mind registers its perceptions of place in graphic detail as well as reverent contemplation and often interrupts the novel's linear organization of plot events to do so. Thus, descriptions of Tregua's frequent walks along the city's streets are typically interspersed with paragraphs that record strings of sense impressions that seem to have no obvious relation to what he is doing or thinking. For example, while he muses about the meaning of life when he is on his way to an appointment, his stream-of-conscious thoughts are suspended while he takes note of the wetness of the sidewalks, the movement of the traffic, the sparkling windows of tall office buildings, and the behavior of women soliciting charitable donations by jingling coins in small earthen bowls.

Although this is to some extent part of the process of scene setting that every writer of fiction undertakes, Eduardo Mallea's approach to this task is a distinctive as well as remarkably effective one. His seamless integration of places and persons represents human nature as inextricably interwoven with the material circumstances in which it originates and develops; the conventional barriers between the mind and the body, the animate and the inanimate, and the real and the imaginary are collapsed by Mallea's assumption that these usually opposed categories in fact interpenetrate one another to the extent that any attempt to separate them can only be artificial. In downplaying the role of abstract thought in humanity's understanding of experience, and in stressing that things must come into being before one can begin to think about what they mean, Mallea has many affinities with such existentialist thinkers as Søren Kierkegaard and Miguel de Unamuno; as a consequence, *Bay of Silence* is generally considered to be an existentialist novel.

***Argentina.** South American nation which, in Tregua's view, is a national entity related to, but distinct from, its major city, Buenos Aires. Whereas the latter is a perhaps excessively civilized milieu that, although complex and confusing, is all too easy to scrape along in, the Argentinean countryside is portrayed as an enigmatic, mysterious, and profound landscape that contains essential truths necessary to individual survival in the modern world. Tregua believes that there is a "submerged, healthy country" slumbering underneath the widespread social and political corruption sanctioned by Argentina's ruling class, and much of the novel's plot is devoted to discussions of how the necessary reforms might be achieved. Tregua's status as a middle-class person who admires the simple authenticity of those beneath him on the social scale, while nonetheless tempted by the material comforts enjoyed by those above him, is conveyed in a number of scenes set in places of amusement: a rowdy strip club and an elegant literary reception are two notable examples of the novel's portrayal of social class distinctions.

***Brussels.** Capital of Belgium in which Tregua lives for several months during a prolonged visit to Europe. This is the first city other than Buenos Aires in which he has spent an appreciable amount of time, and its differences from what he is used to lead him to speculate about the factors that distinguish one urban community from another. Tregua's characteristic sensitivity to the particularities of places leads him to discern a distinctive rhythm to the pulse of life in Brussels, which, as in the case of Buenos Aires, is demonstrated through close attention to details of architecture, landscape, and public behavior.

The most important venue of Tregua's time in Brussels is an abandoned theater in which the city's radical intellectuals debate the public issues of the day. The decrepitude of this building and the brilliant but ineffectual rhetoric displayed there are telling symbols of the helplessness of the European intelligentsia on the eve of World War II—the period in which the novel concludes.

***Lake Como.** Resort community in the Italian Alps. Tregua's view of the fundamental irrelevance of the upper classes is conveyed in another portrait of socialites with too much money and too little sense, and whose frivolity in the face of approaching chaos he finds unendurable.

***Monte Hermoso.** Argentinean coastal town where Tregua and the woman he loves spend an idyllic holiday. This is a modest vacation spot whose cuisine—like its guests—is wholesome rather than pretentious. Both Martín and his companion are spiritually healed by this affirmation of how Argentinean life might be revitalized by returning to the timeless truths exemplified by the country's natural landscape.

— *Paul Stuewe*

THE BEAUX' STRATAGEM

Author: George Farquhar (1678?-1707)
Type of work: Drama
Type of plot: Comedy of manners

Time of plot: Early eighteenth century
First performed: 1707; first published, 1707

Unlike most English comedies of manners, this play is set in the country instead of in London. As a result of this setting, emphasis is placed on low characters—innkeepers, servants, and highwaymen—instead of fashionable society. Archer and Aimwell, however, are newly arrived from the city, and much of the play's force derives from the contrast between country and city life. The two settings of the play, the inn and Lady Bountiful's house, reflect this conflict.

Litchfield Inn. Way station for travelers coming and going from London to the country that is utterly corrupt. At the inn highwaymen plot to commit crimes with the complicity of the crooked innkeeper, who even tries to corrupt his daughter for money. At the inn beaux from London plot stratagems. It is the forces from the inn that invade Lady Bountiful's house in an attempt to destroy it.

Lady Bountiful's house. In contrast to the world of the inn, Lady Bountiful's house represents the simple virtues and charity of the best of the country. At Lady Bountiful's house benevolence and concern for others dominate. Here the sick are healed and the corrupt are converted to virtue. This world is invaded by forces from the corrupt town by means of the highwaymen from the inn and by means of the beaux from the city. The robbers attempt to steal material goods while the beaux attempt to steal female virtue as well as money from Dorinda's fortune. These corrupt forces eventually are defeated or neutralized while the country values of Lady Bountiful dominate at last.

— Paul Varner

BECKET: Or, The Honor of God

Author: Jean Anouilh (1910-1987)
Type of work: Drama
Type of plot: Historical
Time of plot: Twelfth century

First performed: Becket: Ou, L'Honneur de Dieu,
1959; first published, 1959 (English translation, 1960)

Although much of the action of this play takes place in medieval England and France, its core setting is the medieval Canterbury Cathedral, the ancient religious center of England and home of the archbishop of Canterbury, head of the Roman Catholic Church in England. Here the struggle between the royal state and the medieval church finds its articulation in both the friendship between Henry II and Thomas à Becket and Becket's murder at the hands of Henry's men.

*Canterbury Cathedral. Medieval cathedral located in Canterbury, a city southeast of London. The play both opens and closes at Canterbury Cathedral. The stage directions locate Henry II of England at Becket's tomb at the beginning of the play. The year is 1170. Henry is naked, except for his crown and cloak, and is about to be scourged by monks as punishment for the murder of Becket. That this punishment takes place in the cathedral is particularly important because it symbolizes the power of the Church. Henry's attempt to control not only the state but also the Church through his friend Becket is what has led Henry to this ignominious moment.

The bulk of the play is told in flashbacks and traces the friendship and later the enmity between Henry and Becket. When Henry names Becket Archbishop of Can-terbury, Becket turns from being thoroughly the king's man to being God's man.

When the struggles between Henry and Becket reach their peak, Henry asks of his four henchmen if any of them can rid him of Becket. The men take this as a command and go to murder Becket at Canterbury Cathedral, where he is about to celebrate mass.

Because churches are traditionally places of sanctuary, the murder in the cathedral is particularly horrific and leads to serious repercussions for Henry. Within two years, Becket becomes a saint and his tomb in Canterbury Cathedral becomes the site of miracles and pilgrimages. In killing Becket, Henry creates a martyr, and the holiest site in England.

— Diane Andrews Henningfeld

THE BEDBUG: An Extravaganza in Nine Scenes

Author: Vladimir Mayakovsky (1893-1930)
Type of work: Drama
Type of plot: Satire

Time of plot: 1929 and 1979
First performed: Klop, 1929; first published, 1929
(English translation, 1931)

First staged in 1929 by the avant-garde theater of Vsevolod Meyerhold, this play uses the concept of a character revived from suspended animation in the future to show the growing sterility and emptiness of Soviet society. Prophetically, the real 1979 Soviet Union proved to be a period of notorious stagnation under Leonid Brezhnev.

*Tambov (1929). Russian city located about 260 miles southeast of Moscow that provides the play's principal setting. Ivan Prisypkin, a former Communist Party member, moves among the working-class parts of this city in the year 1929 with casual familiarity. However, when he is thrust fifty years into the future, he is an alien who can have no place. Vladimir Mayakovsky's Tambov is a generic provincial Soviet city, without any hint of the cultural riches of the actual city, which was the home of such eminent figures as Alexander Pushkin and Sergei Rachmaninoff.

Scenes set in 1929 Tambov include such typical settings as a state department store, a workers' hostel, and an enormous beauty parlor. Mayakovsky's stage directions describe these settings only briefly, enough to evoke the images of these stock elements of the early years of Soviet society.

Tambov (1979). By contrast, Mayakovsky provides much more extensive descriptions of sets for his imaginary Tambov of the future. An enormous amphitheater with its long-distance voting system is described in detail, a collection of radio loudspeakers with semaphore arms and colored electric lights taking the place of human voters. This set in particular is the most telling of the dehumanization of Mayakovsky's future Soviet society. Other future sets include a revivification chamber, a plaza with strange metal trees that produce their fruits on plates, and a zoo in which Prisypkin is confined when he proves incapable of functioning in this "perfected" society.

— *Leigh Husband Kimmel*

THE BEGGAR'S OPERA

Author: John Gay (1685-1732)
Type of work: Drama
Type of plot: Social satire

Time of plot: Early eighteenth century
First performed: 1728; first published, 1728

A sense of time and place is vital in recognizing and appreciating John Gay's biting satire. Politics, institutions, and mores of London in the early eighteenth century provided much material for the writer with a sharp eye and a keen wit. Gay uses Peachum's house as a backdrop to the political intrigues, particularly those involving British prime minister Robert Walpole.

*London. Scenes in London places such as Newgate Prison expose hypocrisy and corruption in the justice system and further heighten the invective against deceitful politicians, officers of the court, tastes of society, and the power of money. By exposing the treachery and fraud occurring in these various places, Gay hoped to correct or eliminate the political and social vices that marked London in the early eighteenth century.

Peachum's house. London home of Mr. Peachum, a receiver of stolen goods and an informer. His home is his kingdom in miniature—the place where he conducts his business and gathers his followers. His dwelling acts as sort of a microcosm of what goes on in Walpole's realm and the larger political arena. Peachum is the mock-aristocrat who gains and maintains power through bribery, theft, dishonesty, and treachery, all mechanisms Prime Minister Walpole allegedly used to retain his control over the country. Furthermore, Peachum's house also serves as a mock-court, allowing Gay to poke fun at the ills of the court in early eighteenth century London. There seems to be little difference between the actions of the highwaymen and the courtiers; both groups are skilled thieves. Overall, Gay clearly exposes the targets of his political satire within Peachum's domain.

*Newgate Prison.** Notorious London penal institution that was demolished in 1902. Much of the play's business occurring in this prison exposes the corruption in the justice system. Lockit, the jailer, is easily bribed, thereby illustrating the notion that the right price can purchase "justice" and that laws and punishment are class-conscious. Money is important in Newgate, and its importance emphasizes the power of money as a major theme in the play. Furthermore, Macheath's character is most fully exposed after he becomes a prisoner at Newgate, and it is here that many of the play's conflicts are resolved. Macheath is transferred to the Condemn'd Hold to await execution, but since Gay's play is an opera, it must have a happy conclusion. In a satirical turn on the fashionable Italian opera, Gay uses this final scene at Newgate as a departure from the "realism" achieved in the production. Macheath is allowed to live so that this beggar's opera can follow the Italian opera's convention of the contrived happy finale.

— *Michele Theriot*

BEL-AMI

Author: Guy de Maupassant (1850-1893)
Type of work: Novel
Type of plot: Naturalism

Time of plot: c. 1885
First published: 1885 (English translation, 1889)

The hero of this story is a brutal, calculating, duplicitous social climber whose arena is Paris. The novel shows the city's late nineteenth century richness—its glorious monuments, its chic and important cafés (where one sees and is seen), its workers' slums. The novel is one of the most urban of nineteenth century French novels, depicting the relationship between Paris's glamour and luxury and its middle-class inhabitants' greed and opportunistic betrayal.

*Paris.** Capital of France and the social, political, and cultural center of French life. Georges Duroy's rise (and there are passages where he literally climbs stairways to one success or another) is reflected in his material and romantic triumphs. The novel's first chapter shows the beginning of Duroy's career as a boulevardier, an individual who spends a good deal of time going from café to café to see and be seen. In fact, while strolling some of Paris's "grands boulevards" and adjacent thoroughfares, Duroy meets magazine editor Forestier, his future boss and the present husband of Duroy's future wife Madeleine. After realizing that they served in the army together, the two men stroll through Paris, covering quite a bit of territory together.

The opening scenes of the novel are exciting, presenting a kind of panorama of Paris's Right Bank (the north side of the Seine River). Guy de Maupassant alludes to the Opera and to the Church of the Madeleine, where Georges's second wedding will take place. There is an interlude at the Folies Bergère, where a prostitute makes overtures toward Georges, and a scene on the Champs Élysées, perhaps Paris's most famous street. Maupassant creates a powerful sense of the terrain on which Georges will fight for success, from the glamour of this beautiful city's monuments, to its cafés and bistros, to its seamy underside—all of which prove to Georges that, as his friend tells him, it is primarily through women that a man becomes successful in Paris. Later, Maupassant characterizes Paris as a colossus with a life of its own, a life derived from the collective heat, lust, and activity of its inhabitants.

***Church of the Trinity.** Right Bank church in Paris that is the setting of scenes that characterize Duroy and three of his victims. It serves as a trysting-place for Duroy and Virginie Walter, the wife of his publisher, whom Georges brutally seduces and then discards. This seduction is particularly shocking because Madame Walter takes great pride in her Christian virtue and purity. Maupassant makes Madame Walter's moral downfall seem all the more terrible by setting its beginning in a church. This scene will remind readers of a similar passage, in *Madame Bovary* (1857; English translation, 1886), by Gustave Flaubert, one of Maupassant's mentors. In that novel, the heroine's virtue is assaulted in a cathedral.

***Church of the Madeleine.** Another prestigious Parisian church, one that provides a stunning irony: It is there that Georges marries the wealthy Suzanne Walter,

daughter of Virginie Walter, with the cream of Paris society in attendance. However, even during the wedding reception, Georges is planning a rendezvous with a longtime mistress.

***Normandy.** Region of western France in which Maupassant himself was born. After Georges marries Madeleine Forestier, the widow of his boss, they visit his parents in a tiny, primitive village near Rouen. Their short stay here is uncomfortable for all concerned except Georges, who enjoys revisiting his childhood home. This passage emphasizes the contrast between rural France and the glitter of Paris as well as demonstrating the humble background of the soon-to-be powerful Duroy. His mother quickly learns to hate Madeleine as a parasitic city woman; Madeleine is shocked by the crudeness of the villagers and the conditions in which they live. Most of all, however, the visit to Normandy demonstrates the sharp clash between harsh reality (as shown in the presence of factory smokestacks amid the pretty, bucolic landscape) and a kind of poetic naïveté in Madeleine; one evening during the visit, she even experiences a sudden, sharp, spiritual crisis which precipitates the couple's return to Paris.

— *Gordon Walters*

BELINDA

Author: Maria Edgeworth (1767-1849)
Type of work: Novel
Type of plot: Social realism

Time of plot: Late eighteenth century
First published: 1801

The opposition between city and country, between England's world of fashionable dissimulation and its world of natural simplicity, underwrites the entire novel. However, there is no straightforward opposition, for neither world on its own proves to be the path to that prudence Belinda must achieve in order to find happiness.

***London.** The major metropolitan area and capital city of Great Britain, London is also the fall and winter meeting place for the nobility and aristocracy of England's countryside—people whose wealth derives from rents and not from work. The London of Maria Edgeworth's novel is the London of the fashionable world and the primary setting through which she criticizes that world as mercenary, dishonest, dissipated. It is the London of spectacle, of theaters, operas, masquerades, balls,

of "bustle" and "glare." Throughout her descriptions of the city, Edgeworth emphasizes the glittering appearances which, like Lady Delacour's mask as "the comic muse," disguise the sordid reality of disease, disaffection, and dissipation.

Delacour House. Mansion in London's Berkeley Square district that is the home of Lord and Lady Delacour. Here the beauty, wit, and wealth of London gather. However, these revels are merely a "spell," a "thin veil" covering domestic misery. The house conceals a secret, in the form of Lady Delacour's mysterious boudoir, a bedroom locked to all but her and her maid. The boudoir is not the haunt of vice but of disease; even as her wound eats at Lady Delacour's bosom, the secrecy cloaking it—of which her boudoir is the emblem—devours her marriage. Notably, it is Belinda's forcing Lady Delacour to open the locked door to her husband, to remove the veil and reveal her disease that ultimately restores happiness to Delacour House.

Oakly Park. Stately country home of Lady Anne and Mr. Percival that is located near London. Even as Percival House, the mansion in Upper Grosvenor Street, London, is contrasted, in its domestic harmony, intelligent society, and rational pursuits, with the dissipation and dangerous secrets of Delacour House, Oakly Park is contrasted both with London and with the picturesque retreat of Mrs. Ormond's cottage. As Lady Anne notes, Oakly Park and London are two different worlds. Oakly Park provides leisure for reflection and for noble pursuits; London is marred by vicious idleness and by "busy eyes and tongues," whose gossip, like their opinions, is "idle and ignorant." The estate symbolizes a balance between too-knowledgeable society and the too-innocent country.

Mrs. Ormond's cottage. Small house with walled garden in Windsor, a country town immediately west of London. The site of the royal family's Windsor Castle, it is a favorite summer retreat of the aristocracy. Here Clarence Hervey replicates the isolation and simplicity of the former New Forest home of his ward, Virginia St. Pierre (born Rachel Hartley), and her governess. However, this artificially rural retreat itself breeds a dangerous idleness that aligns the country with the city; without the common labor of honest country life, Virginia becomes caught up in novel-reading and romancing, in wild imaginings, which, like the wild gossip of Londoners, ultimately threaten Hervey's happiness and her own.

*New Forest. Largest forest in England, which at the time the novel was written covered much of the land between the seaside towns of Southampton and Bournemouth. Here Clarence Hervey finds his child of nature, Virginia, living a hermitlike existence with her grandmother in a beautiful, glade, surrounded by beehives—a sign of honest country labor—and rose trees, the classic English symbol of cultivated nature and romantic love.

— *Susan Johnston*

A BELL FOR ADANO

Author: John Hersey (1914-1993)
Type of work: Novel
Type of plot: Social realism

Time of plot: 1943
First published: 1944

Set in the fictional town of Adano, one of the first landing points of the American invasion of Sicily during World War II, this novel is permeated with a sense of place; even the buildings in Adano have essential roles in relation to the plot and themes of the book.

Adano (AH-dah-no). Fictional town on the southern coast of Sicily, based on the island's real town of Licata, which was one of the initial landing points of the Allied Occupation of Italy in July, 1943. The fictional town physically mirrors the actual town as a seat of shipping and the sulfur industry, as a fishing port, and even in some of its place names. The town halls of both Adano and Licata are located in squares called "Piazza Progresso," and the principal churches of both towns are called Church of Sant'Angelo. The novel takes its name from an incident that actually occurred after Italy's Fascist dictator, Benito Mussolini, had the real town's seven-hundred-year-old bell melted down so its metal could be used to make munitions. John Hersey's fictional military governor, Major Victor Joppolo, is based on the actual American military governor of Licata during the American occupation.

A typical commercial port for its time and place,

Adano has a population of about forty thousand people. It is large enough to contain thirteen churches and social strata ranging from rich industrialists and politicians, both honest and corrupt, to shopkeepers, poor working people, cart-drivers, and fishermen. However, it is small enough for every resident to know everyone's loyalties, strengths, and weaknesses. The fictional town is at the mouth of the River Rosso, surrounded by hills and rocky promontories in an arid part of Sicily and depends on water carts to carry in drinking water—a fact upon which the plot of the novel revolves.

Palazzo di Citta. Adano's city hall, where much of the important action takes place, especially in Major Joppolo's office. Located on Adano's main square, the Piazza Progresso, the building and Joppolo's office are described in detail in the first chapter of the book. The building both projects a look of authority and represents real authority throughout the novel. Major Joppolo's office is also described in detail, from its oversized furniture to its painting of the incident of the Sicilian Vespers on the wall. The Palazzo is an old stone building, with a second-floor balcony that is the location of many public speeches and a clock tower with a baroque frame designed to hold a bell. However, there is no bell, and the occupied town needs a new bell as much as it needs food and fair government.

As the headquarters of Major Joppolo, the Palazzo is the scene of the townspeople's petitions and Joppolo's just decisions. When Joppolo announces that he will countermand an unjust order of a general, a cartman exclaims that "there has never been a thing like this—that the poor should come to the Palazzo di Citta, and that their request should be granted." On the other hand, Tomasino, the head of the fishermen, avoids the Palazzo precisely because it represents authority to him, and he hates all authority.

Albergo dei Pescatori. Restaurant with the best food in Adano. Major Joppolo and Captain Purvis of the military police regularly eat eggplant and pasta lunches together at this restaurant. In the days before the war stopped the fishing, the Albergo specialized in fish for fishermen, and when the fishing boats are able to go out again, there are huge crowds celebrating at the restaurant. A lunch at the Albergo is the setting of the tale of the death of Giorgio, an Italian soldier and prisoner of war who had been the lover of Tina, daughter of the fisherman Tomasino and sympathetic female friend of Major Joppolo.

Villa Rossa. Quattrocchi's grand town house, one of the finest in Adano and a symbol of Italian culture that is filled with beautiful antiques. A number of American engineers and military police are billeted in the villa. After several soldiers get drunk and smash valuable objects, Joppolo demands that they care for the house as if each object belonged to their own mothers, thus insisting on respect for the Italian people and their culture. Later the house is the site of the farewell party in honor of Major Joppolo.

— *Susan Butterworth*

THE BELL JAR

Author: Sylvia Plath (as Victoria Lucas, 1932-1963)

Type of work: Novel

Type of plot: Psychological realism

Time of plot: 1953

First published: 1963

Set in the 1950's, this novel chronicles a promising female college student's struggles with depression. Since many elements of the book closely parallel events in the author's own life, including a similar bout with depression that ended in a period of institutionalization, most readers approach the novel as a loosely disguised autobiography. In fact its author, Sylvia Plath, was so concerned those close to her might recognize themselves in the characters of the novel, she published it overseas under the pseudonym Victoria Lucas. The novel did not appear in the United States until after her death in 1963.

New York City. Approximately the first third of *The Bell Jar* is set in the urbane, cosmopolitan environs of Manhattan, where Esther Greenwood—a young, ambitious college junior from a sheltered Boston suburb—is a summer intern for *Mademoiselle* magazine after winning a writing contest. Filled with aspirations of entering a magazine publishing career after college, Esther welcomes the opportunity to get her feet wet in a major New York publishing house a full year before her graduation from college. However, shortly after she settles in New York, a host of disillusioning events tarnishes her view of the city and her romantic dreams of seeking fame and fortune there. Although painfully aware that she is "supposed to be having the time of [her] life" in Manhattan, Esther cannot cope with the intensely competitive, highly chauvinistic atmosphere of New York publishing in the 1950's. She suffers an emotional and physical collapse that ends in her return to her mother's home in suburban Boston weeks before the scheduled end of her internship. Esther likens her untimely breakdown and forced retreat from the city of her dreams to "watching Paris from an express caboose heading in the opposite direction."

Boston suburbs. Esther's family home, to which she returns from New York. Rather than providing her with the peace and quiet she needs to regain her bearings before returning to college, Esther's time in her mother's home furthers her descent into a debilitating depression. Her unsympathetic mother offers little in the way of consolation, unable to see her daughter's condition as anything more than a case of pre-graduation jitters. However, Esther regards her return home with even greater foreboding than she does her time in New York. Whereas most disillusioned city-dwellers might welcome the stability and familiarity of a retreat to the suburbs, Esther sees their "white, identical clapboard houses" as "one bar after another in a large but escape-proof cage."

Not only is she uncomfortable at work, but similarly disillusioned in her relationships with men. After finding out that her fiancé has secretly been having an affair with another woman, she feels betrayed and finds it difficult to trust the other men she meets. Isolated from productive influences while cloistered in her mother's home, Esther begins to obsess over what she sees as a fateful chain of personal failures. After only a few weeks there she attempts suicide.

Esther's college. Unnamed New England women's college famous for its academic rigor that is modeled after Plath's own alma mater, Smith College, in Massachusetts. None of the novel's scenes are expressly set at this college, because Esther's depression prevents her from returning there for her senior year; however, she repeatedly reflects on a number of things that happened there earlier that set the stage for her breakdown. She has maintained straight A's at the college but regards her academic achievements as meaningless in the personal and professional world that beckons her after graduation.

Walton Hospital. Private asylum in which Esther is institutionalized after her emotional condition worsens. There she initially fails to respond positively to electroshock therapy—which she finds so violent and frightening she likens it to electrocution—but eventually begins to improve with the help of a sensitive, compassionate psychotherapist. At the end of the novel she stands at the threshold of gaining release from the institution. Although she remains emotionally fragile, Esther is confident that she has gained a reprieve from "the **bell jar**" her illness lowered mysteriously and unmercifully around her.

— *Gregory D. Horn*

BELLEFLEUR

Author: Joyce Carol Oates (1938-   )
Type of work: Novel
Type of plot: Gothic

Time of plot: Mid-sixteenth to late twentieth centuries
First published: 1980

Place creates a Gothic atmosphere that drives this novel's entire narrative, as the story moves without constraint between past, present, and future events. The novel's unity is found not in a linear chronological development, but in its physical setting in a region of the northeastern United States near the Canadian border.

Bellefleur Manor. Ancestral home of the Bellefleurs, a large American clan whose roots go back to the American Revolution. The family mansion sits on the shores of mythic Lake Noir near the Canadian border, a region similar to the Adirondack Mountains of New York State. Over the years, the family gains control over a vast part of the region. As its wealth and influence grow, it advertises its power by building the manor as a grand castle. However, the great structure is both castle and prison, for it binds all the Bellefleurs—living and dead, past and present, young and old—together forever. To be a Bellefleur is to be a captive in Bellefleur Manor and its region, forced to live with all manner of oddities brought on by a family tradition of intermarriage among cousins.

An eerie, coppery pink in color, the house is a huge structure with "innumerable walls and towers and turrets and minarets," like "a castle composed in a feverish sleep." By the late twentieth century, the castle has fallen into serious disrepair, along with the fortunes of the family. It is leaking, broken, and occupied by cats, rats, ghosts, a vampire, and a mass murderer. The house and family fortune are eventually rescued by Leah Bellefleur, but the manor is then destroyed by her husband, Gideon, in a violent act that kills most members of the clan, including Gideon and Leah themselves. However, their children are spared, and the manor's destruction frees them from the hold it has long exercised on their family.

Along with many rooms and suites for family members and their wives and children, the manor contains a nursery for the children, in which they are tutored by Hiram Bellefleur, and a walled garden where the children play. It is from this garden that a huge bird—the Noir Vulture—one day snatches one of the Bellefleur children and carries her off. A particularly more mysteri-ous area of the manor is the Turquoise Room, also known as the "Room of Contamination," in which Samuel Bellefleur locks himself, never to reappear again. Young Bromwell Bellefleur claims one of the manor's towers as his laboratory, and he eventually becomes a famous astrophysicist. Another room is occupied by the vampire Veronica Bellefleur.

Cemetery. Family burial place, located just beyond the manor's walled garden, near Mink Creek. Mink Pond, created by Mink Creek, is the favorite hideout of Raphael Bellefleur, who one day is attacked by a tenant farmer's son (or perhaps a dog); he is saved from dying when the pond's waters close over him. Later the pond mysteriously dries up, and Raphael disappears. Yolande Bellefleur is also attacked by the same boy (or dog) in the cemetery. She flees and hides in the barn, where her brother Garth saves her from the attacker by burning the barn.

Lake Noir. Dark and mysterious body of water on which the manor sits. The lake claims the lives of several members of the Bellefleur clan. It is said to be inhabited by humanlike creatures who live just below its surface and walk upside down on the water. Their activity can be seen most easily during the winter, when the Lake is covered with an exceptionally thick coat of ice.

Nautauga County. Mountainous region surrounding Lake Noir. Its Mount Blanc is the home of Jedediah Bellefleur, a hermit who dedicates himself to worshiping God. Ewan Bellefleur is the sheriff of the county, which, in addition to Bellefleur Village, contains such towns as Nautauga Falls, Port Oriskany, Mount Kittery, Paie-des-Sables, and Innisfail, in which Jean Pierre commits his mass murders.

— *August W. Staub*

BELOVED

Author: Toni Morrison (1931-   )
Type of work: Novel
Type of plot: Psychological realism

Time of plot: Late nineteenth century
First published: 1987

Opening in the year 1873, this novel covers events unfolding over the preceding eighteen years but denies readers signals with which to distinguish among different periods. Its protagonist is Sethe, once a fugitive slave who murdered her first daughter, Beloved, rather than let her become a slave. After being imprisoned for her crime, Sethe begins life anew but is slow to come to terms with her guilt. While working as a cook in Cincinnati, Sethe is visited by a man from her slave days in Kentucky. Before she can avail herself of the opportunity for renewal and emotional health that he represents, she must find peace with her past—a peace that seems to be threatened by the very house in which she lives.

*Ohio River. River separating the slave and free states that Sethe crosses while fleeing from Kentucky to Ohio. She gives birth to Beloved as she crosses the river. Years later, the child reappears to Sethe in mortal form along a riverbank. Toni Morrison's choice of the Ohio River for these events is significant. One of America's major maritime shipping routes, the Ohio extends from the confluence of the Allegheny and Monongahela Rivers in Pittsburgh, Pennsylvania, and flows for nearly one thousand miles before joining the Mississippi River at Cairo, Illinois.

In the nineteenth century, the Ohio river was filled with passenger-carrying flatboats and paddle-wheel ferries and served as a central conveyance for families moving west to capitalize on the frontier's promise of prosperity. In slave narratives from the same period, however, the Ohio River symbolized freedom. For slaves, crossing the Ohio River and making one's way into the "free" state of Ohio was tantamount to entering a land in which one's citizenship was honored.

Sweet Home. North Kentucky plantation on which Sethe begins her life as a slave. Her flight from slavery in Sweet Home to Cincinnati is based on the historical story of a fugitive slave named Margaret Garner, who began killing her own children when it appeared she would be recaptured. When Garner was tried for her crime, she was charged not with murder but with theft— for violating the Fugitive Slave Act of 1856 by destroying the legal property of her family's slave master.

That the Ohio River represented a physical demarcation between one way of life and another for so many African Americans in the nineteenth century is treated ironically by Morrison, for in no meaningful sense can Sethe be regarded as "free" in Ohio. Although she may be legally free there under the law, she is very much a prisoner of her experiences as a slave in Sweet Home. This is why Morrison presents the story not as a linear narrative but rather as a quilt, a tapestry. The kind of time that one can read on a clock and the kind of space that one can calculate on a map are of less importance in the novel than the protagonist's experiences within a space-time continuum in which the past constantly intrudes upon the present. For instance, the novel distinguishes between "memory," that is, the human capacity consciously to recall events that transpire in one's life, and what Sethe experiences as "re-memory"—things that "just stay."

Bluestone Road house. Sethe's Cincinnati home. The most important place in the novel, 124 Bluestone Road figures into every section of the book. Each of the novel's three sections begins with a description of the mood of the house, as if the house itself were a living, breathing creature. The first part opens by describing the house as "spiteful"; the second part calls it "loud," and the third part calls it "quiet."

By the time the story begins, Sethe's male children have been driven from her house by a paranormal presence that seems to haunt its timbers. The arrival of Paul D appears, at first, to signal a return to a more normal state of affairs. However, he soon also senses spirits hovering above the house's stairwell that resent his presence and his command of Sethe's attentions and do not wish him well. By the novel's midpoint, the house drives Paul from Sethe's bed. Later, he is driven from the house itself. Only after struggles in the novel's last third is he able to return to the house.

With such a haunted house, *Beloved* might seem to be part of a long and honorable tradition of gothic tales, aligning it in particular with the nineteenth century psycho-gothic ghost stories of Edgar Allan Poe and Henry James. However, this is only superficially true, as *Beloved* is about dramatizing the psychic pains of its protagonist. Beloved's spiritual presence in the house is, effectively, Sethe's own grief and guilt taking on something approaching perilous dimensions. The house has height, mass, and an architectural design to be sure.

Sethe herself is no more delusional than her house is a fantasy. The house has all the things that one associates with what is "real." However, the "reality" of 124 Bluestone Street in Cincinnati far exceeds what is normally meant by a "place," for Morrison reminds readers that the most important places are those that one cannot leave behind.

— *Jay Boyer*

BEN-HUR: A Tale of the Christ

Author: Lew Wallace (1827-1905)
Type of work: Novel
Type of plot: Historical

Time of plot: Time of Christ
First published: 1880

Backdrops in this sweeping, panoramic novel set during the time of Jesus Christ span the ancient Mediterranean world, from Italy to Palestine, and involve cities as large and varied as Rome, Antioch, and Jerusalem and cultures as diverse as those of the Romans, Greeks, Jews, and Christians.

*Roman Empire.** The broad context of the novel is the Roman Empire during the Golden Age of the Julio-Claudian emperors, who ruled from 27 B.C.E. to 68 C.E. This empire, the largest the world had yet known, extended more than eighteen hundred miles from west to east and included parts of three continents—Europe, Africa, and Asia. With more than 50,000,000 subjects under its protection, the empire was comparable in size to the continental United States.

In Lew Wallace's novel, as in history, Rome has an ambiguous role. It represents both hostility and opportunity. Its hostility is exemplified in the crucifixion of Christ, the destruction of Jerusalem, the annihilation of the temple, and the expulsion of the Jews from their homeland. Opportunity is exemplified in the empire's toleration of its Jewish subjects, who flourish in its cities. Ben Hur, the novel's hero, is a Jew who obtains Roman citizenship and prospers within the Empire. Meanwhile, Christianity spreads rapidly over Roman highways and in the cities.

*Rome.** Capital of the Roman Empire. This city, which ultimately will become a Christian Jerusalem in which Peter and Paul will preach and be martyred, is a powerful image throughout the novel. Rome and Jerusalem were founded around the same periods: Rome in the eighth century B.C.E. and Jerusalem about two and a half centuries earlier. One was the City of David, the other, the City of Caesar; Lew Wallace wanted to show both as "Cities of Christ."

*Holy Land.** Eastern Mediterranean region corresponding roughly to the area of modern Israel and Palestine that was the center of many of the stories of the Bible. The region has strong religious significance to Jews, Christians, and Muslims. In *Ben-Hur*, the Holy Land is Judea, the home of the Jewish people in general and the prominent Jewish family Hur in particular. For Wallace, the Holy Land has the mixed imagery of birth (of Jesus and of Judaism) and death (crucifixion of Christ and destruction of Palestinian Jewry by the Romans).

The Hur family name means "cave" in Hebrew, and cave images appear several times in the novel, climaxing in the construction of secret underground worship spaces for Christians in the Roman catacombs.

*Jerusalem.** Chief city of ancient Palestine whose name means "city of peace." Since the time of King David, Jerusalem has been the political, religious, and cultural center of Judaism. The Jerusalem of *Ben-Hur* has been transformed by Roman occupation and has a Roman theater, a hippodrome, and an amphitheater—all of which help make it resemble a Greco-Roman metropolis. Because of this, the city was often known as Antioch Jerusalem (a symbolism not to be missed in the novel). Jerusalem has an ambivalent role in both the life of Jesus and in the novel. It is both home, or a place of allies—but it is also an alien element. The Hur family home, the leper caves, and the court of the Roman procurator Pontius Pilate all reflect the ambivalence of the place.

*Antioch. Rich and important city situated on the Orontes River in Syria, some fifteen miles from the Mediterranean Sea, that was the cement holding together the classical world. Antioch was the second-most important city of the eastern Roman Empire, eclipsed only by Alexandria in Egypt. Not only did it command sea lanes to the west and south, it also was the terminus for transcontinental highways to Mesopotamia, Persia, and the East. Antioch attracted a diverse population, including many Jews and Christians. In Antioch the disciples of Jesus were first called "Christians" in a church founded by Peter, served later by Paul and Barnabas. As in history Antioch serves as a place of transition and maturation for Christianity (a kind of Second Jerusalem for the Early Church), it is also a town of transition for Ben-Hur. Antioch is a place of new beginnings, whether at a well (frequented by Balthasar, one of the Three Wise Men), or the arena, where old enemies can be humbled. The famed chariot race of *Ben-Hur* takes place in Antioch.

— *C. George Fry*

A BEND IN THE RIVER

Author: V. S. Naipaul (1932-   )
Type of work: Novel
Type of plot: Psychological realism

Time of plot: Early 1970's
First published: 1979

A grim exploration of postcolonial Africa, this novel never specifies its exact location. Its primary setting—the interior of a large tropical country—resembles the former Belgian Congo, which became the Democratic Republic of the Congo (and was known for a time as Zaire), which V. S. Naipaul visited during the 1960's. However, the precise location is not significant, as the story pertains not only to all of postcolonial Africa but to all postcolonial nations.

River. Unnamed river that connects the tropical African country's interior to the outside world. It provides the major means for travel and transporting goods to the town in which the central character and narrator, Salim, settles. When progress first comes to the town, Salim finds the steamers with their first-class cabins an impressive contrast to the old barges and dugouts that were long the only means of transportation. However, by the time the novel ends, with Salim leaving the town for good, the steamer on which he travels has become dingy, and his first-class cabin is merely a travesty of luxury. The river itself is gradually filling with water hyacinths that hamper navigation. Like the town and the Domain on its banks, the river is a major symbol of the emptiness that pervades the novel.

Town. The town in which Salim settles by a bend in the great river, also lacks a name. Once home to a thriving European community, it is half-destroyed during the nationalist war for independence. Salim travels there from an unnamed country on Africa's east coast to set up a hardware-variety store. A keen observer, he reports on the town's condition in such a way that he integrates its ruined monuments, dilapidated villas and shops, rutted-out streets, and overgrown gardens into the overall theme of desolation.

Bush. Term widely used in Africa for open country. The bush surrounding the town is seen by Salim as encroaching on the settlement and gradually obliterating its last traces of civilization. His description of the bush, like his description of the town, is dispassionate. He does not long for the return of European civilization; he simply records its passing. To European colonists, "bush" could mean forests, deserts, jungles, or mountains and was something to be feared and conquered. For Africans during the colonial era, the bush served as a refuge from the European presence. All of Africa was originally bush, and Naipaul shows how thoroughly it consumes the faint marks that European colonialism has left behind.

Domain. Next to the town lies the Domain, which was built as a symbol of modern Africa. Intended first as an international conference center, or possibly as an agricultural showpiece, the Domain eventually became a polytechnic university and research center. Underneath its glittery appearance, however, the establishment is shoddy. Its buildings are poorly constructed and deteriorating, its flashy furniture is tawdry, its gigantic swimming pool is unusable, its grounds are neglected. When Salim first visits the Domain and enters one of the houses built for staff, he is impressed. However, he soon realizes that the place, like everything else at the bend in the river, is a mockery—nothing more than a feeble attempt to show that this African country could be European. Its failure makes it merely one more monument to desolation.

— *Robert L. Ross*

BENITO CERENO

Author: Herman Melville (1819-1891)
Type of work: Novella
Type of plot: Adventure

Time of plot: 1799
First published: 1856

By using a fictitious island off the southern coast of Chile as a symbol of the Southern Hemisphere's destructive involvement with slavery and by placing in direct contact with a slave revolt a Massachusetts ship's captain symbolizing the Northern Hemisphere's idealism and optimism about slaves, this novel ironically reverses the values and assumptions about slaves, slaveholders, and abolitionists reflected in Harriet Beecher Stowe's Uncle Tom's Cabin *(1851-1852). The result is a depiction of abolitionists as dangerously naïve, slaveholders as heroically tragic victims of historical forces beyond their control, and black slaves as dangerous enemies often masquerading as the best friends of their white owners.*

*Chile. South American country off whose coast the American whaling ship *Bachelor's Rest* encounters the Spanish slave ship *San Dominick*, whose slaves have mutinied and taken control, in the harbor of a small island. By setting his story in the southernmost extreme of the known world, Herman Melville dramatizes the racial tensions inherent in the southern United States during the same period. In an attempt to gain the confidence of Captain Amasa Delano of the *Bachelor's Rest*, the rebel slaves pretend still to be prisoners and slaves.

Babo, the ostensibly devoted slave of the *San Dominick*'s captain appears to behave as a quintessential "Uncle Tom," doing everything he can to meet his master's needs. The narrator's description of the slaves is of "natural valets and hairdressers" whose docility arises from the contentment of their limited minds. This is the same view of black slaves depicted in Harriet Beecher Stowe's *Uncle Tom's Cabin*, which was published a few years before Melville's story. However, in *Benito Cereno* Melville powerfully depicts this view of slaves as a fantasy, with the reality the oppressive violence and savagery of Babo and his allies, who have killed most of the Spanish crew.

In Melville's view, this is the pragmatic reality of the Southern Hemisphere's centuries-long involvement with slavery, and the effect upon slaveholders, represented by Benito Cereno, is that of oppressive pessimism, fatalism, and horror. This is Melville's view of the psychological reality of slaveholders in the American South. Even after being freed from the black rebels, Benito Cereno cannot function or regain equilibrium; when asked what has cast such a psychological shadow upon him, he replies simply, "the negro." A few months later, he is dead, having followed his leader as tragic victim of the historical burden of slavery. That is the reality of the Southern Hemisphere's slaves and slaveholders.

*Lima. Capital of Peru where the rebel slaves are tried after the *San Dominick* is recaptured. Once Babo leaps into Captain Delano's boat in pursuit of Benito Cereno, he is captured and the revolting slaves are defeated by the crew of Delano's ship. The captured rebels are then taken to Peru for trial and, in the case of Babo, executed. Significantly located between the hemispheric

extremes of southern Chile and Duxbury, Massachusetts, Lima, Peru, acts as a symbolic middle ground of justice and morality between the blind optimism and idealism of New England abolitionism and the horrific degradation of Southern Hemisphere slavery. Here, real spiritual awareness and assistance are available to those victimized by historical evils such as slavery, epitomized by a monk who devotes himself to attempting to help Benito Cereno recover. However, to the conservative and cynical Melville, even such justice, spirituality, and practical morality cannot overcome the destruction wrought by humanity's historical excesses. Thus, Peru's symbolic middle-ground justice can kill Babo, but it cannot save the doomed Benito Cereno, who can only follow his leader.

— John L. Grigsby

BEOWULF

Author: Unknown
Type of work: Poetry
Type of plot: Epic

Time of plot: Sixth century
First transcribed: c. 1000

This epic poem's major actions on land unfold in the great hall of the Danes, Heorot; the terrible wild surrounding Heorot, including the great underwater cave of Grendel's mother; and the cave of the dragon in Beowulf's native Geatland. These places contrast the fragile civilized world of the Danes and Geats (Geets) with the unknown world. Water, as sea and as dark, dreadful pools, makes a kind of place that is yet another world of threats and danger to humans.

Heorot (HEH-oh-rot). Headquarters of the aging Danish ruler Hrothgar. The great timbered hall is elaborately described, for only here can human beings be, within limits, civilized. (The unnamed great hall of the warrior-hero Beowulf's uncle, King Hygelac of the Geats, resembles Heorot.) A great open hall with smaller divisions, Heorot is adorned with gold. Its approach is by a stone-paved road. It has benches and tables at which the retainers of Hrothgar sit. At night it is lit by torches, and its light reaches out to the surrounding wild. It is only within the king's hall that court poets can tell and retell the heroic and dreadful tales of the northern peoples, for these tales demand a proper setting for their force and meaning. The stories give the values of the culture, both positively and negatively. They teach about the importance of loyalty and about the consequences of both loyalty and betrayal.

Here the people, or rather the nobles, carry on all the activities of human life; it is where they eat and drink and where many sleep. But it is nevertheless also close to the wild, not only in being made of wood, but in its name, for Heorot means "Hart," or male deer—a noble animal but still animal. In being wood, like others mentioned in the poem, it can be and will be burned, with great slaughter. The humans who live here can and will be terrible to one another. Moreover, Heorot's bright lights and noises offend Grendel, a monstrous descendant of Cain who is condemned to wander alone in the wastelands. Grendel visits Hrothgar's hall regularly and carries off warriors to devour.

Wasteland. There is no description of farming or herding activities in the land around Heorot; indeed, there seem to be no human inhabitants there. Beowulf and his companions are alone as they pass through it. The great hall contains everything human in this world. Outside, the world is a great wasteland, dark forest, mists, moors, narrow dangerous paths, great, gray crags, and no animals or birds, except terrifying water monsters.

Grendel's cave. This underwater home of the monstrous Grendel and his mother is the opposite of Heorot. It is home to only two beings, and everything about it is unnatural. Although the entrance to the cave is by way of water, the cave itself is dry. It too is lit by a fire, but its fire is certainly uncanny. After Beowulf kills Grendel's mother, the cave is suddenly illuminated by a magical light. Like the cave of the dragon, it is filled with many treasures; however, they do not seem to be connected with human activity in any way, not even the sword that Beowulf finds there and uses.

Dragon's lair. The dragon lives in a dark cave from which a dark stream of water issues. He guards a great treasure of precious materials, goblets, bowls, cups, dishes, rings, weapons, and armor. The swords are partially eaten away by time since they are iron, but most of the objects are made of gold. The hoard was accumulated and left behind by the last man of a long-forgotten community. All the treasures were created by men and are thus products of "civilization." While they seem to give off a kind of light, they are slowly reverting to the darkness of the nonhuman.

Sea. The waters of the sea are dangerous for travelers, largely because of sea monsters but implicitly because of threat to the ships that carry men. Beowulf tells the story of his dreadful battles with these monsters. He wins these battles, but all bodies of water are nonhuman and perilous as in Beowulf's terrifying descent into the great pool or mere where Grendel's mother lives.

— *L. L. Lee*

BÉRÉNICE

Author: Jean Baptiste Racine (1639-1699)
Type of work: Drama
Type of plot: Tragedy

Time of plot: 79 C.E.
First performed: 1670; first published, 1671

Although there is only one set for this play, upon which all the scenes are enacted, there are several significant places within the Roman Empire that are mentioned and are familiar background to the participants.

Titus's palace. Residence of Roman emperor Titus in Rome. Although such a place existed, the play's action takes place entirely within a fictional chamber between the apartments of Titus and those of Bérénice, the queen of Palestine. The halls of the palace are described as furnished with splendor and so, therefore, is this chamber. It is stately and withdrawn from the rest of the palace so that Titus and Bérénice can meet privately. It has three doors, one to Titus's apartments, another to Bérénice's, and a third for the entrance and exit of other characters. There is at least one chair or couch here, and it is decorated with festoons in which the names of Titus and Bérénice are intertwined.

*****Palestine.** Eastern Mediterranean country, between Syria in the North and Arabia in the south—both of which Titus adds to Palestine's territory as compensation for casting Bérénice aside. Palestine is subject to Roman rule. Bérénice is its queen and Agrippa, her brother, is king. Judea is the southern part of Palestine. Titus and Antiochus fought together to subdue a triple-walled city. This is probably Jerusalem.

*****Commagene** (kahm-ah-JEE-nee). Small province on the west bank of the Euphrates River in northeastern Syria that was annexed by Rome. It is bounded by Cilicia to the west, and this territory is given to Antiochus, king of Commagene, to add to his governance.

— *Pauline Morgan*

BERLIN ALEXANDERPLATZ

Author: Alfred Döblin (1878-1957)
Type of work: Novel
Type of plot: Social realism
Time of plot: 1927-1928

First published: Berlin Alexanderplatz: Die Geschichte vom Franz Biberkopf, 1929 (English translation, 1931)

Alfred Döblin's exhaustive description of life around Berlin's Alexanderplatz is the key element that gives his great modernist novel its particular narrative force. Bustling with activities and constantly under construction, the central square gives a distinctive, modernist shape to fate and life of all the characters passing by. The streets, shops, cafés, and pubs surrounding the place also epitomize life in modern, urban Germany after the country has lost World War I and shortly before the onset of the Great Depression and Adolf Hitler's takeover of power would change life in that place forever.

*Alexanderplatz. Large, central square in the east central part of Germany's capital city, Berlin. During the late 1920's in which this novel is set, this square was a center of commerce, traffic, and working-class neighborhoods from which streetcar lines connect the entire city. Alexanderplatz is also the center of the novel, which revisits it countless times. The area is constantly under construction; a subway station is being built, and existing shops and houses are torn down to make room for new ones.

Döblin successfully captures the full atmosphere of the square, with its fast life, advertising slogans, popular songs playing in its cafés, and the cries of street vendors and newspaper agents, as well as random conversations among the passersby. This modernist collection of episodic slices of life fully evokes the bustle of human activities in Alexanderplatz, where life is hectic, transitory, and often devious. Burglary plagues Berlin, where no place is safe from plunder. The unwilling presence of the ex-convict Franz Biberkopf at one of these locations changes his life for the worse. Places outside Berlin have a remote quality; they tend to be locations of retreat or violence.

Alexanderplatz's public houses of food and drinking serve as homes away from home for many characters. Many social activities occur in these places, all of which Döblin describes with a keen eye for atmosphere. These places typically have backrooms in which shady deals are negotiated. At Henschke's, Biberkopf is thrown out for selling right-wing newspapers, and a police raid at Alexander Quelle has him arrested. Döblin also provides a graphic description of a central slaughterhouse and often refers to its slaughters when his characters encounter misfortune.

Dwellings of most characters are relatively drab, uninviting places, especially those of men living alone. The presence of their girlfriends brings them more liveliness. Important conflicts take place in some of these rooms, which see much mayhem and human despair. In general, Döblin's characters prefer the streets or bars to their homes.

*Tegel prison. Penal institution in northwest part of Berlin, behind whose redbrick walls and black iron front gate, Döblin's protagonist, Franz Biberkopf, has spent four years for killing his girlfriend Ida. The prison's strict order distinguishes this place from the chaos of modern city life. Biberkopf has a hard time leaving the prison on the streetcar. His imagination cannot let go of the place. Later, he twice returns to look at the prison from the outside. Tegel is less severe than the rural penitentiary at **Sonnenburg**, the eventual home to Biberkopf's false friend Reinhold. Its name, which means "castle of the sun," is bitterly ironic.

Rabbi's apartment. Home of a Jewish man who takes in the freshly released Biberkopf. Located in the former Jewish quarter of Berlin, adjacent to Alexanderplatz, the apartment has a comfortably arranged living room with a large sofa, chairs, and a plush carpet. The rabbi's home is open to his friends. As Biberkopf sinks into Berlin's underworld, his visits to the apartment eventually cease.

*Freienwalde (fri-ahn-VAHL-dah). Idyllic resort town outside Berlin whose nearby forest is the site of Reinhold's grisly murder of Mieze, Biberkopf's girlfriend. Reinhold buries and reburies her in the summer woods, until her corpse is found and laid to rest in a Berlin cemetery.

*Buch Insane Asylum. Located in a bleak, rural landscape outside Berlin, this place signifies the historical geographic and social ostracism of the mentally ill, kept at the margins of cities. Biberkopf nearly starves himself to death here before he overcomes his shock at Mieze's murder. Suffering a symbolic death, he reenters the city a new man.

— *R. C. Lutz*

THE BETROTHED

Author: Alessandro Manzoni (1785-1873)
Type of work: Novel
Type of plot: Historical

Time of plot: Seventeenth century
First published: I promessi sposi, 1827; revised, 1840-
 1842 (English translation, 1828; revised, 1951)

Alessandro Manzoni's preoccupations with weaving a literary work into a historically accurate background has produced a novel concerning the suffering of the disenfranchised that is caused by tyrannies of the seventeenth century: factional warlords, corrupt noblemen, unstable political climate, and natural disasters. The novel's star-crossed lovers, Lucia and Lorenzo, travel through many places as they flee from a villainous nobleman. While separated, each of them faces riots, famine, plague, political chaos, and personal dangers throughout northern Italy.

Milan. Northern Italian city that was a place of authoritarian rule and Spanish and Austrian domination during the seventeenth century, in which this novel is set. Milan experiences one crisis after another. When the young peasant hero Lorenzo becomes separated from his betrothed, Lucia, he enters Milan, initially unaware that it is experiencing a devastating famine. Price-fixing and tariffs on bread provoke rioting and disorder. A gullible countryman, Lorenzo gets caught up in the rioting and is arrested. After escaping from the city, he later returns to look for Lucia and finds Milan looted, barren, death-ridden, almost like a ghost town, Moreover, plague has hit the city so hard that Lorenzo finds its streets littered with dead bodies. Manzoni's grim description of Milan is an accurate picture of its condition during the seventeenth century.

Village. Unnamed village, about one mile east of Lecco, near Lake Como, in which Lucia lives with her mother. In this village lies the source of all troubles that prevent Lucia and Lorenzo from marrying. They must first escape from the villainy of a local nobleman, Don Rodrigo. Lucia's departure from her home village is painful to her because it contains all that she knows and loves in life. Don Rodrigo has Lucia captured and taken to a castle, where Lucia bemoans her separation from Lorenzo.

This village is a poignant locale because Lucia and Lorenzo are betrothed and are supposed to be married as planned, but the simple act of taking a marriage vow is thwarted and the lovers have to leave the place for safety elsewhere. This village is also a common theme concerning country people who are prone to gossip and rumors, as is often the nature of country and rustic ways of life. The lovers' sudden departure in the middle of the night is a great cause for villagers to speculate and gossip from one ear to the other until the news reaches the nobleman. His wrath provokes an all-out scheme of capturing and separating Lorenzo and Lucia at all costs.

*Bergamo. Italian city about nine or ten miles from the River Adda. Lorenzo comes here under a false name and takes a labor job after fleeing from Milan. Eventually, he finds a way to communicate with Lucia.

— *Hanh N. Nguyen*

BETWEEN THE ACTS

Author: Virginia Woolf (1882-1941)
Type of work: Novel
Type of plot: Psychological realism

Time of plot: June, 1939
First published: 1941

All the action of this novel takes place on the English estate of Pointz Hall and in its immediate surroundings. The hall and its farm are the solid, but paradoxical, representation of English and world history, so that this place, this center, radiates outward, with place becoming time.

Pointz Hall. Ancestral home of the Olivers in southern England. As the house bears a weight of historical symbolism, it needs to be seen clearly. It is middle-sized, as English manor houses go, whitish, attractive to passersby, but oddly situated, facing north, away from the sun, and standing low in its meadow so that it suffers in winter. In that way, it is atypical, not quite fully English. Its furniture is mid-Victorian, and thus out of date—contrasting with the furnishings and modern bathrooms that the newly rich coming down from London, such as the Manresas, have put into the old houses they have bought.

Pointz Hall has a principal staircase, but the other staircase is not much more than a ladder at the back of the house, intended for the servants and therefore making a statement about the English class system. On the bottom floor of the hall is a main room, looking out to the garden, where guests are entertained. There is also a library containing histories of England and the world, histories of the local world, and volumes of English poetry. However, there are also pulp novels that houseguests have left. Thus, the past and the present (seemingly a decline) are put side by side. Also downstairs are the kitchen and the larder. However, before the Reformation the larder had been a chapel, so that the house connects with the old religion, Roman Catholicism, and once more shows the passage of time. Upstairs are bedrooms and a nursery. Here is Lucy Swithin's room, where she is reading an outline of history that tells her that England had been, millions of years before, one with Europe. Lucy's book and the nursery, with its children, are once more contrasts and connections between the past and the present.

Sitting in its hollow, the house faces a terrace that is the stage for the village pageant. However, the terrace is surrounded by trees and shrubs that continually remind one of ties to the land. When the villagers act out their pageant of English history, they continually move in and out among the trees, once again connecting the present with the past and with the sacred.

Barn. The estate's barn is immense, possessing a great central room that is lit brilliantly when its doors are opened. Made of the same stone as the village church, it has been likened to a temple by visitors who have been to Greece. The barn is the centerpiece of the farm, the old agricultural and somehow sacred world, but a world gradually being eaten away by the modern.

Village. Unnamed village near Pointz Hall; it is never seen in the novel—apart from its church tower—but is continually referred to, especially in telling what the actors in the village's historical pageant do in their real lives. The village has elements of modernity—shops anda post office, for instance. However, the villagers' roots go back for centuries, and their names can be found in the eleventh century Domesday Book of William the Conqueror—in contrast to the newly arrived Manresa family, representatives of the modern. Even the surrounding countryside, with an old Roman road where the county council proposes to build a communal cesspool, rather ironically puts past and present side by side.

Terrace. Area directly in front of Pointz Hall on which members of gentry sit to watch the villagers' history play. However, as the play itself takes place on this terrace, the lower-class actors are directly in contact with their audience. Therefore, the last scene of their play, the "Present," in which the actors, almost among the audience, carry mirrors that reflect that audience, emphasizes the relationship of audience and actors, gentry and the lower classes, almost satirically. However, the "stage," through the scenes of the play, is the present and also the past, so that this place becomes time itself.

— *L. L. Lee*

THE BIG ROCK CANDY MOUNTAIN

Author: Wallace Stegner (1909-1993)
Type of work: Novel
Type of plot: Historical realism

Time of plot: 1905-1932
First published: 1943

Arising from author Wallace Stegner's youth in Canada and the American West, this novel follows the migrations of a family dragged by its father from one place to another in search of easy wealth and explores the consequences of his inattention to his family's need for an attachment to place and to community.

Whitemud. Canadian town, based on the real town of Eastend, in southwestern Saskatchewan, Canada, where Stegner lived for about five years when he was a boy. The real town's name derives from its location near the eastern end of the Cypress Hills, a prominent geographical feature that lies parallel to the U.S.-Canada boundary. In the fictional Whitemud and at a nearby wheat-farming homestead used only during the growing season, the Mason family has its only long-lasting home and experience of community.

The family's Whitemud home is a two-story, eight-room house built by Bruce's father, Bo Mason, in an attempt to salvage his marriage to Elsa, whom he had earlier deserted in Washington State. The theme of the importance of having a lasting, secure and affectionate home is the emotional core of *The Big Rock Candy Mountain*, and the five years the Masons spend in Whitemud are the center of the novel's exploration of this theme. Bo chooses the town simply as the latest target of his ambition to get rich quick. He regards it as a dirty little "dung-heeled sagebrush town," but Elsa views it as a place to settle down and live respectably, if modestly. For Bruce and his older brother, Chet, Whitemud is the site of typical childhood adventures, but for Bruce, especially, it represents society and civilization, a warm place in which his precocious intelligence is molded both by culture and the natural world.

In the novel's most lyrical episode, Bruce and his parents spend a day making an automobile trip from their homestead to the Bearpaw Mountains, which lie sixty miles to the south across the international boundary. Although the Bearpaws are actually only modest in height and extent, to the nine-year-old Bruce they seem like "Mountains of the Moon." The day's journey is a holiday not merely from the routine of homestead life but also from Bo Mason's chronically bad temper brought on by the failure of his money-making ambitions.

*****Salt Lake City.** Utah city founded by Mormon pioneers in the mid-nineteenth century, to which Bo Mason takes his family after turning from various failed legitimate ventures in Saskatchewan to an illegal liquor business. When his bootlegging ambitions finally outgrow Whitemud, he uproots his family, moving first to Great Falls, Montana, and then to Salt Lake City. There he thrives on the margins of respectable life in a city widely known for its upright character. Though he accumulates money from his illegal activities and sometimes invests it sensibly, he remains incapable of sharing his wife's yearning for a stable home and family life. His shady business and heedlessness corrode the family, with only Bruce surviving a decade of constantly moving from one dwelling to another in advance of the authorities.

Stegner later published *Recapitulation* (1979), a novel that continues Bruce Mason's story. Like *The Big Rock Candy Mountain*, it is semi-autobiographical but embraces a greater range of Stegner's own experiences as a teenager in Salt Lake City.

Big Rock Candy Mountains. Mythical land of plenty. Stegner's characterization of Bo Mason is aimed at analyzing and discrediting an aspect of America's westward migration, in which many people sought not merely opportunities but excessive wealth and advantage, at the expense of resources and other members of their communities. A gentle parody of these attitudes appeared in a song that became popular in the 1920's titled "In the Big Rock Candy Mountains," and Stegner adapted the song's title to his novel. The song celebrates a place where the "hand-outs grow on bushes" and a bluebird sings to a lemonade spring. Stegner's novel shows in painful detail how a quest for an easy land of plenty can drive wedges between a man and his wife, between a father and his children, and between an individual and his community.

— Clyde S. McConnell

THE BIG SKY

Author: A. B. Guthrie, Jr. (1901-1991)
Type of work: Novel
Type of plot: Adventure

Time of plot: 1830-1843
First published: 1947

This panoramic novel recounts aspects of the frontier experience of the American West in the years preceding the great western migrations that began in the mid-1840's. Its protagonist is a young Kentuckian, Boone Caudill, who flees westward from his family home following a violent confrontation with his father. Caudill becomes a "mountain man," trapping beaver and moving freely within the northern Rocky Mountains. Though he gains a sense of belonging to the landscape, he loses his capacity for living among his own people at the same time they are beginning to pour into the western frontier.

***Missouri River.** Great river of the upper Midwest and northern Great Plains that provides the first stage of Caudill's route to the West. It also serves as a test during his passage from youth to adulthood. As a crew member on a small trading vessel, a keelboat, he experiences the daily toil of rowing, poling, and dragging the boat against the unpredictable and often dangerous currents of the river. He also witnesses the unequal relationship between the European American traders and the Native Americans whose lands and ways of life are threatened by the westward expansion of white commerce and settlement. The constant potential for violence between whites and Indians contrasts with Caudill's growing love for the pristine landscape of river, bluff, hill, and prairie. The sky and the earth soon seem to him "the ceiling and floor of a home that was all his own."

Although the Missouri is a tributary of the Mississippi River, it is longer than the Mississippi. It also passes through more varied terrain and has more picturesque tributaries—most notably the Yellowstone River. However, the literary importance of the river is the fact that it has its source in the Rocky Mountains, whose majestic peaks and serene valleys are Caudill's unspoken goal. The river is a road to both worldly and spiritual fulfillment, though Boone himself is unable to put his yearnings into words for himself or his companions.

***Teton River** (TEE-tawn). Tributary of the Missouri River that rises in northwest-central Montana. The captain of Caudill's keelboat sets out from St. Louis intending to reach the most northern tributaries of the Missouri, where he could trade with the feared Blackfeet Indians, who are known for their fighting skills and courage. He stakes his success upon bringing from St. Louis a young Blackfoot girl, Teal Eye, who was separated from her people during a raid by the Crow people. Teal Eye steals away from the boat not long before it is ambushed and destroyed, but several years later Caudill realizes that he loves her and sets out to find her in the broad valley of the Teton River, near present-day Choteau, Montana.

***Montana.** Region (later a territory and state) in which much of the novel is set. If the great Missouri is the heart of the adventure in *The Big Sky*, the Teton—a small but picturesque river—is the object of the author's deepest affection. A. B. Guthrie grew up in Choteau and returned there in later years. His novel celebrates not only the Choteau area but also the entire state of Montana, whose nickname is **Big Sky Country**. Caudill voices the author's own sentiment that Montana's Teton Valley is a place in which a man could spend his entire life and "never wish for better." Guthrie's writings return again and again to Montana. His writing's passion for the region is matched only by the paintings of the celebrated Montana artist Charles M. Russell.

***Kentucky.** State that is Caudill's childhood home until he leaves as an adolescent. As a man of middle years he returns there to visit his family and finds Kentucky physically and psychologically oppressive. An element of his unease lies in his dislike of the very notion of settled homes, places that are closed in and "full of little stinks." For Caudill, houses smother men who have the "feeling of the mountains" in them.

***St. Louis.** Missouri's largest city, just below the confluence of the Missouri and Mississippi Rivers, which for some years before 1830 was a point of departure for both overland western journeys and those by river. The historic Lewis and Clark expedition started from near St. Louis in 1804 and returned there in 1806, after following the course of the Missouri River for much of its journey, which extended to the Pacific Coast. The journals of the expedition have served as a literary background for all subsequent accounts of the Missouri River's hinterland, and the expedition itself is often characterized as an early expression of the national doctrine of manifest destiny—the inevitability of American expansion into the West—a sentiment repeatedly expressed by the characters in *The Big Sky*.

— *Clyde S. McConnell*

THE BIG SLEEP

Author: Raymond Chandler (1888-1959)
Type of work: Novel
Type of plot: Detective and mystery

Time of plot: 1930's
First published: 1939

Raymond Chandler was one of the first fiction writers to see the literary potential of Los Angeles, a vast, sprawling city of one- and two-story stucco buildings, where nearly everybody is from somewhere else. Chandler saw that Los Angeles was the ideal setting for his hard-boiled brand of fiction because the city's vastness, cultural poverty, diversity, and anomie foster lawlessness and perversion.

Sternwood Mansion. Los Angeles home of General Sternwood, which Chandler uses to represent money—the motivating factor in all the skullduggery that follows. General Sternwood is being blackmailed because he is known to be a multimillionaire. His two daughters are being exploited for the same reason. Private investigator Philip Marlowe becomes involved in the family's troubles because the general needs to protect his money and his daughters. Chandler dramatizes the presence of enormous wealth by describing the size and luxury of the estate, the number of servants required to maintain it, the general's private greenhouse, Vivian Regan's all-white bedroom, and the family's expensive automobiles. Chandler also uses the opening scene at the Sternwood Mansion to introduce many of the principal characters of his novel. Chandler skillfully introduces the characters of Carmen Sternwood, the nymphomaniac who is the source of most of the trouble; Norris, the butler; the general, who represents the dying moral values of a past era; the chauffeur, who will eventually murder Arthur Gwynn Geiger; Vivian Sternwood; and Vivian's faithful maid. The dialogue also gives a preliminary introduction to characters who will appear later: Bernie Ohls, the assistant district attorney; Geiger, the blackmailer and pornography peddler; Eddie Mars, the gambler; Mars's beautiful estranged wife; and Rusty Regan, who never actually appears but is essential to the story. The Sternwood Mansion is described in detail because it serves as an important setting for the events of the novel.

Geiger's bookstore. Shop in the heart of Hollywood, symbolizes the cancer that lies hidden in the heart of an ostensibly peaceful city where the sun shines most days. The front of the store displays leather-bound classics, but in the back room lurks the most lucrative merchandise—pornography. Chandler uses this setting to introduce two other characters, Agnes Lozelle and Carol Lundgren.

Geiger's house. Bungalow home of the pornographer and blackmailer Arthur Gwynn Geiger on Laverne Terrace, in the Hollywood Hills, that suggests Geiger's corrupt mind, decadent lifestyle, and acquisitive mentality. As always, Chandler makes maximum use of his settings. Here Marlowe discovers Geiger's corpse and later meets Eddie Mars. Toward the end of the novel, he brings Carol Lundgren here for a scene set against the home's exotic Asian decor.

Brody's apartment. Home of the blackmailer Joe Brody. The apartment is interesting historically because it shows how inexpensive housing was during the Great

Depression. Though practically broke, Brody is able to live in a spacious, beautifully furnished apartment for approximately forty dollars a month. Chandler's economical use of setting is revealed here, as he uses Brody's apartment repeatedly: Marlowe gets Carmen's pictures, learns about the events of the night of Geiger's murder, and sees Carmen at her worst when she appears with the gun that killed Rusty Regan. With Brody's murder, Marlowe has seen and heard enough to be able to deduce the truth underlying the complicated web of guilt, mental illness, and deception.

Cypress Club. Eddie Mars's gambling casino, which is situated many miles from the heart of Los Angeles. A rambling mansion, it has been converted into a crooked enterprise designed to fleece affluent patrons. The Cypress Club is another elaborate setting and is used for three important chapters.

Realito. Fictitious town among the orange groves that have yet to be cleared to make way for post-World War II tract homes. Just as the Cypress Club is about thirty miles to the southwest of central Los Angeles, Realito is about thirty miles to the east. All the intervening space would soon become part of an awesome megalopolis. Here Marlowe finally meets Eddie Mars's missing wife and has a dramatic shootout with Canino, who has murdered Harry Jones in a seedy office building near downtown Los Angeles, sending him to join the other deceased characters in what Chandler euphemistically called "the big sleep."

— *Bill Delaney*

BILLY BUDD, FORETOPMAN

Author: Herman Melville (1819-1891)
Type of work: Novel
Type of plot: Symbolic realism

Time of plot: 1797
First published: 1924

The novel is set aboard a fictional British warship on duty in the Atlantic Ocean in 1797, when Britain and France were at war, when the natural rights of man versus the supremacy of the state was being hotly debated, and when the Royal Navy had experienced several incidents of mutiny over the issue of impressment. The physical and temporal settings, then, reinforce a political theme as Captain Vere sacrifices an individual for what he perceives to be the good of society.

HMS *Bellipotent.* Seventy-four-gun warship onto which seaman Billy Budd is impressed to serve in the British Navy. In earlier versions of the story, this ship is called the ***Indomitable***. Both names suggest power as a means of preserving order. The ship, one of many in Britain's Mediterranean fleet, represents the authority of the state and also serves as the guardian of the state's citizens' welfare. At the same time it is a microcosm of the society it is designed to protect. It consists of a variety of social types and a range of social classes all governed by the ultimate authority, Captain Vere. Class stratification and character type are reflected in the various deck levels and compartments of the ship, where the men live and work. Billy, for example, works on the foretop while Claggart works on the lower gun decks. A particularly important location on the ship is Vere's cabin, the scene of Claggart's death and Billy's trial. It represents Vere's irreproachable authority and is the place where he makes his decision about Billy's fate and society's welfare. While the mission of the *Bellipotent* is to protect the British from the French, British society is also threatened by anarchy, a threat stemming from rights-of-man theories and preceded by actual mutinies in the British fleet, namely that of April, 1797, at Spithead in the English Channel, and May, 1797, at the Nore in the Thames Estuary. To protect society from anarchy, Vere, despite his personal feelings, decides Billy must die for committing this most serious of naval offenses and orchestrates his trial in the confines of his isolated cabin.

Rights of Man. Merchant ship from which Billy is taken to serve on the *Bellipotent*, this vessel is named for Thomas Paine's 1792 book on the natural rights of man.

The contrasting names of the two ships reflect this political theme as Billy, for the good of the state and its citizens, is impressed into the Royal Navy, surrendering his natural right to freedom. He is forced to give up a life in which he can act to defend himself or his dignity without fear of government reprisal (the striking of Red Whiskers) and accept the complex social life aboard the great warship, with its reliance on displays of authority against perceived derelictions of duty (the whipping of the after-guardsman).

Upper gun deck. Location on the *Bellipotent* where Billy is kept after he is condemned to die. Herman Melville juxtaposes the natural innocence of Billy against the machinery of war located in this space. Furthermore, the space is lit by lamps fueled by oil provided by war contractors, begging the question, who are the true beneficiaries of war? For whom is Billy being sacrificed? It would seem to be the war contractors rather than the citizens of Britain. This room also stands in stark contrast to the foretop with its relative freedom and natural light.

Mainyard. Spar from which Billy is hanged. Normally, men are hanged in the foreyard but Vere uses Billy's execution as a special lesson in the exercise of state power, after which any threat of mutiny is squashed and life aboard the ship returns to routine.

— *Michael A. Benzel*

THE BIRDS

Author: Aristophanes (c. 450-c. 385 B.C.E.)
Type of work: Drama
Type of plot: Social satire

Time of plot: 431-404 B.C.E.
First performed: Ornithes, 414 B.C.E. (English translation, 1824)

This play's imaginary setting in relaxed and festive Cloudcuckooland is contrasted deliberately with Imperial Athens, the site of the play's performance, through dramatic action and choral interludes.

Cloudcuckooland. Imaginary city-state of the birds, located in the sky and invented by Aristophanes, who set another play, *The Frogs* (405 B.C.E.), in another imaginary place, mythical Hades. Two humans leave their own city of Athens and seek Hoopoe, the bird king, at a desolate cliffside vaguely described as a "hundred-mile hike" from home. Hoopoe's roost is a leafy thicket wheeled onstage with its master; the humans must sprout wings to accept Hoopoe's offer of hospitality inside. Hoopoe satisfies his guests' quest for a perfect city-state of rest and relaxation by agreeing to help them establish such a utopia for the birds. Various charlatans from Athens are subsequently driven off as they seek selfish advantage in the new city.

*****Athens.** Democratic ancient Greek city-state at the height of its imperial power when this play was produced during a major state religious festival. The chorus of birds shifts its focus from the imaginary setting of the play to the real location of the production by addressing the audience directly in choral interludes which allow Aristophanes, himself a citizen of Athens, to express his political views to the assembled citizenry and delegates from subject allies. Throughout the play, places are mentioned relevant to Athens's contemporary political situation, such as the Greek city-states Sparta and Corinth, Athens's enemies; Persia and Babylon, representing an imperial eastern threat; Lydia and Phrygia, Asiatic regions that supplied slaves; the Aegean islands of Chios and Melos, subject allies of Athens, and so on. Some obscure towns are named solely for humorous effect, such as Olophyxia or "Groansville" in the northern Aegean, and Corinth's neighbor Orneai or "Birdland."

Mount Olympus. Mythical mountain dwelling of the Greek gods, located somewhere above the birds' territory. Rest and relaxation triumph over politics when the gods cede their universal sovereignty to Cloudcuckooland in order to continue receiving men's sacrifices, which must pass through its territory.

— *Elizabeth A. Fisher*

THE BIRTHDAY PARTY

Author: Harold Pinter (1930-   )
Type of work: Drama
Type of plot: Absurdist

Time of plot: Mid-twentieth century
First performed: 1958; first published, 1959

Like the single-room flats in plays by John Osborne and Shelagh Delaney, the tawdry seaside boardinghouse in which Harold Pinter's play is set focused attention on characters from a social class that had previously long been ignored or treated only with condescension on stage before. The setting of Pinter's play was disparaged by some critics in the 1950's and 1960's as "kitchen-sink realism." Shabby settings, deliberately banal dialogue, and often menacing silences and pauses in Pinter's plays contrasted starkly with the wit and stylishly elegant settings of contemporary British playwrights such as Noël Coward.

Seaside town. Unnamed coastal English town. Long popular with English vacationers, many English coastal towns featured amusement parks and other entertainments, along with public beaches. Some of the smaller coastal towns gained reputations for seedy raffishness as their old seafront hotels and tourist accommodations lost much of their former grandeur due to neglect and the ravages of time. They have been satirized in a number of literary works, including *The Birthday Party*, which is apparently set in one of them.

Boles boardinghouse. Dilapidated seaside establishment run by Meg and Petey Boles. For some time, it has had only one tenant, Stanley Webber. The play's primary set is the Boleses' living room, which has a table and chairs at its center and a square porthole in the wall separating it from the kitchen. That the home is cheaply run is apparent from the meager breakfast that Meg serves. Although she boasts of the house's cleanliness and says it is on an approved list of such accommodations, her claims are probably exaggerated. Petey supplements their income by collecting paltry fees from people who use seaside deck chairs. The arrival of oddly menacing strangers, Goldberg and McCann, suggests the presence of something sinister beyond the household, but neither the name, the nature, nor the purpose of this menace is ever disclosed. As in the fiction of Franz Kafka, the lives of seemingly ordinary characters are intruded upon by inexplicable, sinister happenstance.

— *William Hutchings*

THE BLACK ARROW: A Tale of the Two Roses

Author: Robert Louis Stevenson (1850-1894)
Type of work: Novel
Type of plot: Adventure

Time of plot: Fifteenth century
First published: 1888

An English countryside of woods, marshes, small farms, and scattered villages is the setting on which characters in this novel move. A fictionalized Suffolk County, along the coast of the North Sea in southeastern England, provides a colorful backdrop for a historical adventure novel set during the Wars of the Roses. Its landscapes are picturesque but not as important to the story as character and plot.

*Tunstall Forest. Hardwood forest dotted with knolls and hollows and crossed by numerous dirt trails that lies in Suffolk, though the county is never named in the novel. The forest was larger in the fifteenth century than it is today. Since at least the time of the Robin Hood legend, woods have often played a romantic role in English literature. In Robert Louis Stevenson's novel, Tunstall Forest stands in for the Sherwood Forest of Robin Hood. The woods provide hideouts for the heroes, young Dick Shelton—the protagonist—and the honorable "outlaw" band known as the "Black Arrow." It also serves occasionally as a source of threat when it cloaks potential ambushes.

Lawless's den. Den excavated under a giant beech tree in the forest that is partially uprooted during a storm that is the hiding place of Dick Shelton's accomplice Will Lawless. Although the cave has a hearth that gives it a homey feel, its roof is of roots, its walls of sod, and its floors of dirt.

Tunstall Moat House. Castle of Sir Daniel Brackley, Dick Shelton's guardian and the story's chief villain, located within the forest. This moss-covered fortress of the woods is complete with guard towers, a lily-strewn moat, a supposedly haunted room, and secret passageways that are both narrow and dank. It is heavily romanticized, even to the point of helping to reinforce what later become literary clichés about medieval castles.

St. Bride's Cross. Crossroad point within the forest where two major plot advancements occur. There, Dick Shelton meets Lord Foxham, who helps in his quest to marry Joanna Sedley, and Richard "Crookback," who will one day be King Richard III of England. Shelton saves Crookback in a battle beneath the cross, then joins the future king to fight for the House of York against the House of Lancaster—Sir Daniel's side—in the civil war.

Shoreby-on-the-Till. Fictional small town on the river Till near where the river supposedly empties into the North Sea. Shoreby is the site of a battle between the forces of Lancaster and York. Its streets serve as battlefields, its taverns as command centers. After the battle, the town is sacked. The division of the town during the battle serves as a metaphor for the division of England during the Wars of the Roses, although it is unclear if Stevenson intended such a connection. The sack of Shoreby may well represent the devastation of England caused by the wars.

At the edge of Shoreby stands a beach house in which Joanna Sedley is held captive by Sir Daniel during portions of the narrative. This is actually a collection of buildings lying amid sand-hills and patches of grassy upland dotted with brush. A more important building in Shoreby is the abbey church where Dick is trapped after escaping from Sir Daniel's house in town. The church itself is a holy place, but not all of its human representatives are holy. This contrast between the sacred and the corrupt may be a comment on the politicizing of religion, particularly during the Wars of the Roses.

*Tunstall Hamlet. Small village of scattered houses at the edge of Tunstall Forest. Stevenson describes it as lying within a green valley that rises from a river. There are farms on the outskirts of Tunstall Hamlet, including that of Nick Appleyard, an old soldier who is the first to die by the Black Arrow. Tunstall Hamlet was a real place but is heavily fictionalized by Stevenson; the name is still known to local inhabitants but is not officially recognized by the government.

River Till. Wide and sluggish stream whose many fens and marshy islets provide both atmosphere and a barrier to travel for the characters in the novel. (England has at least three rivers named Till, but none of them appears to be close enough to the real Tunstall Forest to be the river Stevenson uses in his story. However, a tributary of the River Tweed in Northumberland that is named Till matches the physical description of the River Till in *The Black Arrow*.)

— *Charles A. Gramlich*

THE BLACK SWAN

Author: Thomas Mann (1875-1955)
Type of work: Novella
Type of plot: Symbolism

Time of plot: 1920's
First published: Die Betrogene, 1953 (English translation, 1954)

This, Thomas Mann's last work of fiction, records an older woman's passion for a young man. Its setting lacks romance, as the story takes place in the ordinary and obscure German city of Düsseldorf and the surrounding countryside. The city itself plays a minor part in the narrative, but the luxuriant landscape so full of flowers and greenery takes on a symbolic role, as does the castle.

*Düsseldorf. City on the Rhine River in western Germany's Ruhr region, which was the nation's industrial heart in the 1920's. At one point in the narrative, the characters, who live in the best part of the city, unwittingly pass through a district given over to industry and lined with workers' houses, an area they usually avoid. The genteel Düsseldorf described in the novella is a place of tree-lined streets and rows of apartment buildings with ornamented facades. It could be any provincial city in Germany during the 1920's; as one character notes, it lacks the sophistication of Berlin or Munich. Nevertheless, it seems exactly the right place for the unfolding of Frau Rosalie von Tümmler's poignant story. Like the city she inhabits, she is ordinary and provincial, yet possesses a touch of beauty and gentility.

Mann himself spent time in Düsseldorf, where, according to his biographers, he engaged in a homoerotic affair with a young man.

*Ruhr. The western German landscape that Frau Tümmler so loves stands in sharp contrast with the area's industrialization, where weapons factories, steel mills, and coal mines dominate. Although crisscrossed with the heaviest concentration of railways in the world, the Ruhr has rich soil and a temperate climate that nurture such an abundance of trees and shrubbery and flowers that they tend to obscure the traces of heavy industry. In every season, each one distinct, Frau Tümmler celebrates what she reverently calls "Nature," and takes long walks in Düsseldorf's fine parks and the surrounding countryside. Having been born in the spring, she associates this season of rebirth with her own renewal as a woman when she falls in love with the handsome young American, Ken Keaton, who is tutoring her son in English.

The Ruhr landscape with its subdued beauty serves effectively to draw parallels between the everlasting cycles of nature and the temporal condition of human life. It also enlarges Frau Tümmler's strong belief in a woman's closeness to the organic world, which, in an ironic twist, leads to her destruction. Her deification of "Nature" and her willing surrender to emotion separate her from the conflicting force of the intellect, which her impassive daughter represents. The opposition between emotion and intellect emerges as a central theme in all of Mann's fiction.

Holterhof Castle. Apparently imaginary castle beside the Rhine, whose banks, from Düsseldorf to Koblenz, are dotted with castles, some ancient and in ruins, others more recent and preserved. Holterhof Castle assumes its own reality, as the climactic scenes take place there. First, the group visits the castle's pond to feed the black swans, the source of the novella's title. When Frau Tümmler teases a swan, pretending to withhold bread, it hisses at her—an incident that she later recalls as a prediction of her death. The black swan, with its phallic neck and its feminine body, is also suggestive of the desired sexual union. Once inside the castle Frau Tümmler and the young American separate from the rest of the tour group. They wander through dank and dark passageways, where she confesses her love for him and they kiss for the first time. In a daring metaphor, the castle's ravaged interior foreshadows the clinical description of Frau Tümmler's cancer-ridden female passages.

— *Robert L. Ross*

BLACK THUNDER

Author: Arna Bontemps (1902-1973)
Type of work: Novel
Type of plot: Historical realism

Time of plot: 1800
First published: 1936

This novel is a fictionalized account of a historical slave revolt that occurred in Richmond, Virginia, in 1800. Poor weather and the difficult terrain of creeks, swamps, and low-lying fields shape the leader Gabriel's strategy for his slave attack on Richmond and symbolize the insurmountable forces that led to his uprising's defeat.

Richmond. Capital city of Virginia, located in plantation country on the James River. At the time in which this novel is set, Richmond has a population of around six thousand people, with scattered shops, a notary's office, a jail, a public watering trough, hitching bars for horses, and huge oak trees for shade. Horses, coaches, and slaves on errands for their owners travel the unpaved streets, while barefoot women with baskets on their heads stride along the footpaths. The town has a dancing school for white children and a printer's shop, both run by Frenchmen, in which political liberty is a frequent topic of conversation. The surrounding peninsula between the James and York Rivers consists of swamps and meandering creeks that rainstorms can suddenly transform into raging, impassable torrents.

Creuzot's printshop. Richmond gathering place for supporters of the French Revolution. Its owner, Monsieur Creuzot, a French Jacobin, is labeled as a radical, along with Alexander Biddenhurst of Philadelphia, who advocates a classless society. Overhearing the "strange music" of their conversation about "liberty, equality and fraternity," the slave Gabriel, who is the coachman for a man named Prosser, becomes bewitched by the idea of freedom. He rallies the slaves who are angry about their fellow slave Bundy's death at Prosser's hands, and takes charge as "general" of an army of slaves to attack Richmond and kill all its white people—"except the French."

Prosser plantation. Gabriel's home, located on the outskirts of Richmond. In the low cornfields of his plantation, Thomas Prosser beats to death an old broken-down, drunken slave named Bundy. This act of cruelty ignites the simmering rebellion, with Prosser's giant coachman Gabriel as its self-proclaimed general.

Sheppard plantation. Plantation of Moseley Sheppard that is home to Old Ben, a trusted slave who presides over the great house with its broad staircase and "cavernous" rooms that are "dark as death" at night. The morning mists stream over the house and the vast fields where "gleaming birds" crow up the sun. Old Ben keeps the household running and also keeps secret the meetings of the planter's son Robin with a mulatto girl.

Mingo's house. Home of a black freedman and saddlemaker who knows how to read. There, on Sundays some black men, Gabriel among them, gather to hear Mingo read from the "good book" about how the Lord proclaims liberty for the strangers in Egypt that were oppressed by their masters. Mingo's words persuade others, like Old Ben and Pharaoh, to take part in the slave uprising.

Brook Swamp. Gathering place outside Richmond for the slaves. There eleven hundred men and one woman are to begin their assault on Richmond. Gabriel directs three columns to approach the town from different directions and quickly kill all white people. However, a sudden storm of wind and heavy rain makes creeks and pathways impassable, so that only four hundred reach the gathering place. Rising stream and low fields make the region a sea of islands and bays with reefs and currents. Many of the slaves interpret the storm as a sign of God's displeasure and stay away from the rising. After the rising fails, many say that the stars were not right—an opinion with which Gabriel agrees shortly before he is executed.

— *Marguerite R. Plummer*

BLEAK HOUSE

Author: Charles Dickens (1812-1870)
Type of work: Novel
Type of plot: Social realism

Time of plot: Mid-nineteenth century
First published: 1852-1853

This, Charles Dickens's most structurally complex novel, has two independent narrators and a large number of plots, including several search-and-hunt detective plot lines. Esther Summerson's narrative centers around Bleak House and the homes of her numerous friends in London; the anonymous third-person narrator focuses on Court of Chancery and lawyers' offices and slum areas of London. Occasionally, the narratives reach out into the English countryside, especially around Lincolnshire, where both narratives converge.

Bleak House. Home of John Jarndyce, the novel's elderly hero-benefactor, and his cousins Ada Clare and Richard Carstone, and ward, Summerson, the novel's heroine. Situated in the region of St. Albans, a town some twenty miles north of London, Bleak House is portrayed as a refuge, not only from the corruption of the *Jarndyce v. Jarndyce* lawsuit, but from the corruption of London itself. It is a large old rambling house, as eccentric as its owner. Yet, as its very name suggests, it is not all sweetness and light. The *Jarndyce* case affects Richard, and he leaves to take up lodgings with a lawyer. Undesirable visitors come for John's handouts. Finally, disease spreads there through the young street sweeper Jo, striking Esther down and disfiguring her. Nearby lie the Brickfields, with their wretched hovels for the laborers.

*Lincoln's Inn. Seat of Great Britain's High Court of Chancery, presided over by the Lord High Chancellor. It is situated off Chancery Lane, in central London. Here are heard all the disputed cases over inheritance—including the *Jarndyce* case—some of which drag on for years. Dickens portrays such hearings through his descriptions of the court and its environs: fog-bound, dark, labyrinthine, corrupt. Nearby, in Lincoln's Inn Fields, the spider-like solicitor Tulkinghorn has his chambers and house. His threads spread out everywhere into London, seeking particularly to entrap Lady Dedlock and capture her secrets. At his chambers, he is murdered by Hortense, Lady Dedlock's dismissed maid.

Also near Lincoln's Inn lies a labyrinth of back streets containing Krook's Rag and Bottle junk shop, full of old legal documents, which are meaningless to Krook since he cannot read, but among which is the document that finally settles the *Jarndyce* case. His shop is a parody of the Court of Chancery; his spontaneous combustion there is a warning to it. Nearby is **Sol's Arms**, a low-life pub that doubles as a music hall, where a coroner conducts an inquest into the death of Captain Hawdon in the dingy shop's garret room.

Chesney Wold. Ancestral home of Sir Leicester and Lady Dedlock, located in Lincolnshire, some 160 miles north of London. The house is built on a low, swampy area and is consequently damp, decaying, and miasmal.

The decaying house reflects its owners, just as Miss Havisham's decaying **Satis House** does in *Great Expectations* (1860-1861). The inhabitants of Chesney Wold are depicted as being bored almost to death, but the house's most emphasized feature is its Ghost's Walk, symbolizing Lady Dedlock's wretched secrets, her secret lover and her illegitimate child. It is here that mother and child finally meet, through Esther's visit to the Dedlock's neighbor, Boythorne, whose house, by contrast, is always seen in sunny weather.

Tom-all-alone's. Dirty and disease-ridden part of London that is a symbol of the vulnerability and victimhood of the lowest classes. Caught up in a Chancery case, this neighborhood is the refuge for the sweeper Jo, a key figure in the detective plot, but, more significant, in Dickens's protest at the neglect of the poorest by a so-called charitable society. Dickens sees the area as the breeding-ground of the contagion that eventually affects every layer of society. Nearby lies the Burying Ground, a filthy and contaminated cemetery where Captain Hawdon is buried and where Lady Dedlock is found dead.

*London. The novel mentions more places in London—some named, some not—than can be easily cataloged. However, these places can be grouped by which of the two narratives they figure into. The legal quarter centers round Lincoln's Inn, but also includes the Temple, just north of the River Thames, and the area between the two consisting of the Strand and Holborn Hill. Fictitious names include Symonds Inn, the chambers of Mr. Vholes, Richard's lawyer, just off Chancery Lane, and Cook's Court in Cursitor Street, the home of Mr. Snagsby, the law stationer, where Mr. Chadband also holds his religious meetings.

The geography within Esther's narrative is far from clear but centers on the slightly more fashionable areas of London to the west, including Newman Street, where the Turveydrops Dance Academy is situated, off Oxford Street, near Esther's own London lodgings. Near Leicester Square lies George's Shooting Gallery, where Jo dies. George himself often goes south of the river where lies the Bagnet's house, down Blackfriars Road.

— *David Barratt*

BLESS ME, ULTIMA

Author: Rudolfo A. Anaya (1937-   )
Type of work: Novel
Type of plot: Bildungsroman

Time of plot: 1943
First published: 1972

In this novel place reflects the split in the young Antonio Marez himself between his two family traditions: the llano *or plains where the men of his father's pastoral family have always been* vaqueros *or cowboys, and the town, where his mother's farming family has always lived. By the end of the novel, Antonio blends the two traditions into a workable identity for himself. The rich, religious symbolism of the novel can be understood only in the context of this southwestern cultural geography.*

Guadalupe. Small town in eastern New Mexico where Antonio lives. Tony's family has moved from Las Pasturas (a smaller town where he was born) to Guadalupe, where he will spend these crucial years growing up. The town is dominated by three symbolic structures: the Roman Catholic church where Tony receives his catechism, the school he attends, and the water tower. Many of Tony's adventures will be on water: It is at the river at night where he watches the death of Lupito, in a pond where he sees the golden carp, in a snowstorm where he witnesses the death of Narciso, and in Blue Lake where he finds his friend Florence drowned.

Tony and his family live on a hillside outside of town, where Tony does traditional chores, feeding the livestock and tending his mother's garden, and it is from his mother's family that he learns some of his most lasting lessons: "From my mother I had learned that man is of the earth, that his clay feet are part of the ground that nourishes him, and that it is this inexplicable mixture that gives man his measure of safety and security. Because man plants in the earth he believes in the miracle of birth, and he provides a home for his family, and he builds a church to preserve his faith and the soul that is bound to his flesh, his clay."

Ultima, a *curandera* (or healer) and grandmother-figure who was present at Tony's birth, introduces him to the beauty that surrounds Guadalupe: "the wild beauty of our hills and the magic of the green river" that surround the town. Thus, Tony's location just outside of town, and his adventures in the hills and on the river there, show a merging of the two familial traditions through the help of Ultima.

Llano (YAH-noh). Plains on which Tony's father works all of his life as a cowboy. The *vaquero* tradition is a dying one, being eliminated by fences and highways and the modern farming equipment which changes the face of the Southwest in the twentieth century. The *llano* also symbolizes not only an older way of life, but a sense of freedom that Tony's father and others still cherish in the modern world: From "my father and Ultima I had learned that the greater immortality is in the freedom of man, and that freedom is best nourished by the noble expanse of land and air and pure, white sky."

Agua Negra ranch. Between Guadalupe and Las Pasturas. Tony accompanies Ultima when she goes to the simple adobe home of Tellez to lift a curse that has caused stones to rain down upon it. It is the last act before her death.

El Puerto (de los Lunas). Small town that is Tony's mother's birthplace. Every fall, Tony and his family make a pilgrimage to "the adobe houses of the peaceful village. . . . We always enjoyed our stay at El Puerto. It was a world where people were happy, working, helping each other." By the end of the novel, Tony says, "Take the llano and the river valley, the moon and the sea, God and the golden carp—and make something new." He will weave together, in short, the various strands of his family traditions: not only the "moon" and the "sea" (the Luna and Marez families), but also his orthodox Catholic heritage with the native spiritual traditions of the Southwest, including the magical folk religion and history represented by Ultima.

— *David Peck*

BLITHE SPIRIT: An Improbable Farce in Three Acts

Author: Noël Coward (1899-1973)
Type of work: Drama
Type of plot: Comedy

Time of plot: Late 1930's
First performed: 1941; first published, 1941

A conventional English living room becomes the scene of a supernatural battle between two women, one dead, one alive, for the affections of a man who does not particularly care for either of them.

Living room. Central room in the Condomines' house in Kent in which the entire action of the play takes place. The home is situated somewhere between the southeastern English towns of Folkestone and Hythe. The room is described as being attractive and comfortably furnished, though it is not clear whether this reflects the tastes of Charles Condomine's first wife, Elvira, or his second, Ruth. Elvira implies that the room was designed by her and laments that it has been "spoiled" by Ruth, whose taste is "thoroughly artsy-craftsy." Significantly, the room is the one in which Elvira died, but she seems not to be tied to it and is able to leave as she wishes.

By setting the play in one room, Noël Coward brings to the fore the claustrophobic nature of the relationship between Condomine and his current wife. Ruth is not convinced of her husband's affection for her, and the gulf between her and her husband is emphasized by her being unable to see or hear Elvira, obliging her to address the empty air and frequently the wrong spot when she attempts to talk to the ghost, whereas Condomine can see and hear his first wife perfectly.

The living room becomes the focus first of the two wives' resentment of each other, manifested in their constant rearrangement of vases of flowers. Later, after Ruth's death as a result of Elvira's tampering with her car, it becomes the focus of their joint resentment of Charles, once he realizes that he is free of both of them, at which point they begin to destroy the room.

— *Maureen Speller*

THE BLITHEDALE ROMANCE

Author: Nathaniel Hawthorne (1804-1864)
Type of work: Novel
Type of plot: Psychological realism

Time of plot: Mid-nineteenth century
First published: 1852

Nathaniel Hawthorne opens this novel with the familiar premise that cities are sites of corruption while bucolic rural retreats offer regeneration and renewal. His characters leave the city to found Blithedale, Massachusetts, an experimental farming commune begun to reject the classism, competition, and materialism of city life. The opposition of city and back-to-nature settings ultimately defies conventional associations, however, as Blithedale becomes plagued by jealousy, artificiality, competition, and betrayal.

Unnamed city. Anonymous city representing the corruption of "civilization" from which the idealists who go to Blithedale come. For the affluent utopians (Coverdale and Zenobia), city life is soft and artificial, full of comforts, glitter, and social conventions that mask true feelings. For the poor (Moody and Priscilla), city life is a constant struggle marked by rigid class lines, poverty, and ill health. Wealthy and beautiful Zenobia leaves Blithedale periodically to resume her social life in the city. When Coverdale becomes disillusioned, he also returns to the city, where he indulges in comforts, eavesdrops on neighbors, and tells his friends he was never serious about the experimental commune. The city also supports popular and exploitative public entertainments. Here Priscilla becomes the Veiled Lady, a kind of slave to Westerveldt.

Blithedale. Experimental farm commune in Massachusetts that is founded to model life without class boundaries or competition, and one day, perhaps, without gender roles. The utopians want to live in harmony with one another and with nature. They assume such lives will ennoble them spiritually and will lead to heightened artistic and intellectual accomplishments.

Almost immediately, however, it becomes apparent that the Blithedalers are naïve and that the main characters are merely "playing" at being social reformers. They are uncomfortable treating the farming couple they live with as equals and had not understood that even farmers must compete in the financial market. Moreover, their lives quickly begin to revolve around worldly concerns. Zenobia and Priscilla become competitors for Hollingsworth's affection, while he secretly plans to subvert the social experiment to his own obsessive project, the reformation of criminals. Coverdale, the narrator, is a complicated mix of idealism and ironic pessimism. He yearns to be bold enough to commit to utopian aims, but usually his ironic pessimism wins out and his emotional commitment to life remains shallow. Coverdale fails to form deep friendships with either Zenobia or Priscilla, despite his desires. He is befriended by Hollingsworth, but his refusal to help Hollingsworth betray the Blithedalers costs him this friendship, which he doubts was ever real. Priscilla, a poor, victimized, city girl, flourishes at Blithedale, but her simple response has nothing to do with the philosophy behind the project, and her belief in women's inferiority aligns her with conservative, not revolutionary, social forces. Her unquestioning acceptance of Hollingsworth's ideas eventually implicates her with his plan to take over Blithedale and with Zenobia's death. The Blithedale experiment ends with Zenobia dead, Hollingsworth a broken man, and Coverdale returned to his city life unchanged. Priscilla's life has a conventionally happy ending, including marriage and inherited wealth, but she seems content only because she is too shallow to be affected by the experiment's failure or by life's ambiguities.

Coverdale's tree. Coverdale's secret retreat when he wants time alone, away from the community of Blithedale. This retreat shows he is not comfortable with communal life, and it reveals his preference for spying on others' lives rather than committing to a full emotional life of his own.

Hollingsworth and Zenobia's hill. The Blithedalers assume Hollingsworth and Zenobia have picked this site for their house. Secretly, though, Hollingsworth plans to build his reformatory here, with Zenobia's financial backing. After Zenobia's death, the hill becomes her burial site. Like many other people and things in this novel, the hill was never what it seemed and did not turn out as planned.

Eliot's Rock. Most important feature at Blithedale and the site of two confrontations involving the four main characters. Here Zenobia abandons her beliefs in women's rights in order to win Hollingsworth's approval. Later, Hollingsworth puts Zenobia "on trial" here, apparently accusing her of a relationship with Westervelet and of abetting Priscilla's subjugation to him. Zenobia in turn accuses Hollingsworth of wooing her for her money and of using philanthropy for egoistical ends. That night Zenobia dies, an apparent suicide, and Hollingsworth takes on the guilt for her "murder."

— *Grace McEntee*

BLOOD WEDDING

Author: Federico García Lorca (1899-1936)
Type of work: Drama
Type of plot: Tragedy

Time of plot: Early twentieth century
First performed: 1933; first published, 1935 as *Bodas de sangre* (English translation, 1939)

This first play in Federico García Lorca's dramatic trilogy is set in southern Spain's Andalusia region, where the author was raised, and treats the lives of Gypsy women. However, Lorca does not specify the setting of his play and thus opens it up to universal themes of love, frustration, honor, and revenge. The three-act play unfolds in a village over one month, as preparations are made for a wedding.

*Andalusia. Vast region of southern Spain that Lorca knew best and uses as the setting for many of his works. Inhabited by Moors from Northern Africa for nearly eight hundred years, it retains their cultural influences in many areas, especially in architecture, vocabulary, place names, poetry, and music. Some Moorish descendants also still remain, as do the Spanish gypsies, whose cultures combined to produce flamenco songs, music and dance.

Homes. Locations of many scenes, using minimal stage settings and direction, limited scenery. Rooms are painted yellow or pink or white and are decorated with flowers and simple furnishings.

Cave. Dwelling in which the bride lives. Caves were often used as dwellings in mountainous parts of southern Spain, notably by Gypsy families. The interior of the bride's cave is comfortably and tastefully decorated. However, its exterior is "as hard as a landscape" on ceramic decorated with white, gray, blue and silver colors.

White house. Building with arches and white stairs, walls, and floors that resemble those of a church. Neighbors meet here to discuss the ill-fated wedding and its deadly aftermath.

— *Margaret V. Ekstrom*

THE BOHEMIANS OF THE LATIN QUARTER

Author: Henri Murger (1822-1861)
Type of work: Novel
Type of plot: Sentimental

Time of plot: Mid-nineteenth century
First published: Scènes de la vie de Bohème, serial, 1847-1849; book, 1851 (English translation, 1901)

Four artistic friends living in Paris's Latin Quarter form their own "Bohemian Club" and try to be creative while carousing and chasing women. All four of them are unknown in their fields, none has a regular source of income, and all tend to scorn those who do. To them art is more a matter of faith than profession. They routinely meet in favorite haunts in the student section of Paris.

*Latin Quarter. District of Paris on the south bank of the Seine River surrounding the University of Paris's Sorbonne College. Predominantly populated by students and artists, the Latin Quarter is the primary setting of the novel, which unfolds during the closing years of France's July Monarchy and the advent of its Second Republic. At a time when middle-class values are officially prized and honored, the young intellectuals of the novel resist and drop out of the "official world" to lead an impecunious existence among the lower classes. They think nothing of welshing on their debts and are consequently frequently ejected from their apartments. Almost as a matter of pride, the young poet Rodolphe

sometimes sleeps in a box at the Odéon Theater and sometimes outdoors, once even in the branches of a tree on the Avenue St. Cloud. Despite their irregular living arrangements, the young friends stay in constant touch, having favorite places in which to engage each other in endless talk, primarily about what is wrong with society and about their relationships with women.

Café Momus. Quintessential Paris bistro where the members of the Bohemian Club are known as the "Four Musketeers." It is located at the Carrefour de Buci in Paris's Saint-Germain-des-Près area, a center of Left Bank activities. There the four friends meet alone in a room large enough to hold forty customers, but because these fellows are so obnoxious, they drive everybody else away. Rodolphe monopolizes the house newspapers and bullies the café's owner into subscribing to *The Beaver*, a unknown journal that he edits himself. Colline plays backgammon from morning until midnight. Marcel paints, moving all of his equipment into the café: easel, oils, brushes, male and female models. Alexander Schaunard uses the café as a place to advertise music lessons. If all this were not enough, these intruders even brew their own coffee and do not always pay what they owe. When the owner stops giving them credit, they stop frequenting his café.

The bonding among the Bohemians is a male practice, overcast with adolescence exuberance. Such characteristics have no specific local or time period, but Henri Murger suggests that his characters' raffish behavior goes hand and hand with the permissive, artistic milieu of the Latin Quarter, a place where free spirits can play by their own rules.

Paris. The story of the Bohemians lies mainly in Paris's sixth arrondissement, but some of the novel's action occurs in other parts of Paris, particularly the historic downtown area. Colline lives on the Ile St.-Louis in the fourth district; Rodolphe lives for a time in Montmartre in the eighteenth district; Musette, Marcel's mistress, holds court near the Bois de Boulogne in the sixteenth district. The four friends sometimes meet in a restaurant on the rue St.-Germain l'Auxerrois in the first district. However, no matter where they are, the spirit of Bohemia invariably goes with them.

Murger's sympathy with his characters is personal—he puts himself in the story in the personage of Rodolphe; he knows the Paris of the period intimately and could not have conceived of his story's being set in any other city. The Bohemian spirit, he claims, is possible only in Paris. However, Murger's tale is about universal attitudes. There is nothing exclusively Parisian about bad manners or bloated egos. The novel reveals little about its characters' backgrounds, except to suggest that the characters come from the very bourgeois class they deride. However, even while explaining behavior more through environmental than personal forces, Murger produces some unintended social commentary about the Paris of the 1840's.

In the nineteenth century, poor girls from the provinces flocked to Paris in droves to find their fortunes, many discovering, or realizing, that their chief assets were their young bodies. They thus became the prey of men willing to take advantage of their desperation and hopes. Murger pretends his heroines are equal partners in the search for love with the men, but his Bohemians are predaceous. Rodolphe, for example, expects Mimi to wait on him, and he expects to enjoy sex whenever he wants it. Moreover, he is furiously jealous and tyrannical. Schaunard is hardly more sympathetic, sometimes hitting his mistress Phémie with his walking stick. Yet, despite these attitudes, Murger still pretends that the women are as free spirited as the men because this is the way things are done in the Latin Quarter in Paris.

Despite his intentions, Murger unwittingly demonstrates that there are no exclusive places in the world for lazy freeloaders, and that life in Paris, especially for his male characters, is more determined by style than environment. When his Bohemians tire of their hand-to-mouth existence and decide to grow up, they join the "official world," in Paris, but far from their old haunts.

— *Wm. Laird Kleine-Ahlbrandt*

THE BOOK OF LAUGHTER AND FORGETTING

Author: Milan Kundera (1929-   )
Type of work: Novel
Type of plot: Psychological realism

Time of plot: 1948-1980
First published: Le Livre du rire et de l'oubli, 1979
    (English translation, 1980)

Through the emotional and intellectual void that consumes the lives of its characters, this novel vividly depicts the fearful emptiness of Eastern European life under communist management. Set in Czechoslovakia, the novel opens in Prague as the country's communist regime comes to power, but it progresses forward in a nonlinear sequence that includes flashbacks and flash-forwards, to places both real and imaginary, as it traces what the momentous political change means in the lives of Czechs and how it confounds their place in the history of Europe.

*Prague. Capital of Czechoslovakia, an Eastern European nation that was created after World War I, that was occupied by Nazi Germany through World War II, and that fell under the Soviet orbit in the late 1940's. Seen through the perspectives of different characters at diverse places and times, the city becomes an emblem of the wrongs endured by the people of Czechoslovakia under communist rule. For example, in 1971, three years after the Russian occupation of his homeland, Mirek—under surveillance by the not-so-secret police—seeks to retrieve his letters from a former lover.

The novel opens in February, 1948, as the communists are taking control of the country. After describing events at the ceremony held in Prague to commemorate the event, the narrator introduces two significant and re-occurring ideas. First, that history may be altered in service to power; second, that human imagination offers escape through an element of magical realism, a communal dance in a ring. In 1950, despite the fact that several artists have been hanged by the communists, Kundera observes that the people of Prague still dance in rings—a fact that further demonstrates the contrast between the restrictive regime and the blind-to-it-all, free-spirited people of Czechoslovakia whom the regime seeks to suffocate. This tension between the controlling forces of governmental censorship and the natural forces of human emotions is reflected in the history of the characters (which some of them seek to alter) and the altered history of Czechoslovakia itself.

*Bartolomejska Street. Short but famous Prague street, on which all but two buildings belong to the police. The novel's narrator, now an excommunicated horoscope writer, takes a one-room apartment there in 1972, after the Soviet occupation of the country makes it impossible for him to work legally. From his apartment, he can see the towers of Prague Castle above, representing the glorious history of the Czech kings, and, in the police courtyards down below, the not-so-glorious history of the current Czech prisoners. This juxtaposition of past wealth and political grandeur and present oppression and penury sharply accents the decline in Czech culture that Kundera blames squarely on the communist occupation.

*Riviera. Resort region on southern France's and northwestern Italy's Mediterranean coasts where the American girls Michelle and Gabrielle take a summer-school course for foreigners in a small, unnamed town. Under Madame Raphael's tutelage, they study Eugène Ionesco's play *Rhinoceros* (1959). Kundera depicts the girls making their giggling preparations for a shallow presentation, and they provide him an opportunity to define different types of laughter. The girls laugh in their bedrooms, they laugh in the stationery store in which they buy cardboard to make rhinoceros noses for their presentation, they laugh as they imagine how their teacher will respond to their presentation. As her pet students, they know that no unpleasant reality can cloud the illusions of their laughter. At the disastrous presentation itself, the girls' ridiculous efforts are mocked by the class, and they even receive a kick in the behind from another student. As their laughter dissolves into tears, the girls do not slink to their seats in mortified silence; instead, their teacher joins them at the front of the class, and, once again, the magic dance intervenes, offering escape as the girls and their teacher turn into angels and spiral up on high. Serving as a sort of parallel universe, this place and its characters serve to indict the callous indifference of the rest of the world, particularly Europe and the United States, for their failure to acknowledge or confront the atrocities committed by the communist regime in Eastern Europe.

Provincial town. Unnamed town in Western Europe in which Tamina has been working at a small café since she and her late husband, Mirek, left Czechoslovakia illegally. The displaced Tamina urgently tries to retrieve memories of her husband and their past together in Czechoslovakia's Bohemia region—memories recorded in notebooks that she has left in her mother-in-law's house in Prague. In her quest to remember, Tamina, guided by the unlikely angel Raphael, is taken by boat to an unreal island where she has erotic encounters with squirrels and children, and effectively forgets Prague and its past, which is her past, as well. When the darkness of the water takes her in its embrace, her final forgetting is complete.

Nudist beach. Place where the novel ends, with the doctor Jan and his lover, Edwige, taking a final holiday at a nudist beach before Jan leaves Europe for the United States. Jan dreams of pure arousal innocent of physicality, while Edwige invokes a return to pagan sensuality; they assent to each other's visions in mutual misunderstanding. In a discussion with a group of naked people, a paunchy man raises the subject of the end of Western civilization; this is received with enthusiasm by the others.

— *Kathleen M. Bartlett*

THE BOOK OF THE CITY OF LADIES

Author: Christine de Pizan (c. 1365-c. 1430)
Type of work: Novel
Type of plot: Allegory

Time of plot: Early fifteenth century
First published: Le Livre de la Cité des Dames,
c. 1405 (English translation, 1521, 1982)

The narrator Christine sits in her study in early fifteenth century Paris, while receiving three visitors: Reason, Rectitude, and Justice. These allegorical "ladies" aid her in constructing an allegorical City of Ladies from examples of women of the past. Christine mentions women from a great many places, though France and ancient Rome provide the greatest number. Although the work is devoid of a developed sense of place, the qualities of womanhood that make up the allegorical city lend it an air of righteousness and virtue.

***Paris.** France's capital city and Christine's home. Parisian society of her time is typically misogynist, or antifeminist at best, with its attitudes fed by religious, philosophical, and cultural arguments against the virtue and worthiness of women. Numerous examples of worthy women in Christine's recitations derive from French history. This probably serves to support the *traditio* theory, whereby ancient Rome's greatness was translated to Christian France.

Christine's study. Surrounded by books on all kinds of subjects, while "solitary and separated from the world," the widowed Christine ponders the role of women in western intellectual and literary history. Her visitations by the allegorical ladies are not a matter of a dream, but of a conscious struggle against the social prejudices of her age, as symbolized by her own books. She is thus both isolated from the world's opinions, yet intimately fenced in by them.

City of Ladies. The "city" that Christine is to build with her pen ("mix the mortar in your ink bottle") will be gorgeous, peerless, everlasting, ever prosperous and unconquerable. Each of Christine's three visitors provides her with a long list of examples of worthy women with whom she is to build the city. It is to be constructed on the flat, well-watered, fertile, and fruitful Field of Letters. Reason helps Christine with the ditches, foundations, and walls by refuting the misogynistic claims of male authors and by reporting on a long list of powerful and inventive women. Rectitude helps her lay out streets, build edifices, and populate the place by reciting a litany of worthy and virtuous women who were seers, loving and faithful wives, saviors of their nations, well educated, chaste, and who loved overmuch. Roofs of gold, as well as a queen, are provided by Lady Justice, in the forms of female saints and the Virgin Mary. Like the **City of God** of St. Augustine, Christine's city is a community of virtuous people past and present, whose personal qualities segregate them from the common fold.

Amazonia. Vibrant empire ruled and defended by women. Located by tradition and by Christine in southwestern Russia (Scythia), Amazonia has deep roots in Western mythology. Christine uses it as a fount of powerful, exemplary women, as an example of a place ruled successfully by women, and as a fully female society like that of her own city, which surpasses it.

*Rome. Ancient capital of the Roman Empire. True to her culture, Christine finds many of her heroines in the ancient city of Rome. Even this early in the Renaissance much was known of the valor and virtue of ancient Roman men and women, as celebrated by their historians, especially Livy. Rome's special place in Western culture as the root of both secular and Christian empires made the stories of her chaste maidens, bold matrons, and female martyrs especially compelling.

*Troy (Ilium). Ancient city celebrated by Homer and Vergil and discovered in western Turkey by Heinrich Schliemann in the late nineteenth century. Troy provides Christine with a number of heroic women, both on the battlefield (Penthesilea) and within the walls. Christine seems to compare Troy's foundation and fate with those of her city.

*Carthage. Powerful ancient city-state, located on the coast of northern Africa in what is now Tunisia, and enemy of the young Roman republic. According to Christine, Carthage was founded by its female ruler, Dido. It serves as backdrop to Christine's recounting of Queen Dido's career.

— *Joseph P. Byrne*

THE BOOK OF THE COURTIER

Author: Baldassare Castiglione (1478-1529)
Type of work: Didactic

First published: Il libro del cortegiano, 1528 (English translation, 1561)

This didactic novel is written in the form of a grand conversation over four evenings among courtiers and guests of the duke of Urbino. Evoking elements of works such as Giovanni Boccaccio's Decameron *(1349-1351), Niccolò Machiavelli's* The Prince *(1532), and contemporary idealist literature on education, nobility, and women, these dialogues explore characteristics of the ideal courtier, his function at court, women, and human virtue. The setting of the conversation is itself a court—a place with which Baldassare Castiglione was quite familiar—and the speakers are all real historical figures. The circumstances and setting gives the work both its full flavor and its limitations.*

*Urbino. City in central Italy that was the center of the duchy of Urbino, in whose court Castiglione's dialogues are set. The duchy is a small state whose court is among the most splendid in central Italy during the period in which the dialogues are set. The Montefeltro family had ruled the city and its hinterland since 1374. Urbino's small size and isolated location meant that its dukes derived at least part of their income from mercenary military service. The famous portrait of Federico da Montefeltro, father of the last Montefeltro duke, in which he sits in his simple study reading a large book while dressed in armor, sums up the family's combination of the martial with the humanistic. Both his court and Castiglione's participants reflect this dual ethic, one not unusual at similar courts of its time.

When Federico died his young son was but ten years old, thus unable to sign contracts for military service, and proved to be sickly. Castiglione sets the conversation in 1507, the year before the young duke's untimely death. Thus, the last Montefeltro duke was still alive, though absent, and his court in decline. Early on, Castiglione touches on the theme of nostalgia for better days. The air in the mid-fifteenth century palace is rarefied, demanding both the expectation and provision of courtesy and fine manners. The group is essentially discussing who it is that belongs in their very select company. The isolation of the court from the surrounding world allows for the idealism on which the conversation is built and ensures that few practicalities intrude into the discussion. Court life is dominated rather by music, dancing, dining, and fine conversation.

*Italy. In the early sixteenth century, when this book was written, Italy was a patchwork of republics and monarchies. Wars between France and Spain drew Italian states into shifting and destructive alliance systems, and began the disintegration of the genteel world that Castiglione presents in these dialogues. Small states, such as the duchy of Urbino, were threatened with extinction, and the idealism about politics one finds in the dialogues was already undermined forever by Machiavelli's darker vision. In 1507, however, the courts represented or discussed by the participants in Castiglione's dialogues were still working entities, and the issues posed not yet muted.

Participants in the dialogues viewed republics, such as those of Florence, Venice, and Siena, as unstable places where even sworn enemies might have to govern side by side. Bereft of true court life, the republics were run by merchants, who were fickle, opportunistic, and ignoble—in all ways uncourtly. Nonetheless, Tuscany was a cultural center, whose dialect of Italian was becoming dominant, and Venice was a center of ostentatious noble life and political stability, combining elements of a ducal court and republican offices.

*Bergamo.** Town in northeastern, subalpine Italy that was noted for its lack of culture and the general oafish-ness of its people. Like Castiglione, William Shakespeare uses the *bergamasque* dance as a low form fit only for peasants.

*Rome.** The early ancient city provides examples of virtuous behavior worthy of nobility, while the few references to later events are generally negative. Little is said about contemporary Rome.

*France** and *Spain.** These huge players on Italy's chessboard appear as entities casting long shadows, rather than as settings for narrative action. France had invaded Italy in 1494 seeking unsuccessfully to dominate Naples. In 1499 French forces returned and established hegemony in Milan and surrounding areas, imprisoning Duke Ludovico Sforza and impairing court life. Spain's Aragon kingdom had conquered Naples in 1504 and established a fine, if somewhat somber, court life there.

None of the participants in the dialogues are crass enough to discuss the politics of the day, but the references they make to the French and Spanish are generally negative, such as the distaste of French nobles for letters and the presumption of French and Spanish courtiers.

— *Joseph P. Byrne*

BOOK OF THE DUCHESS

Author: Geoffrey Chaucer (c. 1343-1400)
Type of work: Poetry
Type of plot: Allegory

Time of plot: Indeterminate
First published: c. 1370

This work moves from a dream, to a dreamlike location, to a direct reference to Richmond, John of Gaunt's estate. It uses place to create a series of scenes that are alternately real and unreal. The situation the poem describes, the death of Blanche, is, however, very real.

Narrator's bedroom. The poet's persona begins by describing the unhappiness in love that prevents his sleep. This introduces the story of Seyx and Alcione, the dead husband appearing to his beloved wife as adapted from Ovid's *Metamorphoses* (c. 8 C.E.; English translation, 1567). Rehearsing this myth allows correspondence of the bereaved Alcione and the bereaved Black Prince (Edward, Prince of Wales). Seyx's ghost appears in Alcione's bedroom, thus interlocking the locations of the mythic figure and the narrator.

When the narrator awakens, it is a brilliant spring morning, and he sees on his bedroom windows scenes that recall the Trojan War as rendered on Dido's walls in Vergil's *Aeneid* (c. 29-19 B.C.E.; English translation, 1553). This creates a linkage with the forest scene through appearance of Vergil's patron, the emperor Augustus, here called Octavian.

Forest. Location derived from Paradys d'amours in *Le Roman de la rose* (thirteenth century; *The Romance of the Rose*), an Old French allegory. As the narrator's windows show Troy's fall, so his walls portray the Guillaume de Lorris and Jean de Meung poem. Octavian appears on horseback to hunt a hart, the lover's hunt through its wordplay on "heart." The poem thus moves among literary, dreamlike, and real locations through these interlocking scenic details.

The bereavement of the Black Prince corresponds to the solitary condition of the narrator, but the narrator's windows and walls make him see his life in literary rather than real terms. This could explain the inability of narrator and prince to communicate, though it is also true that no person can completely appreciate the sorrow of another.

— *Robert J. Forman*

THE BOOK OF THESEUS

Author: Giovanni Boccaccio (1313-1375)
Type of work: Epic
Type of plot: Romance

Time of plot: Antiquity
First transcribed: Teseida, c. 1340-1341 (English translation, 1974)

The structure of this first epic poem in the Italian language is straightforward. Book 1 explores how the Amazon woman Emilia comes to be in Athens, and book 2 shows how her suitors Arcites and Palaemon arrive there.

*Athens. Boccaccio's mythologized version of the ancient Greek city, in which conflicts are resolved by heroic wisdom. It is to Athens that the Theban widows of Creon's victims come for justice, and it is there that the ruler Theseus brings the Amazon leaders Hippolyta and Emilia. Athens is also home to the temples of Mars, Venus, and Diana, shrines that figures in Boccaccio's epic frequently visit. Theseus's presence in Athens, where he is a model of wisdom and heroism, indicates that the city has a civilizing influence on this many-adventured hero.

Grove. Pleasant cluster of trees just outside of Athens where Palaemon, escaping from prison, meets Arcites, a regular visitor to the grove, to fight for the right to court Emilia until Theseus intervenes.

Scythia (SEHTH-ee-ah). Mythical home of the Amazon nation of warrior women, apparently located somewhere north of the Black Sea. Theseus leads an army against Scythia and, after a spirited resistance, the Amazons surrender.

Theater. Athenian arena in which Arcites and Palaemon meet in battle to determine which shall have the hand of Emilia. Each man leads one hundred warriors before a noble audience of Athenians and distinguished visitors.

— *Robert W. Haynes*

BORIS GODUNOV

Author: Alexander Pushkin (1799-1837)
Type of work: Drama
Type of plot: Historical

Time of plot: 1598-1605
First published: 1831 (English translation, 1918); first performed, 1870

This play was Alexander Pushkin's attempt to create a Russian historical play in the style of William Shakespeare. To find a subject that was not overtly political and unlikely to arouse the wrath of censors, Pushkin reached deep into Russia's past, to the Time of Troubles following the death of Czar Ivan IV, "the Terrible."

Moscow. Russia's capital city in the period during which this play is set. Pushkin wrote the play during the period when he was exiled from the royal court at St. Petersburg, which Czar Peter the Great had made Russia's capital in 1712. (In 1918 the Bolsheviks would return the government to Moscow.)

Kremlin. Enclosed fortress at the heart of Moscow and the seat of the historical czar Boris Godunov's government. The word *kremlin* is an anglicization of Russian's *kreml'* for "fortress." Many old Russian cities were centered upon similar fortresses, but the Kremlin of Moscow became the seat of the Russian government. Because of great architectural changes in the Kremlin since 1598, it is almost impossible to correlate the palace

of Godunov's time with any modern Kremlin palace. Pushkin's minimalist stage directions depend upon the director's and players' familiarity with Russian history to recreate the scene on stage.

Red Square. Open area in front of the Kremlin. In Russian, the same word means both "red" and "beautiful"; what was originally understood as the "beautiful square" acquired its modern name. In Pushkin's play, the square is the site of several key interactions among the leaders and the common people.

Kraków. Polish city that is the location of the house of Wisniowiecki, supporter of the False Dmitri, pretender to the Russian throne.

— *Leigh Husband Kimmel*

THE BOSTONIANS

Author: Henry James (1843-1916)
Type of work: Novel
Type of plot: Psychological realism

Time of plot: 1870's
First published: serial, 1885-1886; book, 1886

A character is nothing without a setting, as the narrator says in this novel, but in its opening two-thirds the novel itself is curiously lacking in settings, and its three major characters seem divorced from what settings there are (mostly houses and neighborhoods in Boston and New York). This situation changes in the last third of the novel, which contains extensive descriptions of new settings; however, the imagery of even these descriptions is highly ambiguous, reflecting the ambiguity of the novel's conclusion.

Boston. Massachusetts's capital and leading city, known in this novel mainly as the city of reform and feminist views, which one character refers to as "Boston ideas."

Charles Street. Fashionable Boston street on which Olive Chancellor, the novel's central feminist figure, lives. Near the even more fashionable Beacon Street. Because of where she lives, the wealthy Olive is expected to move in fashionable circles, but she has cut herself off from that milieu in order to be a reformer.

Olive's house. Boston residence of Olive Chancellor; a place of strange, narrow rooms, perhaps suggesting something strange and narrow about Olive's life and ideas. The house is full of books and fashionable objects, and yet seems not entirely comfortable, as if embodying a conflict in Olive between expensive tastes and a self-denying dedication to a cause. Olive's windows provide

a view of distant, ugly, impoverished parts of Boston, perhaps to show, by contrast, how comfortable Olive is materially. Somewhat oddly, Olive's companion, Verena, finds the view lovely, perhaps suggesting that however impoverished those parts of Boston may be, they are richer metaphorically than Olive's house of narrow rooms.

Miss Birdseye's rooms. Site of a feminist meeting in Boston to which Olive takes her cousin, Basil Ransom, and where they both meet the inspirational speaker, Verena Tarrant. The rooms, which belong to Miss Birdseye, an old reformer in decline, are in a boardinghouse in the South End, a part of Boston in decline. They are much less elegant than Olive's house, and Olive thinks that Birdseye lacks taste. However, the point seems to be that Birdseye is quite at home in plain rooms because she is more interested in causes than in taste—unlike Olive, who is in conflict because she is interested in both.

Ransom's neighborhood. Ugly yet somehow appealingly alive neighborhood, where Basil Ransom rents shabby rooms on the upper East Side of New York City near the corner of Second Avenue. The narrator says, however, that the neighborhood had little influence on the southern-born Ransom, who seems quite out of place in both New York and Boston.

Tarrants' house. Shabby little house where Verena Tarrant lives with her parents in the Boston suburb of Cambridge on a street ironically called **Monadnoc Place**. Monadnoc is the name of a New Hampshire mountain often called sublime, but there is nothing sublime about Monadnoc Place. However, Verena herself does seem sublime, and thus very much separate from her surroundings, though in a more positive way than Basil and Olive.

*Memorial Hall. Harvard University building commemorating students who died while fighting for the Union during the Civil War. Verena takes Ransom to see it. It is described in the novel as a noble, solemn place celebrating honor, sacrifice, duty, and generosity. Ransom feels a spirit of reconciliation between North and South when he sees it. The mood is broken, however, when Verena criticizes the memorial for glorifying war.

*Central Park. Pastoral oasis in the middle of New York City where Verena and Ransom go for a walk. The park and its surroundings are described in great detail, but in contradictory terms. On one hand, the area is fresh and fragrant, with a glow over it. Verena enjoys herself, and Ransom's voice seems to merge into the distant hum of the city, as if finally he is fitting in somewhere. However, when Ransom and Verena leave the park they encounter disappointed, unemployed men propped against a wall; and even within the park, the narrator says that the landscape is artificial.

*Cape Cod. Slender peninsula extending from southeastern Massachusetts into the Atlantic Ocean. It is such a restful vacation spot that the novel's narrator calls it the "Italy of Massachusetts." Ransom and Verena court on Cape Cod, near the fictional town of **Marmion** on the real Buzzard's Bay, amid scenery that is described in detailed but contradictory terms. The scenery is both rocky and shrub-covered, bright and dim, shining and hazy. There is sweetness and peace in the air, but the landscape also contains decaying shipyards and tough orchards that promise to bear only sour fruit.

*Boston's Music Hall. Vast auditorium that is filled with people waiting to her Verena speak at the end of the novel. Ransom sees the audience as a raving rabble and compares the hall itself to Rome's great Colosseum, which had been the site of horrific blood sports in ancient times. The climactic scene at the music hall, in which Ransom spirits Verena away before she can make her speech, is fraught with agitation, conflict, and uncertainty.

— Sheldon Goldfarb

THE BRAGGART SOLDIER

Author: Plautus (c. 254-184 B.C.E.)
Type of work: Drama
Type of plot: Comedy

Time of plot: Third century B.C.E.
First performed: Miles gloriosus, c. 200 B.C.E.
(English translation, 1767)

The setting of Plautus's comedy utilizes the architecture of the typical urban Roman dwelling more thoroughly than other Roman comedies of its time, probably because its plot hinges on an architectural feature of Roman homes. Only the fronts of two houses are seen in the play; however, the other parts of the houses are described in the prologue, and events crucial to the play's plot that occur within the houses are reported on stage.

Periplecomenus's house. Home of the old gentleman Periplecomenus in Ephesus, a Roman town in Asia Minor. The front of this house appears stage right (to the au- dience's left); its front door opens onto the street, which is represented by the stage, on which all the action takes place. The stage right exit, right of the house, leads to the harbor. It is clear that the houses share a common wall through which a clever servant has made a secret opening, which is a key to the plot. The house's roofs are also connected, since the soldier's servant Sceledrus is able to move from one to the other while chasing a monkey.

Pyrgopolynices' house. Home of the braggart army captain, Pyrgopolynices, adjacent to Periplecomenus's house. The description of this house gives much more detail on the structure of Roman houses. From the roof of Pyrgopolynices's house, his neighbor's servant vio-

lates his privacy by peering into his living quarters. This is possible because the roof slopes inward to an opening (*impluvium*) below which a courtyard or patio (*atrium*) is open to the sky. Here the slave observes the mistress of Pyrgopolynices kissing the houseguest of his neighbor Periplecomenus. This house is situated stage left (to the right of the audience), and the stage left exit next to it leads to the forum.

— *John R. Holmes*

BRAND

Author: Henrik Ibsen (1828-1906)
Type of work: Drama
Type of plot: Social criticism

Time of plot: Nineteenth century
First published: 1866 (English translation, 1891); first performed, 1885

The settings of this closet drama revolve around three churches: the ice church, the old village church, and the new village church—all of which embody religious and highly symbolic elements. Other important settings include the Norwegian village, a glacial mountain, and the parsonage in which Brand, his wife, and son live.

Ice church. Naturally formed, domelike place of peace made entirely of ice that is the main setting of acts 1 and 5. Located high in an unspecified region of the mountains of Scandinavia, this "church" symbolizes the inflexible side of Christianity and materially exemplifies Brand's belief that salvation must come through total suffering and sacrifice. Predictably, this religion is not merely cold and heartless, but also ruthlessly unrelenting.

Village church. Presumably, a small, Lutheran state church. While this church is meant to be the center of village life, religion here has grown lifeless and ritualis-

tic and meaningless. Henrik Ibsen uses it to symbolize the lack of warmth and love among Christians. It is thus torn down by Brand and his followers.

New church. Replacement for the previous village church. Built by Brand, the mayor, and the village people, this new building and new church are immediately rejected by them at the opening ceremony and the key is thrown into the river. It is meant to be a church where all the congregants will worship God in an "all or nothing" fashion; however, this proves impossible after Brand realizes that God is one of love and not of law.

— *Carl Singleton*

BRAVE NEW WORLD

Author: Aldous Huxley (1894-1963)
Type of work: Novel
Type of plot: Dystopian

Time of plot: 632 years After Ford
First published: 1932

To further its satirical purposes, Aldous Huxley's novel of the future substitutes new institutions for many pillars of English society. Its religious centers are replaced by "community singeries," its schools by "conditioning centers," its architectural marvels by vast rectangular blocks. The story ventures outside England only once, when Bernard and Lenina visit the United States, not as a pilgrimage to the land of Our Ford's birth but to investigate another inglorious example of American inventiveness: an Indian reservation.

*Great Britain. In Huxley's dystopian future, the British Isles are part of Western Europe, one of ten administrative divisions of the world supervised by resident controllers.

Central London Hatchery and Conditioning Centre. Place where new citizens of London, the one-time capital of Britain, are produced. It has four thousand rooms. Life begins in the Fertilizing Room, after which cloned embryos are implanted in artificial wombs in the Bottling Room. Treatments administered in the Social Predestination Room determine the future status of the individuals delivered in the Decanting Room. The building's upper floors contain the Infant Nurseries and Neo-Pavlovian Conditioning Rooms. The center includes pleasant gardens, where children are allowed to play, but their games are carefully designed to supplement their careful education. The hatchery is the core of Huxley's sarcastic extrapolation of the principles of American automobile pioneer Henry Ford's assembly-line production system and Frederick Winslow Taylor's theories of applying scientific management to the organization of entire societies.

*Fleet Street. Real London street on which most British national newspapers were produced at the time Huxley wrote *Brave New World*. In the year A.F. ("after Ford") 632 (the twenty-seventh century by regular calendars), the street is dominated by a sixty-six-story building whose lower floors accommodate the Bureau of Propaganda—encompassing Television, Feeling Pictures, and Synthetic Voice and Music as well as the three remaining newspapers—while the eighteen uppermost floors house the College of Emotional Engineering.

*Westminster Abbey. One of the two most famous churches in London in the twentieth century, the abbey is situated close to the Houses of Parliament, near the River Thames. In A.F. 632 it has become a cabaret serving a vast apartment complex. The site of the other famous London church, St. Paul's Cathedral—at the top of Ludgate Hill—is occupied in A.F. 632 by the huge Fordson Community Singery, whose seven thousand rooms are used by Solidarity Groups for fortnightly services.

New Mexico Savage Reservation. Fictional Indian reservation west of Albuquerque, New Mexico, encompassing the Malpais Valley. It is one of several set aside for the use of people—including Native Americans—who remain stubbornly dedicated to squalid, inefficient, and chaotic ways of life that have been rendered obsolete by Fordism. Its 560,000 square kilometers are divided into four sub-reservations, each surrounded by an electrified fence.

*Eton. Real village north of Windsor in England's Berkshire region, the site of what is probably England's most famous preparatory school. The school still exists in A.F. 632; it, the School Community Singery, and the fifty-two-story Lupton's Tower form three sides of a quadrangle in whose center stands a chrome-steel statue of Our Ford.

Park Lane Hospital for the Dying. Sixty-story building externally decorated with primrose-colored tiles, overlooking Hyde Park. Visits to such institutions are a routine part of the existential process, so that children may become accustomed to the idea of death—against which patients are not encouraged to put up undignified struggles.

*Cyprus. Large eastern Mediterranean island. In the novel, it is mentioned as the site of an experiment undertaken in the year A.F. 473, when twenty-two thousand Alphas were allowed to create a society of their own, unsupported by the ranks of mentally inferior Betas, Gammas, Deltas, and Epsilons, who were eight-ninths of the population in Fordist society. When nineteen thousand Alphas died in civil wars caused by their reluctance to do the menial work needed to maintain their society, the survivors petitioned the World Controllers to resume their government over the island.

Lighthouse. Ferroconcrete edifice intended for the guidance of air traffic, erected on a hill between the towns of Puttenham and Elstead in the English county of Surrey, south of the Hog's Back ridge. In this improvised "hermitage" John the Savage tries, unsuccessfully, to isolate himself from the England of A.F. 632.

— *Brian Stableford*

BREAD AND WINE

Author: Ignazio Silone (Secondo Tranquilli, 1900-1978)

Type of work: Novel

Type of plot: Social realism

Time of plot: 1930's

First published: German translation, 1936 as *Brot und Wein*; Italian original, 1937 as *Pane e vino*; revision, 1955 as *Vino e pane* (English translation, 1962)

This second volume of Ignazio Silone's Abruzzi Trilogy explores the experiences of an Italian political organizer who for health reasons spends time in a remote mountain village disguised as a priest. There he learns first hand about the poverty and lack of political consciousness that controls these village people and develops a genuine compassion for them and the hardships of their lives.

***Abruzzi** (ah-BREWT-see). Region of south-central Italy on the eastern side of the country, opposite Rome and near the Adriatic Sea. An area of plains, hills, and mountains, it is the setting for all the volumes in Silone's Abruzzi Trilogy. Silone chose this region because he was born in southern Abruzzi in Pescina and because he needed a poor region in which to set his novels of peasant, or *cafoni*, life. Abruzzi is an area of vast feudal estates where a large number of *cafoni* eke out a subsistence farming a harsh, unforgiving terrain. Most of the peasants live in squalid one-room houses with their livestock, who provide a needed source of heat in the winter. It is also an area isolated from the outside world and therefore still primitive socially, politically, and religiously. Since *Bread and Wine* is about exploitation in a rural region, the Abruzzi provides an exemplary locale for the novel.

***Pietrasecca** (pee-eh-trah-SEHT-chah). Remote Italian village nestled in the hills of Abruzzi. Pietro Spina, a communist agitator, retreats there disguised as a priest seeking the mountain air for his lungs. Silone's depiction of the poverty, superstition, and isolation experienced by the local *cafoni* carries the social message of the novel. The locals are depicted in many ways as grotesques, even though Silone clearly feels compassion for their plight. Here, Pietro discovers the futility of his quest to politicize the country people as their subsistence living precludes them from any activity that does not directly contribute to their survival. Politics, he says, is for the well fed.

***Fossa** (FAHS-sah). Town closest to Pietrasecca. Despite its small size, Fossa is the "town" in the novel. Silone uses it to contrast with the village, where living is on the most basic level. In Fossa there are the markers of civilization: a doctor, lawyers, civil servants, all of the accouterments of the modern state. There, also, Pietro Spina would be recognized even in his cassock, for readers learn that he is a famous local son. In this town Silone dramatizes the effect of the newly formed Fascist government in Rome as the residents are being forced to compromise their political and social beliefs in order to retain their jobs and gain preferment. Unlike many of his former friends, who have caved in to the pressures, Pietro has remained true to his youthful ideals.

***Rome.** Capital and largest city of Italy. Don Paolo travels there to reconnect with his communist group. After shedding his priestly clothes in a bathhouse, he emerges once again as Pietro Spina, and although he is careful about his contacts, he can once again walk the streets without disguise. It is in Rome that his political commitment begins to change as a result of his experiences in Pietrasecca, which have helped him to recognize some of the silliness propounded by the organized left.

***Orta.** Another of the small towns spotted throughout the hills of Abruzzi, Orta is the ancestral home of Pietro Spina and where his grandmother still lives in the family home. The family, well-to-do and conservative, would seem to be an unlikely source for a revolutionary like Spina.

— *Charles L. P. Silet*

THE BRIDE OF LAMMERMOOR: A Legend of Montrose

Author: Sir Walter Scott (1771-1832)　　　　*Time of plot:* Late seventeenth century
Type of work: Novel　　　　　　　　　　　　*First published:* 1819
Type of plot: Gothic

This novel is an account of the enmity between Scottish families, whose conditions are symbolically reflected in their homes: Ravenswood Castle and Wolfscrag. The contrasted fortunes of the Ravenswoods and their successors, the Ashtons, embody an account of the underlying pattern of Scottish history as the remnants of an ancient feudalism surrender power and influence to a new political class.

Ravenswood Castle. Gothic fortress occupying a significant pass in Lammermoor (or Lammermuir) Hills, which straddle the border between the counties of Berwickshire and East Lothian in southeastern Scotland. A baronial seat in feudal times, the castle has deteriorated along with its resident family, passing out of their hands in the late seventeenth century, when Allan Lord Ravenswood was forced by a combination of political and financial misjudgments to sell the castle to the Lord Keeper, Sir William Ashton. Although Sir William undertakes considerable renovation work—in the course of which the banqueting hall is transformed into a library filled with legal commentaries and histories—the restoration of the house is temporary; it has fallen into ruins by the time that the tragic tale of Lucy Ashton is passed on to Jedidiah Cleishbotham by Richard Tinto.

Wolfscrag. Isolated tower on a narrow and precipitous peninsula jutting out from Scotland's desolate North Sea coast between Eyemouth—a fishing village about eight miles north of Berwick-upon-Tweed—and Saint Abb's Head, another five miles to the north. One of the first acquisitions of the Ravenswood family, the tower becomes their last when Allan Lord Ravenswood forfeits his title and removes himself there after losing the castle. Wolfscrag thus becomes the sole heritage of Allan's son Edgar, who retains the ironic title of Master of Ravenswood as a matter of courtesy.

The tower is in a horribly dilapidated state, its rough stone-work exposed by the ragged black wall-hangings whose deteriorated state is responsible for the fire that eventually destroys its interior. It is significant that Edgar provides refuge at Wolfscrag to Hayton of Bucklaw, his eventual rival for Lucy's hand, before Bucklaw inherits the estate of Girnington.

Wolfshope. Hamlet near Wolfscrag, whose name is said in the text to be equivalent to Wolf's Haven. Although its inhabitants no longer owe any formal allegiance to Ravenswood and are keen to assert their right of independence, they are quick to rally round to help when Wolfscrag catches fire.

Alice Gray's cottage. Humble dwelling on the Ravenswood estate, constructed out of turf and stones. It has a small garden, crudely hedged by elder bushes, which includes a turf seat shaded by a mournful birch tree, and several beehives. The cottage is overhung by a menacing rock—one of numerous ominous symbols contained in Ravenswood's surrounding landscape—for which reason its situation is called **Craig-foot**.

Mermaiden's fountain. Spring on the Ravenswood estate not far from Alice's cottage, associated with a legendary nymph or naiad. It was once enclosed by a Gothic construction, but this has long fallen into ruins by the time Lucy is carried there by the Master of Ravenswood after an unfortunate encounter with wild cattle.

Tod's-hole. Alehouse situated between Ravenswood Castle and Wolfscrag, some five or six miles from each, which makes a convenient meeting place for characters inclined to conspiracy. It is near a churchyard called the Armitage or Hermitage, in which some Ravenswoods and their loyal followers are interred and where Alice Gray wishes to be buried. "Tod" is a dialect term for a fox.

*****Edinburgh** (EDH-en-behr-oh). Capital of Scotland, where the Master of Ravenswood stays for a while as the guest of the unidentified marquis of A—— (probably Atholl) after the destruction of Wolfscrag

Langdirdum. Village in western Scotland that is the home of the artist Richard Tinto, from whom the novel's narrator obtains the tale. "Lang" is Scots for long, while "dirdum" signifies commotion or admonishment.

Gandercleugh (GAN-der-clew). Village in which Jedidiah Cleishbotham, the notional collector of the "Tales of my Landlord"—the series to which *The Bride*

of Lammermoor belongs—is the parish-clerk and school-master. "Cleugh" means gorge or ravine, while a gander is a male goose.

— Brian Stableford

BRIDESHEAD REVISITED: The Sacred and Profane Memories of Captain Charles Ryder

Author: Evelyn Waugh (1903-1966)
Type of work: Novel
Type of plot: Social realism

Time of plot: Twentieth century
First published: 1945

A strong sense of place is central to this novel, whose settings range widely over the Western world. However, it is Brideshead Manor, the English home and seat of the Marchmain family that stands at the heart of the work and anchors the affections of the main characters. The great estate contains and evokes memories that form the lives and characters of the Marchmains and their intimates.

Brideshead Manor. Imposing English country estate of the Marchmain family where troops are to be quartered in the early days of World War II and the location where this frame novel opens. The bulk of the novel comprises flashback memories of the house and its family of Charles Ryder, an army captain when the novel begins. Earlier, while a student at Oxford University, he befriends Sebastian Flyte, the younger son of Brideshead's Lord Marchmain. From Charles's first visit to Brideshead as a young man he senses the place's importance to the Marchmains as he is drawn into their family circle. In addition to the home's strong family associations, Charles comes to realize that it and its art nouveau chapel are emblematic of the strong Roman Catholic faith that guides the family even when their behavior is anything but exemplary.

*Oxford University. Historic English university that is novel's second great anchor. There Charles meets Sebastian and most of the friends he retains through the rest of his life. The heady charm of Oxford's dreaming spires and intense friendships of youth influence Charles more than the university's intellectual opportunities. The unimaginably wealthy and charming Sebastian introduces Charles to a new world of art and pleasure. Although Charles leaves Oxford without taking a degree and becomes a successful artist, Oxford continues to inspire him and remain a touchstone of his youth.

Ryder family home. Charles's childhood home and his life there with his widower father serve as a counterpoint to the glamour of Brideshead and Oxford. After blowing his allowance too quickly at Oxford, Charles returns to a dull life with his father. Eventually it becomes clear his father's bemused detachment is the model for his son's inability to attach to his own wife and children, as the glamour of the Marchmains becomes his only reality.

*Venice. Italian city in which Lord Marchmain has lived with his mistress, Cara, for years. After Charles escapes the tedium of his family home, he and Sebastian decamp to Venice, where he finds that Sebastian's father and mistress are a sedate middle-aged couple who are received in the best homes. The wise Cara is a counterpoint to the manipulative and devoutly religious Lady Marchmain at Brideshead. Charles's Venice sojourn, like his earlier experiences at Oxford and Brideshead, are important learning experiences. Moreover, the lush beauty of all three places helps form Charles's sensibilities as an artist.

*London. Capital of Great Britain and cultural and commercial center of the British Empire. Charles spends much of his adult life in London, where his Oxford contacts help advance his artistic career. Evelyn Waugh depicts London and Charles's friends there as stagnant and without the allure of Brideshead, Oxford, Venice, and exotic places on which Charles bases his art. The chief characters of *Brideshead Revisited* do not thrive in London.

Ocean liner. Ship on which Charles and Sebastian's sister Julia are reunited during a transatlantic voyage. At sea, attached to no firm ground, Charles begins an affair with Julia while his seasick wife is confined to her cabin.

*North Africa. After Sebastian becomes a confirmed alcoholic, he roams around North Africa, supported by family funds. He gains a sense of purpose caring for a German boy fleeing conscription by the Nazis but continues to drink. He finally turns up on the doorstep of a monastery in Tunis. Although he appears to be at the point of death, the monks nurse him back to life. He joins the remote monastery as a lay brother. The monks tolerate his alcoholism and come to believe him a holy man. Sebastian's final fate and home in Tunis force Charles to ponder anew the connections between charm, religious faith, and a love of beautiful places in the Marchmain family.

— *Isabel Bonnyman Stanley*

THE BRIDGE

Author: Hart Crane (1899-1932)
Type of work: Poetry

Type of plot: Epic
First published: 1930

An exquisite mesh of art, modern engineering skills, steel, and granite, New York City's Brooklyn Bridge is a transcendental symbol of the interconnectedness of the American experience and represents modern humanity's inexpressible longing for the Divine. Of the many locations mentioned in Hart Crane's sixteen-part poem, the major sites are New York City, New England, North Carolina, and the Midwest. Various mythological places such as Atlantis and Cathay connect the individual pieces and expand the theme of America as the promised land.

*Brooklyn Bridge. Steel suspension bridge connecting New York City's boroughs of Manhattan and Brooklyn that opened in 1883. Considered a masterpiece of modern architecture and engineering, it serves Crane's poem as a symbol of unimaginable, divinelike power, as well as a bridge to the past, the America of Crane's time, and to the future. Crane opens with a paean, or hymn of praise, to the bridge, While composing this poem, Crane rented the apartment in Columbia Heights from which the bridge's designer, John Augustus Roebling, had overseen its construction. The section titled "Proem" takes the angle of vision of that apartment window, which looked down at the bridge, and follows a sea gull as it rises up over the top of the bridge and disappears—a metaphor for imaginative flight.

*New York City. Crane's vision of America's largest city is ambiguous. On one hand, "Proem" and "The Tunnel" depict a city resembling London in T. S. Eliot's 1922 poem "The Waste Land," which contrasts a sordid contemporary urban environment with an idealized past. In Crane's poem, many of New York's famous streets exemplify a similar contrast: Avenue A, Broadway, Fourteenth Street, Chambers Street, Bleeker Street, and Prince Street. On the other hand, in "Proem" and "Atlantis," New York's Brooklyn Bridge represents the greatest achievement of modern man.

*Cathay. Medieval name for northern China, the fabled Orient and a land of spices and riches. Crane uses it here as the first of a series of "promised lands," including **Atlantis**, **Avalon**, and America. These idealized places are backdrops for the modern mechanical age, which, too, has enormous potential and great dangers.

River. The central image of "The River" is the Mississippi River, which flows past Cairo, Illinois, where it is joined by the Ohio River and symbolizes freedom and continuity. Although most of the section actually is set first on a train and among hoboes crossing the country, the river, like the bridge, connects past and present America.

*Cape Hatteras.** North Carolina promontory where Orville and Wilbur Wright flew their first airplane from the hill at Kitty Hawk. Crane speculates both on the awesome power of modern machines, embodiments of the creative power of the imagination and, potentially, destructive of human values.

Quaker Hill. New England location with an old hotel called the Mizzentop, a beautiful relic of a more glorious time sullied by modern commercialism that has replaced the earlier peace and tranquillity of the Quaker religious meeting.

— *Richard Damashek*

THE BRIDGE OF SAN LUIS REY

Author: Thornton Wilder (1897-1975)
Type of work: Novel
Type of plot: Philosophical realism

Time of plot: Early eighteenth century
First published: 1927

The primary setting of this novel is colonial Peru at a time when the Roman Catholic Church wields a powerful influence over the local people's lives, and they experience a community tragedy, when a bridge collapses, killing five people. The narrator tries to reconstruct the lives of the five victims from a book written by a Spanish friar who was burned at the stake for trying to prove that the bridge's collapse was an act showing the wisdom of God.

Bridge of San Luis Rey. Colonial Peru's most famous bridge, an old rope suspension bridge in the region between Lima and Cuzco that collapsed on July 20, 1714, sending five travelers to their deaths in the deep gorge below. Their deaths would have been forgotten, were it not for the fact that a Roman Catholic priest, Brother Juniper, who narrowly missed being among the dead, questioned why the others died and he was spared. His questions sought to demonstrate the importance of place in the shaping of human lives. After devoting his life to investigating the lives of the five victims, he published a book showing that God had reasons to send each of the victims to their deaths at that moment. The book was condemned by Church authorities, and he was burned at the stake for going too far in explaining God's ways to humanity. The one surviving copy of Brother Juniper's book fell into the hands of Thornton Wilder's fictional narrator, who tells the stories of the five bridge victims' lives and examines the effect their deaths had on the people whom they left behind.

The bridge has become a memorial to despair. For example, Madre Maria, who seemed to be the one physical connection among the five victims, felt great despair because her children were lost in the fall. She felt that she had to overpay for her placing her wards on that bridge at that moment. Only she remembered the orphans whom she had so carefully reared. She retreated to her memories at the place of the convent.

Cathedral. Roman Catholic cathedral in Lima, where a great service was held after the tragedy for its victims. Everyone in attendance considered the incident an example of a true act of God, and many reasons were offered for the various deaths.

— *Robert L. Wyatt III*

THE BRIDGE ON THE DRINA

Author: Ivo Andrić (1892-1975)
Type of work: Novel
Type of plot: Historical realism

Time of plot: 1516-1914
First published: Na Drini ćuprija, 1945 (English translation, 1959)

This sweeping panorama of life on the Drina River at Višegrad, on the border between Bosnia and Serbia, spans four centuries. During this time many changes take place, brought about mostly by the existence of the bridge.

***Drina River** (DREE-nah). Ancient river located entirely within Bosnia and Herzegovina that forms part of the boundary of the modern Yugoslavian republic of Serbia. It is significant in that its banks represent the division between East and West in this frequently war-torn region.

***Bridge.** Unchanging heart of the novel. While everything else changes, the bridge remains constant. It was built between 1566 and 1571 by the Grand Vezir Mehmed Pasha Sokolli. He ordered a bridge to be built near Višegrad. He hoped to link the eastern and western parts of the empire and improve the region economically. These goals were accomplished during the life span of the bridge. The unusually beautiful edifice quickly became the focal point of the area, where the various local inhabitants—Serbian Orthodox, Bosnian Muslims, Roman Catholics, and Jews—would gather on the two small terraces in the middle of the bridge to discuss matters of mutual concern. The bridge was witness to everything that befell the town's inhabitants: harmonious cohabitation, wars and struggles, floods and fires, attempts to blow up the bridge, and changes such as the building of a water duct and local railroad.

The bridge's significance is dramatized by events that occur during and after its building. According to legend, a pair of Serbian twins had to be immured in the bridge to ensure the success of the project. The main builder, the Serb Rade the Mason, was impaled on a stake in order to frighten local saboteurs, who frequently destroyed overnight what had been built during the day because they feared the consequences of tampering with nature, especially by an occupying "evil" force. Several deaths took place on or near the bridge; there were also several attempts to destroy the bridge, the latest during World War I.

The bridge on the Drina is not merely a utilitarian structure, however. Throughout the novel Ivo Andrić emphasizes three symbolic meanings of the bridge: its linking, permanence, and beauty. Despite the changes in the area surrounding it, the bridge has withstood the centuries. Andrić concludes several chapters by emphasizing the durability of the bridge, while its beauty attests the artistic, creative spirit of human beings. These three qualities make the bridge function like a character who exists among the people for generations.

***Višegrad** (VEE-sheh-grad). This town by the Drina was a small settlement before the bridge was built. It grew constantly as the impact of the bridge effected not only the town but also the entire region. The town practically owes its existence to the bridge, growing out of it as if from an imperishable root. Thus, the chronicle (as Andrić calls it) of the centuries-old bond between the townspeople and the bridge reaches beyond a mere historical and geographical coincidence.

— *Vasa D. Mihailovich*

BRITANNICUS

Author: Jean Baptiste Racine (1639-1699)
Type of work: Drama
Type of plot: Tragedy

Time of plot: 55 C.E.
First performed: 1669; first published, 1670 (English translation, 1714)

This tragedy unfolds within a single large room in the palace of Emperor Néron, who was infamous for his brutality. His palace is a closed space in which violent crimes may be committed at any moment, making the play's moral characters understandably terrified whenever they enter it.

Néron's palace (nay-ROH[N]). Imperial palace in Rome within whose public area the tragedy takes place. In his preface to the play—which bears the name of Néron's half-brother—Jean Racine wrote that Néron was never a virtuous man and that his play would portray him as a "monster." The crimes of Néron (more commonly known as Nero) are so well known, even to those with only a superficial knowledge of Roman history, that Racine's audiences not only expected unspeakable crimes to be committed within the palace, they sensed Néron's evil presence even when he was physically absent from the stage. Néron is both voyeuristic and sadistic. His pure evil is everywhere in his palace. In the play's second act, he attempts to seduce the young Junie, whom he tries to force to renounce her love for Britannicus. Later, as Junie and Britannicus talk together, audiences are aware that Néron is offstage listening. Almost any course of action they take will get Britannicus killed. Both lovers are in grave danger.

Because of a convention associated with seventeenth century French theater, physical violence could not be depicted onstage. However, this restriction actually serves to make the public area of the palace seem even more threatening, as audiences cannot know what horrendous crimes Néron and his henchman, Narcisse, are committing offstage.

When Néron, Britannicus, and Junie finally meet together onstage for the first time, near the end of the third act, it is clear that Néron intends to kill Britannicus and rape Junie, but the audience does not know the order in which these crimes will be committed. Eventually, Néron calls in guards to arrest Britannicus, who is marched offstage to await his death. The only uncertainty is the form that Britannicus's execution will take. Later, Néron gives a glass of poisoned wine to Britannicus, who dies instantly in front of numerous witnesses, who immediately look at Néron. The virtuous Burrhus, who has tried in vain to teach moral values to Néron, returns to the stage and describes the murder in a short funeral oration. When Junie hears his speech, she flees. In the play's final scene, Albina, who is the confidant of Néron's mother, Agrippina, returns to the same public room and announces that when Narcisse chased after Junie on a public street, he was killed by a mob protecting the innocent Junie, who is to remain in the Temple of the Vestal Virgins, where she will finally be safe from the emperor. Although no physical violence is depicted in the public room, this scene is filled with violence in the minds of both the spectators and the moral characters.

— *Edmund J. Campion*

BROAD AND ALIEN IS THE WORLD

Author: Ciro Alegría (1909-1967)
Type of work: Novel
Type of plot: Social realism

Time of plot: 1912-1926
First published: El mundo es ancho y ajeno, 1941 (English translation, 1941)

This novel personalizes the generic concept of the mistreatment of conquered peoples by conquerors through the physical setting and associated inhabitants. In South America's northern Andes Mountains the physical and mental spaces of the indigenous peoples who inhabit them are overwhelmed and displaced by the descendants of the Spanish conquerors, who continue the exploitation process over the centuries. This is the story of mutually exclusive world views, one integrated into nature and the other determined to tame nature to its own ends.

***Andes.** Great mountain range that runs through Peru and the other countries of South America's west coast. Within the novel, the mountains' peaks are personified by the indigenous peoples: Urpillau, Huarca, Huillac, Puma, Suni, Mamay, who are inextricably tied to nature. Geography is always a silent presence in the novel. At times, it is almost a dominant character, reflecting the importance of geography in Peru's culture: the lofty Andean sierra with its crisp, thin air, its gaunt landscapes, sparse vegetation, and rocky soil. Ciro Alegría was born and reared on a hacienda in the same region in which he sets this novel.

Rumi. Small Peruvian Indian village in which the novel is primarily set. The village is physically defined by Lombriz Creek, the plateau of El Alto, Lake Yanañahui, and the cliffs over Yanañahui; its space defines its inhabitants' sense of self and order. Rosendo Maqui, the mayor, represents the inhabitants of Rumi at their best at the same time as the Rumi community, people and space, represents the ideal of nature. Rumi is a pastel-colored place, with cobbled, windswept streets and huddled houses. Its people grow potatoes and tend their llamas. They chew coca to cope with hunger and the cold, and their chests are like those of pouter pigeons since their high-altitude air has little oxygen.

Umay Ranch. Private ranch adjoining Rumi that is owned by Don Alvaro Amenabar, a greedy and unprincipled *patrón* who uses force and legal trickery to wrest the best farmland of the villagers away from them. His greed diametrically opposes every tenet of the Rumi community's philosophy and practices. Amenabar represents the worst of the latter-day conquerors.

Yanañahui (yah-na-NYAH-wee). New and higher altitude location to which Rumi's people move their village after Amenabar forces them off their original land. After going through great suffering and loss to rebuild in this location, they eventually lose even this less desirable space, as the conquerors' space has no room for them, physically or psychologically. Nowhere under the Peruvian flag is there a place that is not hostile to Indians.

Cities. The large Peruvian cities that figure into the story, such as the provincial capital, Trujillo, and Lima, the national capital, are centers of primarily European institutions: banks, a law school, the seat of government. Imposed upon the landscape, rather than integrated into it, the cities represent not only the continuing physical and mental encroachment of the descendants of the original conquerors upon the indigenous inhabitants but also the unbridgeable gap that still separates them.

Jungle plantations. Rubber tree collecting camps and coca plantations in Peru's jungle backlands are perceived by Indians as places of hope where they can earn money; however, they prove to be hellholes. Both courageous and cowardly Indians try to bridge the gap between the cultures or escape their fate in their communities by taking jobs on the plantations. However, these profit-making enterprises—like the cities—are imposed on, not integrated into, nature, and the Indians who work on them are generally overwhelmed.

— *Debra D. Andrist*

THE BROKEN JUG

Author: Heinrich von Kleist (1777-1811)
Type of work: Drama
Type of plot: Comedy

Time of plot: Late eighteenth century
First performed: 1808; first published, 1811 as *Der zerbrochene Krug* (English translation, 1830)

The setting of this play is the united provinces of the Netherlands, a republic depending on the ability of its civil servants to uphold the law and maintain public trust. In addition to the defendant Ruprecht being on trial for breaking a jug, the judge and court inspector are metaphorically on trial as civil servants. The courtroom of Huisum remains the backdrop for the action from start to finish, underlining the question of justice and how well the society's institutions can serve it.

Huisum (HI-sum). Fictional Netherlands village, surrounded by cultivated fields, not far from the real city of Utrecht. Its occupants, who farm the land and raise livestock, are mostly illiterate. Characters need to make frequent trips to Utrecht for goods and services as well as for business. Economic dependence on Utrecht reflects its political position as provincial seat, location of the superior court.

Courtroom. Heinrich von Kleist has noted that the inspiration for this play came from a Dutch etching that showed a courtroom with a trial in progress and included a broken jug as well as characters analogous to those in this play. The courtroom serves also as Judge Adam's living room. The cabinets in the courtroom contain a messy mix of cheese, ham, and sausage interspersed with or wrapped in various legal files. The confusion of private and public realms, which compromises Adam as a civil servant, is indicated.

Frau Martha's house. From the garden, Eve's bedroom window on the second floor is visible. Posts, reaching from the ground to Eve's window, support a trellis covered with grapevines. As the scene of the crime, this geography becomes important during the trial. The grapevine hints at sensual desire and entanglement; and Eve's room, like the jug in it, is a symbol of her chastity and honor, which appear to have been violated by an intruder who broke the jug during his hasty retreat.

— Julie D. Prandi

THE BRONZE HORSEMAN

Author: Alexander Pushkin (1799-1837)
Type of work: Poetry
Type of plot: Historical realism

Time of plot: 1703 and 1824
First published: Medniy vsadnik, 1837 (English translation, 1899)

This poem's introduction deals with Peter the Great's founding of St. Petersburg in 1703, while the remaining two parts occur in Alexander Pushkin's time, detailing the flood of St. Petersburg in 1824. The flood becomes more than an abstract historical event when Pushkin describes the plight of a simple clerk, Yevgeny, and the insanity brought on by his fiancé's drowning.

*****St. Petersburg.** Russian city built by Peter the Great in which the poem's entire narrative is set. Czar Peter moved his capital to St. Petersburg in 1703 after capturing the formerly Swedish territory. His intent, in addition to claiming the conquered territory, was to create a "window to the West" and modernize Russia by providing her with a western port. Russia at that time was a deeply tradition-bound country, suspicious of western influences. Peter's iron will clashed with entrenched societal forces such as the church, landed gentry, and peasants. Those opposing Peter the Great bristled at his total disregard for tradition and his vaunting pride—even to the point of blasphemy. A theme in Russian literature is that St. Petersburg is a cursed city. The legend is that Peter the Great established the city, rashly built on a marsh and at such a northern latitude, solely to impose his will on the Russian people. In his overweening pride, he rebelled against God and nature, and the city and its inhabitants must suffer as a result. As proof of this "curse," the city is said to be built on the bones of the 100,000 men who died during its construction. The city is considered "cold" in comparison to Moscow, center of old Russia. Additionally, the city floods at the whim of the Neva River, showing that although Peter could build a city, it is still subject to forces superior to any human.

*****Neva River.** River running through St. Petersburg. Just as the river runs through the great Russian city, it also threads through the poem, responsible both for giving life to the city, as well as destroying Yevgeny.

*****Senate Square.** Government center in St. Petersburg. In the poem, called "Peter's Square," after the statue of Peter the Great, "The Bronze Horseman," overlooking the Neva. Yevgeny waits out the flood here and after discovering that his fiancé has perished in the city's low-lying, poorer regions, he returns half-crazed for his final encounter with the "Horseman." Yevgeny's plight echoes that of Pushkin. Socially liberal military officers and friends of Pushkin staged a putsch on this square de-manding the emperor enact wide-ranging social reform. They were brutally suppressed, though Pushkin was un-scathed due to his social proximity to the emperor.

— *Paul John Schmitt*

THE BROTHERS ASHKENAZI

Author: Israel Joshua Singer (1893-1944)
Type of work: Novel
Type of plot: Historical realism

Time of plot: Late nineteenth and early twentieth centuries
First published: Di brider Ashkenazi, 1936 (English translation, 1936)

Most of the action in this novel is set in the Polish city of Lodz during the period when Poland was controlled by—and even considered a part of—Russia. After the Russian Revolution and World War I, Poland became an independent nation, a fact that has dire consequences for Lodz in this novel.

*Lodz (lewj). Industrial city in central Poland, about seventy-five miles southwest of Warsaw, in which the novel is set. The growth of the city from a sleepy village to the center of Poland's textile industry is important to the novel. During the nineteenth century, the Russian government encouraged weavers in Germany and Moravia to come to Poland, where they were given free land, special conditions, and ready markets. The government's goal was to establish an industry that could take advantage of Poland's natural resources. As a consequence, many weavers settled in Lodz. As the textile industry expanded, Lodz's Jewish community rose from a few dozen people to thousands as Jews arrived from Poland's countryside and Russia—from which they were expelled. Some of these people prospered in the weaving trade; most, however, remained poor and lived in Balut, an impoverished, working-class section of Lodz, which author Israel Joshua Singer describes as "Russia's greatest manufacturing centre of textiles and revolutionaries."

The novel ends shortly after the Soviet Union comes into existence, and Poland struggles to regain its independence. Meanwhile, Lodz experiences alternating periods of boom and depression, and the novel ends with a period of great depression as Polish independence means that Lodz loses its vital Russian markets for its textiles. The workers' movements that arise do not win new rights for the workers but instead engage in pogroms against Lodz's Jewish community.

The Ashkenazi brothers, Simcha Meyer, later known as Max, and Jacob Bunim, later known as Yakob, are born in Lodz and live most of their lives there. Both survive the pogroms and economic downturns and make fortunes. At one point, Max becomes so wealthy and powerful that Singer calls him, the "new king of Lodz."

*Petrograd (PEH-treh-grad). City in northwestern Russia also known as St. Petersburg and, after the Russian Revolution, as Leningrad. Throughout most of the novel, Petrograd is the capital of Russia. Max Ashkenazi travels there to bribe government officials to achieve his goals as an industrialist. During World War I, shortly before the German occupation of Lodz, he moves his factory to Petrograd and establishes the "new Lodz-in-Petrograd," of which he is hailed the "uncrowned king." However, the Revolution ends Max's good fortune, and he is thrown in jail.

Railroad station. Station several miles inside Poland where Yakob is killed by police while he and Max are trying to change trains while returning to Lodz from Petrograd. Because they are Jews, Polish policeman arrest them and order them to shout, "To hell with all the Yids," and to dance. Max complies, but Yakob does not and is shot.

Warsaw. Capital city and cultural center of Poland to which Yakob goes to live with his new wife's wealthy family. However, because he spends much of his time in Lodz, he eventually divorces his first wife and marries his niece. Warsaw is also the city to which Max's son Ignatz goes with his wife at the same time Max is trying to get Ignatz to take over his textile business in Lodz. However, Ignatz feels oppressed in Lodz, which he considers a cultural wasteland, and believes that Warsaw is somewhat like Paris, France—to which he and his wife eventually return.

*Carlsbad. Austrian vacation resort and watering place where many wealthy Jews from Lodz spend their summers, taking the baths, gambling, and otherwise enjoying themselves. Yakob goes to Carlsbad, but Max, seeing the place as an example of terrible waste, refuses to accompany his wife and in-laws there.

— *Richard Tuerk*

THE BROTHERS KARAMAZOV

Author: Fyodor Dostoevski (1821-1881)
Type of work: Novel
Type of plot: Psychological realism

Time of plot: Nineteenth century
First published: Bratya Karamazovy, 1879-1880
  (English translation, 1912)

Fyodor Dostoevski's last and greatest novel returns to the heartland of Russia to examine a family in disarray. This novel is not so much a literal description of Russian rural life under Czar Alexander II as it is a symbol of it.

Skotoprigonyevsk (sko-to-prihg-ON-ih-ehfsk). Russian town in which the Karamazovs' home is located and the location of the worst debauchery commonly blamed on Fyodor Karamazov—the rape of the mentally disabled Lizavita. Dostoevski's narrator withholds the name of the town until almost the very end of the novel, at the beginning of the trial of Dmitri Karamazov. Otherwise, the narrator refers to it only as "the town" or "our town." The name Skotoprigonyevsk is most likely derived from the Russian word *skotoprigony*, meaning a stockyard. It is a generic Russian rural town of the time, located somewhere in the broadleaf-forest belt that is the heart of old Russia. For the people of Skotoprigonyevsk, the bright lights and Western fashions of the capital in St. Petersburg are almost unimaginably distant, talked about but never seen.

Karamazov home. Dwelling of Fyodor Pavlovich Karamazov, patriarch of the Karamazov family. As befits a wealthy landowner, it is a spacious house, tended by a faithful servant and his wife. However, it is also in notable disrepair, with crumbling wallpaper. These signs of decay reflect the moral dissolution of the elder Karamazov and are likely a deliberate touch of Dostoevski's art. Although the house is the family home, it is not a place where Karamazov's sons find nurturing or comfort. All three of his legitimate sons are fostered by maternal relatives. As Karamazov's degeneracy makes him progressively more paranoid, the effects of his house also become a sort of quasi-prison for him, and he locks himself within his room. The house eventually becomes the site of Karamazov's death—the circumstances of which are mysterious as a result of Karamazov's progressive isolation.

Monastery. Spiritual retreat of Alyosha Karamazov and of the saintly Father Zossima. Located not far from the Karamazov home, this monastery is an important spiritual center of the region. Thus, when Fyodor Karamazov quarrels with his son Dmitri over a supposed inheritance which Dmitri accuses his father of having squandered, the two men visit the monastery, where they appeal to Father Zossima to adjudicate their dispute. The monastery is a symbol of Christian salvation. Fyodor Karamazov is so morally degenerate that he is insensitive to the presence of the holy and behaves in his usual shameful fashion, thereby destroying any hope of reconciliation with his son. Another son, Alyosha, finds the monastery his key to spiritual peace and helps the troubled Grushenka to reach moral regeneration and forgiveness.

Dostoevski's monastery reflects his Slavophile politics. Unlike Russians who believed that Russia's future lay in adopting Western innovations like democracy or socialism, Dostoevski and other Slavophiles believed that Russia must look to its own roots for moral and spiritual rebirth. The key to this revitalization, Dostoevski believed, lay in the Russian Orthodox Church.

— *Leigh Husband Kimmel*

BRUT

Author: Layamon (fl. c. twelfth century)
Type of work: Poetry
Type of plot: Epic

Time of plot: c. 409-689
First published: c. 1205

This poem tells the story of the settlement of England from the end of the Trojan Wars to the final Saxon victory over the Britons in 689. Although covering a vast period of time, it focuses primarily on the story of Arthur and his court at Camelot, the central element in all Arthurian stories.

***England.** Provides the overall setting for *Brut*, which is the story of the kings of England from the supposed first English king, Brut, through one of the most legendary English kings, Arthur. Since this work focuses mainly on the story of Arthur, such Arthurian settings as Cornwall; **Tintagel Castle**, where Arthur was born; and **Camelot**, the site of Arthur's court, supply the locales for the events illustrating Arthur's rise to power and the development of the code of chivalry and the brotherhood of the Round Table. Layamon also recounts Arthur's battles and victories in France, Ireland, Scotland, Iceland, Norway, and Denmark. As do most versions of the Arthur story, *Brut* concludes with Arthur's fatal battle with his son Modred at Camelford and his being spirited off to the mystical island of **Avalon**, where he will stay until he is again needed in England.

— *Tom Frazier*

BUDDENBROOKS

Author: Thomas Mann (1875-1955)
Type of work: Novel
Type of plot: Social realism

Time of plot: Nineteenth century
First published: Buddenbrooks: Verfall einer Familie,
   1901 (English translation, 1924)

Most of this novel is set in Lübeck, a German port city where Thomas Mann was born and spent his childhood. The stern realities of city life are offset by Mann's beautiful descriptions of the Buddenbrooks' brief but significant holidays in the nearby seaside resort of Travemünde.

***Lübeck** (LEW-behk). German city in which the novel is set. Although the novel does not identify the city by name, its four-story house at 4 Meng Street is clearly the house that belonged to Thomas Mann's grandparents. All but the elegant facade and cellar were destroyed when Lübeck was bombed in 1942. These have been preserved in the new building, the Buddenbrook House, the Heinrich and Thomas Mann Center purchased by the City of Lübeck in 1991. As in the novel, Meng Street intersects Breite Street and stands in the shadow of the medieval twin towers of St. Mary's Church.

Most of the action is set within the walls of the Buddenbrooks' two homes, not only because of the damp, cold climate on the Baltic Sea but also because the family is perhaps unconsciously insulating itself from the social upheaval that has been sweeping Europe since the French Revolution. Two rooms in particular define their protected living space in the Meng Street residence. The salon is called the "landscape room" because it is hung with large tapestries of idyllic scenes; and the formal dining room is called the "room of the gods" because statues of Greek gods are set into the walls.

The Meng Street house, which is purchased by the Buddenbrooks at the height of their prosperity, is still closely connected with the family business and has grain storage facilities on the premises. However, the fact that the family has let the back wing of the house fall into ruin is a sign that the Buddenbrooks' fortunes are in decline. Stray cats inhabit the space over rotten floorboards.

Their opulent new home on Fischergrube has attractive features, which reflect the family's aesthetic and philosophical preoccupations. There is a large music room with a grand piano, and the garden has a fountain. Thomas Buddenbrook goes there to reflect upon the meaning of life and death. The house is no sooner built than he has second thoughts about it, and the business wanes. Thomas becomes irreversibly depressed and dies prematurely following a botched tooth extraction.

When the business must be liquidated at a loss, Thomas's widow and son move to more modest accommodations, where the son dies of typhus. One by one, the Buddenbrooks are laid to rest under their large memorial slab in a graveyard that borders on a copse of trees.

The Buddenbrooks bought their Meng Street house from a family whose business had failed. The Latin inscription over the door, "Dominus providebit" (God will provide), becomes more an ironic epithet than an assertion of faith as the Buddenbrooks meet their demise. It is a bitter irony that the house is quickly bought by the Buddenbrooks' business rival, the unscrupulous upstart Hermann Hagenström, whose family is thriving.

Thomas Mann mentions the outer world only when it relates directly to events in the Buddenbrook family. Flags fly from every house when the Buddenbrooks celebrate one hundred years of business. Johann Buddenbrook disperses an angry crowd before parliament by addressing them in Low German. On a cold winter night, Antonia Buddenbrook waits in the town square to hear whether her brother Thomas or the hated Hagenström is elected to the senate. At the market, dying fish gasp for air, echoing Elizabeth Buddenbrook's painful death from pneumonia and foreshadowing Thomas's fatal collapse on Breite Street.

*Travemünde (tra-vuh-MEWN-duh). German seaside resort just north of Lübeck where Mann spent the happiest times of his life. For Antonia Buddenbrook, Travemünde comes to represent a lost opportunity, a promise of love and prosperity in a new social order that she was not quite ready to embrace. While she was resisting an arranged marriage that would supposedly enhance the family, she stayed here with the Schwarzkopfs, simple people with a healthy lifestyle. In the course of long walks on the beach, Antonia fell in love with their intelligent son Morten, a medical student and politically active bourgeois.

Real appreciation for the place is expressed later in the novel by her frail nephew Hanno, who can watch the waves endlessly and is glad he will not be quizzed on the names of the boats. His joyous summer holidays in Travemünde are contrasted sharply with his feelings of hopelessness in school.

Significantly, when his ailing father Thomas is told to take a holiday in Travemünde, it rains for days. Thomas has lost the will to live.

— *Jean M. Snook*

BULLET PARK

Author: John Cheever (1912-1982)
Type of work: Novel
Type of plot: Psychological realism

Time of plot: Mid-twentieth century
First published: 1969

The setting in this novel is an upper-middle-class bedroom community near New York City—the kind of place that is a frequent target of satire and social criticism. In this scene of presumed materialism and superficiality, is revealed the unconditional love that Eliot Nailles, a merchandiser for Spang mouthwash, has for his son. Into this peaceful community the rootless and demented Paul Hammer moves for the sole reason of killing Eliot's son. The improbable conjunction of setting, characters, and events demonstrates that the depths of the human condition cannot be understood by a facile psychology and sociology.

Bullet Park. Suburban area of stately homes, manicured lawns interrupted by swimming pools, and the buzz of chain saws and lawn tractors. At the heart of the town is the train station where the commuter railroad connects residents to New York City, the great magnet of purpose, reputation, and money. At 7:46 A.M. every weekday morning, the commuters, in their business uniforms and with their folded newspapers, obeying the code of privacy that allows them only to nod to each other, rush into the city. Aboard their trains, they zoom past local stops and past the bedroom windows of Harlem into Manhattan's Grand Central Station, from which they run to their various subways and taxis. In the evening, the reverse migration is more relaxed. The train's bar car is open, and more cocktails await them at home in the company of wife, children, and dog. On weekends, cocktail parties, with all kinds of dalliances within them, dot Bullet Park's landscape. Local police keep an eye out for those who drink too much and obligingly guide them home.

So goes John Cheever's satirical portrait of Bullet Park—overprivileged, overindulgent, and empty of significant feeling, which at first the author seems to confirm. At the train station one morning, Mr. Shinglehouse is sucked up by the Chicago Express barreling through—literally lifted out of his loafers. However, no one on the platform knows him well enough to allow the strange event to alter his day. Mr. Shinglehouse disappears with the same anonymity with which he lived.

Within the milieu of Bullet Park, advertising executive Eliot Nailles is generally happy and content, loving his wife, his son, his home, and his job. He has his discontents. He drinks too much, and is worried about his son's adjustment to school and career. But his commitments make him whole. The first half of the novel generally confirms the satirical expectations readers have of Bullet Park. However, those expectations are a strategic misdirection to contrast with the strange madness of Paul Hammer.

Hammer's world. In contrast to Nailles's powerful sense of identity with a place, the world of the crazed killer Paul Hammer is a phantasmagoria of images taken from around the globe: famous sights of London, Rome, and Paris, mixed with a compulsive detailing of all the hotel rooms in which he has stayed. He travels everywhere and belongs nowhere, obsessively seeking the "yellow rooms" that he thinks will satisfy him. He is psychotic, but it is a moral, rather than a clinical psychosis, for he is clear-headed enough to pursue his murderous purposes. He selects Eliot Nailles, whom he has never met, as his victim (he later shifts his focus to Eliot's son, Tony) because his mother, an ideologue who hates America, tells him he should pick out a place like Bullet Park, disguise himself as an ordinary resident, find a representative of American capitalism, and nail him to the door of the church. Hammer is so spiritually empty that this threadbare and merciless comment sponsors the only direction in his life.

Church. Bullet Park Episcopal church in which Hammer intends to kill Tony Nailles on the altar. It is the same church in which Tony was christened and in which the Nailles family worships each Sunday, an image of Eliot Nailles's thoroughly conventional view of life. In a moment of heroism, Eliot attacks the church door with a chain saw and rescues his son.

— Bruce Olsen

THE BULWARK

Author: Theodore Dreiser (1871-1945)
Type of work: Novel
Type of plot: Social realism

Time of plot: 1890 to the mid-1920's
First published: 1946

This novel preserves the force of its narrative of family conflict by evoking only sparingly a sense of physical environment—a strategy in accord with the fact that the book's main characters are Quakers, who in varying degrees seek to live according to the dictates of an "inner light" rather than everyday experience. The Quakers' spiritual aspirations deeply condition their notions of natural beauty and worldly goods, but with the passing years many in their circle turn away from the precepts of their faith and toward the expansive mainstream of American life.

Thornbrough. Home of the Barnes family near Dukla, Pennsylvania. The novel's main character, Solon Barnes, is a native of Maine, where his father farmed and had a modest business in town until he moved the family to Pennsylvania to aid his widowed sister-in-law. His family soon occupies Thornbrough, a decrepit pre-Civil War home along a country byway. Restoration of the house to its former elegance prompts reflection upon the spiritual legitimacy of material comfort, prosperity, and wealth. Because Quaker belief endorses simplicity, not merely in dress but also in living arrangements, the restoration of Thornbrough is acceptable to the family only because they can view it as an act of stewardship rather than one of material indulgence.

Theodore Dreiser offers descriptions of the house and its surroundings, but they are brief and often schematic. Although Solon's father enjoys the small creek that runs through his land, he never troubles to learn where the stream ends. Later, Solon, now married to the daughter of his wealthy employer, decides to move his family from their home in town to Thornbrough, not because of its beauty, but because the children would be better protected from undesirable influences of the more worldly families in the town by living among the green fields and free spaces of the countryside. However, this countryside is threatened by development. Though located in a pastoral region, Dukla is well on its way to becoming a suburb of Philadelphia. Solon himself is able to commute to work from the Dukla station to the city in twenty-five minutes.

The transformation of countryside into suburb and the transition from the age of the horse and buggy to that of the automobile are topics of considerable significance to

Dreiser. He is both an admirer of modernity and a critic of capitalism, and Solon Barnes is the vehicle of his ambivalence. Solon refuses to give up his horse and buggy and does not even contemplate buying an automobile. Even the bicycle, "with its tendency to take boys and girls into the streets and along the roads unchaperoned," embodies an unwarranted freedom. Mobility and dispersal, hallmarks of American life, are inherently questionable: When Solon's oldest daughter, Isobel, goes away to college, a school is found for her that has the "advantage of being not too far distant."

*****Madison.** Capital city of Wisconsin. Much of *The Bulwark* concerns the various kinds of conformity, indifference, and rebellion toward Solon's values and moral precepts shown by his five children. The most clearly delineated of the children is Etta, whose rejection of her father's world has both an intellectual and a geographical element. Stimulated by the intimate friendship with a fellow student at her boarding school, Etta surreptitiously joins her friend in Madison to attend the summer session at the university there. Her friend tempts her with an account of how in the West girls are treated as though they have brains. Solon Barnes's overnight train trip to Madison in a futile attempt to retrieve his daughter is the longest journey of his life.

*****New York City.** In the autumn, Etta travels to New York City, where she intends to study and to immerse herself in the cultural life of the city. This second geographical displacement is another kind of reproach to Solon's world. His family believes that moral peril awaits a single girl in the giant metropolis. Etta's break from the world of rural Pennsylvania is complete when she becomes the lover of a prominent young artist, who, ironically, breaks off the relationship in order to fulfill a commission for a Western landscape.

*New Jersey. A destructively climactic act of revolt on the part of Stewart, the youngest of Solon's children, tellingly involves the automobile, which allows a further degree of unwarranted freedom. Away at a school on the outskirts of Philadelphia, Stewart is kept on a tight budget by his parents but manages to join his fashionable friends on nighttime auto trips into neighboring New Jersey, where they find amorous encounters with girls of lower social status. The young men's misadventures end with the death of a young girl whom they rape after she is given a sedative by Stewart's friend. Stewart, hiding a knife when he is jailed, commits suicide to avoid facing his family.

— *Clyde S. McConnell*

A BURNT-OUT CASE

Author: Graham Greene (1904-1991)
Type of work: Novel
Type of plot: Bildungsroman

Time of plot: Mid-twentieth century
First published: 1961 (first published in Swedish translation from manuscript, 1960)

Set in equatorial Africa during the waning days of European colonial rule, this novel gives dramatic expression, in Greene's words, to varieties of belief in regions far removed from world politics and household preoccupations. More than a specific geographical place, the Congo depicted in this novel is a region of the mind in which spiritual and moral issues become entangled.

Leprosaria. Congolese village located hundreds of miles inland from the provincial capital Matadi and loosely structured upon leper communities that Graham Greene had visited during his travels through the Belgian Congo and what were then the Cameroons. Situated on a tributary of the "great river"—presumably the Congo River—the leprosaria is part mission and part treatment facility for those who suffer not only from Hansen's disease (leprosy), but also from sicklaemia, tuberculosis, or elephantiasis. Its Roman Catholic church and state-supported hospital symbolize the spiritual and medical work being done to comfort the needy who wander among the squalid rows of two-room brick houses that bake in the noonday sun. Sermons about the existence of God and arguments about evolution occur within sight of gross suffering and human deformity, over which darkness mercifully falls. The central narrative of the novel involves a new hospital that is being built in order better to serve the eight hundred people who drift in and out of the village. The struggle against disease is concurrently a struggle for human justice.

Hidden from the world, the leprosaria suddenly becomes a center of interest after Monsieur Querry arrives.

An ex-husband and father, ex-lover, ex-Catholic and ex-architect, Querry abandons Europe for anonymity in a place far removed from civilization. Although he professes to be a "burnt-out case," no longer of use to anyone, this does not prevent others, particularly Montague Parkinson and Marie Rycker, from using him. Ironically, Querry reenters human affairs while at the leprosaria, but his reentry leads to his death. After being shot as an adulterer, Querry is buried alongside other impenitent sinners in the village's unkempt cemetery.

Luc. Regional capital that is ten days' journey by steamship and four days' journey by road from the leprosaria. Its cathedral, government buildings, hotel, and modern pink flats make it a feeble replica of a contemporary European city. At the invitation of the governor, Europeans gather here to socialize under strict rules of propriety and etiquette. Querry goes to Luc on two occasions. First, to locate an electrical apparatus for Dr. Colin, and then months later to bring Marie Rycker to see a doctor about her presumed pregnancy. During his latter visit, he is compromised by being found in Marie Rycker's hotel room at night in order to tell her a bedtime story.

Palm oil plantation. Managed by André Rycker and located some six hours from the capital at the first ferry on the road from Luc to the leprosaria. The "ramshackle factory" is ugly but functional, and the governor has previously "decorated" Rycker for the work he has accomplished here. During his last leave in Europe, Rycker marries a young woman, Marie, and for two years he keeps her isolated on the plantation so he can educate her about her duties as a good Catholic wife. Like his factory itself, Rycker's marriage falls into a shambles, as Rycker squeezes every drop of genuine human love from it. Marie dislikes her husband as much as she dislikes the rancid blasts of hot air that emanate from his palm-oil furnaces. While Rycker patronizes Marie with eloquent speeches about Christian grace, she schemes for an opportunity to escape from Africa, having uncovered more than she had bargained for in the unexplored regions of her heart.

Pendélé (pen-DAY-lay). Village in which Querry's leper servant, Deo Gratias, grew up, that is an elusive symbol of peace and happiness that are never attained.

— *Joe Nordgren*

BUS STOP

Author: William Inge (1913-1973)
Type of work: Drama
Type of plot: Comedy

Time of plot: 1950's
First performed: 1955; first published, 1955

The process of wooing a wife provides the comedy for this drama set in a remote and lonely roadside diner in Kansas. Human loneliness and its effects add a serious contrast to the basic plot.

Kansas diner. Dingy Kansas restaurant where long-haul buses make rest stops. All three acts of the play occur within this setting. The audience understands that the owner's apartment is above the restaurant and there is a privy out back. These facts emphasize the small-town nature and rural setting of the play. A sense of bleakness, isolation, and loneliness pervades the play. The time is an hour after midnight, and snow is falling heavily. Roads are closed, and the bus from Topeka will be forced to lay over.

When the bus arrives and its passengers and driver disembark, the lonely diner becomes alive with people, each of whom reflects the isolation of the location with a similar isolation. Preoccupied by personal concerns, the characters allow little real communication among themselves. Eventually, a few manage to overcome their personal isolation. However, for the most part, the restaurant becomes a metaphor for the lack of meaningful interaction among human beings and for the transitory nature of human relationships. The play is Edward Hopper's painting *Nighthawks*, transferred from an urban to a rural location. At the conclusion of the play, the diner once again stands empty and alone.

— *H. Alan Pickrell*

BUSSY D'AMBOIS

Author: George Chapman (c. 1559-1634)
Type of work: Drama
Type of plot: Tragedy

Time of plot: Sixteenth century
First performed: 1604; first published, 1607; revised, 1641

This play cynically traces public and private corruption tainting a superior individual; fittingly, its action alternates between two centers of corruption: the court of France's King Henry III and the private residence of Count Montsurry, whose wife seduces the seemingly incorruptible Bussy d'Ambois.

Royal courts. In tribute to Queen Elizabeth of England, George Chapman has France's King Henry III contrast the French and English courts. A place of dignity, decorum, and respect, the English court exposes the deficiencies of the French court, whose rooms of state are a rude marketplace, its lords and ladies rural bumpkins. Chapman uses location to satirize the people at the royal courts, who include unprincipled sycophants who exchange insults, seduce married ladies, fawn at banquets, and, in private chambers, formulate plots. The satiric spirit of the play calls for luxury, excess, and signs of decadence and corruption. Reports to the king visually depict offstage violence in Homeric epithets.

Count of Montsurry's home. Multiroomed mansion with secret passageways, and, near the countess's bedchamber, a secret vault. On stage, the main action occurs in or near the vault. There a friar and Bussy d'Ambois enter secretly at the lady's request; d'Ambois beds Tamyra, the count of Montsurry's wife; Montsurry sets a trap for d'Ambois and kills him. Montsurry's house contains a room filled with instruments of torture, including a rack on which Montsurry has his faithless wife stretched.

— *Gina Macdonald*

CADMUS

Author: Unknown

Type of work: Short fiction

Type of plot: Adventure

Time of plot: Antiquity

First published: Unknown

This account of how the Greek city of Thebes was founded by Phoenician colonists depicts a meandering journey from east to west, reflecting patterns of early migration; it reaches its midpoint at the sacred site of Delphi in central Greece, where Cadmus receives his divine command to establish a new city. The act of foundation occurs at a sacred spring, where Cadmus kills a dragon, from whose teeth spring the ancestors of the Theban aristocracy.

***Phoenicia** (fih-NEESH-ah). Homeland of the ancient Phoenicians, in the region along the eastern coast of the Mediterranean Sea now occupied by Syria and Lebanon. Cadmus, whose Phoenician name means "man from the east," was a son of Agenor, king of the Phoenician city of Tyre, and brother of Europa, who gave her name to Europe. When Europa is kidnapped by Zeus, Agenor sends all his sons, including Cadmus, out to retrieve her. They eventually give up the search and create permanent colonies around the Mediterranean. Like them, Cadmus and Europa represent geographical locations in human form, and their journey depicts patterns of Bronze Age migration and settlement. The Cadmus myth is somewhat unusual in its combination of elements from both Eastern and Western mythological traditions. This is reflected in the Phoenician connections of Cadmus' lineage and the probable derivation of his name from a Phoenician or Semitic word meaning "the one from the east."

***Delphi** (DEL-fi). Site of Apollo's oracle in the Greek province of Boeotia that was known as the "navel," or center of the Greek world. Delphi was the meeting place between the divine and human realms, where the Pythia conveyed the will of the gods to men. When Cadmus arrives at Delphi while still searching in vain for Europa, oracle tells him to give up his quest, then follow a cow—

a symbol of female fecundity—and found a new city where it lies down to rest and call the city Thebes. These instructions from the most famous oracle in Greece serve to validate the status of Thebes as a sacred site, while the role of Cadmus may indicate that Phoenicians really did found a colony there in the Bronze Age.

***Thebes** (theebz). Most important city in Boeotia, near Mount Cithaeron. After following the cow to this location, Cadmus kills a dragon guarding a nearby spring. From the dragon's teeth spring warriors, who found Thebes's first aristocratic families. This motif reflects Eastern notions of humans being born from the ground but also ensures that the city's aristocratic families could claim to be genuinely Hellenic in origin. The city that Cadmus founds on this site has seven gates and famously high walls. An alternative story ascribes the foundation of Thebes to twins, Amphion and Zethus, who named the city after Thebe, Zethus's wife. Thebans reconciled these different accounts by crediting Cadmus with founding the higher city on the acropolis, the Cadmeia, and making the twins responsible for walling the lower part of the city.

Thebes ultimately became one of the most mysterious locations in Greek mythology. A site of close encounters between gods and mortals and between East and West, it is the city where the Eastern god Dionysus chose to reveal himself to the Greeks. Although Cadmus enjoyed a happy marriage to Harmonia, the history of their descendants was jinxed by misfortunes; moreover, Cadmus and his wife left Thebes for Illyria in their old age. After they died, they were transported to the Elysian Fields in the underworld. The myth of Cadmus and Thebes suggests that the encounter between Greece and the East was fraught with conflict, and that the foundation of cities is accompanied by violent sacrifice. Thebes is a prime location in Greek mythology for such encounters.

— *David Larmour*

CAESAR AND CLEOPATRA

Author: George Bernard Shaw (1856-1950)
Type of work: Drama
Type of plot: Comedy

Time of plot: October, 48 B.C.E., to March, 47 B.C.E.
First published: 1901; first performed, 1906

This five-act play is built around the historical meeting between Julius Caesar and Cleopatra in Egypt. However, George Bernard Shaw's interests were primarily dramatic, and he made no claim to historical or geographical accuracy in the play.

***Egypt.** North African country in which all the play's action takes place. When Caesar led his Roman troops there in pursuit of his enemy Pompey, he got involved in a power struggle between Egypt's Queen Cleopatra and her brother and nominal coregent, Ptolemy. Caesar took Cleopatra's side, and this civil war forms a secondary conflict in Shaw's play.

***Alexandria.** Egypt's capital city, in which the play's second through fourth acts are set during the six-month period when Ptolemy's forces were besieging Caesar and Cleopatra. In the play, Caesar uses this time to teach Cleopatra how to be a more effective leader. Shaw's description of Cleopatra's royal palace in Alexandria compares its throne room favorably to the home of a rich British industrialist.

Act 3 opens on the quay in front of Cleopatra's palace, which the Roman guards will not let her leave. In order to reach Caesar, Cleopatra has herself rolled into a carpet and smuggled by boat to the harbor's lighthouse, where Caesar has his headquarters. Afterward, Caesar and Cleopatra live together within the palace. The play's final act returns to the quay, where the victorious Caesar says his good-byes to Cleopatra.

***Lighthouse.** Fortress guarding the entrance to Alexandria's harbor in which Caesar and his soldiers station themselves in act 3 so they can guard their retreat to the sea if they need to leave Egypt.

***Sphinx.** Monumental ancient statue of a creature with a human head and a lion's body near Giza, about one hundred miles south of Alexandria, where Caesar and Cleopatra meet for the first time in the second scene of act 1. One of the world's oldest human-crafted monuments, the Great Sphinx symbolizes human progress, which Shaw believed requires the existence of "supermen" and "superwomen." His play depicts Julius Caesar as a superman figure at the height of his powers and Cleopatra as a potential superwoman; it is thus fitting that they first meet at the foot of the Sphinx. After their meeting, Cleopatra takes Caesar back to the throne room of her palace. Not yet realizing who Caesar is, she wants to flee from the Romans. Caesar then begins to teach her how to lead others and reveals to her who he truly is.

Cleopatra's palace. Secondary palace on Egypt's border with Syria to which Cleopatra retreats when her war with Ptolemy goes badly. The first scene of act 1 takes place in the palace's courtyard. Shaw uses the scene to make comparisons with Great Britain's Buckingham Palace and the British army that are unfavorable to the British. This scene is the only one in the play that does not feature either of the play's two title characters; however, Shaw uses it to set up the situation and to have the guards comment on the dishonorable efficiency of Roman soldiers.

— *Thomas R. Feller*

CAIN

Author: George Gordon, Lord Byron (1788-1824)
Type of work: Drama
Type of plot: Tragedy

Time of plot: The period of Genesis
First published: 1821

This post-Fall poem is set outside the Garden of Eden, from which Adam and Eve have been banished, as their son Cain vents his rage at being condemned to die for his parents' sin. Accosted by Lucifer, who takes him on a tour of Hades and other parts of the universe, Cain concludes not only that he has lost paradise, the only place humankind has been happy, but also that every other place reveals that God has not even given humans knowledge to compensate for their loss.

Lands outside paradise. Complaining that his father has been tamed and his mother has forsaken the desire for knowledge that led to her exile from Eden, Cain agrees to go with Lucifer on a tour of the places that will give him the knowledge denied him by God. Lucifer convinces Cain that any place outside paradise is a place of human ignorance. By accompanying him, Lucifer suggests, Cain can satisfy his quest to learn the "mystery of my being."

Abyss of space. Lucifer calls infinite space the "phantasm of the world; of which thy world/ Is but the wreck." The abyss of space represents all places prohibited to man by God but which Lucifer can show to Cain.

Hades (hay-deez). Underworld that Lucifer shows to Cain to prove God's hatred of man. In Hades, many "good, great, glorious things" have been taken from the earth, just as Cain and his family will be taken when they die. For Cain, this knowledge of Hades confirms Lucifer's condemnation of God. Lucifer urges that Cain associate his well-being not with an actual place but rather with "an inner world" composed of his own thoughts.

*Earth. Region outside Eden to which Cain returns from Hades. He is enraged that his brother still worships a vengeful God who will continue to punish generations of innocent humans. He tells his sister Adah he has seen worlds closed both to humans and to God's light. To Cain the earth seems merely a place of dust and toil. Angry that his brother Abel should still want to appease a bloodthirsty God, Cain strikes and kills him. Not only has Cain lost his place in the family, he must travel even farther away from Eden; he is truly a man without a place.

— *Carl Rollyson*

THE CAINE MUTINY

Author: Herman Wouk (1915-   )
Type of work: Novel
Type of plot: Bildungsroman

Time of plot: 1942-1945
First published: 1951

The naval vessel of this novel's title is the heart and linchpin of this story set in the Pacific during World War II. Like many other authors, Herman Wouk uses a straitened setting and extreme situation, in this case a naval vessel caught in a typhoon, to reveal the fundamental natures of his characters. At the same time, he also uses the ship to show the fundamental problem of a democratic nation at war, namely the need to balance a tradition of freedom with the autocratic command structure of a successful military force.

USS *Caine.* U.S. Navy destroyer-minesweeper on which Willis Keith serves and grows from a spoiled and dependent youth to a battle-tested man. The *Caine* is not an impressive ship, a small and rusty vessel that dates from World War I and is acknowledged by its first captain, de Vriess, to be outdated. However, in its very mediocrity it has a power to reveal the best and worst in each of the characters. From the moment Keith comes aboard, he and the other characters are shown through how they handle the various crises they encounter, culminating in the disastrous typhoon. Captain Queeg proves unequal to the task of command time and time again, and finally comes apart entirely when confronted with nature's wrath. Keith grows into his role as a naval officer and ultimately shows heroism in the face of a Japanese kamikaze attack, saving the ship while Tom Keefer, the instigator of the mutiny against Queeg, panics and flees.

With expertise drawn from his own war experience aboard naval destroyer-minesweepers, Wouk uses the multitude of small details of the *Caine*, its various compartments and equipment, to paint a picture of life aboard a steam-powered naval vessel as vivid as the stories of Napoleonic sailing warships created by Patrick O'Brien and C. S. Forester. The *Caine* in essence becomes another character of the novel, complete with its own foibles and peculiarities with which the human characters must deal. Its name, which evokes the biblical figure of Cain and the mark placed upon him by God for slaying his own brother, is regarded by many of the novel's characters as a sign that the ship and everyone aboard are cursed.

***Pacific Ocean.** Region in which the *Caine* operates, moving between California and the Marianna Islands. The novel's pivotal moment comes in the midst of a powerful tropical storm that tests Queeg and his officers to their breaking points. At once both a place of testing and a meteorological event, the incident is based on an actual historical typhoon, one of two through which Ad-

miral William F. Halsey took a U.S. naval fleet in 1944. Because of the extensive damage sustained by Halsey's fleet in those storms, there was serious talk of relieving Halsey of his command. However, these larger historical and political issues are far from the minds of the officers and crew of the *Caine* as they battle the elements. They are concerned only with keeping the ship afloat long enough to get through the storm. Queeg, so demanding of the privileges and prerogatives of his command in ordinary times, fails to act decisively. Believing that his incapacity constitutes an immediate danger to the ship's survival, the executive officer temporarily relieves him of command in an act that becomes the "mutiny" of the novel's title.

***Pearl Harbor.** U.S. Navy base on Oahu in the Hawaiian Islands. Here Keith faces a powerful temptation to dodge the trials of assignment aboard the *Caine*. While waiting for the ship to return from a lengthy mission at sea, Keith plays the piano to entertain at an admiral's party, and the admiral is pleased enough by his performance to offer him a staff position, far from the front lines. Although Keith seriously considers it, a letter about honor and duty from his dying father leaves him convinced that he must not attempt to evade his responsibility to report for duty aboard the *Caine*, where he undergoes the trials that will make a man of him.

***Columbia University.** New York institution of higher learning where Keith trains as an officer candidate and is first introduced to Navy life. In its spartan buildings and parade grounds Keith makes his break from his mother's dominance and learns the Navy way, sometimes illogical but always right by definition.

— *Leigh Husband Kimmel*

CAKES AND ALE: Or, The Skeleton in the Cupboard

Author: W. Somerset Maugham (1874-1965)
Type of work: Novel
Type of plot: Social satire

Time of plot: Late 1920's
First published: 1930

Although Edwardian London, generally, and the Bloomsbury district with its pseudo-sophisticated literary life, in particular, are this novel's main setting, the novel's animating mise-en-scène is the Kentish port town of Blackstable, which serves the novel as a reference point for all the action except a dramatic epilogue that flashes forward to Yonkers.

*London.** Britain's great city, like New York and Paris, hosts the literary marketplace where Edward Driffield, perhaps the last of the great Victorian novelists, has risen from the modest ambience of Blackstable in rural Kent County to eminence largely because he outlived temporary fashions. An opportunist named Alroy Kear—a minor novelist but one seasoned in Bloomsburyan deceptions—finds, in orchestrating the dead Driffield's life, that he must deal with Blackstable and what he deems the unmarketability of the "provincial." Through the sensitive lens of novelist Willie Ashenden, now middle-aged and humanely cynical, W. Somerset Maugham ushers the reader into literary London, a breeding ground for self-importance and false appearances, a wasteland in which one writer's longevity and another's sycophancy can flourish under art's protective canopy.

Blackstable. Class-conscious Victorian village in Kent, where a few ruling families rule the roost. When Alroy Kear, Driffield's fatuous biographer, asks Willie Ashenden as a favor to recall his teenage encounters with the great author and his first wife, a former barmaid named Rosie Gann Driffield, Willie's memories take over chapters 5 to 10. They go far beyond the superficial responses to Kear to become a social guide to Blackstable and its stratified townscape in late Victorian England. Snobbery is rampant and nowhere more prevalent than in the parentless Willie's life in the household of his aunt and uncle, the vicar of Blackstable.

Blackstable is based on Whitstable, which lies six miles north of Canterbury and was the place where at age ten Maugham began the classically deprived life that he dramatized in his finest novel, *Of Human Bondage* (1915). Willie, at fifteen, has long since taken on the snobbish colorations of Blackstable. He shares his uncle's attitude of superiority and his disdain for one of Blackstable's economic props, the tourist trade, which the vicar refers to as the "rag-tag and bobtail" of summer visitors from London. "I accepted the conventions of my class and Blackstable as if they were the laws of Nature," Ashenden admits. In this novel of passage, Blackstable, for all its provinciality, provides the setting for mostly good deeds, London for mostly bad.

It is in Blackstable that the tyro Willie learns that life offers more than conformity to the Calvinistic dictates of the Blackstable vicar. There he learns to ride a bicycle—a joyous new conveyance for late-Victorians—and to do brass rubbings. It is in Blackstable that he first experiences unconditional goodness—an essence in Rosie that he will powerfully defend to Kear and Amy Driffield. Not accidentally, it is in Blackstable, not London, that Willie squelches Kear and Amy with praise for Rosie, whom they hold in contempt, as one "who loved to make people happy [and who] loved love."

Ferne Court. Home of the Driffields in Blackstable where the widowed Amy lives alone but where, to her dismay, fans of Edward visit. This house is the scene of Willie's vigorous defense of Rosie.

*Yonkers.** City, a few miles west of New York which in the early years of the twentieth century was populated by immigrants like Rosie. It is the setting for Rosie's climactic revelations in her book-ending reunion with Willie, who comes to Broadway for the opening of his play. In Yonkers, Rosie finds a place, conveniently remote from England, where she can reveal to the only person who will fully understand the one great sorrow of her life.

— *Richard Hauer Costa*

CALEB WILLIAMS

Author: William Godwin (1756-1836)
Type of work: Novel
Type of plot: Detective and mystery

Time of plot: Eighteenth century
First published: Things as They Are: Or, The Adventures of Caleb Williams, 1794

One of the earliest novels of detection and suspense, this book contains settings symbolizing the author's contention that social forces in England serve only to perpetuate established power.

Falkland's Manor. Country house of the intelligent and well-read English nobleman Ferdinando Falkland. This manor house acts as a focal point for the central theme of the novel: that even the most virtuous and intelligent of people can be corrupted by inherited social power. This house signifies the corruption of Falkland, who personally combines great intelligence with arrogance. When the novel's hero takes a position as secretary to Falkland, his movement through the house symbolizes his growing knowledge that Falkland has committed murder. Falkland's efforts to keep his criminality hidden are symbolized by the locked library and chest at the center of the mansion. In a plot movement similar to a fairy-tale, Caleb unlocks hidden and dangerous knowledge when he sneaks into the locked room; there he learns that Falkland has committed murder and allowed others to take the blame for it.

Village. Unnamed English country village populated by poor but honest farmers and overbearing noblemen, this setting demonstrates William Godwin's concept that people should govern themselves by reason and not by inherited laws and conditions. The landscape of this setting is not described beyond a few simple structures—a few mansions, some simple dwellings, and a few village greens—but the human settings are emphasized. The antagonist in the village is Tyrrel, a vicious and violent nobleman, and it is clear that within this setting Falkland and Tyrrel will eventually struggle for dominance. This struggle is characterized as an abuse of reason and justice, and Falkland—despite his education and civility—is quick to jettison reason if his pride is wounded. A key secondary character cautions Falkland, "You have impetuosity, and an impatience of imagined dishonour, that if once set wrong, may make you as eminently mischievous." After Falkland murders Tyrrel, this prediction comes true with Falkland allowing the blame for the murder to fall onto a poor family that had been victimized by Tyrrel. Falkland's concern for his reputation, instead of for the lives of the farmers, drives home Godwin's point here.

From the execution onward, the later settings of the novel demonstrate Falkland's intention to eliminate Caleb Williams, the only person with certain knowledge of the murder. Falkland marshals the many social institutions of England to control Caleb. As Caleb goes from location to location he learns about the vast extension of noble power in eighteenth century England.

*****London.** Capital and largest city of Great Britain, which Godwin uses to demonstrate that Caleb cannot hide from Falkland's power. London is not extensively described in this novel, giving the sense that the place is intended to function symbolically. Although London may seem like a place of refuge, given its size and mixed population, it does not provide much rest for Caleb. In fact, the paucity of description of the city parallels the futility of Caleb's search for shelter. There is literally nowhere he can hide himself for long. In London, Caleb disguises himself and takes a false identity, yet finds that Falkland has hired a police agent, Gines, and has published wanted posters for his arrest.

Welsh village. Last place of shelter for Caleb, a rural location where he believes he is free from Falkland. Caleb eventually escapes from London and wanders into Wales, where he is initially accepted by the rural people. Although he takes a job and begins to participate in social life, Caleb is soon apprehended by Gines and subjected to Falkland's abusive power.

Caleb's prison cell. Locked cell, containing only a bed and a small table. Caleb dies here under the observation of Falkland's agents. In the first version of the novel, Godwin ended his story with Caleb's death in a locked room, with the strong implication that he had been poisoned by Gines. This scene was cut from later versions of the novel and was replaced by a scene in which Caleb talks Falkland into admitting his guilt and letting Caleb go free. This setting is, however, more appropriate for the original ending. First, it symbolizes Falkland's interest in keeping knowledge of his guilt locked away; as in the first setting, the mansion house, the reality of murder is locked up and controlled. In the second place, it demonstrates Godwin's contention that social power exists in England only to perpetuate itself by whatever means necessary; in this sense, Caleb's locked death chamber signifies the lifelong control society has over the individual, who lives or dies at the command of those with power.

— *Michael R. Meyers*

CALL IT SLEEP

Author: Henry Roth (1906-1995)
Type of work: Novel
Type of plot: Bildungsroman

Time of plot: 1907-1913
First published: 1934

An evocation of the European immigrant experience at the beginning of the twentieth century, this novel is set in two real, crowded, working-class neighborhoods of New York City, Brownsville and the Lower East Side, where indigent newcomers, including young Henry Roth himself, settled.

Ellis Island. Official processing center in New York Harbor, where, like thousands of other immigrants in 1907, David Schearl and his mother Genya first set foot in America. They are met by Genya's husband Albert, who has preceded them across the Atlantic and has been living in Brownsville and working as a printer. Albert accompanies his wife and son on a ferry from Ellis Island to the city, where they begin their lives together as a new American family. Genya's first words, a remark about having arrived in "the Golden Land," highlight the novel's attention to its urban setting.

Lower East Side. Congested section of Manhattan where European immigrants, particularly Jews, settled soon after arriving in the United States. David Schearl and his parents live on the fourth floor of a tenement house on 9th Street and Avenue D. The novel is largely restricted to the consciousness of a frightened, confused little boy who, except for an unfortunate excursion with his father on his milk route, rarely ventures beyond the turbulent streets immediately surrounding his building. In addition to the family apartment itself, significant events occur on the roof of the building. Roth's Lower East Side is a vibrant, polyglot community, terrifying to a young newcomer but inspiring to an author. Roth later credited this urban setting for much of the stimulus to write *Call It Sleep*.

Brownsville. Poor section of Brooklyn, New York, in which the Schearl family lives in a tenement on Bahrdee Street. Later, the family moves across the East River to Manhattan, where Albert Schearl finds work as a milkman. Though David's young friend Yussie talks of having come to Brownsville from Brooklyn, Brownsville is in fact part of Brooklyn, which is in turn one of the five boroughs that constitute New York City. The cellar in the Brownsville building figures significantly in David's heightened imagination.

Veljish. Town in Galicia, Austria, which is David's mother Genya's hometown. Although none of *Call It Sleep* itself is actually set there, Veljish, whose idyllic rural landscape contrasts sharply with urban New York, figures prominently in the wistful memories that David overhears Genya sharing with her sister Bertha in a Polish that he does not entirely understand.

Cheder. School for instruction in the Jewish religion, which is tyrannized over by Reb Yidel Pankower and which David is forced to attend. It is here, in a squalid schoolroom on the Lower East Side, that David reads Isaiah's account of the angel with burning coal.

Candy store. Owned by David's Aunt Bertha and her husband Nathan. When David brings him to the store, on Kane Street on the Lower East Side, his Polish friend Leo makes sexual advances toward David's cousin Esther.

Metropolitan Museum of Art. Destination of a rare uptown Manhattan expedition by David and Aunt Bertha, a temple of high culture in which the two outsiders become hopelessly lost trying to find their way out.

Precinct police station. Young David is brought here when, wandering too far beyond the family tenement in Brownsville, he becomes lost.

— *Steven G. Kellman*

THE CALL OF THE WILD

Author: Jack London (1876-1916)
Type of work: Novel
Type of plot: Adventure

Time of plot: 1897
First published: 1903

The vast Yukon River basin is the main setting in this novel. The sense of place is key to this story, because the harsh realities of survival in this unforgiving environment gradually transform Buck, a thoroughly domesticated family dog, into the ferocious leader of a wolf pack.

*Yukon River basin. Region of mountains, glaciers, forests, and rivers. This place was well known to Jack London, an eager participant in the Klondike gold rush of 1897. Buck, stolen from Judge Miller's place in California, is taken north where he is pressed into service as a sled dog, repeatedly making the grueling round trip between Dyea, on the coast, and Dawson, the rough-hewn territorial capital more than four hundred miles inland. In winter, this trip encompasses 95 miles of ice-packed lakes and 350 miles of frozen river. The lakes (Marsh, Tagish, Bennett, and Laberge), the differing stretches of the river (Thirty Mile, Five Fingers, and Hootalinqua), and the intersections of other rivers (Big Salmon, Little Salmon, and Pelly) become the weary round in which Buck's transformation to wildness evolves. He becomes increasingly aware of the world beyond the sphere of man. Buck senses in the cold and the silence of the vast wilderness surrounding him a primitive call to run free. Eventually the weary dog is sold to Charles, Mercedes, and Hal, hopelessly inept and ill-prepared prospectors. They mistreat their dogs, finally starving them and beating them unmercifully. Buck is saved from death at their hands by John Thornton, a prospector encamped for the winter where the White River flows into the Yukon.

Thornton's river camp. Temporary winter camp at the mouth of the White River. After John Thornton saves his life, Buck begins to heal in body and spirit as the spring thaw weakens the iron grasp of winter on the landscape. John Thornton, unable to accompany his partners earlier because of frostbitten feet, has also healed in this place, and he and Buck form a bond unlike any Buck has ever experienced. As the days lengthen and the air grows warmer, Buck begins to venture more often deep into the forest of spruce and birch, feeling more strongly the call to the life of his ancient ancestors, but always the love he bears Thornton calls him back to John's campfire each evening. Later, John's partners return for him and the prospectors continue their year-round search for gold along the Yukon River, ranging as far away as Circle, more than five hundred miles downstream. During these travels, Buck becomes ever more at home in the wild and remains attached to the world of man only because of his tie to Thornton.

Thornton's valley camp. Lodge in a mountain valley. In their endless search for gold, John and his partners sled up the Yukon River from Dawson. They continue along the Stewart River until it loses itself in the uncharted reaches of the Mackenzie Mountains. High along this backbone of the continent, they wander from valley to valley until in the spring they find a stream rich in gold deposits. Here they stay, working tirelessly, piling up sacks of gold beside the lodge. Buck is free to roam the wild country at will for days at a time, and deeply buried primordial instincts become ever stronger as he encounters free-ranging wolves. Finally, when he returns to camp and discovers John and his partners have been murdered by raiding Yeehats, Buck's last bond with civilization is severed.

Buck kills two of the Indians as they flee the camp and shortly thereafter establishes his dominance over the wolf pack. Among the Yeehats, Buck becomes a legend, a Ghost Dog who runs at the head of the wolves through the high mountain valleys.

— *Beverly Haskell Lee*

CAMEL XIANGZI

Author: Lao She (Shu Qingchun, 1899-1966)
Type of work: Novel
Type of plot: Naturalism
Time of plot: 1930's

First published: Lo-T'o Hsiang-tzu, 1936 (English translation, 1945 as *Rickshaw Boy*; 1979 as *Rickshaw*; 1979 as *Camel Xiangzi*)

This novel of a Beijing rickshaw-puller's unhappy life is set in the city of the author's birth. A member of a poor but respectable family of an imperial guardsman, Lao She knew Beijing intimately. His novel's ironically named protagonist, Xiangzi ("Lucky"), is depicted as a simple, honest, hard-working former peasant who loves the capital city so much that he would never return to the countryside. Lao She peppers his novel with references to various city gates, roadways, and districts both within and without the city walls. All can still be located, but many would be unrecognizable to inhabitants of the 1930's.

***Beijing (Peking)** (bay-zhing). Present-day and historical capital of China. At the time of Lao She's story, Chiang Kai-shek's Nationalist government moved the national capital southward to Nanjing (Nanking), and Beijing (northern capital) was renamed "Beiping" (northern peace). Readers consulting the several translations of this work may be confused by different renderings of this and other place names, but all refer to known places in and around Beijing. Most of the novel takes place in the section of Beijing west of the Forbidden City in the northern walled section where Lao She lived as a boy.

Much of the book takes place on the streets of Beijing where Xiangzi (Hsiang-tzu in earlier editions) contends with the vagaries of Beijing's weather, interference by police, and the aggravation of traffic. Hard, sweaty work punctuates the boredom of waiting for fares at rickshaw stands or teahouses. Indeed working in the streets, Xiangzi is separated from the private lives of both the poor and the rich.

Rickshaw yard. Place adjacent to a section where many large residences of Qing elite families live side-by-side with more modest dwellings of ordinary Manchu bannermen. The large, but not palatial houses in which Xiangzi served as regular employee were found in narrow alleys (*hutong*) of this section and were surrounded by high blackish-gray brick walls entered through stout wooden gates.

— *David D. Buck*

CAMILLE

Author: Alexandre Dumas, *fils* (1824-1895)
Type of work: Drama
Type of plot: Sentimental

Time of plot: Nineteenth century
First performed: 1852; first published, 1852 as *La Dame aux camélias* (English translation, 1856)

This play unfolds in the mid-nineteenth century world of a high-class Parisian courtesan, providing an opportunity for beautiful costumes, lavish scenery, and glamorous actors that reflect the glamour of mid-nineteenth century Paris, which is contrasted to the simpler life of the country.

***Paris.** Already the City of Light at the time Alexandre Dumas wrote this play, France's capital city is the scene of pleasure, artistic embellishment, and, finally, true love. The courtesan Marguerite Gautier (nicknamed "Camille") moves about the city in her fine carriage, provided by wealthy patrons, graces a theater box every evening, adorns herself in cashmere, velvet, and jewels, and pays as much as an average man's wages each day for her signature white camellias. However, Paris, where she plies her scorned trade, is also a city of contagion, jealous lust, gambling, duels, and fatal extravagance that she longs to escape.

*Auteuil** (OH-tei). District on the western outskirts of Paris. In a villa at Auteuil, a few miles from the depravities of Paris, Marguerite and her sincere young lover, Armand, enjoy a brief interlude to savor their mutual love. The health of the consumptive Marguerite improves in this idyllic setting, but even here, one may not live without money, and Armand's humorless and earnest father eventually intrudes to drive Marguerite away from his son. True to the myth of love in the Western world, this ethereal and pastoral existence cannot last. In order not to harm the honor of Armand's family, Marguerite renounces him and returns to Paris and the love-death that awaits her.

— *Allene Phy-Olsen*

CANCER WARD

Author: Aleksandr Solzhenitsyn (1918-   )
Type of work: Novel
Type of plot: Social realism

Time of plot: 1955-1956
First published: Rakovy korpus, 1968 (English translation, 1968)

As is true of many of Aleksandr Solzhenitsyn's works, the action of this novel takes place in a constrained setting, in this case that of a hospital in a provincial city of the Soviet Union. However, in Solzhenitsyn's expert hands this straitened setting becomes a microcosm and a metaphor for the entire Soviet Union.

Ward Thirteen. Ward for cancer patients in a hospital in the Soviet Union's provincial city of Tashkent. The inauspicious nature of the ward's number "thirteen" is noted immediately by the first of the novel's major characters, Pavel Nikolaievich Rusanov, although as a Communist Party member and atheist, he has never allowed himself to be superstitious.

The ward is a long, drab room with eight beds, each occupied by a cancer patient. The iron beds are narrow and creaky with thin mattresses that provide little comfort. Their occupants are a representative cross section of the ethnicities of the Soviet Union, including an Uzbek and a Kazakh, in addition to ethnic Russians. These men have also occupied a wide variety of positions in life, from prison guard to researcher. Rusanov regards having to share accommodations with such lowly persons an insult to his dignity and strives continually to get a private room, which he regards as his due as a party member.

In contrast, the novel's other major character, former prisoner Oleg Kostoglotov, regards the ward's meager accommodations as something to be fought for. Because he has come from his place of exile in a remote village, he has been able to call ahead to reserve a place for himself at the hospital. When he does arrive and is told no bed is available for him, he stretches out to sleep in the waiting room and refuses to leave until he is admitted.

Solzhenitsyn uses this setting and his characters' responses to it to show their inner selves. At the same time, the cancer ward becomes a metaphor of the entire Soviet Union, riddled with the moral cancer of Stalinism and the lies it produced.

*Tashkent.** Provincial city in which the hospital is located. At the time the novel takes place, Tashkent is the capital of the Uzbek Soviet Socialist Republic, one of the fifteen constituent republics that made up the Soviet Union. (After the collapse of the Soviet Union in 1991, Tashkent became the capital of independent Uzbekistan). Here Rusanov is the personnel director of a large industrial enterprise, a position that gives him considerable power and places him in close contact with officials of the Soviet secret police.

Like many cities of the Soviet Union during the period in which the novel is set, Tashkent has a modern Soviet shell built around a much older city core. The modern Soviet city is drab and industrial—a product of centralized planning with no apparent history or character. By contrast, the Old City of Tashkent, whose history goes back to the Turkic tribes who settled along the Great Silk Road, is an Asiatic city with small shops and houses facing enclosed courtyards. When Kostoglotov, newly discharged from the hospital, walks through the Old City, he notes how different these inward-facing Asiatic homes are from the homes of his native Russia, homes with windows facing the street so their inhabitants can look at their neighbors. Yet he finds this a place he can love, a place rich in humanity.

Zoo. Old-fashioned zoo in Tashkent, holding a variety of animals that are kept in small cages or enclosures and arranged according to the taxonomical groups to which they belong. Here Kostoglotov finds evidence that his country's moral cancer is in remission—an unknown man who throws tobacco into a rhesus monkey's eyes is not described with typical Stalinist clichés such as "agent of American imperialism," but rather simply as "evil."

Ush-Terek (oosh-teh-REHK). Settlement in Kazakhstan, Kostoglotov's place of exile. It is never seen in the narration but is frequently in Kostoglotov's thoughts. It is based upon Kok-Terek, the settlement to which Solzhenitsyn was exiled.

— Leigh Husband Kimmel

CANDIDA

Author: George Bernard Shaw (1856-1950)
Type of work: Drama
Type of plot: Comedy

Time of plot: 1894
First performed: 1897; first published, 1897

All three acts of this play are set within the front room of the parsonage of which Reverend Morell is the incumbent. George Bernard Shaw provided detailed instructions for the play's stage settings, not only directing how furniture and fittings should be set within the parsonage but also describing the surrounding area of London so that the play could be appreciated within the social and cultural background as well.

*****Hackney.** Unfashionable middle-class district in northeastern London; an unattractive place, with miles of unlovely brick houses, black iron railings, stony pavements, and gray slate-roofed buildings. Most houses have front gardens whose lawns are divided by pathways from their front gates to their hall doors. Near the end of Hackney Road is Victoria Park, 217 acres of open space fenced by wooden paling. It has plenty of open grass fields, trees, a lake for swimmers, flowerbeds, and a sandpit for children to play in. A bandstand, cricket pitches, and a gymnasium are also among the park's attractions. The parsonage has a good view over the park from its front window.

Victoria Park is still an important open space in Hackney, with most of the features described by Shaw. Mare Street—the location of a public hall in which Morell is to speak on the evening in which the play takes place—is

the left hand roadway at the park end of Hackney Road.

St. Dominic's parsonage. Hackney home of the Christian Socialist clergyman James Morell and his wife, Candida. Located only three minutes by horse-drawn Hansom cab from a train station, the parsonage is a semidetached building with a front garden and a flight of steps leading up from the path. The tradesmen's entrance is down steps to the basement, which has a breakfast room in the front, used for all meals, as the formal dinning room is used as a meeting room, and a kitchen in the back. There are other rooms on an upper floor, including bedrooms.

The drawing room on the ground floor, where Morell works, has a large window overlooking Victoria. This room is furnished with a long table across the window with a revolving chair at one end where Morell habitually sits so that he can gaze at the park. The table is littered with pamphlets, letters, journals, nests of drawers and an office diary. A smaller table at the other end bears a typewriter, and Morell's typist, Miss Proserpine Garrett, sits at the table with her back to the window. There is a chair for visitors in the center of the room.

The parsonage's furniture is unpretentious, as would be expected in the home of a parson of limited means. The wall to the left of the window is fitted with bookshelves containing theological books. On the opposite wall is the entry door, and next to it, opposite the fireplace is a bookcase standing on a cabinet, near a sofa. A generous fire is burning in the fireplace with a comfortable armchair and a black japanned coal-scuttle to one side of the hearth; a miniature chair for children stands on the other. The hearth is surrounded by a fender and a rug lies on the floor before it. The mantle piece is made of varnished wood with neatly molded shelves, tiny bits of mirror let into the panels, and a traveling clock in a leather case on it. Above the fireplace hangs an autotype of the chief figure in Titian's painting *Assumption of the Virgin*, chosen because Morell imagines a spiritual resemblance between the Virgin and his own wife that indicates the moral purity he believes his wife has.

Apart from the cluttered table, the room is neat and clean. This indicates a difference in the personalities of Reverend Morell and his wife.

— *Pauline Morgan*

CANDIDE: Or, The Optimist

Author: Voltaire (François-Marie Arouet, 1694-1778)
Type of work: Novel
Type of plot: Social satire

Time of plot: Eighteenth century
First published: Candide: Ou, L'Optimisme, 1759
(English translation, 1759)

This novel is an attack on the philosophy of Optimism, which asserted that because Earth was created by a loving, perfect, omnipotent, and omniscient God, it must be the best of all possible worlds. Voltaire's young traveler, Candide, visits most of what in the eighteenth century was the known world: Europe, South America, North Africa, and the Near East. With only brief exceptions, he everywhere encounters human hypocrisy, corruption, and superstitious irrationality, and he gathers a wealth of evidence that Earth was far from being the best of all possible worlds.

Castle of Thunder-ten-tronckh. Castle in Westphalia of Baron Thunder-ten-tronckh, Candide's presumed father, in which Candide is born and from which he is eventually expelled. Voltaire's ironic description of the castle sets the tone for the entire text. According to Candide's mentor, the Optimist philosopher Pangloss, the castle is the best of all castles in the best of all possible worlds. Voltaire immediately undercuts this notion by "supporting" it with carefully chosen ironic details. For example, the castle is a fine one because it has windows and a door, and a piece of tapestry in the great hall. A fine castle would have many windows and doors, and tapestries everywhere to insulate its occupants from the cold stone walls. Voltaire's narrator goes further, describing the castle's 350-pound baroness of Thunder-ten-tronckh, a pack of ordinary dogs that doubles as the baron's hunting pack, and household servants who double as huntsmen. If the castle truly were the best of all possible castles, its baroness should personify grace and beauty, it would have dogs used for hunting only, and would have servants dedicated to training and managing the hunting dogs. The greatest irony lies in Pangloss's insistence that stones were made for building castles, so man has castles. Castles were built for defense; in an ideal world, there would be no need for defense.

El Dorado. South American utopia that Candide and his servant, Cacambo, discover by accident during their flight from Jesuit missionaries in Paraguay. Unlike other locales in the novel, El Dorado truly is the best of all possible worlds, the very antithesis of corrupt European civilization. Gold, which the people of El Dorado call "yellow mud," is everywhere, and precious stones litter the ground, but the inhabitants care nothing for these riches. Travelers in El Dorado—even outsiders like Candide and Cacambo—are welcomed and entertained sumptuously at government expense. The people do little but praise God, as if with one voice, and the king of El Dorado is the very model of the modern enlightened monarch. No one wants to leave this paradise—except the two irrational European visitors, who want nothing more than to exploit its wealth.

*Lisbon. Capital city of Portugal, in which thirty thousand people were killed by an earthquake on All Saints' Day in 1755. Lisbon's earthquake forced Optimists to re-examine their beliefs, in part because it occurred on a religious holiday and candles used in the celebrations caused countless fires. How could a benevolent God permit such a tragedy in the best of all possible worlds? In the novel, Lisbon symbolizes all that is wrong with Pangloss's beloved Optimism. The most generous man in the novel, Jacques the Anabaptist, drowns in the harbor, while the brutish sailor he rescues survives unscathed.

Candide and Pangloss help the people of Lisbon extinguish fires and care for the injured while the rescued sailor, who epitomizes the evil in human nature, robs the dead, gets drunk, and fornicates with a prostitute amid the stench of the burning city and the moans of the dying. To prevent more earthquakes, the leaders of the Inquisition (also leaders of the university and therefore some of the best educated men in Europe) try to appease God by burning to death supposed heretics, none of whom is actually guilty. After rain—perhaps a sign from God the Inquisitors choose to ignore—extinguishes the fires, Pangloss is hanged for nothing more than discussing free will over dinner, and the naïve Candide is flogged merely for listening to Pangloss. Later that same day, another earthquake strikes, revealing the vanity of this "civilized" human sacrifice. For Voltaire, this great capital represents greed, cruelty, and superstition, the real bases of European "civilization."

Land of the Oreillons. Region bordering Paraguay that Voltaire uses to build an attack on his bitter rival, Jean Jacques Rousseau, an Enlightenment philosopher who believed that people were inherently good but were inevitably corrupted by society and its institutions. In a pure state of nature, Rousseau argued, mankind would be governed only by its goodness. The land of the Oreillons has no recognizable social structure or institutions, and Voltaire describes it as the pure state of nature envisioned by Rousseau. Its people, however, far from being good, practice bestiality and cannibalism.

*Surinam. Dutch colony north of Brazil in which Candide encounters a slave who has endured the hell of the Caribbean sugar plantations, arguably the worst place in the world in which to be a slave. The slave has had all of his limbs amputated as punishment for his various escape attempts and now can do nothing but lie in the dust, waiting for his master. Despite his uselessness, he is still kept as a slave. Candide's brief visit to Surinam exposes the European sugar consumers' responsibility for the cruelty of Caribbean slavery.

Turk's farm. Twenty-acre farm in Turkey run by an old man who ignores the outside world and lives contentedly on what he and his family can produce on their own land. This farm illustrates the primary theme of the novel: rather than try to reform or to explain away the evils of the world, Voltaire suggests, people should cultivate their own gardens, that is, improve conditions in their own immediate spheres. The Turk's farm is a model, self-sufficient society in microcosm, wherein each member satisfies a need and each member's needs are satisfied. Candide buys a similar farm nearby on which he and his friends form their own "family," and he ends his travels.

— *Craig A. Milliman*

CANE

Author: Jean Toomer (1894-1967)
Type of work: Poetry and short fiction
Type of plot: Experimental

Time of plot: Early twentieth century
First published: 1923

Panoramic rotating geographical settings—from South to North and from Washington, D.C., to Chicago—are presented in a self-expressive lyrical style. Jean Toomer intersperses poetry and prose narratives that give voice to the invisible and the unspeakable aspects of his African American heritage. The changing settings complement Toomer's exposure to a diversity of lifestyles and relationships amid pluralism, which endorses his claim to an American heritage that reflects the pain of slavery and racial hatred.

*American South.** Although Toomer lived in the South only for a brief period, the experience had connected him to his ancestral roots. He knew that his father was from the South even though he had never seen him. His poem "Song of the Son" expresses nostalgia for the past. Toomer seeks solidarity with his African heritage as he mentions "souls of slavery" and "cotton bales," to record a way of life that was shared by his ancestors. The first part of his book includes prose sketches of southern women whose sexual lives provide a common thread despite their individual differences. For example, Fern is an attractive and available woman who leaves an impression on the males that she is "above them." She becomes a metaphor of a fluid identity that transcends conventional constraints. She can call upon Jesus Christ and also sing like a Jewish cantor; in spite of their regional and racial divisions in lifestyles, all men are eager to please her. Toomer can imagine her in different settings—as a prostitute as well as the wife of a lawyer or a doctor.

*Washington, D.C.** Capital of the United States and the urban setting for the second part of Toomer's book. In "Seventh Street," Toomer's imagery includes streetcar tracks and Cadillacs.

*Chicago.** Great midwestern city that is the setting for the last story in Toomer's book, "Bona and Paul," which brings together a southern white and a northern African American in a transient relationship.

— *Mabel Khawaja*

THE CANNIBAL

Author: John Hawkes (1925-1998)
Type of work: Novel
Type of plot: Allegory

Time of plot: Twentieth century
First published: 1949

This novel presents a nightmarish vision of post-World War II Germany, a nation whose history is characterized by cyclical violence and human predation, and the novel's landscapes are potent symbols of decay and sterility.

Spitzen-on-the-Dien. Imaginary German village in which the new Germany is to be born. The novel opens and closes in 1945 in Allied-occupied Germany with a first-person, neo-Nazi narrator, Zizendorf, declaring that the town is an idyllic place. Ensuing descriptions, however, are anything but idyllic. The season is winter, and a thick fog hovers over everything. The town's architecture has been destroyed—broken mortar and bricks are strewn about, walls are pock-marked and smashed, and buildings teeter at precarious angles. Supporting beams are charred, and a sense of permanence has given way to instability. In fact, the very earth has been scorched and rendered unproductive.

Fires burn along the town's curbs, and excrement pits smolder and send noxious gases through the air. Wells have been poisoned, and the nearby canal is thoroughly polluted and odious. Carcasses of animals and flimsy tar-paper shacks dot the landscape. Banners, which once celebrated warriors marching off to victory, now lie in mud, and a few of those same soldiers, now ragged and defeated, trudge home with venereal disease. All the citizens are clothed in drab gray, and the prevailing imagery suggests feebleness and sterility.

Most inhabitants stay indoors, but those who are active suggest a society of cruelty and destructiveness. Two parallel plots unravel in the night. In the one Zizendorf and three accomplices string wire across a road to snare the motorcycle-bound Leevey, a lone Jewish American soldier in charge of a third of Germany's territory. In killing this overseer, Zizendorf believes he is inaugurating a new, invigorated Germany, free of oppression. At the same time, a figure named the "Duke" chases a child through the streets, eventually murdering the child and serving the flesh to his family for dinner.

John Hawkes served as an ambulance driver for the American Field Service in Italy and Germany during the war and was inspired to write the novel after reading a magazine article about a cannibal in Bremen, where he had been stationed. Thus, the novel's title refers not only to the Duke but, more important, to Zizendorf and the German nation itself. All are predatory creatures scavenging in a blasted landscape and feeding themselves on their own carcasses. To emphasize the circularity of despair and predation, Hawkes shifts the temporal setting in the middle section to 1914 and follows one of the characters from that time to the novel's present.

Sportswelt Brauhaus (sportz-VELT BROW-hows). Chic restaurant and bar patronized by the wealthy and Germany's military elite. Stella Snow, an elderly woman in 1945, appears as a young singer in 1914, singing at the Sportswelt Brauhaus. The season shifts to summer, and Stella is an object of sexual desire. The restaurant is bucolic, with a garden of fragrant flowers. It is decorated by trellised vines and filled with the calls of night birds. Linden trees adorn the horizon, and the rising sun casts disarming blue shadows.

To all appearances, the place is edenic, but a serpent inhabits this garden in the form of jealous lovers and a self-satisfied military. The seeds of Nazi Germany have already been sown in the aristocratic elite of pre-World War I society and are most evident in Stella's marriage to Ernst Snow, son of the restaurant's owner.

Upper World. Mountain hotel to which the privileged escape. After a chaotic courtship, the two retreat to the mountains, where they honeymoon and temporarily leave the growing national tension behind. This geographically elevated place is compared to Valhalla, the residence of divinity, and is characterized as being near to God. For a brief time the new couple appear contented, but reminders of the lower world intrude in the figure of a decrepit horse and stark icons of Christ's crucifixion and death, which Ernst compulsively buys and uses to decorate their marriage bed. No sooner do they return to the troubled world below than Ernst dies and the first World War begins.

Hawkes's Germany is country of terror and destruction, with each generation instructing its young on the arts of self-ruination. Stella and Zizendorf represent the social extremes of the nation—one a crass, amoral survivor and the other a deluded megalomaniac who will surely lead the nation into another military disaster.

— David W. Madden

THE CANTERBURY TALES

Author: Geoffrey Chaucer (c. 1343-1400)
Type of work: Poetry
Types of plot: Romance, farce, fable

Time of plot: Antiquity through the fourteenth century
First transcribed: 1387-1400

Geoffrey Chaucer's greatest work comprises a virtual encyclopedia of medieval literature, exploring almost every genre, theme, subject, and social milieu known to his time, over a historical period spanning ancient Greece to then-contemporary England. One notable symptom of this scope is reflected in the extraordinarily broad range of Chaucer's interest in places, from Africa and Arabia to Yorkshire, from Genghis Khan's Asia to Theseus's Athens. (A published gazetteer of Chaucer's works lists 325 separate places.)

Tabard Inn. English tavern that is the starting point of the poem's pilgrimage, located in Southwark, a borough across the River Thames from and just south of London, at the beginning of the main road to Canterbury—the pilgrims' destination. The owner of the inn, Harry Bailly, proposes and serves as judge for the storytelling contest that makes up *The Canterbury Tales*. The tavern location is an appropriate entryway into Chaucer's world for a number of reasons. It is a place of hospitality and conviviality, in which men and women of a variety of social classes and backgrounds might realistically mingle informally and in temporary equality (as done on the pilgrimage itself). The historical Southwark was a neighborhood that was not entirely respectable, known for its brothels as well as its taverns, and many of the tales represent immoral characters and bawdy incidents. Indeed, in Chaucer's time, many people viewed pilgrimages with some suspicion, as opportunities for rowdy vacations rather than as pious religious journeys. Finally, the first four tales have often been seen as unified by the theme of "herbergage," of the use and misuse of dwelling-places and hospitality.

*****Canterbury.** Destination of the pilgrims in England's southeastern Kent region. The pilgrims undertake the journey to visit the shrine of St. Thomas, located in the Trinity Chapel in Canterbury's great cathedral. The collection ends just before they arrive at Canterbury; its penultimate tale, of the Manciple, is delivered at "Bobbe-Up-and-Down" (usually identified as Harbledown, two miles from Canterbury). The prologue to the final tale, that of the Parson, makes explicit the allegorical significance of the location as the Parson undertakes to show the pilgrims that their physical journey from London to Canterbury is an emblem of their spiritual pilgrimage as Christians from this world to heaven.

*****London.** England's capital city. While the pilgrims themselves leave London immediately, the various prologues and tales mention some fifteen or twenty specific buildings, streets, and landmarks within the city and reinforce the contemporary and local atmosphere of a work whose tales themselves are often set in distant times and places. For example, the "Cook of London" sets his fragmentary tale among the working (and even unemployed) classes in "our city." What exists of his tale suggests that it was to have been an exploration of the seamier side of the city in Chaucer's day.

*****Canterbury Way.** Route taken by the pilgrims along the course of the old Roman Watling-Street, roughly congruent with modern England's A2 highway that connects London to Canterbury. The work mentions some ten towns or place-names along the way, which some scholars have seen as offering clues to the organization of the work as a whole, under the theory that Chaucer must have meant to present these places in the correct geographical order in which the pilgrims would have passed them. Other scholars caution that the fact that not one of the fifty-five relatively complete manuscripts of the *Tales* is organized so as to present these places in their proper sequence constitutes a warning not to press this point too literally.

*****Athens.** One of the chief cities of ancient Greece and the scene of most of the Knight's tale, the epic's first and longest tale. The most important locations within the Greek city are the tower in which Palamon and Arcite are imprisoned and the adjacent garden in which Emelye takes her walks. The men's rivalry for Emelye's hand is finally resolved at the third important location, a circular stone stadium a mile in circumference built to contain a tournament at which they will fight for Emelye's hand. At the main gates to this stadium are three shrines, to Venus, Mars, and Diana. All of these locations fulfill important thematic functions for the poem. The prison and garden are metaphors for life's spiritual and psychological prisons and gardens, which are shown to be far more significant than physical ones. The stadium represents the efforts of the governor of Athens, Theseus, to impose order and structure upon the chaos of the (pagan) world, and each of the three temples is associated with, and revelatory of, one of the three members of the romantic triangle.

*****Troy.** Ancient city in Asia Minor made famous in Homer's *Iliad* (c. 800 B.C.E.). It is by far the most frequently used geographical name in Chaucer's work, although the vast majority of those references occur in another work, his long historical romance *Troilus and Criseyde* (c. 1382), which is set in and around Troy at the close of the Trojan War.

— *William Nelles*

CAPTAIN HORATIO HORNBLOWER

Author: C. S. Forester (1899-1966)
Type of work: Novel
Type of plot: Historical

Time of plot: June, 1808-June, 1811
First published: 1939; *Beat to Quarters*, 1937; *Ship of the Line*, 1938; *Flying Colours*, 1939

Most of the action in the first two parts of this trilogy is set aboard ships commanded by C. S. Forester's British naval hero—first along the Pacific coast of Central and South America, then off France's Mediterranean coast. Through most of the first two books, Hornblower operates at such a distance from his naval superiors that he has the independence of an unfettered sovereign. In the third book, however, he becomes a fugitive in France, longing to return to the relative freedom of the seas.

HMS *Lydia*. Three-masted, thirty-six-gun frigate of the British Royal Navy commanded by post captain Horatio Hornblower on a secret mission to the Pacific. Hornblower is the unquestioned authority over about 380 men and officers, and his ship is so far from higher naval authority that Hornblower has vastly more independent authority than typical naval captains. Operating off the coasts of hostile Spanish colonial territories, the *Lydia* represents the only connection Hornblower and his crew have to their homeland.

*****Central America.** Apart from the *Lydia*'s long voyage to and from this region, all the action in *Beat to Quarters* takes place along Central America's Pacific coast, which the novel depicts as being at the extreme edge of European civilization. Its coastline is volcanic with a chain of slate-pink peaks and vivid green forests on the lower slopes fringing the sea. Forester got his inspiration to write his first Hornblower novel when he sailed down this coast in the early 1930's and thought about how difficult it would have been for Imperial Spain to enforce its authority over a rebel faction in that wild region.

*****Gulf of Fonseca.** Bay on the Pacific coast of what is now Guatemala. The gulf can be recognized by the active volcanoes flanking its entrance. Hornblower makes a perfect landfall after four months at sea out of sight of land. His mission is to make contact with the region's rebel commander, El Supremo. The squalid disorder and repressive political situation ashore contrast sharply with the cleanliness and order aboard Hornblower's ship.

HMS *Sutherland*. Seventy-four-gun ship of the line on which Hornblower commands about 450 men in *Ship of the Line*. Like most large British naval vessels of its

era, the *Sutherland* is part of a squadron commanded by an admiral; however, through much of this novel, it is on detached missions similar to those that Hornblower commands in most of Forester's eleven novels about his exploits. A Dutch-built ship captured from the enemy, the *Sutherland* has a shallower draught and more rounded prow than typical British-built ships, thus allowing Hornblower to fool the enemy into thinking it is French. After the French capture the ship in a desperate battle at Rosas, Napoleon Bonaparte uses Hornblower's ruse as an excuse to charge him with piracy and have him taken to Paris to be executed.

*****Rosas.** French-held Spanish port near France's Mediterranean coast. Here Hornblower surrenders the *Sutherland* to the French after the most intense naval battle in his entire career. His ship is ruined, but it inflicts enough damage on enemy ships to enable the rest of the British squadron to come in and complete their destruction at the beginning of *Flying Colours*. Captain Hornblower, First Lieutenant William Bush, and coxswain Brown are then put in a coach that will take them overland to Paris.

*****Loire Valley** (leh-wahr). Valley in central France that is the main setting of *Flying Colours*. En route to Paris, Hornblower and the others escape their captors and flee down the Loire River on a stolen boat in the black of a frigid winter night. After their boat overturns, they have the good fortune to find succor in the home of a French nobleman. As they rest and recuperate, Bush and Brown build a boat on which the three fugitives continue their flight during the following spring. Their boat trip follows the same river route taken by Forester himself several years before he wrote this novel. In contrast to the sailors' frightening middle-of-the-night escape on the river from French soldiers at the beginning of the novel, their journey to the Atlantic coast at its end is leisurely and almost idyllic.

Château de Graçey (sha-TOH duh gray-SAY). Home of Comte de Graçay, who shelters the sailors through the winter and equips them for their spring voyage down the river. Standing on a bank of the Loire River, the château is about nine miles south of Nevers. During the months that Hornblower stays there, he experiences a genteel and luxurious lifestyle opposite that of the naval life with which he is familiar, and he has an affair with the count's widowed daughter-in-law, Marie. His commitment to his military responsibilities eventually pulls him away, however. The château is a major setting again in *Lord Hornblower* (1946), in which Hornblower visits the Graçays after Napoleon's first abdication.

*Nantes (nahnt). French port at the mouth of the Loire River on the Bay of Biscay. The British naval blockade has left Nantes a dying town, and many of its warehouses alongside the river are deserted. As the point of entry into the open sea, which represents true freedom, Nantes is the goal of the sailors' boat trip, although they are uncertain what they will do after they arrive there.

HMS *Witch of Endor*. Ten-gun British naval cutter on which Hornblower and his men complete their escape from France. Captured a year earlier by the French, the small ship is resting idly in Nantes when the sailors arrive there. Wearing uniforms of Dutch officers tailored by de Graçay's servants, the sailors hijack a work crew of prisoners of war, who help them take the *Endor* out to sea, where they meet a British squadron.

— *Pauline Morgan*

CAPTAINS COURAGEOUS

Author: Rudyard Kipling (1865-1936)
Type of work: Novel
Type of plot: Adventure

Time of plot: 1890's
First published: 1897

A classic nineteenth century morality fable, this novel is the story of a millionaire's pampered son, Harvey, who is saved by the crew of a fishing boat after falling off an ocean liner on the Atlantic's Grand Banks. Rudyard Kipling's strength as a writer lay in his ability convincingly to evoke exotic places and cultures. Although this story is set in North America, it transports its readers to a setting as alien as any of his stories of India.

Grand Banks. North Atlantic Ocean region off the coast of Newfoundland that is the novel's primary setting. Once the richest fishing area in the world, the 150,000-square-mile region mixes the frigid waters of the Labrador Current from the north with the warm waters of the Gulf Stream from the south. The mixture fosters a heavy plankton growth that makes it an ideal habitat for the fish such as cod, haddock, herring, and mackerel that Kipling's schooner catches. At the time Kipling wrote, thousands of schooners from New England and Canadian ports annually converged on the Grand Banks, creating what Harvey calls in the novel a city on the sea. The southern part of the Grand Banks straddled the late nineteenth century shipping lane between Europe and North America, making plausible the premise of the novel's plot. Indeed, collisions and close calls among ocean liners and fishing schooners were a common occurrence.

We're Here. Gloucester, Massachusetts, fishing schooner that rescues Harvey and transforms him into a seaman. Much of the novel's action occurs within the cramped quarters of the boat. Built for both speed and cargo-carrying capacity, the *We're Here* leaves little space for its crew's living quarters. When Harvey first boards the boat, its hold is almost empty. Three months later, when it returns to Gloucester, it may hold as much as 150 tons of salted fish. The schooner's deck is equally crowded with fishing dories, tackle, and other paraphernalia. Harvey's world is thus suddenly transformed from spacious luxury to a few square feet of living space in which privacy is nonexistent. Although the boat's captain maintains a well-disciplined and clean boat, the contrast between the boat and the fastidious upper-class milieu from which Harvey comes is wrenching to him.

— *Nancy Farm Mannikko*

THE CAPTAIN'S DAUGHTER

Author: Alexander Pushkin (1799-1837)
Type of work: Novel
Type of plot: Historical

Time of plot: c. 1774
First published: Kapitanskaya dochka, 1836 (English translation, 1846)

This novel is the story of Piotr Andreitch Grineff, a young nobleman, and his coming-of-age during the violent peasant rebellions led by Emelyan Pougatcheff in late eighteenth century Russia. The story unfolds on the wild, untamed military frontier of the Russian Empire, somewhat resembling literary representations of the Wild West in the mid- to late nineteenth century.

*****Simbirsk** (sihm-BEERSK). Russian town (later renamed Ulyanovsk) on the Volga River 485 miles east of Moscow. In one of Simbirsk's surrounding rural regions, Piotr's father received a plot of land, probably after his career of military service. The town's distance from the civilized cities of Moscow and St. Petersburg serves to show that his military service was, although honest, perhaps less than brilliant. This is also suggested when he reads in the "Court Calendar" that his peers are now high-ranking general officers. In a Simbirsk tavern, the young Piotr loses one-hundred rubles in a drunken gambling bout at the first stop en route to his military assignment. Through this experience, Piotr breaks free of his parents' control and takes his first steps toward independence.

*****St. Petersburg.** Capital of Russia and center of imperial power, high society, and culture. As a nobleman, young Piotr was registered here on paper, though he lived in Simbirsk, as a sergeant with the largely ceremonial Semyonovsky Guards Regiment. When his father realizes that young Piotr is learning little in Simbirsk from his expensive, foreign tutor, he decides it is time to allow life experience on Russia's frontier to educate the young boy. Piotr's father refuses to approve an easy capital assignment and requests that an old friend assign Piotr to service in Orenburg—a town geographically and culturally remote from St. Petersburg.

*****Orenburg.** Russian town in the southern Ural mountain range roughly three hundred miles to the southeast of Simbirsk. In the eighteenth century, Orenburg was the regional military and administrative center of this turbulent province on the Russian frontier. Serfs seeking freedom from horrible working conditions on European estates competed with ethnic German settlers, Yaikian people indigenous to central Asia, and Cossacks for limited arable land. This mix of influences made the region, tenuously under the control of the Russian Empire, unstable.

Bailogorsk fortress. Outpost to which Piotr is assigned and where most of the story's action occurs. It is located approximately twenty-five miles from Orenburg, the term "fortress" being a rather exaggerated description of the small, walled village. The fortress is where Piotr meets the captain's daughter, Maria Ivanovna, a shy, but stalwart woman, representing the best qualities of the simple Russian. The fortress quickly falls to Pougatcheff's men after widespread desertion by the local troops and a minor skirmish. It is recaptured just as easily during the suppression of the rebellion.

*****Tsarskoe Selo** (TSAHR-skoy-ye sih-LOH). Location of the royal summer palace, approximately twenty miles south of St. Petersburg. Translated literally, its name means "Czar's Village." Coincidentally, the town was later renamed "Pushkin," in honor of the novel's author. Alexander Pushkin often frequented Tsarskoe Selo and would have been very familiar with the gardens and palaces that he describes when Maria Ivanovna meets the empress. Although Tsarskoe Selo was the actual place where the empress would have resided, its location so close to St. Petersburg is ironic in that Piotr's salvation comes from the very place that his father was certain would lead to his ruin.

— *Paul John Schmitt*

THE CAPTIVES

Author: Plautus (c. 254-184 B.C.E.)
Type of work: Drama
Type of plot: Farce

Time of plot: War between Aetolia and Elis
First performed: Captivi, second century (English translation, 1767)

A war between Elis and Aetolia, both regions in Greece, is the backdrop for this comedy of mistaken identities. It is set in Aetolia, outside the house of the wealthy Hegio, which went from home to prison to home again for Tyndarus, the long-lost son of the testy Hegio.

*****Aetolia** (ee-TOH-lee-ah). Ancient city-state in western Greece, near which Hegio lives close to an unnamed harbor town. Aetolia is at war with Elis, another city-state, located on southern Greece's Peloponnesian Peninsula, which is home to Hegio's son Tyndarus, a captive since his boyhood.

Plautus's historical sources, if any, for this drama are unknown, but it is likely that any two warring Greek regions would have met his dramatic needs. The war that threatens to separate Hegio from his sole remaining son in fact reunites his family. The Greek setting is typical of the Roman playwright Plautus, who used many Greek plots, characters, and plot devices, though the story's mores are more Roman than Greek. By using Greek settings he could comment on Roman foibles from a distance.

Hegio's house. Though the audience never sees inside it, Hegio's house stands as a symbol of the captivity of his sons, Tyndarus and Philocrates. For Hegio's houseguest Ergasilus it is a place to practice his parasitism, and for the plot is it a convenient meeting place for the various characters. For the Roman audience, the home, placed a short distance out of town, is symbolic of family and the high value it held in that culture. From the beginning, however, it is also symbolic of the disguised homecoming of Hegio's lost son, as well as of the errant slave Stalagmus, who can and does identify him.

— *Joseph P. Byrne*

THE CARETAKER

Author: Harold Pinter (1930-   )
Type of work: Drama
Type of plot: Surrealism

Time of plot: Twentieth century
First performed: 1960; first published, 1960

While Harold Pinter was undoubtedly influenced by Samuel Beckett and the Theater of the Absurd, his plays are sufficiently different to be classified as comedies of menace. As with most of his work, this play is set in a single-room London flat that may be owned by one or both of two young brothers, Aston and Mick. An older man,

Davies, is brought to the room by Aston and given a bed for the night but is threatened and later offered the job of caretaker for the property by Mick. The naturalism and occasional surrealism of the dialogue goes hand in hand with uncertainty of plot.

London flat. One-room setting for the play's entire three acts. The time setting is contemporary with the writing. The room is in a run-down house in a run-down area in the west side of London, several of whose districts are mentioned—Shepherd's Bush, Camden Town, and Finsbury Park. The poor state of the room is instrumental to the plot. A bucket catches rainwater dripping through its leaking roof. The room has no washing or cooking facilities, and there is no heat. The only window is half-covered with a sack, letting in a draft and the rain.

Only Aston's bed is visible; Davies' bed is covered by mundane items that form a surreal collection when heaped together. They include a kitchen sink (a nod to the "kitchen-sink" realism of British playwrights of the period), a stepladder, a coal bucket, a lawn mower, a shopping trolley, boxes, and the drawers of a sideboard.

All these items must be moved before Davies can sleep on his bed. Beside the bed is a gas stove. Though it is clearly not connected, Davies complains about its presence and the danger of fire or explosion.

Elsewhere in the room are a cupboard containing such items as a clothes horse upon which Davies sometimes hangs his trousers at night, piles of boxes and newspapers, and an electric toaster, which Aston tries to fix throughout the play.

There are other rooms "along the landing" that also belong to the brothers; they are apparently in even worse condition. Beyond the window, to the rear, is an overgrown garden for which Aston has plans—he wants to clear it and build a shed; however, it seems obvious that he never will.

— *Chris Morgan*

CARMEN

Author: Prosper Mérimée (1803-1870)
Type of work: Novella
Type of plot: Psychological

Time of plot: Early nineteenth century
First published: 1845; revised, 1847 (English translation, 1878)

Prosper Mérimée's novella opens with a preamble in which its detailed and pedantic archaeologist-narrator describes searching for a historical site; it is meant to establish an atmosphere of normality in which the hero, Don José Navarro, will gradually but naturally come to take front stage in what becomes a lurid portrayal of destructive passion and violence. Much of the geographical descriptions of Spain's rugged southern landscape flow from impressions of Mérimée's own travels there in 1830 and 1840.

Andalusia. Southern province of Spain that is the story's principal setting. Don José's narrative to the scholar from his jail cell forms the main body of the tale; he dwells on his recent life as a smuggler and thief for a gang in which his lover, Carmen, acted as a lookout. His story moves from location to location in a wild landscape made up of hills and gorges where he and his fellow brigands pursued a criminal existence.

As he had done in his first experiment with the novella genre in his acclaimed *Colomba* (1841) set in Corsica,

so now Prosper Mérimée again uses an exotic and colorful setting, not faraway places but rather those with sharply different cultures. Indeed, the Spanish landscape becomes part of the very fabric of *Carmen*. For all that, to avoid offending Spanish friends and sensitivities, Mérimée makes Don José Navarro a Basque and Carmen a gypsy. His 1847 revision of his novella concludes with a chapter on gypsy customs and dialects, but not before identifying the locations in southern Spain (and elsewhere) where gypsies are to be found.

The archaeologist-narrator meets Don José for the first time at a grassy, watery ravine that stands in contrast to the wildness of most other sites mentioned in the story; it is symbolic of the tempo of the novella, which speeds up as its denouement approaches. Eventually, locations in this action-packed drama barely flash by. Thus, this picturesque gorge near Córdoba in Andalusia is described as a green patch of grass near a swamp in which a rivulet gets lost. The entrance of the gorge leads to a sort of natural circus completely shaded by the steep surrounding cliffs.

***Córdoba.** Andalusian city on the Guadalquivir River, where Carmen lives after stabbing a fellow worker at the Seville cigar factory where she worked when Don José met her. Her dwelling in an outlying district consists of a large room with a small table, two stools, and a chest. It is the same place where the narrator meets Don José for the second time. Months later, the narrator visits Don José in a Córdoba jail cell, where he is being held after killing Carmen.

Stag Inn. The *venta* is also described in detail, suggesting the poverty of Andalusia and thus, in some perverse way perhaps, justifying the fairly widespread brigandage then existing in the province and involving the main characters. This inn is in fact a single-roomed shack which serves as bedroom, dining room, and kitchen both for its operators and their guests. In the squalid room, there is a fire burning in the center, with the smoke emerging through a hole cut in the roof. The "beds" consist of five or six mule blankets which travelers wrap around themselves as they lie on the floor. There is a shed serving as a stable some twenty feet away.

— *Peter B. Heller*

CARMINA

Author: Catullus (Gaius Valerius Catullus, c. 85-c. 54 B.C.E.)

Type of work: Poetry

First transcribed: c. 50 B.C.E. (English translation, 1894)

The setting of most of Catullus's poetry, best known for its passionate lyrics about a woman named Lesbia, is the ancient world of republican Rome. Just as Catullus uses a variety of meters and themes in his poetry, his poems also reflect the geographic diversity of this Roman world, which extended from Lesbia's Rome to the Mediterranean region and beyond.

*****Rome.** Center of Roman civilization that is the backdrop for most of Catullus's poems. His verses include descriptions of the cosmopolitan circle in which he lived and wrote. When he describes the Spaniard Egnatius or his Roman friends Furius and Aurelius, for example, he does so from the perspective of an urban and urbane Roman.

*****Verona.** Catullus's birthplace in northern Italy. His affection for Verona is reflected in the poems in which he mentions visits to the city or people and things associated with Verona. Catullus uses Verona and other towns as opportunities to celebrate his love of Italy and to satirize features of Italian life.

*****Bithynia** (bah-THIHN-ee-ah). Roman province in what is now Turkey, where Catullus spent an unsuccessful period as a minor administrative official. It provides the poet with occasion to laugh at himself and his unfulfilled ambitions of fortune-hunting there. In one poem, he presents Bithynia as an exotic place where a Roman official might acquire slaves to carry a litter.

*****Troy.** Region in Asia Minor associated with the ancient city of Troy that was, for Catullus, a place for mourning. In several poems he mentions the death and burial of his brother there, and one poem describes how he grieves at his brother's tomb, dampening the soil of Troy with his own tears.

— *Thomas J. Sienkewicz*

CASS TIMBERLANE: A Novel of Husbands and Wives

Author: Sinclair Lewis (1885-1951)
Type of work: Novel
Type of plot: Social realism

Time of plot: 1940's
First published: 1945

The importance of place in this novel is manifest in the space it devotes to descriptions of fictional Grand Republic, Minnesota, its various neighborhoods, and the other locations where action occurs. One soon sees the many parallels between those staid and somber sites that reflect Timberlane's character and the unconventional and more exciting places to which his young wife, Jinny, is drawn.

Grand Republic. Minnesota hometown of District Judge Cass Timberlane, located in fictional Radisson County, eighty miles north of Minneapolis, more than seventy miles from Duluth, with a population of 85,000. Having lived a large part of his life in the real town of Duluth, Sinclair Lewis describes his fictional epitome of middle America as large enough to have a painting by Jean Renoir, a school-system scandal, and both millionaires and a slum. The city has the prejudices and small-mindedness of smaller towns and the caste system of the bigger cities. Cass reluctantly concedes the imperfections of Grand Republic but nevertheless loves it. He sees it as a new kind of city, a city for everyone, a city of "decency and neighborliness." He feels secure there, but the pull of the city on him is part of the reason that his marriage to Jinny begins to crumble.

Bergheim. Cass's family home. Built in 1888, it is a somber dark green structure with a circular tower and an octagonal conservatory, Some people consider it a "monstrosity" and remember that both of Cass's parents died in it, but Cass himself loves the house. His first wife Blanche hates the house. His second wife appreciates his attachment to it, but when Cass comes into a substantial sum of money and asks Jinny how they should spend it, her first suggestion is that they buy a new house. Left empty for months after the Timberlanes move out, Bergheim becomes the site of yet another tragedy when the Timberlanes' pet cat is killed there by dogs on the day Cass visits the house one last time.

New Timberlane home. Modern house in the Country Club district near Dead Squaw Lake. Built in a modern "streamlined" development, the house is everything that Jinny likes, and has little that Cass appreciates. Its furnishings include new gray furniture, mulberry-colored carpets, and paintings of flowers in an Impressionist style. It has fewer and smaller rooms than Bergheim, and Cass is never truly happy or comfortable in it. He accepts it, secretly hoping that living there will help tame Jinny's restlessness.

Baggs City. Florida community near Palm Beach to which Cass takes Jinny on their first honeymoon. Baggs City is a re-creation of Grand Republic in Florida: staid and stodgy, full of older people who resemble Cass more than his young wife. They stay at the Bryn-Thistle-on-the-Bay Inn, far removed from the bright lights and diversions of nearby Palm Beach. Baggs City provides the privacy that Cass desires, but Jinny bears it for only a few days before persuading him to take her to Palm Beach. There Jinny revels in what Lewis calls the "American Cannes," all of whose people are beautiful, whose houses all made of gold, and whose ocean water is imported from the Riviera.

*New York City.** Site of Cass and Jinny's second honeymoon. Hoping to expand Jinny's horizons and doing everything he can think of to show his devotion, Cass takes Jinny to New York, a city that he has visited before but for which he has no affection. He dislikes the city's hustle and bustle. However, Jinny is both frightened and entranced by New York and loves it. The city becomes for her a solution to her growing dissatisfaction with her marriage. She persuades Cass to agree to move there, giving up his judgeship, and going into private legal practice. However, Grand Republic's hold on Cass is too great, and he soon returns to his hometown.

Hatter boardinghouse. Jinny's residence before marrying Cass. Described as "the hobohemia of Grand Republic," it consists of a dozen bedrooms above the Lilac Lady Lunchroom. Young and not-so-young so-called intellectual, working class, educated nonconformists live there, and Jinny feels at home there. Cass feels out of place when he goes there to court her, but he perseveres.

— *Jane L. Ball*

THE CASTLE

Author: Franz Kafka (1883-1924)

Type of work: Novel

Type of plot: Allegory

Time of plot: Early twentieth century

First published: Das Schloss, 1926 (English translation, 1930; restored German edition, 1982; new English translation, 1998)

This enigmatic and unfinished novel about a man's confrontation with an inscrutable bureaucracy is set in an unspecified country village at the foot of a great castle—a setting that emphasizes the essentially feudal relationship between the villagers and the castle. Wholly dependent on the castle for their land and livelihoods, the villagers live by the castle's rules and are subject to the whims of castle officials. The juxtaposition of ancient and modern images—the feudal castle on the one hand and a nightmarish modern bureaucracy on the other—adds a timeless and dreamlike quality to the narrative.

Bridge. Wooden bridge connecting the main approach to the village on which the protagonist, K., pauses in the opening moments of the novel. The bridge is a transitional point between K.'s previous life, about which only a few details are provided, and his new life in the village. For a long time he stands on the bridge, "gazing upward into the seeming emptiness." Although K. is ostensibly a traveler with no immediately identifiable goal, his gaze upward into apparent emptiness foreshadows the presence of the castle.

Bridge Inn. Named after the bridge near which it stands, this inn is K.'s first point of contact with the villagers and the castle. His unannounced arrival creates suspicion among the peasants and elicits a rebuke by a castle official, who explains that he cannot stay on castle property without permission. The inn, normally a welcome place for travelers, instead becomes the initial source of K.'s alienation in the village.

Village. Unnamed place in an unspecified country in which the narrative is centered. Franz Kafka never elucidates K.'s reasons for going to the village. Although K. claims to have been summoned there by the castle's Count Westwest to do surveying work, he does not know, or pretends not to know, of the castle when an official interrogates him on his arrival. From the moment his position within the village is challenged, K. begins to defend his presence; he claims an affiliation with the castle in his capacity as a commissioned land surveyor and tries to legitimize his position by becoming engaged to Frieda, a barmaid at the Gentleman's Inn who is the former mistress of Klamm, a high castle official.

The village also represents a community from which

K. is excluded on the most fundamental levels. K. attempts to create a place for himself within that community, which leads him to his interminable and ultimately unsuccessful efforts to reach the castle.

Westwest's Castle. The castle represents a legitimizing authority, whose approval is necessary for K.'s future as a citizen of the village. Throughout the novel, the castle is both the focus of his ambition and an enemy that must be conquered. His efforts to gain access to the castle and its officials resemble, in comic and tragic ways, the efforts of a knight to breach a fortress. That his goal is misplaced seems evident from his initial examination of the castle's physical structure. His early impressions about its grandeur are contradicted when he gets a closer look and finds that it is "neither an old knight's fortress nor a magnificent new edifice, but a large complex, made up of a few two-story buildings and many lower, tightly packed ones." As the story progresses, K. discovers more details about the castle and its officials that undermine their largely self-proclaimed authority. However, he remains undeterred in his desire to reach the castle.

Gentleman's Inn. Village inn frequented by castle officials that affords K. his closest proximity to the workings of the castle. From the inn, K. almost reaches the castle but is overcome by sleep during an interview with Bürgel, a castle secretary. The Gentleman's Inn also provides the only substantive information about castle procedures. Following his interview with Bürgel, K. witnesses clerks delivering and retrieving files from castle officials in their sleeping chambers. Kafka's repeated use of bedrooms as settings for business affairs suggests a blurring of the distinction between public and private life.

Chairman's bedroom. Prior to his visit to the chairman of district number ten, K.'s provisional supervisor, K. meditates on the relationship between life and work within the village. Nowhere else has he ever seen official and private lives so closely intertwined, so closely in fact, "that it sometimes seemed as though office and life had switched places." This point is illustrated by K.'s interview with the chairman, who receives him in his bedroom because he is too ill to get out of bed. There, K. discovers the chaos and inefficiency of the castle's administrative officials. Paperwork is strewn throughout the chairman's house. The chairman also informs K. that his summons as a surveyor was based on an administrative error, which was explained in a memo that has since been lost.

Klamm's sleigh. Horse-drawn vehicle for traveling on snow owned by Klamm. K. tries to initiate a meeting with the mysterious Klamm by waiting for him inside the sleigh by the Gentleman's Inn. Sumptuously appointed with pillows and furs, the sleigh represents the wealth and comfort of the castle's highest officials. K.'s invasion of the sleigh symbolizes his failure to reach the castle by force or deception. After K. refuses to abandon his vigil, the sleigh is eventually unyoked, and K. goes back in the inn feeling that his small victory in standing up to Klamm's coachman and secretary was a hollow one.

Schoolhouse. Village school in which K. gets a janitorial position after being denied his surveyor post. There, he and Frieda, along with his two assistants, move into the cramped quarters of the schoolhouse, establishing some semblance of a family household. However, K.'s quarters are daily intruded upon by the arrival of the students. After being frustrated in his attempt to legitimate his position as a surveyor, K. seeks to establish himself as a needed member of the village community in his role as school janitor. However, his continued efforts to reach the castle eventually drive away Frieda.

Gerstäcker's cottage. Dimly lit home in which the unfinished novel suddenly ends. Although it is unclear what kind of ending Kafka envisioned for the novel, it is evident in K.'s willingness to accept Gerstäcker's invitation to stay in his cottage that he is still looking for any opportunity to gain an advantage in his quest for the castle, despite his continued failures and growing exhaustion.

— *Philip Bader*

THE CASTLE OF OTRANTO

Author: Horace Walpole (1717-1797)
Type of work: Novel
Type of plot: Gothic

Time of plot: Thirteenth century
First published: 1765

Place plays a concrete role in this seminal gothic novel. There would be no story at all without the building itself, the castle of Horace Walpole's title, and this image has come to represent all the subsequent haunted and haunting castles in gothic fiction.

Otranto. Large estate dominated by a castle in Sicily. The massive details of the medieval castle and the rich surrounding territory, ruled by Manfred, prince of Otranto, represent the haunting presence of the past in modern times. Part of the castle's armament falls on Manfred's son, crushing him, and the castle itself crumbles to the ground. Through these actions Walpole dramatizes the inescapable burden of the past. This reveals the pressure of the father on the son and the obligation that the younger generation always assumes to forge something new from what the past generations have done. Moving portraits of ancestors in the castle as well as the dungeons, dark chapels, and other hidden recesses in the Gothic architecture also express this nightmare obligation to prevail, to escape, to make something artistically and culturally meaningful. A new Otranto emerges at the end of the story out of the crush of the old in the same way that Walpole's invention of the gothic novel is forged out of old materials.

Strawberry Hill. Real country estate near London that Walpole himself remodeled into a fake, or forged, "Gothic" castle. His new building looked like the fictional castle, but it was constructed out of modern materials of the time rather than medieval stone. Walpole wrote his story in this house following several nights of haunting nightmares that were probably brought on by overwork. His father was the famous prime minister Robert Walpole, so that the weight of the past was felt personally and artistically.

Church of St. Nicolas. Otranto church. On the title page of the novel, Walpole identifies this location in the Otranto principality as the place where the original text in Italian was published. This literary hoax, or forgery, is supported by significant front matter written by Walpole about the finding and translation of the medieval story for his English audience. It is all wonderful misplacing, or literary artifice, and as such is a textual equivalent of the artificial and yet genuinely haunting pleasures of the Strawberry Hill estate where, in an adjoining personal printing house, Walpole produced the first edition of the book.

Holy Land. Eastern Mediterranean region in which Christianity arose that is the target location for the medieval Crusades. It is also the place where the crushing events that drive the story took place. The exotic East was always of importance in the writing of the eighteenth century.

Falconara. Sicilian principality that neighbors Otranto in which there is no crushing ancestral pressure. Thus by contrast the civility of this estate expresses the heavy emotionalism of Otranto.

— *Donald M. Hassler*

CASTLE RACKRENT: An Hibernian Tale

Author: Maria Edgeworth (1767-1849)
Type of work: Novel
Type of plot: Regional

Time of plot: Eighteenth century
First published: 1800

In this novel, the physical decay of Rackrent Castle in Ireland parallels four generations of the crumbling Rackrent family and the Anglo-Irish social class system that the family represents. In addition, Castle Rackrent corresponds to the era's popular gothic novel convention of imprisonment.

Castle Rackrent. Irish home of the Rackrent family, the novel's primary setting. The castle symbolizes the relationship of England and Ireland during a historical period when a harsh debate over union of Ireland with Great Britain creates a split among the Irish upper classes.

Regarded as the first regional novel in English, *Castle Rackrent* spans four generations of the Rackrents, an Anglo-Irish landed gentry family. Although the class of people known as the Anglo-Irish, the wealthy protestant landowners, had ruled Ireland for generations, many spent their lives in England and on the European continent living in luxury while reaping profits from their ag-

ricultural lands in Ireland. They often left the management of their estates in the hands of corrupt overseers who failed to keep up the property. This absentee landlord system, coupled with a greedy emerging Irish middle class exploited the disenfranchised and aggravated the impoverishment of Ireland's peasant class.

Rackrent Castle's very name emulates the sound of disintegration: The *rack* was a medieval instrument of torture on which victims were physically stretched past the limits of their endurance; *rent* is a word for splitting apart. Indeed, the castle literally disintegrates as the novel develops. At the same time, the Rackrent family, a picture of four generations of the absentee landlord system, sinks into decay as each generation uses dishonesty and trickery (directed particularly toward victimized women) to acquire more money. Intent on realism, Edgeworth spares nothing in utilizing Castle Rackrent as a symbol to reveal the corruption inherent in the Anglo-Irish social system and to call for the overthrow of Ireland's absentee landlord system.

Many late-eighteenth and early nineteenth century gothic novels feature castles, or castlelike houses, to characterize people who are locked within or without. The suggestive atmosphere of Rackrent Castle emphasizes the era's popular gothic principle of imprisonment and the terrifying aspects of women's place in society at the end of the eighteenth century. Sir Kit Rackrent's wife—who, significantly, does not have a first name—is locked within the castle's walls because she refuses to surrender her jewels, particularly a diamond cross, to the estate after she marries into the family. Ultimately, after being imprisoned in a room for seven years, she escapes only because Sir Kit dies. The theme of imprisonment, all-pervasive in nineteenth century literature, is spoken of as ordinary by the novel's unreliable and irrationally loyal narrator, Thady Quirk. After Sir Kit dies, he blames all the trouble on Lady Rackrent's refusal to do her duty, especially when her husband made no secret of the fact that he married her for her money. After the Rackrents go bankrupt, Thady's son Jason, a sharp attorney, exploits the family's weaknesses and winds up with their land.

Moneygawl estate. Home of Isabella Moneygawl, whose father locks her in her chamber when she disobeys him. The novel's second estate, Moneygawl re-emphasizes Edgeworth's political view of the decaying Anglo-Irish social order and her pervasive gothic theme of incarceration. Although Isabella is freed after Sir Condy Rackrent marries her, her marriage only traps her once again—this time at Castle Rackrent, which has become a tumbledown eyesore.

— *M. Casey Diana*

CAT AND MOUSE

Author: Günter Grass (1927-   )
Type of work: Novella
Type of plot: Bildungsroman

Time of plot: World War II
First published: Katz und Maus, 1961 (English translation, 1963)

Like The Tin Drum *and* Dog Years, *the two other novels in Günter Grass's Danzig trilogy, this novella is set in wartime Danzig, a Polish port on the Baltic Sea. Elements of place and time reflect the corroding influence of Germany's National Socialist government and wartime on society's conventional values.*

*Danzig** (DAN-zik). Polish city (now known as Gdansk) on the Baltic that was occupied by Nazi Germany during the time in which this novella is set. Grass re-creates the city of his youth by using such specific place names as Osterzeile and Westerzeile, streets in a working-class neighborhood. Here, look-alike, one-family homes with copycat yards illustrate the sterile, conformist society easily conquered by National Socialism.

*Neufahrwasser Harbor** (noy-FAHR-wahser). Danzig harbor near which the *Rybitwa*, a partially submerged Polish minesweeper, provides the major setting for the story's action. The ship's bridge, which rises above the surface of the water, covered by rust and gull droppings, illustrates the long-lasting destructiveness of war. Joachim Mahlke, a Danzig schoolboy, and his schoolmates spend their summers playing on and swimming around the ship's bridge. Mahlke brings his prized possessions, an assortment of religious items and cultural artifacts, from his dry attic room to the ship's radio room. The narrator sees this transfer of possessions as an act of absurd and "deliberate destructiveness." The minesweeper becomes the last refuge for Mahlke after his rejection by his school's principal.

*Conradinum** (kohn-rahd-EEN-um). Mahlke's school, whose neogothic windows infuse its gymnasium and dressing room, dubbed the "Sacristy," with a "mystical light." The new martial religion as preached by the returning war heroes stands in contrast to the school's humanistic foundation. The appearances of the returning heroes foster Mahlke's desire to win the Knight's Cross.

St. Mary's Chapel. Converted gymnasium, which, in contrast to the school, has bright lights and lacks the "mystical light" and is rendered impotent by wartime Danzig.

— *Wilma J. Schmeller*

CAT ON A HOT TIN ROOF

Author: Tennessee Williams (Thomas Lanier Williams, 1911-1983)
Type of work: Drama

Type of plot: Psychological realism
Time of plot: Mid-twentieth century
First performed: 1955; first published, 1955

This play is set in the second-floor bedroom/sitting room of a rural Mississippi plantation house that is the home of Brick and Maggie. Brick, an alcoholic who has broken his leg in a drunken effort to jump hurdles at the high school athletic field, is confined to his bed. He can hobble about on crutches but cannot go downstairs to the main part of the house.

*Mississippi Delta.** Fertile farming region of the western part of the state of Mississippi that is bordered by the Mississippi River. Brick and Maggie's plantation is located in this region, which is dominated by large cotton plantations and strong family traditions. One of these traditions is to pass family plantations from fathers to eldest sons, but only to sons who have children to continue the tradition. In Tennessee Williams's play, Brick's father, Big Daddy Pollitt, is dying. He wishes to leave the plantation to Brick but hesitates because Brick has become a drunkard, and his wife, Maggie, has yet to produce the necessary grandson to carry on the Delta tradition.

Plantation house. Home of Brick and Maggie, whose large and beautiful bedroom opens on a veranda that encircles the second floor of the house. The room is clearly fit for important people to occupy and hold court; by the end of the play, the entire seventeen member cast has been received there. Also the place in which marriages are celebrated, the room is ironically a soft and beautiful prison in which Maggie's desire for Brick goes unrequited. No matter how she appeals to Brick to make love, he rejects her, thereby turning their bedroom into a place where Maggie feels tormented, trapped like a cat on a hot tin roof.

— *August W. Staub*

CATCH-22

Author: Joseph Heller (1923-1999)
Type of work: Novel
Type of plot: Metafiction

Time of plot: 1944
First published: 1961

This sometimes surreal antiwar novel and black comedy examines the linguistic underpinnings of modern human beliefs, morality, and logic within a realistic setting in a combat zone of World War II. The "catch-22" of the title not only refers to the sense of being trapped by military and other bureaucratic institutions but also signifies a larger "trap" of absurdity that characterizes modern life—indeed the belief that human beings are somehow trapped and powerless in the face of forces beyond their control. A masterpiece of satire, the novel utilizes its setting to emphasize both the basic absurdity and horrific costs of war and to link geographical place to the novel's themes.

Hospital. Military hospital in Pianosa in which the novel opens and to which it periodically returns; it is the refuge to which Army Air Force captain John Yossarian, the protagonist, escapes whenever the stress of dealing with the war and "catch-22" overcomes him. The hospital operates as a symbolic representation of a haven from the madness of the outside world that the war has created. It is immediately evident, however, that the hospital's own activities are every bit as inane and insane as the world from which Yossarian is fleeing. Feigning an indefinable liver ailment, Yossarian utilizes the hospital for many of his shenanigans—such as censoring the correspondence of enlisted men erratically, impersonating other patients, and playing jokes on enlisted men.

The hospital serves as a microcosm of the larger world of war—replete with absurdity upon absurdity. The "craziness" of the hospital is exemplified in patients such as the "Soldier in White," who has interchangeable intravenous tubes connected to his elbows and groin, and the "Soldier Who Saw Everything Twice." These absurdities reflect the nonsense outside the hospital that terrifies Yossarian, who is convinced that people are trying to kill him.

*Pianosa (pee-ah-NOH-sah). Tiny island in Tuscan archipelago, off the west-central coast of Italy, near Elba and Corsica, in the Mediterranean Sea, on which Yossarian's bomber squadron is stationed. The island is the central location for much of the action that occurs—in a nonsequential order—within the novel. The absence of an ordinary fixed chronology gives the novel's settings a larger significance because they are the only features of the narrative that remain fixed.

During World War II, Joseph Heller himself was stationed on nearby Corsica, and may have chosen Pianosa for its obscurity, thereby undercutting and satirizing the self-aggrandizing officers who appear in the novel who direct the squadron's bombing raids from the island. Pianosa also functions as a counterpoint to other locations because its beaches provide some rare moments of tranquility for Yossarian and his friends. Thematically, Pianosa is also the setting for the pivotal and gratuitous death of Kid Sampson and the culminating climax when

Milo Minderbinder actually bombs his own men in a perverted twisting of capitalistic ideals into war rhetoric that at the same time parodies the Machiavellian concept of the end justifying the means.

Yossarian's tent. Living quarters on Pianosa that Yossarian shares with fellow officer Orr. His tent is a site where bureaucratic absurdity invades his personal life, as during the episode when a dead body cannot be removed from his tent because it does not officially exist. Yossarian's tentmate, Orr, baffles Yossarian throughout most of the novel with nonsensical circumlocutions and non sequiturs but finally becomes one of the few men actually to escape both the war and "catch-22." Symbolically, Orr defines the concept that responding crazily to a crazy situation (such as a war) is a valid response while sanely planning one's escape. Yossarian's tent is thus the locus for one of the novel's basic truths and a perception of how to respond to such a truth.

*Bologna (boh-LOH-nyah). Industrial town in north-central Italy, at the foot of the Apennines, that becomes the major target of squadron bombing raids. Whereas almost all chapters in the novel take their titles from characters, the fact that chapter 12 is titled "Bologna" has a special significance. With its long history, dating back to the Etruscans, and its noted Renaissance university, Bologna functions as a symbol for humanist civilization, providing a thematic contrast to the wanton destruction of the bombs, which are often erroneously and erratically dropped.

The concern Yossarian has about bombing Bologna becomes a focal point for the men, who are seen as both willing and unwilling pawns in an American assault on the city. The issue that war gives arbitrary power to some to send others to their death is echoed in the general agreement that it is Yossarian's "job" to get himself killed over Bologna. Through trickery, Yossarian manages to postpone the raid the first time it is scheduled. The second time, he gets his plane to turn back, thereby avoiding the conflict. Ironically, the raid turns out to be a "milk run," and Bologna afterward haunts him, because of his own sense of mortality and his inability to subscribe to a system that insists one be killed.

*Rome. The capital of Italy is the subject of the novel's thirty-ninth chapter, titled "The Eternal City," in which Yossarian goes to Rome after it is liberated from Axis control. This is a defining chapter that culminates in Yossarian's realization that all of society—not just the military—is permeated by the principle of "catch-22." Besides depicting a nightmarish Rome fallen prey to all kinds of brutality and victimization of humanity that a state of war allows, the chapter portrays a city, long a place where the airmen came for rest and recreation (mostly with prostitutes), as a mental state for Yossarian where some sanity (love, pleasure, sensuality) could exist, but which is now in shambles. As Yossarian seeks the kid sister of Nately's whore, hoping to save and protect her, Rome becomes a rich symbol for human suffering and for what the truly human must summon from within in order to survive. There, Yossarian finally realizes that the "catch" of the book's title does not exist; however, that realization does not greatly matter because people believe that the catch exists. Rome, like Bologna, signifies human history and culture perverted and destroyed by war, yet it manifests how civilians, rather than military personnel, are so tortured by its costs.

Yossarian's airplane. Bomber in which Yossarian acts as bombardier during bombing raids. The plane is setting for much of the air action and is the place where Yossarian experiences horrendous fear and horror—such as the bombing raid over Ferrera in which Kraft is lost, or the recurring motif of Snowden and his grisly death. The plane functions as a telling emotional portrayal of the true reality of war and the singular, actual, human beings who engage in it.

— *Sherry Morton-Mollo*

THE CATCHER IN THE RYE

Author: J. D. Salinger (1919-   )
Type of work: Novel
Type of plot: Social realism

Time of plot: Late 1940's
First published: 1951

J. D. Salinger's masterpiece takes place primarily in New York City, where the adolescent Holden Caulfield experiences a painful awakening. The city that Holden comes to know is full of dirty thoughts and dirty people, and the only innocents in a world of "phonies" are children like his sister Phoebe.

*New York City. Primary setting for most of Salinger's writings. Salinger knew the city well; while he grants New York the "big-city" aura for which it is famous, he also paints a picture of the city's darker side. Instead of having Holden attend fancy cocktail parties, Salinger has him staying at the seedy Edmont Hotel and sleeping in Grand Central Station. According to Salinger, New York is a place that brings out the worst in people.

*Upper East Side. Manhattan neighborhood in which Holden's family lives. While his parents are away, he visits with his sister Phoebe in the family apartment. For Holden, Phoebe is the only person who is not a phony, and Salinger paints a portrait of her as pure innocence. Everything in her room is neat and orderly, including her schoolbooks. The whole apartment suggests normalcy and structure, the two things Holden needs more than anything else.

Edmont Hotel. Rundown hotel in which Holden stays. The building represents the uglier side of New York City, and its ugliness is reinforced in a scene involving a prostitute named Sunny and one in which Holden makes unsuccessful sexual advances toward two women at a nightclub.

*Rockefeller Center. New York City landmark with a public ice skating rink to which Holden takes Sally Hayes on a date. While ice-skating should be a happy endeavor, Holden cannot get over the feeling that there are phonies all around them. Holden's feelings are so overwhelming that they begin to spill over into his relationships with others, including Sally.

Pencey Prep. Residential military school in Agerstown, Pennsylvania, that Holden attends. Salinger based the school on Valley Forge Military Academy, his old military school in Pennsylvania. Although these students are in military school, Salinger shows them to be like other children; for example, Ackley's room is as much a mess as Ackley himself. Nevertheless, Holden is impelled to rebel against the school's attempts at military discipline.

Taxicabs. On his way to the Edmont Hotel, Holden asks the cabdriver what happens to the ducks in the wintertime. On his way to Ernie's nightclub, he asks another cabdriver the same question. This suggests that, like the ducks, Holden feels the urge to leave in the wintertime but does not know where to go for safety and shelter.

*Museum of Natural History. New York science museum that Holden visits while searching for Phoebe. There he experiences one of the few places in which he feels truly happy. What he finds there are walls covered with graffiti; no matter how desperately he wishes to hold on to the innocence of childhood, the sight of the graffiti reminds him that he cannot.

Sutton Place. Home of Mr. Antolini, a former teacher, that Holden tries to crash after leaving his parent's apartment. Even here he sees the dark side of life, as he interprets Antolini's behavior as a sexual advance. Even here in the home of a trusted friend, he finds no escape from the predators of the world. He flees to Grand Central Station, convinced that he is the only person who understands what the world is really like.

Wicker Bar. Posh setting in which Holden meets one of his former schoolmates, Carl Luce, to discuss Eastern philosophy. Holden tries to behave like one of the phonies he despises and eventually finds himself drinking alone, disgusted with himself for his posturing. The bar and the people in it are posh and well-to-do, something Holden is not, and his attempt to fit in fails.

*Central Park. Large public park in central Manhattan in which Holden wanders around, looking for Phoebe, before meeting Luce. The children playing happily at the park are, for Holden, a picture of innocence.

*California. The novel is framed by a narrative that begins and ends with Holden speaking to a psychiatrist somewhere in California. Before leaving New York, Holden says good-bye to his sister, telling her that he plans to head westward.

— *Kelly Rothenberg*

CATILINE

Author: Ben Jonson (1573-1637)
Type of work: Drama
Type of plot: Political

Time of plot: 62 B.C.E.
First performed: 1611; first published, 1611 as
    Catiline His Conspiracy

As he had done in composing Sejanus His Fall *(1603), Ben Jonson turned to classical sources for both the plot and theme of this, his second major tragedy. The story of Catiline's plot to overthrow the government in Rome and the heroic efforts of the famous orator and statesman Cicero to foil his plans gives Jonson the framework for a story about a civilization in danger. Hence, the setting of the story in Rome has important thematic significance.*

*Rome. Ancient capital of Roman civilization. Jonson uses a well-known plot to overthrow a government as a means of demonstrating the danger that individual ambition poses to a stable civilization. Here, the city of Rome is more than merely a geographical locale for the play's action. It symbolizes all values that are good, holy, and ordained by the gods. What Catiline's evil machinations threaten is not simply the transfer of power within a city. Rather, the fall of Rome would mean the end of a civilization created on principles of law and reason, in which citizens are treated with dignity and governed through the collective consent of the majority,

expressed through elected representatives. To emphasize the importance of the city, Jonson frequently has characters refer to Rome as "Mother," noting how, symbolically, the city has nurtured its citizens; consequently, Catiline's plot is tantamount to rape. Such vivid imagery helps personify the city and engage playgoers and readers emotionally in the elected leaders' struggle with the conspirators.

— *Laurence W. Mazzeno*

CECILIA: Or, Memoirs of an Heiress

Author: Fanny Burney (Madame D'Arblay, 1752-1840)
Type of work: Novel

Type of plot: Social realism
Time of plot: Eighteenth century
First published: 1782

The title character of this novel is an heiress with no control over her inheritance until she comes of age, and even then she faces a difficult restriction that limits her choice of suitors. Meanwhile, the fortune that she is to come into is overseen by three male guardians, through whose homes she passes, as her inheritance shrinks.

Bury (BIHR-ee). Rural Suffolk town in which Cecilia grows up and where her family has a long history of being rich farmers. Her background is thus one of wealth earned by physical labor, not one of old family name and old money—an important distinction in eighteenth century England. The town of Bury, its inhabitants and environs, represents goodness and innocence, and contrasts with the more sophisticated and duplicitous life of London. After spending some time in London, Cecilia seeks refuge in Bury and stays with her old friend Mrs. Charlton, while her own home is being readied for her.

London. Political, cultural, and social center of England, to which Cecilia goes when she is about to reach her "majority" and must prepare for her "coming out" as a young lady of society. There she stays in a succession of her guardians' home and finds each objectionable for a different reason.

Portman Square. Location of the London home of Cecilia's guardian Mr. Harrel and his wife. Their extravagant house, which is always undergoing some kind of physical improvements that involve contracts with architects and laborers, reflects their own dangerously profligate lifestyle, a way of living Cecilia has never experienced and finds distressing. For example, to prepare for a masquerade party, the Harrels redecorate their entire home.

Violent Bank. Summer villa of the Harrels—another example of how they live beyond their means, while compromising Cecilia's inheritance. The importance that the Harrels place upon external appearances of wealth and position is emphasized by the ostentation of both their homes.

Mr. Briggs's home. In contrast to the Harrels, the London home of the miserly Mr. Briggs, another of Cecilia's guardians, is a painful reflection of its owner's frugality. This home, which Cecilia finds completely comfortless, exemplifies the error of valuing money for itself alone, with no thought to the needs of others in society.

St. James Square. Location of the London home of the third of Cecilia's guardians, Mr. Delvile, and his wife. This home reflects the old name and social standing of the Delvile family and the overwhelming pride that the Delviles have in their family name and position.

Delvile Castle. Country estate of the Delviles. Owned by the Delvile family for generations, the castle is situated on a large tract of parkland. Though impressive from a distance, it shows wear and needs repair. While its past history is impressive, its former glory has dimmed. Nevertheless, Mr. Delvile views the estate as an important part of his son's birthright and as an emblem of the social stature of his family, even though the family no longer has the resources needed to maintain the estate properly.

— *Linda L. Keesey*

CELESTINA

Author: Fernando de Rojas (c. 1465-1541)
Type of work: Novel
Type of plot: Tragicomedy
Time of plot: Fifteenth century

First published: Comedia de Calisto y Melibea, 1499;
revised edition, 1502, as *Tragicomedia de Calisto y
Melibea* (English translation, 1631)

This novel caustically explores how courtly love might have been experienced in Spain in the early sixteenth century. At that time, through such institutions as the Inquisition, Spain was carrying out a massive restructuring of its society. Before 1492, the region was religiously, politically, and ethnically diverse; afterward, all Moors and Jews were expelled, executed, or forcibly converted to Roman Catholicism, and religious orthodoxy was imposed through an increasingly centralized government on all aspects of Spanish life, including literature. It is no surprise, therefore, that the two lovers of the story, who are more concerned with erotic than heavenly love, pay with their lives for their sins.

***Spain.** Although the novel makes no specific mention of where it is set, it is clear that its setting is in Spain during the fifteenth century, when it was written. The author, Fernando de Rojas, was a *converso* (a Jew who publicly converted to Christianity) and therefore a member of a group that was treated with suspicion and subjected to public humiliation. Although the novel was approved by the Inquisition's censors because it offers, on the surface, a straightforward account of the wages of sin, its bitterly ironic denunciation of all forms of hypocrisy and pretense is hard not to associate with what Rojas presumably experienced personally.

Tradition has it that the story takes place in Spain's university town of Salamanca, where Rojas himself studied. Indeed, a walled garden there is known as the Garden of Melibea—a place that figures in the novel. However, these traditional associations are of little consequence in understanding the novel, except perhaps to note that its popularity may be seen as an indication that its views were widely shared in Spain.

Celestina is a strongly moral work, and each place in it is presented in a moral light. These places include the garden, the street, and the various private abodes of the characters. The difference between the public declaration of the street and private desires expressed in private is emphasized by a central literary device in the novel, which (except for short summaries at the beginning of each chapter) consists entirely of the speech of the characters. The novel's frequent use of asides and soliloquies allows the reader to see what the characters are saying only to themselves as well as what they say to one another.

When characters appear in public areas, such as the street, they speak with two voices. One is the public voice, which tends toward elaborate courtesies and big promises. The other is the voice of the aside and of talking to oneself. This voice often offers an immediate cynical reinterpretation of what has just been said, or, in the case of the love-struck Calisto, who talks to himself as he walks down the street, is cause for gossip among onlookers.

It is behind closed doors that people are at their frankest, and the novel is filled with incidents of doors being closed in people's faces, visitors coming to the doors of houses asking to enter or pass along messages, and speech being passed through closed doors. In private areas, Calisto and Melibea hatch plots with their servants and converse or pass along information to Celestina, the go-between and title character.

Although Celestina is an old woman without the education that has benefited the young nobles whom she seeks to illicitly unite, she is by far the novel's ablest rhetorician. She is the personification of hypocrisy, always ready with the high or low speech and argument that will be to her tactical benefit in her greedy pursuit of financial reward for helping the two young rich people achieve their goal. Fittingly, she is killed at home, the place of her plots, cons, and conspiracies.

Garden of Melibea. Place where Calisto first sees Melibea. It is no mistake to associate this garden with the biblical Garden of Eden, for in the first moments that Calisto sees Melibea, his love is at its purest. It will soon be corrupted by the urgencies of his lust and the impatience of his pride, making him ineligible for a return to the edenic state of a lasting union there with Melibea. She, too, will fall short, for similar reasons, of the innocence required of an inhabitant of Eden.

The garden also clearly represents the earthly ideal of romantic, courtly love. In the tradition of courtly love, all that is pastoral and natural is pure and uncorrupted and stands in favorable contrast to society and the city, where deceit, greed, and corruption flourish behind respected facades. In *Celestina*, this traditional comparison is most richly explored.

The garden is also an oasis in which the lovers may speak to each other directly and honestly, in marked contrast to all the other locations in the novel, where speakers' true aims and desires are usually base rather than loving and sugar-coated rather than plainspoken. In this sense the garden retains an element of the romantic ideal and offers an indirect attack on the hypocrisy of Spanish society, and thus, by implication, its program of enforced religious correctness.

Stairs. Calisto falls to his death on some stairs. They may be symbolized as the place between two places, neither heaven nor earth, where it is difficult to keep one's balance. He is a flesh-and-blood man who tries to achieve an ideal courtly love. He fails, falling into lust, sin, and death.

Tower. After Calisto's death, Melibea shuts herself away in a tower, and she soon leaps to her death. The tower has long been a symbol of an affected removal from the nitty-gritty of ordinary life, as for example the ivory tower of academia. In this respect, Melibea's retreat to the tower may be seen as an attempt to remove herself from her desires and her pain. She does not succeed, however, and succumbs to her despair, which is itself a mortal sin, and commits suicide.

Towers are also symbols of patriarchy and social organization, as represented in church towers and modern skyscrapers, which embody the most central and powerful institutions of a city. In this regard, Melibea's attempt to live in the tower may be seen as an attempt to make herself again a part of her society instead of its willing outcast. Her failure to live by society's rules, however, in particular its sternly enforced rule of female chastity before marriage, makes this impossible.

— *Eric Howard*

THE CENCI: A Tragedy in Five Acts

Author: Percy Bysshe Shelley (1792-1822)
Type of work: Drama
Type of plot: Tragedy

Time of plot: Sixteenth century
First published: 1819; first performed, 1886

Based on a historical incident, this drama is faithful to locales in and on the outskirts of Rome, where the historical events took place. Although set mostly indoors in private residences, it repeatedly evokes a sense of the city through descriptions of political intrigues and alliances that shape the tragedy and develop Percy Bysshe Shelley's ideas on tyranny and the indomitable human spirit.

*Rome. Great Italian city in which the primary palace of the Cenci family is built. Outwardly, the palace reflects the grandeur of Rome at the end of the Renaissance. Its accommodations are sumptuous, and it is a scene of great pomp and pageantry. However, the palace is home to Count Francesco Cenci, a decadent and selfish tyrant determined to break the spirit of everyone in his family, in particular his strong-willed daughter Beatrice. Cenci flourishes in Rome, which suggests the city is tainted with the spiritual corruption he represents.

This is revealed by Cenci's relationship with the Vatican, seat of the papal government. Shelley depicts the Vatican, which represents both the religious and political character of the city, as corrupt and hypocritical because its accepts the bribes Cenci pays to avoid prosecution of murders.

Beatrice's perceptions of the city are the most telling. She knows that she can easily find assassins with no regard for life who will murder her father. When her mother begs the pope's legate not to return them to Rome to be tried for Francesco's murder, Beatrice soothes her with this mocking appraisal: "There as here/ Our innocence is as an armed heel/ To trample accusation." Beatrice knows full well that this idealized Rome does not exist and that they are likely to be executed for a type of crime for which Francesco regularly bought absolution.

Castle Petrella. Castle in the Apennine mountains outside Rome that presents Beatrice and her family with a refuge beyond Rome's influences, where Francesco can be more easily killed. Its setting in the wilds expresses the savagery of the murder committed on its premises and the extremes to which Francesco has driven his family.

— *Stefan Dziemianowicz*

CEREMONY

Author: Leslie Marmon Silko (1948-   )
Type of work: Novel
Type of plot: Social realism

Time of plot: Shortly after World War II
First published: 1977

Leslie Silko's first novel describes the crisis of identity that an orphaned, half-breed Indian experiences when he returns home after surviving a prisoner-of-war camp in World War II and has problems finding a place for himself in either Indian or Anglo society. Eventually, he realizes that only by returning to the values and practices of traditional tribal life can he ultimately find balance and a sense of personal peace. The arid landscape of western New Mexico provides not only the setting but also a poignant theme for the work, which emphasizes a strong, tribally based sense of place.

*Gallup. Northwestern New Mexico city on the Puerco River that is the seat of McKinley County. With Navajo communities to the north and west, Zuni to the south, and various Pueblo tribes to the east, Gallup is an important regional center for Indian arts and crafts, as well as an area headquarters for the Bureau of Indian Affairs. The protagonist, Tayo, goes to Gallup to ask a medicine man named Betonie for a special ceremony. Betonie cures with elements from contemporary culture, such as old magazines and telephone books, as well as with native ceremonies. He explains Tayo's sickness as due to witchery.

*Laguna. Tayo's home, the center of Laguna Pueblo culture, located about fifty miles west of Albuquerque, to which he returns after the war. Historically, Laguna Pueblo became one of the most cosmopolitan pueblos because of its position on a major east-west route that later included a train line; the pueblo is also the birthplace of author Leslie Silko.

*Philippines. World War II combat zone in which Tayo served before returning to New Mexico. Recalling that he was unable to fire upon Japanese soldiers because they seemed to resemble his uncle, Tayo begins the novel thinking himself insane and begins his quest to find a ceremony that will cure him of his madness.

*Mount Taylor. Snow-capped New Mexico mountain northwest of Laguna Pueblo that is usually visible from the town. Known to the Laguna people as "Tsepina" (woman who walks in the clouds), the mountain is considered a holy place. Tayo eventually actualizes much of his personal ceremony in the wilderness area by the mountain.

*Paguate. Small village about six miles north of Laguna Pueblo that is believed, in Laguna cosmology, to be the Place of Emergence—the place where human beings emerged into the present world from the worlds below. Flooded underground uranium mines near Paguate represent an evil re-rendering of the natural landscape that Tayo struggles to overcome throughout the novel.

— *Richard Sax*

THE CHAIRS

Author: Eugène Ionesco (1912-1994)
Type of work: Drama
Type of plot: Absurdist

Time of plot: Indeterminate
First performed: 1952; first published, 1954 as *Les Chaises* (English translation, 1958)

Using a single stage setting, this absurdist drama employs place to reinforce the impression that human life is radically mysterious, unpredictable, and strangely comical. The setting that initially greets the audience is fairly realistic and somewhat comforting; however, the characters, action, and dialogue of the play are so frequently bizarre and purposely confusing that the audience soon feels a conflict between the play's ostensible setting and its substance. Finally, as the play ends, the setting itself becomes bizarre, and the audience recognizes that life is uncomfortably mysterious.

Tower. Structure in the middle of a circular island surrounded by a stagnant sea in which an Old Man and an Old Woman live. Eugène Ionesco describes this, the play's setting, in meticulous detail; it is half of a circular room with basically symmetrical windows and doors. The play's initial dialogue indicates that the room is above a vast expanse of water. Two unusual but real people appear and soon there are real chairs on stage, along with realistic sound effects from outside the tower. However, the increasingly bizarre dialogue soon claims that the action takes place in an unbelievably futuristic setting 400,000 years after the destruction of Paris. When guests arrive from the outside world—accompanied by realistic sound effects of boats and doorbells—they are invisible. Strangely, after dozens of chairs are added to accommodate the invisible guests, the room begins to seem realistically crowded and theaterlike, and the play's real audience seems to become an extension of the fictional audience on stage. It is a surprise when the long-awaited orator is not invisible and even more surprising when the orator is a deaf-mute incapable of communicating the main character's important message to the world. However, the most chilling effect is saved for last. After the stage turns to darkness, but before the final curtain falls, the invisible audience makes laughing, murmuring, and coughing sounds, just like a real audience. The imaginary stage audience is thus drawn into the bizarre fictional world, making imaginary and real and certain and uncertain difficult to discern.

— *Terry Nienhuis*

CHAKA

Author: Thomas Mofolo (1875?-1948)
Type of work: Novel
Type of plot: Historical realism

Time of plot: Early nineteenth century
First published: 1925 (English translation, 1931)

This historical novel is set in nineteenth century South Africa, when much of the country was still ruled by black African peoples. The mostly natural land, with its vast open expanses, abundant vegetation, and roaming wildlife, dotted by indigenous African settlements, provides an impressive natural backdrop against which unfolds the life and death of the Zulu king Chaka. The author deliberately relates the wild nature of a land untamed by European influences to the abundance of gratuitous violence, bloodshed, all-encompassing superstition, belief in supernatural forces, and frequent death that characterizes his presentation of traditional tribal life and war.

*South Africa.** The interior of what is now the Republic of South Africa provides a realistic backdrop for the quasi-historical story of the rise and fall of the Zulu founder-king, Chaka (also known as Shaka) in the early nineteenth century. Thomas Mofolo depicts South Africa as a relatively wild country, in which the influence of the European settlers is not yet pervasive. The narrative focuses on the northeastern corner of the country occupied by the Zulu, the richest and most agriculturally advanced area of African settlement. Most of the novel takes place here, but comparisons to the poorer regions serve as an internal frame of reference to show how fertile land gives rise to a more warlike people than the regions where finding food is a more pressing concern.

*Kafirland.** Mofolo's term for the northern part of Natal Province more generally known as Zululand Africa. ("Kafir" derives from an Arabic word for "infidel" that white South Africans transformed into a pejorative term for Africans.) Kafirland lies between the Indian Ocean to the east and a mountain range traversed by rivers to the west. The region is depicted as lusciously green and fertile, without the life-threatening droughts found elsewhere. This part of the country is relatively densely populated and has given rise to large, numerous, and prosperous villages. In the novel, Kafirland is also a place of pervasive witchcraft. Masters in the art possess special knowledge of medicines for enchantment, bewitchment, murder, and killing enemies, as well as love potions. During his rise to power, Chaka relies heavily on witchcraft.

Many natural geographical features in Kafirland are imbued with supernatural powers and linked to magic phenomena. An example of a special feature of the landscape being singled out to explain a magical occurrence occurs at an unnamed spring by a tall tree, where Chaka meets a mysterious man who calls himself the diviner. This man seems able to read Chaka's mind; together, he and Chaka come to wield great power. The novel's straightforward narration of these events bestows on its landscape a supernatural element of mystic proportions.

Qube. Kafirland village of Nandi, Chaka's mother. It consists of many individual kraals—as the walled enclosures built around individual houses are known in South Africa. The huts provide shelter to people and domestic livestock, and their walls are intended to keep out human and animal intruders. Because his mother's village lies so close to the wilderness of the African bush, young Chaka is able to distinguish himself as a hunter. He begins building his reputation by killing a lion that enters his mother's kraal. Through the well-developed communication system that links the villages, his fame spreads more quickly than it could in less densely settled parts of the country.

*White Umfolosi River** (ewm-foh-LOH-zee). River of the water-snake that flows through Kafirland after rising near what is now Vryheid in Natal. As the Umfolosi runs through the countryside on its course to the Indian Ocean, its water and fish enrich the surrounding land. Because of its central role in sustaining life in Kafirland, the Zulu bestow special legends on it and its water. As with other natural features throughout the land, outstanding geographical features are imbued with supernatural powers and linked to magic phenomena. When Chaka bathes in the river, a huge water snake appears before him. Because he does not flinch, a great future is predicted for him.

*Dingiswayo** (deen-gih-SWAY-yoh). Zulu capital that shares its name with a chieftain who invites Chaka to fight alongside him against neighboring rulers. Dingiswayo rules his capital village with peace and only fights to protect his people. Measured against other settlements, Dingiswayo is a comparatively civilized place. There, Chaka is treated with love and kindness. When he succeeds Dingiswayo as ruler, he gives his people the name "Zulu Amazula" (Heaven and the People of Heaven).

*Umgungundhlovu** (ewm-gewn-gewn-DLOH-vew). New capital village built by Chaka. Mofolo depicts life in settlement in a manner reminiscent of life in the ancient Greek city-state of Sparta. Like the rulers of the warlike Spartans, Chaka decrees that the purpose of all human activity must be war. His capital is walled, and its guards are forever vigilant in their effort to watch all entries and exits to and from the city. In the middle of Umgungundhlovu is a courtyard in which state functions are performed as declared, ordered, or commanded by Chaka. This courtyard sees the manifestation of Chaka's power.

The capital is also the place where Chaka has thousands of his own warriors gratuitously killed for what he deems cowardice. This place becomes a sight drenched by unquenchable blood-lust. The sheer magnitude of violence and blood that occurs in this place is extremely disheartening. The capital of Chaka is not like the capital of Dingiswayo.

— *R. C. Lutz*

THE CHANGELING

Authors: Thomas Middleton (1580-1627) and William Rowley (1585?-1642?)
Type of work: Drama

Type of plot: Tragedy
Time of plot: Early seventeenth century
First performed: 1622; first published, 1653

Set in eastern Spain, this play uses a castle and a madhouse as sites to test wives' morals. The play's setting is Spanish, but its English authors do not strive for realism.

*****Alicante.** Mediterranean port city near Valencia in eastern Spain in which the play is set. The play opens outdoors, near a church by the port, with the Valencian nobleman Alsemero delaying his departure for Malta and getting drawn into Beatrice-Joanna's adulterous and murderous plots. The rest of the play is wholly restricted to interiors, as if to suggest women's domestic confinement.

*****Valencia.** Capital city of the eastern region of Spain from which Alsemero comes. Valencia is about one hundred miles north of Alicante—a distance great enough to make Alsemero a "stranger" to Beatrice-Joanna's father, Vermandero, who hesitates to give him a tour of his castle.

Vermandero's castle. Alicante headquarters of Governor Vermandero and the setting for all the scenes in the play following its opening. The castle citadel into which Beatrice-Joanna invites her lover Alsemero represents Beatrice-Joanna herself, with the underground vault in which De Flores murders her fiancé reflecting her sinful depths.

Dr. Alibius's house. Home of Alibius, a jealous old doctor who keeps his lovely young wife, Isabella, confined at home with his mad patients. The madness and folly observed in Alibius's institution form a grotesque reflection of the madness and folly of the outside world. The determination of Isabella to resist "lunatic" adulterous propositions counterpoints Beatrice-Joanna's moral defeat at the castle. The nominally Spanish madhouse actually evokes England's Bethlehem Hospital, an asylum in Bishopsgate, London—especially in a line referring to "the chimes of Bedlam [Bethlehem]." Thus, virtue triumphs in a more English setting.

Hell. Ultimate destination to which Beatrice-Joanna and De Flores are doomed, evoked twice by reference to a country game called "barley-brake," in which couples hold hands and are forbidden to separate, while trying to catch others who run past them as their replacements in the central space called "hell."

— *Margaret Bozenna Goscilo*

THE CHARTERHOUSE OF PARMA

Author: Stendhal (Marie-Henri Beyle, 1783-1842)
Type of work: Novel
Type of plot: Historical

Time of plot: Early nineteenth century
First published: La Chartreuse de Parme, 1839
(English translation, 1895)

The primary setting of the novel is the Italian town of Parma, where Fabrizio del Dongo becomes the focal point of power struggles among Parma's prince, the nobility, and the del Dongo family. Set in the aftermath of French emperor Napoleon Bonaparte's final defeat at the Battle of Waterloo in 1815, the novel is also an assessment of the historical forces and personalities responsible for the fitful disintegration of royalist rule in Europe.

*****Milan.** City in northern Italy's Lombardy region. Stendhal evokes the atmosphere of this region to explain Napoleon's romantic impact on the novel's main char-

acter, Fabrizio del Dongo. Napoleon entered the city on May 15, 1796, the head of a young army destined to change the face of Europe. It is this Napoleon that awakens Fabrizio's ambitions to fight in what becomes Napoleon's last famous battle at Waterloo two decades later. Milan also represents, in Stendhal's ironic prose, a foil to the jaded sophistication of his French readers. In introducing his cast of passionate characters, Stendhal comments that in Milan, a "region quite remote from our own, a man may still be driven to despair by love."

*Como.** City in northwestern Italy not far from Milan. With its charming lake of the same name, it is one of the most beautiful sites in the country and in the novel is the home of the del Dongo family. Stendhal presents Como as the secluded, stifling setting in which the naïve Fabrizio grows up with visions of sharing in Napoleon's glory.

*Waterloo.** Belgian village south of Brussels, where Napoleon fought his last, losing battle in 1815. Stendhal effectively evokes the country atmosphere and the confusion of battle, including Fabrizio's ludicrous attempts to join Napoleon's forces. Traveling under false papers he is arrested as a spy. His incarceration is the first of several imprisonments that ultimately lead to his self-incarceration in the Charterhouse of Parma.

*Parma.** Northern Italian city south of the River Po that serves as the site of the novel's central action. Here Fabrizio, under suspicion by the prince and the royalists because of his Napoleonic adventures, wins the favor of the clergy and becomes a controversial figure emblematic of the city's factionalism. Dominating the city is the despotic prince, who has ambitions to become the constitutional monarch of Italy. Indeed, it is only his ambition that prevents the prince from summarily having Fabrizio executed for killing (in self-defense) a rival for the love of an actress. Fabrizio is a prisoner in the Farnese Tower, the prison which is part of the city's citadel—a defensive fortress that is mentioned frequently in the novel. Like Parma itself, the citadel is a center of intrigue, where Fabrizio must take care that he is not poisoned by his jailers, and where he survives because he is able to bribe them.

Parma's combination of corruption and thuggery makes the simple, passionate Fabrizio an endearing figure to the public even when they feel he is guilty of murder. However, the prison also becomes a metaphor for his self-confining passions. His devotion to Napoleon leads to his first arrest. His equally devout passion for an actress results in his incarceration in the Farnese Tower. There through a window he observes his jailer's daughter and wishes to stay in prison so he can remain close to a woman with whom he presumes he will never be able to live. Even after she forces him to agree to a daring escape from the tower, he returns to his prison cell in despair over his inability to have her.

*Charterhouse of Parma.** Although it provides the novel's title, this former monastery is mentioned only in the book's last three paragraphs. It is the site of Fabrizio's religious retreat from the world. However, it also becomes another form of imprisonment and exile. Stendhal clearly means to link the Charterhouse of his title to the del Dongo castle at Grianta in Como where Fabrizio grew up and to places like Ferrara, a small ancient town in northern Italy, where Fabrizio hid after killing his rival. Thus the idea of society as a prison house from which Fabrizio cannot escape and the idea of society itself as a place of incarceration suffuse Stendhal's deeply ironic and disturbing novel.

— *Carl Rollyson*

CHÉRI

Author: Colette (Sidonie-Gabrielle Claudine Colette, 1873-1954)
Type of work: Novel

Type of plot: Psychological realism
Time of plot: c. 1910
First published: 1920 (English translation, 1929)

This story of an aging courtesan and her scandalous young lover Chéri is set in France in the legendary period known as the belle epoque. *Colette's nostalgic, satiric reconstruction of the Parisian demimonde concentrates on a piquant May-December romance symbolizing the spirit of the time.*

*Paris. France's capital city is an essential ingredient in the story of Chéri. In this novel, Colette creates a portrait of Paris in the early twentieth century. During that era, France enjoyed a time of prosperity, progress, and brilliant cultural achievements. Pleasure reigned, and the city was filled with cafés, cabarets, and music halls, as well as the famous Folies Bergère. The construction of the Eiffel Tower in 1889 seemed to inaugurate this period of peace and prosperity, becoming a symbol of Parisian accomplishment. In this atmosphere of gaiety, frivolity, and creativity, the different classes of Paris mixed together freely and amused themselves with a variety of entertainments. This free-spirited and imaginative period helped create the legend of the French as a race who loved life and knew how to enjoy it. Glamorous Parisian women piled their hair under huge, decorative hats and met with friends and lovers at fine restaurants for gourmet meals, gossip, and intrigue. A general atmosphere of liberality and leisure permitted largesse to be grandly lavished on expensive cocottes and handsome gigolos. Much of the appeal of this novel comes from its evocation of this elegant and hedonistic era. This era in France is remembered by Colette as a shimmering golden time before the onset of the problems of modernity, as demonstrated by World War I and its aftermath. It is in this period that Colette herself was a young woman, enjoying success as a writer and actress. Her novel is based on memories of the era that are both bitterly rueful and sweetly nostalgic, suggesting that the author is looking back on her own youth during a time of plenty and pleasure in a city that was her home for most of her life.

Lonval town house. Home of Lèa de Lonval on the Avenue Bugeaud in Paris. Although this novel is named after the handsome young gigolo known as Chéri, the character of the forty-nine-year-old courtesan Lèa de Lonval is its true heart. Lèa has been a triumphant success as a frivolous woman, whose many lovers validated her desirability. She has devoted herself entirely to her own beauty, to a life of pleasure, and to running her well-appointed and charming house. Much of the novel deals simply with the sensuous joys of Lèa's love affair with her far younger lover, Chéri, whom she takes under her wing, making her home a pleasure-palace devoted to his whims. Lèa's beautiful home, however, is already getting to be old-fashioned. When Lèa surveys her bedroom, the hub of her universe, she realizes that its ostentatious, over-decorated luxury, especially its large brass-and-iron bed, is rapidly becoming out-of-date. As her bedroom is dated, so too her ornate mirror also tells her that she is growing old, that her time as a great beauty is over. Lèa knows that times are changing, and that things will not always be as they are. Chéri himself, suffocated by Lèa's devotion and beginning to feel the difference in their ages, leaves her establishment for good at the end of the novel, fleeing as if Lèa's pleasure-palace has become a prison.

*Neuilly (noh-YEE). Countrified suburb of Paris, where Chéri's mother and fellow courtesan Charlotte Peloux lives. Like her friend and rival Lèa, Charlotte has made her love life into a profitable venture, but her opulent home has none of the aura of warmth, generosity, or sensuality associated with Lèa's house in Paris.

*Normandy. Region of France bounded on the north by the English Channel. During summers here, Lèa fattens the pasty-faced and underweight Chéri on corn-fed chicken, cream, and strawberries, and gives him boxing lessons, transforming him gradually into a robust young man.

— *Margaret Boe Birns*

THE CHEROKEE NIGHT

Author: Lynn Riggs (1899-1954)
Type of work: Drama
Type of plot: Social realism

Time of plot: 1895-1931
First performed: 1936; first published, 1936

The setting of this play, particularly Claremore Mound, is a constant reminder of the fallen state of the Cherokee Nation. The play literally begins on a night in Oklahoma in 1915, but the title also suggests the spiritual darkness that has enveloped the once proud Cherokees. The theme of the play is rooted in the soil of what had been Indian Territory.

Claremore Mound. Scene of a nineteenth century massacre of Osages by Cherokees in the last big battle between the two tribes. Claremont, chief of the Osages, is believed to be buried there. The play chronicles, through several decades of the lives of selected characters, the subsequent decline of the Cherokees.

*Claremore. Town in northeastern Oklahoma in whose Rogers County jail Bee Newcomb, a one-quarter Cherokee prostitute, betrays Art Osburn, also part Cherokee, who has been arrested for the murder of his older Indian wife. Viney Jones, a former country schoolteacher, has totally rejected her Cherokee heritage and moved to Quapaw, where her husband is mayor.

Whiteturkey farmhouse. Ramshackle home of Kate Whiteturkey, a rich Osage woman who owns three Stutz Bearcats; located in Bartlesville, Oklahoma, near the Kansas state line. Hutch Moree, Viney's former companion, is living with Whiteturkey; he is a "kept man," completely dominated by Kate—an ironic reversal of the Cherokees' great victory at Claremore Mound.

Eagle Bluff. Edge of a sheer cliff overlooking the Illinois River and the town of Tahlequah, seat of the Cherokee Nation, and the fields and woods of the river valley below. Young Gar Breeden, a half-breed Cherokee, climbs the bluff after running away from his "guardeen" in Claremore. He is captured by members of a religious sect who believe themselves to be one of the Lost Tribes of Israel. They steal cattle, hogs, and grain from the Cherokee farms below. In their religion, they worship the sun, rain, and snow as much as they worship Jesus. In one of the most striking ironies in the play, menacing white fanatics have even appropriated the nature worship of the Cherokees.

— *Patrick Adcock*

THE CHERRY ORCHARD

Author: Anton Chekhov (1860-1904)
Type of work: Drama
Type of plot: Impressionistic realism

Time of plot: Early twentieth century
First performed: 1904; first published, 1904 as
    Vishnyovy sad (English translation, 1908)

Set somewhere in central Russia, more than a decade before the Russian Revolution, Anton Chekhov's play shows only an open field, the house of Madame Ranevsky, and her doomed cherry orchard.

Ranevsky estate. Madame Ranevsky's estate is located somewhere in the provinces of central Russia. Three acts of the play take place in her large house. Act 1 is set in what was once the nursery, a large, high-ceilinged room which has become an informal meeting place. The second act is set in a field not far from the house, near an old chapel. The third act reveals the true opulence of the house: Its drawing room with a chandelier is in the foreground, and dancing couples can be seen in the ballroom through arches at the rear. Act 4 returns to the nursery, now stripped of its decorations and ready to be vacated by Madame Ranevsky and her family. Madame Ranevsky's world is doomed by economic and social forces usually identified with offstage places. A station is nearby, from which characters go to Russian cities like Kharkov and Moscow. Madame Ranevsky's problems are made acute by her irresponsibilities with both men and money, both of which are associated with Paris.

Cherry orchard. The most important part of the setting of three of these acts is the visible symbol of the fragile and doomed beauty of Madame Ranevsky's world, the cherry orchard itself. It is revealed in all its blooming spring beauty through the large, tall windows in act 1. In the next act, it is visible at the edge of the field. It can be seen again in the desolation of act 4, denuded now of its blossoms because it is October.

— *George Soule*

THE CHEVALIER DE MAISON-ROUGE

Authors: Alexandre Dumas, *père* (1802-1870), with Auguste Maquet (1813-1888)
Type of work: Novel
Type of plot: Historical

Time of plot: 1793
First published: Le Chevalier de Maison-Rouge, 1846 (English translation, 1846)

In effect, a tale of two prisons, this novel describes two attempts to rescue the French queen Marie Antoinette and her children from the baleful institutions in question, following the death of her husband, King Louis XVI. Although the novel's eponymous chevalier was the prototype of Baroness Orczy's The Scarlet Pimpernel *(1905), and the hero's final gesture foreshadowed Charles Dickens's* A Tale of Two Cities *(1859), the constraints of history force Alexandre Dumas's narrative to a much more downbeat denouement than either of its successors; its inevitable conclusion is the site of the guillotine in the place de la Révolution.*

*****Paris.** Typical of *romans feuilletons*—books published in installments—this novel is full of references to the streets of Paris, which is explicitly characterized here as the sensitive heart of the organism that is France. The story opens with the chiming of the bells of the Cathedral of Notre Dame as heard from the rue Saint-Honoré, and Maurice's first crosstown journey is minutely detailed. The story strays no farther from the capital than the suburb of Auteuil. Apart from those detailed below, the most significant settings in the plot are 24, rue de Nonandières, where the pretended flower girl Héloïse Tison lives, and Noah's Well Tavern at the corner of the rue de la Vieille Draperie, where one of Dixmer's plots is carefully nurtured.

*****Temple.** Fortified dwelling established in Paris by the Knights Templar in 1128 and converted into a prison by the eighteenth century. (The prison was subsequently destroyed in 1810, after which its site was occupied by the Marché du Temple, one of the city's major commercial centers.) In Dumas's novel, the wall of the prison fringing the rue Portefoin supports a wooden construction that functions as an alehouse for its guardsmen. Dixmer purchases a house in the rue de la Corderie (on the site where number 20 now stands) in order that his accomplices might dig a tunnel under the gardens to reach the alehouse, through which Marie Antoinette and her family might escape; it is the discovery of this plot that causes her removal to the Conciergerie.

*****Conciergerie** (kon-see-ehrj-ur-ee). Prison of the Palais de Justice, a group of buildings on the Ile de la Cité in the heart of Paris. The Conciergerie itself had once been a royal palace, built on the site of a Roman prefectorium. At the time of the novel it was flanked by the quai des Lunettes and the quai aux Fleurs. Its gates opened on to the Pont-au-Change, across which those condemned by the Revolutionary Tribunal were transported to the guillotine in the place de la Révolution. At the height of the Terror, commitment to the Conciergerie was a virtual guarantee of a speedy execution, for which reason it was ironically characterized as the "Inn of Death."

Although the rooms occupied by Marie Antoinette and her family were destroyed by the Commune, the rest of the prison is still standing. The large vaulted hall of the Palais de Justice, known as La Salle des Pas-Perdus, is a key setting in the later phases of the novel. The curious ancestry of Paris's prisons, most of which were former palaces or religious houses, is further emphasized by the tour that Maurice makes while searching for Geneviève after her arrest, taking in the Carmelites, the Port Libre, the Madelonnettes, Saint Lazare, and the Luxembourg.

*Old rue Saint Jacques. Street in Paris's Fauborg Victor district, so described to distinguish it from another Parisian street of the same name. Here, not far from the jardin des Plantes, Dixmer's house is located. Although Maurice does not realize its importance when he first offers the mysterious woman safe conduct, it becomes the setting for all the key scenes of his unfolding misfortune. He is imprisoned there, then becomes a frequent visitor as he is unwittingly drawn into Dixmer's schemes. Having previously observed Geneviève secretly from the garden, it is from that vantage point that he finally learns the extent of her involvement with the queen's allies.

*Rue de Roule. Location of Maurice's house, not far from the rue Sainte-Avoie; he is secretary of the rue Lepelletier section of the Civic Guard section, whose base is nearby.

— *Brian Stableford*

CHICAGO POEMS

Author: Carl Sandburg (1878-1967)
Type of work: Poetry

First published: 1916

Carl Sandburg's poems offer readers a graphic and original portrait of the city of Chicago in the heady years before World War I, when skyscrapers began to dominate its skyline, motor cars and jazz bands made their first appearances, and many new ethnic groups moved into the fabled "Windy City."

*Chicago. Illinois's largest city and the industrial and commercial center of the Midwest. Sandburg's poetry depicts Chicago as a mythic figure, a city personified as a kind of superman—optimistic, pugnacious, and indomitable. Ultimately, Sandburg celebrates the city's unquenchable vitality and energy. The most familiar poem in his collection, "Chicago," is most notable for its form, which, like a jazz composition or the expanding grid of the city itself, keeps going on its own momentum. The city and the poem are open-ended structures, and Sandburg's "Chicago" is both utterly real and strangely mythological. The stockyards, railroads, skyscrapers, criminals, prostitutes, and marginal characters it describes are painfully accurate.

Many of Sandburg's poems break Chicago's massive cityscape down into comprehensible lives, in which frustrations, dashed hopes, and unfulfilled longings define the everyday existence of the working-class people, who make up the vast majority of the city's residents. Sandburg's poems are all telling examples of his socially conscious verse. He is also sensitive to the plight of the mushrooming ethnic populations, especially the Italians and Eastern Europeans, as shown in such poems as "Child of the Romans" and "Happiness," the latter celebrating a family of Hungarians enjoying a picnic on the banks of the Des Plaines River.

— *Daniel L. Guillory*

THE CHICKENCOOP CHINAMAN

Author: Frank Chin (1940-   )
Type of work: Drama
Type of plot: Comedy

Time of plot: Late 1960's
First performed: 1972; first published, 1981

Frank Chin's first produced play opens inside a darkened jet airliner, in which the protagonist, Tam Lum, is flying to Pittsburgh, Pennsylvania. The two-act, six-scene play has often been mined for pithy quotations on Asian American themes and concerns, but it has also been justly criticized for undermining certain dramatic conventions with questionable results. Themes of masculinity and the intersection of cultures provide circumstances for characters to launch into lengthy diatribes against racist aspects of popular culture.

*Oakland. Principally African American district of Pittsburgh, Pennsylvania, where the protagonist's friend Kenji has an apartment, in which most of the play is set.

Chinatown. Chinese district of an unspecified American city. Tam Lum comes from California, so he may be from San Francisco or Oakland's Chinatown districts. The "chickencoop" in the title refers to Chin's perception of American Chinatowns as zoos or dirty, noisy, foul-smelling places occupied by people who speak an unintelligible language. In many of his works, Chin depicts the Chinese of Chinatown as insects or frogs. He does not regard Chinatown as an ethnic enclave where the Chinese congregated to preserve their culture. Instead, he sees it as a product of American racism, of discriminatory housing laws.

*Hong Kong. Chinese port city that was a prosperous British colony at the time this play was written. The play opens with Tam conversing with his "Hong Kong Dream Girl," who appears on stage, a beautiful Asian in a drill-team uniform. Tam's conversation with her during his flight to Pittsburgh constitutes the first scene of the play.

— *Richard Sax*

CHILD OF GOD

Author: Cormac McCarthy (1933-   )
Type of work: Novel
Type of plot: Social realism

Time of plot: Early 1960's
First published: 1973

As in many of his novels, Cormac McCarthy elevates the landscape in this novel to nearly character-level status. His depiction of the descent of an East Tennessee mountain man into the depths of degradation is as much an exploration of the land as the man's mental condition.

*Eastern Tennessee. Remote and harsh hill country area dominated by woods, rivers, and fields. Evicted from his home as the result of a false charge of rape, Lester Ballard embarks on a dark journey of survival through a countryside filled with images of nature in its rawest form. It is a setting in which Ballard steadily sheds his last remaining ties to civilized conduct. Instead, he resorts to basic animal instincts as he sets out on an orgy of grotesque behaviors, including incest, infanticide, and necrophilia. With each step back from civilization, Ballard eventually emerges as a creature of the landscape, scavenging the woods for "trophies" to satisfy his strange lusts. So effective is McCarthy in blending Ballard into the harsh landscape that in the end the reader is inclined to draw little distinction between him and the area's other forms of wildlife. From a distance McCarthy's landscape appears as a thing of beauty in its raw natural state. Even Ballard, when viewed from a distance, appears as a sympathetic figure in his lone struggle for survival under harsh conditions. The author is careful, however, not to let the reader slip into a sympathetic state. Depravities are never far away, as McCarthy regularly jars the reader back to reality with close-up views that underscore the obscenities carried out on the natural beauty of his terrain.

Caves. Series of caves located in the limestone country of eastern Tennessee. As they do in McCarthy's novel *Suttree* (1979), caves play a major role in *Child of God*. Ballard's descent is not only a mental phenomenon but also a physical one that takes him from the hills to the fields to the underground caves where he seeks his ultimate withdrawal. Like a pack rat, he collects and hides his "trophies" alongside the bones of other animals. That he had finally reached the underbelly of nature is driven home by the author, when he describes the walls of the cave as having "an organic look to them, like the innards of some great beast."

Frog Mountain. Mountain located in the heart of the hill country where Ballard spends much of his time searching for prey. It also is the site of a road turnaround, which serves as a symbolic collision point of local civilized society and the natural world. It also serves as a prime stalking ground for Ballard to carry out his wanton assaults on unsuspecting residents.

*Sevierville. Small town in eastern Tennessee that serves as the county seat of Sevier County. The city represents the civilized elements from which Ballard becomes totally estranged. Again, his mental isolation is as pronounced as his physical separation, as illustrated in his visit to the local blacksmith shop to have an ax sharpened. As Ballard watches, the blacksmith carefully explains to him each step of the sharpening process, which concludes with him suggesting that Ballard now was able to do it himself. "Do what?" is Ballard's response. It is one of several awkward interactions with the local citizenry, when he is forced to visit the city for supplies.

Ballard's farm. Farmhouse located deep in the Tennessee hills where Ballard lives. The home represents the high point of his existence until the forced sale of his property by county authorities.

Cabin. Abandoned clapboard structure situated on a neighbor's property. Ballard's move into the cabin following the loss of his home represents the first downward step in his journey into degradation. "Were there darker provinces of night he would have found them."

Hospital. County hospital that Ballard checks into after being flushed from the depths of his cave. Choosing not to return to the woods, he instead enters this emblem of civilization, in which he cryptically tells a nurse that he is where he is "supposed to be."

— *William Hoffman*

CHILDE HAROLD'S PILGRIMAGE

Author: George Gordon, Lord Byron (1788-1824)
Type of work: Poetry
Type of plot: Picaresque

Time of plot: 1809-1818
First published: 1812-1818

The four cantos of this long poem record the journey of a pilgrim, Childe Harold, a privileged nineteenth century nobleman who is repulsed by his own dissolute life and seeks rebirth by visiting ancient, classical sites in Spain, Greece, and Italy.

*Spain. In canto 1, Childe Harold departs Albion, or England, and crosses the Bay of Biscay to Portugal and Spain, which has become the battleground for "Gaul's," or France's, "unsparing lord" (Napoleon). Although Napoleon is dramatized as a conqueror justly condemned for his ruthlessness, he also represents a new force for freedom sweeping away Europe's monarchies and rejuvenating its people. Harold himself is seeking precisely this kind of renewal. With Napoleon's defeat "Britannia," or England, "sickens," Byron exclaims. He exhorts: "Awake, ye sons of Spain! awake! advance!" Spain is no longer the land of chivalry; it is ruled by a corrupt king, a "bloated Chief," and will soon be a conquered province over which European nations will squabble. The ebbing strength and nobility of cities such as Seville and Cádiz are lamented as Harold makes his way through the "nerveless state."

*Greece. In canto 2, Harold visits the famous site of the Parthenon, a temple devoted to Athena, the goddess of wisdom. However, like Spain, Greece has been robbed of its glory. British marauders have taken away parts of the ancient building and defaced a shrine. All Greece has become a "sad relic of departed worth." Seeking inspiration in the places of Western greatness,

Harold finds only degradation as he traces Alexander the Great's path through Albania and other parts of the Balkans.

***Belgium.** In canto 3, the "self-exiled" Harold visits the "grave of France, the deadly Waterloo," where Napoleon suffered his final defeat. In the aftermath of that great event, many of Europe's monarchies were reestablished. From this scene of defeat Harold turns toward Switzerland and the places where great writers, such as Edward Gibbon, Jean-Jacques Rousseau, and Voltaire, employed their "gigantic minds" to comprehend the tragedy of humanity. Indeed, Gibbon's great work on the Roman Empire leads Byron to think of the degraded state of Italy, which provides yet another example of humanity's fallen state and of Byron's theme: "We are not what we have been . . . We are not what we should be."

***Italy.** Canto 4 begins in Venice, a magical city of great beauty, which seems to rise out of the water and yet is a site of disintegration with its palaces "crumbling to the shore." Its great buildings, St. Mark's Cathedral, for example, call to mind Venice's history as an independent city-state, but now its freedom and glory are gone.

Certainly Italy remains a source of inspiration as Byron thinks of great writers such as Dante, who was associated with Florence, the Italian version of Athens. Italy is where Vergil wrote his poetry, but here also an empire was born and decayed, a fact that brings to mind Napoleon and France once again. France has "got drunk with blood to vomit crime," but Rome is the very "field of freedom, faction, fame, and blood." Nowhere is the scene of human achievement and defeat better seen than in Harold's visit to the Roman Colosseum, which is an architectural wonder and a place of torture, where gladiators fought for sport.

Indeed Byron's description of Rome's Colosseum coalesces the poem's sense of the importance of place: "While stands the Colosseum, Rome shall stand;/ When falls the Colosseum, Rome shall fall." Each place Harold visits is an emblem of the human desire for permanence and achievement, yet each place is in ruins, an emblem of human defeat. That ruins and some historic structures such as the Roman Pantheon and St. Peter's church and dome still stand evokes in Byron the hope that human greatness can be revived. Viewing St. Peter's, Byron comments that "growing with its growth, we thus dilate/ Our spirits to the size of that they contemplate."

The pilgrim's final resting place is the ocean, Byron emphasizes, which evokes the immensity of the world out of which man struggles to create and endure. Nature itself becomes the titanic force against which all human created places must be measured.

— *Carl Rollyson*

THE CHILDREN'S HOUR

Author: Lillian Hellman (1905-1984)
Type of work: Drama
Type of plot: Problem

Time of plot: 1930's
First performed: 1934; first published, 1934

The culture of New England during the 1930's is central to this play; it is a time when intimate female friendship had been "medicalized" into the potential disease of lesbianism, and a place in which lingering Puritan values required especially rigid and lurid responses to the suspicion that the directors of a girls' school might be same-sex lovers.

Wright-Dobie School. Girls' school, near the fictional town of **Lancet** in rural New England, that is the play's principal setting. A modest but comfortable private residential school, it uses a large converted farmhouse that contains both residential units and classrooms for a small group of middle-school girls. Karen Wright and Martha Dobie, the teachers and owners, also live in the building.

Although the action of the first and third acts occurs in the living room, the layout and location of the school are significant. Especially important is a lack of privacy. The schoolgirls easily overhear adult conversations that can be misinterpreted—to the detriment of Karen and Martha. The malicious schoolgirl Mary Tilford persuasively claims that she and other students have witnessed or overheard a sexual encounter between the two teachers.

The school's rural isolation is important in the third act. The two accused teachers live alone, cut off from the village culture that rejects them and leers at them, making them feel they are prisoners on display. This isolation contrasts with the hope of escaping to Vienna, Austria, that Karen's fiancé, Joe Cardin, offers near the end of the original script. In her 1952 revision of the script for a revival during Congress's infamous House Committee on Un-American Activities hearings, Lillian Hellman changed Joe's proposed escape to a place even bleaker than the empty school—an unspecified American farming country in the middle of nowhere.

Amelia Tilford's living room. Home of Mrs. Tilford, the grandmother of the malicious Mary. The fact that Mrs. Tilford is wealthy but old-fashioned is reflected in her home, which appears to be in the village of Lancet; however, this is not made clear in the script. The size and comparative emptiness of her house are important in the play's second act, when Mary has the opportunity to be alone with her schoolmate Rosalie, whom she intimidates into confirming her own story about Karen and Martha's alleged sexual encounter. The house's location near the center of village life and the visual evidence of Mrs. Tilford's social and moral authority help to establish her power to close the school and to win the libel suit brought by Karen and Martha.

— Terry Heller

CHITA: A Memory of Last Island

Author: Lafcadio Hearn (1850-1904)
Type of work: Novel
Type of plot: Impressionistic realism

Time of plot: Nineteenth century
First published: 1889

The title character of this novel is a young girl who is rescued at sea by a Spanish fisherman when a storm raging over the Gulf of Mexico sweeps her, along with hundreds of other vacationers, into the sea. The fisherman and his wife then raise the girl as their own and teach her to love and yet fear the ocean.

Last Island. Fashionable resort in the Gulf of Mexico that is devastated by the hurricane that kills Chita's natural mother and leaves her adrift in the sea. Filled with well-to-do vacationers from New Orleans, the island has a hotel whose guests enjoy the beach, bathe in warm salt water, relish fine food and drink, dance to the music of well-paid orchestras, and flirt with one another pleasurably. Over pearly dawns and flaming wine-red sunsets is the comforting sky, sometimes divinely blue, often mysteriously luminous or sprinkled with stars. When the storm begins to lash the island, the wind is like a breath, then it howls with sand-filled fury. Water suddenly creeps over the polished dance floor. Lightning crackles. The sea heaves monstrously. In a flash, cottages and native dwellings, and the gorgeous hotel are scoured from the land. Trees and numberless bodies are scattered for a hundred miles along the coasts of the devouring sea.

*****Gulf of Mexico.** Sea off the coast of Louisiana that is a combination of life and death, of beauty and horror. "If thou wouldst learn to pray, go to the sea," readers are advised. Feliu Viosca, Chita's foster father, says that the "world is like the sea: those who do not know how to swim in it are drowned." Those who venture too far into the sea find its water turning colder and may be clutched and drawn in by treacherous undercurrents. However, when Feliu swims through dangerous breakers and rescues Chita, who is floating on a billiard table far from shore and still tied to her dead mother by a scarf, the ocean "lifts up its million hands, and thunders as if in acclaim."

The gulf's coastal environment contains both delights and horrors. As Chita grows up, she loves the sun's splendor and the often-haloed moon, the greens and blues of the sea and the sky transparent or filled with lamplike stars, the fresh and bracing air, the shrieking sea birds, the brown bare-footed fishermen, the quietly busy women. However, the sounds of stormy seas fill her sleep with nightmares of being overwhelmed by mountainous waves. One day she wanders into a swamp behind a grove, encounters insects, weeds, crawfish, worms, and suddenly a sailor's dilapidated makeshift grave. His grinning skull is exposed, and a huge toad puffs nearby. When Chita wonders if her deceased mother looks hideous too, Carmen reassures her that her mother remains beautiful and is in the cloudless sky with God.

Viosca's Point. Location of the Vioscas' home, a rude but clean and comfortable cottage. Inside and nearby is gear for fishing, at which Feliu is so expert that he has two vigorous young assistants. Carmen's most precious possession is her shrine to the Virgin. Its central feature is a waxen image of Mother and Child—a Señora de Guadalupe figure that Feliu brought her from Mexico. In her prayer-book is an illustration, with heavenly lamp, kneeling angels, and caption beseeching protection from "las Tempestades." Carmen often dreams of the dead daughter, Conchita, whom she has left behind in Spain. During the night of the storm she dreams that the Virgin stoops and gives her the Child; its Indian-brown face turns white, and Carmen seems to smell Spanish olive groves.

*****New Orleans.** Louisiana's grand city at the mouth of the Mississippi River is crowded by walls that block Nature, ever young and beautiful, from the view of its harried citizens. These unfortunates are furious, brutal, sick, and bitter, victims of "the more or less factitious life of society." If Chita were back there, she would have to strain "her pretty eyes, for many long hours at a time, over grimy desks in gloomy school-rooms."

*****Barcelona.** Spanish city in which Feliu and Carmen's natural daughter, Conchita, is buried. Initially, Feliu hopes that Chita's natural father will be found and give him a large reward that will allow Carmen to go back to Barcelona to visit Conchita's grave. However, he and Carmen eventually come to love Chita as their own. After eleven years pass, Chita's father, a New Orleans physician, recognizes her when he goes to Viosca's Point to tend a fever patient; however, he himself dies almost immediately in a feverish delirium.

— *Robert L. Gale*

THE CHOSEN

Author: Chaim Potok (1929-2002)
Type of work: Novel
Type of plot: Domestic realism

Time of plot: 1940's
First published: 1967

Set in the New York borough of Brooklyn through a period in which the United States was fighting in World War II and the Jewish state of Israel was coming into being, Chaim Potok's first novel explores the coming of age of two Jewish teenagers—one Orthodox, the other Hasidic.

*****Brooklyn.** Largest of five boroughs of New York City and the setting for the entire novel. The diverse ethnic groups living in Brooklyn's brownstone row houses include many Jews, such as the novel's central characters, who live in the borough's Williamsburg neighborhood.

Malter home. Brooklyn home of Reuven Malter, a teenage Orthodox Jew who lives with his widower father, a teacher in a Jewish parochial school and a scholar of Jewish law. The Malters live downstairs in a brownstone house with a tiny yard on Lee Avenue, which is shaded by Sycamore trees; paintings by famous Jewish artists line the walls in their home's entry hall. Curtained French doors, trimmed with Ionic columns, open into the father's windowless study, where a yellow desk lamp glows. The senior Malter wears a skullcap and glasses as he sits hunched over a large desk covered by a green blotter and stacks of papers, and writes religious articles. Floor-to-ceiling bookcases line walls of his study, where he and Reuven drink tea and discuss the history of two sects of European Jews. They say prayers and eat the Shabbat meal in the kitchen.

During his recovery from an eye injury in a softball game, Reuven sits on the back porch in a lounge chair and inhales scents of grass and flowers. His room has a bookcase, a narrow bed, a desk covered with papers, and a small radio with a program schedule featuring classical music. Its walls display maps of Europe and pictures of President Franklin D. Roosevelt and the scientist Albert Einstein. Reuven's cat likes to sit on the sill of a window facing an alley.

Saunders Home. Brooklyn home of Reuven's new friend, Danny Saunders, a member of a Hasidic Jewish family. His father, Isaac Saunders, is a rabbi who leads a small sect of Hasidic Jews. The three-storied brownstone of the Saunderses serves as residence, synagogue, and counseling office, and the family lives on the second floor. Men in black caftans, black hats, and heavy beards often wait outside.

The large downstairs room in which temple services are conducted contains the Ark, the Eternal Light, and two podiums covered with red velvet. Walls are painted white, and black velvet drapes cover the windows. Light bulbs dangle from the ceiling. Chairs with small tables for scriptures are placed in rows with an aisle down the middle.

A conference room and study occupy the third floor. Here, the senior Saunders discusses Talmud passages with Danny and Reuven. Saunders sits in a red leather chair with carved wooden arms, behind a black desk. Hundreds of musty-smelling leather-bound religious books are shelved in tall bookcases and stacked on chairs and the floor. A quote from the poet John Keats, "Beauty Is Truth, Truth Beauty, That Is All Ye Know on Earth, and All Ye Need to Know," is etched over the door. Murals on walls in the vestibule portray world-famous religious leaders, scientists, and authors. Here, Danny reads forbidden history and philosophy books, especially Sigmund Freud's theories.

Samson Raphael Hirsch Seminary and College. Whitestone school located on Brooklyn's Bedford Avenue, where both Reuven and Danny study. Facing the seminary from across the street is a Roman Catholic church with a statue of the crucified Christ on its lawn. Both Hasidic and Orthodox Jews attend Hirsch. After they graduate, Danny sheds his Hasidic identity and enrolls at Columbia University to study clinical psychology, while Reuven continues rabbinical studies at Hirsch.

— *Martha E. Rhynes*

A CHRISTMAS CAROL

Author: Charles Dickens (1812-1870)
Type of work: Short fiction
Type of plot: Moral

Time of plot: Mid-nineteenth century
First published: 1843

While this story is clearly set amid real nineteenth century London places, its most important places are the miser Ebenezer Scrooge's past, present, and future—which he visits with ghosts after retiring to bed on Christmas Eve.

*****London.** Scrooge's first nocturnal journey is guided by the Ghost of Christmas Present, who whisks him from his bed on a nighttime journey to observe London's joyful holiday season. They oversee Christmas delight in the Cratchit home, located in a poor section of London (where author Charles Dickens himself had once lived).

Before this ghost withers away on the streets of London, he escorts Scrooge to holiday scenes among northern miners and coastal lighthouse keepers; he even whisks him out to sea to watch Christmas's softening effect on rough sailors. Scrooge next visits scenes from the past and future.

Scrooge's bedroom. Room to which Scrooge retreats after Marley warns him about night-time visitors and the place at which his nocturnal adventures begin. The old miser is then spirited from his bed and escorted through the air to his childhood home, west of London in Rochester—which was also Dickens's childhood home. Here they drop down in three locations, designed to soften Scrooge: a sad and lonely schoolroom, a warehouse magically transformed for Christmas fun by the generous Fezziwig, and a park bench where a youthful Scrooge coldly breaks off his engagement.

Churchyard. Cemetery where Scrooge sees his own grave during his journey with the Ghost of Christmas Yet to Come. The callous and bleak atmosphere of a shop where Scrooge sees his own bed being sold and the even greater shock of seeing his own name on a tombstone in the overgrown churchyard complete the reformation of the old miser, especially after he realizes that the future he has been seeing is not immutable. When he awakens back in his bedroom on Christmas morning, he is a very different man from the one who fell asleep there the night before.

Scrooge's countinghouse. Scrooge's London offices; a bleak, cold working place, warmed by the smallest imaginable fire, even on the coldest winter days when the story opens. On the day after Christmas, however, the story comes full circle in this setting, with Scrooge filling his office with both physical warmth and true holiday cheer.

— *Marie J. K. Brenner*

THE CID

Author: Pierre Corneille (1606-1684)
Type of work: Drama
Type of plot: Tragicomedy

Time of plot: Eleventh century
First performed: 1637; first published, 1637 as *Le Cid* (English translation, 1637)

Set in Seville in eleventh century Spain, this play deals with the famous Spanish medieval hero El Cid. The play divides its action between Chimène's house and the royal palace in which the princess Doña Urraque, known as the infanta, lives. The loneliness felt by the two leading female characters in their houses and the isolation on the battlefield of Rodrigue from his own soldiers only serve to heighten in audiences' minds the solitary suffering of the three principal characters.

Royal palace. Corneille portrays the two houses in *The Cid* basically as elegant prisons in which Chimène and the infanta lead apparently comfortable lives but cannot express their deepest feelings to others. One might expect the infanta to be a happy person because she is so wealthy, but such is not the case. The royal palace in which she lives is a marble museum and almost a tomb for her. There she must always act and speak in conformity with the expectations of her social standing.

Chimène's house (shee-MEHN). The home of the daughter of Don Gomez is more modest than the royal palace, but is equally oppressive. Chimène is constantly watched by a female servant who reports to her father. Corneille effectively contrasts the interior spaces occupied by Chimène and the infanta with the open surroundings in which the warrior Rodrigue operates. Rodrigue, like the women, is also profoundly alienated. Once he believes that he can never marry his beloved Chimène, he seeks death in a rash attack to defend Seville against the invading Moorish forces, only to win an unexpected victory. He is no happier on the battlefield than are Chimène and the infanta in their elegant domestic prisons.

— *Edmund J. Campion*

CINNA

Author: Pierre Corneille (1606-1684)
Type of work: Drama
Type of plot: Tragedy
Time of plot: c. 10 C.E.

First performed: 1640; first published, 1643 as *Cinna: Ou, La Clémence d'Auguste* (English translation, 1713)

Rome is a frequently used setting in French classical literature, serving as a trope, or metaphor, for personal virtues, self-respect, and honor, ideals translated into the national context by the policies of the great French chief minister of King Louis XIII, Cardinal Richelieu. Over half of Pierre Corneille's tragedies relate to Roman history; however, in the canon of his greatest plays, only this play is set in Imperial Rome itself.

***Rome.** Center of the ancient Roman Empire and principal setting of this play. *Cinna* mentions "Rome" more than forty times in 1,780 lines of verse, serving to reinforce the ideal of personal responsibility. Scattered mentions of other places recall the huge geographical extent of Emperor Augustus's realm, including not only Italy and Sicily, but also much of Europe, western Asia, North Africa, and the peoples of Macedonia, Greece, Parthia, and Persia.

Augustus's palace. Headquarters and residence of Emperor Augustus. The play's references to the palace supplement the aura of majesty surrounding the personal power of Augustus, among whose courtiers are those whose conspiracy will eventually be uncovered. Almost exactly half the play's action takes place in Augustus's apartment. There, references to Rome and the Romans abound and Augustus meets his advisers, who, unknown to him, are conspiring to kill him. His readiness, how-

ever, to use his private quarters for the seeking of counsel reveals his essential humanity, a quality prominent in the closing sections of the play.

The rest of the play's action occurs in the apartment of Amelia, who is engaged to marry Pompey's grandson Cinna. There, Cinna confronts the realization that unless he kills Augustus, Amelia will not marry him. Just as Augustus's apartment is the appropriate locus for the political action, Amelia's apartment locates the sentimental action and foregrounds the growing conflict between Cinna's personal and political loyalties.

***Tiber River.** Italian river running through Rome. The idea of expiating one's sin by drowning would have been familiar to Corneille's audience. Maximus, Cinna's fellow conspirator, who betrays the plot for reasons of base personal jealousy, is reported to have leaped into the Tiber, the river of Imperial Rome.

— *William Brooks*

CINQ-MARS

Author: Alfred de Vigny (1797-1863)
Type of work: Novel
Type of plot: Historical

Time of plot: Seventeenth century
First published: 1826 (English translation, 1847)

This novel has many settings, and they often change abruptly. Multiple settings and the disjointed, episodic structure of the novel reflect the instability of French political and social life in the early seventeenth century; setting and structure also complement the volatile, unpredictable character of its hero.

Château de Chaumont* (SHAH-toh deh shoh-MOHNG). Home of the novel's hero, Henri d'Effiat, the marquis de Cinq-Mars, sits alone high on a hill near the Loire River, dominating what lies below, distinctly separated from a village and its commoners. Halfway up the slope of the mountain is a church, frequented by both the nobles from the château and the villagers. Alfred de Vigny's descriptions of the châteaux in this story emphasize the fairy-tale ambience of the Loire countryside, a region famous for its many Renaissance châteaux and the romantic legends that surround them. Vigny presents the valley as the scene of peace, prosperity, health, and happiness. The Château de Chaumont is, naturally enough, the birthplace of the love between Cinq-Mars and Marie de Gonzague, an Italian princess who takes refuge there.

The ideals and values that the Château de Chaumont and its setting represent physically are clear: the grandeur of France's hereditary feudal nobility, their traditional independence, their religious traditionalism, and their obligations to the lower classes. In the novel's first chapter, the young, passionate, impetuous Cinq-Mars rides forth from his lofty dwelling, headed for Perpignan to fight in Louis's war against the Spanish—but ultimately to defend the hereditary nobility and his own ambition against Richelieu.

Once Cinq-Mars leaves his mountain castle, however, he begins a physical and moral descent that will end in his execution, in a public square in Lyon beside another river—the Rhône.

Château de Chambord (SHAH-toh deh shahm-BORE). Favorite country estate of King Louis XIII, not far away from Cinq-Mars's estate in the Loire Valley. In direct contrast to the latter, Chambord is dark, sad, and dreary—the estate of a gloomy, duplicitous king. A stunning feature of this château is a double spiral staircase. Here, in a crucial scene late in the novel, Cinq-Mars descends one stairway after attempting to gain the king's support against Cardinal de Richelieu. As he descends, the sinister Père Joseph, Richelieu's confidant, goes up the other spiral. The scene wonderfully illustrates several points: Louis's weakness, indecision, and betrayal of Cinq-Mars; Cinq-Mars's fall from grace; and the motifs of height and depth, ascent and descent, so frequently seen in the novel.

Pierre-Encise (pyehr-en-seez). Château in Lyon that serves as the prison in which Richelieu holds Cinq-Mars after the conspiracy against him has been discovered. In a bitter irony, this prison—like the Château de Chaumont, where Cinq-Mars began his career—sits high atop a peak, and Cinq-Mars is confined to a tower.

*****Richelieu's palace.** Château high in the city of Narbonne in southern France that is the headquarters of the most powerful man in France. The palace's high altitude make it the third counterpart of Cinq-Mars's Château de Chaumont.

*****Perpignan** (per-pee-NYA[N]). City in southern France, near the Mediterranean Sea, that is the scene of Richelieu's exile of a sort. Here, after the siege of the city, the king recognizes the heroism of Cinq-Mars in battle by inviting him to Paris, the seat of the monarchy. Although he is lifting the siege, the king orders Richelieu to remain behind—in remote Perpignan. In seventeenth century France (and even more so during the eighteenth century reign of Louis XIV), the king's court is the center of French culture and artistic, social, and political power. Cinq-Mars is now the king's favorite; Richelieu is furious.

*****Paris.** France's capital city appears, logically enough, at the mid-point of *Cinq-Mars*. During the seventeenth century, the city was France's political, social, and cultural capital to an extent even greater than it is today. Moreover, settings in *Cinq-Mars* are in the epicenter of Paris, in the area around the Louvre (which was the main royal palace in the seventeenth century) and in the Ile de la Cité and the Ile Saint Louis, islands in the middle of the Seine River. It is in the very heart of Paris that the conflict between Cinq-Mars, who comes to represent personal ambition gone astray, and Richelieu, the despotic architect of central government, is played out. In the novel's Paris episode, Vigny devotes detail to the dark, labyrinthine streets of the Ile Saint-Louis, in which a rabble of anti-Richelieu protesters demonstrate angrily. Readers see again, in another way, that the story's critical tensions are between Paris and the provinces: the center versus the periphery, chaos versus order, and individualism versus autocracy.

— *Gordon Walters*

THE CITY OF THE SUN

Author: Tommaso Campanella (1568-1639)
Type of work: Novella
Type of plot: Utopian

Time of plot: Seventeenth century
First published: Civitas solis, 1623 (English
  translation, 1885)

This short work is a prose dialogue between a knight of the Order of Hospitalers of Saint John and a Genoese sea captain—who supposedly sailed with Christopher Columbus—concerning the society of the City of the Sun, a utopian state on an island that the captain has recently visited. The Hospitaler merely asks questions and does not comment on the captain's remarks.

City of the Sun. Utopian society on the island of Taprobane in the Indian Ocean, on the equator. The island is entirely fictional, but Tommaso Campanella may have been thinking of Ceylon (now Sri Lanka) when he wrote this dialogue. A Dominican friar with reformist ideals, Campanella hoped that some of his utopian principles would be introduced in his native Calabria, in southern Italy, and was imprisoned and tortured by the papal government for his beliefs.

The City of the Sun is two miles across, built on a hill above an extensive plain, in the form of seven concentric rings. Each ring has gates to the north, south, east and west and is heavily fortified with earthworks, ditches, towers, and cannons. Within the city are palaces, marble steps, and richly decorated rooms. At the center is a circular temple supported on columns and surmounted by a dome.

The prince who rules over the city is also the high priest, called Hoh or Metaphysic. His deputy Pon is in charge of all military matters including defense, the army, and the manufacture of armaments. Another deputy, Sin, controls the arts and sciences; much of the known detail of these is pictorially inscribed on the inner walls of the concentric rings of the city: mathematics and laws, minerals and weather, plants and fish, birds and insects, science and law, respectively. A third deputy, Mor, is responsible for the welfare of the people—breeding, education, food, and clothing.

One of the most important tenets of belief is that property is held in common—though Campanella seems to be thinking more of the organization of a monastery here than of a communist state. Similar togalike clothes are worn by all, being washed each month and renewed four times a year; the clothing is always white in the city, though red is allowed outside or at night; black clothes are forbidden.

Education is formal, carefully prescribed, and obligatory for all (a radical suggestion at the time Campanella wrote). Young people are put into training schemes and professions according to their intelligence and aptitude—not their fathers' professions, as was customary in Italy at the time. Because everything is done for the greater common good, and this is accepted by the people of the City of the Sun, there is no jealousy.

Because nutrition is centrally controlled to be balanced and healthy with sufficient food for everyone, and because physical exercise is obligatory, the women are strong of limb, tall, and agile. People with disabilities are put to work at jobs they can excel at, for example, the physically lame are employed as guards, the blind sort wool, and those with crippling disabilities serve as spies for the city. Both men and women are trained for war. Although the city is peaceful, with no intention of invading other states, it is also prepared to fight to right wrongs committed against other states. The army has a particularly skillful and well-armed cavalry.

The city trades by barter rather than money. Visitors are welcomed for short stays and may apply for citizenship. Agriculture is so efficient that people work only four hours a day. Medical facilities are said to be very good. Passing reference is made to ships powered not by oars or the wind, and to the secret restoration of life after the age of seventy.

There is a highly developed judicial system, based on the decisions of the people themselves. It is harsh only on criminals who are trying to harm the liberties enjoyed by fellow citizens. However, the system uses no prisons or torture—a subject of personal interest to Campanella, who was a victim of both in Italy.

— *Chris Morgan*

CLARISSA: Or, The History of a Young Lady

Author: Samuel Richardson (1689-1761)
Type of work: Novel
Type of plot: Sentimental

Time of plot: Early eighteenth century
First published: 1747-1748

Setting is of practical and symbolic importance in this novel, whose wicked seducer, Lovelace, tries to maneuver the innocent young Clarissa Harlowe out of her father's home and into a place where she will be at Lovelace's mercy. The novel's English places—especially homes—are characterized in terms of what they mean to the heroine's peace of mind and safety of body; they are prisons (literal or figurative), refuges, or traps.

Harlowe home. Country estate of wealthy English gentry, near the village of St. Albans, to the northwest of London, it is presided over by a tyrannical patriarch, and its gardens are enclosed by an iron gate. It represents an Eden from which the heroine is lured by the satanic Lovelace into disobeying her father. It also represents the heroine's virginal body and mind, locked against Lovelace. Eventually, she is tricked by Lovelace into opening the gate and is abducted by him in the fatal error that begins her tragedy. The Harlowe home should offer a haven from the world for Clarissa, but it is so fraught with conflict that it becomes her first site of persecution when her siblings turn against her in jealousy, and her father tries to force her to marry a wealthy but odious man. After she forfeits her father's protection, she is never perfectly safe from Lovelace again.

St. Albans inn. The first stop after Lovelace abducts Clarissa in a coach. Lovelace pretends that they are brother and sister and makes up a story to explain why Clarissa has no luggage and is angry at him. Clarissa is frantic to get herself out of Lovelace's "protection," while Lovelace himself, peeved by her romantic resistance of him, resolves to carry her to a location that he controls.

Mrs. Sinclair's brothel. House on London's Norfolk Street. Lovelace gives Clarissa a choice of places to go, recommending London, ironically, for the privacy it can offer her. He invents letters attesting the character of the widow Sinclair's house, pretending it is the lodgings of a respectable officer's widow, whereas in fact it is a private brothel presided over by an intimidating, elderly, and grotesque woman who uses the name "Mrs. Sinclair" as a pseudonym. Here Clarissa is surrounded by unsavory people who resent her for her virtue, almost as though the brothel is a parody of the Harlowe home. Clarissa is at pains to defend herself against Lovelace's elaborate ruses to "test" her virtue.

Mrs. Moore's house. Lodgings of a respectable widow in London's Hampstead Heath neighborhood, and the place to which Clarissa escapes when she becomes suspicious of Lovelace's intentions. After tracking her down, Lovelace tells Mrs. Moore that Clarissa is his wife, who has run away from him in a nervous, spoiled fit of pique. He moves into the house with his servants and tries to persuade Clarissa to return to the "Widow Sinclair's." He finally manages to entrap her there by a ruse, and with the collaboration of Mrs. Sinclair and her prostitutes, he drugs Clarissa and rapes her.

Smiths' house. Shop and lodgings of an honest glove-dealer and his shopkeeper wife on King Street in London's Covent Garden neighborhood. Clarissa escapes here from Lovelace and remains safely until she is found out by Sinclair, who has her arrested coming out of church for not paying the bill for her room and board.

Rowland's house. Police officer's home in London's High Holborn neighborhood. Arrested and detained here, Clarissa chooses to stay in the prisoner's room, a "shocking" garret with bars on the windows and a locked door. She is subjected to persecuting visits from the spiteful prostitutes and is generally humiliated and dejected by the experience. When Lovelace learns what has happened he is furious and sends his friend Belford to tell Clarissa that she is permitted to return to the Smiths' without any danger of harassment from him. Worn out and disheartened by her persecutions and tired of life, Clarissa begins to waste away and becomes bedridden. As one of her final actions she orders and designs her own coffin. She dies in her room at the Smiths' with the coffin beside her, dreaming of returning to and being received as a prodigal daughter in "her father's house," that is, her Heavenly Father's house.

— *Elise Moore*

THE CLAYHANGER TRILOGY

Author: Arnold Bennett (1867-1931)
Type of work: Novel
Type of plot: Domestic realism

Time of plot: 1870-1895
First published: Clayhanger, 1910; *Hilda Lessways,*
1911; *These Twain,* 1915

This trilogy is set in what Arnold Bennett called the "Five Towns," a fictional version of England's industrialized Midlands region that serves as the background of much of his work. The individual stories of Edwin Clayhanger and Hilda Lessways are covered within the first two volumes, while These Twain *describes their life as a married couple. Since Bennett conceives of human nature as inextricably linked to the material conditions under which it grows and develops, the physical circumstances of life in the Five Towns play a major role in determining the actions of his characters.*

Clayhangers' first home. Combination dwelling and business premises in which Edwin Clayhanger spends his formative years. Situated on a busy square in one of Bennett's **Five Towns**, the fictional English city of **Bursley**, "D. Clayhanger, Printer and Stationer" is an integral part of local commercial life. Darius Clayhanger, Edwin's father, has worked for his living since the age of seven, and as a result has come to believe that one's identity is a function of one's occupation; all of his waking life is taken up with the operations of his printing business, which is described with a wealth of detail that suggests Darius himself has been imprinted with the stamp of the powerful presses he oversees.

Although Edwin does go into the family firm, he refuses to permit his decision to define the limits of his ambitions. He turns his bedroom into a sanctuary from the outside world—a place in which objects such as a model sailing ship can be contemplated and used to fuel the imagining of a life free from constraint. Even after he assumes responsibility for much of the shop's daily operations, he insists on creating a personal "lair" that symbolizes how he conceives of his position in the business: off limits to his employees but able to overhear what they say and do, Edwin preserves a sense of personal identity within the commercial organism that has swallowed the rest of his family.

Clayhangers' new home. Suburban residence to which the family moves when Edward is twenty-four years old. Owning a house that is not a place of business is a step up the social scale for the Clayhangers, and Edwin uses the opportunity provided by this change to create an even more satisfying refuge in his new bedroom. The acquisition of a personal library, which con-

tains many books his family would find incomprehensible or offensive, represents a further step in his efforts to widen the horizons of his existence.

After the death of his father and his marriage to Hilda Lessways in *These Twain*, Edwin asserts his new sense of independence by renovating the dwelling to suit himself. The installation of a radiator in its downstairs hall symbolizes his rejection of the Victorian cliché that cold houses build firm characters, and the physical as well as emotional warmth of his household is sharply contrasted with the frigid climate of his relatives' abodes. Edwin also strives to make his home a sanctuary against the demands of the outside world; just as he made his boyhood bedroom a refuge from his family, so does he make his adult residence a haven from the "varnished barbarism" of surrounding society.

Orgreave home. Residence of a refined middle-class family in which Edwin first meets Hilda Lessways. The Orgreaves' interests in music and literature open up new worlds of enjoyment for Edwin, and their amply furnished household likewise inspires him with the idea that one need not settle for the bare minimum of necessities in life. When the Orgreave parents die, the children go their separate ways, and Edwin is profoundly saddened by the loss of a place that represented his sense of what a cultured and civilized life should be.

*****Brighton.** Resort city on the southern English coast. When Edwin travels here in search of Hilda Lessways, he encounters extremes of wealth and poverty that stimulate his budding awareness of social inequality. For Hilda, who has gone to Brighton to manage an ailing friend's boardinghouse, it is the place where her sexual feelings are awakened by the seductive charms of a ruthless bigamist. As in many other British novels, notably Graham Greene's *Brighton Rock* (1938), the narrative's depictions of pervasive misery and squalor serve as an ironic counterpoint to the city's reputation as a wonderland of pleasure and delight.

Lessways home. Initial setting of the second part of the trilogy, *Hilda Lessways*. Here Hilda and her mother lead a comfortable but sterile existence that Hilda experiences as a prisonlike confinement offering material plenty but no deeper satisfaction. This household is portrayed as being obsessed with appearances, devoted to daily rites of cleaning and scrubbing whose gleaming surfaces mask the untidy realities that lie underneath them. Although Hilda comes from a middle-class background and Edwin from a working-class one, they are both driven by the need to create rewarding lives for themselves out of their spiritually and intellectually impoverished origins.

George Cannon's office. Law firm in which Hilda finds her first job. As is typical of Bennett's approach to character development, the office is presented as a literal embodiment of its occupant's personality: well organized and efficient, flawed only by a toppled volume of romantic poetry, whose presence foreshadows future revelations concerning Cannon's moral failings.

Shawport printing works. New suburban location of the Shawports' growing family business. After the structure has been built, Edwin regrets that he has taken a conservative rather than aggressive view of his economic prospects, and makes a direct connection between the only partial adequacy of the building and the "half-measures" that he sees as characterizing his life as a whole.

*Dartmoor Prison. Penitentiary in which Hilda's bigamous lover, George Cannon, is incarcerated. When Edwin and Hilda visit the prison in company with upper-class relations of the Orgreaves, the contrast between the latters' blithe disinterest in what they see and Edwin's horror at the treatment of the inmates is one of the trilogy's most powerful statements of differences among English social classes.

— *Paul Stuewe*

CLIGÉS: A Romance

Author: Chrétien de Troyes (c. 1150-c. 1190)
Type of work: Poetry
Type of plot: Romance

Time of plot: Sixth century
First published: Cligés: Ou, La Fausse morte, c. 1164
(English translation, 1912)

In this second of five romances by Chrétien de Troyes, one sees the legendary Arthurian court and its refined subjects as in the author's other works, with the dissimilarity being composed of the romance's many adventures having been based on Greco-Byzantine material. Once again, the localities lend to a reading of the historical past, but with a semimythic quality that transcends time. Although references are made to other locales, there are seven primary settings in this work.

*Athens. Greek city in which the Greek prince Alexander is born and where he dies; a place of rich tradition and heritage, but also one that harbors deception and deceit in this work. Alexander wishes to take leave of his family to be properly trained as a knight in Britain under the tutelage of King Arthur. He returns to Greece after his father dies to reclaim his rightful place as emperor; however, that place has been taken from him by his brother Alis.

*Brittany. Province of Celtic origin in what is now the western part of France that has been an important trading center throughout history. Alexander leaves Brittany with King Arthur and his retinue along with the Queen and Soredamors.

*Windsor. King Arthur's knights do battle with Count Angrés and his traitors. Alexander and Soredamors are wed here, and Alexander is made king of a large kingdom in Wales. In addition, this is a place of historical interest, in terms of beauty, culture, and diversity.

***Cologne** (kah-LOHN). German city with roots going back to the Roman era. It serves as the foreign location to which Alis descends in order to fulfill his own needs, while simultaneously breaking an oath with his brother in order to marry the eldest daughter of the German emperor.

***Wallingford.** Ancient English borough near present Oxford where knights go for a tournament. This setting is also the location of many tragedies.

Underground tower. Place where Fenice is kept after she and Cligés feign her funeral and burial. The setting symbolizes secrecy and that which is hidden.

— *Adriana C. Tomasino*

A CLOCKWORK ORANGE

Author: Anthony Burgess (John Anthony Burgess Wilson, 1917-1993)
Type of work: Novel

Type of plot: Dystopian
Time of plot: Indeterminate future
First published: 1962

Anthony Burgess's dystopian novel assigns no specific date to its grim vision of the future, but its world is evoked vividly through the voice of its teenage narrator, Alex. Environment reflects theme: When the "rehabilitated" Alex is released from prison, he finds a city restored to order, but its seemingly peaceful streets are patrolled by brutal police officers recruited from teenage gangs like his own.

City. Unnamed future British city where Alex and his "droogs," or friends, roam. The landscape is cheerless and industrial; echoes of the past and its culture can be seen, but these are largely decayed or corrupted. Streets are named for twentieth century British writers, and Alex and his gang wear masks of "historical" figures including Peebee Shelley (Percy Bysshe Shelley) and Elvis Presley. The Public Biblio, or library, is frequented only by the old and the poor, and the Filmdrome, or cinema, is decaying from lack of use. Giant housing developments, such as the Victoria Flatblocks, are home to most of the population. Past the flatblock developments is **Oldtown**, where Alex and his friends go in search of valuables to steal. Like its aged but elegant houses, the people of Oldtown seem to represent an earlier Britain. They include old men with sticks and old "ptitsas," or women, with cats. While robbing the Manse, a house in Oldtown, Alex beats and kills an old woman. The fifteen-year-old criminal is sentenced to fourteen years in prison.

Staja 84F. State prison in which Alex is imprisoned for robbery and murder. In this overcrowded, depersonalizing environment, he is addressed by number rather than by name. When a seventh man is thrown into Alex's cell, originally built for three, it sparks a brawl

that ends with the new man dead and Alex again accused of murder. Ironically, this incident wins Alex his freedom. Alex is chosen as a subject for Ludovico's Technique, a conditioning treatment designed to reform criminals. Given drugs to make him physically ill, he is forced to watch violent films, accompanied by classical music. Within weeks, Alex cannot see or think of violence or hear music without feeling horribly sick.

Municipal Flatblock 18A. Apartment in which Alex lives with his parents. The building's dingy halls are adorned with a socialist mural showing naked working men and women, their dignity marred by obscene graffiti. The elevators are smashed, so that Alex must walk ten flights up to his small flat. Despite the general dreariness of his surroundings, Alex has made his bedroom an oasis of civilization. Surrounded by stereo speakers on the walls, ceiling, and floors, Alex lies on his bed listening to Bach, Beethoven, and Mozart and dreaming violent dreams. When Alex returns home after his nonviolence conditioning, he is surprised to find the walls free of graffiti and the elevators running, and his stereo and albums sold.

Korova Milkbar. Public drinking place in which the novel opens; a favorite haunt of Alex and his droogs.

The milkbar has no liquor license but sells milk laced with drugs, either hallucinogens or stimulants.

HOME. Cottage in a village outside the city that is the home of the writer F. Alexander. Following a night of violence in the city, Alex and his droogs drive out to the country and stop at a comfortable middle-class cottage with a sign reading "HOME." In the course of their break-in, which ends with the beating of F. Alexander and the rape of his wife, Alex reads part of Alexander's work, *A Clockwork Orange*, in manuscript. The book, which gives Burgess's novel its title and central metaphor, is a condemnation of the attempt to impose upon human beings restrictions appropriate to machines. The writer's home, like the houses in Oldtown, seems a relic of an older, gentler era.

Alex returns to HOME as a victim. Released from prison, he is driven to the country by his former droogs, now policemen, and beaten. He makes his way to F. Alexander's place, where the writer, not recognizing Alex, who had worn a mask during the break-in, welcomes him. F. Alexander's cottage, warm and cozy, seems to offer Alex salvation, but it turns into another trap for him. The writer's political cronies want to martyr Alex to the cause of liberty, even commenting that it would be better for their purpose if he could look worse than he does. They spirit him to another flatblock, lock him in a room, and play music until Alex, maddened from pain, jumps from the window.

— *Kathryn Kulpa*

THE CLOSED GARDEN

Author: Julien Green (1900-1998)
Type of work: Novel
Type of plot: Psychological realism

Time of plot: 1908
First published: Adrienne Mesurat, 1927 (English translation, 1928)

This, Julien Green's second novel and the first he set in his native France, establishes what would become something of a staple in Green's novels: a fictional French town located somewhere between stereotype and caricature, as are many of Green's characters. The small-town setting allows Green credibly to develop and build the feeling of claustrophobia that leads his protagonist, Adrienne Mesurat, toward a nervous breakdown.

La Tour L'Evêque (lah tewr leh-VEK). Fictional French provincial town to which the widowed Antoine Mesurat retires in the company of his two daughters, Germaine and Adrienne. Its buildings tend to be ugly, its residents contentious and impertinent. Its landmarks described are typical of any small French town, with streets named for military figures and patriotic concerts in the town square. As the narrative proceeds, Adrienne feels increasingly hemmed in by a circle of watchful eyes. Before arousing her father's protective instincts, she enjoys walking through the town, unaware that even then, she is doubtless being watched.

Villa des Charmes (vee-ya day sharm). Mesurat family residence, grandly named for two hornbeam trees (*charme* in French) planted in the gated front yard, the closed garden of the novel's English title. Thirty-five year old Germaine, a self-proclaimed invalid, remains house-

bound until her sudden departure; her eighteen-year-old sister, Adrienne, is at first free to leave the house at will, but after the death of their father—in what may or may not be an accident—remains virtually imprisoned inside the Villa des Charmes. The house itself is described as ugly, built economically with more windows than bricks. In the novel's opening scene, young Adrienne is shown cleaning house, moving heavy furniture with apparent ease and casting reproving glances at the ancestral portraits hanging on the walls. Before long, however, her appearance of robust health gives way to delusions and fainting; the house itself, meanwhile, appears to Adrienne in terms of dark shadows and steep staircases.

Villa Louise. Neighboring residence, rented to the enigmatic Léontine Legras, at the very least a "kept" woman, with possible criminal connections. Adrienne occasionally seeks companionship at the Villa Louise with this neighbor, who is by turns friendly and treacherous. After Antoine Mesurat's sudden death, Madame Legras threatens to reveal Adrienne's possibly murderous secret, finally taking advantage of Adrienne's near-catatonic state to rob her of gold and jewels.

From the start of the novel, the Villa Louise stands as an important landmark, at first empty in anticipation of the new tenant's arrival, then as one of the few buildings that can be seen from the Villa des Charmes. At the end of the novel, the Villa Louise again stands empty, Madame Legras having defaulted on her lease and absconded with her plunder.

*Montfort L'Amaury. Town southwest of Paris that is Adrienne's first stop on her ill-fated attempt to escape

from La Tour L'Evêque. From here Adrienne mails her self-incriminating letter to Dr. Denis Maurecourt, the object of her unrequited affections.

*Dreux. Small city west of Montfort on the same train line that is the second and final stop on Adrienne's brief journey. Here Adrienne checks into a hotel, suffers a nightmare in which she fancies herself to have contracted Germaine's illness, and goes to a pharmacy in search of remedies. She then roams the town, admiring its landmarks and markets, briefly attracting the attention of a young workman whom she first sends away, then tries to find. Adrienne's visit to Dreux serves to highlight the increasing severity of her mental condition.

— *David B. Parsell*

THE CLOUDS

Author: Aristophanes (c. 450-c. 385 B.C.E.)
Type of work: Drama
Type of plot: Social satire

Time of plot: Fifth century B.C.E.
First performed: Nephelai, 423 B.C.E. (English translation, 1708)

The stage in this comedy represents the house of Strepsiades in Athens and the building next to it which houses the school of Socrates, which Strepsiades calls phrontistérion, *"the thinkery." The house of Strepsiades is a typical Athenian household, but that of Socrates is crammed with scientific gadgets.*

Strepsiades' house (strehp-SI-eh-dees). Home of Strepsiades, a plodding but solid citizen of Athens who is hounded by creditors because of debts incurred through the excesses of his son Pheidippides. His home appears to be a typical middle-class Athenian household. Pheidippides sleeps in a room next to his father's, and servants are quartered close enough to come when called. Strepsiades' room doubles as an office in which he works his accounts—which mostly concern paying his son's bills.

Thinkery (Thinking-School or *phrontistérion*). House owned by the philosopher Socrates, who is conducting scientific experiments when he is first approached by Strepsiades, who finds him suspended in a basket "contemplating the sun." This laboratory-like environment is a cross between a place of wonder and a madhouse. Groups of students stare into the ground, studying the underworld. Strepsiades sees a number of

scientific instruments used by the students in their investigations. When Socrates appears, he enters from above, lowered down on a winch used in the tragedies for the entrance of gods from the heavens. This is followed by a visit from a chorus of clouds, brought down from the heavens as part of Socrates' politically dangerous examination of things beyond the earth.

*Athens. Cosmopolitan Greek cultural center of late fifth century B.C.E. The Athens revealed by the play's two houses bustles with intellectual activity. It is also a center of commercial activity, and the high level of culture is indicated by the leisure available to Strepsiades' young son Pheidippides, who has squandered a fortune on horse racing. The allegorical figure Right sees the Athenian marketplace and public baths as the source of the boy's corruption.

— *John R. Holmes*

THE CLOWN

Author: Heinrich Böll (1917-1985)
Type of work: Novel
Type of plot: Psychological realism

Time of plot: 1945-1960
First published: Ansichten eines Clowns, 1963
(English translation, 1965)

Set in postwar West Germany, this novel is critical of how the new Germany can so easily have forgotten its bloody wartime past in order to become a booming industrial state. Through the biting observations of the narrator and outcast clown, Hans Schnier, from his Bonn apartment, it becomes obvious that he will never be able to connect with the selfish environment around him.

*West Germany. Federal Republic of Germany, created when Germany was partitioned after World War II. Out of the rubble of the war, West Germany has become a modern industrial state with a vibrant industrial base. A new landscape has been created, one that papers over the tortured past of the Nazi Third Reich and the war. The novel's flashbacks to the Germany that was under the control of the Nazis expose how readily the German state could change from its embrace of Adolf Hitler to its embrace of democracy. Over the years, Hans Schnier's father becomes rich by extracting coal from German soil. The family remains seemingly unaffected by the political and economic turmoil that consumes the country because of this exploitation of the land.

*Bonn. New capital of West Germany that is the hometown of the clown Hans Schnier, who returns there a broken man. To Schnier, Bonn becomes the symbol for all that is corrupt with the new West Germany. He became a successful clown outside Bonn; he returns there disillusioned and takes up residence in the apartment that he previously shared with the love of his life, Marie Derkum. Schnier has not performed in his hometown. He had always ventured to other German cities such as Cologne and Hannover to make his livelihood as a clown. He is thus out of place in this city. By the end of the novel, he is reduced to begging for money at a train station, while hoping that Marie will come back to him.

Apartment. Schnier's home in Bonn. From there he converses on the telephone with the outside world—his parents, other family members, his agent, and childhood friends. Most of the novel is set in this terra-cotta apartment, which in the past Schnier normally lived in only three or four times a year. In his traveling days, he usually feels more at home in hotels than in his own apartment. The isolation of the apartment speaks to the separateness that Schnier feels toward the whole country.

Railway station. At the end of the novel, Schnier puts a thick layer of makeup on his face and carries his guitar to the Bonn train station, where he begs for money and waits for Marie to return from Rome with her new husband. He is determined to wait for Marie in the hope that she will save him from the destitute existence into which he has spiraled. He is most definitely at the crossroads of his life. For Schnier, the past, the present, and the uncertain future will converge at the train station.

*Rome. Capital of Italy to which Marie and her new husband, the prelate Heribert Züpfner, go to celebrate their Roman Catholic faith and their marriage at the center of the Catholic world. They may even hope to have an audience with the pope. When Züpfner takes Marie away from Schnier, he persuades her to rekindle her Catholic faith. Schnier also has visions of himself in Rome asking to see the pope. Rome is a symbol for the religious establishment that creates a wall between Schnier and the woman he loves.

*East Germany. Democratic Republic of Germany, created when Germany was partitioned after World War II. East Germany is depicted as a puppet state of the Soviet Union in which no one is allowed to express views that differ from the Communist Party line. On a visit to East Germany, Schnier cannot bring himself to conform by performing sketches that are critical of capitalism. To do so would run counter to his integrity as an artist.

— *Jeffry Jensen*

THE COCKTAIL PARTY

Author: T. S. Eliot (1888-1965)
Type of work: Drama
Type of plot: Comedy of manners

Time of plot: Mid-twentieth century
First performed: 1949; first published, 1950

This play is set in two London places: a couple's flat and a psychotherapist's consulting room. The cocktail party that opens the play ironically lacks the hostess, Lavinia Chamberlayne, and its guests are only people who Edward Chamberlayne does not know are coming and cannot un-invite after his wife disappears. The result is an awkward social occasion for many. The play's setting thus emphasizes dysfunctional relationships that are only beginning to heal by the end of the play.

Chamberlayne flat. London apartment owned by the Chamberlaynes, in whose drawing room most of the play is set. Although the apartment has an offstage kitchen, there appears to be virtually nothing eat in the apartment, except for a few eggs. The lack of food for the party, or even ordinary meals, symbolizes the lack of provision for any life in this shell of a home. As the play unfolds, both Chamberlaynes prove to live hollow existences that each of them has come to loathe. Relationships that Edward starts with Celia Coplestone and that Lavinia starts with Peter Quilpe prove fruitless and unsatisfying. Once the pretenses of husband and wife are unmasked, they learn to love each other, and are at last "lain" in their "chambers," as their last name suggests. The last cocktail party held in this home shows that Edward and Lavinia have grown closer together, and Guardians toast to the partial success they have had.

Harcourt-Reilly's consulting room. Office of the psychotherapist Sir Henry Harcourt-Reilly. The office is arranged so that Sir Henry can manipulate the entrances and exits and meetings of people at his will. His consulting room functions like the central office for a spy network. Along with the other two Guardians, Mrs. Julia Shuttlethwaite and Alexander MacColgie Gibbs, these three function like the Greek Fates who shared an eye between them as they wove the tapestry of people's lives. Sir Harcourt-Reilly sings about "One-Eyed Riley" and Mrs. Shuttlethwaite—whose name suggests weaving—is constantly looking for her glasses with only one lens. Alex completes this seemingly all-knowing trio with his globetrotting habits for gathering information about patients. Sir Henry ultimately sends Celia to her martyrdom, while salvaging the marriage of the Chamberlaynes, and trying to help Peter, whose future remains uncertain at the end of the play. For all of their insights and schemes, the Guardians prove limited in their ability to shape and direct lives.

— *Daven M. Kari*

COLD COMFORT FARM

Author: Stella Gibbons (1902-1989)
Type of work: Novel
Type of plot: Parody

Time of plot: Early twentieth century
First published: 1932

Throughout this novel, the heroine Flora Poste contemplates her life in the light of books she reads, even asserting that she is much like the nineteenth century writer Jane Austen. These references invite readers to read the novel as a parody following the struggle between Flora's Austenesque virtues of efficiency, orderliness, cleanliness, and irony and the old-fashioned attitudes of her rural relatives. As Stella Gibbons satirizes the regional novels of authors such as Mary Webb, Sheila Kaye-Smith, Thomas Hardy, and D. H. Lawrence, her descriptions of places support her themes of common sense and female ability.

Cold Comfort Farm. Starkadder family farm to which Flora Poste moves. Taking its name from a line in William Shakespeare's play *King John* (1596-1597), the farm is located outside the village of Howling, near Beershorn in southern England's Sussex region. One of the characters believes the farm is cursed, as seeds do not grow and the cows do not reproduce. However, this opinion is negated by the fecundity of the maid and the hearty growth of the sensual sukebind (a fictional plant), just as the austerity of the farm's name is undercut by the primal passions seething beneath the characters' forbidding personalities.

The farm is described in long, adjective-filled phrases reminiscent of the lush description in regional novels of the period. These descriptions include anthropomorphized animals, plants, and buildings that serve as symbols of the human passions. The farm is symbolic of a sentimentality toward the rural and old-fashioned, a place where a dishwashing "mop" is considered innovative and even a newspaper is disconcerting. The heavy regional style is made comic, for example, by Gibbons's use of modern and fanciful names for the farm animals, such as bull named "Big Business," the misconceived metaphors and similes (the sun "throbbed like a sallow lemon"), and the casual approach to calamity (the hired hand fails to notice when a cow loses a leg). The farm is populated by stereotypical rural types, from the domineering matriarch to the hell-fire-and-brimstone preacher to the loyal family retainer.

Dark and dirty, the farmhouse is a maze with nooks, crannies, hidden doors, and inaccessible attics. It is not necessary to know that Gibbons is directly parodying the farmhouse in Mary Webb's *The House in Dormer Forest* (1920) for readers to realize that the house embodies the darkness and complexity of the human relationships in the novel.

Howling. Town one mile away from Cold Comfort Farm. It has no train station and only one pub, the **Condemn'd Man**. Even to reach Beershorn, the closest train station (which is seven miles from the farm), takes four and a half hours by train from London, even though the Sussex region is only about fifty miles from London. The cheerless names and the slow transportation emphasize the isolation of the Starkadders and their farm.

Woodshed. Place where the family matriarch, Aunt Ada Doom Starkadder, saw "something nasty" when she was a little girl. Ada uses this ugly memory as an excuse to impose her will on the family; if any one crosses her, she threatens to have an "attack." The woodshed symbolizes all evil for Ada, evil from which she must protect herself and her family. The nasty incident is never explained, and the reader never gets a description of the actual woodshed (it is not on Cold Comfort Farm, since Ada came from elsewhere when she married into the Starkadder family), but its presence haunts the novel.

*****London.** Great Britain's capital city is mentioned but never lavishly described; London provides a contrast to Cold Comfort Farm. To Flora, the great city represents normalcy in dress, action, speech, and attitude. Therefore, it is to London that she takes Elfine to transform her into a woman fit for Richard Hawk-Monitor and where she takes Judith for psychiatric help.

The Downs. Grassy, treeless upland expanse between Cold Comfort Farm and Hautcouture Hall (pronounced "Howchicker Hall" by the locals), the family estate of her higher-class boyfriend, Richard Hawk-Monitor. Elfine spends a lot of time outdoors, both in the Downs and elsewhere; Flora indicates that Elfine's poetry celebrates nature in an honest, unself-conscious way, unlike both the Freudian descriptions of Mr. Mybug and the sentimentalized descriptions in rural novels of the period.

*****Hollywood.** California motion picture industry center to which Flora dispatches Seth, who loves the "talkies." While Hollywood does represent modernity, it is not depicted as a center of normalcy. Instead, it offers a lifestyle at the opposite extreme from that of Cold Comfort Farm. The narrator calls it the "Kingdom of Cockaigne," which is an imaginary land of delight and luxury.

— *Kathryn A. Walterscheid*

THE COLLECTOR

Author: John Fowles (1926-   )

Type of work: Novel

Type of plot: Psychological realism

Time of plot: c. 1960

First published: 1963

This novel's settings help to portray and contrast the two main characters and to investigate themes of freedom, personal responsibility, and class. Frederick Clegg and Miranda Grey move separately to London and then together to the outskirts of a small village not far from Lewes in East Sussex. The geographic movements portray their temporary rise in situation and then their separation from society. The misfit Clegg's desire for isolation symbolizes his static nature and class consciousness. Miranda's longing for freedom symbolizes her desire to grow and experience life.

Fosters. Secluded cottage in southern England's East Sussex region built in 1621. After winning a fortune in a football pool, Clegg buys the house because of its isolation and particularly because it has a large cellar complex. Its location, two miles from the nearest village and three quarters of a mile from the nearest neighbor, provides a perfect locale for Clegg to follow his dream, to "collect" Miranda as he has collected butterflies. After he kidnaps Miranda, he confines her in his cellar. During her two months of imprisonment, Clegg lives upstairs while Miranda lives underground in her whitewashed cellar room with no fresh air. Her claustrophobic cellar existence symbolizes Clegg's darker nature and the unconscious desires that he cannot integrate into his personality.

The cottage's cellars are described realistically, the outer room equipped as a kitchen and the inner cellar as a bed-sitting room. Miranda refers to her stone-and-concrete chamber as the "crypt" and longs for sunlight and fresh air and freedom, which lie outside her locked door. The cottage is surrounded by fields of alfalfa (lucerne), gardens, hedges, and woods. Clegg himself is impervious to the natural beauties of his home but Miranda's artistic nature leads her to admire the main house's upstairs rooms, with "crossbeams and nooks and delicious angles," which she gets to visit only occasionally. Miranda struggles against her imprisonment. Though unsuccessful in all her escape attempts, she has some success in transcending the cellar as she mentally matures.

*****London.** Great Britain's capital and great city, in which Miranda grows, personally and artistically. Before being kidnapped, she attends the **Slade School of Art**, lives with her aunt in Hampstead, and comes to know George Paston (G.P.), an artist who functions in the novel as a foil for Clegg. In contrast, London serves

as a reminder to Clegg that he does not fit in socially; he is obsessed by class differences. His pleasures in London are limited to stalking Miranda and buying "books of stark women" in Soho.

G. P.'s Studio. George Paston's art studio in northern London's Hampstead district. As a symbolic contrast to Miranda's cellar room, G. P.'s studio represents freedom. In her cellar room, Miranda daydreams about G. P. and his studio, recollecting what she has learned there of art and music and relationships and herself. The studio is modest, but everything in it expresses G. P.'s true nature, thereby contrasting with Clegg's cottage, whose inherent charm is compromised by the way he has decorated it with what he thinks represents respectability.

Ladymont. Miranda's London boarding school before she wins a scholarship to the Slade School of Art. Throughout the novel, Miranda matures beyond the "suffocating atmosphere" of Ladymont, where middle class social propriety rules over individualism. Miranda begins to think for herself instead of blindly accepting the values of her background.

Town Hall Annexe. Clegg's government office workplace in London before he wins the football pool that allows him to quit his job and move to Sussex. A misfit even in the government office, Clegg only finds respite from the boring and repetitive work of clerking by staring out the window at Miranda's family home across the street.

*****Lewes** (LEW-ihs). Sussex town in which Clegg shops after moving into Fosters. He avoids the nearby village in order to preserve his privacy, but his neurosis about how people regard him causes him discomfort even in Lewes.

— *Marion Boyle Petrillo*

THE COLOR PURPLE

Author: Alice Walker (1944-)
Type of work: Novel
Type of plot: Social realism

Time of plot: 1920's-1940's
First published: 1982

The structure of this novel follows the expulsion of the main characters, Celie and Nettie, from their childhood home to a final triumphant return to that same place. Similar to Harriet Beecher Stowe's Uncle Tom's Cabin *(1851-1852), Walker uses domestic motifs and especially the places of domesticity, houses and homes in a poor rural southern community, as a subversive trope to counter chauvinistic and racist attitudes. By using these places, the author is able to present female characters in a stereotypical role which makes their transformation all the more dramatic and admirable.*

Pa's home. Rural Georgia home in which Celie and Nettie live together as young sisters. This place serves as a frame for the novel, which begins and culminates in this small, frame house. Despite the severe psychological and physical abuse to which the girls are subjected in this place, the home is where their formative bonding occurs. Although the girls are treated like slaves in their own home, this place of origin endures throughout the novel as a constant reminder of their only identification as family and the primary source of motivation for a desperately hoped for reconciliation.

The culmination of the novel is directly linked to this place. At the end of the novel, Celie takes possession of the home. The significance of this act is threefold. First, it serves as a validation of her hard-won independence. The house becomes a place in which she makes the important decisions concerning upkeep. After this change occurs, the home becomes prosperous and its inhabitants are at peace, in contrast to Celie's early years in the home under male leadership. The house also serves as a reward for the faithful endurance of the sisters. Their long suffering results in a happy reunion in the place of their childhood trauma. Finally, the place is a symbol of transformation. Its inhabitants are emotionally transformed into vibrant characters, symbolized by the house's physical and structural reconstruction.

Mr. _____'s house. Celie's home after she marries the unnamed Mr. _____. Representing the nadir of her existence, this house becomes her descent into hell, though the hellishness of the place is masked by its outward appearance within a social context that prohibits a woman from rising to the level of her abusive husband. What goes on behind closed doors in this home is pro-

tected by the sham of traditionally accepted behavioral norms and social custom. Within this house, Celie is continuously mistreated by Mr. _____, the ultimate insult coming when he brings his ailing mistress, Shug Avery, into the home and Celie is expected to care for her. In her marriage home, as in her childhood home, Celie has no control over her destiny and receives no more affirmation as a person than a slave might have.

*Memphis. Tennessee city famous for its night life, where Shug Avery, a singer and performer, makes her home. In Memphis, Celie lives with Shug in relative luxury, enjoying the amenities of Shug's healthy income. Celie learns a trade, and with Shug's support and economic sense, eventually makes great strides toward becoming financially successful as the owner and manager of her fashion business. Celie's tenure in Memphis is important because it is the first time in her life that she is free from the bondage of abusive men. For the first time, Celie becomes aware of her options and begins to see herself as a valuable human being.

Olinka village. West African village where Celie's two children are raised by Nettie and the place where Nettie spends most of her life separated from her beloved sister. The primitivism of this jungle place contrasts with the modernization of America, but more important, despite the obvious contrast, this place is used to parallel the journeys of Celie and Nettie. In both places, the ramifications of female subjection to men are indicated. This village also serves to presuppose the limitations of paganism, apparently contrasting with the Christian background and home of Nettie. However, the reality suggested by the author is that American Christianity, when reinforcing traditional relationships that obscure abuse and prevent female ascension and equality, is suspect.

Harpo's home. Another ordinary home in the impoverished rural southern setting of this novel, and a place in which female retaliation to physical abuse occurs. Like his father, Harpo abuses his wife; however, Sophia fights back before eventually leaving him. Her action contrasts with Celie's endurance of mistreatment. Left alone, Harpo transforms his home into a juke joint. Shug later sings there, and Squeak also begins her singing career at this place, so this is one place where a woman can be celebrated, provided she is talented and attractive. In contrast to the abusive family relations, the juke joint becomes a place where men in the community gather to celebrate their existence; however, their celebrations are little more than masks to cover the serious mistreatment of women.

Miss Millie's home. Home of the white mayor and wife, where Sophia finds herself unjustly sentenced to twelve years of maid service for refusing to cower to Miss Millie. This home serves to remind readers of another layer, beyond the home, in a social nexus that encumbers a black woman seeking validation and independence. Readers see the awful price of racism that Sophia endures because she has sufficient dignity to stand her ground, but her stance contrasts with Celie's tranquil endurance.

Samuel's home. Home of a local minister, who will become a missionary to Africa, which becomes Nettie's home when the girls are separated. It is the closest thing to a positive traditional view of domesticity in the novel. However, even this home, despite its overt piety and compassionate motives, reinforces female subjection.

— *Kenneth Hada*

THE COMEDY OF ERRORS

Author: William Shakespeare (1564-1616)
Type of work: Drama
Type of plot: Farce

Time of plot: First century B.C.E.
First performed: c. 1592-1594; first published, 1623

By setting this play in Ephesus, William Shakespeare transformed Plautus's third century B.C.E. play Menaechmi *from a brilliant secular Roman farce into a complex play imbued with wonder and deepened by many allusions to Christianity. His addition of a second plot from John Gower's fourteenth century poetical version of the Greek romance* Apollonius of Tyre *changes Plautus's cynicism to a miraculous recovery in which grace and mercy prevail over fateful loss and harsh justice.*

*****Ephesus** (EF-ah-sas). Ancient Greek port city in Asia Minor that was later the capital of Roman Asia; it is now an archaeological site near Smyrna in Turkey. Elizabethans were familiar with Ephesus from the New Testament, and as an ancient seaport and location of the temple of Artemis (Diana to the Romans), which is one of the Seven Wonders of the World. The commercial pagan center for the cult of Diana became a place of Christian conversion in the first century.

While St. Paul was living in Ephesus, he wrote his Epistle to the Ephesians, which makes strong statements about marriage and domestic relations—themes that are at the core of Shakespeare's play. St. Paul described

Ephesus as a place of sorcery and exorcists—a description that match's the play's depiction of the city as a "town full of cozenage" with "sorcerers" and "witches." It is an apt location for the farcical confusions that arise from the twin masters (Antipholus of Syracuse and Antipholus of Ephesus) and twin servants (Dromio of Syracuse and Dromio of Ephesus); Doctor Pinch tries to exorcise Satan and cure madness. In contrast, Aegeon accepts the enmity between Ephesus and Syracuse and his sentence of death. Only humility and submission to God's will suffice in a world of human errors.

The play features four locations within Ephesus: the houses of Antipholus of Ephesus (Phoenix), the courtesan, and the Priory; and the street—a fluid space for the frenetic encounters in which identities are mistaken as all assume acquaintance and prior actions. The setting was especially effective on Elizabethan stages, which had large open spaces with two pillars, entry doors, and an upper stage.

*Syracuse. City in southeast Sicily founded by Greeks in the eighth century B.C.E. At the time in which this play is set, Syracuse and Ephesus were enemies and it was forbidden for citizens of one land to journey to the other—a point around which the play's plot revolves. The penalty for the crime was execution or a payment of a thousand marks. Aegeon, a merchant of Syracuse who has recently traveled to Ephesus, is to be put to death because he cannot raise the thousand marks.

— *Velma Bourgeois Richmond*

THE COMPANY OF WOMEN

Author: Mary Gordon (1949-   )
Type of work: Novel
Type of plot: Social realism

Time of plot: 1963-1977
First published: 1981

The narrative in this novel shifts between New York City and a town in western New York State. Using memory as a method of storytelling, the author follows five women's devotion to Father Cyprian Leonard, a Roman Catholic priest, with whom they keep in touch long after he moves upstate.

Convent of Our Lady of Sorrows. New York City convent at which five working women of different backgrounds come together on a retreat in 1932. The retreat is the creation of the dynamic priest Father Cyprian Leonard. Though he is as rigid as the church he represents, his faith and charisma endear him to the women, and they begin a lifelong devotion to him. Meeting throughout the 1930's the women develop close friendships with one another outside of the convent, but Father Cyprian is the linchpin that holds them together.

*New York City. City in which four of the women in the retreat group work and live, and two of them marry. Populated with millions, New York City is a lonely place for single women, and loneliness is one of the things that drives the five women to the religious retreat, where they become friends.

Orano. Fictional farming town in western New York State that is the birthplace of Father Cyprian and his home after he returns there in 1959. A few years later, the women from his New York City retreat begin spending their vacations in Orano. Its small-town warmth is a contrast to the indifferent atmosphere of the big city. During the tumultuous 1960's and 1970's, Orano is also an oasis from the troubled demonstrations and stormy political environment of the city.

Though tranquil and peaceful on the surface, however, Orano has its underlying realities as evidenced by Father Cyprian who, in a moment of cruel pique, forces Felicitas to experience the foul stench of farm animal excrement. Also, the beautiful countryside belies the underlying poverty of the community and reflects the underlying emotions of the protagonists, each jealous of the other, each vying for Cyprian's attention during their vacations. Eventually, Orano does measure up to the positive image of small towns everywhere and brings solace and refuge to Felicitas, the daughter Charlotte conceives while she is a student at Columbia. At the story's end, the women settle in the farming community and find the peace they sought in New York City, where they first met at the religious retreat.

*Worcester (WEW-ster). Massachusetts city in which Muriel lives. The only woman of the group who does not reside in New York City, Muriel lives with her mother, whom she takes care of, and works as a typist. She is as lonely in Worcester as the women who live in New York City. After her mother dies, she builds a house in

Orano and lives next door to Cyprian for six months of the year.

*Columbia University.** New York City university to which Charlotte's daughter, Felicitas, transfers from St. Anne's College during the late 1960's. Her pursuit of classical studies—the reason for her transfer—becomes less important to her than experiencing real life and fitting in with her peers. Her sheltered background of Catholic schools and vacations spent with her mother, her mother's women friends, and an aging priest do not prepare her for college life in a big city. In 1970 the Vietnam War is on, and the word "hippie" is new to the language. Naïve Felicitas revels in her new-found friends and freedom but is seduced by a professor. Surprisingly, her resulting pregnancy is not only supported by the older women, but Father Cyprian welcomes them all back to live in Orano.

— *Anne Trotter*

THE COMPLETE POEMS OF EMILY DICKINSON

Author: Emily Dickinson (1830-1886), edited by
Thomas H. Johnson

Type of work: Poetry
First published: 1960

Emily Dickinson never married, seldom traveled, and lived her entire fifty-six years in her parents' home in Amherst, Massachusetts. Though she profoundly probes the human soul, her vistas seldom stretch beyond her immediate environs.

*Amherst.** Massachusetts town where Dickinson lived, about ninety miles west of Boston. Although her poems mention Amherst by name only twice, it is organic to Dickinson's poetry. She absorbed the old-fashioned Calvinism of nineteenth century Amherst. At the congregational church she attended in childhood, sermons depicted a wrathful God and threatened everlasting punishment. Dickinson frequently chose religious subjects, and yet, with the contrariety endemic to New Englanders, she rebelled far more than she acquiesced. In a few instances, she seems to have been influenced by the New England Transcendentalists.

*Homestead.** Dickinson family home on Main Street in Amherst. Most of Dickinson's poems employ the imagery of the domestic sphere. Yet she possesses the New England Puritan typological imagination that beholds cosmic meanings in homely images. Everyday events become, through metaphor, intense psychological states. She can comment that "The Bustle in a House/ The Morning after Death/ Is solemnest of industries/ Enacted upon Earth—." The household imagery used to describe feelings so profound provides much of the impact of her poems. Home was, to Dickinson, her natural place, and to her imaginative vision, the source of the "types" of ineffable psychological states.

*Homestead grounds.** Garden and meadow near the Dickinson home. Dickinson's store of images brims over with the natural phenomena of her gardens. The robin, she declares, is her "Criterion for Tune—/ Because [she] grow[s]—where Robins do—." Daisies, roses, and bees abound in her poetic garden, as well as berries, carnations, maples, gentians, butterflies, anemones, orioles, whippoorwills, and violets—all found in the immediate surroundings of the house.

*Amherst cemetery.** Community graveyard that is within walking distance of the Homestead. Dickinson must have contemplated the cemetery many times as funeral processions passed, as some of her poems testify. A few are spoken from the grave, as shown in lines "I died for Beauty," and "I heard a Fly buzz—when I died."

— *Jo N. Farrar*

COMUS

Author: John Milton (1608-1674)
Type of work: Drama
Type of plot: Allegory

Time of plot: Age of myth
First performed: 1634; first published, 1637

Although this play uses real seventeenth century English and Welsh locations, its main action unfolds in a world of myth.

*Ludlow Castle. Norman fortress built on the Welsh border to maintain English imperial power in the eleventh century. The castle served as the residence of the fifteenth century king Edward IV, who was the first prince of Wales. During John Milton's youth, the castle was home to the lieutenant general (also known as president) of Wales. When the earl of Bridgewater was appointed to that office in 1634, Milton wrote "A Masque [to be] Presented at Ludlow Castle" at the time of his formal installation. Readers have given the masque the name of its most eloquent character, the handsome tempter Comus.

Wild Wood. Forest that is home to Comus. As the drama begins, a guardian spirit descends into a forest where travelers are always in peril. He has been sent by Jove. (The mythology is classical, but the theology is Christian.) He explains that Jove takes special interest in Great Britain, and in the nobleman sent "to guide" the Welsh. The spirit has come to protect the nobleman's children as they travel to their new home. He is especially watchful because the forest is home to Comus, the son of Circe. Just as Circe turned men into swine in

Homer's *Odyssey* (c. 800 B.C.E.; Eng. trans., 1616), Comus has gathered a "rout of monsters."

There are three siblings, a lady and her two brothers. When they become separated, Comus moves in, disguised as a shepherd offering the lady food and shelter. But his home develops into a place of misrule, where he entices the lady to drink from his magic cup. She resists until the spirit leads her brothers to the rescue.

*Severn River. Longest river in Wales, flowing from England to the Atlantic. After the brothers chase off Comus, the spirit needs further assistance and summons a river nymph named Sabrina, whose home is the Severn (which is also known as the Sabrina River). Attended by water-nymphs, she rises and sings a song that releases the lady.

*Ludlow. Market town in Herefordshire. The play's final scene shows Ludlow and its castle, which the children approach. The country folk welcome them in dance, and the children greet their parents. After an evening of festivities, the spirit bids farewell, urging everyone to "love virtue."

— *Thomas Willard*

CONFESSIONS OF AN ENGLISH OPIUM EATER

Author: Thomas De Quincey (1785-1859)
Type of work: Essays
Type of plot: Fantasy

Time of plot: Early nineteenth century
First published: 1821

Thomas De Quincey's stylized reflections on his opium addiction recall his youthful vagrancy in England, after he ran away from his grammar school, and the growing importance of his hallucinogenic dreams as his addiction grew stronger.

Manchester Grammar School. School in the city of Manchester in England that is roughly equivalent to an American prep school. There, the adolescent Thomas De Quincey's already delicate health is strained by the arduousness of his experience and his boredom with the school environment and his guardians and mentors. He begins grappling with his health problems and bodily pains, especially of the liver. The gloomy climate and rains of Manchester make his educational experiences even more dismal. After some deliberation, he resolves to leave the school and becomes a vagrant.

London. Capital city of Great Britain in which De Quincey eventually settles after running away from Manchester Grammar School. Getting by on borrowed money, he lives precariously by wandering cold streets by night and sleeping by day. His poor health and disillusionment grow, forcing him to live frugally and in a period of intellectual decline and aimlessness. Despite being Britain's greatest city, London does not improve De Quincey's outlook on life or his prospects.

Worcester College (WEW-ster). College of Oxford University in which De Quincey enrolls at the urging of his family. While developing a deep interest in German philosophy and literature at Oxford, De Quincey begins using opium, initially for medicinal purposes, to ease his physical pains, but he eventually becomes addicted. He leaves Worchester College without completing his degree.

Grasmere. Village in England's Lake District in which De Quincey settles. There, his addiction to opium reaches its height. He leads a sedentary life in his small cottage, where he succumbs completely to the power of opium. In the first stage of his addiction, opium gives him peace and harmony. He has a great affection for his cottage, which he adorns with old books, draperies, and other accoutrements. He is content to live in his cottage, using opium and reading great literature. This languid lifestyle initially seems ideal to De Quincey, who attributes his happiness to the freshness and natural beauty of Grasmere. In the second stage of his opium habit, however, De Quincey begins experiencing depression, melancholy, and hallucinations. His life becomes even less active as he slowly realizes that opium addiction creates more health problems than it cures, and he experiences fantastic and disturbing dreams.

De Quincey depicts Grasmere with such poetic affection and picturesque seriousness that he thinks the village's fresh air should revive his health and remove his melancholy.

— *Hanh N. Nguyen*

CONFESSIONS OF FELIX KRULL, CONFIDENCE MAN: The Early Years

Author: Thomas Mann (1875-1955)
Type of work: Novel
Type of plot: Picaresque
Time of plot: Early twentieth century

First published: Bekenntnisse des Hochstaplers Felix Krull: Der Memoiren erster Teil, 1954 (English translation, 1955)

Writing his memoir from jail, Felix Krull reflects upon a lifelong concern to know "which is better, to see the world small or to see it big?" Though his question is directed not to geography but to the fulfillment of his fantasies and dreams, intuitively he knows from childhood that his cunning ambition requires the broadest possible stage. Leaving his youth and his native German language behind, he embarks on a life of bold yet light-hearted deception in Paris and beyond.

Lisbon. Portugal's capital city was to be only a brief stop on a world tour that Felix undertakes using an identity he has traded with an aristocratic Parisian friend. Because of a chance encounter on the Paris-to-Lisbon train with a distinguished paleontologist, his visit is extended for many weeks so that he can exploit his new identity in attempting to seduce the man's wife and daughter.

Lisbon is one of many southern European destinations found in Thomas Mann's fiction; the most celebrated occurs in *Death in Venice* (1912), but a more compelling literary source for the notion of a sojourn in a southern region is the Italian journey of the German poet Johann Wolfgang von Goethe (1749-1832), whose life and work permeated the consciousness of writers like Mann. For both authors, southern Europe represents not merely a gentler climate but also the warmth and grace of classical and Mediterranean cultures as well as a relaxation of the cultural and sexual inhibitions of home.

Lisbon is the one locale in *The Confessions of Felix Krull* evoked with any great degree of topographic detail; its hills and streets, people and dwellings—and a bull ring still in use today—are colorfully described. However, Mann had little interest in visual detail for its own sake. In his last year he observed, "The world of the eyes is not my world." The vividness of Krull's description of Lisbon is Mann's masterful interpretation of his character's evolving experience. Though the beauty and grandeur of the city predictably fail to have an effect on Felix's character, at last his love of luxury and sensuous pleasure is in harmony with the physical environment.

If Mann had lived to continue his tale of Felix Krull, the episode in Lisbon would likely have been a point of transition to even more exotic escapades in South America, but the novel's abrupt conclusion, with a scene in a garden followed by a hilarious seduction, makes the city itself seem to be a true consummation of Felix's desire.

*Paris. Felix arrives in the capital of France virtually penniless and leaves it a year later as an aristocrat, albeit a fake one; he is transformed *in* the City of Light, but not by it. Although he takes in the circus and the opera, and enjoys other modest pleasures that he can afford as a low-paid hotel worker, he gives little attention to the city's famous monuments and other cultural riches, instead preferring to assume the role of a *flâneur*—a detached and idle denizen of the city's boulevards and cafés. The most vivid excursion Felix offers his readers is a furtive mission to "rue de l'Echelle au Ciel"—Ladder to Heaven Street—to fence some jewelry he has pilfered only days earlier on his train journey to Paris. When he alludes to the "spaciousness and splendour" of Parisian scenes, his thoughts only serve to remind him of his disgraced late father exclaiming *"Magnifique!"* and "almost fainting at the memory" of his happy student days in the French capital.

The mainspring of life in Paris for Felix is his work in the Hotel Saint James and Albany, a first-class hotel in which he is first an elevator boy and later a waiter. The varied spaces of the hotel are brilliantly rendered in both their physical and social dimensions, and Felix is as much at home in the dreary workers quarters as in the fashionable dining room. In the busy hotel, unlike the bustling but anonymous streets of Paris, every motion and interaction must be negotiated with staff, bosses, and guests. Felix, who imagines himself as a spiritual and physical descendent of the god Hermes, moves gracefully into and out of astonishing relationships with men and women both young and old. The most poignant of these brief encounters is with Lord Strathbogie, who invites Felix to accompany him to his ancestral home near Aberdeen, Scotland, to be his valet and, ultimately, his heir. The character of Strathbogie is thought to be a partial self-portrait by Mann, as is the figure of Felix himself. From this perspective, one can see the geographical symbolism of the episode: the author's youthful surrogate is destined for sun-drenched Southern climes, not the cold mists of the North.

*Frankfurt. German center of commerce and wealth. With the virtual collapse of the Krull family following the elder Krull's suicide, Felix and his mother are forced to move to Frankfurt, a "great, cold-hearted city." While his mother contrives to start a boardinghouse, Felix undertakes his self-education in the ways of the urban metropolis, but he must be content with pressing his face "against the magnificent gates of a pleasure garden."

If *Confessions of Felix Krull* is a late, satirical form of the novel of personal development, or *Bildungsroman*, it is no longer nature or culture that is the classroom, but rather the modern industrial city with its alienation and class distinctions, which Felix absorbs and then transcends. In his enchantment at the city's material treasures and his "eagerest desire to learn," Felix is a harbinger of urban, consumerist culture.

Krull home. Located in a town slightly to the west of Mainz, on the Rhine River in western Germany, the Krull home stands on a slope "happily exposed to the summer sun." To the young Felix, the family's bourgeois home stuffed with knick-knacks is a virtual Eden of sensuous pleasures; this is a condition that extends to the town, where as a youngster he engages in an act of theft of candy from an unattended delicatessen.

Around the turn of the twentieth century, when this novel is, roughly, set, travel is mostly by boat, carriage, or railway car; the automobile does not appear in the novel. Felix's cherished first memory of an excursion is from age eight, when the family travels to Wiesbaden to attend the theater. There he sees and is enraptured by an operetta set in Paris, thus prefiguring his later experiences in the French capital.

— Clyde S. McConnell

THE CONFESSIONS OF NAT TURNER

Author: William Styron (1925-   )
Type of work: Novel
Type of plot: Psychological realism

Time of plot: c. 1810-1831
First published: 1967

Based closely on the real-life story of Nat Turner's 1831 slave revolt, this novel is set firmly in antebellum Virginia, where Nat's perceptions of his condition and plans to mount a slave revolt evolve as he is transferred from owner to owner.

***Virginia.** Southern state in which the historical Nat Turner (1800-1831) led the revolt on which William Styron's novel is based. Following the historical record, the novel is set in various locations in Southampton County, in the state's southeastern corner. Styron suggests that Virginia's "relatively benign" atmosphere may have made it the only state in which a revolt such as Turner's could have occurred, as conditions in states south of Virginia were so dehumanizing that slaves had little leisure with which to contemplate their condition and consider changing it. By contrast, many slave owners in Virginia were mild enough to permit slaves the leisure to contemplate their slavery, and even, in the case of Turner, permit them to learn to read. Indeed, it is through reading the Bible that Turner is inspired to mount his revolt.

***Jerusalem.** Site of the Virginia jail where Turner awaits his execution and dictates the confessions that form this novel after his revolt collapses. During his last days, the "gray dawn" approaches "stealthily," and the "pale frost" awakens Turner to the "hard clay" of his cell's floor and to the "mournful" sounds of the city and the "hysteria" that hangs over Jerusalem "like thunder." Ironically, when Turner begins his revolt, its ultimate goal is to reach Jerusalem, where he intends to seize the armory so he can supply weapons to his incipient army. Jerusalem becomes his final destination, though not in the way he originally plans. In this depressing atmosphere at the end, under the "gray impermeable sky," Turner feels, for the first time, not closer to God in Jerusalem, but utterly separated from the God whose will he originally believes he is obeying.

***Dismal Swamp.** Large swampy area overlapping southeastern Virginia and northeastern North Carolina. Turner plans for his followers to take refuge there after wreaking their vengeance on white people, who he believes are incapable of following black people into the swamp. He never reaches the swamp, but the outcome of his revolt proves to be as dismal as the swamp itself.

Turner farm. Place where Nat is born and reared and where he experiences his greatest happiness. When he is young, he is unconscious of his slave status, thanks to belonging to masters who object to slavery on principle. There Nat is taught to read and is promised that he will learn a trade and be emancipated when he reaches the age of twenty-five. He later remembers this farm as a big house with the "golden light" of spring and the smell of newly plowed ground. He remembers flowers, ferns, and the "brilliant fuss of chattering birds."

Eppes farm. Nat's second home, located near the western Virginia town of Shiloh, a "grim and pious" little community, where Nat is the only slave and leads a life of dull drudgery. Nat later remembers the community as a place of small farmers, a "bleak and undone brotherhood" of failures from a depression era, along with their "goiterous women" and "worm-infested children."

Moore farm. Nat's third home. Here he is whipped for the first time and learns more of the cruelties of slavery. He remembers his first introduction to this place during a bleak winter. There he sleeps in a "dark little cupboard" where he learns to live with "emaciated mice" and spiders. Nat's plans for killing the white masters begins to take shape while he is living on this farm.

Travis farm. Nat's final home, which he remembers as "more pleasant acres" than those on which he previously has lived and on which his living accommodations, his "bachelor quarters," are "cozy." His memories include a "balmy climate." Nat feels that he possesses some dignity under his masters, the Travises, whom he regards as basically decent people who let him ply his

trade of carpentry. However, it is in the nearby woods that he first experiences a vision of God, which he interprets as divine sanction for his mission.

*Norfolk. Large coastal Virginia town. At both the beginning and end of the novel, Nat dreams about the ocean and his own stark white temple nearby, which he says must have been based on his dreams of Norfolk, which he never actually sees. He dreams of a "barren, sandy cape" with the winds "benign and neutral." On the promontory stands a serene white temple. This mysterious temple, without doors or windows, seems to represent the ultimate mystery of God, near the ocean of the cycle of life and death.

— *Jo N. Farrar*

THE CONFIDENCE MAN: His Masquerade

Author: Herman Melville (1819-1891)
Type of work: Novel
Type of plot: Satire

Time of plot: Mid-nineteenth century
First published: 1857

In contrast with the varied, exotic, and often far-flung settings Herman Melville employed in much of his other work, the action in this novel is restricted to one day aboard a steamboat that is beginning its trip from St. Louis to New Orleans. Nonetheless, in this philosophical/theological satire setting is important both symbolically and in terms of plot. Melville represents the steamboat as a microcosm of American culture, just as the Pequod *in* Moby Dick *(1851) was a microcosm of world culture. The steamboat's many niches provide ample space for the title character to meet victims, ply his trade, and change disguises; the steamboat offers all the amenities found on land, yet it inhabits water, ever moving, rooted to no single place. Like its passengers with their mutable ethics, the ironically named boat is unmoored, complex, full of secrets.*

Fidèle. Mississippi river steamboat on which the entire novel is set. The *Fidèle*'s main cabin is a large, opulently appointed room in which passengers spend their time drinking and gambling. Melville seems to use the frivolity of these pastimes as both a commentary upon superficial pleasures and upon the intoxicating, risky nature of financial speculation. At times the unnamed Confidence Man, though considered a criminal, seems to differ from the other passengers only in his superior skill at dissembling and risk-taking. In his guise as Mr. Truman, he meets a merchant in the main cabin and sells him shares in the "Black Rapids Coal Company."

The merchant tells the story of a young man who leaves his jealous, possibly demented wife, only to be

sued by her and eventually ruined. This is one of several stories told in the course of the novel, usually by the Confidence Man's intended victims; the stories revolve around trust, morality, and money, major themes of the novel. Elsewhere in the text, in one of many literary allusions, Melville compares the passengers of the *Fidèle* to the pilgrims in Geoffrey Chaucer's *Canterbury Tales* (1387-1400); their story-telling is an obvious connection to Chaucer's masterwork, but unlike Chaucer's pilgrims, Melville's steamboat passengers do not even pretend to share a sacred destination but are driven solely by self-interest and greed.

Emigrants' quarters. Dark, confined area of the steamboat in which the poorest passengers sleep. There the Confidence Man talks a miser out of a hundred dollars, engaging him in a theologically tinged, mostly one-sided dialogue about trust, a subject to which he returns often in his many encounters with the boat's passengers. Melville compares the emigrants' quarters to purgatory and to Hell; some modern critics see the Confidence Man as a satanic figure, and his ease in these infernal surroundings may lend credence to this interpretation. The shabbiness of the emigrants' quarters contrasts with the gentlemen's cabin, where the novel's final scene takes place.

Settee. Long wooden bench on the steamboat's main deck. Although located in the open, it affords a semiprivate place to talk. The longest continuous scene in the novel takes place here, as the Confidence Man, in his final guise as the foppish Frank Goodman, talks with, in turn, a passenger in a violet vest, a character named Mark Winsome (a stand-in for Ralph Waldo Emerson), and a character named Egbert (a stand-in for Henry David Thoreau). The man in the vest tells the Confidence Man about Colonel John Moredock, who devoted his life to hating Indians; they discuss whether Moredock's pure hatred is a kind of virtue. With Winsome and Egbert the Confidence Man debates some of the tenets of Transcendentalism, concluding that Emersonian "self-reliance" is little more than tight-fisted economic and emotional self-interest. Of all his encounters on the boat, the Confidence Man comes closest to meeting his match in the loquacious and obstinate Egbert.

Barber shop. Salon located in an arcade on the steamboat's main deck. After his disputations with Winsome and Egbert, the Confidence Man goes to the barber shop for a shave as he prepares to retire for the night. He tricks the barber into giving him a shave on credit despite the latter's prominently displayed sign, mentioned here and in the book's opening scene: "NO TRUST." In Melville's time barber shops were associated with cosmetic artifices such as fake moustaches, toupees, and the dyeing of hair; thus the Confidence Man's duping of the barber, who makes his living fooling people, conveys particular irony.

Gentlemen's cabin. Sleeping compartment containing berths and a table, lit by a single lamp on whose glass shade is emblazoned the altar of Moses as described in Exodus. Here the Confidence Man encounters an elderly man reading the Bible. They talk about the Apocrypha, raising the question of whether it is possible to have confidence in even the word of God. A young peddler enters and persuades the old man to buy a money belt. The novel ends with the Confidence Man extinguishing the symbolic lamp and leading the old man to what the reader assumes will be a swindling, if not an outright robbery.

— *Hayes Hampton*

THE CONFIDENTIAL CLERK

Author: T. S. Eliot (1888-1965)
Type of work: Drama
Type of plot: Comedy of manners

Time of plot: Mid-twentieth century
First performed: 1953; first published, 1954

This play is set in a grand London house. Its first and third acts take place in the house's business room; the second act is set in the flat redecorated for a business assistant and situated in the meadow, near the main house. Life in the world of this play is conducted as if it were a business.

Mulhammer's house. Stately London home that represents high society while also housing many illusions and self-deceptions. Although most of this house is not shown in the play, its grand business room gives the impression that the entire house is similarly grand. One entire room is devoted to Sir Claude's own pottery and his dream of becoming a first-rate artist—a goal he knows he will never achieve. The house is thus devoted to his attempt to overcome his artistic failings with business successes. Colby Simpkins is brought into the home to be the new confidential clerk, largely because Sir Claude thinks Colby is Sir Claude's illegitimate son, and in part because Sir Claude thinks Colby is another second-rate artist who must find his success in the business world.

By the end of the third act of the play, again set in the business room, all characters' illusions are dispelled, and the play's changelings have found their true identities. Colby proves to be the son of a disappointed church musician, so Colby pursues a church profession in Joshua Park, the part of London in which Mulhammer's former confidential clerk, Eggerson, lives. Barnabas Kaghan is the misplaced foundling of Lady Elizabeth, so he proudly joins the family as Lucasta's fiancé. Only Sir Claude, who at first seems most in charge, ends in speechless despair as his illusions crumble around him at a hearing he himself has called.

Mulhammer's flat. Bachelor's apartment renovated for Colby Simpkins. The main room's most prominent furnishings include a fine piano and a desk with a typewriter, thus symbolizing the tension in Colby's life between the world of art and the world of business. It is in this apartment in the second act that Colby realizes that his world contains too many illusions and that he must find the truth before he can choose his profession.

— *Daven M. Kari*

CONINGSBY: Or, The New Generation

Author: Benjamin Disraeli (1804-1881)
Type of work: Novel
Type of plot: Bildungsroman

Time of plot: 1832-1840
First published: 1844

This novel about the lives, loves, friendships, and struggles in British upper-class society around the time of the great Reform Bill treats the emergence of the industrial class to political power. Harry Coningsby's life experiences, from sitting at a desk in a preparatory school to sitting in his first seat in Parliament, mark the emergence of a new English elite that is more accommodating of political and social change.

***Eton.** Fashionable boys' preparatory school, located near Windsor, outside London, to which the protagonist, Harry Coningsby, is sent after he loses both parents at age nine. Founded in the fifteenth century, Eton is the most prestigious public school (equivalent to an American private school) for boys in Britain. The novel portrays the school as a scenic place at which bells ring merrily as boys advance in age, while forging influential bonds of friendship that are to last lifetimes. The boys also run the famous Library at Eton, an experience intended to serve as a participatory model for governance of free institutions. Coningsby reads much, and by the age of eighteen is ready to complete his education at Cambridge University, which ranks with Oxford University as the finest institution of higher learning for the elite of British society.

Monmouth House. Magnificent mansion and residence of Coningsby's grandfather, the Marquis of Monmouth, at which Coningsby renews his acquaintance with his grandfather, along with an assortment of uncles and aunts. Lord Monmouth tells young Coningsby to regard the house as his own. Coningsby's own family home, **Beaumanoir**, is also a vast and ornate mansion in which even mundane things, such as the serving of breakfast, can evolve into a ceremonious occasion.

Forest Inn. Traveler's hostelry in England's Midlands region where Coningsby first makes the acquaintance of the wealthy young Jew, Sidonia, a believer in the Hegelian omnipotent individual and the omniscience of youth. Sidonia is also a firm believer in the power of intellect and Coningsby renews their acquaintance at a later dinner arranged by his grandfather at Monmouth House.

*****Paris.** Capital of France in which Coningsby again meets Sidonia while on vacation when he is twenty-one years old. Coningsby meets with great social success in Paris but falls in love with Edith Millbank, who is already engaged to Sidonia.

*****Manchester.** City in northwestern England in which Coningsby briefly lives that the novel portrays as a center of the country's Industrial Revolution and a beacon of technological progress, as symbolized by the fact that Coningsby's bedroom is lighted by gas. Coningsby finds much to admire in Manchester.

Hellingsley. Estate adjoining Monmouth that Lord Monmouth dreams of owning that is bought out from under him by the wealthy manufacturer Oliver Millbank, who represents the new British aristocracy of merit, talent, and industrial-based wealth. The purchase also gives Millbank control of a parliamentary seat in the next election.

Darlford. Constituency in which Coningsby stands for election to Parliament, at his grandfather's suggestion. The novel ends with his election, which places him on the threshold of public life as a symbol of a new generation of political leaders.

— *Irwin Halfond*

A CONNECTICUT YANKEE IN KING ARTHUR'S COURT

Author: Mark Twain (Samuel Langhorne Clemens, 1835-1910)
Type of work: Novel

Type of plot: Social satire
Time of plot: Late nineteenth and early sixth centuries
First published: 1889

This pioneering time-travel story sends a modern American, a New England "Yankee" who happens to be both a mechanical whiz and a fervent believer in American republicanism, back to the feudal world of sixth century England during the legendary King Arthur's time. The clash of cultures that ensues pits past against present and English cultural conservatism against American progressivism.

*England. Apart from the frame that surrounds the main narrative and a brief interlude in Gaul toward its end, the entire novel is set in southern England during a roughly ten-year period that begins in June, 528 C.E. Before selecting this time period, Mark Twain contemplated writing a novel contrasting the feudal institutions of the Hawaiian kingdom, which he had observed in the 1860's, with those of the modern West. He decided instead to set his story in England of the sixth century after reading Sir Thomas Malory's *Le Mort d'Arthur* (1485). As is typical of literary treatments of Arthurian legends, Twain's depiction of sixth century England is far from realistic. What interested him was not the details of any specific period, but resistance of old and entrenched institutions to change. He was particularly critical of the Roman Catholic Church, which dominated England through the Middle Ages. His Yankee's noble efforts to implant modern technology and democratic social and political institutions in medieval England meet the implacable resistance of the Church and end in apocalyptic failure.

*Warwick Castle. Castle on the Avon River, near modern Birmingham, in which the novel begins and ends. The castle links distant past and present and may be seen as Hank's emotional portal to the sixth century. In the book's prelude—set around 1889—the frame narrator meets the "Yankee," Hank Morgan, at the castle. Later, at an inn, Hank begins telling his story and lets the narrator read his manuscript, which becomes the core of the novel. The novel ends with the narrator revisiting Hank just before the latter dies. Connections between the historical Warwick Castle—which Twain visited and admired—and Arthur's Camelot are entirely Twain's invention. The castle's location is several hundred miles north of the novel's sixth century settings.

*Connecticut. New England state that is home to Hank, who styles himself "a Yankee of the Yankees." As befitting the stereotype of a no-nonsense New Englander, Hank calls himself "practical . . . and nearly barren of sentiment." Twain was born and raised in the South but lived in Hartford, Connecticut, at the time he

wrote *A Connecticut Yankee*, and he strongly admired New England culture and values.

*Hartford. Connecticut city in which Hank is head superintendent in the great Colt Arms Factory until he is sent back in time by a blow on the head he receives in a crowbar fight with a factory ruffian. Hank's job makes him even more versatile and inventive than the typical Yankee. At the factory, he "learned to make . . . anything in the world, it didn't make any difference what; and if there wasn't any quick new-fangled way to make a thing, I could invent one." These skills give him the confidence to try to make over early England's technology.

Hank mentions Hartford several times in his narrative and has a wistful nostalgia for a young West Hartford telephone operator (a "hello-girl") that tends to pull him emotionally back to his own time.

Camelot. Legendary seat of England's **King Arthur's court** and principal setting for the novel's earliest and last chapters. Though the subject of intense research, Camelot's historical location—if it actually existed—is unknown, and *Connecticut Yankee* itself provides only vague clues to its location. Its Camelot appears to be about fifty or sixty miles southwest of London and nowhere near Warwick Castle. The novel depicts Camelot as a large city on a plain overlooked by a hilltop castle. In common with other renditions of Arthurian legends, the novel describes a castle with towers, turrets, and vaulted ceilings more characteristic of the architecture of the High Middle Ages than of the much earlier period in which the story is set. Under Hank Morgan's leadership, Camelot begins to develop into a truly modern city, only to revert to its primitive condition when Hank's new civilization collapses.

Valley of Holiness. Home to several hundred monks and ascetic hermits who represent a concentration of early England's most backward beliefs. After rescuing imaginary princesses from imaginary ogres, Hank arrives in the valley to find that its famous holy fountain has stopped flowing. He uses the crisis to mount his most spectacular demonstration of modern technology, when he uses a rocket display to punctuate his triumph over the magician Merlin in a competition to restart the fountain's water flow. Modernism's other triumphs over backwardness in the valley include the appearance of the

first issue of Hank's Camelot newspaper. However, the tenuous line between old and new belief systems is strained when Hank is nearly upstaged by a second-rate conjurer whose crude magic impresses the local monks almost as much as his own real science and technology. The incident shakes Hank's confidence in his ability to transform England.

Abblasoure (ab-lah-sewr). Village about ten miles south of the Valley of Holiness near which Hank and King Arthur—traveling incognito—visit the home of a family wiped out by smallpox and then spend several days in the home of the charcoal burner Marco. During this sojourn, Hank and the king have their first extended exposure to the everyday lives and concerns of the lowest rungs of English society. Initially, Hank is favorably impressed by the people he meets; however, careless remarks that he and the king make elicit the villagers' deep fear of new ideas and turn the villagers savagely against them.

Cambenet (kam-beh-net). Village where Hank and the king are sold into slavery by the Earl Grip. From there, they begin a month-long march to London as members of a slave caravan—an experience that moves the king to begin modifying his views on the institution of slavery.

*London. Little more than the small trading center founded by Romans several centuries earlier, London is the principal setting of chapters 35-38. Hank and the king arrive there as slaves but are rescued by a brigade of knights who ride in from Camelot on bicycles.

Sand Belt. Site of an apocalyptic battle after the Church's Interdict forces the collapse of Hank's civilization. The belt is a defense perimeter around **Merlin's Cave**, where Hank and his few remaining allies confront more than twenty-five thousand knights. The first knights who enter the belt are blown to bits by mines. When a second wave of knights enters the depression created by the explosions, they are drowned by a stream that Hank suddenly diverts into the new ditch. Hank's victory is pyrrhic, however, as the immense numbers of dead bodies surrounding the cave make his stronghold a death trap from which he is the only person to escape, and he escapes only because Merlin casts a spell that makes him sleep for thirteen centuries.

— *R. Kent Rasmussen*

THE CONSCIENCE OF THE RICH

Author: C. P. Snow (1905-1980)
Type of work: Novel
Type of plot: Psychological realism

Time of plot: Early twentieth century
First published: 1958

This novel focuses on the life of a wealthy Anglo-Jewish family, the Marches, as observed by their impecunious friend Lewis Eliot. Their splendid London residence lies at the heart of the narrative, providing a setting for the novel's many elegant dinner parties and family gatherings. Symbolic of a traditional, opulent, and hierarchical way of life, their Bryanston Square home is juxtaposed with the humbler Pimlico dwelling chosen by Charles March after his marriage to the communist Ann Simon, as well as with the obscure midland home of the narrator, resembling the provincial Leicester of C. P. Snow's birth.

***London.** Great Britain's capital and leading city. On his arrival in London, the narrator, young provincial lawyer Lewis Eliot, is fascinated by the metropolis, whose life takes on a glamour of its own, and whose restaurants, theaters, and clubs are "invested with a warm, romantic haze." The London summer pleasures of his wealthy friend Charles March include such typical upper-class amusements as the ballet, Wimbledon, coming-out dances, and parties in the prestigious neighborhoods of Grosvenor Square, Knightsbridge, and the Park. With the Marches, Eliot visits the splendid home of the Holfords, with its beautiful garden and extravagant display of fireworks, the fashionable house of Herbert March, and, above all, Leonard March's Bryanston Square residence, all of which allow him to observe closely the exotic milieu of the rich. Lewis himself rents two small rooms at the top of a lodging-house on Conway Street, near Tottenham Court Road.

As both Lewis and Charles study law, they frequent the legal London of chambers and courts. Charles's decision to abandon his career in law for the less prestigious one in medicine provokes one of the central conflicts of the novel.

Bryanston Square. London home of the patriarch Leonard March (Mr. L.) and his two children, Katherine and Charles. Bryanston Square is a stronghold of the traditional upper-class Anglo-Jewish way of life, with its lavish parties and elegant Friday dinners designed to consolidate the family. Most social events take place in the large, dazzlingly bright drawing room and even larger dining room, which contains family portraits dating back to 1730. The house's study, with its dark brown wallpaper and bookshelves of ancestral leather-bound

collections, is the refuge of the master of the house. Lewis Eliot's awe at the splendor of the March residence highlights the contrast between his lowly origins and the wealthy Jewish merchant class into which Charles was born and from which he is trying to escape.

Despite its traditional character, Bryanston Square is not immune to the social changes taking place in the 1930's. To the displeasure of its household servants, the opulent guests of the past are being replaced by people without connections or wardrobes. Even Mr. L.'s children turn away from the customs of their elders; their rebellion takes many shapes, from relaxing the once-rigid dinner dress-code to choosing controversial life partners. When Katherine and Charles leave Bryanston Square with their spouses, they abandon the social order represented by their father and his brilliant residence. The last part of the novel, aptly titled "Alone," closes with an image of Mr. L.'s solitude: After testing the latches and switching off the lights, he would be left in his own company.

***Pimlico.** London neighborhood in which Charles March establishes his medical practice and lives with his wife Ann. His father disapproves of his choices of both a career and a spouse and repeatedly refers to his new place as "Pimlico and similar unsalubrious neighborhoods." Lewis Eliot describes the house as dingy on the outside but featuring a bright interior, marked with Ann's taste. The cozy brightness of the house corresponds to the happiness of Charles and Ann's marriage.

Note **office.** Located on London's Charing Cross Road, the office of the communist newspaper to which Ann contributes. The building's murky stairwell reeks of shavings and mildew, and the *Note*'s neighbors include "art photographers," dingy solicitors, and a questionable-looking trading company. When Lewis visits the office, he gets a glimpse of a world of which Mr. March would rather not know.

Haslingfield. Hampshire country house of Mr. L. that provides the setting for the long, lazy summer days that the Marches spend with friends. It is here that Ann and Charles fall in love. With its bay windows, tennis courts, terrace, and lush wooded view, Haslingfield is every inch the traditional English summer estate. Mr. L.'s migration between his two houses has been marked with unfailing regularity for the forty years since the purchase of Haslingfield. His premature return to London in the year of the *Note* affair betrays the turmoil caused in the patriarch by his son's disloyalty.

— *Magdalena Mączyñska*

THE CONSCIOUS LOVERS

Author: Sir Richard Steele (1672-1729)
Type of work: Drama
Type of plot: Sentimental

Time of plot: Early eighteenth century
First performed: 1722; first published, 1723

This play is set in London, but unlike earlier comedies, the London presented in this play is the world of the middle class, not the fashionable world of coffeehouses, periwigs, and elaborate dress.

Bevil's house. London home of Sir John Bevil. Contrasts in the play may be seen in the different lodgings of the characters since all the scenes but one take place indoors. Sir John Bevil's house is the house of a wealthy merchant replete with a full staff of servants. It is a house designed for practical uses and plain taste. Much of the comedy in the play comes from the scenes with servants, especially Tom and Phillis.

Indiana's house. Home of Indiana and Lucinda, a small, simple dwelling that fronts the street in Charing Cross. When Mr. Sealand enters the house searching for Indiana he has no difficulty finding her. Nevertheless, Indiana's house, despite her state of relative poverty, is a genteel dwelling suitable for one of her class. It is not a dwelling of the lower classes such as would have been common in the historical London of the day.

***St. James Park.** Large London park. Only one scene is set out of doors. The setting of act 4, scene 2, is the fashionable Mall area of St. James Park. The Mall was a long tract in St. James that was formerly used for playing pall-mall. By the time of this play it was known as a fashionable park used for walking, for meeting lovers, and for displaying the latest fashions. It is often confused with Pall Mall, another park close by.

— *Paul Varner*

CONVERSATION IN THE CATHEDRAL

Author: Mario Vargas Llosa (1936-   )
Type of work: Novel
Type of plot: Social realism

Time of plot: 1960's
First published: Conversación en la catedral, 1969
      (English translation, 1975)

In this complex novel, two men meet in the "Cathedral," a shabby bar in Lima, Peru, to spend an afternoon telling each other stories and talking about power, politics, and the past. Their conversation, which goes on for four hours, gradually reveals a scathing portrait of the corruption and immorality of the city's ruling classes.

*Lima. Capital city of Peru. Mario Vargas Llosa often draws from his personal experiences to write about corruption and injustice in modern Latin America. In this novel he uses his intimate knowledge of Lima as the basis for his story. As a young man, he spent two years at Lima's Leoncio Prado Military Academy, where his father sent him after discovering that he wrote poetry, to him, an unmasculine pursuit. Vargas Llosa found the school's restrictions, discipline, and bullying atmosphere unbearable. His first novel, *The Time of the Hero* (1962), portrayed the institution, and many of his works focus on father-son relationships.

In the 1950's, Vargas Llosa worked as a journalist at Lima's *La Cronica* and Radio Panamericana. *Conversation in the Cathedral* draws on the political atmosphere in Lima during this period. Lima is Peru's cultural and business center. It runs at a slower pace than many South American cities; its rhythm is more traditional and its people reflect a steadier, calmer constitution. Lima's atmosphere has been described as dreamlike, partly because of the mists that settle over the city between May and October. Under its blanket, residents meet at bars offering folk and Creole music, shop at open marketplaces, and dine at Lima's celebrated restaurants.

Cathedral. The "Cathedral" of the novel appears to be a bar or cheap restaurant. There, Santiago Zavala, a thirty-year-old journalist, meets with Ambrosio, a man working at the dog pound, where Santiago has gone to collect his own dog, which had been seized in a roundup of rabid animals. As their conversation progresses, Santiago gets drunk from drinking too much beer and taking in the oppressive memories and shocking revelations arising in the conversation. For example, he learns that his ostensibly respectable upper-class father has been cheating his chauffeur, who happens to be Ambrosio. Moreover, Ambrosio has murdered a woman who was blackmailing Santiago's father.

Gradually, their conversation reveals a cast of interrelated whores, maids, ministers, bureaucrats, generals, senators, businessmen, cops, madams, and strong-arm men who fit together to fill out the jigsaw puzzle that is Lima and the nation of Peru itself. Although the conversation in the Cathedral is never reported in full and thus never clears up all the questions it raises, it does let loose a kind of labyrinth of memories and associations that form the novel's narrative.

— *Elaine Laura Kleiner*

CORIOLANUS

Author: William Shakespeare (1564-1616)
Type of work: Drama
Type of plot: Tragedy

Time of plot: Third century C.E.
First performed: c. 1607-1608; first published, 1623

William Shakespeare's plays were originally performed with settings indicated only by brief stage directions and lines within the scenes. This is set during the time of early Rome, on the outskirts of the towns of Corioli and Antium. Shakespeare adapted this story from the Greek historian Plutarch's writings; however, the historical Coriolanus lived in the fifth century B.C.E., not in the third century C.E., in which this play is set.

*Rome. Capital of the Roman Empire on the banks of Italy's Tiber River. It is a walled city built on seven hills, one of which is the Capitoline or Capitol Hill. The senate house, where the tribunes meet and new consuls are sworn in is on Capitol Hill. Here, too, is Rock Tarpeian, a precipitous rock from which traitors are flung to their deaths—a fate suggested for Coriolanus. The market place, or Forum, is a meeting place for citizens where Coriolanus solicits the voices of the people in his attempt to become consul.

*Corioli. Walled city in the territory held by the Volsci, who are enemies of Rome. The Roman army is camped in trenches before Corioli's walls as the play begins. The gates in the wall, where Coriolanus enters alone to fight Tullus Aufidius, face the encampment. The real battle of Corioli took place in 493 B.C.E., but no traces of the town remain, and its exact location is unknown.

*Antium. Volsci town on the Italian coast south of Rome where the Volsci general Tullus Aufidius flees after the battle of Corioli. Coriolanus goes to his house there after his exile from Rome.

— *Pauline Morgan*

THE CORSICAN BROTHERS

Author: Alexandre Dumas, *père* (1802-1870)
Type of work: Novel
Type of plot: Adventure

Time of plot: 1841
First published: Les Frères corses, 1844 (English translation, 1880)

The setting of this story about supernaturally bonded twins is split between their homes in Paris, the sophisticated capital of France, and Corsica, an island of vitality and primitive traditions.

*Corsica. Mountainous French island in the Mediterranean Sea. Smaller than Sicily, Sardinia, or Cyprus, Corsica is just over one hundred miles south of mainland France. The novel opens with the Parisian narrator, a fictionalized Alexandre Dumas, arriving in Corsica after a visit to Elba, a much smaller French island northeast of Corsica. From Corte and Ajaccio, Corsica's capital, he travels south to Sartène. Whereas the itinerary the narrator recommends to fellow French travelers emphasizes Corsica's geographical proximity to Toulon, on the French mainland, the rest of the novel dwells on the gulf between life and customs in France and in its island department, Corsica. The narrator remarks that Corsica is a French department but is far from being France.

While extolling the island's picturesqueness, its marvelous horses, its famous bandits, and its old-fashioned hospitality, the narrator notes its two supreme differences from the French mainland: its people's constant use of the Italian language and their belief in the vendetta, a blood feud between families or clans, which originated in Sicily and other parts of Italy.

Corsica is also famous as the birthplace of French emperor Napoleon Bonaparte, and nearby Elba was the island of his first exile. Clearly some of the narrator's admiration for Corsica comes from Dumas's Bonapartist sympathies. Writing twenty-three years after Napoleon's death, Dumas brings Napoleon into the story indirectly by making Lucien de Franchi the owner of a saber given by Napoleon to his grandfather at a 1798 battle in Egypt. Fittingly, Lucien associates his and Napoleon's former island home with space and liberty, refusing to leave it for any city.

*Sartène (sahr-TEN). Southern Corsican province in which the narrator enjoys the hospitality of the de Franchis through the first half of the novel. During his stay with them in the obscure village of Sullacaro—which has exactly 120 houses—he admires Lucien as a fine specimen of manhood and applauds his success in eradicating vendettas. Lucien, in fact, seems almost a cultured noble savage, someone who could play the Parisian gentleman, as does his twin brother, but who prefers to live according to the rhythms of nature in his homeland.

Château of Vincentello d'Istria (vihn-sen-TEL-oh dihs-TREE-ah). Ruined family castle to which Lucien and the narrator journey by night to meet a feuding bandit. The landscape is imposing, almost Gothic, with the moon shining down on the ruins, on the Mediterranean in the distance, and on the ridges of Mount Cagna, which divides the island in two—in a manner reminiscent of the twins—unity in separation. In one of the novel's pointed contrasts between Corsican and Parisian life, Lucien follows the narrator's praise of agility in climbing steep rocks with a joking reference to the capital's own hill, Montmartre—a hill in north central Paris, and definitely an elevated urban location with its stairways and residing artists.

***Paris.** Capital of France in which the second half of the novel is set, most notably in Louis's apartment, which the narrator visits immediately on his return to the city. Through deliberate contrasts with the many outdoor settings in Sartène, the action here unfolds mostly in interiors, such as restaurants, elegant bachelor residences, salons of bourgeois households, thereby capturing the capital's emphasis on fashionable living. Whereas in Sullacaro the narrator accompanies Lucien on a moonlit rendezvous in the mountains with a bandit, here he joins Louis at the young man's romantic assignation at the Ball of the Opéra, under the clock in the green room. One outdoor site is the place where Louis is buried, Père Lachaise cemetery, established in 1804 in the eastern part of the city.

***Bois de Vincennes** (bwah deh vihn-senz). Forest east of Paris enclosed in the twelfth century as a royal hunting preserve; the accompanying chateau was used as a royal residence between the fourteenth and seventeenth centuries. The large forest area became a popular site for duels, and there both Louis and Lucien duel with Monsieur de Château-Renaud. The final chapter offers a dramatic fusion of Corsican and Parisian customs when Lucien kills his brother's opponent in a duel that he conducts in the spirit of a vendetta. Despite Lucien's earlier complaint about France's tastes and habits diluting Corsican values, it is his Corsican honor that triumphs in the end.

— *Margaret Bozenna Goscilo*

THE COSSACKS

Author: Leo Tolstoy (1828-1910)
Type of work: Novel
Type of plot: Psychological realism

Time of plot: Nineteenth century
First published: Kazaki, 1863 (English translation, 1873)

In this classic portrayal of the "superfluous man"—a common figure of nineteenth century Russian literature, a character alienated from society and unable to attain any accomplishment that gives him true satisfaction—Leo Tolstoy takes his hero Olenin to a Cossack village in the northern slopes of the Caucasus Mountains. Although Olenin finds the lives of these vital, semibarbaric people intensely alluring, he cannot make a place for himself among them and ultimately brings disaster on them.

***Caucasus Mountains.** Mountain range south of Moscow between the Black and Caspian Seas that has historically been regarded as the dividing line between Europe and Asia. Now divided among several former Soviet republics, the region was under Russian domination in the nineteenth century. With its picturesque mountains and many fiercely independent tribes, the region occupies a place in Russian literary tradition similar to that of the Wild West in American literature. The various tribes of Tatars, Chechens, Circassians, Azeris, Georgians, Armenians, and others were often regarded as "noble savages" in a manner similar to the literary romanticization of Native Americans.

The Chechens in particular were renowned as fierce fighters, and the appellation *dzhigit* is often compared to the expression "brave" for a Native American warrior, although it is inextricably linked to expert horsemanship in a way that even the great Plains Indians never attained. The Chechens were also far more successful at resisting Russian overlordship than any Native American societies were at resisting the westward expansion of the United States. Indeed, since the breakup of the Soviet Union in the early 1990's, the Chechens have continued to resist Russian domination.

Although Tolstoy's novel is to some degree the Russian equivalent of an American Western story, Tolstoy tempers the romantic imagery of the half-wild Cossacks and Chechens with knowledge taken from his own experiences as a soldier serving in the Caucasus. In fact, Tolstoy has Olenin thinking of how the reality of the area differs from the romantic stories he heard and dreamed about while living in Moscow.

*Terek River (TEH-rehk). Dividing line between the Christian Cossacks and the various Islamic tribes including the Tatars and Chechens. The Grebenskiye Cossacks were granted an area along the northern bank of the Terek to build their villages, with the understanding that they would defend the area against the depredations of Chechen bandits who rejected the czar's authority.

Novomlinsk (no-vom-LIHNSK). Cossack village where Olenin is stationed. It is a typical village of the Grebenskiye Cossacks, larger than the peasant villages of central Russia, with neat thatch-roofed houses raised on pillars. The houses do not huddle close together as in a typical Russian peasant village, but all have ample space around them, and are located along several streets and lanes instead of a single central street. By each house is a small vegetable garden, orchard, and grape arbor, all carefully tended. The village is surrounded by an earthen berm upon which prickly hedges grow, and at the gates a sentry stands. In many ways the Cossack village resembles a military camp, with its watchposts and patrols of Cossack men bearing weapons; however, there is little of the spit and polish of a regular military installation. Rather, this is a sort of rough camaraderie of warriors who fight at one another's back against tribes they often respect more than the regular soldiers of the czar, who are regarded as oppressors and intruders. It is believed that Starogladovskaya, a village in the area, home of a Tolstoy museum, served as the basis for Tolstoy's fictional village.

*Moscow. Traditional capital and largest city of Russia. To Olenin it represents everything that is wrong with his life, effete and over-civilized. At the time the story takes place, Moscow is not Russia's political capital. Peter the Great moved the seat of government to his new city of St. Petersburg in 1712, and it would not return to Moscow until 1918, when the Bolsheviks rejected the northern capital as too risky strategically. However, even during the period of this novel, Moscow remained in many ways a cultural capital.

— *Leigh Husband Kimmel*

THE COUNT OF MONTE-CRISTO

Author: Alexandre Dumas, *père* (1802-1870)
Type of work: Novel
Type of plot: Historical

Time of plot: 1815-1838
First published: 1844-1845 (English translation, 1846)

This novel focuses on a post-Restoration France where corrupt anti-Bonapartist lawyers, military men, bankers, and politicians thrive, while their victims struggle for livelihood and justice. Set in three major locations— Marseilles, Rome, and Paris—that open up to offstage events in far-flung, exotic places such as Calcutta and Constantinople, the narrative has an epic sweep appropriate for its hero's seemingly omniscient and omnipotent quest for revenge against those responsible for sending him to prison.

*Marseilles (mar-SAY). Southeastern French city in a bay on the Mediterranean coast, popularizer of the French revolutionary anthem, "La Marseillaise," and the home of Alexandre Dumas's hero, Edmond Dantès. Dumas depicts Marseilles as a romantic gateway to such exotic Mediterranean ports as Smyrna and Algiers, as host to a Catalan (Spanish) community—where the heroine lives—and as a loyal supporter of Napoleon Bonaparte during his hundred-day return from exile in 1815. Like Gascony in Dumas's *The Three Musketeers* (1844), this Marseilles provides the hero with southern liberalism, nobility of heart, and passion.

Pharaon. Ship on which Dantès serves as mate. Its stop at Elba dooms him even while its name foreshadows the "Arabian" wealth and power that is later at his command.

*Porto-Ferraio. Largest town on the island of Elba, off the west coast of Italy, to which Napoleon was exiled in 1814. Dantès's visit to this island enables his enemies to accuse him of Bonapartism.

*Château d'If. Fortified castle on If, one of several small islands in the bay of Marseilles. Lying about two miles out to sea, the island presumably takes its name from its dominant tree, the cypress (*if* in French). Built in 1524 by King François I, the historical château eventually became a prison. Dantès's fourteen-year imprisonment here—through reigns of three French kings—indicates the repressive injustice of the post-Napoleonic Restoration governments. His imprisonment also partially parallels Napoleon's years of exile, first to Elba and later to St. Helena in the South Atlantic. Like the Corsican outsider who conquered much of Europe, Dantès transforms himself from a plebeian into a fabulously powerful figure who dominates his world. By making Dantès's fellow inmate the Abbé Faria, imprisoned in 1808 for espousing Italian unity, Dumas parallels the reactionary injustices in Italy and France in the first decades of the nineteenth century.

*Corsica. Mountainous French island in the Mediterranean—smaller than Sicily, Sardinia, and Cyprus—located 105 miles from southern France and 56 miles from northwestern Italy. In the novel, the island is thematically important as Napoleon's birthplace and as home of the Italian blood feud known as the *vendetta*—related to both the count's complex plot and his Corsican servant Bertuccio's simpler vengeance.

*Monte-Cristo. Tiny Mediterranean island south of Elba. Here Dantès discovers a treasure that the novel repeatedly links to the fabulous tales of the fifteenth century *Arabian Nights Entertainments*—an association typical of late-Romantic era Orientalism. Moreover, the island's name—literally, "Christ's Mount" in English—conveys religious connotations suitable for a protagonist who first pretends to be dead in order to escape prison, then is rebaptized in the sea, and finally hopes for rebirth in abandoning his vengeful path. In real life, Dumas celebrated the phenomenal success of this novel by building himself a château he named Monte Cristo, where he played host on a scale matching that of his fictional hero.

Pont du Gard Inn (POHN-dyu-gahr). Lowly French hotel owned by one of Dantès's treacherous friends, situated between Nîmes and Beaucaire in southern France, west of Marseilles. Whereas a Parisian veneer of elegance and wealth covers the other conspirators' criminality and self-interest, here baseness appears in cruder, provincial form.

Sinbad the Sailor's grotto. Dantès's palatial hideaway on the isle of Monte-Cristo. Here he welcomes a French visitor dazzled to find a sumptuous establishment on a tiny island that is believed to be inhabited only by wild goats and visited only by pirates and smugglers. The hideaway consists of a boudoir filled with ankle-deep Turkish carpets and luxurious fabrics; a dining room with marble walls and magnificent statues holding huge baskets of pineapples from Sicily, pomegranates from Malaga, oranges from the Balearic Islands, peaches from France, and dates from Tunis; a waiting room whose walls, floor, and ceiling are decorated with skins from Bengal tigers, Siberian bears, and Norwegian foxes. Besides reflecting the period's sea commerce, the grotto's furnishings—like the name that Dantès adopts from one of the heroes of *The Arabian Nights' Entertainments*—contributes to the novel's fairy-tale exoticism.

*Rome. Largest and richest city of Italy. Crowded with carnival festivities, Rome is the appropriate stage for Dantès's first appearance in the guise of the "count of Monte-Cristo," one of several masks he wears. In chapters 31-39, Dumas invests the city's renowned tourist attractions with colorful melodrama as the count meets with an Italian bandit at the moonlight Colosseum, rescues a Frenchman held for ransom in the Catacombs of Saint Sebastian, and attends an execution on the Piazza del Populo. Just as Monte-Cristo associates Dantès with smugglers and pirates, so Dumas's picturesque, brigand-filled Rome showcases the count as a master among bandits.

*Paris. In chapters 40-112, Dumas recreates the Paris of 1838 with a specificity based on his own daily experience of life in the capital during and after this period. Thus, realism prevails as characters visit the opera to hear *Wilhelm Tell*, go for carriage drives on the Champs Élysées, buy houses in the suburbs, and follow the stock market with an eye on Spanish politics. At the same time, a Gothic atmosphere of evil broods over the luxurious homes of the count's enemies. For the most part, the novel's Paris is that of the privileged classes, among whom a deadly concern with wealth, prestige, and power has atrophied morality and passion—except in the younger generation. Toward the end of the novel, Paris appears through the departing count's eyes as "this modern Babylon."

*Auteuil (OH-tei). Parisian suburb in which Dantès buys and refurbishes a house, complete with a huge library and a conservatory with exotic plants. Here the count gives a fabulous "Oriental feast [. . .] one would attribute to Arabian fairies," with food and drink from the four corners of the world, including sturgeon from the Volga river in Russia and lamprey from Lake Fusaro in Naples. The story of a newborn buried on the grounds reveals the corruption at the heart of this respectable Parisian milieu.

*Janinna. City on the shores of Lake Janinna in northern Greece, governed by the Greek Pasha Ali Tebelin until 1822 despite Turkish domination of his country. Whereas Dumas uses most exotic locations in the novel simply to suggest the count's cosmopolitanism, he lends Janinna some historical dimension as a site of French treachery and Turkish repression during the Greek war for independence. The historical Ali's death at Janinna at the hands of the Turks in 1822 is a matter of record—and although Dumas invents the sale of Ali's wife and daughter as slaves to a sultan in Constantinople, it is a scenario based on Turkish custom. The novel's sympathetic representation of Greek nationalism accords with its endorsement of French liberalism and Italian unity.

— *Margaret Bozenna Goscilo*

THE COUNTERFEITERS

Author: André Gide (1869-1951)
Type of work: Novel
Type of plot: Psychological realism

Time of plot: Early 1920's
First published: Les Faux-monnayeurs, 1925 (English translation, 1927)

Set mainly in Paris, this novel focuses on the bourgeois family and school as repressive institutions from which deceit, lack of authenticity, and corruption spread into society at large.

*Paris. Capital of France that provides the background for the first and third parts of the novel, which unfold in summer and fall, respectively. André Gide concentrates the ills of contemporary France into its capital, transposing other cities' real scandals—including schoolboy suicides in Clermont-Ferrand and counterfeiting activities in Rouen—to his fictionalized Paris. Concerned more with his characters' moral environment than their physical environment, Gide sketches in the cityscape not with descriptive details but with place names and specific itineraries. At the heart of his map is the Left Bank of the Seine; however, Bernard Profitendieu wanders the entire city in search of freedom and adventure, while the novelist-protagonist, Édouard, traces old contacts both there and across town.

*Rambouillet (rah[n]-bew-YAY). French town about twenty-eight miles southwest of Paris. Gide's modernist minimizing of realistic description is at its most extreme in chapter 17's vague evocation of Rambouillet, a town with a fourteenth century château, a large park and a forest. When Vincent Molinier joins two aristocratic friends for dinner, they simply "sat down to table on the terrace of a hotel overlooking a garden where the shades of night were gathering." Only the chapter title, "The Evening at Rambouillet," pins down the locale and suggests upper-class indulgence.

*Luxembourg Gardens. Spacious gardens attached to Paris's Luxembourg Palace, built on the Left Bank by King Louis XIII's mother in the seventeenth century. This site is at the center of the urban landscape, with the first chapter taking Bernard from his parents' home near the gardens to a path overlooking the Medici fountains, where his schoolmates congregate for intellectual discussions. In his working notes for this novel, Gide planned a "'poetic' description of the Luxembourg—which must be as mythical a place as the Forest of Arden is in the fantasies of Shakespeare." The gardens assume their most "poetic" aspect as the setting for Bernard's meeting with an angel, which concludes the travels and encounters that mature Bernard from a reckless runaway into a prodigal son happy to return home.

Vedel-Azaïs School (ved-el-a-ZA-ee). School and boardinghouse close to the Luxembourg Gardens run by the Protestant Monsieur Azaïs. Between the criminal influence of an adult boarder and the "poisonous air that reigns in it, under the stifling cover of morality and religion," the school initiates its youth into lies, theft, counterfeiting, sadism, blackmail, and homicide. This environment's festering evils push Boris, an alienated little boy born out of wedlock in Poland, to a public suicide.

*****Sorbonne.** Heart of the University of Paris, located on the Left Bank near the Luxembourg Gardens. It is at this prestigious center for learning, founded in 1257 as a theological college for the poor, that Gide has artistic, intellectual Olivier Molinier and Bernard pass their matriculation exams.

*****Saas-Fée** (sas-FAY). Swiss resort at the foot of the Dom, Switzerland's highest mountain, in Zermatt, in the southern canton of Valais. In the second, shortest part of the novel, Édouard, Laura Douviers, and Bernard visit the Swiss village, escaping the oppressive summer heat of Paris and gaining perspective on the complications of their lives in France. After climbing the Hallalin mountain, Bernard describes Saas-Fée as a purifying retreat "out of sight of all culture . . . of everything that reminds one of the avarice and stupidity of men." By escorting Boris from Saas-Fée to Paris, and specifically to the Vedel-Azaïs school, Édouard exposes the vulnerable boy to such social corruption.

*****Vizzavona.** Small village halfway up one of the highest mountains in Corsica, a large French island in the Mediterranean Sea. Olivier's summer vacation in Vizzavona with the predatory Count Passavant counterbalances, and results from his jealousy over, Bernard's Swiss getaway with Édouard.

*****Casamance** (KA-sa-mohns). Region of Senegal in West Africa, lying south of what is now the Gambia, along the Casamance River. This is Vincent's offstage retreat after he kills Lady Griffith, whose tale about sailors from the shipwrecked *Bourgogne* hacking off the hands that clutched at their lifeboat captures her own and other characters' brutal survival tactics.

*****England.** Another country that Gide keeps on the periphery of the novel—like Poland and Africa—to suggest the greater world lying beyond Paris and the oppressive nuclear family.

— *Margaret Bozenna Goscilo*

THE COUNTESS CATHLEEN

Author: William Butler Yeats (1865-1939)
Type of work: Drama
Type of plot: Allegory

Time of plot: Indeterminate
First published: 1892; first performed, 1899

William Butler Yeats's play is set in rural Ireland in a time before the country became independent. During a country-wide famine demons, fairies, and preternatural spirits inhabit this mystical land, and the poverty-ridden peasants believe in a combination of paganism and Roman Catholicism. The play contains Irish myth and legend and supernatural magic and examines such motifs as sacrifice and regeneration and Irish Nationalism prevailing over British colonialism.

*****Ireland.** Island west of England occupied and governed by Great Britain during the time of this play. The seat of power resides in London, and England controls the wealth and the land. Lack of land and money causes economic hardship as extreme poverty and famine looms over the country. The impoverished peasants, who previously lost their cattle, farm implements, and fields, sell their souls to demons for food and money. Yeats believed that Ireland should be filled with holy symbols, not only from an orthodox religion but also from poetry and mysticism. These symbols reveal the mystical spiritual realities not found in degenerate Europe.

Rua cabin. Home of Shemus and Mary Rua, a hut warmed and lighted by foul-smelling sod fires in which the play opens. A door leading into the farmyard allows the peasant couple to watch over their few chickens and see the surrounding trees and woods. The cabin walls and trees are painted in flat colors without much light or shadow. This gives an otherworldly aura and diminishes any realism which may enter the drama, conforming to Yeats's belief that dramatic scenery should be symbolic and decorative. The small and rocky fields cannot support a family; the economically and spiritually impoverished peasants remain superstitious, fearful, and easily duped.

Cathleen's castle. Home of Countess Cathleen, located in the woods not far from where the Ruas' cabin stands. The old castle has turreted walls painted in a flat gray color against a diapered or gold background. Its great hall contains kegs of gold (coveted by the English) and an oratory with an altar, where Cathleen prays. Her grace and nobility make her superior to both the powers of darkness and the English overlords whom they represent. Her wealth and her faith allow her to save the peasants. As a symbol of Ireland, Cathleen gives everything she has, including her soul, to save her people.

— *Ronald L. Raber*

A COUNTRY DOCTOR

Author: Sarah Orne Jewett (1849-1909)
Type of work: Novel
Type of plot: Bildungsroman

Time of plot: Mid-nineteenth century
First published: 1884

The characters in this novel are strongly influenced by their landscapes and history, and the book's New England settings exemplify Sarah Orne Jewett's view of the ideal conditions under which a nineteenth century woman might grow up.

Oldfields. Fictional Maine farming community, probably modeled after the environs of Jewett's birthplace, South Berwick, Maine. Jewett's father, a physician, often took young Jewett along on patient visits, pointing out for close observation features of the people and landscape. As a child, Nan flourishes on the farm. Local society—with its Puritan heritage—tends to be narrow, formally pious, and conservative. The opening chapters tell several stories of talented people thwarted by the limited life choices available there. Nan, however, is allowed to grow up "naturally"; she rafts on the river, roams the fields day and night, and plays with farm animals. She develops the self-reliance to resist the limits usually imposed on girls. From the local people she picks up the virtues of a work ethic and mutual helpfulness. Nan returns to rural Oldfields to begin medical practice despite opportunities to work and study in major city hospitals and in Europe.

River. Unnamed river that is a key place in rural Oldfields—the Salmon Falls and Piscataqua Rivers join below Jewett's South Berwick. Nan's despairing mother nearly drowns herself and the infant Nan near a graveyard along the river. Nan returns to the spot twice: when she decides to become a doctor and again at the end of the novel, when she meditates on the providential guidance she has felt.

The fictional village of Oldfields resembles Jewett's childhood home. Oldfields differs from Jewett's South Berwick in the absence of modern manufacturing. The narrator specifies that the village is untouched by the hurry and shoddy building of the industrial revolution.

When Nan's grandmother dies, Nan moves to Dr. Leslie's house in the village, which is much like Jewett's home in its central location, spaciousness, and somewhat exotic furnishings, such as a medical library. The village offers the adolescent Nan new resources for growth, while not depriving her completely of her free, rural life. Nan's adventuresome habits are curtailed in the more watchful village, but Oldfields also brings her into daily contact with liberal mentors. Dr. Leslie teaches her to study patients' whole selves in deciding upon treatments. Mrs. Graham teaches adult manners and proper feminine taste, preparing her to interact well even with people opposed to her vocational choice. Thus she becomes ready to embark upon medical studies.

As in other works, Jewett here implies that knowing both rural and urban life is important to becoming a whole person. This was her own experience growing up in a rural village, roaming the countryside, learning self-reliance and social skills, and becoming a professional writer who divided her year between South Berwick and Boston, Massachusetts.

Dunport. Fictional New England town, probably modeled on Portsmouth, New Hampshire, at the mouth of the Piscataqua River. Dunport is an Atlantic commercial port—with law firms, shipbuilding, and other businesses—and with a substantial number of leisure-class women. One of these is Anna Prince, Nan's aunt.

Much larger than Oldfields, Dunport has an active social life but lacks a city's resources for entertainment and education. Again, the river is a key location—possibly the same river that flows through rural Oldfields.

Here the local youth entertain themselves with rowing parties and picnics. On the river, Nan becomes acquainted with a suitor and receives his proposal. In the harbor for repair, two ships with entangled rigging become an extended metaphor of unfortunate marriages.

Nan visits Dunport, partly out of gratitude for her aunt's financial support, to end the feud that began when her gentleman-physician father married an ambitious farm girl. The places associated with her father and the amenities of the town extend Nan's understanding and test her resolve. The fine houses and women's social life offer a relaxing routine in contrast to the hard work of medicine. The leaders of society oppose her vocation. An attractive suitor opens this way of life to her, but she tactfully turns him away. Seeing her father's childhood environment and mementos helps to confirm that she is carrying on his own medical ambitions and hopes. Assured that she has chosen rightly, she is ready to begin her career.

— Terry Heller

THE COUNTRY OF THE POINTED FIRS

Author: Sarah Orne Jewett (1849-1909)
Type of work: Novella
Type of plot: Social realism

Time of plot: Late nineteenth century
First published: 1896

This novella is an evocative homage to a Maine village that the narrator visits one summer. By focusing on the fishing village and surrounding islands, she writes about the native people whose lives are profoundly affected by the dramatic landscape in which they reside. First-hand knowledge that author Sarah Orne Jewett gleaned from the summers she spent in the Penobscot Bay area provides an intimate view of coastal Maine before it became a popular spot for vacationers.

Dunnet Landing. Fictional Maine fishing village where the narrator boards with Mrs. Almira Todd and around which his story revolves. The tenacity of the coastline's tall pines, spruces, and firs, often rooted in rocks, and the always-changing sea, providing bounty one day and tragedy the next, reflect the strength, integrity, and patience of Maine's people, who make their homes on the rugged yet strikingly beautiful coastland. The sound of the sea is ever present throughout the narration. Visitors, including the narrator, are hospitably received and become privy to the islanders' family histories, idiosyncrasies, joys, and sorrows. The fishermen from this village are strong, weather-beaten, for the most part silent on shore. Taciturn sea captains are often surprisingly well read. In wooden boats, these men have traveled around the Cape of Good Hope and battled the ferocious seas of Cape Horn. Their women are sociable, creative, and compassionate. They appreciate the wild roses and make use of the berries and herbs covering the mid-summer hillsides. Mrs. Todd, who includes her visitor in her summer activities, is a wonderful teller of tales, both real and embellished. Many of the wives living in small weather-beaten houses have traveled to distant ports with their seagoing husbands, bringing back exotic small souvenirs.

Green Island. Outer Maine island accessible only by boat and the birthplace of Mrs. Todd and home of her mother, Mrs. Blackett. Mrs. Blackett lives in a house on the only level area of a large sloping green field, a steep climb from the sea where Mrs. Todd and her visitor land their dory. The small farm sits below dark spruce woods. The tops of these conifers are sharply outlined against a deep blue sky. Eastward, toward the ocean, a flock of gray sheep grazes among the sparse pasturage among the large gray rocks. The island is described as a "complete and tiny continent." From the top, where the air is fresh with the fragrance of sea and scattered bayberry bushes, one can see the ocean surrounding the island. In the distance hundreds of other small islands and the far mainland ap-

pear. This island, in its silence and loneliness, contrasts with Dunnet Landing, the busy, noisy fishing village.

Shell-heap Island. Small and lonely island, three miles from Green Island and eight miles from the mainland, that is difficult to visit because of strong winds and tricky tides. Even when the conditions are favorable, the island is a difficult place on which to land. Self-exiled Joanna Todd lives on this island, which takes its name from piles of shells left by earlier Indian residents. Other evidences of past Indian occupation include stone tools they have left behind.

Black Island. Island closest to Shell-heap Island. Its residents often spy on the movements of Joanna Todd with a spyglass.

Fessendon. Town inland and a full day's sail from Green Island. To reach Fessendon from Green Island, one has to go down the coast to Cold Spring Light and around a long point of land.

— *Anne Trotter*

THE COUNTRY WIFE

Author: William Wycherley (1641?-1715)
Type of work: Drama
Type of plot: Comedy

Time of plot: Seventeenth century
First performed: 1675; first published, 1675

This play builds on a contrast between London manners and "country" attitudes, which are displayed by Mr. Pinchwife and his young wife Margery, to present a sharply comic picture of sexual behavior in Restoration London.

*****London.** Capital and leading city of England. The play depicts fashionable London, in which wives are expected to be ready to deceive their husbands and take lovers and where gentlemen are considered potential or actual rakes. This is a world in which country manners and morals are regularly derided and feminine chastity is associated with lack of London sophistication, except by Margery Pinchwife's sister, Alithea, who is the play's true heroine.

Horner's lodging. London bachelor apartment of Mr. Horner; a key setting in the play, as the place where Horner's scheme of pretending to be impotent in order to gain access to other men's wives is announced in the

first act. The lodging is later the scene of various seductions and the notorious "china scene," in which Horner uses the metaphor of "inspecting his china" to describe his conquests of various women. In act 5 the apartment is the setting for the play's denouement, in which Alithea chooses Harcourt over her naïve suitor, and Pinchwife's suspicion about Horner's successful seduction of Margery is refuted by the repetition of the lie about Horner's supposed impotence, which is reaffirmed by his mercenary doctor.

Pinchwife's house. Home of the old cuckold Mr. Pinchwife and his young bride, Margery Pinchwife. The house is a virtual prison for Margery, whom Pinchwife is determined to hide from fashionable London and potential seducers. The location also provides a scene for his debates with his sister-in-law, Alithea, who consistently argues that his effort to "protect" Margery from meeting amatory rakes will produce the opposite effect and make her determined to escape from his zealous confinement of her.

New Exchange. One of many fashionable meeting places for rakes and ladies, it is the setting for Margery's rebellious adventure away from the house, where disguised as a boy, she encounters Horner, which leads to her seduction.

— *Edgar L. Chapman*

THE COURTSHIP OF MILES STANDISH

Author: Henry Wadsworth Longfellow (1807-1882)
Type of work: Poetry
Type of plot: Sentimental

Time of plot: 1621
First published: 1858

The setting for this poem is Plymouth, which was founded by English Pilgrims near Cape Cod in Massachusetts. Henry Wadsworth Longfellow uses the hardships of frontier life in an area previously occupied by Native Americans to create the feeling of loneliness that is so crucial to the circumstances of this poem.

*****Plymouth.** First English settlement in North America. A village at the time in which this poem is set, Plymouth was built on the vacant townsite of the Pawtuxet Indians on the southeast coast of what became Massachusetts. Longfellow describes the village in such a way as to make the reader feel a part of it. The site's earlier Pawtuxet occupants died from smallpox, which had apparently been contracted though contact with English fishermen in the area. The wooded areas mentioned indicate the widely scattered nature of the settlement, allowing room for gardens and growth, both of which were vital to the frontier setting.

Longfellow uses the region's rugged coastline to es-

tablish a feeling of finality among Plymouth's colonists. The rocks, especially famous Plymouth Rock, represent both stability and hope for John Alden.

Wheat field. Longfellow's use of this field is a constant reminder of the danger posed by local Native Americans. In early 1621 the field was planted over the graves of settlers who had died during the winter, supposedly so that the Indians would not know how many English settlers had perished. This dead reportedly included Rose Standish, the wife of Miles Standish, and most of the family of Priscilla Mullins.

— *Glenn L. Swygart*

COUSIN BETTE

Author: Honoré de Balzac (1799-1850)
Type of work: Novel
Type of plot: Social realism

Time of plot: Early nineteenth century
First published: La Cousine Bette, 1846 (English translation, 1888)

This novel is about passion and passions, not only physical, but also material—the passion for status, the lust for revenge. The characters all inhabit a rather small area of a huge city; they cannot escape one another as they attack others and defend themselves. The city, Paris, presents temptations of all kinds.

*Paris. Political, social, and cultural center of France, even more so in the nineteenth century than in the twenty-first. *Cousin Bette* is set entirely in central Paris—indeed, the claustrophobic settings of the characters' scheming change only to the extent that the characters visit one another or move from one dwelling to another. In the mid-nineteenth century, as in the twenty-first, Parisians' social status was often indicated by the location of their homes. In *Cousin Bette*, a change in living quarters represents a character's move, deliberately or not, from one social or moral level to another. In Honoré de Balzac's vision, the reign of King Louis-Philippe (who ruled France from 1830 to 1848) was characterized by the transcendence of material appearances over moral attributes.

Hulot home (ew-LOH). Located in a fashionable area of Paris (on the rue de l'Universite on the Left Bank of the Seine River.) The Seine literally and figuratively divides Paris. The novel opens with an important scene in which the Hulots are struggling to maintain signs of high status, but the descriptions of their furnishings indicate the extent to which their material—and moral—fortunes have declined. While the Baroness remains virtuous, her husband throws his money away on loose women.

Bette's quarters. Lisbeth Fischer ("Bette") is Madame Hulot's cousin. Although she moves several times during the story, at first she lives on the rue du Doyenné, on the Right Bank of the river. Bette lives in a shabby house in this dark, seedy, dangerous area, which reflects her loneliness and the dark quality of violence seen in her own character. She falls in love with one of her fellow tenants, a young artist. Baron Hulot's future mistress, Valerie Marneffe, also lives here. Later, when Bette moves to more respectable quarters, in the rue Vanneau, Baron Hulot arranges for Valerie to live there as well. Thus develop Bette's various roles in the novel, of go-between, procuress, confidant, and spy. She uses all her acquaintances and family members to satisfy her own longing for vengeance, status, and material comfort. Bette comes to have free access to the homes (and confidence) of all the major characters and pits them against one another. Her ultimate personal target of material and social success is Baron Hulot's brother, Marshal Hulot—a hero of the Napoleonic Wars and one of the novel's few admirable characters. She gains entry to the Marshal's home, in the prestigious rue du Montparnasse, as his resident housekeeper, and eventually coerces him into marrying her.

Josepha Mirah's home. Josepha, an actress, was one of Baron Hulot's first concubines, and she used his money and influence in her quest for success and position. The luxury of her home near the Palais Royal, on the Right Bank of the Seine, stuns Baroness Hulot. The contrast between the opulence of what Josepha has earned by the sale of her honor and what the Baroness has been left with in defending her moral and Christian principles is a striking juxtaposition. The lesson is, then, that money buys status, immorality prospers in the Paris of King Louis-Philippe, and goodness and Christian conduct meet with pain and humiliation.

Passage du Soleil (pah-saj dew soh-lay). Paris slum in which Baroness Hulot finds her fallen husband. Having changed his name more than once and fled the authorities because of acts of political corruption, Hulot has purchased a young girl (something he has done more than once). Balzac's description of the neighborhood offers an interesting version of nineteenth century Parisian urban renewal. The Passage du Soleil is the scene of property speculation; rents are rising, and the area's poor are being forced out. Again, money matters a great deal in this city. At the novel's end, in keeping with the story's cruel pessimism, Balzac's Baron returns home with his loving wife, leaving his distraught adolescent lover in the care of a friend.

— *Gordon Walters*

COUSIN PONS

Author: Honoré de Balzac (1799-1850)
Type of work: Novel
Type of plot: Naturalism

Time of plot: 1840's
First published: Le Cousin Pons, 1847 (English translation, 1880)

Set in a variety of homes throughout Paris, this novel is a sharply observed study of an old man who is treated with contempt by wealthy relatives who cheat his friend and legatee out of a fortune in artworks after he dies.

Marville's house (marh-VEEL). Home on Paris's rue de Honoré of Monsieur Camusot de Marville, Sylvain Pons's cousin-in-law and a presiding judge of the Royal Court of Justice. This house is described in scant detail. Although it faces north and presents a gloomy aspect to the street, it has a south-facing inner courtyard and an attractive garden. The novel emphasizes the house's tranquillity and respectability, as befits the home of an important magistrate, and this is reflected in its furnishings—imposing green draperies, tapestries, thick carpets, and sober furniture. It is, however, an uncomfortable house to Pons, an elderly musician and amateur art collector, because it lacks works of art.

An upper floor of the house is rented to an old woman, but later Marville and his wife move there, leaving the lower floor to their daughter now married at last, with the mansion as part of her wedding dowry.

Pillerault's house. Home of Monsieur Pillerault on rue de Normandie in the Marais district of Paris. The building is a former town house, described as a lodge, an upper floor of which is rented to Pons and his friend and fellow musician Pons Schmucke. The building, in two parts, consists of three double-depth flats, plus three smaller flats, one of which Pons and Schmucke occupy. The house also contains a shop belonging to the iron-monger-turned-bric-a-brac dealer Remonencq.

The lodge is run by Madame Cibot and her husband, who are systematically defrauding its residents in numerous small ways in order to supplement their incomes. As the lodge keeper, Madame Cibot controls other people's access to Pons when he becomes ill; she is also well placed to allow people to enter his rooms without his knowledge.

Remonencq's shop (reh-moh-NANK). Curio shop of the rascally Remonencq, who is Madame Cibot's accomplice. Originally a coffeehouse, the shop has not been altered since Remonencq took it over as a bare shell, with a kitchen, back premises, and a small bedroom, the attached flat being rented separately. After starting out as an ironmonger, Remonencq gradually changes trades. After initially filling his shop with cheap goods, he gradually stocks it with better quality antiques as he moves up in the world.

The shop's location enables Remonencq to overhear information about the quality and worth of Pons's art collection. After Madame Cibot becomes widowed, she marries Remonencq, who then accidentally poisons himself, leaving her to inherit the shop.

Magus's house. Home of the art collector Elias Magus on Paris's Chaussée des Minimes. The house is an old mansion, in which an entire floor has been lavishly restored to accommodate Magus's collection, with brocade curtains at the windows and expensive carpets on the floors. The ground floor is used as storage for works of art and contains an art restorer's workshop. Magus's daughter, Noémi, also has a suite of rooms in the house and is, like the treasures, closely guarded. Magus himself lives in two shabby, poorly furnished, and ill-kept rooms on an upper floor.

Pons's flat. Rooms of Sylvain Pons in Marville's house. Although the novel mentions bedrooms, a dining room, and a drawing room, it does not describe them. The only room described in any detail is the one housing Pons's art collection. Originally panelled in white and gold, this room has colors that have softened to yellow and red. Its upper walls are covered with paintings, and its lower walls are lined with ebony sideboards containing many curios. Tables in the middle of the room display other valuable objects.

Poulain's flat (poo-LAN). Home on rue d'Orleans of Dr. Poulain. This is a small flat, consisting of two rooms and two bedrooms, plus a kitchen and a servant's bedroom, part of a much larger building, a mansion during the time of the French Empire. It has remained untouched for forty years, and though tiny is expensive to rent. Nevertheless, it conveys an air of respectable poverty, of struggling to make ends meet, which is at odds with Dr. Poulain's aspirations, to be a successful and wealthy man. It is no surprise, therefore, that when he learns that Pons's art collection is worth a fortune, he determines to make some money for himself from Pons's illness.

Fraisier's flat. Home on rue de la Perle ("pearl") of the rascally attorney Fraisier. Described as the "man of law," Fraisier helps Madame Cibot in a complicated series of transactions designed to defraud everyone involved with the illicit disposal of Pons's wealth, including Pons's friend Schmucke, to whom he leaves the collection.

Much at variance with a street named "Pearl," Fraisier's home is in a house described as suffering from leprosy. The house's stairwells are strewn with refuse that indicates that most of the occupants are engaged in manual work. The door of Fraisier's flat is shabby and dirty from being handled by so many people. Inside, the metalwork is tarnished, the wood unpolished, and the legal files are covered in dust, reflecting Fraisier's dubious moral character.

Topinard's flat (toh-pee-NAHR). Home of Monsieur Topinard and his family in Paris's Cité Bordin; a flat with two rooms, a kitchen, and a small attic. Although they live in a shabby flat in a Parisian slum, Topinard and his wife keep their flat spotlessly clean, reflecting their good characters. Topinard is a supernumerary at a theater where Pons and Schmucke used to work. He inquires after the two men every day during Pons's final illness but is not granted admission by Madame Cibot. When Schmucke is turned out of the flat, Topinard and his wife take him into their home and offer him their best room, their private bedroom. However, he refuses the offer and takes up residence in their attic, where he dies shortly afterward.

— *Maureen Speller*

CRANFORD

Author: Elizabeth Gaskell (1810-1865)
Type of work: Novel
Type of plot: Domestic realism

Time of plot: Early nineteenth century
First published: 1851-1853

Originally published in brief magazine installments, the early chapters of this novel offer an almost sociological portrait of a country town and its conservative female society—a portrait that is simultaneously nostalgic and gently satirical. The second half of the book moves toward a more closely plotted novel in answering questions and dramatically reuniting long lost siblings. Place is everything—and nothing—in an all-enveloping culture and state of mind with little physical description of scene.

Cranford. English village modeled on Knutsford in Cheshire, where Elizabeth Gaskell spent part of her childhood, A country town larger than a village, Cranford is "in possession of the Amazons," in that its patterns of social life and mores are dictated almost exclusively by widows, spinsters, occasional younger unmarried women visitors, and maid servants. Husbands, if they exist, are away on business all week in the neighboring commercial city of Drumble. However, as Drumble is only twenty miles away by railroad, the creation of a railroad line nearby threatens to destabilize the comfortable routines of morning needlework, afternoon calls, and early evening tea parties followed by serious card playing. None of the women, with the exception of Mary Smith, the youthful narrator and frequent visitor from outside, seems ever to leave the town. However, Cranford is, in fact, large enough to possess an inn and a number of shops, including a millinery establishment and a century-old assembly room attached to the inn, which once held balls and parties of county families but is now rarely used. Mary Smith notes that Cranford's aging population does not read or walk much, so the settings the reader encounters most often are modest cottage interiors, usually at tea time.

Woodley. Country estate of Thomas Holbrook, whom Miss Matty might have married except for her sister's disapproval of his modest social rank. When Miss Matty and Mary visit the estate in June after a chance encounter only a few months before Mr. Holbrook's death, readers are treated to roses, currant bushes, feathery asparagus, gilly-flowers, and an old-fashioned but comfortable house. Here is a setting for a wider and fuller life than Miss Matty can live in Cranford, whose social strictures are so stiff and precise that Holbrook for many years made Misselton, four or five miles in the opposite direction from his estate, his market town after Miss Matty refused his offer of marriage.

Drumble. City about twenty miles away from Cranford. It is probably modeled on the large industrial English city of Manchester, which bears the same relationship to Knutsford that Drumble bears to Cranford. In contrast to Cranford, Drumble seems to be an almost entirely masculine destination, although Mary Smith does shop there after returning to her father's house and before coming back to visit Miss Matty again. The city is never pictured directly but is often spoken of, albeit with a certain ambivalence, a place to be viewed both warily and respectfully.

*****Paris.** France's capital city, like Drumble, remains a distant, even more remote presence, and again primarily a masculine one. In the minds of the Cranford ladies, Holbrook's death is probably a consequence of his having visited there. In a later episode set in Cranford, the former Jessie Brown and her husband visit Paris and send as a gift to a Cranfordite a newly chic hoopskirt; the local residents are so baffled by the alien elegance of the metal framework that they believe it to be a parrot cage.

— *Nan C. L. Scott*

THE CREAM OF THE JEST

Author: James Branch Cabell (1879-1958)
Type of work: Novel
Type of plot: Satire

Time of plot: Twentieth century
First published: 1917

In this novel two worlds are first set in opposition and later united: author Felix Kennaston's vivid dream world and his dull but comfortable waking life in early twentieth century America. Through the power of a magical signet (the "sigil of Scoteia"), Kennaston moves through myth and history, always seeking Ettarre, the divine woman who can never be possessed. However, Ettarre proves to be incarnate in Felix's wife, and he eventually discovers that everyday life can be filled with the "exquisite wonderfulness" he has been seeking in his dreams.

Poictesme (PWA-tem). Imaginary medieval French realm whose name is derived from the cities of Poictiers (modern Poitiers) and Angoulesme (modern Angoulême), although it lies in the south of France, along the Mediterranean coast, on the Gulf of Lions. It corresponds geographically to the modern district of Gard, overlapping Herault and Bouches-Du-Rhone. It is a central location in many works of James Branch Cabell's eighteen-volume *Biography of the Life of Manuel* (1927-1930), the story of the pig-keeper who ruled Poictesme and of how his "life" continued on for twenty-odd generations of descendants.

Based in part on country resorts in Virginia where Cabell passed time as a young man, Poictesme is a pleasant country of fields, forests, and mountains. Among its walled cities and castles is the capital, Storisende, the home of Manuel's heirs. They hold Poictesme in feudal bond from Horvendile, an immortal demiurge, who may be senior to the creator of the world. Horvendile is also, however, the alter ego of Felix Kennaston, the author of the fiction in which Horvendile appears at the beginning of the book. But it is not clear if Horvendile is Kennaston's representative or Kennaston Horvendile's, nor is it clear if Poictesme is purely a fancy of Kennaston's or if, in his world, it is a historical place. He calls it the "one possible setting for a really satisfactory novel," but he himself is a descendant of Manuel and returns to Poictesme at the end of the book, at least mentally, bringing the life force of Manuel full circle.

Alcluid. Kennaston's inherited country home, presumably in Virginia, though Cabell never makes this certain. The place may be based on Cabell's own country home, Dumbarton. **Lichfield**, the nearest town to the fictional Alcluid, is a stand-in for Richmond, Virginia, Cabell's hometown. Kennaston lives with his long-time wife, Kathleen, in the ambivalent mix of dull but relished comfort and discontented longing that assails Cabell's heroes again and again. Home is one pole of his existence, where he has found half of the sigil of Scoteia in the garden; he also received it, as Horvendile, from Ettarre in Poictesme. The real and fantastic are united in Alcluid when Kennaston realizes that his unquenchable love for Ettarre has in fact been consummated by his indivisible bond with his wife, and that the sigil is part of the seal of her cold cream jar.

Nephelococcygia (neh-feh-lah-KAH-kee-gee-ah). Land of dreams that Kennaston enters by hypnotizing himself with the sigil of Scoteia before he goes to sleep. The imaginary place takes its name from a Greek expression that may be translated as "cloud-cuckoo-land"—the name of the city built on air in Aristophanes' *The Birds* (414 B.C.E.). Kennaston visits various times and places, historical and imaginary, usually as Horvendile, and usually in the company of Ettarre, whom he desires endlessly but may never touch. He observes William Shakespeare, Oliver Cromwell, Napoleon Bonaparte, Pontius Pilate and the day of Christ's Crucifixion, the death of Tiberius Caesar, the invention of gunpowder, and many other people, events, and exotic places.

— *William Mingin*

CRIME AND PUNISHMENT

Author: Fyodor Dostoevski (1821-1881)
Type of work: Novel
Type of plot: Psychological realism

Time of plot: Mid-nineteenth century
First published: Prestupleniye i Nakazaniye, 1866
 (English translation, 1886)

Almost all the action in this novel takes place in St. Petersburg, founded by Peter the Great as the new capital of a modernizing Russia. Fyodor Dostoevski uses the real names of streets and landmarks in writing not only a psychological masterpiece but also a brilliant work of city description. The rooms, streets, bars, hotels, narrow alleys, wide squares, bridges, canals, and rivers of mid-nineteenth century St. Petersburg become part of the thoughts of major characters as well as the environment in which decisions are made and actions take place.

*St. Petersburg. Capital of Imperial Russia. Deep within the glittering outer facade of St. Petersburg's state buildings, elegant promenades, and gilded mansions is a central core of filth, stench, poverty, despair, and depravity. The outside order is mere cover for the horror and disorder within. Dostoevski lived in St. Petersburg for twenty-eight years, moving during this period into twenty different apartments. Minute details about places where Dostoevski lived appear in *Crime and Punishment* to provide descriptive realism along with significant symbolism. On the micro level, the scenes of Dostoevski's novel unfold in the vicinity of the apartment he was renting at the time. On the macro level, St. Petersburg is symptomatic of the split in the Russian psyche between the cold Western rationalism and capitalistic materialism of the new Russia and the traditional Muscovite values of the old Russia. Like the city itself, the major character Raskolnikov (whose name means "split" or "schism") must struggle to discover his identity in a battle between cold rationalism, which leads him to double murder, and his Russian soul, which seeks repentance and resurrection. As a student, Dostoevski himself fell into Western-style radicalism and was sentenced to death in 1849 by the repressive regime of Czar Nicholas I. After being placed before a firing squad in St. Petersburg, Dostoevski was pardoned and his sentence commuted to eight years in Siberia. Back in St. Petersburg, Dostoevski remained aware of a continuing inner struggle. As he says in *Crime and Punishment*, St. Petersburg has "gloomy and queer influences on the soul of man."

*Haymarket. District filled with vendor stalls, peasant stalls, bars, hotels, and brothels that developed in St. Petersburg during the last quarter of the eighteenth century. It was filled with alleys and crammed with all sorts of people from the lower classes. It was bordered by slums (where Raskolnikov, Sonya, and the pawnbroker live), yet it was only one-half mile from St. Petersburg's fashionable Nevskii Prospect. All types of people pass through the Haymarket; it is here that an accidental encounter with the pawnbroker's half-sister (Lizaveta) convinces Raskolnikov that the time is right to murder the pawnbroker. Here, too, he bows down to kiss the ground (a sign of connectedness to mother earth and traditional values) and then goes to the police to confess that he is a murderer.

Stolyarny Lane. Street located near the Haymarket on which the main character, Raskolnikov, lives. The poverty-stricken former university student has a single shabby room with low ceilings, in an almost cavelike dwelling. Here, on a dilapidated couch-bed in his tiny, windowless room, Raskolnikov falls under the influence of the sinister plot to kill the pawnbroker and steal her ill-gotten gains. Although his room is a world unto itself, Raskolnikov always keeps the door unlocked, providing the opportunity for others to enter and for him to exit into the wider, ominous world of St. Petersburg.

*Sadovaya Street. Street not far from Raskolnikov's building on which the pawnbroker Alonya Ivanovna and her half-sister, Lizaveta Ivanovna, live in the fourth-floor apartment. Their two rooms are kept clean due to the efforts of Lizaveta, who works as a virtual slave. Raskolnikov visits three times before murdering the pawnbroker and Lizaveta, who unexpectedly walks into the apartment shortly after the pawnbroker's axe murder. A fortuitous set of circumstances allows Raskolnikov to leave the apartment unnoticed. Later, he returns to the apartment to relive the event.

Sonya's room. Home of the prostitute Sonya Marmeladov, in a three-story house on the Ekaterinsky Canal. The room has many windows that let in light and overlook the canal, although the walls are yellowed, and the room is nearly barren. It is here that Raskolnikov tells Sonya about the murders, unaware that Svidrigaylov, an unscrupulous suitor of his sister, is in an adjoining room, listening to his confession through the door.

*Neva River. Major river of St. Petersburg which also boasts a tributary, the Little Neva. Bridges and water in general play an important symbolic role in *Crime and Punishment*. The Neva is the courier of rebirth but also of death. It brings discord but also calmness. Thus Raskolnikov thinks of throwing what he has stolen from the pawnbroker into the Neva but chooses instead to bury it under a stone. He throws the last of his money into the Neva as a symbol of his rejection of materialism. It is on Tuchkov Bridge, over the Little Neva, that Raskolnikov enters a mood of tranquillity and decides not to kill the pawnbroker. (The decision changes, however, when he enters Haymarket Square.) For evil characters such as Svidrigaylov, the river brings coldness and depression. After an excursion on Tuchkov Bridge, Svidrigaylov decides to kill himself.

*Siberia. Vast, desolate region of eastern Russia. After confessing his crime, Raskolnikov is sentenced to eight years imprisonment in Siberia. The faithful Sonya follows him into this frozen wasteland. Yet the prison, on the bank of a river, is the place of rebirth and salvation for Raskolnikov, where he discovers love and traditional Russian values. His apartment in St. Petersburg was more a prison than his cell in the wide-open spaces of Siberia. While here, he patiently looks forward to his future life with Sonya. Dostoevsky himself spent eight years in Siberia, four in a prison camp and four in military service, after which his life and beliefs took dramatic new shape.

— *Irwin Halfond*

CRIMES OF THE HEART

Author: Beth Henley (1952-   )
Type of work: Drama
Type of plot: Comedy

Time of plot: 1974
First performed: 1979; first published, 1981

This play is set primarily in a small southern town that symbolizes the limitations traditionally placed on women of the South. Although two sisters travel to other places, they cannot escape these limiting roles until they reunite with their third sister in the old Mississippi home of their patriarchal grandfather and face the challenge together.

*Hazlehurst.** Southern Mississippi town near the state capital, Jackson, where playwright Beth Henley was born. The play unfolds the lives of three granddaughters of Granddaddy MaGrath, the family patriarch who strongly believes in traditional southern roles for women. Lenny, the oldest sister, is to become the "old maid" who cares for aging relatives. Babe, the youngest, is to be a dutiful wife—the preferred role for southern women. Meg, Granddaddy's favorite child, is to be "the Southerner who leaves the South and makes it big."

*Biloxi.** Mississippi coastal port. As a teenager Meg temporarily escapes Hazlehurst and, by extension, the role that she is supposed to fulfill by going to Biloxi with her boyfriend during Hurricane Camille.

*Hollywood.** California town symbolizing the center of the glamorous film industry to which Meg goes in the hope of achieving Granddaddy's dream for her: becoming a singer so renowned that she transcends those in even the highest social class of the South. However, like most young people dreaming of finding fame and fortune in Hollywood, she fails; she is so afraid of disappointing Granddaddy that she eventually loses her singing voice and goes insane.

*Memphis.** Tennessee city to which Lenny briefly escapes from her caretaker role. She goes there to see the pen pal she met through a Lonely Hearts Club ad. Once she returns to Hazlehurst and Old Granddaddy, she relinquishes her newfound dream of love and returns to the idea she will never be able to give a husband happiness. The drama's resolution involves the eventual rejection of these roles by all three sisters, and by play's end the old maid caretaker, the senator's wife, and the aspiring singer are free to develop their own identities.

— *Jo K. Galle*

THE CRISIS

Author: Winston Churchill (1871-1947)
Type of work: Novel
Type of plot: Historical

Time of plot: 1860's
First published: 1901

Drawing closely on historical events, this novel examines the effect of the Civil War on the lives of people in St. Louis, in a state split between secession and Union supporters.

*St. Louis.** Major Mississippi River port city and principal city of Missouri, a border state that was occupied by Union troops before it could declare itself for the Confederacy when the Civil War began in 1861. Union generals Ulysses S. Grant and William T. Sherman spent many years in St. Louis before the war. South St. Louis had a large proabolition population of Germans, who had left Germany after the failure of the revolutions of 1848. However, St. Louis was also a city in which many southern aristocrats lived, along with others who had relocated from the South. St. Louis was also the birthplace of author Winston Churchill.

Mrs. Crane's boardinghouse. St. Louis establishment where many of the novel's major characters, such as Eliphalet Hopper, the Brices, and the Cranes, visit or reside. The house is a center of considerable debate bordering on "mad delirium." It is here that Stephen Brice, who has relocated from Boston to St. Louis in order to have a better chance in a legal career, brings a female slave he has just purchased with his last dollars, to free her from the horrors of slavery.

Carvel house. St. Louis home of Colonel Carvel and his daughter Virginia. Located on Locust Street, this family house and its possessions are seized over Christmas in 1861, along with the possessions of other secessionist families. Judge Whipple, a New England transplant and ardent abolitionist, purchases the property for his friend, Colonel Carvel. Nevertheless the colonel moves to his picturesque summer home in Glencoe, Missouri, to the southwest of St. Louis. Judge Whipple visits there, and it is at Glencoe that Stephen Brice meets Virginia Carvel.

Bellegarde. Residence of the pro-secessionist Colfaxes; located on Bellefontaine Road outside St. Louis.

It is here that Clarence Colfax gives a huge ball to announce his betrothal to Virginia Carvel. Stephen Brice is intentionally not invited.

*Camp Jackson.** Confederate army camp and arsenal set up in St. Louis by Missouri's pro-secessionist governor Claiborne Jackson. Confederate volunteers, including Captain Colfax, attempt to gain control of the city, but five German regiments from South St. Louis surround the camp and force the Confederate sympathizers to surrender. In the novel not a shot is fired; however, in the actual historical event, twenty-eight people were killed.

*Wilson's Creek.** Ten miles southwest of Springfield where the fiercest Civil War battle in Missouri is fought on August 10, 1861, Although Union forces lose the battle, they retain control of Missouri.

*Vicksburg.** Mississippi town on the Mississippi River where Union and Confederate forces meet in a major battle to determine control over traffic on the river. There, Lieutenant Stephen Brice sees General Sherman, renewing an acquaintance made earlier in his civilian days. Brice also meets with General Grant, who soon promotes him to captain. The novel provides considerable detail about the battle and Grant's heroic steadfastness in pursuing the campaign. After Confederate captain Clarence Colfax is badly wounded, Brice uses his influence to have Colfax sent to St. Louis for medical attention, as fate brings the two friends together.

*White House.** Home and headquarters of U.S. president Abraham Lincoln, before whom Virginia Carvel successfully pleads for the life of her fiancé, Clarence Colfax, who has been convicted as a Confederate spy. Later, while visiting the president, Major Stephen Brice proposes marriage to Virginia Carvel within Lincoln's office; the coming merging of pro-Union and pro-Confederate families symbolizes the future reuniting of the divided nation.

— *Irwin Halfond*

THE CROCK OF GOLD

Author: James Stephens (1882-1950)
Type of work: Novel
Type of plot: Fantasy

Time of plot: Indeterminate
First published: 1912

Set in Ireland, this novel is replete with images of confinement: narrow, dark spaces that sometimes enclose even narrower spaces, including tombs. The process of emergence from these prisons is a difficult one, requiring the guidance of mythical creatures. Like most paradisal constructions, the wider world into which this escape may be made is as vague as it is dazzling.

*Ireland.** Island nation west of Britain that was united under British rule in 1912—the same year James Stephens published *The Crock of Gold*. (In 1922, Ireland was partitioned into the Republic of Eire and Northern Ireland, which remained part of the United Kingdom). The Ireland depicted in the novel, however, is an Ireland of the imagination, carefully repopulated with all the lost idols of local mythology (and one visitor from overseas, the Greek nature-God Pan). Like William Butler Yeats and other champions of the so-called Celtic Twilight, Stephens believed that the soul of the Irish people was contained within its myths, and the territory mapped by his novel is a figurative internal landscape rather than a mere figment of geography.

Coilla Doraca. Pine wood, in whose heart stands the small house in which two Philosophers live with their ambivalent wives, the Grey Woman of Dun Gortin and the Thin Woman of Inis Magrath. Except for one small clearing a short distance from the house, the wood is a very dark and still place, because neither the sun's light nor the wind can penetrate the close-set branches. The hearthstone of the house eventually becomes the tombstone of one of the Philosophers and his wife, the Grey Woman of Dun Gortin.

Gort na Cloca Mora. Rocky field where a crock of gold is buried, having been hidden there by the Leprechauns (Leprecauns in the novel), one of six clans of fairies in the neighborhood of Coilla Doraca. The tree under which the crock was hidden sits atop an underground chamber, which becomes the temporary hiding-place of the kidnapped children of the two Philosophers. A neighboring field, which extends toward the top of a mountain, has a similar covert: the cave to which Pan takes Caitlin Ni Murrachu, where the Celtic god Angus Og comes to see her.

Cloca Mora was transformed into Glockamorra by E. Y. Harburg in the Stephens-inspired musical comedy *Finian's Rainbow* (1947; film version, 1968); the song "How Are Things in Glockamorra?" has convinced many an American tourist that there really is a place of that name, but it has not yet appeared on maps of the real Ireland.

Cave of the Sleepers of Erinn. Resting-place of the gods of Ireland, located on a mountain, to which the Philosopher goes in search of Angus Og. When he leaves it again, he bears messages for Mac Cul and MacCulhain—the legendary heroes more usually known as Finn McCool and Cuchulainn.

Police station. Station to which the Philosopher goes in order to surrender, rather than hiding in the Leprechauns' lair, resembles a military barracks. It has a walled garden, used as an exercise yard, but little can grow there save for creepers because the surrounding walls are so high. The cell in which he is confined is a subterranean cellar with a bench running around its walls, whose only window is a ground-level iron grating admitting a meager light. The cell's only means of access is a wooden ladder extended from a hole in the ceiling.

*Kilmasheogue (kihl-ma-SHOHG). Hill south of Dublin that is transformed within the story into a mountain decked with fairy forts. On its heights the Thin Woman of Inis Magrath gathers a host of the Shee, representing every part of Ireland. (*Shee* is a phonetic spelling of *Sidhe*, the Gaelic word for the residual spirits of the ancient Irish dead.) The assembled host greets Angus Og and Caitlin before the entire company sets off on a delirious journey into bright and boundless space, seizing the Philosopher from his prison as they go—thus, symbolically, liberating human intellect from all the cruel jailers who stand guard over the realm of the mundane.

— *Brian Stableford*

CROME YELLOW

Author: Aldous Huxley (1894-1963)
Type of work: Novel
Type of plot: Social satire

Time of plot: c. 1920
First published: 1921

Like the various venues provided for flirtatious philosophical conversation by the nineteenth century writer Thomas Love Peacock, the country house called "Crome" is a symbolic embodiment of England, fabricated over the centuries by the eccentrics of the past in order to play host to all manner of contemporary eccentrics. Although it is a parodic image, it is also an exceedingly affectionate one: an authentic home whose loss or destruction—though probably inevitable, one way or another—would be irreparably tragic.

Crome. English country house that is the seat of the Wimbush family. Formerly a monastery, it was rebuilt in the Elizabethan era by Sir Ferdinando Lapith in accordance with his eccentric theories of sanitation, which involved obtaining a maximum separation of distance between bathrooms (privies)—those at Crome being initially situated at the tops of its three towers—and the sewers into which they empty their wastes. Further rebuilding in the eighteenth century resulted in more practical plumbing facilities, although Sir Ferdinando was by no means the last eccentric to inflict his originality on Crome's architecture. The estate is still capable of further change—as illustrated by the yearly fair to which it plays host, which brings about a periodic transformation and enlivenment. However, there is a sense in which it is inescapably wedded to a lost past.

A turfed terrace in front of the house has a summerhouse at either end. The beautiful garden that slopes rather dangerously away from the terrace, encompassing a swimming pool, seems strangely monochromatic when viewed from the house, but the high-hedged flower garden conceals a blaze of color. Crome's interior is a patchwork of obsolete styles: Its long gallery is decorated with Italian primitive paintings and Chinese sculptures; its paneled drawing room is equipped with capacious chintz-upholstered armchairs; its modernized morning room features lemon yellow walls and rococo tables; its dining room is decked out with eighteenth century furniture and art. Similar variety is displayed in the many different kinds of antique beds with which the house's guest rooms are equipped. Crome also has a library, because no English country house would be complete without one, but none of the fashionable texts about which the assembled houseguests love to talk are contained therein.

The name Crome is obviously a variation of "chrome"; however, the name is not intended to recall the bright metal finish associated with that metal. Chrome yellow is a pigment (neutral lead chromate) that was once familiar to every English child as a staple of watercolor painting boxes. Aldous Huxley invokes that color here because of its autumnal associations.

Camlet-in-the-Water. Railway station situated on an insignificant branch line in the rural heartland of England on which Crome is most easily reached. The station's name recalls King Arthur's legendary **Camelot**, mischievously but not irreverently.

Home farm. Part of Crome's estate most intimately linked to the house, by virtue of the contiguity of its fields with the gardens. One of its unused granaries is appropriated by the painter Gombauld as the studio in which he paints a portrait of Anne Wimbush.

Rectory. Gloomy abode of the stern Mr. Bodiham, the clergyman entrusted with the care of the parish in which Crome is situated. Although the rectory is of more recent construction than Crome, its architectural affiliation with the Gothic revival embodies more ancient and more stubborn values. However, Bodiham's censorious brand of Protestantism makes no more impact on Crome's inhabitants than the rectory building itself does on the local landscape.

Rational State. Hypothetical future society sketched out by Mr. Scogan. It is the antithesis of Crome, and also—allegedly, at least—the destiny to which the house, and the quaintly crazy England it symbolizes, are ultimately bound; it was to be much more elaborately described and condemned in Huxley's 1932 novel *Brave New World*.

Gobley Great Park. Stately Georgian home, far more modern than Crome, featured on the picture postcard that Mary receives from Ivor, to add to the other temptations that seem likely to lure her away from her past-mired home. It is, however, merely one more staging-post on the way to the Rational State.

— *Brian Stableford*

CROTCHET CASTLE

Author: Thomas Love Peacock (1785-1866)
Type of work: Novel
Type of plot: Fiction of manners

Time of plot: Nineteenth century
First published: 1831

The "castle" of this novel's title is not actually a castle, but rather an English villa whose name reflects its recently enriched owner's delusions of grandeur. As Lady Clarinda observes, however, a castle is, in essence, a place of safety "even if Mammon furnished the fortification." Thomas Love Peacock's novel pays more attention to the progress of learning than his other novels, and this is symbolically reflected by the range of its settings.

Crotchet Castle (kroh-SHAY). House in England's Thames Valley. Not a true castle, it stands on the summit of a hill whose slopes are wooded, overlooking a grassy valley punctuated with juniper bushes. The hill still bears slight but clear traces of ancient Roman occupation. The opinion that it was once a military station or *castellum*—a theory robustly defended by the Reverend Dr. Folliott—provides a further excuse for its misleading name, although it is commonly referred to in the text as a mere camp.

Within the house the breakfast room is the arena of the first of the philosophical discussions conducted in the text, whose principal focus is—as is usual in Peacock's fictions of contemporary manners—the inexorable march of social progress. Subsequent discussions take place in the main dining room, the library, and the music room. The library houses a large collection of books, both ancient and modern (the older ones carefully sorted by Dr. Folliott), while the music room is equipped in a similarly egalitarian spirit with the scores of classical operas and more fashionable tunes.

The reader is told neither the name of the village adjacent to Crotchet nor the name of the inn where Dr. Folliott is taken to see the Charity Commissioners after his violent encounter with ruffians in the vicinity of the Roman camp. This unusual vagueness is symbolic of the judgment that Crotchet Castle and its surroundings are typical of social changes that have overcome the whole of England. The past is retained, in the Roman camp, the library, and the music room, but it has become detached from the present, relegated to the status of a collection tended by amateur curators.

Hautbois farm ([H]OH-boy). Ancient property near Crotchet Castle that has long been taxed to pay for the upkeep of an almshouse on the edge of the unnamed village. This farm is the only place in the vicinity of Crotchet Castle that is named in the novel. The almshouse its taxes support is derelict, although the tax is still collected, having been absorbed into Mr. Folliott's salary—the underlying allegation is that the church no longer passes on the welfare that it collects.

*Oxford. Historic university town on the River Thames. A further reflection of Crotchet Castle's emphasis on matters of learning is provided by an expedition up the River Thames and across the River Severn into Wales. The characters are tourists in Oxford, continuing their discussions as they stroll around observing "curiosities of architecture, painted windows, and undisturbed libraries."

Lake in Meirion. Wild spot in western Wales that the romantically inclined Mr. Chainmail eventually reaches at the end of his long expedition, having parted company with his fellows; there he sees the "vision" of a lovely girl rowing a coracle that leads to his marriage. The lake is close to the seashore, where the ruins of a real castle can be found, providing a sharp contrast with Crotchet Castle. This part of Wales had a special mythical significance for Peacock, who set his Arthurian romance *The Misfortunes of Elphin* (1829) there shortly before writing *Crotchet Castle.*

Chainmail Hall. Mr. Chainmail's home, which receives all of Crotchet Castle's guests, as well as its own, on Christmas Day, is a far more imposing building than Crotchet Castle. Its vaulted ceilings, stained-glass windows, and other anachronistic embellishments—especially its medieval armory—embody Chainmail's great regard for the long-gone feudal era of chivalry. It is here, steeped in nostalgia, that the novel ends. Although the sadly ironic postscript makes further reference to the symbolic location of **Dotandcarryonetown**—the world of commerce—its final phrase suggests that the greater part of the world is now a "rotten borough." (Rotten boroughs were parts of England no longer inhabited by more than a handful of individuals, but which still had the right, in 1831, to elect members of parliament.)

— *Brian Stableford*

THE CRUCIBLE

Author: Arthur Miller (1915-)
Type of work: Drama
Type of plot: Historical

Time of plot: 1692
First performed: 1953; first published, 1953

As a work depicts a historical occurrence, this play relies heavily on place for the development of its themes. By choosing to set the play in Salem, Massachusetts, in the late seventeenth century, Arthur Miller is invoking the Puritan way of life adhered to by its settlers. Historically the witch persecutions occurred in Salem Village (now Danvers, Massachusetts) rather than in present-day Salem, a distinction not made in the play.

Salem. Small Massachusetts town on the Atlantic coast, about twenty miles northeast of Boston. A small community sandwiched between the ocean and the wilderness, Salem felt itself surrounded by danger, a danger that could be combated only by hard work, perseverance, and strict religious observance. The Native Americans living in the area presented a threat, but the devil, who lurked in the nearby wilderness, was a far greater threat, tempting villagers to worship him. The theocracy that governed Salem was designed to prevent this from occurring; thus any departure from orthodoxy was condemned, and any opposition was summarily crushed.

Parris's house. Home of the Reverend Parris in Salem. It is symbolically appropriate that the home of Parris, the congregation's minister, is the site of the first outbreak of witchcraft hysteria. Act 1 occurs in an upstairs bedroom of the Parris house. The room contains only "a narrow window," a metaphor for the narrowness of Puritan beliefs, through which not much light is allowed to shine. The somber room "gives off an air of clean spareness," and the "raw and unmellowed" nature of the wood coincides with the nature of Puritan life.

Proctor home. Farmhouse five miles from Salem. Act 2 takes place in John and Elizabeth Proctor's home. The room where the act is set seems cold; although it is spring, John declares, "It's winter in here yet," signifying the emotional distance between John and Elizabeth. Court officials travel five miles to arrest Elizabeth, indicating how widespread the witch hysteria has become.

Salem meetinghouse. Church building in Salem in whose vestrom act 3 is set. It is a "solemn, even forbidding" room with heavy timbers, now used as the ante-room of the court. A symbol of the religion, the gloomy meetinghouse is where people are condemned rather than brought to the light of God. Although churches traditionally offer sanctuary to even the lowest of criminals, the church in Salem is where innocent people are condemned. Ironically, at the end of the act, a bird (not the dove of the Holy Spirit, but a demoniac bird) appears in the high rafters of the room.

Salem jail. Act 4 takes place in a jail cell, a dark place that looks empty even though two prisoners are kept here. All the prisoners are filthy, cold, and weak from hunger. The play ends in the jail, indicating that death is the ultimate outcome of such a cruel and narrow religion.

Forest. Wilderness west of Salem. The forest represents humankind's pagan instincts, which the Puritans have set out to suppress. In spite of their role in the church, Parris has caught his own family members dancing with the devil in the forest. Although John Proctor cultivates the earth right to the edge of the forest, the forest itself remains wild and uncultivated.

Andover. Massachusetts town a few miles from Salem in which rebellion against the court is rumored to be afoot. Parris fears it will spread to Salem.

Boston. Leading Massachusetts city, located about twenty miles southwest of Salem. The judges come from the General Court of Boston, and Boston carries a great deal of weight with Salemites. A witch had been hanged in Boston two years before the opening of the play.

Beverly. Massachusetts town a few miles from Salem from which the Reverend Hale comes. The town seems to be slightly more enlightened than Salem.

— *Jo N. Farrar*

CRY, THE BELOVED COUNTRY

Author: Alan Paton (1903-1988)
Type of work: Novel
Type of plot: Social realism

Time of plot: Mid-twentieth century
First published: 1948

Alan Paton's novel depicts mid-twentieth century South Africa as a country at once beautiful and full of grim destitution, corruption, disenfranchisement, and racial inequality, which combine to make life harsh for the country's native African citizens.

*Johannesburg.** South Africa's biggest and most advanced city and center of the country's prosperous gold mining industry. During the period in which the novel is set, Johannesburg, like the rest of South Africa, is governed by increasingly rigid racially discriminatory laws and customs, all of which favor the country's white minority. Nevertheless, black Africans flock to the city and its mines from impoverished rural areas to find wage employment and other opportunity. However, even in the great city, jobs are hard to find.

The novel focuses on the quest of Stephen Kumalo, an educated Zulu man ordained as an Anglican priest, to find his son in Johannesburg. After he reaches the city, he discovers his sister working as a prostitute and selling bootleg liquor, and his brother, who has become a corrupt political activist. Meanwhile, he observes the downtrodden condition of the city's African residents and the extreme racial inequalities in economic and political conditions. He yearns to be back in his own village, back to the innocence and the simple way of life.

Paton uses the modern city to accentuate Kumalo's naïve expectations of city life. As Kumalo explores Johannesburg, he sees the worst of humanity: extreme poverty, prostitution, crime, filth, destitution, and deprivation. The city is the worst place he can imagine. However, even within this great center of racism and distrust, he encounters kindness and humanity—mostly from fellow African and white clergymen, who comfort and support him when his religious faith and optimism begin to leave him. Through their small kindness, Paton redeems the city.

Parkwold Ridge. Johannesburg home of Arthur Jarvis, a tireless activist for African rights who has been murdered by Kumalo's son, Absalom, during a burglary attempt on the house. After Jarvis's death, his father, James Jarvis, for the first time begins to understand his son's dedication to African rights through his exploration of his son's study, which is filled with books and his writings on the need for African reforms. Gradually, father gets to know his son better in death than he ever did in life. He learns that his son loved the land of South Africa itself. Although he fought almost alone in his cause and his principles, he was passionate about the sufferings and disenfranchisement of the majority of his country's peoples. It is within his home that his life's work on African reforms exists.

Ndotsheni (en-doh-TSHAY-nee). Arid and impoverished Zulu village in South Africa's Natal Province in which Stephen Kumalo and his wife live in a simple home. Kumalo's son, sister, and brother have all fled the village for the big city in search of better opportunities, and Kumalo, in turn, finally leaves the village to search for them. Only after seeing Johannesburg does he fully appreciate the simple and truthful ways of his home. The novel's descriptions of Ndotsheni underscore the jarring differences of Johannesburg. Kumalo's faith in humanity is restored after he returns home and sees the changes brought by James Jarvis's material contributions to Ndotsheni's welfare and agricultural development: daily milk supplies for children, a new dam, and other improvements.

High Place. Prosperous farm owned by James Jarvis, the father of Absalom's murder victim. Although Jarvis's farm is near Ndotsheni, Jarvis and Kumalo never cross each other's path until they become aware of each other through their shared tragedy. Indeed, Jarvis has always isolated himself from the lives of his native African neighbors, and his interest in their welfare is minimal until after he meets Kumalo. The aptly named High Place is where James Jarvis isolates himself from Africans.

The time and energy Jarvis devotes to his farm also prevents him from understanding his son in his true light until after his son is dead. In honor of his son and moved by his growing understanding of the desperate economic problems of his African neighbors, Jarvis draws on the resources of his farm to make substantial contributions to the agricultural development of Ndotsheni.

— *Hanh N. Nguyen*

CUPID AND PSYCHE

Author: Unknown

Type of work: Fable

Type of plot: Mythic

Time of plot: Antiquity

First transcribed: Unknown (first English translation, probably 1566)

Most stories that have come down from antiquity were initially part of oral traditions. The first written version of this collection forms part of The Golden Ass *by the second century North African Lucius Apuleius. Descriptions of places in the work are sketchy and vary among different sources.*

Home city. Place where Psyche, the daughter of a Greek king, was born, possibly on the island of Crete. The city has many altars and temples dedicated to Venus that are neglected as the pilgrims from many countries who throng the streets throw flowers at Psyche's feet. Outside the city is a cliff top which is reached by climbing a steep hill. It overlooks a deep valley. This arrangement is typical of many ancient Greek cities. Psyche's bier was laid at the highest point.

Cupid's mansion. Place where Psyche lives as Cupid's wife. Situated in a valley carpeted with flowers and soft grass, it is surrounded by pleasant meadows, a grove of trees, and a clear-water spring. The mansion's roof is made of costly woods supported by golden and ivory pillars. Inside, the splendid hall is paved with marble on which there are pictures made from small blocks of colored stones. Golden lamps hang from the roof and stand in niches all around it. Golden statues stand on pedestals, and many other precious things lie around. A bath of silver is provided for Psyche's comfort. Food is served on a golden table. It is populated by invisible servants.

Temple of Ceres. One of the places that Psyche visits in search of help to find Cupid, the temple is located on the hills above Crete's plain of Cisamos. It resembles many Greek shrines, with pillars supporting the roof and steps leading up to the temple door. Inside, Psyche finds corn ears lying in heaps and others plaited into garlands; sickles and other tools are strewn about in confusion where worshipers have left them.

Venus's house. Place on **Mount Olympus** where Psyche is given impossible tasks to perform by Venus.

In one room, the servants heap all kinds of seeds for Psyche to sort out. Holes, cracks, and crannies in the walls and floor allow ants to enter the room and sort the seeds into neat heaps for her. Cupid is locked up in another room of the golden-gated house. Outside the house, a river runs along the edge of the woods, in which Venus's fierce, golden-fleeced sheep are allowed to wander. Scraps of fleece adorn the bushes against which the sheep have rubbed. Beside the river grow the sacred reeds from which the god Pan makes his pipes.

From Venus's house can be seen a mountaintop waterfall that is the source of the **River Styx** which flows through the **underworld**. It is called the Cocytus while it is above ground. The mountain face is a precipice of black rock. The waterfall dashes into a narrow gorge at the foot amid clouds of spray, and its water runs steeply over rocks and stones into a black cavern. In the sides of the gorge the heads of dragons peer from holes, watching with unblinking eyes.

Tartarus. Moss-covered tower that Psyche visits on her way to the underworld, in the mountains near the Laconian shore. Here Psyche is told that the route to the entrance is southward along the Taenarian promontory and near the cape bearing Poseidon's temple. The entrance to the underworld is through a cave. At the end of the path is the River Styx and the ferry crossing manned by Charon, who ferries across the souls of the dead for a penny. The gate of the underworld is guarded by the three-headed dog Cerberus.

— *Pauline Morgan*

THE CUSTOM OF THE COUNTRY

Author: Edith Wharton (1862-1937)　　　　　*Time of plot:* Late nineteenth century
Type of work: Novel　　　　　　　　　　　　　*First published:* 1913
Type of plot: Social realism

New York and Paris—the major locales for this novel's action—are used to demonstrate how New World commerce and energy conflict in subtle ways with Old World sophistication and tradition. Undine Spragg, a shallow, ambitious woman, uses culture only for self-ornamentation and the economy as a source of money for her indulgences. Her string of marriages reveals hidden levels of both cities' upper social strata. The ironically named Apex City represents midwestern values she wants to forget, but also the brashness and creative finagling which enable her financier husband to rise in American business.

*New York City. On the eve of the twentieth century, New York City is the focus of young Undine Spragg's dreams. Her determination to marry into the top level of American society is attained there by slow, deliberate, steps, culminating in her marriage to Ralph Marvell, the scion of an old New York family. Once their incompatibility and the Marvell family's diminished fortunes become clear, she flails about, looking for excitement and a more advantageous arrangement. What she learns of New York "society" mores enables her eventually to succeed. She knows where one needs to be seen in New York: at the opera house, at the painter Claud Popple's studio, at fashionable milliners', and at fine restaurants.

Although Edith Wharton provides short, vivid descriptions of New York City scenes, the role she gives to place in this novel is as much about "social space" as about the details of actual physical settings. Undine's New York City includes only Manhattan, and only people with recognizably northern European-derived names and appearances—this in an era when immigrants from southern and eastern Europe were pouring into the city.

*Washington Square. New York neighborhood in which the Marvell family town house is located. Undine views it as a symbol of Old New York aristocratic society, whose strictures and values she can neither accept nor understand.

Stentorian Hotel. New York hotel in which Undine and her parents are living when the novel opens. The hotel represents at least two things: the uprooting Undine's parents endure in order to launch her socially, and Undine's first, mistaken groping toward attaining social status, as when she asserts that the best people live only in hotels, not fixed abodes.

Spragg's office. New York office of Undine's father. It is shown in brief scenes as a place that only men enter. Business arrangements, both legitimate and questionable, are made there, in a setting far from the eyes—and interests—of their wives and daughters.

*Paris. France's leading city is the site of fashionable Americans' annual migration for holidays. Social displays, entertainment, shopping, and meeting the more disreputable or daring of Europe's remaining nobility are the main attractions of such sojourns. Undine likes Paris and tries to go there when she tires of New York. However, in Paris too her activities are largely confined to shopping, café-going, and nightlife, with occasional motoring trips into the countryside. On one occasion, when she worries about being perceived as a bore in conversation, she spends a morning at the great art museum known as the Louvre, but her experience there confuses her more than it enlightens her.

Chelles home (shehl). Spacious old Parisian house belonging to Raymond de Chelles; most of it is rented out. After marrying Raymond, Undine discovers that an entire proud, tradition-bound world of French aristocrats exists behind the gaudy attractions that delight rich Americans. Raymond is not averse to mounting occasional social events in the city, but he expects Undine to spend most of her time at the remote château of Saint Desert, where constant rain and ancient tapestries intensify her frustrations at being bored and trapped.

Apex City. Fictional town in which Undine grows up and where she meets Elmer Moffatt, her first and fourth husband. Critics have speculated that Apex City's location could be either Kansas or Nebraska; however, Wharton was not familiar with the Midwest and probably had no specific city in mind for a model. Apex City is a mix of small city stereotypes, such as its Baptist church and the walk down Main Street. Paradoxically, the small-town values from which Undine escapes later enable her to come full circle and remarry Moffatt when she tires of life with her French husband. When she pro-

tests that the Roman Catholic Church forbids divorce, Elmer points out that she was born a Baptist, and that "we're differently made out in Apex;" he wants her as a wife, not a mistress.

— *Emily Alward*

CYMBELINE

Author: William Shakespeare (1564-1616)
Type of work: Drama
Type of plot: Tragicomedy

Time of plot: First century B.C.E.
First performed: c. 1609-1610; first published, 1623

Although William Shakespeare's plot has several strands and a number of characters in disguise or under assumed identities, most of the action takes place in various sites in Great Britain shortly after Romans conquered it under Julius Caesar. When the play's action moves to Rome, these scenes are suggestive of Italian Renaissance courts; their atmosphere seems intended to establish a contrast between a primitive kingdom and a sophisticated but aging empire.

*Great Britain. Island of which Cymbeline is the king during the reign of Roman emperor Augustus Caesar and which is nominally governed by Rome, thanks to the earlier military incursions of Julius Caesar, whose name is invoked in the verse. Shakespeare deliberately refers to Cymbeline's realm as "Britain" rather than "England," which he uses routinely in his medieval history plays. Clearly, Cymbeline's primitive Britain resembles the pre-Roman Britain of Shakespeare's earlier *King Lear* (1606); however, the insistent use of "Britain" may be due, in part, to Shakespeare's efforts to stress the unity of Great Britain to please his patron, King James I. Whereas *Lear* portrays disasters ensuing from dividing the kingdom, *Cymbeline* stresses the importance of the unity of Britain, affirming its sovereignty by a surprising British victory over Rome's legions as a result of unexpected help given by three warriors from the mountains of Wales.

Lud's Town. Ancient name of London, which is presumably the site of Cymbeline's court. The name "Lud's town" evokes the archaic period in which the play is set, as well as the ancient origin of England's chief city, supposedly founded as a fortress by King Lud. In the play's first three acts, the court is tainted by intrigue and favoritism, mainly resulting from the queen's plotting and the

petulant behavior of her spoiled son, Cloten, although the courtiers are mostly decent people who mock Cloten behind his back. While the court seems provincial in contrast to Imperial Rome, its inequalities and injustices clearly present a strong contrast to the Welsh mountains and the hardy, kidnapped princes who have become self-reliant mountaineers.

*Rome. Capital of the ancient Roman Empire. The language of the play emphasizes the "Italian" character of the city and links it with the intrigues of Renaissance Italy of Shakespeare's time through the scheming figure of Iachimo (or Giacomo). When the action moves to Rome during Posthumus's exile, a proper staging should use the city to project an atmosphere of cosmopolitan cynicism provoking Posthumus to make his wager on the invincible chastity of Imogen. By contrast with scenes of gossip and intrigue in Rome, later scenes showing the courage of Roman soldiers in Britain establish the aura of Rome as a powerful adversary, whose military defeat by the Britons seems miraculous.

Imogen's bedroom. Sexually charged setting of the crucial scene in Iachimo's plot to destroy Imogen's reputation. As Imogen prepares for bed, her bedroom assumes an erotic aura intensified by the emergence of the concealed Iachimo and his voyeuristic inspection of her, which suggests a symbolic rape, as allusions in the verse to the stories of Lucrece and Philomela are intended to suggest.

Belarius's cave (beh-LAY-ree-uhs). Hideaway of the banished nobleman Belarius in the mountains of Wales. The cave and its environs are a rugged wilderness setting that contrasts sharply with cosmopolitan Rome and the injustices of the court's atmosphere. Clearly, the two princes who have grown up in the Welsh mountains have not been spoiled by the royal favoritism which has corrupted Cloten, as Polydore's easy defeat of Cloten illustrates. The mountainous setting not only stimulates the young men's courage and prowess, it also is conducive to poetry, as the dirge they sing at the supposed death of Fidele (the disguised Imogen) illustrates.

Milford Haven. Welsh seaport that is introduced somewhat anachronistically as the chief port of arrival and departure for both the Britons and Romans and is the goal of Imogen's flight. In Shakespeare's earlier work, the port is associated with the successful expedition of Henry Tudor to defeat Richard III, which is virtually a providential event. Shakespeare's invocation of such favorable associations here underscores the nationalist tone of the play; but his use of Milford Haven also ensures that some of the action will take place in Wales, which has mythic associations with Arthurian legend and with the prophecies of Merlin as well as with the poetry of numerous oracular bards.

— *Edgar L. Chapman*

THE CYPRESSES BELIEVE IN GOD

Author: José María Gironella (1917-2003)
Type of work: Novel
Type of plot: Historical realism

Time of plot: 1931-1936
First published: Los cipreses creen en Dios, 1953
   (English translation, 1955)

The geographical focus of this novel of Republican Spain before the Civil War is the coastal Catalonian city of Gerona, which serves as a microcosm of the many competing ideologies influencing Spaniards at the time. The conflicts dividing Spain are further symbolized by the divisions within the Alvear family, whose members include an anticlerical father, his conservative Catholic wife, a deeply religious son, and another son, whose character derives from the author himself, who is desperately seeking to construct a meaningful life in a nation descending into chaos.

Gerona. Town tucked away in the northeast corner of Catalonia near Spain's border with France. Gerona might at first seem an unlikely place to carry the symbolic weight of all the forces sweeping through Spain during the tumultuous years of the young republic. Barcelona, also in Catalonia, about sixty miles southwest of Gerona, is a larger city that played a more important role in the Spanish Civil War than Gerona; however, José María Gironella was born in Gerona and, following the traditional advice given to young writers, wrote about what he knew intimately. For him, Gerona stands for all places in Spain, and each locale in this city has a symbolic meaning.

Alvear apartment. Gerona home of the Alvears, a typical Spanish family living on the second floor of a flat overhanging the Onar River. Because of the river's seasonal floods, the neighborhood is seen as unattractive, though the Alvear residence is better than the flats the family occupied earlier in Madrid, before Matías Alvear, a Republican, was transferred to Gerona to work as a clerk in the telegraph office. Because Alvear is from Madrid and his wife, Carmen Elgazu, is from the Basque provinces, events occurring in the rest of Spain influence family members. For example, one month after the Republic is proclaimed, Matías's brother, a radical, participates in the burning of churches and convents in Madrid.

Seminary. Religious institution in Gerona that the eldest Alvear son, Ignacio, enters at the same time the family settles in the city. The seminary occupies the heights of the city; it, the cathedral, and other churches of Gerona represent the overpowering presence of Roman Catholicism in Spanish life. However, the seminary proves to be only an interlude in Ignacio's search for himself, and he leaves the religious vocation for the secular life. Coinciding with Ignacio's loss of vocation is the proclamation of the Spanish Republic. Later, his young brother César, who is deeply devout, becomes a happy and successful seminarian.

Gerona slums. Ignacio spends more and more time in these Geronese slums, which both attract and repel him. He sees the dilapidated houses, smells the rotting garbage, and hears the growls of the half-starved dogs, but he also gets to know the people, who have an innate happiness that bubbles to the surface in their saloons and cafés. His walks from one part of Gerona to others are like his attraction first to one political ideology, such as socialism, then to another, such as Falangism, as he struggles to find a rational mean between irrational extremes.

Political headquarters. Gerona's many political parties have their particular realms. For example, Izquierda Republicana, the left republican party, has the best hall in town. The Liga Catalana, the conservative Catholic party, holds its social events in church halls. The Confederación del Trabajo, whose objective is the establishment of anarchism, meets in the largest of the city's three gymnasiums. The monarchists gather in the editorial office of *El Tradicionalis*, and the communists, who are poorly organized, meet in a barbershop.

Cemetery. Tensions between Catholics and communists, between the poor and the privileged, and between right-wing and left-wing parties lead to increasing violence and the piling up of corpses in the local cemetery. Communist and anarchist crowds burn eight churches and three convents in Gerona in less than two hours. Doctors and lawyers are forced from their homes and priests from their rectories. Charged with being "fascists," they are dragged to the cemetery and shot. Among the victims in the cemetery is the young seminarian César Alvear, and the final beat of his heart ends the novel.

— *Robert J. Paradowski*

CYRANO DE BERGERAC

Author: Edmond Rostand (1868-1918)
Type of work: Drama
Type of plot: Tragicomedy

Time of plot: c. 1640-1655
First performed: 1897; first published, 1898 (English translation, 1898)

Set in France and based on the life of the historical Cyrano de Bergerac in the seventeenth century, Edmond Rostand's play evokes a time of poets and musketeers, living for honor. Each act of his play has a different primary setting that evokes a strikingly different mood.

Hôtel de Bourgogne (oh-TEL deh Bur-GOIN). Parisian mansion whose main hall is normally used for tennis, but which on occasion is set up as a theater with a stage. Act 1 of Rostand's play opens in this theater, where its play within a play focuses the audience's attention on drama. Cyrano's own lifelong pursuit of honor makes him seem like a combination actor and playwright, composing and delivering his lines for the applause of his peers.

Ragueneau's pastry-shop (rah-geh-NOH). Large Parisian kitchen that provides the location of act 2. The shop symbolizes the search of the pastry chef and would-be poet Ragueneau for honor as a poet and his inability to produce well. Overflowing with food, the room reflects his true talent—that of a chef.

Roxane's house. The primary locale of act 3, Roxane's house has a vine-covered wall and balcony that are meant to remind audiences of a similar setting in

William Shakespeare's *Romeo and Juliet* (1595-1596). The house stands in a conservative district of Paris that contrasts with the daring of the young lovers, Roxane and Christian de Neuvillette. The knocker on Roxane's door "is bandaged with linen like a sore thumb," as if the house, injured by too many suitors seeking Roxane, will irritably resist any future ones.

*Arras (ah-RAS). Spanish-held city in northern France retaken by the French after a siege in 1640 that provides the setting for act 4 of *Cyrano de Bergerac*. There Christian and Cyrano risk their lives for king and honor and are visited by Roxane immediately before Christian is killed by a sniper. The scene in which Roxane brings a wagon of food to the starving soldiers of the Gascon Guards found a receptive audience in Paris, which had suffered through a horrifying siege and famine during the Franco-Prussian War of 1870-1871.

Sisters of the Holy Cross convent. Parisian nunnery in whose garden Cyrano and Roxane meet in act 5, fifteen years after the battle at Arras. Falling leaves accord with Cyrano's advancing age, while the solitary, "enormous" tree in the middle of the stage stands apart, like Cyrano in its size and loneliness. Neither the tree nor Cyrano is on a straight path to the chapel, which symbolizes Heaven. It is here that Cyrano finally reveals to Roxane that he wrote the love letters she received from Christian many years earlier.

— *James Whitlark*

DAISY MILLER: A Study

Author: Henry James (1843-1916)
Type of work: Novella
Type of plot: Psychological realism

Time of plot: Mid-nineteenth century
First published: 1878

In this novella, Henry James uses the settings of Vevey and Rome to symbolize two attitudes of upper-class society. Although Geneva is not an actual setting in the story, it is referred to and represents more conservative, old-fashioned social behavior.

***Vevey** (vuh-VAY). Small resort city on the northeastern shore of Switzerland's Lake Geneva, a large lake in the Swiss Alps. Daisy Miller, a seventeen-year-old American girl from Schenectady, New York, is traveling with her mother and younger brother. The Millers are vacationing in Europe to acquire some culture and because that is what they think rich people do. They are staying at an elegant resort hotel. Also staying at the hotel is American Frederick Winterbourne. Winterbourne went to school at Geneva and spends most of his time with other wealthy Americans in Europe. It is Winterbourne's consciousness that readers follow through the story. Miss Miller and Mr. Winterbourne meet casually on the grounds of the hotel because of Miss Miller's young brother Randolph. Ordinarily it would be improper in high society for a young lady to make the acquaintance of a gentleman without being formally introduced by a mutual acquaintance. At a resort, however, people are more relaxed about social formalities. When Miss Miller suggests that she is eager to see the nearby Castle of Chillon, Winterbourne offers to accompany her. Afterward, Winterbourne leaves Vevey for another social engagement. All of the action in part 1 takes place at Vevey. Winterbourne and Miller agree to see each other in Rome, where many wealthy Americans will spend the winter.

***Castle of Chillon.** Ancient castle in Vaud on the shore of Lake Geneva. Miller expresses a desire to see the castle because it is a major tourist attraction and many people have told her of its beauty. The two take a steamer to the castle. His aunt, Mrs. Costello, does not think this proper, but Daisy and her mother do not seem to know that. Their guide, Eugenio, does not approve of the outing, but Miller goes anyway. In her immaturity she does not appreciate the history of the castle, but Winterbourne finds her charming nonetheless.

***Rome.** Capital city of Italy. Most of the action of part 2 takes place at the Miller's hotel, Mrs. Walker's home, the Pincio (a large public garden), the ruins of the Colosseum, and a Protestant cemetery. The Americans living abroad are harsher in their judgment of the provincial Americans than the Europeans are. The ruins of the Colosseum are particularly important. Though they are a beautiful and significant historical ruin, it is a dangerous place to go after dark. First, for a young lady to be alone there with a gentleman would damage her reputation. Second, being out in Rome at night leaves one vulnerable to what is called "Roman fever," probably malaria.

***Schenectady** (skeh-NEHK-ta-dee). City in the northern part of New York State. No action takes place here, but this is the Millers' home. Their provincialism and lack of education are emphasized throughout the story. The society in which the Millers wish to move regards Schenectady as something of a backwater.

Geneva. Large French-speaking Swiss city on Lake Geneva. It is implied that Winterbourne, the character through whose eyes readers see the story, is having an affair with a married woman even though the social mores are conservative. He returns here at the end of the story, having realized that Daisy Miller admired him and that, because of his reserve, he has lost a chance for love.

— *Toni J. Morris*

DAME CARE

Author: Hermann Sudermann (1857-1928)
Type of work: Novel
Type of plot: Domestic realism

Time of plot: Nineteenth century
First published: Frau Sorge, 1887 (English translation, 1891)

This novel is set in an unnamed Prussian village in the most remote province of Germany and revolves around two homes—a large estate and a neglected farmhouse—and the families who live in them. This setting, well known to the author, who was born in the same region, serves as the geographical and psychic center of the protagonist's existence. Growing to maturity in an isolated, heavily forested, conservative community, Paul Meyerhofer, an impoverished farmer's son, is unprepared to deal with tensions of social class, sexual awakening, and religious fundamentalism. His brooding inwardness is seen as a mark of the isolated locale, which is known for producing writers and characters of introspective and mystical inclination.

East Prussia. Province in the extreme northeastern part of Germany that bordered on Russia when the novel was written and extended to the Baltic Sea. (It was divided between Poland and Russia after World War II.) Primarily agricultural, the province had only one large city, Königsberg, its capital. Hermann Sudermann was intimately familiar with the area, and his novel offers realistic descriptions of its landscape, its seasons, and its rituals, which included the observance of midsummer night.

Mussainen (moos-SI-nen). Poor farmhouse of the Meyerhofer family in a fictional village in an outlying region of Germany. The house is located on a moor some distance beyond the village, perhaps to emphasize its remoteness. After having been abandoned by its former owner, it is in desolate condition, and its new residents, the Meyerhofers, are too poor to afford anything better. The Meyerhofers are in dire circumstances; the father does not work regularly and squanders his meager resources on financial speculations and alcohol. The mother is physically and emotionally frail and is completely dominated by her husband. Of their five children, only Paul cares about the farm. It is he who rebuilds it after it is burned down by a disgruntled farmhand. At the end of the novel Paul himself burns the house down to distract his father, who is about to set a nearby estate, Helenenthal, on fire to avenge his eviction by the estate's new owner.

There seems to be a curse on Mussainen, though not explicitly uttered. An allegorical figure, Dame Care—in the meaning of worry, concern, or anxiety—hovers over the mother and Paul, an apparition in gray who personifies misfortune and who appears at crucial moments, but only to those two figures. Perhaps they are being tested because, as the deeper figures, they are capable of love, selflessness, and humility. The mother dies in the prospect of a better life for her son, and Paul is released from Dame Care by a loving woman. This explanation conforms to the many fairy-tale allusions in the text: The humble suitor finally wins the princess.

A more worldly explanation of the house's evident curse may be that it is haunted because the father does not fulfill his obligations. The Meyerhofers are forced to move into the house because of his mismanagement. A complicating factor is the impending machine age that invades this house and, by extension, this pastoral region. Max Meyerhofer, Paul's father, acquires a steam engine, which he keeps in a shed next to his house, to help him harvest the peat on his land; however, it is not in working condition. After Paul repairs it, it crushes the flute that his beloved has given him to encourage his self-expression and musical talent—a victory of mechanization over art. After Paul burns down Mussainen, he feels free for the first time in his life, as he has no possessions left to worry about.

Helenenthal (heh-LEE-nen-thawl). Grand estate in the same fictional East Prussian village as Mussainen. It is bought by a wealthy man named Douglas after Meyerhofer can no longer afford to keep it. Meyerhofer's resentment of Douglas for dislodging him leads to the climax of the story—his thwarted attempt to set Helenenthal afire and the destruction of his own home. A major theme of the novel is the relationship between the two families, which is basically socioeconomic. Forced to move to Mussainen, the Meyerhofers can still see Helenenthal from their new home. While remaining physically near, its social distance is great.

Helenenthal is an elaborate, fenced-in property with numerous buildings, a large garden, and a white house, in which Paul was born. To him this house is "the lost paradise," mainly because he admires Elsbeth, the daughter of the house, whom he is too shy to approach. He abandons a garden party at Helenenthal, to which Elsbeth has invited him, because he feels uncomfortable in society. Ironically, Paul ultimately inherits Helenenthal when he marries Elsbeth—an unconvincingly happy ending to the novel.

— *Henry A. Lea*

THE DAMNATION OF THERON WARE

Author: Harold Frederic (1856-1898)
Type of work: Novel
Type of plot: Social realism

Time of plot: 1890's
First published: 1896

The town of Octavius, the primary setting for the novel, significantly contributes to the moral disintegration of young Methodist minister Theron Ware. Poor, humble, sincere, simple, and innocent, Theron succumbs to the temptations embodied in the sensuous aestheticism of Celia Madden, the sophisticated cynicism of Father Forbes, and the scientific skepticism of Dr. Ledsmar. Each is represented by a signature locale—Celia's chamber, Father Forbes's dining room, and Dr. Ledsmar's home/laboratory. Theron's impulsive pursuit of Celia to New York City reveals his ironic self-delusion in his own capabilities.

Octavius. Fictional small town in the Mohawk Valley of New York State based loosely on Harold Frederic's hometown of Utica in the same region. There the young Methodist minister Theron Ware is given his first congregation. Octavius proves to be both a disappointment and an opportunity for Theron Ware. He is disappointed in not being posted to the larger and more prosperous town of Tecumseh but is grateful to leave the provincial village of Tyre behind him. Octavius represents an opportunity for him to develop his talents on a bigger stage. However, in Octavius Theron confronts both an ultra-conservative congregation and the unorthodox opinions of the Irish Catholic Celia Madden, the Roman Catholic priest Father Forbes, and Dr. Ledsmar. Octavius develops into a battleground for Theron's soul, as he faces puzzling and unsettling temptations from each of his three new acquaintances.

Celia Madden's chamber. Celia's "sacred chamber" is her bedroom and sitting room. Furnished with nude statuary, paintings of the Madonna and Child, candles, and flowing draperies, her chamber reflects her "Greek" philosophy and sense of the exotic and beautiful. The room also intensifies the heady pleasure that Theron finds with Celia. She intoxicates him with her beauty, with her liberated philosophy of life, and with the emotional intensity of Frédéric Chopin's music.

Forbes's home. Roman Catholic church and rectory in Octavius. Theron compares his role as a Protestant minister with Father Forbes's role as a Catholic priest. Forbes is a patrician autocrat, in command, living in luxury, and idolized by his female parishioners. He leaves parishioners waiting for hours while, in contrast, Theron is always at the disposal of his congregation. In his dining room, the priest sits in a circle of light, surrounded by wine, candles, and books. His erudition, sophistication, and cynicism offer Theron an appealing alternative view of religious callings.

Ledsmar's home. Dr. Ledsmar's cluttered home on the outskirts of Octavius reflects his prolific intellectual explorations, as well as his skepticism and amorality. No experiment goes beyond the purview of scientific curiosity, not even the experiment on a "Chinaman" to see how much opium he can tolerate. Ledsmar's home on the fringes of society houses wide-ranging experiments on such subjects as plants and lizards. Like his home, Ledsmar is nonconformist and beyond the reach of the town's constraints.

Theron Ware's parsonage and church. Small parsonage, church, and gardens in Octavius. In comparison with the homes of Celia, Father Forbes, and Dr. Ledsmar, Theron finds his home stultifying. After visiting Celia's chamber, he sees his own home as "bare and squalid" and "offensive to the nostrils." His home is the scene of meetings with tight-fisted trustees, an unimaginative and unsophisticated wife, a meager bookshelf, and wretched singing.

In another contrast, Alice's garden each day grows more beautiful with flowers and plants donated by the lawyer and church trustee Levi Gorringe, whom Theron sees as competing for Alice's affection. Even enduring the professional fundraiser with the Soulsbys in his own church makes him physically ill. Theron's home painfully reminds him of everything he thinks is wrong with his life—his marriage, his limited scholarship, and his ministerial calling. After being exposed to the ideas of his new acquaintances, everything about his life appears desiccated and paltry.

Woods outside Octavius. Site of a Methodist camp meeting and a Catholic picnic. Religious fervor intensifies Theron's emotions, and he deserts the strictures of the Methodists for a ramble in the woods. The Catholic picnic he attends, with its revelries and beer tent, contrasts with the more sober and somber festivities of his own straitlaced religion. As he meets with Celia in the privacy of the woods, high on a hill above the picnic, seemingly removed from the constraints of his life, he kisses her.

*New York City. At the end of the novel, Theron descends into the confusing and occasionally hellish world of New York City in pursuit of Celia and Father Forbes. He is unfamiliar with the landscape and the world of trains, hack drivers, and hotels. Nevertheless, he confidently imagines that Celia loves him, that he has escaped detection, and that everyone drinks claret for breakfast. Eventually, however, Theron's adventures in New York expose him as an inexperienced provincial minister who has deluded himself into thinking that he is a sophisticate. After Celia rejects and ridicules him, New York becomes the site of his deepest disillusionment.

— *Ann M. Cameron*

THE DANCE OF DEATH

Author: August Strindberg (1849-1912)
Type of work: Drama
Type of plot: Psychological realism
Time of plot: Late nineteenth century

First performed: 1905; first published, 1901 as *Dödsdansen, första delen* and *Dödsdansen, andra delen* (English translation, 1912 as *The Dance of Death I* and *The Dance of Death II*)

Place forces the conflict driving this play, in which three people must confront their needs, desires, passions, and ultimate fate while they are forced to live together in an isolated tower on a remote island off the coast of Sweden.

Tower. Island home of Alice and her husband Edgar, a captain in the Swedish army. Part of an ancient fortress that was once a prison, the tower is still a prison for Edgar and Alice, who are cut off from the mainland and from the other officers and officials on the island. Edgar believes himself superior in rank, intelligence, and general character to any others on the island. It is clear that Edgar and Alice have grown to dislike each other intensely; it is also clear that Edgar is not well. There is so much bickering between the two that all the servants have left. Into this isolated place comes Alice's cousin Kirk, who brings further proof of isolation as he announces that he has been sent by the government to oversee a quarantine of the entire island because of an infectious disease. The sense of isolation and entrapment is intensified when Edgar has a heart attack and it becomes obvious that he is dying. Alice and Kirk renew an old

love interest as they care for the dying Edgar. Alice tells her lover that prisoners used to call the fortress "hell" and that they are now the "devils" living in hell. When Edgar confronts the lovers, Kirk runs off into the night, deserting Alice. She and her husband must now do the final measures of his "dance of death" alone in the fortress known as "hell."

— *August W. Staub*

A DANCE TO THE MUSIC OF TIME

Author: Anthony Powell (1905-2000)
Type of work: Novel
Type of plot: Social realism
Time of plot: 1914-1971
First published: 1976: *A Question of Upbringing,*
  1951; *A Buyer's Market,* 1952; *The Acceptance*

World, 1955; *At Lady Molly's,* 1957; *Casanova's Chinese Restaurant,* 1960; *The Kindly Ones,* 1962; *The Valley of Bones,* 1964; *The Soldier's Art,* 1966; *The Military Philosophers,* 1968; *Books Do Furnish a Room,* 1971; *Temporary Kings,* 1973; *Hearing Secret Harmonies,* 1975

In Anthony's Powell's twelve-volume series of novels, Nicholas Jenkins, a pleasant, intelligent, and self-effacing journalist often uses quite specific locations that were important in his life to tell the story of his life and that of his acquaintances from the time of his childhood until old age.

Public school. School that Jenkins attends as a boy. A British "public school" is equivalent to an American private school; parents pay fees, and only parents with some financial resources are able to afford them. Jenkins's school is unnamed, suggesting that it is not meant to represent one of the great schools of England—such as Eton or Harrow. However, it appears to be of some distinction, as most of its boys are of the affluent middle class, and some have connections with the aristocracy.

The school is a late childhood version of English upper-class society. Charles Stringham has titled connections. Jenkins's father is an army officer, and Peter Templer's father is a successful industrialist. Kenneth Widmerpool is an anomaly; he comes from the lower middle class and was sent to the school by his parents at a great financial sacrifice to make connections that may help him later in life. The cheerful arrogance and social poise of Stringham and Templer differ from the social ineptness and groveling of Widmerpool. The latter's constant striving sets a thematic pattern for the rest of the

work; the indifference of Stringham and Templer to hard work and calculating conduct is set against Widmerpool's determination to succeed, however questionably. Jenkins, slightly below Stringham and Templer in the social and economic hierarchy, but above the vulgarity and slyness of Widmerpool, represents a kind of ideal gentleman, moral, fair-minded, and unassertive.

*Oxford University. One of the great British institutions of higher learning, in which a social hierarchy is again present. Some young men, such as Templer, who could attend, refuse to do so, confident of their connections to get them ahead. Widmerpool, obviously not bright enough to get a scholarship, cannot go on, but gets right to work on his plan to make something of himself.

It is at Oxford that Jenkins meets characters who will people his world when he begins his career in London. At the time of the novel, the university world is more than simply a matter of education; like the public school, connections are to be made, and university dons sometimes wield considerable power in the real world.

*London. Center of political, economic, social, and artistic life in Britain, where Jenkins must make his way in the literary world, and where his connections help him. He is in a good position to watch the characters rise and fall as they move on into middle age and early old age. London follows the European tradition, centuries old, of gathering similar activities in specific neighborhoods. This is particularly so in central London.

*Shepherd Market. London area of small shops, restaurants, and cheap rooming houses, northwest of Piccadilly Circus and bordering on Mayfair, a smart, expensive residential area. It is a well-known assignation point for prostitutes. Jenkins lives there on first coming to London in 1923. He sees it as an enchanted area where the young man in search of adventure and success can live modestly and where, despite its seediness, there is an air of sophistication and a sense of the centers of power, social, artistic, political, and economic, at hand.

*Ritz Grill. Restaurant in the fashionable Ritz Hotel on Piccadilly, a frequent meeting place for Jenkins with characters coming in and out of his life. It is here that he gets involved with the great and disastrous love of his life, Jean Duport, at Christmas in 1932. Le Bas, the schoolmaster, has his Old Boys reunions here.

*Belgravia. London neighborhood area west of Buckingham Palace, a labyrinth of squares of the most expensive housing in London where Jenkins and his young friends, male and female, attend dinners and dances at the homes of the rich and titled. Widmerpool, assiduous in his determination to get ahead, is ridiculed by a debutante at a dinner dance given by Lord Huntercombe of Belgrave Square.

*Victoria. Unfashionable, somewhat run-down area west of Belgravia, where, appropriately, Widmerpool and his mother live in a small apartment. It might be seen as symbolically proper that this pair, determined to achieve success, are hovering on the edge of the more expensive part of central London.

*Soho. London district area northeast of Piccadilly Circus popular for social slumming by artists, actors, and musicians. Soho is symbolic of the raffish nature of young pleasure seekers, and for the obvious excesses of young, talented associates of Jenkins. Several clubs and restaurants patronized by Jenkins and his friends are in this ramshackle, flashy area: Casanova's Chinese Restaurant, Foppa's, Trouville, and Umfraville's Night Club.

*Stourwater Castle. Originally the home of the financial magnate, Sir Magnus Donners, who gives both Stringham and Widmerpool their early chances to succeed in big business. The magnificent house and land, the art collection, and Donners's generosity are at odds with his boring sense of importance, and are part of Powell's satirical view of the dead hand of wealth and power. Significantly, this is where Widmerpool's career begins and literally ends. It is here that the last act of humiliation is imposed upon him by a spurious spiritual thug, and this time acting the fool kills Widmerpool.

— *Charles Pullen*

DANCING AT LUGHNASA

Author: Brian Friel (1929-   )
Type of work: Drama
Type of plot: Psychological realism

Time of plot: Summer, 1936
First performed: 1990; first published, 1990

Rural Ireland in August, 1936, provides the setting for this "memory play" in which the narrator, Michael, recalls how the lives of his mother and her four sisters were altered forever by the events of a few weeks.

Mundy home. Typical rural Irish farm house of the 1930's, with a kitchen serving as a general living and working area. Not just the cooking but all domestic tasks take place here, including the knitting Agnes and Rose sell to a local merchant. The wireless radio, which the sisters have dubbed "Marconi" after the name on its front, occupies a key position; also visible are an iron range, a sturdy table, an oil lamp, and buckets for well water by the back door. As the stage directions note, these austere furnishings are mitigated by flowers, curtains, and other items. The front door opens onto a garden, underscoring the grace with which the five women eke out a living.

Ballybeg. Literally "Smalltown" in Irish, Ballybeg is the village just outside of which lies the Mundy household. Brian Friel has made Ballybeg a symbolic Irish "everytown" in several of his plays, often using it, as he does here, as a microcosm for Irish society at various points in the country's history. As Michael says in his opening monologue, these few weeks in August, 1936, produced in him an unease, a sense of things rapidly changing. Ballybeg, then, marks the threshold between childhood innocence and adult experience for Michael. Similarly, it marks the line between two eras of modern Irish life, as the family dissolves after the sisters lose their respective livelihoods to factory mass production or to the dwindling number of students at the village school.

*Donegal. County in western Ireland; remote even by rural standards, it is one of the last places to benefit from the electrification of the country and part of the Gaeltacht, or Irish-speaking region. It is known for its rough beauty, with wilderness or backwater associations, hence the lingering customs of Lughnasa, the harvest festival honoring the pagan deity Lugh. These agrarian rituals at the village's margins are set against the approaching changes to small village life, just as the Mundy sisters' first wireless radio represents the encroachment of the wider world upon their lives in the mid-1930's.

— *James Scruton*

DANGEROUS ACQUAINTANCES

Author: Pierre Choderlos de Laclos (1741-1803)
Type of work: Novel
Type of plot: Psychological realism

Time of plot: Mid-eighteenth century
First published: Les Liaisons dangereuses, 1782
  (English translation, 1784)

This novel of manners portrays the libertine life of a small segment of the French aristocracy known as the bonne compagnie. *Like other novelists of his era, Pierre Choderlos de Laclos is interested in presenting his novel as a true story, one that actually happened. He uses place to help achieve this end. Paris, country houses, and the convent all played significant roles in the lifestyle of the* bonne compagnie. *Letter headings within the novel indicate dates and places—a device that creates a sense of authenticity, while helping readers follow the action of the story.*

*Paris. France's capital city is the focal point of the novel's action. During the eighteenth century, Paris was the center of social interaction. Laclos's novel portrays the aristocracy of the period, especially the libertine segment of this social group. Paris is thus the only setting possible for Laclos's fiction.

Madame de Rosemonde's château (rohz-MOHND). Country house belonging to Madame de Rosemonde, the aunt of the vicomte de Valmont. The château is important as the place where the notorious libertine Valmont may encounter and interact with a woman of the upper bourgeoisie. Madame de Tourvel is visiting Madame de Rosemonde during her husband's absence from Paris. She has in a sense withdrawn from society and shut herself away from the dangers of Paris. It is also at the château that the unsuspecting Cécile de Volanges is placed in a vulnerable situation that allows Valmont to seduce and morally corrupt her.

In the village near the château Valmont performs a charitable act that helps a miserable villager in order to convince Madame de Tourvel that he is of good character.

Convent. Religious community from which Cécile's mother brings her home to Paris. At the time in which the novel is set, convents were traditional refuges for women and residences for girls of aristocratic families until they reached marriageable age. Totally ignorant of the world when she emerges from the convent, Cécile is ill prepared for what awaits her. At the end of the novel, the convent once again plays a significant, though conventional, role, when both Madame de Tourvel and Cécile withdraw to the convent. The novels of the period abound with heroines abandoned by lovers who seek solace within religious orders. Madame de Tourvel goes there to die, Cécile to take the veil and expiate her sins.

La Comédie Italienne. Popular theater in eighteenth century Paris that is the scene of Madame de Merteuil's public humiliation. At the conclusion of the novel she appears in her box there after the scandalous intrigue resulting in Valmont's death and is ignored and shunned by everyone. Thus Laclos ends his novel in an appropriately moralistic fashion, as evil is punished.

— *Shawncey Webb*

DANIEL DERONDA

Author: George Eliot (Mary Ann Evans, 1819-1880)
Type of work: Novel
Type of plot: Social realism

Time of plot: Mid-nineteenth century
First published: 1876

This complex novel presents scenes of interpersonal encounters emphasizing the saving influences that people can have on others. It counterpoints types of aesthetic and ideological culture, comparing apparently purposeless members of the English aristocratic and landed classes, to their disadvantage, with Jewish characters of talent, vision, and artistic dedication. The sense of place reinforces cultural distinctions: The upper classes are seen finding their pleasures attending outdoor activities or dinner parties on their estates or yachting or visiting cities on the continent, while the Jewish characters are seen demonstrating their superior talents or involved in learning activities that perpetuate their cultural heritage. Social distance prevails among the upper classes, while the Jewish settings are often more domestic and intimate, encouraging sympathy among the characters. Especially for the three marriages in the story, emphasis among the landed classes is on guarding their patrimony, a contrast with the Jewish internationalism and valuing of a spiritual identity.

Offendene. Modest home of Gwendolen Harleth's mother, Mrs. Fanny Davilow; located in Wessex (name of the early kingdom of the West Saxons that grew into modern England). Gwendolen sees Offendene as boring; the place reinforces her narrow perspective and values, identified as a nervous susceptibility, an overwhelming sense of dread, and illusions about the degree of control she can exert over others, while her own life, in fact, is governed by chance, not choice. At the end of the story, after Gwendolen has learned more about herself, she finds Offendene an attractive place to which to return.

Leubronn. German resort where Deronda first meets Gwendolen at a gaming table. The novel opens in the middle of a scene in which Gwendolen becomes dependent on Deronda as a spiritual mentor when he redeems a necklace she has pawned and admonishes her for gambling. Leubronn is a place of escape for Gwendolen,

who is trying to avoid Grandcourt's proposal of marriage, and establishes her character as that of a gambler. It is also the place where she learns of her family's lost fortune. (Eliot based the fictional resort on Homburg, Germany, which she visited in 1872.)

*Genoa. Northern Italian seaport in which the lives of both Gwendolen and Daniel reach their crisis points. As explained in the story, the "grand" city and harbor are significant for their history of accepting Jewish refugees. There Daniel meets his mother and learns of his distinguished racial and religious heritage, which will determine his future marriage and vocation. Gwendolen is saved from the inferno of her marriage, but precipitated into her own purgatory. With Deronda's sympathy, she redirects herself toward a life guided by moral motive.

Quetcham Hall. Estate home of the Arrowpoints, where Gwendolen meets Julius Klesmer, a prominent Jewish German musician, who later destroys her illusions about gaining a living by singing and acting. It is where Catherine Arrowpoint, a dramatic foil for Gwendolen, declares her independence from her parents' and the landed classes' expectations about a proper marriage for an heiress. She and Klesmer are the ideal characters in the novel, partly because they are consummate artists.

Hand and Banner. Public tavern that serves as a gathering place for meetings of the Philosophers' Club. As Mordecai's guest there, Daniel comes to a better understanding of Mordecai's vision for a political and religious reuniting of the dispersed Jews.

*Blackfriars Bridge. Bridge across the River Thames in London where Daniel becomes more fully understanding of Mordecai's belief in the transmutation of souls. The setting is associated with Mordecai's specific vision of his spiritual heir rising out of a flaming sunset, and, significantly, permits Deronda to come to Mordecai by water.

Brackenshaw Park. Place representing landed power that is the scene of the archery meeting, at which Gwendolen wins a gold arrow. Here she first meets and dances with Henleigh Mallinger Grandcourt, whose "impassive" appearance is contrasted with Klesmer's "animation."

*Frankfurt. German city in which Deronda visits a synagogue, his interest stirred by his concern for Mirah, where his likeness to his grandfather is recognized by Joseph Kalonymos, keeper of his grandfather's collections of papers significant to Jewish history and culture.

— *Carolyn Dickinson*

DANTON'S DEATH

Author: Georg Büchner (1813-1837)
Type of work: Drama
Type of plot: Tragedy

Time of plot: March-April, 1794
First published: Dantons Tod, 1835 (English translation, 1927); first performed, 1902

Set in revolutionary Paris at the height of the Reign of Terror—the orgy of executions orchestrated by Georges Danton which tainted the reputation of the French Revolution irredeemably—Georg Büchner's play places the most famous figures of the period in the institutions they established.

*Paris. Capital of France and center of revolutionary activity in which the play is set. The locations of many of the play's scenes are only vaguely identified, such as "a room" and "a street"; however, all the crucial locations of the Terror are carefully included, in telling sequence. One crucial scene in act 1 takes place in a Jacobin Club, and a scene in act 2 is set in the National Convention (the Revolutionary government). Act 3 moves back and forth between the Luxembourg prison, the Revolutionary Tribunal (the court that issued condemnations), a meeting of the Committee of Public Safety (which determined its policy) and the Conciergerie (the prison of the Palais de Justice, whose voluble inmates include Tom Paine, author of *The Rights of Man*). Scenes 7 and 9 of act 4 are set in the place de la Révolution, the site of the guillotine, toward which Danton is irresistibly moved by implacable fate, taking the ideals of the Revolution with him.

The various anonymous rooms and streets used as settings are unidentified because they do not need to be, but the differences between the discussions to which they play host are glaring; the interior debates are thoughtful and mostly idealistic, but insulated from a full awareness of the forces that they have already unleashed; their exterior counterparts are more casual, more abrupt, and more confused. Once Danton is condemned to make his final trip from the interior to exterior, however, he reaches his philosophical conclusion: that the world is chaos, and its god, awaiting birth, is nonexistence.

— *Brian Stableford*

DAPHNIS AND CHLOË

Author: Longus (fl. third century C.E.)
Type of work: Fiction
Type of plot: Pastoral
Time of plot: Indeterminate

First transcribed: Poimenika ta kata Daphnin kai Chloen, third century C.E. (English translation, 1587)

The pastoral content of this novel is what differentiates it from other works written during the same time frame. It contains numerous allusions to Homer and myth that help clarify events occurring in its two protagonists' lives. This work adheres to Aristotle's "unity of place." All its action centers upon a small area on the Greek island of Lesbos, with references to the two major cities on the island as well.

*Lesbos (LEHS-bohs). Greek island in the Aegean Sea on which actions centers on two cities: Methymna and Mytilene. Methymna is a city believed to be named after a daughter of King Makara, who was married to Lesbos of Thessaly, the namesake of the island. Within a century of the time when *Daphnis and Chloë* was written, Methymna suffered from a series of raids. The individuals from this place seem different from Daphnis and Chloë and the rest of the people in their environment; they are outsiders.

The other important city on Lesbos is Mytilene, which is named after another of King Makara's daughters. *Daphne and Chloë* opens here, describing the city as beautiful and idyllic. Like the people in Methymna, Mytilene's people are seen as outsiders and are quite different from the book's main characters.

Philetas's garden (fih-leh-TAHZ). Place described by the old man, Philetas, as the setting in which he sees "Love" in the form of a child. The boy has wings, is handsome, carries a bow, and appears much like the image readers would have of Cupid on Valentine's Day. The old man speaks with the god called Love and is told he is lucky to have envisioned him, because he is the only old man in the world who has seen Love, the protector and guardian of those youths in love whom he seeks.

Cave dedicated to the nymphs. Sanctuary where Chloë is discovered as a baby being suckled by a ewe with her own golden tokens: a girdle, sandals, and anklets. The cave is an important locale because Daphnis and Chloë spend time there talking, bathing, and sacrificing to the nymphs who protect them in times of need. The cave's spring symbolizes new life, rebirth, paradise, and the beauty of nature, as well as Chloë's true origin.

Woods. Place where Daphnis is originally found, as he is being suckled by a goat; and beside him are a little purple cloak, a gilded brooch, and a dagger with an ivory hilt. The location is as vague and uncertain as the origin of Daphnis himself until the end of the work. When Daphnis is finally taught his lesson of love in the woods, the setting seems much deeper and in a thicker area of the woods where Chloë has never been. Through this second description, the reader is made aware that the "deeper" woods and Lycaenion represent the loss of innocence for Daphnis. Since Chloë is still a maiden, this location remains unknown to her.

Dionysophanes's estate (di-oh-nih-SO-fuh-neez). Ground in which Lamon and Myrtale live in a cottage and tend to a farm. Daphnis grows up and reaches maturity here as well. This place is significant because it depicts the true nature of Daphnis's existence. Within the grounds are the temple of Dionysus and a spring named after Daphnis.

*Aegean Sea. The sea surrounding Lesbos signifies all that is tumultuous, violent, and disruptive of a peaceful existence: Pirates invade, and Daphnis is beaten; Chloë is kidnapped; and a boat is lost to sea for which the herdsmen are blamed. This setting simultaneously represents the happiness that Daphnis is to have with Chloë as a result of the treasure he is to find there under the direction of the nymphs in a dream.

— *Adriana C. Tomasino*

THE DARK JOURNEY

Author: Julien Green (1900-1998)
Type of work: Novel
Type of plot: Psychological realism

Time of plot: Early twentieth century
First published: Leviathan, 1929 (English translation, 1929)

This novel continues the portrayal of provincial France that Julien Green established in The Closed Garden *(1927). Its towns are drab and insular, peopled with foul-tempered and strangely obsessed characters; its landscape is heavily wooded, frequently dark, and forbidding.*

Chanteilles (shahn-TAY) and **Lorges** (lorzh). Neighboring French provincial towns within relatively easy access to Paris by train. The towns are framed on both sides by rivers, portentously named the Sommeillante (sleepy) and the Preste (quick). Much of the novel's action takes place on or near bridges that cross the rivers, where Paul Guéret waits for the young laundress Angèle. Guéret has moved to Chanteilles with his wife, Marie, in a futile search for a better life than the one they left behind in Paris. His marriage remains loveless, and the only job that he has found is that of tutor to the slow-witted only son of the wealthy Grosgeorge family.

Restaurant Londe (lohnd). Restaurant that is an important Lorges landmark, owned and managed by the imperious Madame Georges Londe, who maintains and relishes a jealous hold on her exclusively male clientele. Guéret stumbles into the restaurant more or less by accident, instantly arousing the insatiable curiosity of the proprietress, who has never seen him before. Determined to snare Guéret in the same net that holds her other customers, Madame Londe refuses to accept payment for his meal, insisting instead that he open an account by signing his name. Thus armed, Madame Londe also ensures that the newcomer will return because he is now in her debt.

From an elevated perch, Madame Londe presides over her establishment with the demeanor of a stern and scolding teacher, occasionally revealing secret knowledge of a customer's recent purchases, business dealings, or family life. The main source of her information is young Angèle, a nonpaying boarder, who is possibly her niece, whom she regularly sends out on assignations with customers for the sole purpose of collecting gossip to keep them under her control. She does not know, or care, what Angèle has to do to gather the information that she covets; *that*, Madame Londe self-righteously assures herself, is none of her business.

Villa Mon Idée (vee-YAH moh-neh-dee). Large, pretentious home of the Grosgeorge family, where Guéret regularly meets with his pupil, the couple's only child. Eva Grosgeorge, resentful of her older husband and harboring bitterness that is never fully explained, turns her resentment toward Guéret when her son André seemingly fails to respond to Guéret's teaching. Her husband, in turn, shares his own marital and sexual problems with Guéret, inadvertently revealing himself to be one of Angèle's "regulars" and precipitating the crisis that will result in Guéret's beating of Angèle and, later, his murder of an elderly homeless man who stumbles upon his hiding place.

After several weeks at large, Guéret will return to the Chanteilles area, only to be spotted by Angèle and, soon thereafter, by the crafty Eva Grosgeorge, who first offers him shelter at Mon Idée, then hatches a scheme to turn him over to the police while he remains a virtual prisoner in Madame Grosgeorge's upstairs sitting room. The name Villa Mon Idée literally means "my idea."

*Paris. Capital of France, where Guéret and his wife formerly lived and worked. Marie Guéret, still employed as a seamstress by a Paris department store, still makes weekly trips to the capital in order to deliver her finished orders. Guéret himself may well have spent some of his time there while hiding out from the authorities and changing his appearance by growing a beard.

— David B. Parsell

DARK LAUGHTER

Author: Sherwood Anderson (1876-1941)
Type of work: Novel
Type of plot: Psychological realism

Time of plot: 1920's
First published: 1925

Sherwood Anderson's vision of humanity cut off from an original source is embodied in place throughout this novel. People in cities, working in factories and artificial environments such as newspaper offices, have lost connection with the elemental source of life, the river. Humans, "drops of water," find themselves and their elemental passions on the Ohio and Mississippi Rivers, where the dark laughter of African Americans reverberates.

*Ohio River. Major tributary of the Mississippi River that rises in western Pennsylvania and flows southwest nearly one thousand miles before joining the Mississippi. On a boat trip on the Ohio with his parents, Bruce Dudley hears the singing, conversation, and laughter of African Americans for the first time. Their daily connection with the river allows their voices to remain in touch with the world. Bruce's return to the river as an adult spawns a connection with the river and the sense of self he lost while in Chicago.

*Mississippi River. Bruce's trip down the Mississippi awakens his sensibility to the elemental self he lost. He rides the Mississippi to New Orleans, enjoys the shade and sounds of trees on the bank, hears the voices of African Americans, and returns to his childhood home and his place near the Ohio River.

Old Harbor. Bruce's childhood home in Indiana, to which he returns after years in Chicago. Old Harbor is a fictional town similar to the more famous Winesburg, Ohio, which Anderson depicted in greater detail in 1919. Bruce is reunited with the Ohio River and rejects newspaper work. He changes his name from John Stockton to Bruce Dudley, indicating his change of self in his old home, and experiences a personal rebirth, working with his hands varnishing automobile wheels.

Grey home. Home of automobile wheel factory owner Fred Grey and his wife, Aline. Aline is reunited with her lost sense of self in the garden of the home built on Fred's family's acreage. Living with Fred, who is the embodiment of the comfortable bourgeois man, in a home with separate bedrooms, Aline experiences intense restlessness and despair. Hiring Bruce as a gardener, she expresses her forgotten sexual self, which is brought to life in the presence of natural vegetation.

Aline and Bruce's decision to admit that Bruce is the father of her forthcoming child indicates their complete acceptance of themselves as natural creatures, uninhibited by the decorum of artificial, civilized society.

Martin home. Home of Sponge Martin, the first natural human Bruce meets on his journey back to his original self. Sponge lives on the river in an old brick home, a former stable on a dirt road that was the main road of town before the factories took the town away from the river. Sponge fishes with his wife and shares a natural intimacy that is crude by societal standards but refreshing and honest to Bruce.

*Chicago. Great midwestern city in which Bruce, as John Stockton, lives with his wife, Bernice, in a studio apartment. Both write for a newspaper, where they enjoy success. However, Bruce feels adrift in the city. A lack of connection to the fundamental elements of life make him listless and bored. Every city dweller appears bored and frightened to him. Artistic men in the city appear feminine to him, and the women are turning masculine. The artificial living environments of Chicago have altered the natural responses of the people. Bruce does not even have to use his hands to work. He can phone the stories to the newspaper.

*Paris. Capital of France where Aline Grey spends time after World War I. She seeks to develop her artistic abilities, studying painting. However, she is already too removed from her original self to become an artist, and suffers the same fate as Bruce, marrying for security and comfortable compatibility instead of passion. She meets Fred in a studio apartment, denying her interest in a working man at the same party, because he is not of her social standing.

— *Mark Walling*

DARKNESS AT NOON

Author: Arthur Koestler (1905-1983)
Type of work: Novel
Type of plot: Social realism

Time of plot: 1930's
First published: 1940

This novel unfolds almost entirely within a Soviet prison, in which a former Communist Party functionary, Nicolas Rubashov, awaits trial for crimes against the party. As he tries to understand why he is there and observes the horrors being experienced by his fellow prisoners, he reflects on the ruthless acts he committed in the past in the name of revolution. Formerly, he believed that ends justify means—that establishment of worldwide communism would justify violence, deceit, and death. Eventually, he confesses to crimes he never committed.

Prison. Soviet detention center in which Rubashov is being held. With its dark corridors, closed off from the outside world and operating under its own logic, the suffocating prison is a physical manifestation of the communist dystopia and a metaphor for the communist rationale. Outside the prison, seasons change from cold, dismal winter to early spring. Inside its grim multistoried brick structure, prisoners are confined in cells behind thick doors with spy-holes. Barred windows overlook a snow-packed courtyard, where prisoners exercise. Armed guards patrol the ramparts. Down a dimly lit corridor is a barber shop and an unsanitary infirmary that reeks of carbolic and tobacco. The doctor's desk is cluttered with bandages, swabs, and instruments. Beneath the prison is a room where beatings and near-boiling steam baths are used to force prisoners to confess to imaginary crimes against the state. Those found guilty are taken down a spiral staircase, stunned by blows to the head, and shot behind the ears with pistols.

Rubashov's own cell, number 404, has a basin, a cot, and a bucket for his bodily wastes. At first, he hears only muffled sounds and echoes in the prison building. Later, neighboring prisoners communicate by tapping messages on the walls in a simple code. From the window, Rubashov observes other prisoners exercising in the courtyard. Through the spy-hole, guards observe him writing in a diary or lying on a straw mattress. Rubashov gets a limited view of the corridor and cells across the gallery. He observes Bogrov, a naval hero, being dragged down the corridor toward his execution. Prisoners drum the death march on the walls.

Rubashov is interrogated in the office of Warden Ivanov. Ivanov and his assistant, Gletkin, wear military uniforms with pistols in leather holsters; the desks are cluttered with files and reports. A photograph of party officials before Joseph Stalin became head of the Soviet Union is missing from the wall. During Rubashov's seven-day interrogation, he sits on a hard-backed chair while Gletkin shines a spotlight into his red-rimmed eyes.

Art museum. German museum in which Rubashov remembers being arrested by Gestapo officers while meeting with a fellow Communist Party leader to plan a reorganization of the German branch of the party, which the Nazi government has forced to go underground. They are surrounded by paintings of voluptuous nudes. These paintings, which represent worldly indulgence, contrast with a pen-and-ink drawing of the Madonna's hands outstretched toward the needy of the world. After Rubashov was arrested, he was tortured. However, after Germany and the Soviet Union signed a nonaggression pact in 1939, Rubashov returned home to Russia a hero.

Belgian port city. In another of Rubashov's recollections, he meets with Belgian party members in a port city, where he noticed distinctive harbor smells, a town clock, and narrow streets where prostitutes hung out their laundry. The room in which the party met had walls covered with election posters and notices; its windows were smeared with paint, and planks on trestles served as tables for propaganda leaflets. Overhead, a naked light bulb and a strip of fly paper dangled. Five Russian ships, laden with supplies bound for Germany, lay at anchor in the harbor. When Rubashov ordered union members to unload the ships, the communist workers refused, and Rubashov had them expelled them from the party.

Rubashov's apartment. Shabby Moscow residence

of Rubashov, into which armed Soviet soldiers burst when they arrested him. The building's porter, Vassilij, watched silently as they escorted Rubashov to the creaky elevator. An American-made automobile then took them over littered and unpaved streets to the prison.

After Rubashov's execution, Vassilij and his daughter live in the apartment. The old man hides a picture of Comrade Rubashov, his hero, in his mattress and secretly reads the forbidden Bible.

— *Martha E. Rhynes*

DAVID COPPERFIELD

Author: Charles Dickens (1812-1870)
Type of work: Novel
Type of plot: Bildungsroman

Time of plot: Early nineteenth century
First published: 1849-1850

The early scenes in Copperfield's story evoke both the joy and the pain of David's childhood in Suffolk. The crisscrossing of the main characters in Canterbury and London, as well as the shipwreck scene, the European wanderings, and the embarking for Australia, complete the adventures of David and his friends.

Blunderstone Rookery. Suffolk birthplace and boyhood home of David Copperfield, who often associates the place in his mind with the nearby tombstone of his father. Charles Dickens himself grew up in Suffolk and always tied it to childhood innocence. David's earliest memories of happy evenings with his mother and nurse Peggotty soon give way to the strict and cruel house presided over by his new stepfather and aunt. He retreats to his room and finds refuge in his father's books. This same room is a prison for five days of punishment which to the boy seem a nightmare of years. Peggotty tries to send him affection and tenderness through the keyhole, but nothing can forestall Mr. Murdstone's determination to send him away to school.

*Yarmouth.** Norfolk seaport, about 110 miles northeast of London, where Dan Peggotty and his three dependents live in a boathouse. Little David first travels here on a two-week visit, little knowing that he will return to a changed rookery with Murdstone installed as his stepfather. For David, the boathouse is better than Aladdin's palace; he even has his own special room, something that becomes increasingly important to him. In later visits to the Ark, as he calls it, David brings his school friend, Steerforth, unwittingly leading to Little Em'ly's seduction. Her surrogate father, Peggotty, then insists on placing a candle in the window as a visible sign that he welcomes her back home.

Yarmouth's beach is also the scene of the tempest. The foundering ship is Steerforth's "Little Em'ly," and Ham swims out to rescue a lone survivor on its deck. Symbolically, both men are lost as the boat sinks, and when Steerforth's body washes ashore, it lands on the very spot where the old houseboat, now wrecked, stood with its nightly candle.

Salem House. Dr. Creakle's school, where Murdstone sends the recalcitrant David. Dickens powerfully projects the unhappy boy, the lonely schoolroom, the wicked giant of a schoolmaster. When Ham and Peggotty come to visit David, Steerforth suggests that he would like to visit their boathouse. However, tragedy falls, and David is told that his mother and new brother are dead; he is removed from Salem House on his tenth birthday.

*London.** Great Britain's capital city, in which several sections of the novel are set. The first is at Murdstone and Grinby's warehouse in the Blackfriars district waterfront. Here ten-year-old David pastes labels on wine bottles in much the same way the young Dickens had been sent out to work in a boot-blacking factory in London. David feels "thrown away" on a deadening job and unable to express his agony. A lighter note is provided by his stay with the Micawbers, a happy-go-lucky and improvident family. When Mr. Micawber is imprisoned for debt in the King's Bench Prison, David visits them, much as Dickens had done with his own family.

London is also the setting for David's job as a proctor after he graduates from Dr. Strong's school. He takes an apartment in Buckingham Street. It is from here that he courts Dora. After the wedding, they move into their new home in Highgate. It is a sweet, loving home, marred only by Dora's ineptitude as a housekeeper: the food is raw, the pantry is empty, and the servants are ill-managed. Dora and her dog Jip die here.

The tense and unnatural Steerforth home is located in London, which is also the location of the Blackfriars Bridge scene. Here Dickens is powerful in evoking the dismal and defiled riverside, and in linking its miseries to a suicidal Martha Endell. David's encounter with this fallen woman ultimately leads Dan Peggotty to Em'ly, who has come to stay with Martha in a decaying old mansion in one of the worst sections of the city.

*Dover. Southeast England port that is home to Betsey Trotwood. When ten-year-old David can no longer stand the misery of his job at the warehouse in London, he decides to run away to seek out his great aunt Betsey Trotwood. He has never seen her before, but the shred of a tender memory once shared with him by his mother makes him hopeful of finding refuge with her. His six-day journey begins with the theft of his possessions, his nearly starving to death, and his frightening experiences with robbers and a malicious pawnbroker. This journey through the countryside from London to Dover is the occasion for Dickens to display his unique combination of suspense, humor, action, and pathos. In Dover at last, the child is welcomed by his aunt, bathed, and put to sleep in a snug bedroom.

*Europe. Peggotty plods his way through France, Italy, and Switzerland, determined to find and rescue his niece Em'ly. In Naples, when Steerforth tires of his seduction of Em'ly, he gives her over to his valet, Littimer. She manages to escape him and desperately makes her way back to London. David, too, wanders for three years in Europe, unhappy at his wife's death and aimlessly searching for something that is missing in his life. In Switzerland, Agnes reaches him with a letter, and he is encouraged enough to write a novel and then return to Canterbury.

*Australia. Southern hemispheric continent to which Dan Peggotty, Em'ly, Martha, Mrs. Gummidge, and the whole Micawber family go in the hope of finding new beginnings to their lives. Dickens sends his characters there in order to wrap up the novel's diverse narrative threads. At the time in which Dickens wrote, Australia was a collection of British colonies that were notorious as the destinations of convicted scoundrels, rogues, and adventure seekers. Mrs. Micawber suggests that "For a man who conducts himself well . . . and is industrious . . . It is evident to me that Australia is the legitimate sphere of action for Mr. Micawber!"

*Canterbury. Cathedral town in southeastern England to which David goes to attend the excellent school of Dr. Strong. David again has his own room in a house where he is loved. After he leaves here to work in London, he is troubled to hear that Uriah Heep, who is in control of the Wickfields, has taken David's old room. Later, when David ultimately realizes that he loves Agnes, he returns from Europe and finds his old room is in readiness for his arrival. Like a little ragged boy heading to a safe harbor, David is at last home.

— *Marie J. K. Brenner*

THE DAY OF THE LOCUST

Author: Nathanael West (Nathan Weinstein, 1903-1940)
Type of work: Novel

Type of plot: Social realism
Time of plot: 1930's
First published: 1939

As a quintessential Hollywood novel, this book provides a unique glimpse into the motion picture capital as a land of illusion. The protagonist often finds himself negotiating an alien landscape of the bizarre and the surreal.

*Hollywood. District of Los Angeles, California, and the symbolic center of the American film industry. The novel opens with Todd Hackett, a graduate of Yale University and cinematic set designer, traversing the National Films studio lot on his way home. He walks among a wild collection of historical and national artifacts—Russian hussars, Scottish warriors, French grenadiers, and a Mississippi steamboat. For the time being Hackett takes the place for granted; its contradictions are simply the norm. However, later in the novel, when he chases Faye Greener across the lot, he is struck by its improbable diversity. A recreation of the 1815 Battle of Waterloo commences beside a Western saloon, which in turn gives way to a Parisian street, a Roman courtyard, and a Greek temple. These sound stages eventually dissolve into a ten-acre field of cockleburs where discarded sets have been left to rot, and their disorder and sheer anomalousness suggest a sea of imaginative dreams. The lot acts as a perfect metaphor for the surreal assemblage of people, lifestyles, and aspirations, all of which are either created or encouraged by Hollywood, the dream factory.

San Bernardino Arms. Hollywood rooming house in which Hackett resides. Given the garishness Hackett finds all about him, this is a rather unprepossessing place: three stories of unpainted stucco and unadorned windows. The rooms are small and dirty, but Hackett tolerates the place because of his fascination with Faye and her restless aspirations. Like his rooms, Hackett does not draw much attention to himself; he would rather observe and record the world about him than actively participate in it.

Jennings house. Residence of Hollywood's most distinguished madam, Mrs. Jennings. Her house is an elaborate affair with a careful, tricolor decorating scheme, expensive furniture, and a private screening room. Jennings has pretensions to cultured aristocracy, entertaining only the wealthy and influential and reserving her girls for sophisticated clients. These people stand in marked contrast to those Hackett finds on the street, figures in ill-fitting clothing who hunger for titillation and cheap excitement. Their aspirations and achievements are mundane and unoriginal; their houses are cheaper imitations of Jennings's opulence.

Simpson cottage. Humble house in Pinyon Canyon, outside Los Angeles. Homer Simpson's cottage acts as a fitting example of how Hollywood's other half live. The place is inexpensive and oddly constructed. Its parts are faux versions of something else—shingles that appear to be a thatched roof and a gumwood door painted to look like oak. Simpson's house becomes a model for all the other garish architecture that Hackett finds: Mexican ranch houses, Samoan huts, Mediterranean villas, Egyptian and Japanese temples, Swiss chalets, and Tudor cottages. These monstrosities further underscore the theme of Hollywood's illusoriness and the related contrast between essence and appearance which lies at the heart of social scrutiny.

Hollywood churches. Houses of worship of a variety of cults. Hackett quickly concludes that California is where the nation comes to die from boredom with their miserable lives and demeaning jobs. In their desire for excitement and a heightened sense of significance, they are prey to the machinations of imposter religions, which combine dietary practices, superstition, and folklore. One of these, the Tabernacle of the Third Coming, is a direct parody of Aimee Semple McPherson's Angelus Temple.

Kahn's Persian Palace Theatre. Elaborate movie theater that hosts a film premiere. With huge neon signs, elaborate architecture, and spiraling search lights, the theater draws a huge crowd. Here is the destination of the bored, here is the sanctuary of illusion, and here Hackett's prophetic painting finally is realized. Nathaniel West clearly draws on the practice in 1930's Los Angeles of creating elaborate theaters and giving them exaggerated names, such as the Cathedral of the Motion Picture and the Sanctuary of the Cinema. By locating the riot in front of a theater, West suggests that America's diet of illusory satisfaction will produce a volatile dissatisfaction that will erupt in gruesome violence. Theaters, as the venues of those illusions, are symbols of the culture's emptiness and instability.

— *David W. Madden*

DEAD SOULS

Author: Nikolai Gogol (1809-1852)
Type of work: Novel
Type of plot: Social satire

Time of plot: Early nineteenth century
First published: Myortvye Dushi, part 1, 1842; part 2, 1855 (English translation, 1887)

Tracing the travels of adventurer Pavel Chichikov through the highways and byways of provincial Russia, this novel offers an unusual view of Russian provincial life. The settings Chichikov describes serve not so much to provide an accurate portrait of physical reality as to conjure up the peculiar and often unsavory approaches to life displayed by the inhabitants of those settings. The landscape and architecture of each estate that Chichikov visits tend to mirror the psychological or emotional state of its owner.

Provincial capital. Unnamed Russian city in which the novel opens with Chichikov's arrival. The city serves as the base from which he makes a series of trips into the countryside to visit local landowners. Nikolai Gogol's descriptions of the town, with its poor sidewalks, unimpressive architecture, and sparse vegetation, highlight the pretentiousness of its officials and merchants, as readers may contrast the essential meagerness and inanity of the physical locale with the exaggerated claims made about the site in official plaques and shop signs.

Manilovka (mahn-eh-LOHV-kah). First estate that Chichikov visits. Manilovka is distinguished by a striking lack of vegetation and a superfluous pavilion called the Temple of Solitary Meditation. Its unimpressive landscape reflects the personality of its owner, Manilov, a bland and colorless person who is given to idle and useless dreaming.

Sobakevich estate (soh-BAH-keh-vihch). Everything at the Sobakevich estate echoes the physique and mind of its owner, Sobakevich, a man described as looking remarkably like a bear and who evinces a powerful, authoritarian attitude toward his surroundings. His house is solidly built, somewhat like a military fort, and all its furnishings seem to call out with their heavy construction that they, too, are part and parcel of their owner's personality.

Korobochka estate (koh-roh-BACH-kah). Home of the widow Korobochka, a defensive, fearful woman. The layout of her estate reflects these qualities. The estate is surrounded by fences, and a sea of mud that may be the debased equivalent of a moat. The name

"Korobochka" is derived from the word for "box," and the widow's penchant for mindless acquisition and retention is mirrored in the behavior of one of the sows on her estate: As the animal feeds on a pile of garbage in the yard it consumes a baby chick without even noticing it.

Pliushkin estate (plee-EWSH-kihn). Home of the miser Pliushkin, whom Gogol describes as embodying the horrifying effect that age and isolation can have on humans. He is a desiccated, grasping man, and the rampant decay apparent on his estate offers direct evidence of its owner's withdrawal from life. A distinctive feature of this estate is its overgrown garden, in which a battle between the engulfing forces of nature and the planned designs of humans is played out. The haphazard intermingling of the natural and the artificial carries a strange beauty that may be emblematic of Gogol's own art.

Nozdryov estate (NOHZ-dryof). Home of the gambler and liar Nozdryov, who is the most threatening person Chichikov meets during his travels. The decorations of Nozdryov's home display its owner's militaristic inclinations. Nozdryov shows his guests a collection of daggers, guns, and swords. His penchant for hyperbole and exaggeration shows up when he gives Chichikov a tour of the estate: As he approaches the boundary of his land, he boasts that all the land on his side of the boundary belongs to him and that all the land on the other side belongs to him as well.

The road. The theme of the road itself is one of the most important in the novel. Chichikov uses the road to make his visits to landowners, but more important, it offers him a means of escape when his dubious scheme to get rich is exposed. The narrator of the novel praises the road and the possibilities for new adventures that it implies. One senses that for Gogol too, the lure of the road, of movement, provided an attractive alternative to the prospects of stasis and decay which he evoked in many of his descriptions of the places and people visited by Chichikov.

— *Julian W. Connolly*

DEATH COMES FOR THE ARCHBISHOP

Author: Willa Cather (1873-1947)
Type of work: Novel
Type of plot: Historical realism

Time of plot: Mid- to late nineteenth century
First published: 1927

This novel is set in the American Southwest after the Mexican American War. The harsh desert climate proves a challenge for two French missionary priests who bring together Americans, Mexicans, and Native Americans, who live together but never truly understand one another's cultures.

***Vatican City.** Enclave in Rome that is the center of the Roman Catholic Church and headquarters of the pope. There the novel opens in a prologue that describes an elegant garden in which three Italian cardinals select the new bishop of Santa Fe as they drink fine French wines. This scene contrasts sharply with the harsh world that the relocated priests will find in the American Southwest.

***Canada.** Mission field from which Bishop Latour and Father Vaillant are removed and sent to New Mexico. The Italian cardinals who make the decision to relocate the missionaries express concern about the tendency of priests in the Southwest to lead dissolute lives and agree that the diocese's new bishop must come from a different culture so that he can impose order and orthodoxy in this new diocese. The cardinals are oblivious to the difficulty of the transition they are asking the French missionaries to make by moving from the cold climate of Canada to the hot arid deserts of the American southwest. The novel then describes the missionaries' harrowing trip across inhospitable mountains, rivers, oceans, and deserts in their journey from Canada to Santa Fe.

***New Mexico.** Territory in the American Southwest that the United States occupied in the late 1840's, after winning the Mexican-American War. Most of the novel is centered in this arid region, particularly around the north-central town of Santa Fe, where Father Jean Marie Latour arrives in 1851 after a long and difficult journey from his previous missionary station on the Canadian shores of Lake Ontario. The novel concludes with Latour's death in Santa Fe after he has a cathedral built there.

The ability of the new missionaries to adapt to harsh climates prepares them to undertake even more daunting challenges in the Southwest. When they learn that lazy priests will not travel to distant corners of the diocese, Bishop Latour and Father Vaillant make the journeys themselves, by mule. Cather eloquently describes the physical suffering the priests endure as they travel to small desert villages.

For the first time local Indians and Mexican Americans encounter missionaries who do not exploit them. Remaining faithful to their vow of poverty, Bishop Latour and Father Vaillant teach by example and live in humble houses that contrast markedly with the elegant houses of the corrupt priests, gaining the respect and admiration of Catholics and non-Catholics alike in their large diocese. In a powerful scene, Bishop Latour leads a group of peasants and Native Americans up a mesa to expel a corrupt priest from his fortresslike home and turn over to the church the property he has stolen.

This beautifully written novel deals not only with Bishop Latour's life in Santa Fe from 1848 until his death in 1889 but also with the spiritual growth of his diocese. Even after his retirement, he never leaves his adopted home to return to his native France. He lives on a small farm, says mass in local churches, and helps train newly arrived missionaries.

— *Edmund J. Campion*

A DEATH IN THE FAMILY

Author: James Agee (1909-1955)
Type of work: Novel
Type of plot: Domestic realism

Time of plot: 1915-1916
First published: 1957

This novel is set entirely in eastern Tennessee, but differences in place of only a few miles between city, small town, and mountains underline gaping social and cultural differences within the marriage of Jay and Mary Follet and between their respective families, the Follets and Lynches. The differences in place also give a symbolic dimension to this basically realistic novel.

*Knoxville. Tennessee city that is the novel's main setting, as the home of Jay and Mary Follet and their two children. The novel begins with a short section titled "Knoxville: Summer 1915," a poetically evocative description of summer evenings that breaks into free verse. After supper, as daylight fades and children run around yelling and playing, relaxed fathers, collars removed and shirt cuffs peeled back, are outside watering their lawns with hoses. This scene competes with the natural sounds and sights of locusts, crickets, frogs, and fireflies, which gradually increase as the night comes on. One by one the men coil their hoses and retreat inside their homes. Not even the man of the house—husband, father, and breadwinner—can hold back the night. Thus the short descriptive section serves as a poetic foreword to the whole novel, which develops the effects on a family of its father's sudden death.

The opening section also introduces a subtheme of the novel—the social and cultural tensions between the Follet and Lynch families. Jay, Mary, and children live in a lower middle-class neighborhood of similar houses and families, and the Lynches (Mary's parents, brother, and aunt) live nearby in a slightly older middle-class neighborhood. The middle-class way of life is identified with the city, and the Lynches, who are comfortable, somewhat cultured, and Roman Catholic, assume that their own way of life is the desirable norm. To them, people outside Knoxville are merely hillbillies.

The Lynches admire Jay for having raised himself out of his background (though at first they are aghast when Mary marries him). Jay himself, thoroughly domesticated by the time of the novel (and even cured of a drinking problem), seems to share his wife's and her family's middle-class outlook. Yet every now and then he has to slip himself a drink, and he sometimes finds himself gazing north toward the mountains of his birth and feeling something missing from his life. To some extent, Jay appears to fill this void through his relationship with his young son, Rufus, who idolizes his manly father.

It is probably Jay's manly qualities that attract Mary to marry him. However, her middle-class assumptions and religion make her want to tame those very same qualities in him. In general, the women in the novel seem to take to middle-class life, and its ally religion, more readily than do the men. Even the Lynch men chafe against religion and priests, while the Lynch women embrace them and submit. Like middle-class life, Catholicism is associated more with the city in that part of Tennessee. In the novel, then, the city is the locus of the good life, a stage that expands women's possibilities but that may constrict men.

*LaFollette. Small Tennessee town in the mountains about forty miles north of Knoxville that is the home of the Follet family, whose name links them to the place, LaFollette at the time was primarily a trading center for farmers from the nearby Powell River Valley. To the Lynches, LaFollette epitomizes backwardness, as do the Follets who live there: Jay's drunken brother (an undertaker), their shiftless father, and their downtrodden mother. Jay's ties to his family and the place finally claim him: A speeding driver, he dies in an automobile accident at Powell Station on the way back from visiting his supposedly sick father.

*Appalachian Mountains. Range that includes the Cumberland Mountains around LaFollette and the Great Smoky Mountains east of Knoxville. People living in these rugged mountains are so backward that they are romanticized in the novel. The Follets make a pilgrimage to the family home in the Cumberlands, and Jay takes his family on a scenic tour of the Great Smoky Mountains. Out of touch with modern times, the mountain people exemplify a seemingly idyllic life close to nature and the land, a definite alternative to the middle-class norms of Knoxville. Thus the mountains create a certain ambiguity in this autobiographical novel (Jay's young son, Rufus, seems to be based on Agee), perhaps an ambiguity that the author felt about his own background.

— *Harold Branam*

DEATH IN VENICE

Author: Thomas Mann (1875-1955)
Type of work: Novella
Type of plot: Symbolic realism

Time of plot: Early twentieth century
First published: Der Tod in Venedig, 1912 (English translation, 1925)

As the novella's title may suggest, Venice plays a pivotal role in this story. The central character's transformation from a staid German writer into a man tormented by passion, as well as his untimely death, is inextricably bound to this grand, yet decadent, Italian city. Thomas Mann's novella is a sustained metaphor that reveals the dual nature of the artist, and place is essential to the fulfillment of that metaphor.

***Munich** (MEW-nihk). Well-ordered, proper city in Germany's Bavarian region, in which the story opens around the turn of the twentieth century. There the great writer Gustav von Aschenbach lives. Weary of Germany's cold and damp northern spring and the dullness of his surroundings, Aschenbach decides to spend a summer in a warm place and goes to Italy. Although briefly described, cold Munich serves as a contrast to the warmth and extravagance of Venice, and it represents the writer's discipline and respectability.

***Venice.** Port city in northern Italy where Aschenbach arrives after a few false starts and checks into the Hôtel des Bains on the Lido, an island across the canal from the main city. With a private beach facing the Adriatic Sea, this grand hotel has spacious rooms, well-tended gardens, elegant public areas, a spacious veranda, and an obsequious staff—all of which suits Aschenbach's aristocratic tastes. He then settles into his comfortable room and looks forward to a refreshing holiday.

Drawn to Venice, he takes a boat across the canal to the city, relishing even "that slightly foul odor of sea and swamp." At first glance, "that most improbable of cities" appears beautiful with its fabulous towers and ornate palaces and churches shimmering in the sunlight. On closer examination, however, Aschenbach finds that the city is crumbling. Its once magnificent structures are sinking into the water, the paint everywhere is peeling and moldy, elaborate carvings are half eaten away. Nevertheless, the decay, the odors emanating from the fetid canals, the dank passageways, and the stale air seduce Aschenbach as he wanders through the city.

The twofold character of Venice—its dilapidation and its outward magnificence—foreshadows Aschenbach's own decline. It begins at dinner in the Hôtel des Bains when he watches a Polish family take their seats and admires the beauty of their preadolescent son Tadzio. Soon the admiration turns into an obsession, and Venice assumes a new role, evolving into a place of subterfuge and baseness as Aschenbach sneaks around the passageways to catch glimpses of the boy. At first he remains an ostensibly respectable man, but gradually he gives over to his passions, and like the city he is visiting he begins to deteriorate. He resorts to dyeing his hair and wearing makeup to hide his age—much like the city that covers its deteriorating buildings with fresh coats of paint.

Before long, Aschenbach learns that a cholera epidemic has infected Venice, much as his irrational attraction to Tadzio has infected his state of being. Hotel guests begin to leave, but Aschenbach and the Polish family stay on. Instead of visiting the city, the remaining guests spend more time on the hotel beach, with its brightly colored tents, comfortable chairs, and umbrellas. Aschenbach takes his place on the beach daily, pretending to write but actually watching the graceful movements of Tadzio as he plays in the sand and wades in the ocean. At this point, the city of Venice loses some of its importance as the setting, and "the death in Venice" actually takes place on the beach—a stretch of civilization at the edge of the untamed sea.

The metaphor is complete when Aschenbach at last grasps the dual nature of the artist—that it is one part intellect and the other part sensuality. When he leaves orderly Munich his intellect dominates, but it is later set in conflict with his sensual side through the seductive qualities of the decadent but "improbable" Italian city and through the exquisite but tempter-like Tadzio. No other setting could be imagined for this symbolic analysis of the balance that the artist must maintain. Without that balance, the artist will, like Venice, decay.

— *Robert L. Ross*

DEATH OF A HERO

Author: Richard Aldington (1892-1962)
Type of work: Novel
Type of plot: Political

Time of plot: World War I
First published: 1929

Primary locations include rural England, London, and the World War I battlefields of France. The protagonist George Winterbourne, a young English painter from a small town on the English Channel, is gradually destroyed by the mindlessness and chaos of the European war. The contrast between London and the No Man's Land of the war's battlefront emphasizes the absurdity of the situation.

No Man's Land. Constantly shifting zone between the trenches of the opposing combatants on the French battlefront. This realm of fearsome devastation represents the nightmarish consequences of political blindness and the misapplication of technology. Soldiers struggling here face elemental agony, terror, and exhaustion, and George is transformed by this experience. Upon returning to London, he is appalled by the ignorance and superficiality of those who have not seen the war at first hand. The intense bitterness shared by George and the novel's narrator is a pessimistic response to the naïve or egotistical optimism of Great Britain's prewar generation. Although George learns to value comradeship in the trenches, he is also constantly reminded of the diminished value of human life in this environment. The tremendous strain of staying alive finally makes his life intolerable. No Man's Land is a place of sudden fragmentation of life, of Nature, of architecture, and, finally, of George's sanity, and its image dominates the novel as an emblem of the mindless suffering generated by human stupidity.

Hill 91. Hotly contested area of No Man's Land marked by extreme devastation. George notes that possession of such areas is largely a matter of "prestige."

***Dorsetshire.** Rural county of southwest England that George and Elizabeth Winterbourne visit in their happier days. Later, George is sent to undergo officers' training (along with the narrator) at this same place.

Dullborough. Located near Martin's Point, this is where George attends "The School," and develops an antipathy for conventional perspectives.

***London.** Great Britain's capital city, to which George goes after being forced from his parents' home by their obtuse expectations. He survives there by writing articles and meets members of influential circles within the literary world as he pursues a career in painting. His writing career is based largely upon the actual experience of author Richard Aldington in prewar London; several characters in this novel are thus fictionalized versions of people whom Aldington knew, and many of the novel's London locations reflect places where he lived or which he frequented. George's friends represent literary London, and as he confronts the reality of the war in France, he increasingly sees the London literati as pretentious and irrelevant.

***Hampton Court.** Tudor palace on the banks of the River Thames, west of London, built by Cardinal Thomas Wolsey and later used by King Henry VIII. The novel's generally negative picture of artistic and political London is quietly counterpoised by a passage that emphasizes Aldington's own profound regard for the great city. In the early stages of their affair, George and Elizabeth visit Hampton Court, where they feast their eyes on the magnificent flowers growing in the gardens. This scene forms a significant contrast to the desolation George encounters in France, where he later notices the absence of flowers on the battlefield.

M-. Ruined town on the French battlefront where George is stationed. It is a particularly dangerous place because it is a regular target of heavy artillery.

Maison Blanche. French village near which George is killed. Although the Germans are retreating and the Allies are winning the war, George, who has just lost several members of his unit, leaps to his feet in the face of heavy machine-gun fire.

Martin's Point. Town on the English Channel where George spends his school days and develops his initial artistic aspirations. Aldington modeled the town on his youthful memories of Dover.

— *Robert W. Haynes*

DEATH OF A SALESMAN

Author: Arthur Miller (1915-   )
Type of work: Play
Type of plot: Tragedy

Time of plot: Late 1940's
First produced and published: 1949

Although the primary setting of this play is merely the house and yard of the title's salesman, Willy Loman, it is clearly organic—and not simply background—to everything that happens, as the alienation themes of this mid-twentieth century urban tragedy are embedded in place.

Loman home. Modest house in Brooklyn, New York. Despite the play's fixed location, playwright Arthur Miller makes it clear that Willy's alienation and loss of meaning are afflictions of any modern American city. The introductory stage directions he wrote for act 1 state that the "small fragile-seeming home" is surrounded on all sides by "towering, angular shapes," which have sprung up around it. Throughout the play, the audience is visually aware of a gap between past and present: The house which once stood on a pleasant street of similar homes is now dwarfed by "a solid vault of apartment houses." Like Willy himself, the house has been made insignificant by progress.

Jo Mielziner, who designed the play's original stage setting, framed the house so that it was "wholly, or, in some places, partially transparent." Miller's stage directions explain that whenever action occurs in the present, "actors observe the imaginary wall-lines, entering the house only through its door at the left." By contrast, "in the scenes of the past these boundaries are broken, and characters enter or leave a room by stepping 'through' a wall onto the forestage." The stage setting thus represents the two halves of Willy's life: the realistic present, in which his breakdown is unfolding, and the dreamlike past, where most of his problems originated. "An air of the dream clings to the place," Miller writes, "a dream rising out of reality." Examples of the nature of these two halves pervade the play, concluding in the short "Requiem" in which Willy is buried. All those who hold onto their past, Miller implies—and all the Lomans are guilty of doing this—will have trouble adapting to the present.

***Brooklyn.** New York City borough in which the Lomans live. Willy's failed career, his splintering family, and the materialism that has overtaken his life are also real problems audiences can recognize in the city that has arisen around his house. The play's setting perfectly grounds its themes: No trees or grass grow in Brooklyn, only "the hard towers of apartment buildings." Throughout the play, Miller contrasts this harsh urban environment with the country—such as Willy's New England sales territory, his memories of his rural childhood, and his son Biff's wanderings in the American West.

Willy clearly lacks the tools for success in this modern urban world. Values on which he grew up—represented by his brother Ben and salesman Dave Singleman—are those that came out of a nineteenth century world in which frontiers were still open and the American Dream was a reality. The modern world has been transformed into a consumer culture (represented by products such as cars and refrigerators that Willy complains about), leaving little room for men like Willy. The success myth Willy has followed his whole life is dead. In the end, his son Happy takes up his false dreams, but Biff frees himself from this urban tragedy. The city, the play shows, holds little promise for those who cannot understand themselves and the world they inhabit.

*Boston. Massachusetts city to which Biff rushes in a flashback scene late in the play to get Willy's help so he can finish high school. When Biff discovers his father with a woman, his idealized image of his parent collapses, and his nomadic life begins. The scene could take place in almost any city; however, the Boston hotel room effectively represents both the life of the salesman on the road, and the location for his son's loss of innocence.

— *David Peck*

THE DEATH OF ARTEMIO CRUZ

Author: Carlos Fuentes (1928-   )
Type of work: Novel
Type of plot: Social realism

Time of plot: 1889-1959
First published: La muerte de Artemio Cruz, 1962
(English translation, 1964)

Although Carlos Fuentes's protagonist, Artemio Cruz, is confined to a hospital bed throughout this novel, his reconstructed memory gives readers views of various stages of his life. His memory especially traverses his participation in and reaction to the Mexican Revolution of 1910 in which reformation of land ownership is a major issue. Cruz's flashbacks show how the Mexican landscape characterizes the texture of the novel.

*Mexico City hospital. Mexico's capital and largest city, where Cruz is dying in a hospital bed. Fuentes confines his main character to this restrictive place to illustrate Cruz's descent into near madness from the powerful, aggressive but tragic personality he once exhibited. Due to the limitation of the hospitalization, readers understand the conflict of a man brought face to face with his own mortality. Cruz's decline contrasts with the character who earlier seemed to embody the spirit of Mexican nationalism. His suffering parallels the uncertain outcomes and failed idealism of the Mexican Revolution.

Cruz's seclusion allows Fuentes to focus on his suffering protagonist's interior life. Cruz's memory functions as a very real place in the novel. In stark contrast to his decaying body, his memory is active, and through it readers see a number of poignant binaries: past and present, heroism and cowardice, loyalty and betrayal, love and lust, poverty and wealth, cynicism and opportunism, isolation and socialization.

Cocuya. Large estate in Mexico's province of Veracruz with cultural ties to the nineteenth century dictator Antonio López de Santa Ana. Cruz's mother (of African descent) was driven from this place after giving birth to her illegitimate son. This place reveals the humble origins of Artemio Cruz and may then help to explain his later drive for power and his own betrayal of the revolutionaries. Cocuya metaphorically represents the author's view of the unfortunate, even adulterous, relationship of Mexican aristocracy with imperial forces. That relationship failed to appreciate and respect the attempted land reforms of the revolution.

*Veracruz. Mexican port city on the Caribbean coast and the place where Cruz is educated by Sebastian, who teaches him the ideals of social reform. Cruz recalls on several occasions his teacher and his ideals that seem to have become unraveled in the reality of warfare and class conflict.

***Mexico.** Cruz's flashbacks fill the novel with constant references to landscape, with such vivid images as red deserts, hills of prickly pears and magueys, dry cactuses, lava belts, limestone and sandstone cities, adobe pueblos, reed-grass hamlets, and so on. Such passages reinforce a powerful underlying motif found throughout the novel. The land that has been hoarded and fought over and promised and betrayed endures, despite the manipulative destruction of man. The landscape of Mexico functions for the author as a character-like force that stands in eternal mockery to the short-sighted and ego-driven possessiveness of man. The landscape connects mythic Mexico to the revolutionary period of the early twentieth century and finally to the modern-day society governed by growing technology and industrialization. The soul of Mexico is found in its natural order, and Cruz's fluctuating relationship with the natural environment of his country tragically seems to become appreciative of her eternal quality only when his own life has passed its opportunity to protect and venerate the places so poignant in his mind.

— *Kenneth Hada*

THE DEATH OF IVAN ILYICH

Author: Leo Tolstoy (1828-1910)
Type of work: Novella
Type of plot: Psychological realism

Time of plot: 1880's
First published: Smert Ivana Ilicha, 1886 (English translation, 1887)

The explicit settings in this novella, Petersburg and several unnamed towns in "the province," are all really the same "place" since Leo Tolstoy's interest is in the amorality of the middle-class officials that his characters, Ivan Ilych and his family, symbolically represent. Thus the sketchy physical descriptions all reflect the idea of the "inauthenticity" of the lives of the class to which Ilych belongs. None of the settings in this truly outstanding moral tale is treated in any significant physical detail; yet the reader comes away with a sense of intimate familiarity with the story's characters that is rare in fiction and even, perhaps, in life.

*****Russian provinces.** Settings in flashback episodes. After a brief introduction set in Petersburg in which it is revealed that Ivan Ilych has died, the story moves rapidly through three anonymous provincial towns of the character's past. Lacking physical detail, these merge into one another. The very lack of specific character of the places that Ilych inhabits allows Tolstoy to suggest that it is, ironically, the very ordinariness of Ilych's life that explains its final horror.

As Ilych graduates from the Petersburg School of Law and prepares to take his first post in the "provinces," Tolstoy announces the story's moral theme: "Ivan Ilych's life had been most simple and most ordinary and therefore most terrible"; Ilych "was neither as cold and formal as his elder brother nor as wild as the younger, but was a happy mean between them—an intelligent, polished, lively and agreeable man." He has chosen a life of comfort, security, and social conformity, and Tolstoy's condemnation of this amoral conventionality is the story's core moral idea.

Ivan Ilych is a fascinating caricature of the ordinary man of competence and duty but of no particular passion, who chooses to lead what a later generation would call an "inauthentic life." While Ilych performs his professional legal duties, attends the usual social gatherings, has the infrequent love affair, and finally drifts into a marriage of convenience, the settings in which all this occurs are presented with great economy—readers simply "see," now and then, a comfortable room in which are leather chairs and cigar smoke, or the sparkling lights, the formally dressed men and the well-dressed ladies of a social gathering. That is all, but it is so well done that it conveys, in an ironically understated way, Tolstoy's passionate moral condemnation of modern middle-class conventionality.

***St. Petersburg.** Russia's nineteenth century capital is identified only as "Petersburg" in this story, but its identification is not of great importance. The Petersburg of the story could be any great Russian city of its era. Like the "provinces," it is treated primarily as an artificial and "unnatural" place in which life is reduced to petty bickering and social climbing. The story opens here and, after the interlude in the provinces in which Ilych establishes himself in his legal trade, returns to focus on his last months of life and the "absurd" accident that leads to his slow, debilitating, and painful death.

At the end, Ilych is middle-aged and increasingly dissatisfied with his life: he and his wife squabble constantly, his relations with his children are strained, and he is stalled in his career. To escape his disillusionment, he undertakes the repair of the family's new home in Petersburg. Taking an irrational delight in the task, he imagines that the house marks him as a man of exceptional taste and intelligence. Tolstoy underscores the delusion of Ilych's happiness, however, and, in the only descriptive scene of any length in the story, writes that

> In reality it was just what is usually seen in the houses of people of moderate means who want to appear rich . . . : there were damasks, dark wood, plants, rugs, and dull and polished bronzes. . . . His house was so like the others that it would never have been noticed, but to him it all seemed to be quite exceptional.

This image of pretentious clutter is the story's single lengthy description, and it conveys Tolstoy's moral condemnation of modern materialism. This is clear at the end, when Ilych's illness—caused by a fall he has taken while refurnishing his new house—causes him endless and intense pain, leading him to question the conduct of his whole life. He comes to the conclusion that the intensity of his despair is the result, finally, of the false values by which he has led his life. He has not "lived well" and realizes that, indeed, in living for comfort and pleasure, he has not lived at all; his effort to be as conventional as possible has resulted in a wasted and even, Tolstoy suggests, a "sinful" life. To underscore this point, Tolstoy creates a counterpoint character, the peasant Gerasim, a servant whose simplicity, kindliness, and unaffected selflessness stand in stark contrast to the socially successful and conventionally dutiful but ultimately selfish and amoral members of Ilych's "sophisticated" middle-class circle. It is Gerasim's example which at last persuades Ilych to accept the "rightness" of his fate.

— *Ronald Foust*

THE DEATH OF THE HEART

Author: Elizabeth Bowen (1899-1973)
Type of work: Novel
Type of plot: Psychological realism

Time of plot: After World War I
First published: 1938

Set primarily in London, this story of a young woman's search for a home is suffused with a terrible desolation compounded by a cast of rootless city characters who can offer her little consolation or security.

***London.** Capital and largest city of Great Britain. As one of the novel's characters walks through Covent Garden during the evening, the narrator describes a feeling of desolation, which is representative of a city "full of such deserts, of such moments, at which the mirage of one's own keyed-up existence suddenly fails." In this instance, the keyed-up character is Eddie, a dashing young man who has attracted sixteen-year-old Portia, the novel's protagonist. She wants to believe that he represents an antidote to the cold, staid life she encounters in her brother Tom's home near Regent's Park.

Portia has come to stay in London after her father's death. She is a love child, born of her father's liaison with a woman outside his marriage. His legitimate son Tom has honored his father's desire to have Portia come to live with him for a year in London. Neither Tom nor his wife Anna, who dislikes Portia and invades her privacy by reading her diary, really wants to make a place for her in their lives.

*Regent's Park. Large public park in London. The whole Regent's Park area is described in terms that enclose Portia in a dehumanizing vacuum. The novel opens with a description of the Regency buildings at dusk: "colourless silhouettes, insipidly ornate, brittle and cold." These very words might be used to describe Tom and Anna, who never take a warm or colorful interest in Portia's feelings or experiences.

*Seale. Resort town on southeastern England's Kentish coast which provides Portia with a respite from her dour London life. Tom and Anna have sent her there to stay with Mrs. Heccomb, Anna's former governess, while Tom and Anna are in France for a summer holiday. Portia enjoys the more sympathetic Mrs. Heccomb, who does not have the reserve that Portia finds so alienating in London. Mrs. Heccomb's children respond to Portia more forthrightly and expansively, energizing her and prompting her to ask permission to invite Eddie to come down from the city. Eddie's visit proves to be a disaster, however, for he pays more attention to Daphne, Mrs. Heccomb's daughter, than to Portia. Portia's seaside idyll is destroyed as she realizes that Eddie really is no different from other secretive, duplicitous Londoners.

Returning to London, Portia learns that Anna has discussed Portia's diary with Eddie and another male friend, St. Quentin, a writer. Feeling that she has no place in the city, Portia refuses to return to Regent's Park and calls upon Major Brutt, an unlucky Englishman who has hoped to secure employment from Anna's friends.

*Karachi Hotel. Residence of Major Brutt in the Kensington section of London in which the novel concludes in an agonizing scene. The hotel has been formed out of two houses. It is as grim and heartless as Tom and Anna's Regent's Park home. The bare windows, the poor moldings, the feeble lighting of the rooms, the "unsmiling armchairs" express the dimness of Portia's prospects. The hotel is a space of "extensive vacuity," and like other hotels in the area, "no intimate life can have flowered" inside such walls, even when they were homes.

Portia has come to Major Brutt because she believes he is as desperate and isolated as she is. When he tries to make her return to Regent's Park, she refuses, pointing out that Tom and Anna have as much scorn for him as for her. In his austere, remote attic room, she offers to marry him, but he responds by calling Tom and Anna, who send their servant Matchett to fetch her.

— *Carl Rollyson*

THE DEATH OF VIRGIL

Author: Hermann Broch (1886-1951)
Type of work: Novel
Type of plot: Philosophical

Time of plot: 19 B.C.E.
First published: Der Tod des Vergil, 1945 (English translation, 1945)

The setting of this novel, which is seen through the eyes of the great Roman poet Virgil, progresses from the outer world to the metaphysical inner world of Virgil when he is dying. Vivid images are evoked through memory, dream, and conversation. Hallucinatory visions anticipate the birth and life of Christ. At the end, Virgil's perceptions transcend everyday reality, he enters the "second immensity" and experiences creation in the reverse, right back to the word with which it began.

*Brundisium (brewn-dee-see-uhm). Busy Roman port city on the Adriatic Sea (now Brundisi, Italy). Brundisium is shown first from the sea. On a sunny September evening, the sky is mother-of-pearl over the steel-blue waves of the Adriatic, and the flat hills of the Calabrian coast come gradually nearer on the left. A convoy of seven imperial vessels is carrying Augustus Caesar and Virgil from Athens to Brundisium, where

Virgil dies eighteen hours later. As slaves carry him on a litter from the harbor to the citadel, he identifies parts of the city by their distinctive smells: the stench of fish-market stalls, the sweet smell of fermentation from the fruit market, the dusty dryness of grain-sacks, and the shavings and sawdust from carpentry shops. Virgil's entourage then takes an unexpected turn and goes through an alley, where young and old people live in abject poverty: Misery Street. There is a nauseating stench of excrement, and Virgil finds himself the butt of obscene and nasty jeering. It is unclear how much of Misery Street is real and how much a figment of Virgil's fever. The young boy leading the litter is visible only to Virgil.

Citadel. Building in Brundisium in whose southwest wing Virgil occupies a guestroom with a window overlooking the city and the distant hills. The room has a mosaic floor, a flowing fountain, and a candelabrum decorated with laurel. There is an armchair, a commode, and a bed surrounded by mosquito netting. Alone and awake during his last night alive, Virgil struggles to the window. Below him are the black tile roofs and lighted streets of the city. Above him the constellations Archer and Scorpion shine in the southern sky. A watchman passes regularly. The city then reveals its sordid side to the silent witness. Three drunken citizens argue and fight about the price of room and board, agreeing with each other only when reviling Augustus.

*****Roman Empire.** Mediterranean civilization that is at its peak at the moment in which this novel is set. Four million citizens of the empire are enjoying a time of peace under Augustus, who has no desire to expand the boundaries of the empire beyond their natural limits. Virgil has glorified the history of the Romans in his unfinished *Aeneid*, but he senses that Roman rule will be replaced by something that is not quite here but at hand, something that governs by the law of the heart, the real-ity of love. He is disturbed by the unruliness of the mob and by the crucifixion of thousands of the slaves.

*****Andes.** Village near Mantua that was Virgil's birthplace. Virgil feels uncomfortable in urban surroundings. He is a peasant by birth and longs for contact with the earth and the peace of rural life. In his dying fever, it often seems to him that he is back home in Andes. He sees its elm trees, its waving wheat fields, and the Mantuan plain. He smells the wet clay of his father's pottery and hears his parents' voices. The nostalgic images of Andes spring from Virgil's inner landscape.

Fore-court of reality. Virgil's term for everyday perception and experience. He is convinced that something greater lies beyond. All his life, he has been fascinated with death and has sought to recognize where it may lead. As he lies dying, while still quite cognizant of his surroundings, his universe begins to shift. The light comes and goes, the candelabrum swings, and he becomes aware of things and people who are not subject to the normal restrictions of time and space. He is unexpectedly reunited with Plotia, a woman he did not marry, but whose ring he wears. A star appears in the east, a guiding star that shines night and day. Virgil is on the threshold between life and death.

Second immensity. Place of truth accessible only to the dying. All is seen from within. As Virgil loses all earthly memory, he glides through space and witnesses the entire animal world and then the plant world striving toward the star in the east. The circle of time explodes, and the light plunges into the darkness. Only then is he permitted to turn around and survey once more all of creation. An approaching rumbling sound turns into the word, the word of the oath, the pure word that he cannot retain because it is beyond speech. Hermann Broch takes this view of creation from the Gospel of St. John.

— *Jean M. Snook*

THE DEATH SHIP

Author: B. Traven (Berick Traven Torsvan, 1890?-1969)
Type of work: Novel
Type of plot: Social realism

Time of plot: 1920's
First published: Das Totenschiff, 1926 (English translation, 1934)

Setting provides a symbolic framework for Traven's expedition into the dark estrangement from human values and principles experienced by so many following World War I. Traven's waste land is a grail-bereft world, fallen, loveless, extinct while still living. Gerald Gales, an American sailor initially marooned in Antwerp without papers, is deported throughout Western Europe by the authorities as he vainly seeks work on a ship. No papers, no identity, no employment, he is officially without a country, and the bureaucratic world denies his existence as a human being. Comic social satire and savage absurdity collide mercilessly when Gerry Gales finds himself aboard a "death ship" bound for scuttling, a hell on water that serves as a powerful symbol for the world between the great wars.

Yorikke. Aged cargo ship on which the young American sailor without documentation, Gerry Gales, signs on as a crew member in Amsterdam. This ship represents the darker side of the world's seagoing commerce: slavery, piracy, gun-running, and contraband. Its current voyage appears to be headed toward its deliberate destruction for insurance purposes, and conditions for its crew are appalling. The name "Yorikke" echoes the figure Yorick in William Shakespeare's play *Hamlet* (1600), whose skull in the graveyard fuels Prince Hamlet's speculations on the nature and meaninglessness of existence. Traven's ship resembles poor Yorick's skull in being abandoned in the grave of the world. Moreover, just as there is something rotten in the state of Denmark in Shakespeare's play, so is there something rotten within the *Yorikke*—a microcosm of the universe.

As an archetype, the *Yorikke* calls to mind the *Pequod* in Herman Melville's *Moby Dick* (1851), Dante's Inferno in *The Divine Comedy* (1320), and any of the myriad underworlds in literature that represent the unconscious mind and darker side of human experience. The ship is a symbolic womb of death and potential transformation; an inscription over the crew's quarters states, "He who enters here will no longer have existence." To make matters worse for Gerry, he is assigned to the most appalling job on the death ship: that of fireman. His days and nights cycle through misery and an odd sense of joy as he comes to understand that his position in the cosmos, while tormented and absurd, also has depth and meaning in the bowels of this hell, which he grows to love and cherish because it teaches him how to survive in spirit.

With its hierarchy and cruelties, the *Yorikke* serves as a metaphor for a world driven by economics and power at the expense of sharing and compassion. When Gerry is shanghaied and put aboard the *Empress of Madagascar*, one has the sense that the *Yorikke* will continue its scuttling run forever, as will the indignities and indecencies that human beings perpetrate upon each other, and yet continue to endure.

Empress of Madagascar. Newer ship, onto which Gerry is shanghaied. Eventually, this ship does sink, leaving Gerry floating on the ocean as the book ends. The *Empress* initially appears to be a sound ship, but it is not seaworthy, and the entire crew and its officers are killed in an act of deliberate sabotage—a further comment on the deceptions and ironies of modern life. The *Empress* represents a system willing to destroy itself if that will ensure its material gain. The world is doomed, but the human spirit, in all this hell, will survive.

*Europe. Except for Spain, the governments of Western European nations—as well the United States, through its diplomatic representatives in Europe—are bureaucratic nightmares with no respect for individuals unless they have papers and money. Gerry is threatened with prison and denied by his own countrymen because he cannot prove he exists, and his situation becomes a comic and terrifying metaphor for the individual trapped in the modern web of indifference and alienation. By contrast, Spain is a haven; however, the threat of fascism looms even there. Posing as various nationalities on his misbegotten odyssey, Gerry offers the reader an understanding of the consequences of mistrust and propaganda, and how people are so often judged merely because of what they may appear to be and not who they really are. Like the *Yorikke* and the *Empress of Madagascar*, Europe is an Inferno, a hell in which people may breathe but are dead and not living, yet their indomitable spirit and tenacity to endure even this allows them to survive and hold on, even if it is only to a broken spar in a vast ocean.

— *Erskine Carter*

DECLINE AND FALL: An Illustrated Novelette

Author: Evelyn Waugh (1903-1966)
Type of work: Novel
Type of plot: Social satire

Time of plot: Twentieth century
First published: 1928

This brief novel shows the stages of decline and fall in the morality of its naïve young antihero, Paul Pennyfeather, through his exploits in an Oxford college, a North Wales boys school, and a prison and nursing home. Evelyn Waugh uses his settings to satirize the British class structure of the period.

Llanabba Castle School. Small privately owned school in North Wales attended by fifty or sixty boys, ages ten through eighteen. Despite Waugh's protestations to the contrary, it is most likely a fictionalized version of the North Wales school where he taught after leaving Oxford University. The essence of the school is falseness: The building is a country house altered to resemble a medieval castle, while the school's claims to high academic standards and upper-class pupils and staff are similarly false. Pennyfeather is not impressed by the school's dinginess or the meanness of its meals.

In a scene involving Llanabba's annual sports competition, most of Waugh's targets for satire are attacked: the chaotic organization of the school; the way in which the school's owner and headmaster, Dr. Augustus Fagan, fusses over the few titled parents; whether the nouveaux riches can ever be as good as the old-fashioned titled families; a general air of hypocrisy; and even the position of blacks in society. In sports, cheating by staff and pupils is rampant.

Waugh makes use of this section of the novel to satirize the Welsh people, showing them as mercenary subhumans. In particular he describes (in insulting terms) a local brass band hired to play during the sports competition. Several of the scenes set in Wales take place in a local village public house, which is patronized mostly by the working class.

Scone College. Fictional Oxford University college that is based on Hertford College, which Waugh attended. Pennyfeather is a hard-working, middle-class student, who intends to become a clergyman. He is attacked by a drunken crowd of titled students, who remove his trousers. It is much easier for the college authorities to indict Pennyfeather, who is "of no importance," than to punish the real culprits. After his dis-

grace, Pennyfeather returns to Scone College, claims to be a distant cousin of himself, and continues to pursue his education.

Blackstone Prison. Penal institution in which Pennyfeather is sentenced to a term of seven years after he pleads guilty to white slaving to protect the real criminal, his fiancé Margot. The prison is an exaggerated example of the British penal system of the period. There, Pennyfeather is treated like a stupid and illiterate member of the working class and threatened with violence, just as he had threatened his pupils earlier. Yet, he is quite content with the solitary confinement, poor food, and harsh regime because, Waugh notes, "anyone who has been to English public school will always feel comparatively at home in prison."

Pennyfeather is transferred to **Egdon Heath Penal Settlement**—whose name is an allusion to Thomas Hardy's *Wessex Tales* (1888) and presumably located in Dorset, England. Later, he is taken to a private nursing home, **Cliff Place**, for an appendix operation he does not need. This nursing home, run by Fagan, who has sold the school, is located near the real town of Worthing, on England's south coast. There Pennyfeather feigns death in order to escape.

King's Thursday. Hampshire country house owned by Margot Beste-Chetwynde. Pennyfeather meets Margot at Llanabba's sports competition. She is a wealthy widow, whose son is one of Pennyfeather's pupils, and soon becomes Pennyfeather's fiancé. Margot's traditional Tudor home, unmodernized for centuries, is being completely remodeled in concrete and aluminum by an avant-garde architect. Margot also owns a London house and a villa on the Greek island of Corfu, both of which are briefly inhabited by Pennyfeather.

— *Chris Morgan*

THE DEERSLAYER: Or, The First War-Path, a Tale

Author: James Fenimore Cooper (1789-1851)

Type of work: Novel

Type of plot: Historical

Time of plot: 1740

First published: 1841

This novel unfolds in the environs of the fictional Glimmerglass—a region that is barely inhabited, lushly beautiful, spiritually enriching, and perilous. Thomas Hutter and his two daughters Judith and Hetty live in a log "castle" on an island surrounded by the lake, a place of sanctuary and solitude. As in James Fenimore Cooper's other Leatherstocking novels, the natural setting here becomes a political, familial, and romantic battleground that helps delineate character, highlight human conflict, and pose moral and cultural questions.

Glimmerglass Lake. Imaginary lake closely modeled on the real Lake Otsego, near Cooperstown in upstate New York. Glimmerglass plays a complex role in *The Deerslayer.* On a basic level, it displays rare and unspoiled beauty. Its shimmering waters, dazzling sunlit and starry skies, and lush overhanging trees provide solace, solitude, and beauty for humans weary of the world or hoping to escape detection. The lake offers a wilderness unspoiled by humans, an environmental paradise.

As the name "Glimmerglass" suggests, the lake is a mirror of the universe. It reflects not only the Milky Way, but also the spiritual and moral aspects of God. For Deerslayer, the frontiersman who is a man of "white blood and white gifts," the air is God's "breath, and the light of the sun is little more than a glance of His eye." God is not only the creator, but is an immanent presence. Similarly for his Native American friend Chingachgook, with his red gifts, the Great Spirit is everywhere: in the lake, in the forest, in the clouds. The lake is a temple of God's creation but also an embodiment of God himself.

As an embodiment of God, the lake provides instruction, especially in a moral sense. If this book of nature is read correctly, it nurtures religion, morality, love, and education. Deerslayer and Chingachgook both believe this, as does Chingachgook's love, the Indian maiden Wah-ta-Wah. In an eloquent passage she refuses to leave Chingachgook and her own people, comparing a woman to the honeysuckle, the robin, and the willow, all of which thrive only in their natural environments. Nature is thus emblematic of the way people ought to live their lives. For Deerslayer, nature is his most loving and faithful companion. When Judith coyly asks him where his sweetheart is, he replies that she is "in the forest," in the trees, in the rain, in "the dew on the open grass." Thus nature is God, mentor, moral touchstone, and even lover.

In a measure of how complex Glimmerglass really is, however, Cooper does not limit the setting's connotations to those that are solely positive and morally uplifting. After all, Mingo Indians populate the forest as well. Both good and evil inhabit Cooper's Glimmerglass, and the forest is the site of a surprise attack, scalping, kidnapping, bondage, and murder. The overhanging boughs on the bank are equally capable of hiding friend or foe. As such, Glimmerglass is the site of intense drama, and Cooper treats it as a stage.

Muskrat Castle. Log cabin home of the Hutters on an island in the middle of Glimmerglass Lake, which Thomas Hutter claims to own. Throughout the novel the castle is described as being under scrutiny—all the hidden figures on the dark shores are able to observe the movements to and from the castle, as if it were center stage in the theater of the lake. At night the moon sends a pathway of light down the center of the lake, like lights in a stage setting. Early in the novel Chingachgook dramatically makes his appearance at the rock on the lake, again almost as if he is making an entrance on a stage.

The castle stages the family drama. Buried in the lake at the end of the shoal lies Judith and Hetty's mother; at the end of the novel the lake becomes a cemetery for Tom Hutter as well. In fact, almost as if it is an identifiable character, the lake acts as the priest at Hutter's burial. The castle is the primary home his daughters have known, and family ties them to this consecrated place. The center of the lake is the focal point of the novel. It showcases the strategic battles between the Mingos and the whites, it is the locale in which Judith learns truths about her family, it serves as the site for her romantic encounters with Deerslayer, and it is the burial ground for her family.

Tom Hutter attempts to claim ownership of the lake, but ultimately the lake overshadows all of the humans who serve as transitory specks on its surface. At the conclusion of the novel, Deerslayer and Chingachgook return many years later to Glimmerglass. The lake is very little changed, but the castle and other remnants of human presence have gone to ruin. In Cooper's complex portrait of the wilderness, nature has endured and remains a majestic presence that reflects but also transcends the small concerns of humankind.

— *Ann M. Cameron*

DEIRDRE

Author: James Stephens (1882-1950)
Type of work: Novel
Type of plot: Folklore

Time of plot: Heroic Age
First published: 1923

This novel is set in the Heroic Age of Ireland, in the first centuries of the Christian era. Deirdre, King Conachúr mac Nessa's foster-child and intended bride, elopes with Naoise but later is lured back and betrayed by the jealous king. Deirdre may be seen as an incarnation of Ireland itself. In the early Irish folklore, fertility of the land, livestock, and people was assured by the local goddess of territorial sovereignty, who chose a just consort. Conachúr's attempts to manipulate Deirdre into marriage are acts of betrayal whose outcome can only be the ruin of the kingdom.

Emania. Capital of Conachúr mac Nessa's Ulster kingdom; located near modern-day Armagh in Northern Ireland, where Conachúr has Deirdre raised after it is prophesied that a retainer's child named Deirdre, "Troubler," will bring evil to Ireland. The girl's witch-like foster-mother Lavarcham teaches her respect for the king, but the attempt to train her in isolation from human society fails when Deirdre makes friends with the old guards in the castle in which she is kept. As she develops a sense of herself and makes her first forays into the outside world, she meets Naoise and his brothers, young warriors related to and serving under Conachúr. Deirdre and Naoise become lovers.

***Scotland.** After Deirdre coerces Naoise into elopement, she and her lover and his brothers go to Scotland, turning their backs on their community and civilized space. While a free life in the Scottish wilderness brings joy, the fugitives cannot rest, for Deirdre's beauty has attracted the king of Scotland.

Red Branch. Conachúr's lavishly decorated Ulster fortress, in which he has Deirdre and Naoise stay after their return to Ireland. When Conachúr breaks his promise and lays siege to the building, it becomes a death trap. Deirdre and her warriors make brave sorties among the troops before the six great doors in the belief that Fergus will come to their rescue. Eventually the Red Branch is burned down, and the defenders must flee. The forces thus set in motion conclude in the cattle raid of Cooley and the apocalyptic clash between Ulster and the remainder of Ireland.

— *William Sayers*

DEIRDRE

Author: William Butler Yeats (1865-1939)
Type of work: Drama
Type of plot: Tragedy

Time of plot: Antiquity
First performed: 1906; first published, 1907

This recasting of the ancient tale is set in a "Guesthouse in a wood," carefully described by William Butler Yeats. The story unfolds in Ireland's mythical age of heroes—a period romanticized by Yeats. The house's role as a trap or cage in which the deceitful High King snares the illicit lovers is tantalizingly hinted at until finally revealed in the lovers' final sacrifice.

*Ireland. Yeats's version of the hoary tale must be set in Ireland, as its antagonists are part of the island's rich mythical tapestry. The wandering musicians, reference to the "invisible king of the air," and evocation of another old Irish tale add a patina to this product of the Irish Renaissance.

Woodland house. Roughly constructed timber building that is situated in a deep wood. No one's home, it serves as a resting place, a meeting place, and a place of confrontation and execution. Yeats establishes clearly that the house is royal property firmly controlled by Conchobar's men, who—dark both in complexion and mission—lurk in the shadows beyond the walls. The view from the windows allows glimpses of those who choose to approach and be seen, but deny any broader perspective, as does the lowering night. Yeats writes that the "landscape beyond suggests silence and loneliness," and midway through the lighting of torches increases "the sense of solitude and loneliness." The lovers who had roamed free like birds on the wing have set down and been "limed" as the old stories would have it: snared and placed at the mercy of the hunter. Naisi is specifically netted, "taken like a bird or a fish." The symbolic nature of the house, and especially of the curtained space in the room's center, is fully unveiled as Fergus declares upon seeing the dead queen, "What's this but empty cage and tangled wire. . . ."

— *Joseph P. Byrne*

DEIRDRE OF THE SORROWS

Author: John Millington Synge (1871-1909)
Type of work: Drama
Type of plot: Tragedy

Time of plot: The past
First performed: 1910; first published, 1910

With its origin based on Celtic mythology, the locations in this unfinished play often center on rural Irish lands. In this way, place transcends time; the regions that once existed in the past and in myth have endured. Although there is mention of other areas, there are four primary settings in this tragedy: Lavarcham's house on Slieve Fuadh, Emain Macha, Alban, and the grave below Emain Macha.

Lavarcham's house (LOWR-chamz). Located on Slieve Fuadh, this is Deirdre's home, where Lavarcham, her nurse, raised her. Deirdre's beauty, happiness, and carefree lifestyle are mirrored in the admiration that she has of the wonders of nature; she is to remain here until her marriage to King Conchubor.

*Emain Macha (AE-min ma-HA). Ancient capital of Ulster, where pre-Christian kings of Ireland are thought to have been crowned; presently the seat of the primate of the archbishop of Ireland and now known as Navan Fort, west of Armagh. Emain Macha is mentioned frequently in the play and is the place where King Conchubor insists upon taking Deirdre to be married to him. This place symbolizes everything that is foreign to her: a wealthy life, an older husband, and an unhappy future. When Deirdre and Naisi, her beloved, decide to meet with the king, it is with the full knowledge of their impending doom. In the process, Emain Macha is destroyed.

*Alban. Deirdre and Naisi spend a blissful seven years here, in what is now Scotland. This temporary home sig-

nifies the short-lived love and happiness that Deirdre and Naisi share.

Grave. Located just below Emain Macha, this place is an image representing the mortality of humankind and the permanence of death. Deirdre kills herself just before falling into this grave, where Naisi and his brothers have already been buried.

— *Adriana C. Tomasino*

A DELICATE BALANCE

Author: Edward Albee (1928-   )
Type of work: Drama
Type of plot: Absurdist

Time of plot: October, in the mid-1960's
First performed: 1966; first published, 1967

This play is set in the comfortable, upper-middle-class, suburban home of Agnes and Tobias, which fails to provide refuge from its inhabitants' familial problems or from the terrifying existential emptiness outside it.

Agnes and Tobias's home. Home of a married couple whose living room is the setting for the entire play. Edward Albee's stage directions describe the set as the "living room of a large and well-appointed suburban house." This room contains a library, chairs, a supply of liquor bottles, and an arched entryway. Albee provides remarkably few other details about the set, but the fact that the room is "well-appointed" indicates that it should reflect its residents' affluence, class, and taste. However, their affluence provides no protection against a family implosion—the imminent psychological collapse that Agnes fears, the gray ineffectualness of Tobias, the failure of their daughter Julia's four marriages, the alcoholism of Agnes's sister Claire.

Outside the walls of the house looms an equally terrifying if less readily definable menace that draws Agnes

and Tobias's friends Edna and Harry into their home to seek haven as well. After eating dinner at their own home, they suddenly and unaccountably became frightened and can no longer endure remaining alone in their house. Agnes offers them Julia's room for the night, and they retire. What troubles Edna and Harry is an overwhelming meaninglessness, a realization of the "absurd," a glimpse of the existential void.

Other playwrights treated similar themes in the decade preceding *A Delicate Balance*. What Albee did was to domesticate this theme, presenting a more affluent American setting and characters from whom, presumably, primarily middle-class theatergoers in the United States would feel less estranged and by whom they would be at least initially less discomfited.

— *William Hutchings*

DELIVERANCE

Author: James Dickey (1923-1997)
Type of work: Novel
Type of plot: Bildungsroman

Time of plot: Late twentieth century
First published: 1970

This novel is unusual in its use of realistic detail, which extends to the descriptions of its four principal settings, which include an unnamed city, the small towns of Oree and Aintry, and the wild and powerful Cahulawassee River. Dickey's treatment of these places creates the novel's structural principle of opposition between the moral force of order and the amoral force of chaos. Thus the long episode on the river is sandwiched between the Oree and Aintry chapters, which serve to introduce the reader to the theme of the descent of the characters from civilization to savagery. Finally, all three of these places rest comfortably between the opening and closing chapters, which describe the separation from and the return to the city, to the comforts of marriage, home, law-fulness, and work, all of which satisfy the unheroic but real need that ordinary people have to live peacefully with one another.

The city. Unnamed city in northern Georgia in which the novel's four friends live and work. Although this place frames the main story, it is never named or treated as anything other than a normal, middle-class (sub)urban place. This technique effectively maintains Dickey's realistic intention. Unlike antirealist novels, which distort reality in order to draw attention to the place as a symbol of something else, Dickey's undogmatic use of "the city" allows readers merely to sense that this place is, in some real but undefinable way, a mythical place that represents all of modern, existential life. It is a metaphor for the alienation of the contemporary middle-class, which is treated as both materially successful and spiritually empty.

With its anonymous and interchangeable business complexes, shopping malls, fast-food joints, and suburbs, the city could be any modern American city. This technique underscores Dickey's intention to present the extreme violence of the friends' wilderness canoe trip as a universal human experience: Violence, the novel suggests, is the "normal" experience of modern American men. After the river, the city is the most important of the novel's four places, since its job is to create an image of the modern American place, the most desirable, if flawed, image of order and civilization available to modern humanity.

Oree (OH-ree). Staging area for the characters' whitewater river trip. Oree is not a major setting in the story but is a necessary one. As the first rural stop after the city, it serves to prepare readers for the movement from civilized urban life to the dangerous, anarchic freedom and inhumanity of nature, experienced at its most raw.

Cahulawassee River (ka-hool-a-wash-e). Georgia river on which the four men undertake their canoe trip. That this is the most important of the places in the story is made plain by the fact that it is treated at far greater length than the other three places taken together, as well as by the subtle lyricism of the description of the journey of Ed, Lewis, Bobby, and Drew. The beauty and the anarchic freedom that the river represents to the characters is soon countered and then eradicated by the extraordinary violence and hardship of the episodes that follow: the homosexual rape of Bobby, Lewis and Ed's killing of the mountain men involved in the rape, the death of Drew, the breaking of Lewis's leg, and the exhausting and sobering journey of the three battered survivors the rest of the way to Aintry.

Within the river chapters Dickey contrasts the city with nature. His use of this device implies a value judgment that, finally, favors the flawed city against the perfect, if brutal and dangerous, amorality of nature.

Aintry (AYN-tree). Town at which the river trip ends. The last of the novel's four places, Aintry serves as a sort of decompression device. That is, the story moves from the city, to Oree, to the river itself, and then to Aintry, where Ed concocts a plausible set of lies for the authorities that allows the men to avoid arrest, to heal, and to return to civilization. From Aintry they return to the city and their separate, ordinary lives.

— *Ronald Foust*

DELTA WEDDING

Author: Eudora Welty (1909-2001)
Type of work: Novel
Type of plot: Regional

Time of plot: Early 1920's
First published: 1946

Recounting the reunion of a family around the occasion of a wedding, this novel is the story it is because it takes place in the Mississippi Delta. The Fairchilds are the family they are because they are the Delta Fairchilds. Like any wedding, Dabney's marks both a beginning and an end, as her new life with Troy at Marmion must be born from the end of her old life as a Fairchild of Shellmound.

Mississippi Delta. Broad alluvial plain bordering the Mississippi River, stretching on the Mississippi side from Memphis in the north nearly to Vicksburg in the south. A delta is any land built up from the mud and sand deposited by a river; however, in *Delta Wedding* the term defines a culture as well. Life in the Delta is different from life in Ellen Fairchild's native Virginia, different from life in Troy Flavin's Mississippi hill-country to the east, different from life in Laura's nearby Jackson.

Shellmound. Name of both the cotton plantation owned by the Delta Fairchilds and the sprawling plantation home that is the center of communal life for dispersed Fairchilds, such as George and Laura, as well as for Shellmound residents. The plantation is so large that little Laura repeatedly asks, "Is this still Shellmound?" Its fields have names, like Mound Field (with the remains of Indian mounds), East Field, Far Field, the Deadening (where the first Fairchilds to settle the land cleared away the trees). The house at Shellmound is home to Battle and Ellen's ever-growing brood, a house of numberless rooms sufficient to shelter Battle and Ellen's nine, along with young dependents like the handicapped Maureen and the motherless Laura and old dependents like Battle's eccentric Aunt Mac and mad Aunt Shannon.

Marmion. Empty since its completion in 1890, Marmion lies beyond the bustling life of Shellmound literally and figuratively. Although near Shellmound in distance, it is physically removed because it is on the far side of the Yazoo River, so that one must follow the river to the bridge at the town of Fairchilds in order to reach it. It is part of the Fairchilds' family mythology, the house built by Battle's father just before he was killed in a duel of honor, the house from which George and his orphaned siblings left to be raised by aunts at the Grove.

Now Marmion will become home to Dabney and her new husband Troy Flavin, the Fairchilds' overseer. This house so removed from Shellmound symbolizes the exile that Dabney chooses when she marries beneath her.

Grove. Fairchilds' former home, now home to Battle's unmarried sisters Jim Allen and Primrose. Close enough to Shellmound to accommodate visits to and fro, the quiet Grove was once what busy Shellmound is now.

Memphis. Tennessee city located at the northern tip of Mississippi's Delta, Memphis is the cosmopolitan city of the story. When shepherds' crooks and wedding cakes are needed for Dabney's wedding, it is to Memphis that the Fairchilds look. When the family's beloved George marries beneath him and leaves the Delta, it is to Memphis he moves, although it can never be home to him. To leave the Delta is to leave not just a region but a way of life, and Memphis symbolizes this life in exile.

Jackson. Mississippi's capital city, Jackson, is Laura's home, located roughly fifty miles southeast of the Delta's southern edge. In spite of the fact that Jackson was the author's own well-known and well-loved home by choice for nearly all her life, Jackson is portrayed here as a faceless void into which the now-dead Annie Laurie dropped and out of which her young daughter Laura is to be plucked and given identity at Shellmound. Laura herself recognizes that although Jackson is a big town of 25,000 and Fairchilds nothing more than a handful of buildings in the middle of nowhere, she is the one who feels like the country cousin.

Fairchilds. Mississippi hometown of the Fairchild family is aptly named, being little more than a cotton gin owned by the Fairchild family, a store owned by the Fairchild family, a church and its adjacent cemetery where Fairchilds are buried. Located near Shellmound on the banks of the Yazoo River, Fairchilds is the site of the only nearby bridge crossing the Yazoo River, which separates Shellmound from Marmion.

Brunswicktown. African American community near Shellmound, home to field workers and house servants who move around the central story like an outer wheel. In the face of criticism for her portrayals of persons of color, Eudora Welty's response was that her role as a writer was to hold up a mirror of the time and place, to reflect what *was* in order for readers to make judgments. If so, Brunswicktown is such a mirror. Often visited but poorly known by the younger Fairchilds, Brunswicktown's inhabitants live lives in striking contrast to the Fairchilds'.

— *Diane L. Chapman*

DEMOCRACY

Author: Joan Didion (1934-   )
Type of work: Novel
Type of plot: Political

Time of plot: Mid-1970's
First published: 1984

In the mid-1970's, the Pacific region and Southeast Asia were major concerns for United States foreign policy. The winding down of the Vietnam conflict was as bloody and chaotic as the war itself, and American relations with neighboring countries included various mixes of latter-day colonialism, grandstanding, covert activities, and tragedy. Joan Didion's ironically titled Democracy *shows these forces as they play out in the life of Inez Christian Victor, the wife of an American senator and failed presidential candidate. Although the characters' travels span the entire globe, all the significant events in this novel occur in the Pacific basin or in Southeast Asian cities.*

Honolulu. Hawaii's capital city, in which Inez Christian was born and grew up during the 1930's and 1940's. Her college experience on the U.S. mainland led to her marriage to Harry Victor. Despite his political career as a senator from California, and years of residence in Washington, D.C., and New York City, both family ties and fate keep pulling her back to Hawaii. In part this pattern may symbolize the tensions in American life in this era, when formerly East Coast-oriented political "actors" kept being drawn into obligations and conflicts in the Pacific arena.

Even into the 1970's, life in Honolulu for Inez and her relatives retains many of the perks and institutions of its colonial past. Daiquiri poolside lunches and visiting ballet companies, investments in container corporations and Sea Meadow housing developments all play a part in the family's illusion of a protected life. However, the occasional presence of Jack Lovett, a mysterious agent with covert, unspecified business all across the Pacific region, shows a different face of the island state. This is underscored by the scene at Schofield Barracks in which Jack and Inez watch television coverage of the simultaneous evacuation of several Southeast Asian capitals. Airfields are jammed with trans-Pacific commerce and rescue missions, and a faint sense of decay as well as luxury reminds the reader that Honolulu is a tropical city not entirely unlike the others that loomed so large in the decade's disastrous events. When Inez's father, Paul Christian, shoots her sister Janet Zeigler and a congressman on the rim of the Zeigler's indoor koi-fish pool, the intrusion of reality is complete.

The book is sparing of descriptive detail. Hawaiian scenic vistas play little part, either in the narrative or in Inez's memories. Strangely enough, the few scenes she remembers as places and times where she might have been happy took place elsewhere—a hotel room in Chicago with snow piling up outside; a lunch *en famille* on a rainy day in Paris. These spotty recollections echo her belief that the price public life exacts is a loss of memory, but the memories also reflect settings where she is out of cameramen's and reporters' range. Because of her family's and her husband's prominence, she seldom attained this happy situation in Honolulu.

Kuala Lumpur. Capital city of Malaysia, situated

on the eastern coast of the Malaysian peninsula, which served as a way station and refuge for people fleeing persecution in Cambodia, Vietnam, and other Southeast Asian countries. In the novel, Inez visits a refugee camp in Kuala Lumpur when her husband's travels take them to Malaysia. As a "special interest" it is considered too controversial by his political advisors, but when she leaves Honolulu with Jack Lovett on the eve of her sister's funeral, she ends up working in the camp on a semipermanent basis. Inez thus finally puts her husband's liberal principles into practice, while he is still flailing around, changing positions every time a poll result shifts.

*Saigon. Capital of South Vietnam before the reunification of Vietnam. Of all the places mentioned in

Democracy, Saigon is the only one Inez never visits, but it serves as a storm center and catalyst for many events in her life. Jack Lovett goes to Saigon sporadically on unspecified missions. When Inez's daughter Jessie refuses to attend her Aunt Janet's funeral, she flies to Saigon instead, seeking a waitress job or perhaps a reliable drug connection. This is during the final days of the American pullout from the city. Inez, frightened for Jessie, asks Jack to go to Saigon, as he is the only person who knows his way around the embattled capital. Miraculously, he goes and forcibly puts the young woman on a U.S.-bound flight just as American troops are abandoning their mission in Vietnam.

— *Emily Alward*

THE DEPTFORD TRILOGY

Author: Robertson Davies (1913-1995)
Type of work: Novel
Type of plot: Moral

Time of plot: 1908-1971
First published: 1983: *Fifth Business*, 1970; *The Manticore*, 1972; *World of Wonders*, 1975

This wide-ranging trilogy opens in Ontario, Canada, then moves to France, England, Mexico, and Switzerland. The first book in the trilogy is the life story of Dunstan Ramsey; he and three other central characters come from the same small town. The interweaving of lives is a central premise throughout the trilogy, as is the idea that adult lives have their origins in childhood and youth. All three novels are remembered lives, so their primary settings—St. Gall, Zurich, and London—are the places where people tell their stories, in writing or through conversations with others.

Deptford. Imaginary small rural Ontario town in which the series opens. Robertson Davies patterned Deptford after Thamesville, in which he lived as a small boy. The central characters Dunstan Ramsey, Boy Staunton, Paul Dempster, Mary Dempster, and Leola Cruikshank are first encountered in Deptford and from there move through the paths of their lives. Deptford is a portrait of a small Canadian rural town from about 1905 until 1920, marked out with the excitements and strange horrors of childhood that form the roots of adult life. Like all locations in the trilogy, Deptford provides a specific quality of time and place; however, Dunstan Ramsey's narration gives readers an awareness that there is a quality to the place that makes it a universal picture of childhood and young adulthood.

*Toronto. Ontario city to which Dunstan goes after World War I to study at a university. He then begins his forty-year career teaching at Colborne College, a boys' school partially modeled on Toronto's Upper Canada College. Boy Staunton also studies in Toronto and embarks on his rise to riches and fame in that city. The climax of *Fifth Business* occurs when Boy Staunton dies in circumstances that leave a mystery not resolved until the end of the trilogy.

*Sankt Gallen. Also known as St. Gall, a Swiss city that is a principal location in all three novels. There Ramsey "writes" *Fifth Business* and lives with Liesl Vitzlipützli and Magnus after that novel's mysterious denouement in Toronto. Liesl's nineteenth century castle-house, **Sorgenfrei** ("free-of-care"), is perched on a mountainside outside St. Gall. There David Staunton, Boy's lawyer-son, comes at the end of *The Manticore*. *World of Wonders*, Paul Dempster's life story retold, is largely set in the house on the mountain as well, although the latter part of that narrative takes place in London.

*Zurich (ZEW-rihk). Swiss city to which David Staunton, Boy's son, goes when he is forty to undergo Jungian analysis because he feels he is losing his self-control. His analysis elucidates his life story, his boyhood in Toronto, his schooling at Colborne College and Oxford, and his adult life in Toronto. His analysis features a courtroom of the mind in which he becomes prosecutor, defender, and judge.

The Cave. Cavern in the mountains near St. Gall where Liesl takes David Staunton at the close of *The Manticore*. The cave is the most clearly mythic location in all three of the novels. Despite learning much about himself in analysis, Staunton is still a thinking rather than a feeling person. Deep in the cave, he and Liesl find evidences of ancient bear worshipers. Staunton fails to grasp the holiness of the location, but when he and Liesl leave the cave, their flashlight fails, and he experiences an agonized quarter-mile crawl in the dark that leads him to a psychic conversion.

*Passchendaele (PAHS-en-dahl-ah). French battlefield in World War I on which Dunstan Ramsey per-forms an act of heroism in a 1917 battle in which he loses a leg. While lying in the mud on the battlefield, he sees images of the Virgin Mary and Christ child in a ruined church and believes he has seen Mary Dempster, the mother of Paul, whom Ramsey comes to believe is a fool-saint, a holy innocent.

*Collége de Saint-Michel (koh-LAYJ deh sahn-mee-SHEHL). Center of the Roman Catholic Bollandist order in Brussels, Belgium, to which Dunstan Ramsay goes after the war. His vision of the Madonna on the battlefield leads him to the study of the saints, and he travels Europe in search of statues and legends. Eventually, he becomes an associate of the Bollandists, the order responsible for assembling the histories of all the saints. His visits with them in Brussels help him clarify his ideas about the meaning and function of sainthood. His study of sainthood becomes a doorway into his larger understanding of human history and psychology.

*Guadalupe. Mexican city famous for its Madonna, in which Dunstan encounters Paul Dempster while he is searching for the miraculous Madonna. Dempster, now transformed into Magnus Eisengrim, is an elegant magician. Liesl, who is financing Dempster's show, becomes Dunstan's lover and friend.

— *Peter Brigg*

DESCENT INTO HELL

Author: Charles Williams (1886-1945)
Type of work: Novel
Type of plot: Moral

Time of plot: June and July in the 1930's
First published: 1937

The plot of this novel concerns the production of a play in the suburban community of Battle Hill, thirty miles north of London. The action is split between this location, where some of the characters experience visionary landscapes, and London.

*Battle Hill. This setting is an actual hill with a long and bloody history, from legends of human sacrifice among the Britons and Saxons to that of a dejected construction worker who hanged himself while working on the suburban estate that now covers most of the hill. The hill also includes a manor house, currently owned by the poet and playwright Peter Stanhope. This manor house is the site on which a martyr was burned to death. Thus,

Charles Williams writes, life and death are closer in Battle Hill than elsewhere, the membranes between the worlds thinner. Williams also refers to Battle Hill as a place of skulls, recalling Golgotha, the site of Jesus' crucifixion.

Much of the action occurs in the houses and yards of Battle Hill residents. Not far from the manor house lives Lawrence Wentworth, whose home (unknown to him)

holds the ghost of the construction worker. Elsewhere in town, Pauline Anstruther lives with her dying grandmother. Near them lives Myrtle Fox, another young woman in the play.

Although Lily Sammile seems to visit everyone, no one knows where she lives. The reader is shown the woman's supernatural nature and learns that she lives in a shed by the town cemetery. In the apocalyptic moments after the climax of the play, some graves literally open, their tattered inhabitants gravitating toward Lily Sammile. She attempts to lure various living residents of Battle Hill, and when she fails, her shed, which is also referred to as a cave, collapses around her.

Williams makes much of gates, doorways, and other entrances. Wentworth encounters a female demon (a succubus), but she falls down at a threshold. Lily Sammile is often seen by a gate—Margaret Anstruther's house's gate, the cemetery gate—waiting for people she can talk into becoming like her. Since the novel is about choices of modes of being, a gate can represent choice, the definite border between one place and another, and, more specifically, the entry to heaven or hell.

Wentworth spies on Hugh Prescott and Adela Hunt at a train station, and at the end, a train takes both him and Pauline Anstruther to London. Just as gates mark a choice between two places, trains are vehicles from one place to another, representing movement and change.

London. Capital of Great Britain to which Pauline goes at the end of the novel in order to enjoy her new life. Wentworth takes the same train, but will not sit with her.

In fact, he has forsworn all human community, and in London he completely loses any comprehension of the people and world around him.

London is also a spiritual destination, symbolic of heaven, or at least some desirable afterlife, when the ghost of the construction worker asks Pauline for directions to London. London is also the city of eternity, and by asking to be directed there, the ghost has begun the path to redemption and travel to his next existence.

Garden of Eden. Biblical paradise in which Adam and Eve live until their Fall. When Wentworth takes the demon into his house, his arms, and his bed, he has an illusion of Eden, with him in the role of Adam and the demon as Eve. What he perceives as paradise is actually closer to the experience of being lost in the woods, which the tree and leaf imagery also supports. Moreover, Williams describes the garden as if it encloses Wentworth; instead of being banished from a garden, he has consigned himself to be its prisoner, as he grows more and more infatuated with the demon and will not leave his home.

Gomorrah. Ancient Palestinian town near Sodom that was, according to the Old Testament, destroyed by God because of its wickedness. Williams alludes to Gomorrah, which symbolizes spiritual sterility and avoidance of life, just as its companion town Sodom is symbolic of sexual perversion. When the real Adela faints outside Wentworth's house, she is said to have fallen by the wall of Gomorrah.

— *Bernadette Lynn Bosky*

DESIRE UNDER THE ELMS

Author: Eugene O'Neill (1888-1953)
Type of work: Drama
Type of plot: Tragedy

Time of plot: 1850
First performed: 1924; first published, 1925

The stark setting of this naturalistic tragedy perfectly represents its themes. With the brooding elms above it, the farmhouse embodies the power of human passion, the "palpable force" which human emotions can become.

Cabot farmhouse. Isolated New England farm, originally belonging to Eben Cabot's mother, that becomes the property of her widower Ephraim Cabot and his two sons after Ephraim works her to her grave, as Eben claims. Life on the farm, as on so many farms in New England in the mid-nineteenth century, is a challenging existence, which is one reason why Eben is able to bribe his half brothers to leave. After Ephraim arrives home with his new wife Abbie Putnam, who will inherit the farm if she produces a son, Peter and Simeon leave for

California, and the passionate psychological struggle among the remaining three characters begins.

The action takes place in various rooms of the green and "sickly grayish" Cabot farmhouse: the kitchen, the porch, the bedrooms, and the parlor, described in stage directions as a "grim, repressed room like a tomb." This room has been preserved as Eben's mother left it and is where Abbie's seduction of Eben takes place. At the end of the play, Abbie kills their love child to prove her love to Eben. The sheriff who comes to arrest them admires the farm and concludes, ironically given the tragedies the farm represents, that he wished he owned it.

Much of the action of the play takes place outside: by the gate, where characters stand at sunrise and sunset, and in the barn, where Ephraim sometimes sleeps with his cows. The most important features outdoors, however, are the "two enormous elms" which bend over the roof of the farmhouse and whose "sinister maternity" represents the spirit of Eben's dead mother.

***California.** Home of the gold strikes of 1849. Although never seen in the play, California represents escape for the inhabitants of the Cabot farmhouse. "They's gold in the West," Peter Cabot says to his brother Simeon at the play's opening, and the dreams of "fields o' gold" soon draw these two characters away from this farm strewn only with stones.

— *David Peck*

THE DEVIL UPON TWO STICKS

Author: Alain-René Lesage (1668-1747)
Type of work: Novel
Type of plot: Picaresque

Time of plot: 1707
First published: Le Diable boiteux, 1707; revised 1720, 1726 (English translation, 1708)

The central notion of this novel was taken from a Spanish original, so it is apt that the story is set in Madrid. However, Alain-René Lesage is careful to make continual comparisons between Madrid and Paris to emphasize the fact that all the follies, vices, and deceptions revealed by Asmodeus are similarly endemic in Madrid, as well as every great city.

***Madrid.** Capital of Spain whose secrets are stripped bare by the grateful Asmodeus, the demon of luxury, after Don Cleofas delivers him temporarily from captivity in a phial in an alchemist's laboratory. While they look down upon the city Asmodeus makes the roofs and walls transparent so that Don Cleofas can see all the mean, lewd and ridiculous activities that people ordinarily conceal from their neighbors. Don Cleofas finds the demon while fleeing four men hired by his lover Donna Thomasa to force him to marry her, but he is somewhat surprised to learn that his own propensity for sin is not merely reflected but exaggerated in the great majority of his fellow citizens. Although Madrid is almost as grandiloquent a center of culture and civilization as Paris, its pretensions amount to little more than an architectural veneer overlaid upon barbarian motives and desires.

***Alcala.** Town northeast of Madrid, famed for its university founded by Cardinal Ximenes. Don Cleofas is a student there, as is Don Pedro de Crespides, who is likewise engaged in a romantic excursion to the city.

Don Lewis de Crespides's house (krehs-PEE-dehs). Primary setting of the first interpolated tale, which offers the back-story of the wedding taking place there. It is one of many houses from which silken ladders are let down from high balconies to enable secret lovers to climb up to the bedrooms of young ladies.

La Chicona's house (lah CHEE-koh-nah). Secondary setting of the first interpolated tale, lent by the procuress to Count Belflor in order that Leonora may be lured into the supposed sickroom where Belflor is concealed behind the curtains. La Chicona is visited there by her colleague La Penrada, who keeps a catalog of handsome foreign visitors, which she peddles to interested widows. One of her neighbors is a printer who produces libels in secret; another has a room tapestried in crimson cloth where young women flock to the bedside of an indisposed inquisitor, bearing gifts of medicine. Three doors away is the palace of a deeply indebted marquis, whose steward labors in a book-lined room to repair his master's fortunes by plagiarism.

Prison. Asmodeus and Don Cleofas follow Donna Thomasa and the survivors of the fight between her hired bravos into the prison so that Asmodeus can reveal the stories of the other people justly or unjustly confined there.

Casa de los Locos. Madhouse that provides as much raw material as the prison for Asmodeus, who delights in relating how each lunatic was driven insane—accounts which provide a new basis for assessing the mentality of many other citizens who deserve to be confined there.

Church. Splendid edifice filled with monuments to the illustrious dead, whose impostures are uncovered by Asmodeus while they lie in their tombs, or walk abroad

as phantoms, as easily as those of the living. It is after visiting it that Don Cleofas first sees Death approaching Madrid with his scythe at the ready.

Monastery de la Merci. Reception-point of three hundred Spanish slaves ransomed from Algiers by the Fathers of the Redemption, whose belated homecomings are cynically anticipated by Asmodeus.

Don Pedro de Escolano's house (PEH-droh deh ehs-koh-LAH-noh). Magnificent residence reduced to ashes by an accidental fire. The owner's offer of a huge reward for anyone who can rescue his sixteen-year-old daughter, Seraphina, provides Asmodeus with a means of rewarding the generosity of Don Cleofas.

*****Valencia.** City in eastern Spain, one of several far-flung settings featured in the interpolated tales. Other settings include Siguença, the once-independent kingdom of Castile and Mezzomorto's palace in Algeria. These are, however, far less significant than the sites included in the exemplary "cross section" of Madrid.

— Brian Stableford

THE DEVIL'S ELIXIRS: From the Posthumous Papers of Brother Medardus, a Capuchin Friar

Author: E. T. A. Hoffmann (1776-1822)
Type of work: Novel
Type of plot: Fantasy
Time of plot: Eighteenth century

First published: Die Elixiere des Teufels:
Nachgelassene Papiere des Bruders Medardus,
eines Kapuziners, 1815-1816 (English translation,
1824)

Although a few place-names are mentioned in this novel, the main events of its plot are distributed along an imaginary route drawn between Bamberg and Rome, whose tortuousness is symbolic of a confused spiritual odyssey in which the redemptive power of the Roman Catholic Church proves difficult to attain by those whose divided selves cannot avoid the sidetracks by temptation.

Holy Linden. Remote monastery in Prussia in which the monk Medardus (whose given name is Franz) spends his first eighteen months. At its center is a linden tree whose silver-covered trunk is inscribed with an image of the Virgin Mary. The colorful decorations in its chapel are the work of a mysterious foreign painter. (Hoffmann's own birthplace, Königsberg, was in Prussia).

B. Although this name is unexplained in the text, B. undoubtedly stands for **Bamberg**, the German town in

which Hoffmann worked as a theater producer from 1808 to 1813, before bankruptcy forced him to move on. It is the location of two crucial religious establishments, the first being the Cistercian convent where Franz's mother obtains refuge, near to which he spends the remainder of his childhood, and where Aurelia eventually takes the veil. The other is the Capuchin monastery where Franz becomes Brother Medardus under the tutelage of Leonardus, eventually assuming responsibility for the relic chamber, whose treasures include the diabolical wine acquired by Saint Anthony in the course of his temptation. The monastery's chapel has an altar dedicated to Saint Rosalia, which bears the image of Medardus' temptress. The monastery is the final destination of Peter Schönfeld as well as Medardus.

Baron F.'s palace. House situated in an Alpine valley where Medardus plays a dual role after seeing his *doppelgänger*, Count Victor, apparently fall to his death. There he encounters Aurelia again, recognizing her as Saint Rosalia's double. In the painter's narrative it is the location of the Blue Room where a mysterious portrait—allegedly of the Devil—hangs. When Medardus passes through the estate on his return journey he finds it neglected and decaying.

Devil's Seat. Projecting rock at the summit of an Alpine crag, which overhangs a black and seemingly bottomless pit, the **Devil's Gorge**, from which poisonous fumes rise. It is from there that Count Victor apparently falls to his death.

Inn. Tavern in an unnamed town whose sign depicts a golden lion with wings. There Medardus first encounters the barber Peter Schönfeld, alias Pietro Belcampo, and hears more news of the foreign painter.

Gamekeeper's house. Forest residence where Medardus encounters his *doppelgänger* in the guise of a mad monk.

Prince von Rosenthurm's palace. The town in which the prince's relatively modest residence is located is much smaller, quieter, and more orderly than the city. The edifice is surrounded by a charming park decorated with numerous grottos, chapels, pavilions, and temples. Here Medardus plays faro, hears tales told by the physician which explain the origin of Count Victor, and is recognized by Aurelia as her brother's murderer—although she is in a very different frame of mind when she meets him again in the park.

Prison. Room in which Medardus is confined following Aurelia's accusation. The room is not uncomfortable, but its barred window is set high, and precautions are taken to prevent him from looking out. Before his release he is taunted by the mysterious voice of his *doppelgänger* and fettered to the wall, where he suffers nightmares of torture.

Hospital. Religious establishment in Italy, administered by the Order of Hospitallers, to which Medardus is brought by Schönfeld after fleeing from his wedding, thinking that he has murdered Aurelia.

*****Rome.** Italy's leading city and center of the Roman Catholic faith, to which Medardus is sent on a pilgrimage by Leonardus. After he finally arrives there, he prays in Saint Peter's and many other churches and sees Schönfeld acting in a puppet show in the Piazza du Spagna. However, he spends far more time in a Capuchin monastery outside the city, where he finds another portrait of Aurelia as Saint Rosalia; it is there that he makes his confession and does painful penance, that he reads the wild tale of hereditary misfortune and visitations from Venus recorded in the painter's manuscript, and that he encounters his *doppelgänger* for the last time, during his return journey.

— *Brian Stableford*

DIANA OF THE CROSSWAYS

Author: George Meredith (1828-1909)
Type of work: Novel
Type of plot: Psychological realism

Time of plot: Nineteenth century
First published: 1885

The eponymous heroine of this novel owns a house called the Crossways in Sussex, England, that she struggles to hold onto through a difficult marriage, and she struggles in another kind of crossway as well, as she is torn between her English and Irish roots. The novel presents nature as a refuge and haven for personal growth, and Diana has her most important personal enlightenment while sailing and sightseeing along the Mediterranean coast.

The Crossways. Redbrick country house in Sussex, England, that is home to the protagonist, Diana Antonia Merion. The Crossways, which she has inherited at her father's recent death, is her only source of income, through rentals to tenants. The house takes its name from being near the crossroads to Brasted, London, Wickford, and Riddlehurst; it also symbolizes the transitional, or crossroads, period in Diana's life.

Keeping the Crossways is an important part of Diana's marriage agreement with her first husband, Augustus Warwick. When he loses money on the railroads, he attempts to pressure her to sell the house, but she instead arranges a government position for him because of her friendship with the influential Lord Dannisburgh. That relationship leads to accusations of adultery and Diana's separation from Warwick. She escapes to the Crossways when the pressures of the divorce case become too great. In the end, her attempt to become a novelist fails, and she is forced to sell the Crossways. Until near the end of the novel, she is unaware that she will be able to keep the Crossways, after all, for the man she is about to marry, Thomas Redworth, is the secret purchaser of the house.

Copsley. Country home of Lady Emma Dunstane, Diana's surrogate mother figure, located in Sussex, near the Crossways. Diana socializes at Copsley, where she experiences the love and friendship of Lady Emma. Lady Emma's feelings about nature are contrasted to Diana's because she is an invalid and because she does not enjoy living in a secluded rural setting. Symbolically, she has no need for the sublime qualities of nature because she is already married and thereby, in Victorian terms, fulfilled. In contrast, Diana is still seeking marital happiness and fulfillment. Various characters, including Diana, walk the grounds and sail the property's lake, which gives them the chance to be renewed by contact with nature.

*London. Capital city of Great Britain, in which Diana lives during her marriage to Warwick and after her separation. Their London house represents Diana's imprisonment in a loveless marriage, as she is required only to be beautiful, to be witty, and to entertain important male friends of her husband. After Diana and Warwick separate, Warwick remains in the London house and later dies from complications of a stroke. Meanwhile, Diana takes up residence in another London house that she cannot afford to maintain as she attempts to launch a writing career. This second house also becomes a prison to her.

Clarissa. Yacht on which Diana sails on the Mediterranean Sea with her friends after her divorce trial ends. The cruise gives her a chance to reflect on what has happened and what she wants to do with her life, now that she is free of Warwick. She joins Thomas Redworth in Cairo, with Sir Percy Dacier, nephew to Lord Dannisburgh, and Dacier falls in love with her.

*Italy. Country that Diana visits during her Mediterranean cruise. There she travels along the shores of Lake Como and Lake Lugano, below the Italian Alps, a region that Meredith prized for its restorative powers and exquisite beauty. There, Diana finds herself "reawakened, after a trance of a deadly draught, to the glory of the earth and her share in it" merely by hiking in the mountains, picking flowers, eating local food, and spending time alone in nature.

Meredith found it unnecessary to explain why British travelers went abroad, taking for granted readers' knowledge and experiences of the Grand Tour of the Continent, as well as the class-based expectation that going abroad provided personal growth. Diana experiences nature both as a spiritual force and as a loving companion. Her sensibilities and the narrator's descriptions of the landscapes mirror the expressions of Meredith's nature-themed verse, as the narrator states, for example, "Lugano is the Italian lake most lovingly encircled by mountain arms." Later, while Diana is struggling to write novels in London, she fantasizes about "flying straight to her beloved Lugano lake, and there hiding, abandoning her friends, casting off the slave's name she bore, and living free in spirit."

*Ireland. Country from which Diana's father comes. As an Anglo-Irish person, Diana is torn between the England of her mother and the Ireland of her father. She describes herself as Irish in the novel, and many of her political opinions support government policies that should be favorable to Ireland. When she is about to marry Redworth, she remarks, "Old Ireland won't repent it" as she sees "Old England" (Redworth) coming to greet her. Diana gains a new home in Dublin as Redworth is named Irish secretary, giving her the happiness she seeks.

— *Beverly Schneller*

THE DIARY OF A COUNTRY PRIEST

Author: Georges Bernanos (1888-1948)
Type of work: Novel
Type of plot: Psychological realism

Time of plot: 1920's
First published: Journal d'un curé de campagne, 1936
(English translation, 1937)

Although the principal setting of this novel is a small village in northern France, the real location of all that happens is the soul of the parish priest; the places of his short public life, Ambricourt and Lille, reflect his spiritual journey from suffering to salvation.

Ambricourt. (ahm-breh-kohrt). French parish located on a hillside whose priest sees its miserable little insignificant houses huddled together as a symptom of Christianity in decay. Like the village, the lives of its people seem consumed by boredom. He unfavorably contrasts the place where he will live out his vocation with a Carthusian cloister, where monks create an island of order in the midst of a sea of chaos. His parish is poor, but its poverty is not evangelical, unlike the poverty of Jesus Christ, and the few wealthy parishioners conceal their greed beneath a facade of false humanism, and so their wealth never manifests its full cruelty.

Parish church. Like the village, the parish church and the priest's lodging are coarse and poor. He needs to pay a boy to fetch water for him since he has no well, and his food consists mainly of bread and inferior wine. The church, with its broken windowpanes, is where the priest says mass and encounters the broken lives of his parishioners. The church school, where he catechizes the parish's children, becomes another place of alienation since his young charges are either bored or cruel. Despite his sufferings in dealing with all his parishioners, he sees his parish as part of the everlasting presence of Christ in the world. Like all human communities, Ambricourt is caught in the great spiritual river sweeping all souls into the deep ocean of eternity.

Château. Estate of a count and countess where the central struggle of the novel occurs. Walled and gated, the château stands on a heavily wooded hill, where the priest sees it as turning its back on the village and all its people. Although the château represents a life of privilege and prosperity, the priest discovers there lives of great spiritual poverty. The count is involved in an adulterous relationship with his daughter's governess, and his daughter is so unhappy over her father's affair that she threatens suicide or murder. The countess, whose life has been broken by the death of her son, has withdrawn into a cold hatred of humanity and God. Through a long, agonistic conversation, the young priest is able to break through the wall of isolation that the countess has constructed around her. She becomes reconciled to God, and during the night, after the priest leaves, the countess dies. The priest walks back to his church along Paradise Lane, a muddy pathway between hedges.

*****Lille** (leel). City in northern France where the parish priest's odyssey ends. Lille is a major industrial area, but it, like Ambricourt, is infected with a malaise and indifference to the spiritual life. The priest travels to Lille to consult a doctor about his severe stomach pains, which have been accompanied by the vomiting of blood. Though the city, with its ordered streets and elaborate buildings, offices, and residences, stands in stark contrast to Ambricourt's poverty, the priest finds the city similarly alienating. He feels confused while wandering its streets, just as he has confused the name of the doctor he was supposed to see. The physician he does see, a drug addict, bluntly diagnoses the priest's problem as stomach cancer.

The final place in the priest's life is the decrepit lodgings of a former priest, a friend from his seminary years, who is now a commercial traveler living with a mistress. The priest reaches his friend's apartment by climbing a dark staircase, and the former priest provides him with a camping bed set up not in a room but in a narrow passageway that smells of drug samples. The place is one of ugliness and loneliness, but the priest seems to lose himself in this foulness and misery, the only shelter in his misfortune. As he dies, his friend hears the young priest's final exclamation of his faith.

— Robert J. Paradowski

THE DINING ROOM

Author: A. R. Gurney, Jr. (1930-   )
Type of work: Drama
Type of plot: Comedy

Time of plot: Approximately 1930 to 1980
First performed: 1982; first published, 1982

Because every scene in this play takes place in a dining room, the room takes on a symbolic function as it unifies the characters and illustrates their common struggles.

Dining room. Formal dining room in an upper-class or upper-middle-class home in an unspecific place in the United States. Although the play's eighteen scenes involve eighteen different sets of characters conversing in eighteen different houses, A. R. Gurney's stage directions call for one set of dining-room furniture—a table, some chairs, and a sideboard—to shape the room for all of the scenes. The room, therefore, has symbolic value beyond mere setting: It demonstrates that although the groups of characters are individual, they are also bound together through a commonality. Whatever the small or large dramas of their lives, they are all a part of a larger culture, bound by the same conventions and rules, and sitting at a common table.

From the opening scene, Gurney points out that the people who inhabit these dining rooms are part of a culture on the wane. The client and the agent both admire the dining room, but the client realizes that he will never use it. In the second scene, Sally and Arthur both long for their mother's dining-room set as a symbol of their cherished past. The third scene shows a father trying to raise his children to be the sort of people who eat in dining rooms, and the fourth shows a woman who has returned to school against her husband's wishes. She has dared to use his mother's dining-room table to type on. For these characters and for many others, the dining room itself represents the pull of tradition and family against the new demands of modern life.

— *Cynthia A. Bily*

THE DISCIPLE

Author: Paul Bourget (1852-1935)
Type of work: Novel
Type of plot: Philosophical realism

Time of plot: Late nineteenth century
First published: Le Disciple, 1889 (English translation, 1898)

The objective quality of the rural landscapes described in this novel is less important than the way they are viewed; they are informed with a particularly powerful set of meanings by the scientific attitudes of Robert Greslon and his father, but they also retain a certain stubborn symbolic significance. Paris, by contrast, is described almost entirely in terms of the social connections embodied in its streets and districts.

*****Paris.** Capital of France. The chief Parisian locale featured in the novel is the Rue Guy de Brosse, where Adrien Sixte lives, and its immediate environs. The Rue Guy de Brosse connects the Rue de Jussieu to Rue Linné, at the heart of a humble but respectable district bordered by the Jardin des Plantes and Hospital de la Pitié. Sixte's fourth-floor apartment commands a good view of Père-la-Chaise, Orléans station, and the dome of La Saltpétrière, as well as the Jardin des Plantes, but the last-named is by far the most important; Sixte often takes long walks through the gardens, often as far as Notre-Dame, and his relationship with Robert Greslon is firmly grounded there.

Other Parisian locations briefly but significantly featured in the novel include the Palais de Justice, where Sixte is interrogated by Valette regarding his relationship with Robert, and the Hôtel de Sermoises in the Rue de Chanaleilles, where the Marquise de Jussat, her sister and Charlotte take up residence for a while.

*Clermont-Ferrand. Capital of the department of Puy-de-Dôme in the Auvergne mountains of central France. Robert spends his early life there, in a house built of Volvic stone, whose grey darkens with age to give the city itself a rather a forbidding aspect. Because the house is near the railway station Robert grows up haunted by the whistling of trains. Within the house, Robert's father—an engineer—draws formulas on blackboards and writes at an architect's table; he has a clock in the form of a geographical globe and astronomical maps—but his study looks out over the plain of the Limagne, bounded in the distance by the mountains of Forez, and he loves to walk in the surrounding countryside. Robert and his father undertake frequent long excursions, following paths to Puy de Crouël, Gergovie, Royat, Durtol, Beaumont, and Gravenoire, where the elder Greslon's scientific knowledge illuminates the landscape, giving names to everything and explaining the natural roles of animate and inanimate entities. The meaning this landscape has for Robert changes completely after his father's death because his mother—who has previously only taken him to mass at the Church of Capuchins—does not know the names of the flowers and thinks all insects are filthy and venomous; this is the beginning of Robert's philosophical isolation.

Château Jussat-Randon. Country house on the shore of Lake Aydat, near the former capital of Puy-de-Dôme, the town of Riom (situated nine miles north of Clermont-Ferrand). Robert goes there after obtaining a position as a tutor to the marquis' younger son, Lucien; his manuscript describes the surrounding landscape several times, most memorably when his unrequited love for Charlotte has driven him almost to despair—at which time the lake is thinly sheeted with ice, majestically encircled by snow-capped volcanic mountains, their slopes darkened by the forest of Rouillet. The château is not far from the village of Saint-Saturnin, from which it is separated by Pradat wood, where Robert and Charlotte are briefly lost. The later scenes of the novel are mostly set in Riom, where Robert is charged with Charlotte's murder; after his acquittal he meets his mother and Sixte in the Hôtel de Commerce, where Charlotte's older brother André shoots and kills him.

*Nancy. City in northeastern France that is the birthplace and residence of Adrien Sixte until he moves to Paris in 1872 after death of his father, mother, and aunt. Although Nancy and the family residence are not described in any detail, the fact that Sixte's father was a watchmaker is as crucial to the development of Sixte's character as the fact that Robert's father was an engineer. Fortunately or unfortunately, Sixte's father did not have the same love of the countryside as Robert's, thus confining him to an abstracted and thoroughly mechanical way and view of life.

— *Brian Stableford*

THE DIVINE COMEDY

Author: Dante Alighieri (1265-1321)
Type of work: Poetry
Type of plot: Allegory

Time of plot: The Friday before Easter, 1300
First transcribed: La divina commedia, c. 1320
(English translation, 1802)

Midway through his life, Dante takes this imaginary excursion through Hell, Purgatory, and Heaven. Even the name "comedy" derives from the place where the action culminates, "the endless bliss of Heaven." Dante chose the title in accord with Aristotle's classic definition of comedy; others, reflecting upon the monumental achievement, would add "divine." The poem's diction also springs from its milieux. Instead of the elevated language of Latin, Dante chose to write in the vernacular tongue of his native Tuscany. Two-thirds of this narrative takes place in Hell and Purgatory, and it is not surprising that the sinners there use words that sometimes shock the reader. In the third part of his comedy, which takes place in Paradise itself, Dante goes on to prove that the most sublime poetry could also be written in his mother tongue.

Hell. Dante begins his journey in the grim nether regions. "Abandon hope all ye who enter in," is inscribed on the gates of Hell. With Vergil, the most noble of pagans, as his guide, Dante enters the concentric circles of Hell, where sinners are mired eternally in the crimes that have brought them there. Each punishment cruelly fits the sin. Sowers of discord are eternally rent asunder by demons; violent souls steep forever in streams of blood. There are degrees of punishment in Hell. On the outer regions of Hell, swept perpetually by a whirlwind, Dante finds the tragic adulterous lovers from his own time, Paolo and Francesco. The depths of Hell are reserved for the most heinous of sinners, those who betrayed their masters. Here Dante finds Judas and Brutus, frozen in the Devil's mouth.

The Divine Comedy provides not only a poetic summa of the literature, philosophy, and religion of the Middle Ages, but a medieval Christian interpretation of all human history. Borrowing freely from Ptolemaic cosmology and the speculations of Church leaders, Dante also found the epic poets, particularly Homer and Vergil, enlightening when it came to describing the realm of the dead. Only here could Dante freely mingle fictional personalities from earlier literature with semilegendary characters from epics and real figures from the Italian city states. Only within this locale, constructed from his borrowings and own dreams and visions, could he hope to succeed in his acknowledged goals: to compose a Christian epic celebrating Italian civilization; and to honor Beatrice, the woman he had loved from childhood.

Purgatory. The pangs of purgatory are mitigated by hope. All souls here will eventually be released. Some of these penitent shades discourse on the transience of human fame and the vanity of human wishes. Others answer Dante's questions about free will and the influence of the stars upon earthly lives. Amazingly, even in this place, despite the urgency of purgation, the affairs of the Italian city states remain pressing, and several of these penitents have political discourse with the visiting poets. Dante uses the unique setting not only to exercise his satiric vision but to air some of his own political opinions.

Paradise. Final destination in Dante's journey—heaven, a place of perfect happiness, populated by saints, that calls on Dante to employ all of his powers to make interesting. In Paradise, Vergil is no longer Dante's guide, having had the misfortune to be born shortly before the redeeming advent of Christ. Beatrice now takes his place. Paradise thus becomes the only setting in which Dante could truly have absorbed the great lesson of Christian neo-Platonism. On earth he had worshiped this woman from childhood, and she had inspired his art, even after her death. To see her again in Paradise had been his abiding hope. Yet as he progresses through the Heavens—meeting apostles, doctors of the Church, the Virgin Mary herself—Beatrice's own presence slowly fades and at last Dante is able to perceive the ultimate reality toward which Beatrice's image has always beckoned. He is to contemplate the radiance of Divinity and to submerge himself in the most ecstatic of mysteries, the Triune God and the God-Man.

— *Allene Phy-Olsen*

THE DIVINE FIRE

Author: May Sinclair (1863-1946)
Type of work: Novel
Type of plot: Psychological

Time of plot: 1890's
First published: 1904

This novel takes place primarily in two London locations: a boardinghouse in Bloomsbury and the ancestral home of the Harden family. Through these limited settings, the novel develops a contrast between the urban, or suburban, and the rural. The young writer Savage Keith Rickman begins his poetic career writing Decadent-style lyrics inspired by his urban environment, but he eventually moves on to more pastoral sources of inspiration. The city is the site of suffering, poverty, disease, and stifled creativity, while the country provides a healthy environment that inspires intellectual and creative freedom.

Court House. Home of Lucia Harden; an idealized English country estate in Harmouth that contains the valuable Harden Library. After Lucia's father dies in Italy heavily in debt, she sells the library at an undervalued low price to the father of the gifted young poet Savage Keith Rickman, who then begins an eight-year quest to earn enough money to return the library to its rightful owner and nearly dies from starvation and overwork in the process. At Court House, Rickman discovers both his love for Lucia and, simultaneously, his greatest poetic inspiration. The emergence of this inspiration in a rural, natural environment establishes an urban/pastoral motif that runs throughout the novel.

*London.** City in which Keith Rickman and several other characters live and work. It is often referred to throughout the novel as simply "the City." Rickman's poetic inspiration, like many of the so-called Decadent poets of the 1890's, comes first from the urban environment of London. Rickman both works and socializes within the world of literary magazines and journalism on Fleet Street, where petty rivalries between the editor of *The Planet* and the editor of *Metropolis* damage Rickman's potential literary success. Gossip about Rickman is often circulated at the Junior Journalists' Club, an organization of newspapermen, editors, and literary critics located in the Strand. The city also represents the source of Rickman's struggles between his artistic genius and various mundane requirements: his moral obligations to others, financial security, and his desire for physical love.

Rickman's Book Store. Bookstore owned by Isaac Rickman, Keith's father, that is located in the Strand, an area of London known for its publishing houses and bookstores. Poorly lit and oppressive, the store has a strong odor of old books. Early in the novel, Keith is torn between his poetic career and his familial obligations to his father's business. His father has built a successful business and secure reputation selling new and rare books to the London literati, thanks in large part to Keith's unfailing judgment in appraising books. However, his business begins to fail after he has a falling out with Keith over his purchase of the Harden Library. After he dies, Keith inherits both the store and the debt incurred through the mortgaging of the Harden Library, which he must pay off in order to salvage the library for Lucia.

*Bloomsbury.** London suburb known for its close-knit artistic community in the early part of the twentieth century. After Rickman's work at Court House is completed, the novel shifts location to Mrs. Downey's boardinghouse on Tavistock Place. Mrs. Downey imagines that her boarders represent the elite of London intellectual society, with Rickman as her house's jewel, and she fashions her dinners and nightly gatherings as cultural events. Rickman is eventually reunited here with Lucia when she makes an extended visit to her former tutor, Miss Roots, another boarder at the house. Rickman's later physical decline, when he commits almost all of his finances to the recovery the Harden Library, is marked by his progressively diminishing living arrangements, from the boardinghouse in Bloomsbury to a cheap attic room on Howland Street that he shares with a prostitute.

*Hampstead.** Fashionable northwestern suburb of London in which Horace Jewdwine, the editor of the successful literary periodical *The Metropolis*, lives. His gracious accommodations contrast with Rickman's decline into poverty.

*Ealing.** London suburb where Rickman buys a house for his planned marriage to Flossie, whom he meets in the boardinghouse. After Flossie breaks off the engagement, Rickman maintains the house as a small source of rental income, and he and Lucia eventually decide to live there at the end of the novel.

— *Andrew J. Kunka*

DIVING INTO THE WRECK

Author: Adrienne Rich (1929-   )   *First published:* 1973
Type of work: Poetry

Not only Adrienne Rich's personal birthplace but also the region that was the birthplace of a nation, the eastern states, including Ohio and New York, are used as reference points for the poetic landscape of this collection.

Moreover, the poetry is inclusive, using common yet universal symbols of place, such as river, sea, and cave, to embrace all its readers.

*New York subway. "The Phenomenology of Anger" describes the subway of New York City moving toward Brooklyn. The journey through the speaker's anger takes place against the city landscape, while "walking on Broadway," or while riding the subway. The dreamlike state depicted in the poem dramatizes the female psyche that Rich is determined to awaken.

*Southern Ohio. In "When We Dead Awaken," the phrase "lovely landscape of southern Ohio" is juxtaposed against the devastation left by strip mining, which the region has had to endure. The mining process is used as a metaphor for the stripping away of female power. Moreover, the area becomes a place of betrayal.

Wrecked ship. Ruins of a wrecked ship at the bottom of the sea are explored in "Diving into the Wreck," the title poem of the collection. Although it is not named, the Atlantic Ocean is probably the sea that houses the wreck that the speaker of the poem explores. The wreck and the sea are not named because they must be inclusive, not exclusive. The primary symbol of the poem, representing unrecovered female history, seeks to identify with all its readers, as the final stanza reinforces: "We are, I am, you are/ . . . a book of myths/ in which/ our names do not appear."

— Cynthia S. Becerra

DOCTOR FAUSTUS: The Life of the German Composer
Adrian Leverkühn as Told by a Friend

Author: Thomas Mann (1875-1955)
Type of work: Novel
Type of plot: Philosophical
Time of plot: 1885-1945

First published: Doktor Faustus: Das Leben des deutschen Tonsetzers Adrian Leverkühn, erzählt von einem Freunde, 1947 (English translation, 1948)

The novel depicts a panorama of Germany from its farms and forests to its towns and cities from 1885 to 1945. The countryside is pristine and beautiful and urban life is refined, creative, and intellectual. Beneath it all lurks a demoniac force that undermines Germany and corrupts the composer Adrian Leverkühn. As Serenus Zeitblom is writing his biography of Adrian, Germany is near military defeat at the end of World War II. With rats grown fat on corpses in the rubble, Germany is a landscape of hell.

Buchel (BEW-shihl) Family farm on which Adrian was born in the heart of Germany, not far from Weissenfels. It is an idyllic German farm with abundant land and forest to sustain three generations of the Leverkühn family. In typical German fashion, the timberwork residence, barns, and stalls are built together to form a courtyard. In the middle is a giant old linden, a Germanic symbol of the cosmic tree at the center of the world connecting heaven and earth.

For ten years, Adrian and his friend Serenus play with the farm animals, feast on wild berries and blossoms, swim in a pond, and hike to the top of a hill. It is an edenic picture of German country life. Yet there is

something eerie about the charm of Buchel. Adrian's father has a streak of a morbid magician. The buxom dairymaid teaches the boys gruesome folk songs. Adrian has an odd disturbing laugh. As Serenus suggests, beauty conceals poison.

Buchel is Adrian's cradle and grave. In the care of his loving mother, he spends the final ten years of his life at his home debilitated and lost to the world.

Kaisersaschern (KI-zurz-AHSH-urn). German town to which Adrian moves to attend school, about thirty miles from Buchel. Kaisersaschern, whose name means the "emperor's ashes"—namely those of Otto III—is a composite of several German towns but is most similar to Lübeck, Mann's birthplace and home in northern Germany. It is a modern commercial and industrial town of 27,000 inhabitants at a major railway junction and along the river Saale, the lifeblood of the area. At the core of Kaisersaschern is the medieval: a cathedral, a castle, faithfully preserved residences, and storehouses. Behind this picturesque facade lurks the medieval spirit of irrationality, superstition, magic, insanity, torture—in a word, the demoniac. Serenus traces the political catastrophe of Nazism to the hysteria of the dying Middle Ages especially evidenced in the practices of zealot Christians. In Kaisersaschern as in all of Germany, the past is only veneered with the present. The devil tells Adrian, "Where I am, there is Kaisersaschern." In other words, the town represents a general psychic malaise in Germany, one that infects Adrian's mind for the rest of his life.

After schooling in Kaisersaschern, Adrian studies theology with a concentration on the devil at the university in the nearby medieval city, Halle along the Saale. In Leipzig, Adrian studies music and has his fateful encounter with Esmeralda, the prostitute from whom he voluntarily gets a venereal infection.

Schweigestill (schwi-geh-STIHL). Fictional baroque cloister converted into a boardinghouse close to the fictional town of Pfeiffering, modeled on Polling, a village among the hills of Bavaria. While living in Munich, Adrian discovers the place on one of his expeditions into the countryside. After his encounter with the devil in Palestrina, Italy, he retreats to Schweigestill in part because it resembles Buchel with a pond, a bench on a hill, a house with courtyard, and an old giant tree. The landlords are like his parents and their dog like his own.

As well as an escape into his childhood, Schweigestill also provides Adrian with a sinister retreat. For the next eighteen years, he composes his most important works in an abbot's study similar in ambiance to the one in which the medieval Faust conjured the devil and performed his magic.

Schweigestill means to keep silent and still, to be discreet and even to conceal. It represents Adrian's seclusion and his diabolical secret. Ostensibly for a performance of a new composition, *The Lamentation of Dr. Faustus*, Adrian invites thirty prominent friends and acquaintances to Schweigestill, who gather in a large formal hall with a massive table, deep window nooks, and a plaster Winged Victory of Samothrace. Instead, Adrian announces his pact with the devil. During his confession, he breaks down upon the brown square piano and never recovers his sanity or health. The devil has exacted his price.

— *David Partenheimer*

DOCTOR FAUSTUS

Author: Christopher Marlowe (1564-1593)
Type of work: Drama
Type of plot: Tragedy

Time of plot: Sixteenth century
First performed: c. 1588; first published, 1604

Faustus is a medieval scholar, and as such he requires the attributes of the scholarly existence. This entails the fixed sedentary existence of the scholar's room—his study and books and related context—a campus atmosphere. He moves away from this as he gains power but returns after satisfying the range of his modest imaginings.

Faustus's study (FOWS-tuhs). Lodgings at Germany's University of Wittenberg of Dr. Faustus, a learned scholar and theologian who seeks boundless knowledge. Most of the play takes place here. Characters enter and exit the study frequently, and on many occasions, other characters converse in Faustus's rooms while he is away. The study is faintly described—it contains books of various sorts, and presumably the paraphernalia of scholarly and clerical work. It is a large area, sufficient to entertain as many as nine characters at a time. The fact that the specific university is Wittenberg may be correlated to the fact that it was in this city that

Martin Luther posted his ninety-five theses, heralding the Protestant separation from the Roman Catholic Church and the beginning of the Reformation.

Fantastic travels. At the outset of the third act, the chorus informs the audience that Faustus has traveled above the clouds, on dragons, to see the world from a higher perspective. Faustus notes that he has traveled from Wittenberg through Naples and Campania. Later, he chooses to walk rather than rely on demoniac magic.

*****Papal palace.** Court of the pope in Rome, the seat of the spiritual power of the Roman Catholic Church. Mephistophilis, the agent of the devil that Faustus calls forth, magically transports Faustus to the privy chamber of the pope. In addition to holding audience with male-factors, the pope has dinner brought into the room. Faustus and Mephistophilis hide and wear the clothes of cardinals, and later Faustus becomes invisible and plays tricks on the pope.

Court of German emperor. Seat of political power where Faustus is feasted and treated well by Germany's Emperor Charles. In making sport of some of the retainers, Faustus angers them and they try to waylay him in a suggested outdoor setting. Other scenes also suggest the use of the stage area to imply outdoor or rural settings. Faustus's high aspirations take him to select and rarefied locales, but he returns from these to the byways and rooms of the commons.

— *Scott D. Vander Ploeg*

DOCTOR PASCAL

Author: Émile Zola (1840-1902)
Type of work: Novel
Type of plot: Naturalism

Time of plot: Late nineteenth century
First published: Le Docteur Pascal, 1893 (English translation, 1893)

This novel portrays the domestic life of a doctor and his young new wife up to the time of the doctor's death. Set in the French provincial capital Aix-en-Provence, the novel takes full advantage of the various hues and shades of Aix's fountains and squares, as well as the surrounding countryside, to depict a calmness in the relatively secure life of the residents of the city.

Soleiade (sal-ayd). Aix-en-Provence residence of Doctor Pascal, located about fifteen minutes by foot from the Cathedral of St. Sauveur, and the center of the town's diverse social life. The novel's descriptions of the home are filled with the warm contrasts between shadows and light, stone and vegetation, so characteristic of the private lives of its occupants. More important than the interior, usually closed off from the sun, is Soleiade's terraces and balconies overlooking the garden, where Pascal and his niece Clotilde spend a good part of their time.

*****Aix-Plassans** (aks-plah-SANZ). Quarter of Aix-en-Provence in which Pascal lives; it looks out on the beginnings of the countryside, which offers Pascal and Clotilde a refuge from daily social contacts during their frequent strolls. The soft valley of Plassans seems timeless, shaded by century-old cypress trees. As the region opens onto the countryside, the yellowness of its dusty soil recalls again the contrasts between shade and light. As for Aix-Plassans itself, Émile Zola probably chose this quarter because of his own father's association with it, as an architect and builder of a prominent town fountain.

*****La Viorne** (vjorn). Stream running through Aix-Plassans that is visible from the outer terrace of Doctor Pascal's residence. Its shaded banks seem to draw the viewer's attention away from the stone architecture and fountains of the city's squares and toward one of Zola's favorite symbols of the Provençal countryside, the immense horizon arching over the rocky sides of the many valleys, none famous enough to be known to the outsider, but bearing names familiar to the town's inhabitants.

*****Aix-en-Provence** (AK-sahn-proh-vahns). Old city north of Marseilles in southeastern France. Although Aix-en-Provence has many architectural attractions that

318 / *Doctor Thorne*

make Pascal's residential quarter pale by comparison, Zola concentrates on the single image of the city's cathedral. The area around Aix, because of its natural beauty and the varied hues of its soil, rocks, and valleys, draws his protagonists most often into the countryside.

***Mount Sainte Victoire** (sant vik-TWAHR). Craggy mountain outcropping jutting up in the distance northeast of Aix-en-Provence that is visible from most parts of the city's outskirts. Sainte Victoire's shadows and gleaming rockface were captured on canvas by Impressionist painter Paul Cezanne.

***Cathedral of St. Sauveur** (sant sah-vewr). Prominent medieval church in the traditional center of Aix-en-Provence whose splendid stone carved facade and belfries seem to represent an almost physical force drawing both the eyes and social activities of the town's residents. Zola mentions the church in almost every section of his novel.

***Route de Nice** (nees). Panoramic roadway leading eastward from Aix-en-Provence through the long valleys separating the rocky chestnut- and pine-forested interior from the Mediterranean coastal range. The road seems to represent the direction toward which Zola's characters turn their view if they think of the world beyond. It is, however, the road itself, with its shades of light and colors that is depicted, not its travelers' distant destinations.

***Marseille** (mar-SAY). Port city on the Mediterranean. Although not very distant from Aix-en-Provence, this busy urban port seems to belong to another world entirely. On the occasions when Pascal travels there on professional business, there seems to be an interruption in the novel's rich Provençal imagery, leaving readers with no more than the city's name to imagine how distinct it is from Aix.

— *Byron D. Cannon*

DOCTOR THORNE

Author: Anthony Trollope (1815-1882)
Type of work: Novel
Type of plot: Domestic realism

Time of plot: Mid-nineteenth century
First published: 1858

In this novel of political, economic, and class divisions, locales serve to establish boundary lines that separate the De Courcy, Gresham, Scatcherd, and Thorne families, whose homes themselves are not entirely distinguishable from one another. The attitudes emanating from within the homes become representative of each setting's role in the plot. Estate values, ranging from "old money" to "scant money" to "new and plentiful money," are inextricably interwoven with moral values as the characters frequently travel to and from one another's homes.

Greshamsbury Court. Ancient ancestral home of the Gresham family in Anthony Trollope's fictional **Barsetshire**. Despite extreme economic hardship, the home represents Barsetshire's wealthy landowners. To pay his debts, Squire Gresham sells one-third of his estate to Roger Scatcherd. Gresham welcomes nonaristocrats to Greshamsbury, in which the penniless orphan Mary Thorne is long treated almost as one of the Gresham children. Even Scatcherd, the wealthy but alcoholic stonemason, is not shunned by the squire.

The squire's son, Frank, is heir to the Gresham title and estate, but he comes to hate Greshamsbury and his obligation to marry money to avoid financial ruin. If in-

heriting the family means losing Mary's love, he prefers to reject it and instead become a lawyer, doctor, or farmer. Frank sees Greshamsbury as a burden; Mary sees it as a home no longer welcoming to her. To the squire, the estate symbolizes his failure to protect Frank's inheritance.

Greshamsbury stands as a barometer of the characters' attitudes. Like De Courcy Castle, Greshamsbury falters and nearly crumbles while its finances and pedigree are controlled by Squire and Lady Gresham. Unlike De Courcy Castle's undiluted aristocracy, however, Greshamsbury is revived by a healthy mix of people with and without social pedigrees, old wealth, or newly inherited wealth. The involvement of Mary, Dr. Thorne, and Roger Scatcherd rescues Greshamsbury from ruin. As Greshamsbury's newest owner, Mary returns it to the Gresham family instead of using it for revenge.

De Courcy Castle. Ancestral Barsetshire home of the noble, wealthy, and highly pedigreed De Courcy family. The estate symbolizes one extreme of social attitude—nobility and superiority over others, an unyielding adherence to rigid standards of class distinction. The castle's presence is additionally required as a mechanism for bringing Frank Gresham and Miss Dunstable together, until Frank realizes that he values true love over wealth and social standing.

Located in West Barsetshire, the castle is seen by Frank as "dull" and a "huge brick pile." It appears anachronistic, uninviting, and architecturally unimpressive. Forced by his aunt and mother to visit De Courcy Castle in the hope that he will fall in love with wealthy Miss Dunstable, Frank regards the castle as the embodiment of barrenness of heart. There, he is expected to forget his true love for Mary Thorne and marry the much older heiress, thereby restoring the requisite wealth and position to Greshamsbury.

De Courcy Castle's apparent coldness resurfaces when Augusta Gresham later seeks cousin Amelia De Courcy's wisdom concerning Mr. Gazebee, a young attorney; from within the castle's emotional sterility, Amelia counsels Augusta to reject Gazebee's proposal because he is merely a laborer, not a landed nobleman. (Ironically, Amelia later realizes the value of Gazebee's character and marries him herself.)

Gatherum Castle. Satirically named home of the duke of Omnium and the site of Frank Gresham's disillusionment with upper-class manners. Frank sees the castle as a grand, oversized, fancy, but usually uninhabited shell of a home. Through his eyes, readers see that—like the aristocracy—Gatherum Castle is magnificent and noble when seen from a distance, but up close it lacks any inviting warmth or the simple courtesies of human interaction. Frank desires neither such a home nor such a social circle as those represented by Gatherum.

Boxall Hill. Estate of Roger Scatcherd that is literally and metaphorically the halfway point between Greshamsbury and the city of **Barchester**. Formerly constituting one-third of the Greshamsbury estate, Boxall Hill becomes Scatcherd's property as repayment for his loan to the squire. The ownership shift, and the relative ease with which it takes place, marks the Gresham family's gradually changing attitudes. Significantly, Boxall Hill lies directly between two extremes of locale and of status. As the home's new owner, Scatcherd is as comfortable with wealth as with the working classes, and in owning such a home sets an example for the "laboring classes" and the upper classes alike.

After Scatcherd's death, Boxall Hill provides a sanctuary to Mary Thorne, who moves in with Lady Scatcherd briefly when she is exiled from Greshamsbury. Away from the tensions and aristocratic posings of Greshamsbury, Mary relaxes enough to accept Frank's marriage proposal. However, the comfort and sanctuary she finds at Boxall Hill are greatly diminished with the return of prodigal son Louis Scatcherd, who shares his father's dangerous alcoholism. After Louis dies, Mary inherits Boxall Hill, and it later becomes her and Frank's permanent home, still representing a comfortable midpoint between two extremes of class distinction.

— *Cherie Castillo*

DOCTOR ZHIVAGO

Author: Boris Leonidovich Pasternak (1890-1960)
Type of work: Novel
Type of plot: Social realism

Time of plot: 1903-1943
First published: 1957 (English translation, 1958)

This panoramic depiction of the Russian Revolution dwells on the impact of this upheaval on a few highly educated and sensitive characters, presenting an intellectual, almost spiritual view of the conflict through their experiences.

*Moscow. Russia's greatest city, in which the two most important families in the novel, the Zhivagos and the Gromekos, lead a life of privilege. Yuri Zhivago, the son of a late profligate millionaire, is a young doctor with a bright future. Tonia Alexandrovna, a friend of his early youth and his future wife, belongs to a well-to-do family with an estate in the Ural Mountains. Zhivago is bent on ministering to the needy, while Tonia is a typical wife in love with her husband and supporting him in every way. There is another woman, Lara, whom Zhivago meets coincidentally in Moscow during a patient visit. He gradually falls in love with Lara, who comes from an impoverished family. She is drawn into a love affair with an older man, a lawyer named Khomarovsky, whom she tries to kill at a Christmas party given by another well-to-do family. Thus the paths of the two classes—the wealthy upper class and that of the poorer inhabitants of Moscow—are interwoven, auguring the fateful events that eventually overwhelm Russia. Through the depiction of the affair between Yuri and Lara, Pasternak shows the diverse makeup of Moscow along with the willingness of a member of the upper class to mix freely with those less privileged.

When revolution reaches Moscow, the well-to-do citizens are threatened with a loss of their privileges. In addition to shortages and deprivations of all kinds, homes and apartments are requisitioned by the military, and the Gromekos are forced to squeeze into two rooms of their spacious house. Yuri and Tonia are finally forced to leave Moscow and travel to their family estate in the Ural Mountains, again underscoring the difference between the Zhivagos' stature and that of the revolutionaries, most of whom come from the lower classes. When they return to Moscow much later, separately and at different times, they find that their old way of life has come to an end. Tonia and her family emigrate to France, while Yuri dies of a heart attack in a packed Moscow trolley, symbolizing suffocation under the new communist rule.

Varykino (vah-RAH-kee-no). Country estate belonging to Tonia Zhivago's family in the Ural Mountains. The Zhivagos find peace and serenity at the beautiful estate in the Russian countryside. However, because of the revolution swirling around them, Yuri and Tonia are forced to raise their own crops, a departure from their easy lifestyle in Moscow. Moreover, Yuri, a poet since his student days, returns to writing, inspired not only by the beauty of the surrounding countryside but also by the dramatic, often dangerous events taking place around them. It is the last home Yuri and Tonia share and the place where Yuri and Lara later separate permanently. The heavy snow covering the mansion and the howling wolves, who draw nearer and nearer each night, epitomize the isolation of the Zhivagos and the perils of the encroaching revolution.

Yuriatin (yur-YA-teen). Fictitious town in the central part of the Ural Mountains. It is the final stop after the Zhivagos' long journey from Moscow. It is also the native town of Lara, who plays a fateful role in Yuri's life. The similarity of Yuri's name with the first part of the town's name is not coincidental. The name "Yuri" is equivalent to "George," and Yuri is equated to St. George, who was reputed to have bravely slain a dragon. Yuriatin is an old town with beautiful buildings that boasts a House of Sculpture, a beacon of culture in the destructive days of the revolution. It is also significant that, after escaping from communist forces, Yuri returns to Yuriatin, where Lara is living, and not to Varykino, where Tonia and their child are waiting.

Highway. Road near Yuriatin, on which many events concerning Yuri take place. Controlled mostly by communist forces, it is here that they capture and hold him, forcing him to work for them for several months. From the highway, Yuri witnesses many atrocities taking place. Although as a physician he is morally opposed to bloodshed, Yuri is forced to participate in a skirmish between communists and their opponents, mostly young men. Zhivago nurses a wounded soldier from the opposing side, as if to show that he does not sympathize with the communist cause.

Railroads. Trains play an important role in the novel. They not only crisscross the huge expanses of both Europe and Asia but also figure at crucial points in the story. These include the mysterious death of Yuri's father, which occurs on a train; the days-long journey of the Zhivagos from Moscow to the Urals; and Yuri's meeting Strelnikov, Lara's husband and a revolutionary firebrand, who knows about Yuri's tryst with Lara and implicitly warns him of the consequences. The trains also have a symbolic meaning in that they connect people in the days of the revolution, when individuals and groups tend to drift apart.

— *Vasa D. Mihailovich*

DODSWORTH

Author: Sinclair Lewis (1885-1951)
Type of work: Novel
Type of plot: Social realism

Time of plot: 1920's
First published: 1929

Sinclair Lewis uses Fran and Sam Dodsworth's European travel to satirize American cultural deficiencies. Sam's artistic taste improves as he experiences the culture of England, France, Germany, Spain, and Italy, while Fran's snobbishness prevents her from responding adequately to European reality.

Zenith. Fictional midwestern city in which the novel opens. Lewis created Zenith in *Babbitt* (1922), a novel in which the Dodsworths are a leading pioneer family and Sam creates a major automobile manufacturing company. In *Dodsworth* Sam is proud of his city, but Fran is dissatisfied with its cultural and social life. After selling his business, Sam agrees to spend a year touring Europe. Zenith provides the background to the novel and an implicit counterpoint to Europe.

***England.** For Sam, England is the land of his ancestors, the country whose literature fills his imagination, the place where he believes he will feel most at home. Some things are as expected—coaching inns reminiscent of Charles Dickens's *Pickwick Papers* (1836-1837), quaint London shop-fronts, and double-decker buses. However, he has much to learn—some English accents are incomprehensible to him; even in the theater he can understand only two-thirds of what the actors say. He replaces his evening clothes and hat to match British styles. Fran has little interest in sightseeing, but British society fascinates her. The high points of her visit are the weekend she and Sam spend at the home of a real English lord, arranged by a shipboard acquaintance, and taking tea with the aristocracy of England at the palatial manor house of a member of Parliament. When Sam is uncomfortable at the tea, Fran accuses him of carrying Zenith with him wherever he goes.

***France.** Sam finds France strange, yet appealing in its foreignness. This time the local language is almost totally incomprehensible. Nevertheless, he finds the people astonishingly human, not the stereotypes he has anticipated. Sam enjoys the sights recommended by guidebooks; Fran sneers that fashionable people avoid such places. Lewis remarks that "Paris is one of the larg-

est, and certainly it is the pleasantest, of modern American cities," as he and Fran encounter many expatriates. Sam learns from the journalists and businessmen he meets in Paris's famous New York Bar. Fran admires the socially and culturally pretentious Americans attracted by her beauty and income, and arranges to spend the summer in Switzerland with them, while Sam returns to the United States to attend his thirtieth class reunion at Yale.

***New York City.** Entering New York harbor as a fog lifts, Sam is stunned by a vision of the towers and spires of an enchanted city. After landing, however, a different reality soon sets in, and Lewis uses Sam's reactions to express his own dislike for many aspects of American cities, which he sees as overcrowded, dirty, and noisy. Restaurant food is terrible. Prohibition has ruined the pleasure of drinking. No longer a relaxed, agreeable activity, drinking has become a grim struggle to consume as much alcohol as quickly as possible.

***Europe.** Sam returns to Paris to find Fran guiltily repentant over an adulterous episode. Taking charge, he leads her on a tour of Spain and Italy, which bores Fran, while he enjoys visiting all the standard attractions. Fascinated by European domestic and monumental architecture, Sam carefully studies the structures on his route. From Italy the Dodsworths go to Germany to visit Fran's relatives. Both enjoy their stay, and their sightseeing, guided by young Count Kurt von Obersdorf. The only exception is a brief, shocking visit to a homosexual bar while exploring Berlin's nightlife. Nevertheless, Sam feels at home; he considers the Germans, like the English, to be his kind of people, and believes he understands how they think and act. Meeting German aristocrats especially thrills Fran.

When Fran asks for a divorce, Sam travels to Paris

and Venice, then visits Naples with Edith Cortwright, who will become his second wife. Sam finds Europe more enjoyable as he relaxes among friendly Italians, and explores Capri, Sorrento, and Pompeii with Edith.

Together they plan to return to Zenith and, using what Sam has learned during his European trip, build elegant suburban houses.

— *Milton Berman*

A DOLL'S HOUSE

Author: Henrik Ibsen (1828-1906)
Type of work: Drama
Type of plot: Social realism

Time of plot: Nineteenth century
First published: Et dukkehjem, 1879 (English translation, 1880); first performed, 1879

The house of Torvald Helmer is the focal point of Henrik Ibsen's play. Its various rooms reinforce the image of wife Nora Helmer as a captured doll, or plaything, in a home that could exist not only in Norway, but in any century and on any street in any city where women oppressed by men search for freedom to find themselves.

Helmer house. Home of Torvald Helmer, a successful bank manager, and his wife, Nora. The dwelling contains comfortable and stylish furniture and such items as a china cabinet, a bookcase with well-bound books, and a piano on carpeted floor—all of which demonstrate a stable financial situation. However, the house is a mere container, or doll's house, for Nora, who spends her time entertaining or nervously accommodating (as her nickname "the squirrel" implies) her demanding husband—rather than decorating, designing, or even "taking charge of" her own life.

Sitting areas in the house realistically capture the limitations on Nora's growth as a woman. For example, in these staged sitting areas, Nora secretly eats macaroons to escape her husband's upbraiding; she has threatening conversations with Krogstad, concerning his reinstatement at her husband's bank; and she prepares her costume and practices the tarantella for a Christmas ball she must attend with Torvald. All of these situations in closed rooms psychologically and emotionally demonstrate the manipulation and oppression of this doll in the house, filled with rooms of deception and corruption.

When Nora finally decides to leave her husband, she goes out of the house and slams its downstairs door shut. In so doing, she physically, mentally, and spiritually enters a new space: the unknown. For here she can truly "find herself" now and discover what she wants to do as a woman without Torvald's rules and codes of behavior.

Helmer's office. Torvald's efficiently furnished banking office, which is an emblem of his kingdom—the room in which he makes the rules of conduct for his home and for his little doll, Nora. Ibsen's social realism is evident as in his studio many despotic decisions that further emphasize the theme of female injustice are made. For example, in act 2 Torvald writes a letter dismissing the bookkeeper Nils Krogstad, who has been blackmailing Nora since she forged her dying father's signature to a bond at the bank, when she needed money to take Torvald to Italy when he was seriously ill.

— *Connie Pedoto*

DOMBEY AND SON

Author: Charles Dickens (1812-1870)
Type of work: Novel
Type of plot: Social realism

Time of plot: Early nineteenth century
First published: 1846-1848

Although this novel, like the majority of Charles Dickens's novels, is set in London, it contains many allusions to the sea—an unusual feature in Dickens's writings. The sea stands literally for a shipwreck, the seafaring life of

Captains Cuttle and Bunsby, and the commercial ventures of Mr. Dombey. Figuratively, the sea signifies death and the boundless life beyond. The ultimate shipwrecks are the fall of Dombey's firm, the failure of his marriage, and the betrayal of his manager.

*London. The British capital portrayed in this novel is a curiously fragmented city. One part barely seems to connect to another. The isolating effect of money is its theme, and the geography bears this out. Many houses are described, however, each one symbolic of its occupants. The novel is dotted with a vast array of houses in and around London, of all social classes. Many, like Mrs. MacStinger's house near the India Docks represent entrapment, both relationally and economically. Others suggest the pretence of shabby gentility, such as Miss Tox's house and Cousin Feenix's house in Brook Street. Virtue can exist only in homes outside the city, such as the home of Dombey's agent John Carker and his sister, Harriet, or later, in the new home of Dombey's daughter, Florence, and her husband, Walter Gay, to the west of London. The separateness of each house suggests the lack of nexus, of community, in London. Each house represents the strangeness of the modern city, its unreality.

Dombey's house. Home of the merchant Dombey in a fashionable part of London, between Portland Place and Bryanstone Square. Within the novel, the term "house" means both "home" and "business." Because Dombey cannot separate the two meanings, his family relationships become riffed, and possibilities of life are thwarted by death and separation. His house is gloomy and sunless; the images Dickens uses are of death, prison, enclosure, and decay. Within the house, both Dombey's son Paul and his mother die, and the charade of his second marriage is enacted with all its attempted refinements and moving upscale socially. The house's contents are finally auctioned off as part of the collapse of the commercial "house" of Dombey and Son. It then becomes a lonely prison for Florence, attended only by her faithful servant, Susan.

Dombey's offices. Headquarters of Dombey's merchant business, located within the City of London, Greater London's financial center, near the Royal Exchange and the Bank of England. The complex contains separate offices for Dombey, Carker, and the third manager, Morfin. The offices represent the betrayal of family values: Carker's insulting enmity to his older brother John is an example, as is Walter's being consigned to the West Indies, thus depriving his uncle of his only family and Florence of her "brother." The final stages of Carker's undermining the house also take place here.

Gill's shop. Small shop of the nautical instrument maker Sol Gill, near Dombey's offices. The entrance is guarded by a wooden midshipman, a nautical rank. Gill's stock is mostly outmoded and unsalable. However, the shop represents the true hearth of warm family ties, a place of safety, refuge, and celebration. It is fitting that Dombey's daughter Florence finds refuge here—both when she gets lost as a young girl and later when as a young woman she is rejected by her own father. Gill's hearth becomes her reconstituted family, and her reunion with Walter marks this. As the novel develops, it becomes more and more focused on the polarities of Gill's shop and Dombey's house, as true and false homes for Florence.

Stagg's Gardens. Poor street in London's Camden Town where the members of the Toodles family first live. The neighborhood is torn down to make way for a new northern railroad line out of London, on which Mr. Toodles finds employment. There is a certain ambiguity in Dickens's depiction of the railroad: its speed kills Carker, but it also brings redevelopment and employment opportunities to a poor area. The ambiguity suggests the double edge of rapid industrial progress.

*Brighton. Fashionable resort town, some fifty miles south of London, on the south coast, to which Paul and Florence are sent to attend a boarding school. There Paul receives his education at Dr. Blimber's house, a school that spells the death of learning, just as the ocean's waves become a requiem for Paul's death. Mrs. Skewton also dies there. Florence's presence in the place, however, redeems it somewhat. Life can be lived there, though distorted and emotionally unhealthy.

*Leamington. Another fashionable spa town, north of Oxford, where Major Bagstock introduces Dombey to the woman who becomes a new wife, Edith. In the artificiality of culture here, this new relationship becomes riffed as a desirable transaction, to the ultimate ruin of Dombey.

— *David Barratt*

DOMINIQUE

Author: Eugène Fromentin (1820-1876)
Type of work: Novel
Type of plot: Psychological

Time of plot: Nineteenth century
First published: 1862 (English translation, 1932)

The story of Dominique de Bray's life moves among three key locations: the village of his birth and early childhood, the town where he is educated and falls hopelessly in love, and the city in which he can find no sense of belonging. Having moved through them in series then makes the journey in reverse, always driven by regret rather than desire.

Château des Trembles (SHAH-toh day TRAHN-blay). Dominique's birthplace at Les Trembles, close to the town of Villeneuve. (Villeneuve, meaning "new town," is a common place-name in France; however, the town with that name in this story does not correspond to any actual example.) The surrounding landscape is suggestive of the terrain extending south from Eugène Fromentin's birthplace, La Rochelle; it is a drab plain denuded of trees, checkered by vineyards, marshlands, and fallow fields, bordered by the sea. The château itself, however, is situated in a wooded covert whose environs are full of life.

The house is built in a Flemish style, with irregular windows, slate-covered gabled roofs, and several turrets. A farmhouse of more recent construction and its associated outbuildings are clustered around it. A long water-meadow leads directly from the house to the sea. When the narrator first meets Dominique, who is the mayor of the local commune, the château is the site of various social occasions involving the local vintners in such activities as outdoor dancing, but Dominique's childhood memories recall it as a quieter place. The narrator is particularly fascinated by Dominique's relic-filled study, whose walls and windows are covered in pencilled graffiti, haphazard in character but all carefully dated.

Les Trembles brackets Dominique's story as well as the novel; as a young boy he knows every detail of the house and the garden, and is intimately familiar with the effects of the changing seasons on the surrounding farmlands. At the end of the story he fervently insists that his business is with the land—an echo of the final line of Voltaire's *Candide* (1759), in which cultivation of a narrow plot becomes symbolic of a philosophical attitude of resignation. Dominique revisits his home for two

months late in the novel, when he takes Madeleine and her husband to the top of the local lighthouse in bad weather—the only occasion in which Les Trembles lives up to its name, both literally and metaphorically.

Ormesson. Town about thirty-five miles from Villeneuve. Dominique lives there in Madame Ceyssac's house: a large but cold and empty residence in which traditional formality holds sway. Its rooms seem airless and viewless, its stone staircase forbidding. The house is surrounded by convents, and the overall impression of the town is one of clustered steeples whose bells ring in cacophonous competition, strongly contrasted with the single authoritative chime of the church at Villeneuve.

The dismal river flowing through Ormesson adds to a general atmosphere that is squalid, if not actually fetid. Olivier, Madeleine and Julie live in the Rue des Carmélites, in a house not dissimilar to Madame Ceyssac's but much enlivened by their presence.

There is a real French town called Ormesson-sur-Marne, near Villeneuve-le-Roi, but its local geography is radically different from the one in the story.

*****Paris.** France's capital city figures into the story as a distant prospect long before Dominique actually goes there. His tutor Augustin has correspondents in Paris, and Olivier has just come from Paris when Dominique first meets him in Ormesson. As Madame de Nièvres, Madeleine spends more time there than at Nièvres. Dominique's arrival in the city stands in stark contrast to the enthusiasm with which first glimpses of the capital are usually greeted in French literature. The city's endless avenues of houses seem bleak, and Dominique's first impression is that the whole city reeks of gas. Even the torchlit convoy attending the opera-bound king, glimpsed on his very first evening, fails to impress him. Dominique persists in thinking of Paris as a sort of vast inn, an essentially temporary residence, and does his utmost to avoid any social friction that might erode his personality. He avoids the landmarks that pepper most literary descriptions of Paris, although he takes long walks along the Seine with Augustin.

Château de Nièvres (SHAH-toh deh NYEV-ray). Country house, surrounded by woods, where Madeleine and her husband live when they are not in Paris. Dominique visits it when he hears that Julie is ill and that there is some cause to be anxious about Madeleine's health. They walk to the village, where they find the child Julie had befriended dead—an omen of their final parting.

— *Brian Stableford*

THE DON FLOWS HOME TO THE SEA

Author: Mikhail Sholokhov (1905-1984)
Type of work: Novel
Type of plot: Historical
Time of plot: 1918-1920

First published: Tikhii Don, 1928-1940 (partial English translations, 1934 as *And Quiet Flows the Don*; 1940 as *The Don Flows Home to the Sea*)

This novel chronicles the fortunes and misfortunes of a Cossack family, the Melekhovs, mainly the protagonist Gregor Melekhov, during the latter part of the Russian Revolution.

Don River. River flowing south in central and southern Russia and emptying into the Black Sea. The events move along the lines of its predecessor volume, *And Quiet Flows the Don*. The grandeur of the Don continues to reign. During a flood, the river creates a small island in its middle that serves the civil war combatants as a final refuge. Even though the villagers, especially the Melekhovs, who live directly on the bank, are by now, in the fifth year of the war, exhausted and almost crushed by their constant sorrow, they seem to find solace and invigoration in the Don. Furthermore, some villagers, including those from the Melekhov family, find their tragic end in the waters of the river. When Gregor finally comes home after years of fighting all over the Don region, he crosses the river to get to his hut. He throws into the river his rifle and ammunition, as if finally making peace with himself and his friends and foes.

Tatarsk. Fictional village on the Don. In the later stages of the civil war between the Reds and the Whites it becomes a ghost village. Many of its inhabitants have perished or are on the verge of extinction. The sons of Tatarsk fight several battles, with variable success, but it is the Reds who prevail. The new winds of the revolution are blowing, but, unfortunately, they take with them many villagers, especially the leaders. The magnetism of one's native village draws home Gregor, who returns to Tatarsk and the new rulers whom he had fought bitterly. Only his young son is waiting for him, as if to ensure the survival of the family name no matter what fate awaits Gregor.

Vieshenska (VYE-shen-ska). District center near Tatarsk. Like practically all Russian towns and villages, it changes hands several times in the civil war. In the latter stages, the Whites make the last effort to rise against the Reds, only to be crushed. It will continue to be the focal point of the area, although under different circumstances.

Yagodnoe (YA-gohd-no-ee). Country estate of the richest family in the Tatarsk region, now in its last days as a nobleman's nest. The death of its owners signals the fundamental changes in Russia.

Novocherkask (NO-vo-cher-KASK). Russian port on the Black Sea, where thousands of the opponents of the Reds, having been defeated completely and driven to the edge of a precipice, are boarding ships to go into exile. Gregor refuses to board, after his long-standing companions are rejected because of lower rank. Gregor turns back and joins the Reds.

Island on the Don. Island created by the river during a huge flood, that serves as a hiding place for brigands whom Gregor joins out of desperation after he being rejected by the local Reds, even though he has fought with them against the Poles. The island brings on the last catharsis for Gregor, who realizes that his character is above that of the brigands and decides to return home for good, come what may.

Battle front. As in the first volume, *And Quiet Flows the Don*, the front lines move steadily and furiously. Now they are moving farther south until the last remnants of the Whites are conquered. Many warriors are forced to change sides, like Gregor, with greater or lesser success. The toll, however, continues to rise. Mikhail Sholokhov does not chronicle the battles; he sticks with Gregor until his final decision to return home and face the consequences. The author leaves open the final fate of Gregor, as though unwilling to have him killed. Gregor becomes the symbol of the unspeakable tragedy of the Russian people, especially the Cossacks and peasants.

— *Vasa D. Mihailovich*

DON JUAN

Author: George Gordon, Lord Byron (1788-1824)
Type of work: Poetry
Type of plot: Satire

Time of plot: Late eighteenth century
First published: 1819-1826

Don Juan, the hero of this epic satire ranges from Spain to a Greek island to Turkey to Russia and finally to England—the latter becoming the primary target of Lord Byron's witty attack on his native land's reactionary politics and stuffy social conventions.

*Seville. City in southwestern Spain. Calling it "a pleasant city,/ Famous for oranges and women," Byron sets the tone and theme for his treatment of place. The poet is deliberately light-hearted about his legendary hero, pointing out how the provinciality of the city and of his upbringing makes him ignorant of sex and therefore susceptible to the charms of beautiful women. The restrictions of place stimulate the hero to seek a larger world of experience.

Greek island. Exiled from Seville, where he has been caught making love to another man's wife, the hero falls in love with the ruler's daughter in a setting that resembles an erotic paradise. Because Haidee's father is away, the lovers are free to indulge themselves—although Don Juan finds himself exiled again when the father returns. The Greek island becomes another example of the world as a place that conspires against lovers.

*Constantinople. Turkish capital to which Don Juan is taken by sailors who rescue him after he is abandoned at sea. There he becomes a subject of the Ottoman rulers and continues to attract the amorous attentions of noble women. Byron uses Constantinople to place his hero at the crossroads of the Christian and Turkish empires, demonstrating that for all the differences in customs between East and West, his hero's desire to keep his dignity intact while enjoying himself never slackens. Places threaten to change the hero, but his spirit proves remarkably resistant to the coercions of environment.

*Russia. Even after Don Juan is captured by Russians besieging the Turkish city of Ismail and he becomes a lover of Russia's ruler, Catherine the Great, he remains stubbornly his own person and not merely the plaything of Russia's great autocrat.

*England. Sent to England as part of a diplomatic entourage, Don Juan becomes a fixture of English society, fending off women who look upon marriage as a career. Byron provides many satirical descriptions of his superficial native land, admirably summing up Don Juan's journey from "lands and scenes romantic," where lives are risked for passion, to a "country where 'tis half a fashion."

— *Carl Rollyson*

DON QUIXOTE DE LA MANCHA

Author: Miguel de Cervantes (1547-1616)
Type of work: Novel
Type of plot: Mock-heroic
Time of plot: Late sixteenth century

First published: El ingenioso hidalgo don Quixote de la Mancha, part 1, 1605; part 2, 1615 (English translation, 1612-1620)

Set in Spain during the late Renaissance, this novel develops broad satirical commentary on all aspects of Spanish culture, from politics and religion to literary tradition and scholarship. The country of Spain is more than a mere screen on which plot incidents are projected, however; it is ubiquitous and imbues the characters, institutions, and situations that Miguel de Cervantes depicts. Each location becomes a crucible in which the characters interact, revealing the foibles, idiosyncrasies, and singularities of the people and the culture that has given rise to them.

***Spain.** Foremost European military, political, and economic power at the end of the Renaissance—the time in which this novel is set. Spain was then politically unified as a nation but, from its days as a federation of allied kingdoms, it still retained many regional influences that are reflected in the novel. Spain's importance as a center of trade, exploration, and conquest led it to become a watershed of diverse cultural and linguistic influences, in which Spanish, Arab, Basque, Italian, Portuguese, and French influences, among others, could be traced in the idioms, pronunciation, and customs of the inhabitants. These influences were responsible in part for the vigor and inventiveness of Cervantes' satire.

The satirical focus of the novel is on the people of Spain—their values, attitudes, and prejudices. However, it is Cervantes' narrative montage technique, original with him but widely emulated since, that permits him to scrutinize the entire spectrum of character types comprising Spanish society. This technique, referred to as picaresque, is largely a function of changes in place. As Don Quixote moves from place to place, he encounters new people and situations that reflect the exigencies of each location. As the layers of imagery accumulate, an overall impression of Spain emerges, and parallels among places and events become evident.

When Spain's King Phillip II died in 1598, Spain's cultural greatness was undeniable, and would become greater. However, his legacy also included a nearly bankrupt treasury, an exploited and disgruntled peasantry, a bigoted and privileged nobility, and a persecuting, intolerant religious faith. These attributes of Cervantes' contemporary Spain were the objects of his criticism.

*La Mancha.** Autonomous region in central Spain that encompasses the village in which Don Quixote lives (identified by some sources as Argamarilla de Alba, about twenty miles west of the prison in which Cervantes may have conceived the novel). The area is near Toledo, Spain's ancient capital, and Madrid, its capital in Cervantes' day. Cervantes served as tax collector in La Mancha, where he came in direct contact with all levels of Castilian society, from peasants like his fictional Sancho Panza to impoverished members of the hereditary orders of nobility, like Don Quixote himself.

*Montiel** (mahn-teel). La Mancha district that encompasses numerous small communities of farmers and tradesmen. The Plain of Montiel is the site of Don Quixote's first and second sallies. It is also a fitting place for an adventure to begin, as it was well known by contemporary Spaniards as the place where the legitimate king Don Pedro of Castile was killed by his illegitimate brother Henry in 1369. The region of Montiel is formidably hot in the summer, and generally windy. Cervantes makes use of these prevailing conditions in the novel. The circumstances of Don Quixote's first sally into the plain underscore not only his resoluteness in becoming a knight-errant, but also his madness, for who but a resolute madman would wear a suit of armor, complete with helmet, all day through Montiel's legendary July heat? In his second and most famous sally, Don Quixote takes on the famous group of windmills, perfectly natural features of the landscape for the local farmers and tradesmen, who used them to grind their grain.

Inns. Public hostelries figure prominently in the novel because of the centrality of travel to the narrative technique. Inns were important landmarks on all major Spanish thoroughfares or highways, and offered local inhabitants and travelers alike the opportunity to share and discuss local news, enjoy entertainment, encounter new perspectives, and take refreshment and rest. The dining, toilet, and stable areas in the inns of the day were shared by all guests, a feature that allowed Cervantes to bring Don Quixote and Sancho Panza into direct and intimate contact with a wide variety of other travelers without having to resort to contriving artificial or unrealistic situations.

Close interactions among guests in the novel sometimes lead to the sharing of stories, as in the episode with Dorothea and Cardenio, or the episode with the muleteer who tells the story of the Brayers. On occasions when other guests are coarse, vulgar, combative, sullen, or knavish, the interactions occasionally take less pleasant turns, as when Don Quixote is tied by the wrist to an inn's window and left to dangle painfully until morning, or when Sancho is tossed in a blanket.

Inns also served as natural meeting or rendezvous sites for members of civil, military, or ecclesiastical service traveling on official business. Thus, Don Quixote and Sancho encounter members of the Brotherhood, whom Don Quixote attacks before realizing they are serving a warrant for his arrest, for freeing the galley slaves, among whom is Ginés da Pasamonte, whom Don Quixote sees again delivering his puppet show. Setting these encounters at an inn renders at least marginally credible meetings among the many disparate participants in this set of interrelated adventures.

*****Sierra Morena.** Rough and sparsely inhabited mountain range in central Spain that is the site of Don Quixote's penance. The location is appropriate because of its seclusion and harshness. Don Quixote and Sancho initially travel to Sierra Morena to throw off the pursuit by the Holy Brotherhood, which Sancho rightly fears will result from their freeing of galley slaves. The remoteness and roughness of the mountainous terrain are the same qualities that prompt the fugitive galley slaves to hide in the mountains, where they steal Sancho's ass, Dapple. Its suitability as a place of penance also attracts Cardenio.

— *Andrew B. Preslar*

DON SEGUNDO SOMBRA: Shadows on the Pampas

Author: Ricardo Güiraldes (1886-1927)
Type of work: Novel
Type of plot: Regional

Time of plot: Late nineteenth century
First published: 1926 (English translation, 1935)

This classic tale of the South American cowboys known as gauchos takes place in the vast treeless pampas of Argentina. The protagonist and narrator, Fabio, a devilish young man of uncertain parentage, leaves his small village and becomes an apprentice of Don Segundo Sombra, an aging gaucho. Fabio experiences many adventures and traumas as he drives cattle from ranch to ranch across the seemingly endless plains.

Fabio's village. Small Argentine village where Fabio lives with two aunts as a boy. The opening chapters of the novel describe the village as having forty blocks of flat houses and streets as monotonous as a prison. Village life represents order, structure, and civilization. Fabio flees his dull home in search of adventure in the countryside.

La Blanqueada (blahn-KAY-ahdah). Village saloon in which Fabio often hangs out while playing hooky from school. Occasionally, he makes a lot of money by selling his freshly caught catfish to the owner. Otherwise, Fabio wastes time, gossiping and playing pranks on the seedy characters who frequent the bar. The saloon symbolizes the wasteful and destructive side of village life. Ironically, it is here that Fabio first encounters his mentor, Don Segundo.

Galván's ranch (gahl-VAHN). Ranch of Don Leandro Galván, to which Fabio flees from his aunts' home in the middle of the night, following Don Segundo there. He is hired as a ranch hand and taught the ways of the gaucho. After much struggle, he tames his first wild horse and ropes his first steer. Fabio thoroughly enjoys the physically demanding work but is slow to adjust. He tries extremely hard to prove his courage and strength to the gauchos. He admires the camaraderie among these rugged cowboys and soon joins them around campfires for boastful stories, fire-roasted beef, and maté, a hot tea made from shrubs.

At the end of the novel, Fabio returns to Galvan's ranch after an absence of more than five years. After going through life thinking himself an orphan, Fabio learns that a father he never knew, Don Fabio Cáceres, has died and left him his ranch and fortune. Don Leandro becomes the legal guardian of Fabio, who is not yet eighteen. Fabio thus begins and completes his journey toward maturity at Galvan's ranch, which represents a blissful middle ground between the adventure-filled but dangerous pampa and the boring predictability of village life.

***Pampas** (PAHM-pahs). Wide, open plains of Argentina, in which most of the novel takes place. Fabio persuades Don Leandro to let him participate in his first cattle drive, for half salary. Although Fabio initially fails to saddle his first colt and injures himself while trying, he eventually learns to ride like a true gaucho. His strug-

gle to live as a cowboy only strengthens his character. He develops a sense of fairness and gains courage as he wanders across the enormous plains. Fabio often describes the open road of the pathless pampa in idyllic terms. The limitless landscape and the distant horizon represent freedom and the human lust for adventure.

At other times, however, Fabio describes the land as cruel and dangerous. When the dry, yellow land does not have enough water, cattle stampede in fear. In another instance, the gauchos come across a swamp that threatens to swallow man and beast whole. During these battles of man against nature, Fabio struggles, but eventually triumphs over adversity. The day-to-day difficulties of a gaucho's labor mark significant milestones in Fabio's journey toward maturity.

Fabio's mentor, Don Segundo, embodies the mysteries of the pampa. A man of silence, he represents both the danger and the adventure of pastoral life. His surname, Sombra, means "shadow" in Spanish and symbolizes the shadows into which the heyday of the gaucho is passing. Don Segundo is the last of a dying breed. After he helps Fabio establish the ranch the boy has inherited from his father, Don Segundo rides off into the sunset. While Fabio must now accept the sedentary life of a landowner, Don Segundo cannot. He returns to his true home—the pampa.

— *Corinne Andersen*

DOÑA BÁRBARA

Author: Rómulo Gallegos (1884-1969)
Type of work: Novel
Type of plot: Regional

Time of plot: Early twentieth century
First published: 1929 (English translation, 1931)

Doña Bárbara is a novel of the llano—*the vast treeless, grassy plains of Venezuela. The protagonist Santos Luzardo, whose very name evokes the words for saint and light in Spanish, battles both man and nature in this classic tale of civilization versus barbarism. The novel is notable for its use of richly symbolic names of people and places.*

*****Llano** (YAH-no). Great savanna plains region of central Venezuela that represents nature in its wild and unruly state. Although beautiful and powerful, and therefore much like Santos's nemesis, Doña Bárbara, the plains resist the order and discipline of any civilizing

force. Danger lurks in the muddy, alligator-filled quagmires that threaten to consume interlopers whole. Rómulo Gallegos provides a poetic description of the enormous prairie. This region, with its unbroken horizon, conveys a sense of solitude and loneliness.

Altamira (ahl-tah-MEER-ah). Ranch on which Santos grows up and to which he returns after completing his university studies. Santos maintains an ambivalent relationship with his family estate. When he returns to Altamira, he finds it overgrown with neglect and thinks about selling it. Soon, however, he learns of Doña Bárbara's underhanded schemes to cheat him out of his property, and decides to stay and put up a fight. Resolving to end the dispute by civilized means, he attempts to defend his claim legally, through the courts. Meanwhile, he struggles to tame the wild savanna, as well as stem Doña Bárbara's greed. Eventually, he puts up a fence to mark the border of his property. Santos's ultimate triumph over Doña Bárbara represents a victory for civilization over barbarism. In Spanish, Altamira signifies highmindedness. In the novel, the law prevails over unbridled power.

El Miedo (ehl mee-AY-doh). Ranch owned by the Luzardo family's rival, the Barquero family, until Doña Bárbara, a beautiful woman of humble origins and a violent past, swindles Lorenzo Barquero out of its title. Doña Bárbara—whose name resembles the Spanish word for barbarism—dabbles in the occult and otherwise takes advantage of the dark forces of nature.

El Miedo, which means "fear" in Spanish, represents the danger and power of barbarism. Where Santos builds a fence to contain his land, Doña Bárbara sets fire to her fields in an attempt to encourage growth. Her ranch hands steal and brand the stray cattle from Santos's fields and move the boundary posts that mark the division between El Miedo and Altamira. At the end of the novel, Doña Bárbara mysteriously disappears and leaves her estate to her estranged daughter, Marisela. Marisela marries Santos, and El Miedo becomes part of Altamira. Thus, highmindedness, or civilization, triumphs over fear, the ruling principle of barbarism.

*****Caracas** (kahr-AH-kahs). Capital of Venezuela, to which Santos moves as an adolescent, along with his mother. The two flee the Altamira ranch after Don José's violent and deadly rage against his eldest son, Felix. In Caracas, which symbolizes civilization, the passions that led to Don José's and Felix's deaths are constrained by law and order. At first, Santos finds the city dull and longs to return to the adventures of his childhood in the plains. Soon, however, he embraces the discipline and culture of the city and longs to flee his homeland for the civilization of Europe. In Caracas, Santos studies law and excels at many intellectual pursuits. At the university, he first speaks out against the barbarism of the plains.

Barquero house (bahr-KEH-roh). Dilapidated shack in which Lorenzo, once an ambitious student in Caracas, now lives as a pathetic drunk—another of Doña Bárbara's victims whose uncivilized dwelling represents the consequence of unchecked barbarism. Once the owner of the Barquero ranch, El Miedo, Lorenzo lives with Marisela, the daughter he had with Doña Bárbara.

The Lick. Stretch of savanna crossing the creek that Lorenzo Barquero sells to Señor Danger, an unscrupulous American capitalist who wants to usurp the fertile plain. He bribes the addicted Lorenzo with liquor.

— *Corinne Andersen*

DOÑA PERFECTA

Author: Benito Pérez Galdós (1843-1920)
Type of work: Novel
Type of plot: Tragedy

Time of plot: Late nineteenth century
First published: 1876 (English translation, 1880)

The provincial Spanish setting of this novel satirically contrasts Spain's capital city with a fictitious town and its environs, with Don José de Rey ("Pepe") representing urban values and his aunt, Doña Perfecta, rural and regional values. Torn between the two worldviews these conflicting locales represent, Doña Perfecta's daughter, Rosario, becomes literally feverish from the clash between the changes wrought by love and the rigid, static, moral dominance of Orbajosa as epitomized in her mother, who represents the dark soul of Spain.

Villahorrenda (vee-YAH-or-EN-dah). Impoverished, ugly town on the railroad line out of Madrid at which the young engineer José (Pepe) Rey stops while on his way to Orbajosa. Villahorrenda—whose name means "horrid village"—is a gateway to a hell of backbiters, hypocrites, and thieves. Pepe contrasts the poetic beauty of regional names (Flowervale, Lilyhill, Amiable Valley, Richville) befitting his mother's peaceful pastoral memories with the desolate wasteland of prosaic reality, concluding that this region's inhabitants live in the imagination, seeing what they will, not the miserable, arid reality. The worst land of all is his inheritance, untended and diminished by predatory neighbors. His journey progresses from this hellhole to a cold, dark place of ignorance, violence, and bigotry from which there is no return.

Orbajosa (or-bah-YOH-sah). Provincial city that is home to Doña Perfecta Rey and her daughter, Rosario. The town's name is both a corruption of the Latin term *urbs augusta* ("majestic city") and a mocking play on *ajosa*, the Spanish word for garlic. The city looks like a large "dunghill" to the visitor from Madrid, but its 7,324 inhabitants are proud of its cathedral and wealthy homes, such as the seven mansions along the Adelantado, including that of Doña Perfecta. The city lies in a valley famous for its garlic, a symbol of its close ties to the land and of its residents' tendency to focus on the soil, not the heavens, to turn inward, cavernously, not outward.

The Nahara River passes through the valley, providing Pepe with a thwarted government commission to examine its bed for mining possibilities. Orbajosans, some of whom are rebels and guerrilla fighters, oppose the Madrid government and are convinced of the virtues of their own way of life. Also gossips, they exaggerate the importance of local agriculture, which they call the "breadbasket" of Spain, although they have produced little in recent years. At the same time, they see the worst in the most trivial deeds of outsiders. Typical is Don Cayetano Polentinos, whose book of genealogy inflates the city's national significance by citing every former citizen mentioned in any obscure historical record.

Cathedral. Town church that is the embodiment of community solidarity against outsiders such as Pepe, who is deemed an impious atheist because he criticizes the bad taste of the religious art, the individual decorations, the statue of Virgin and child (attired in pretentious modern styles, for which Rosario and Doña Perfecta are responsible), and the music (*La Traviata* for high mass, a drinking song, and a rondeau). The cathedral reflects the town's obsession with propriety, its belief in the infallibility of its extreme religious cult, one unforgiving of dissent and fearful of German Lutheranism and the currents of eighteenth century philosophical thought, including pantheism.

Casino. Orbajosa tavern that is an abstract representation of the masculine center of the town, in which men smoke, argue politics, gamble, and avoid their wives. Pepe's visit there marks him as a wild layabout.

Troya house. Home of Colonel Francisco Troya and his three daughters. Pepe's pleasure in visiting this home signals his moral decline to other Orbajosans, because the young Troya women scorn hypocrisy and delight in mocking city worthies, dressing up during carnival to go masked into the houses of leading citizens to create havoc.

Doña Perfecta's house. Abode that is grand on the outside; inside, the house is a labyrinth of intrigue, with dark rooms, dark colors, and doors shut tight against anything new. As the genealogist studies her library, characters come and go in repetitive scenes of gossip, hatred, plots, and fear of change. From this center of her web Doña Perfecta foments rebellion and deceit. Her garden, where Pepe and Rosario meet secretly by night to pledge their love, becomes an evil trap sprung by a vengeful María Remedios, ambitious to match her son and Rosario. With Pepe murdered and Rosario insane and institutionalized, the possibility of solutions ends, and Doña Perfecta's distorted hopes die.

— *Mabel Illidge and Gina Macdonald*

DOWN THERE

Author: Joris-Karl Huysmans (1848-1907)
Type of work: Novel
Type of plot: Fantasy

Time of plot: Late nineteenth century
First published: Là-bas, 1891 (English translation, 1924)

The title of this novel places its most significant viewpoint in the bell tower from which the characters can look down disapprovingly on the sprawling streets of the Left Bank of the River Seine: Paris's Bohemian quarter. At street level, the city seems to have lost its way, historically and spiritually; the scientific revolution guided by August Comte's positivist philosophy has devastated religious faith but remains impotent against all kinds of impiety, whose logical extreme is active Satanism.

Durtal's apartment. Set of rooms in a house on Paris's rue du Regard; they contain the compact book-lined study where the scholar Durtal works on his dissertation on Gilles de Rais, a French marshal briefly associated with Joan of Arc. The dust is frequently disturbed and redistributed, but never diminished, by a surly concierge. Over the mantelpiece, in place of a mirror, is an old Dutch painting whose principal figure is a kneeling hermit with a cardinal's hat and cloak set beside him. The bedroom is sparsely furnished but decorated with a photograph of a Sandro Botticelli Venus and a print of Peter Breughel's representation of "The Wise and Foolish Virgins." All this is symbolic, as is only to be expected from the author, Joris-Karl Huysmans, a central figure of the French Symbolist movement

Chantelouve's house. Residence on the rue de Bagneaux of a Roman Catholic historian who supplies Durtal with information—and whose wife, Hyacinthe, becomes Durtal's mistress and guide to the occult underworld of Paris. Chantelouve hosts regular "salons" in his drawing room, where disputatious visitors gather to discuss theological matters and the debased state of contemporary society. The house also has a well-stocked library, where more confidential discussions take place.

*Church of Saint-Sulpice (sah[n]-sewl-pees). One of the most famous churches in Paris, built by King Louis XIV. The church became notorious during Huysmans's time for the nearby street-market whose tradesmen specialized in cheap, sordid devotional artifacts (which became known as "Saint-Sulpiceries" in consequence). The lofty situation of Louis Carhaix's **bell tower** places it, symbolically speaking, in clean air, remote from the streets whose literal pollution reflects a deep-seated moral pollution. Below the belfry is a room used now as storage space for obsolete statuary, because it was misused as a rendezvous in the days when it accommodated a swing. In the apartment in the gallery below the church's towers, Madame Carhaix serves wholesome food, ministering to Durtal's body while her husband assists his spirit.

Château de Tiffauges (shah-TOH deh tif-ohj). Castle in Brittany that was the inordinately luxurious residence of Gilles de Rais, the marshal of France and associate of Joan of Arc who became the subject of a sensational early fifteenth century sorcery trial. When Durtal visits the château in Huysmans's novel, he finds it deserted, stripped of every vestige of its former finery. Its walls are overgrown by ivy and viburnum, but are still intact. Its great halls, walled in granite, with arch-vaulted roofs, are cold and gloomy. They are linked by narrow, twisting corridors whose spiral staircases ascend and descend into mazes of smaller rooms. Following the method of the historian Jules Michelet, Durtal populates it again in his imagination and tries to put himself in the shoes of its medieval lord. It is while doing so that he begins his secret liaison with Madame Chantelouve—a meeting that re-emphasizes the symbolic parallel between the alleged corruption of Gilles de Rais and the moral and spiritual predicament of contemporary Paris.

Chapel. Last remnant of a long-suppressed convent of Ursuline nuns. Its exact situation is unspecified, but it must be somewhere on Paris's Left Bank, since Durtal and Madame Chantelouve's route takes them along the rue Vaugirard, a thoroughfare that branches from one of the quarter's two main roads, the boulevard St. Michel, angling away from the other, the Boulevard St. Germain. Here Durtal witnesses a supposed black mass celebrated by Canon Docre, although his conclusion that it is a mediocre and silly sham is far more reliable than the judgment of legions of credulous readers who have taken it as solid evidence that black masses really were being celebrated in late nineteenth century Paris.

— *Brian Stableford*

DRACULA

Author: Bram Stoker (1847-1912)
Type of work: Novel
Type of plot: Horror

Time of plot: Late nineteenth century
First published: 1897

With the creation of Castle Dracula, whose Gothic outline graces both the opening and closing chapters of this novel, Bram Stoker bestowed upon Transylvania a legendary aura that it still enjoys today. Locale possesses such metaphorical and symbolical functions in this novel as to become synonymous with terror; the forbidding lair of the infamous vampire king has become an icon of mystery and dread.

*Castle Dracula. Ancestral home of Count Dracula in Transylvania that is visited by the English estate agent Jonathan Harker at the beginning of the novel. The gate of admittance to the unearthly horrors that are to come, Castle Dracula is the catalyst for the forces of evil in the novel and the place where the young solicitor sent to transact business with the count encounters things worse than any death. An avatar for the loneliness of terror, the castle, "from whose tall black windows came no ray of light," also becomes the setting for one of the most seductive scenes in the novel—Harker's encounter with the three vampire "sisters."

Almost everything that happens at Castle Dracula is chilling or unnaturally suspenseful. What seem to be ordinary circumstances gradually begin slipping into the realm of nightmare, and by the time Dracula leaves his home for England, the castle has already worked its spell, setting the stage for the unholy dread that is then unleashed.

Modeled on Prince Vlad Dracula's real castle (located in Romania), Castle Dracula is eerily like its historical counterpart although the partially restored ruins are actually quite far from Stoker's conceptualized fortress. It is to Stoker's credit that Castle Dracula's haunting spectral form retains its extraordinarily powerful aura both at the novel's beginning and again at the end.

*Whitby. Picturesque Yorkshire fishing port off the coast of northern England and the setting of Count Dra-

cula's dramatic arrival in Great Britain. It is here, in fact, that the Russian schooner *Demeter* runs ashore—its captain dead at the mast—with a horrid account in its log of the crew's disappearance at the hands of a fiend, and it is here that a few nights later, Mina Murray (Harker's fiancé) rescues her sleepwalking friend, Lucy Westenra (Dracula's first victim), in the local churchyard. With its naïve charm symbolically mirroring the girlish innocence of the two young women, Whitby represents the perfect location for the unsuspecting intrusion of evil.

Hillingham. Westenra family mansion in London. This house does not appear to have been modeled on a real location but may be a composite based on Stoker's own residence at Cheyne Walk. This is the scene of Lucy's continued agony at the hands of Dracula after she returns home from Whitby, and it is where the reader is first introduced to Professor Van Helsing, the doctor-philosopher-scientist-metaphysician who later becomes the acknowledged leader and mentor of the group in its relentless pursuit of Dracula. Hillingham not only witnesses the pathetic death of Lucy—despite the countless transfusions she is given—but that of her mother as well, who suffers a massive heart attack when the escaped wolf Bersicker comes crashing through their window in a spectacular *mise en scène*.

Seward's Insane Asylum. Private London hospital for the mentally ill and the residence of Dr. John Seward, this institution appears to have been modeled on the

London County Lunatic Asylum near Chatham Road. It is a location fraught with dramatic events, which begin when Seward struggles to understand the mysterious but astute lunatic Renfield, a patient seeking to attain a unique kind of immortality by devouring progressively higher forms of life. When Dracula moves next door to Carfax (formerly Lesnes Abbey/Lady Chapel), the estate Harker has procured for him, the asylum becomes an even greater pivotal center of activity; Renfield gradually begins to do the count's bidding and allows him to attack Mina after she and her new husband Jonathan join their friends' concerted efforts to destroy Dracula. The asylum also is witness to moments of great personal dilemma as Renfield alternately embraces the vampire's temptations and then attempts to liberate himself from Dracula's omnipresent self. His final abjuration of the count comes at a great personal cost, his own violent death, and leads to one of the most dramatic scenes in the novel—the "blood baptism" of Mina and the searing of her now-polluted flesh with the holy wafer.

Hampstead Heath. Large, wildly beautiful, and hilly area in north London that is the scene of Lucy's attacks on local children, who call her the "Bloofer Lady," after her untimely death.

Kingstead Churchyard. London churchyard clearly modeled on the famed Highgate Cemetery, whose name Stoker diplomatically changed to avoid legal repercussions. The final resting place of Lucy, it is also the site where Van Helsing proves to Seward that she has become a vampire and where they proceed with her destruction, joined by her fiancé Arthur Holmwood and the Texan Quincey Morris. In an emotionally powerful scene, the grieving but determined friends drive a stake through the heart of the woman they have all loved, bringing her "the calm that was to reign for ever."

Czarina Catherine. Ship on which Dracula flees England, bound for the port of Varna. After the ship reaches Varna, Dracula forces it up the Danube River and then proceeds to take an overland route back to his castle. An unusual aspect of this location is that Mina, now under Dracula's telepathic control, is able to report on the ship's whereabouts through Van Helsing's hypnotically induced trances, thereby providing the vampire hunters with daily bulletins regarding Dracula's intended escape route.

Borgo Pass. Mountain gap in Transylvania near Castle Dracula in which the final dramatic scenes of the novel take place in a series of symbolic tableaux devised to convey the message that good ultimately triumphs over evil. It is here that the men finally track Dracula after purchasing a steamship, horses, and provisions, and it is here that Van Helsing and Mina anxiously wait for them while protecting themselves from Dracula's "sisters" by means of a sanctified holy circle. From this secure place, Van Helsing later makes his way to the castle and destroys all three, along with Dracula's lordly tomb, returning to Mina just in time for them to witness the novel's most intense chase, as the gypsy wagon carrying the count's sleeping body races against the desperate horsemen attempting to overtake them. The last deft strokes of the narrative conclude with the mortally wounded Morris plunging his bowie knife into Dracula's heart as Harker cuts his throat. Comparing the surrounding snow to the now stainless forehead of Mina, Morris dies acknowledging that the curse has passed.

When the friends return to this site seven years later, they revisit their terrible memories of Castle Dracula, which "stood as before, reared high above a waste of desolation," but are nonetheless deeply comforted by the newfound joys that have come into their lives, especially the birth of the Harkers' little boy, Quincey, the promise of new life.

— *Kathryn D. Marocchino*

DRAGON SEED

Author: Pearl S. Buck (1892-1973)
Type of work: Novel
Type of plot: Social realism

Time of plot: 1937-1940
First published: 1942

This propagandistic war novel depicts Japanese aggression in China. It never names either the village or the nearby city that are the centers of its action; however, the city is clearly Nanking, China's capital at the time the Japanese ravaged the city. The book emphasizes the wanton cruelty of the Japanese, while depicting its Chinese characters as peace-loving people unprepared for the ruthless enemy they face.

Village. Unnamed Chinese village west of a great city, in which the novel is set. The village has only one main street and a population of fewer than one hundred people, which suggests that it contains perhaps fifteen to twenty households. The village has one teahouse and several households that maintain small shops as a sideline activity. Except for those working in the shops, the inhabitants are farmers. Ling Tan has several male relatives in the village, but it is unclear if his family lineage is dominant. The novel mentions no temples, schools, or lineage halls in the village. The village is close enough to the great city for its residents to see the city walls and to walk there and return in one day. All the village families give some support to the anti-Japanese resistance.

Ling Tan's house. Home of a village family headed by its patriarch, Ling Tan. The family includes five children, three boys and two girls. Ling Tan is a simple farmer who is happy to see his family well provided for through their collective labor. He owns a few cattle, pigs, and chickens. As in Pearl Buck's other novels, *The Dragon Seed* emphasizes her protagonists' deep attachment to their home and fields. The ten members of the Ling family live in a substantial eight-room house surrounded by a wall and secured by a strong gate.

At first, the Ling family members are not harmed as the nearby city falls to the Japanese. Then the invading troops move west and loot Ling Tan's house, wantonly destroying most of the family's possessions, raping and then murdering an elderly woman relative. One of Ling Tan's sons goes west with the retreating Nationalist government but returns. Another becomes a guerrilla leader based in a Buddhist temple in the hills east of the city. Except for the youngest daughter, who flees west to live in a relocated missionary school, all surviving family members gather regularly in their home and village. Although outwardly complying with the Japanese orders, the Ling family turns their home into a site where information and arms are gathered for retaliatory attacks on the Japanese.

*****Nanking.** Capital city of the Republic of China from 1928 to 1937, during which period its population grew from 250,000 to around 1,000,000. Nanking is not mentioned by name in the novel; however, the novel's unnamed big city matches Nanking's description and historical circumstances. Buck lived in Nanking on the grounds of the Jinling University compound within Nanking's walls from 1921 to 1934 and clearly built her descriptions of the city in the novel from the Nanking she knew. Some action occurs in Nanking, especially in a walled Christian compound where women of the family fled in fear of Japanese troops. Other action in Nanking involves a merchant son-in-law who collaborates with the Japanese.

— *David D. Buck*

DREAM OF THE RED CHAMBER

Author: Cao Xuequin (Ts'ao Chan, 1716-1763), with a continuation by Gao Ê
Type of work: Novel
Type of plot: Domestic realism

Time of plot: c. 1729-1737
First published: Hung-lou Meng, 1792 (English translation, 1929; unabridged English translation; 1973-1986)

The primary setting of this Chinese novel—which has been variously translated as "Garden of Enchanted Vision" and "Prospect Garden"—is the place in which the protagonist, Bao-yu, and his female cousins live. The garden is a miniature world, a place that embodies the three main teachings of Chinese culture: Confucianism,

Buddhism, and Daoism. In addition to the garden, there is the transcendental place, or nonplace, variously translated as "Great Void" and "Land of Illusion," that is the true home of Bao-yu. In opposition to this land is the temporal world, known as Red Dust.

Garden of Enchanted Vision. Also translated as **Prospect Garden**, a magnificent garden containing ten gates, archways, and buildings built for the visit of the daughter of Jia, who has become an imperial concubine. To find a name for each of the garden's special features—each of which must allude to places described in classic Chinese poetry—Jia holds a literary contest, which is won by Bao-yu. After her single visit to the garden, the concubine allows her family to use it, rather than keep it as extravagant symbol of enormous wealth. She tells Bao-yu and his cousins to move in.

Each of the quarters of Bao-yu and his cousins, Bao-chai (rendered Black Jade in some editions) and Dai-yu (also called Precious Virtue) represents one of the three main teachings of Chinese civilization. Bao-chai's house is surrounded by bamboo that grows straight up toward the sky. Moreover, it does not have colorful or fragrant flowers to attract people. Most importantly, the inside of a bamboo stalk is empty. These characteristics match the essence of Buddhist teaching that purity and the "emptiness," or absence of desire and fear, lead one to reality and incorruptibility.

Dai-yu's house is named after fragrant herbs. Flowers and trees are absent; only mosses, rare herbs, and trailing plants that exude aromatic perfumes are visible there. In traditional Chinese culture, a person of virtue is compared to fragrant plants. Confucianism concerns itself with social life, and Dai-yu is a completely social person.

Bao-yu's Daoist commitment becomes obvious inside his rooms—from the Daoist authors and texts that he reads to the dominance of mirrors, which are Daoist images of place and spiritual vision. In yin-and-yang fashion, the mirrors show that endings and beginnings are impossible to separate, and that when any reality becomes extreme, it reverts to its opposite. These are Daoist insights. Bao-yu's quarters are alive with spiritual forms; a circular hall contains a number of "mirror doors," forming a pattern that is so confusingly continuous that it is impossible to see where it begins and ends. Each mirror door is an opening into a different spiritual place that cannot be controlled by human will but only

by harmonizing with the Dao. Bao-yu opens himself to the bending and flowing of the Dao represented in the fluid forms carved into the walls of his rooms. Especially at the end of the novel, he gives up everything to return to the Great Void.

When punishment hits its inhabitants, the garden also suffers. The place is brutally searched for evidence of a maid's forbidden affair. In protest, Bao-chai moves out, diminishing the garden's attraction. When Bao-yu is tricked into marrying Bao-chai because one of the garden's trees blooms out of season, his true love Dai-yu dies of grief. Her pavilion becomes haunted, and dread creeps into the garden. After the Ning-guo House is confiscated, the garden is boarded up. Its desertion at the novel's end signifies that the dream of golden days is over.

The number ten in the garden has a special significance. The Chinese character for "ten" is written like a mathematical plus sign; when dots are placed around this character, Chinese readers would regard the result as a complete circle. This shape gives a center and the four geographical directions; the top is considered heaven, while the bottom indicates the earth. This makes it a complete miniature world.

Great Void. Place of "nonplace"; the spiritual realm that both precedes and follows life on earth. Also variously called the **Land of Illusion** and **Paradise of Truth**, a place in Fairyland that coexists with the realistic places. The Great Void is the "place" where souls are located between reincarnations. Bao-yu's two dream-visits there foreshadow and confirm the fate of the female characters. The novel's inclusion of this magical place underlines its idea that life itself is an illusion. A prominent feature of Fairyland is **Greensickness Peak**, at whose foot a Taoist finds a stone bearing a long inscription that turns out to be the text of the novel.

Jinling (Jing-Ling). Fictional capital of China in which most of the novel is set. Using Jinling, the ancient name of Nanjing, to describe a city modeled after eighteenth century Beijing, the author creates a composite place, one that corresponds to his creation of composite characters. Jinling is the essence of the Red Dust of this world because *jing* means gold and *ling* means mound or grave. Near the end of the novel, the coffins of Bao-yu's grandmother and Bao-chai are carried back to Jinling for burial. Jinling is the place of the past and of death. It is also the place where Bao-yu bids farewell to his father and returns to the Great Void, after his awakening from the mortal dream of the Red Dust.

Rong-guo and Ning-guo Houses. Western (*rong*) and eastern (*ning*) compounds of the great Jia family, located on the northern side of one of Jinling's main roads. Facing south, like the imperial palace, both complexes are so vast that carriages are employed for travel among their many buildings. More than three hundred people live in each compound, the vast majority of them servants. Each adult member of the Jia family has a private residence, with the adolescents living in rooms close to one another. The young Bao-yu spends most of his time among his sisters and female cousins. His free travels between the male and female areas of the compounds indicate his special position in the novel. Just as the novel is primarily interested in the Jias' fate, the living spaces of the Jias are described with loving attention to detail. In contrast, the dwellings of servants remain obscure.

The fate of the houses is tied to the family. When two senior male Jias are convicted of misconduct and sent to the remote Mongolian frontier and the pirate-infested south coast of China, Ning-guo House is confiscated. At their lowest point, after the death of Grandmother Jia, burglars break into her apartment, indicating how steeply the Jias have fallen. After the emperor's pardon, Ning-guo House is restored to the family, while the exiled Jias can return.

Aroma's mother's house. One of the few places of ordinary people. Once only, Bao-yu escapes to visit his maid Aroma at home. The singularity of this adventure indicates that rich adolescents and women were virtual prisoners of their families' compounds.

Temple of the Iron Threshold. Temporary burial place of the Jias. Funeral processions to it provide rare opportunities for the young and female Jias to leave their compounds. In keeping with Chinese tradition, after a few years, the bodies of the deceased are transferred to the Jias' family tombs in Nanjing.

Pear Tree Court. Borderline dwelling at the outer edge of Rong-guo House, with easy access to the city outside. This access suits Xue Pan, a young male Jia with erotic designs on the boys of Jinling.

Bottle-gourd Temple. Minor monastery at the end of a blind alley in the river town of Suzhou (near Shanghai). The first place outside of Fairyland, it is accidentally burnt to the ground by a careless monk, indicating the random nature of human experience.

— *An Lan Jang*
— *R. C. Lutz*

DRINK

Author: Émile Zola (1840-1902)
Type of work: Novel
Type of plot: Naturalism

Time of plot: Second half of the nineteenth century
First published: L'Assommoir, 1877 (English translation, 1879)

The atmosphere and the setting of this novel are claustrophobic in both literal and figurative ways. The novel's action is confined mostly to a single neighborhood to the north of Paris. Within this area, the protagonist of the story, the laundress Gervaise Coupeau, is hemmed in a number of physical and metaphorical ways. A second major motif of the novel is seen in Gervaise's false starts and dreadful failures—her ups and downs.

***Goutte d'Or** (goot dor). Neighborhood north of Paris, on the eastern side of Montmartre, a butte on Paris's northern perimeter that is the center of most of the novel's action. The Goutte d'Or is now part of the city of Paris, but during the period in which the novel takes place, it was far from the center of metropolitan life. However, now, as then, the Goutte d'Or is a dangerous, crime-ridden slum.

Several places within the Goutte d'Or district are crucial to Gervaise's frustrated will to improve her lot. Her moral decadence is represented by the very places she inhabits. When she and her family arrive at Goutte d'Or, they live in the Hôtel Boncoeur (whose name means "good heart"). Later, they move to a huge tenement building, in which Gervaise lives in a number of abodes—winding up, most miserably, in a hovel under the stairs.

Other important stages along Gervaise's way in the Goutte d'Or are symbolized by a sleazy tavern and a smelly, dirty, and crowded apartment building.

*Paris. Seen from the Goutte d'Or, metropolitan Paris stands at a distance, its lights and glamour mocking the lives of the poor of the Goutte d'Or. However, beneath both the Goutte d'Or and the city beyond is the gray, oppressive horizon. After Gervaise marries her second husband, a roofer named Coupeau, they and their wedding guests go on an excursion to the cultural heart of Paris. In a comic episode, they visit the famous Louvre Museum. After a rest stop beneath the Pont-Royal over the Seine River, they climb to the top of the Vendôme column, located in one of the city's most exclusive business and residential areas.

Maison ouvrière (may-zon ewv-rih-yer). Workers' hostel in which Gervaise lives. A city-within-a-city, it is a terrifying labyrinth for Gervaise. Zola characterizes the building as a kind of beast that sucks workers into its bowels. Gervaise's gradual fall is ironically prefigured by her climbing a spiral staircase to meet Monsieur and Madame Lorilleux, who will become two of her worst tormentors.

Sainte-Anne Asylum. As a kind of geographical counterpart to the Goutte d'Or section, the hospital-asylum in which Gervaise's husband dies is located on the Left Bank of the Seine, to the far southeast of the city—in an area called La Glacière. The very name of the district, which means "glacier," suggests harsh cold and, by extension, death. It is with considerable irony that Zola's descriptions near the end of the novel emphasize the similarities between the maison ouvrière, where Gervaise's life with Coupeau begins, and the madhouse where her husband wastes away.

— *Gordon Walters*

DRUMS ALONG THE MOHAWK

Author: Walter D. Edmonds (1903-1998)
Type of work: Novel
Type of plot: Historical

Time of plot: 1775-1783
First published: 1936

Striving for a faithful representation of the past, this novel renders a careful portrait of life in central New York's Mohawk Valley during the American Revolution. Readers see an earlier era as people like themselves might have experienced it, with the minutiae of daily life balanced against the historical events of that time and place. With the exception of individual homes of the fictional characters, all locations in the novel are real places.

*Mohawk Valley. Region of what is now New York State surrounding the Mohawk River, which flows west from a point north of Albany to near Lake Oneida. Most of the action takes place here, but characters refer, usually disparagingly, to the machinations of politicians in Albany and Philadelphia, as well as other sites connected with the Revolutionary War, such as Fort Ticonderoga in New York and Connecticut's Newgate Prison, a former copper mine used as a penal colony to hold Tories and Loyalists.

*Deerfield Settlement. Tiny community at the western end of the Mohawk Valley, near Utica, to which the young pioneer Gilbert (Gil) Martin takes his bride, Magdelana (Lana), after their marriage in 1776 at Fox's Mills, where her family lives. Their first cabin, along with the rest of the houses and fields in the settlement, is burned to the ground by raiding Seneca Indians. The novel ends in 1784 when the Martins return to Deerfield, construct a new and larger cabin on the site of the old one, and re-clear and plant their land in wheat and corn.

*German Flats. Village east of Deerfield and south of the Mohawk River where Gil and Lana spend the winter of 1776 in a one-room house within sight of Fort Herkimer after fleeing Deerfield. During the spring they take refuge in Mrs. McKlennar's well-kept farm, which is one of the few fictional places in the novel. There, Gil works as a farm hand, and Lana does the sewing and takes over the milking whenever Gil must respond to militia calls. Mrs. McKlennar's stone house survives an attack by the Destructives, a roving band of Tories and Indians led by General Butler but is later burned by two lone Indians, while Lana hides with her two sons. Mrs. McKlennar survives by shaming the Indians into dragging her in her bed outside the burning house. Later, Gil and his friends build a simple cabin on the site. Although Mrs. McKlennar leaves her farm to Gil and Lana, her will is destroyed in the fire that claims the house, and the farm is forfeited for back taxes. Later, its is given to a Massachusetts veteran as payment for service to his country.

*Oriskany. Village at the western end of Mohawk Valley that is the site of one of the bloodiest battles of the war, with more than half the members of the Tryon County militia killed in a pitched fight with a combined British and Indian force. The losses to the German Flats militia are devastating.

*Fort Stanwix. Fortification at Rome, New York, that was a key to the protection of the Mohawk Valley during the war. Because the settlers doubt the ability of those in charge of the fort, they take responsibility themselves for protecting their farms from Indians, British forces, and Loyalists. Many settlers have good reasons to distrust their own military leaders, who seize their grain and animals for troops and leave them to starve through the harsh winters. Typical of the military's lack of foresight is their failure to leave the settlers with seed to plant new crops in the spring.

*West Canada Creek. Site of the final battle in the novel, here in 1781 the militia, under the leadership of Marinus Willett, kills Walter Butler and disperses his band of Destructives into the woods.

*Onondaga. Indian village at the far western end of the Mohawk Valley that is the site of an attack on the Onondaga Indians led by Colonel Van Schaick, whose troops burn the village and kill or capture all the Indians who have not fled.

— *Paula L. Cardinal*

DUBLINERS

Author: James Joyce (1882-1941)   *First published:* 1914
Type of work: Short fiction

This collection of fifteen stories is suffused with the sights, sounds, and smells of Ireland's capital city, Dublin, making it a powerful evocation of middle-class Dublin life in the late nineteenth and early twentieth centuries. James Joyce depicts the city as a "centre of paralysis," a drab, comfortless place, economically deprived and culturally stagnant; his characters live closed-in lives, paralyzed by material and emotional circumstances and trapped in an environment that offers little hope of escape or renewal.

*Dublin. Ireland's capital city, which had a population of some three hundred thousand people in the early twentieth century. Joyce, who grew up in Dublin, once told a publisher that no writer had yet presented the city to the world, a situation that he hoped this book would rectify. *Dubliners* does indeed give a strikingly detailed picture of the city, with attention to its topography and the texture of its daily life.

In many stories, characters traverse Dublin on foot, and Joyce carefully records their movements, naming actual streets, bridges, public squares, churches, monuments, shops, and pubs along the way. In "Two Gallants," for example, he creates a kind of verbal "map" of central Dublin, tracing the long, circuitous route that the aging Lenehan follows—first with his friend Corley and then alone—during a warm gray August evening.

Lenehan's wanderings give texture to the story, helping create a sense of Dublin as an actual place. He and Corley hear a harpist playing mournful music for a small group of listeners on Kildare Street. Later, Lenehan visits a shabby shop where he eats a solitary meal of grocers' peas and ginger beer. Near the end of his wanderings, he watches the late-night crowds dispersing on Grafton Street, one of Dublin's most fashionable shopping areas. Such details not only give the story a strong sense of place, they also allow Joyce to suggest the frustration and futility of Lenehan's life as a "paralyzed" Dubliner; his route is essentially circular, his journey lonely and pointless. After eating his meager supper, he feels his own poverty of purse and spirit.

Joyce himself was an avid stroller and often spent hours with his friends roaming the streets of Dublin. His walking knowledge of the city is evident not only in *Dubliners* but in all his fiction, especially *Ulysses* (1922), a novel built around the wanderings of Leopold Bloom on a summer day in Dublin.

*North Richmond Street. Principal setting of "Araby," one of the three stories about childhood that open *Dubliners*. The Joyce family lived at number 17 on this street during the mid-1890's, and Joyce incorporates many experiences from that time into his fiction. The unnamed boy narrator of "Araby" describes North Richmond as a quiet street, whose houses gaze at one another with brown "imperturbable faces."

Joyce also evokes scenes of childhood play in the surrounding area—the dark and muddy lanes behind houses and the dripping gardens where odors arose from the garbage dumps. On Saturday evenings, with his aunt, the boy goes marketing in the "flaring streets," jostled by drunken men and "bargaining women." Such passages capture the rough, run-down character of north central Dublin in the 1890's, a poor part of the city with crowded streets and dilapidated buildings. In "Araby" and in the other childhood stories—"The Sisters" and "An Encounter"—these gloomy surroundings weigh heavily on the sensitive young narrator. While he is not yet "paralyzed" by his environment, he feels a growing disillusionment with Dublin and its citizens.

Committee room. Wicklow Street center of political campaign operations for Richard Tierney in "Ivy Day in the Committee Room." A few campaign workers and other men gather here, mainly to escape bad weather and to wait for the bottled stout that Tierney has promised to send. The room is dark, cold, and gloomy, warmed only by a small coal fire that needs constant tending. When one of the men finally lights two candles, the "denuded room" comes into view, its walls bare, apart from a copy of an election address. Joyce uses the bleak room to mirror the dreary lives of his characters, most of whom are poor, unemployed, and cynical about Tierney and municipal politics generally. Those who support the Irish nationalist cause seem ineffectual, more interested in drinking stout and talking sentimentally about their dead political idol, Charles Stewart Parnell (a real person), than in working to end British colonial rule in their country. The fading fire in the Committee Room seems to suggest the dim prospects for political renewal in Dublin.

Morkin house. Home of Kate and Julia Morkin; a dark and gaunt house on Usher Island, a quay running along the south side of the River Liffey, that is the main setting of "The Dead." Joyce modeled this house on the residence of his great aunts at 15 Usher Island. In "The Dead," the final story of *Dubliners*, Joyce somewhat softens the harsh picture of Dublin given in earlier stories. He makes the house of the Morkin sisters a symbol of what he came to regard as a notable Irish virtue: hospitality. The sisters open their house for a lavish Christmas party, with music, dancing, drink, and an ample supper. Nevertheless, for Gabriel Conroy, the story's protagonist, the house becomes a stifling place. Nervous about the speech he must give and flustered by his unpleasant encounter with Miss Ivors, Gabriel twice imagines being away from the house, outdoors in the snowy night, enjoying the outdoor coolness and being able to walk alone. Like many of Joyce's Dubliners, he feels trapped and longs for escape. At the end of the story, after learning of his wife's girlhood love, Michael Furey, Gabriel recognizes his own self-deception and self-centeredness. Joyce hints that Gabriel might now be poised to live with great compassion and self-awareness, recognizing his connection with all the living and the dead.

*Galway. City in western Ireland's Connacht province and girlhood home of Gretta Conroy in "The Dead." While the actual setting of "The Dead" never moves outside Dublin, the west of Ireland—Galway in particular—plays a crucial role in the narrative. Gretta's husband, Gabriel, experiences a crisis of identity at the end of the story that is precipitated by Gretta's disclosure of events from her girlhood in Galway. This revelation sharply focuses an east-west tension in the story, with Dublin (in the east) representing Gabriel's once-secure sense of self and Galway (in the west) drawing

him toward a new identity, one less certain and stable. Thus, in the final story of *Dubliners*, Joyce suggests an alternative to Dublin, a place Gabriel might go, if only in imagination, to restore his sense of self.

— *Michael Hennessy*

THE DUCHESS OF MALFI

Author: John Webster (c. 1577-1580—before 1634)
Type of work: Drama
Type of plot: Tragedy

Time of plot: Sixteenth century
First performed: 1614; first published, 1623

Aside from a dramatic exterior interlude, the setting of this play is that of the interchangeable interiors of Italian courts and palaces, allowing John Webster to stress the importance of the characters and their language.

Malfi's court. Residence of the duchess of Malfi in Italy. Original set descriptions are sparse, and the central importance of the setting is not so much in its physical nature as its function as a location where characters good (the duchess and her husband Antonio) and evil (Duke Ferdinand, the cardinal, and the duchess's brothers) can meet and interact. Without it being specifically stated, there is a clear sense that this tragedy unfolds largely within walls which, by the end of the play, have become the prison of the duchess. As the play unfolds there is increased emphasis on the themes of darkness and light, leading to a greater use of lanterns. The major purpose of all the settings in this play is to provide a physical space where the characters can speak, for ultimately *The Duchess of Malfi* is about the failure of human relationships as shown in the disease of language itself.

Ruined abbey. Abandoned church that has been transformed into a fortification. When Antonio is lured to his

death, the most notable feature of the place is its startling echo, which is so pervasive and realistic that the superstitious believe it is a spirit which speaks to the living. The echo catches and repeats ironic refrains of dialogue which allow Webster to underscore the inexorable fatality that has enmeshed the characters.

Cardinal's residence. At the conclusion of the drama, language again becomes a crucial part of the physical setting as the cardinal strictly orders his supporters not to rush to his aid no matter how loudly he might call for assistance. As the cardinal is killed to revenge the deaths of the duchess, her husband Antonio, and her children, his minions listen above the scene of the action but do not interfere until it is too late. Once again, language and action are fatally separated.

— *Michael Witkoski*

DULCE ET DECORUM EST

Author: Wilfred Owen (1893-1918)
Type of work: Poetry

First published: 1920

The setting of this poem is the no-man's-land of the Western Front in World War I. Gritty realism evokes the horrors of this desolate landscape and contributes to the emotion of despair in the poem.

No-man's-land. Dangerous zone between facing enemy lines that could be on any of a number of World War I battlefields, sites that were fought over for months and years until the land became an eerie moonscape of craters, unexploded shells, and land leached of all nutrients by noxious residues of powders and gas. This gray world is lighted only by phosphorescent gases and flares; its sounds are those of exploding shells and dying men.

An unexpected gas attack turns the soldiers' world a peculiar sea green, and a comrade "drowns" when his lungs fill with blood and other body fluids. This wretched scene is designed to counter those who would coax the young into joining a war out of a mixture of desire for excitement and patriotism. The desolate scene explodes the patriotic lie "*Dulce et Decorum est pro patria mori*," promulgated by the Roman writer Horace in his *Odes* (23 B.C.E., 13 B.C.E.; English translation, 1621). Death in no-man's-land is not sweet and fitting but obscene and painful. A nameless no-man's-land from the battles of World War I provides the depressingly realistic backdrop of Wilfred Owen's poem which hopes to warn against mindless patriotism unconnected to actual war, which is grim and tragic.

— *Isabel Bonnyman Stanley*

THE DUMB WAITER

Author: Harold Pinter (1930-   )
Type of work: Drama
Type of plot: Absurdist

Time of plot: Mid-twentieth century
First performed: 1959, in German translation; first performed and published in English, 1960

The setting of this one-act play is a claustrophobic basement room that suggests the confined lives of the two main characters and the uncertain, mysterious nature of existence generally.

Basement room. Located somewhere in Birmingham, England, this room is furnished only with two beds pushed against the back wall. A dumbwaiter (small serving elevator) comes down between the two beds. A door to the right exits to a hallway, and a door to the left exits to a kitchen and bathroom—rooms that cannot be seen. The basement room resembles a prison cell, suggesting that the play's two main characters (petty killers or "hit men") are already being punished for their crimes by the bleak, confining lives they lead. Waiting to carry out their next job, they represent each other's hell. The two doors suggest the simple mazes in a rat's cage: On the left side, food comes in and goes out; the exit on the right side represents birth and death.

Though not the kind of company many people would like to keep, the two hoodlums are curiously—almost comically—human. While they wait dumbly, they get bored, hungry, and nervous. Their "orders" finally come down from above via the dumbwaiter and a speaking tube, but at first only food orders for dishes they have no way of fixing. However, the person sending the orders is presumably the boss (named Wilson, recalling former British prime minister Harold Wilson), so they must do something.

Their predicament in the basement room suggests human existence generally—life lived mostly without understanding but under pressure, especially when the orders come down from above. These thoughts lead to speculation about the nature of human beings and of God—or perhaps only about the dubious nature of organizations and governments (which seem largely to have replaced religion in modern life).

— *Harold Branam*

THE DUNCIAD

Author: Alexander Pope (1688-1744)
Type of work: Poetry
Type of plot: Mock-heroic

Time of plot: Eighteenth century
First published: 1728-1743

In this dark Tory satire, various places in London symbolize the cultural breakdown from a world of high art, good taste, virtue, and order to one of popular culture, vulgarization, tyranny by an illiterate majority, and chaos. Journeying past these places is an endless motley mass of "dunces"—bad authors, journalists, publishers, critics, scholars, teachers, trivialists, patrons, opera singers, and politicians—fools under the guidance of the Goddess Dulnes and the king of the Dunces. This journey is the basis of three parodies: the political parade of London's lord mayor, the literary journey of Aeneas in Vergil's epic The Aeneid *(29-19* B.C.E.; *English translation, 1553), and the allegorical movement of dullness and folly from the lower classes to the higher.*

*****London.** Capital and largest city of Great Britain. With a population of nearly seven hundred thousand people in the eighteenth century, London is the setting of the final campaign of "The War of the Dunces," which culminates in the obliteration of high cultural standards. At the core of its East End is the old walled section, known as "the City," center for the lower and middle classes, business, the trades, markets, counting houses, the Royal (stock) Exchange, jails, shanties, butcheries, shipping, coal wharves, and tanning factories. The East End was noted for its mobs, crime, jails, poverty, ugliness, dirt, sooty air, open sewers, and foul odors. London's West End is associated with the royal court and aristocratic elegance, leisure, gardens, lovely parks, large squares, and beautiful houses. The mock-heroic journey of the dunces from the East End to the West End and back symbolizes the conquest of high culture by low standards.

*****Smithfield.** Lower-class section of East London, site of a bazaar and the occasional dramatic entertainment "agreeable only to the Taste of the Rabble." The mock-heroic invocation to the muse in the poem's opening lines announces the theme of cultural degeneration: the bringing of "The Smithfield Muses to the Ear of Kings."

*****Rag-Fair.** Located near the Tower of London, a place where old clothes were sold to the poor. It is the site of the cave of Poverty and Poetry, mythical source of low standards and poor taste. References to Grub Street, a lane of unsuccessful authors who pandered to popular tastes, continue the linkage among poverty, crime, and low culture. From her sacred dome of Dulnes

near the Tower, Goddess Dulnes and the dunces begin their evening movement through the City.

*****Guildhall.** Historic city hall of the City of London. Goddess Dulnes's home is her "Guild Hall," literally the seat of the lord mayor, popular government, and trade. It symbolizes the triple alliance of democratic politics, commerce, and vulgar standards that threatens to overwhelm the landed aristocracy and its high culture.

*****Ludgate.** Western entrance to the City of London. Tracing the route of the lord mayor's parade, the dunces leave the City by this western gate, built by King Lud and carved with images of kings whose heads have been scored off by vandals, symbolizing the antiaristocratic and philistine temperament of the dunces. Their move west to found the empire of dullness parodies Aeneas's voyage west to found the Roman Empire.

*****Fleet Street.** London street that was the traditional home of many printing houses that published newspapers and popular reading. Traveling on this street, the dunces pass two jails, Bridewell, for vagrants, prostitutes, and the disorderly, and the Fleet, for debtors. These prisons suggest the criminality of lowering standards.

*****Strand.** Continuing Fleet Street and running parallel with the River Thames to its south, this street is the direct route of the dunces from the City to the West End and back. Places along it symbolize the encroachments of low life. They pass Drury Lane, noted for fighting and prostitution. At Fleet Ditch, a channel of sewage running into the Thames, the dunces hold their mock-heroic games, among them, contests of urinating, catcalling, racing through slop, and diving in filth, symbolic of bad poetry, criticism, journalism, or unethical publishing.

*Elysian Shade. The descent of Goddess Dulnes and the king of the Dunces parodies Aeneas's descent to the underworld. While Aeneas learned of the greatness of the Roman Empire that he was to found, the king hears a prophecy that his dynasty of dullness will rule the world. By the poem's apocalyptic end, this has come to pass, as the arts, learning, virtue, and religion have become imprisoned, have hidden, or have died, and "Universal Darkness Buries All."

— *H. George Hahn*

DUTCHMAN

Author: Amiri Baraka (Everett LeRoi Jones, 1934-   )

Type of work: Drama

Type of plot: Political

Time of plot: 1960's

First performed: 1964; first published, 1964

All the action in this play takes place within a subway car, rattling under the streets of New York City, on which a white woman named Lula confronts a young black man named Clay. Treatment of "place" is highly symbolic: As a specific location, the city is of secondary importance to the subway, a symbolic subterranean setting in which the deeper realities of American life are dramatized.

*New York City. Literally an "overdrop" for the play, the city serves both as the realistic urban setting for highly charged racial dynamics between black and white Americans in the 1960's and as Amiri Baraka's mythic and symbolic setting for a critique of black consciousness and the Black Arts movement.

Subway tunnels. Subterranean passageways for the subway trains that symbolize places in which social and psychological realities are exposed in their true terms through interactions between characters moving underneath the surface of American culture. Below ground, violent truths of American history erupt into stark view, with profound consequences for particular human beings who cannot escape to the surface and its delusions of safety. The tunnels also function as metaphorical space: the interior consciousness of "the black artist," who struggles to create (and literally, to survive) in a world controlled by the norms of white Western culture and aesthetics. At this symbolic level, the subterranean tunnel setting of the play is itself the *action* of the mind of an artist, struggling to freedom.

Subway car. Train car on which Clay and Lula encounter each other. With its passengers literally pressed into close proximity with one another, the car becomes the site of a compressed narrative of American racial history as it passes through the dark subway tunnels. Within this car, explosive conflicts are framed in harsh light and within sharply delineated space. Clay and Lula are trapped within historical roles and identities, on a stage that is speeding forward into time. The intensely philosophical and politicized violence that unfolds between the two characters is also a social violence shared by other riders when they eventually toss Clay's body off the train. On this level, the car *is* America, exposed to light. Within the other symbolic space of the play, the mind of the "black artist," the subway car serves as an illuminated moment of sharp insight into the threats posed to black artistic consciousness in America.

— *Sharon Carson*

EARTH

Author: Émile Zola (1840-1902)
Type of work: Novel
Type of plot: Naturalism

Time of plot: 1860's
First published: La Terre, 1887 (English translation, 1888)

One of the most famous of Émile Zola's Rougon-Maquart novels, this story takes place in the plains of central France, a region whose long tradition of extensive agricultural production based in small villages surrounding cultural centers such as Chartres and Orléans make it an ideal setting for Zola's naturalist style. The story of peasant workers focuses on Jean Macquart and the network of families in and around the village of Rognes, reflecting images portrayed by the nineteenth century French painter Jean François Millet.

***La Beauce** (lah bohz). Extensive flat plains of central France that have historically been the country's bread basket. The finery and wealth of its main cities, especially Chartres, Châteaudun, and Orléans, which Zola describes only occasionally, are based on a higher level of commerce, which entails a variety of associated professionals, such as lawyers and notaries. This novel reflects a different reality, one of extreme simplicity in village life and family relations that make Chartres seem distant.

Zola underlines the monotony of the Beauce plains by describing the main (indeed only) road connecting Châteaudun and Orléans as straight and flat, visible at a distance only because of its neighboring line of telegraph poles. Villages are "islands of stone," whose only identifying marks emerging out of the wheat fields are church steeples. A few windmills, clearly important for agricultural work at harvest time, break the monotony of the flat horizon, but remain practically immobile most of the year.

Rognes (rohn). Beauce village that is the primary setting for this story of peasant family life and labors. Zola modeled Rognes on the real village of Romilly-sur-Aigre, located four kilometers east of the larger town of Cloyes. The area surrounding Rognes does not offer the same guarantees of soil fertility found in the heartland of the Beauce region. Inferior fertility earns it a separate designation in the popular mind as the "lice-ridden" Beauce.

Zola portrays Rognes itself in terms that suggest sparseness. From the distance, only a few peaks of houses appear at the base of the village church, whose gray stone clock tower provides shelter for several "families of very old crows," a hint that the village has little attraction for younger inhabitants. A notable exception to this bleakness occurs in the early fall when, during the harvest season, the whole village reeks of grapes, and a week of gaiety and open drunkenness accompanies the opening of the previous year's new wine. Here images of Dutch Renaissance paintings of peasant debauchery are clearly meant to reappear in the fields around Rognes.

***L'Aigre** (laygr). Small river that runs through Rognes, carving out a narrow valley that forms a dividing line between the distinct regions of the Perche and the plains of the Beauce. Away from the village, the fields on both sides of the river offer Zola many scenes of peasant activities, especially in the season of the grain harvest, when the wheat crop resembles a yellow moving sea, upon which the ribbon of the Aigre seems to float.

Chartres (shart). Town that is the site of one of France's most famous medieval cathedrals, located on the majestic Eure River. Chartres stands in stark contrast to the villages depicted in the novel. Some lesser figures in the village setting, such as Madame Charles, find themselves transplanted from Chartres to the countryside as a consequence of marriage. Madame Charles seeks any opportunity she can find to revisit the quaint Chartres streets of her youth, with their memories of sophisticated facades, mahogany furnishings in mirrored salons, and hints of the perfumed atmosphere of city life.

Le Perche (leh persh). Pastoral region north of the Beauce. Although adjacent to the plains of the Beauce, the soils of the Perche are quite different. The cereal crops that have always guaranteed the prosperity of regional cities like Chartres give way to rich pasture lands ideal for animal grazing. As a result, the very appearance of villages in the Perche is distinct, surrounded by groupings of highly valued horses whose name, "percherons," recalls their native fields.

Bazoches-le-Doyen (bah-ZOSH-leh-dwa-YAN). First village on the side of Rognes opening to the plains of the Beauce. Although most of the novel's activity focuses on Rognes, some images of the even smaller Bazoches appear because the one and only "main" intersection of roads in Rognes leads to Bazoches. Zola combined elements of two neighboring real villages' names, Bazoches-en-Dunois and Ouzouer-le-Doyen, to create the name of this fictive hamlet.

— *Byron D. Cannon*

THE EARTHLY PARADISE

Author: William Morris (1834-1896)
Type of work: Poetry

First published: 1868-1870

Inspired by medieval Icelandic sagas, the tales in this collection are told by Norsemen who have given up after a thirty-year quest for the fabled Earthly Paradise "across the western sea where none grow old." After lengthy wanderings abroad, they gather in a hospitable "nameless city in a distant sea" where the worship of the ancient Greek gods has not died out and spend the rest of their lives, gathering periodically to swap stories drawn from Norse legends with city elders, whose stories derive from classical subjects.

Greece. An unnamed Greek island is the place where the wanderers and city elders gather to tell stories, after one of the elders encourages the Norsemen to recount their adventures. The hosts tell stories from classical mythology, many with specific sites, such as "Atalanta's Race" in the Arcadian woods, "Pygmalion and the Image" in Cyprus, "The Love of Alcestis" in Thessaly, "The Story of Acontius and Cydippe" in Delos, "The Golden Apples" on a ship from Tyre, and "Bellerophon at Argos."

Norway. Native country of the Norse wanderers, who originally sailed away from it to escape a pestilence—a terrifying example of the fear of death that is their impetus for seeking the Earthly Paradise. The wanderers' stories derive from Norse and other medieval tales and reflect William Morris's admiration for Icelandic sagas and the Norsemen's skilled craftsmanship, courage, and endurance. Places in the Norsemen's tales include mythic lands in "Ogier the Dane" and "The Fostering of Aslaug," an identified dreamland in "The Land East of the Sun and West of the Moon," and Laxdaela in "Lovers of Gudrun," a chivalric episode from the historical saga.

England. Morris's inspiration for this collection of tales was Geoffrey Chaucer's *The Canterbury Tales* (1387-1400), and England's King Edward III represents something of his idealized view of the precapitalist world of the Middle Ages. The force that drives Morris in *The Earthly Paradise* is a feeling of despair and hatred for the contemporary Victorian world, with its troubles and cares. Morris sees himself as a dreamer of dreams of other times. The lyrics in *The Earthly Paradise* that introduce each monthly section of tales record seasonal changes and describe the English landscape.

Earthly Paradise. Imaginary place that is the object of the Norse wanderers' desperate and hopeless quest, a place that evokes a mood that swings from melancholy to sensuous ease. Morris's poem was enormously popular when it was published, probably because it offered a refuge from the ugliness, drabness, and tedium of industrial life in nineteenth century England.

— *Velma Bourgeois Richmond*

EAST OF EDEN

Author: John Steinbeck (1902-1968)
Type of work: Novel
Type of plot: Regional

Time of plot: 1865-1918
First published: 1952

The title of this novel is an allusion to the biblical land of Nod—the place to which God banishes Cain after he murders his brother Abel—and the novel's narrative imaginatively parallels the Book of Genesis, with its Salinas Valley representing the Bible's Garden of Eden and Adam Trask's twin sons representing the biblical Adam's sons, Cain and Abel.

*Salinas Valley (sah-LEE-nas). Long narrow depression between Northern California's Gabilan and Santa Lucia mountain ranges. The Salinas River winds its way up the center of the valley and empties into Monterey Bay. In the novel, the Gabilan Mountains to the east are described as lovely and full of light, presenting to the residents of the valley warm and beckoning foothills. The Santa Lucias to the west, standing between the valley and the sea, are dark, brooding, and dangerous. This contrasting setting enhances the conflicts of the plot—between Adam and his half-brother Charles; between Adam and Cathy, the evil mother of the twins; between Cal and his twin brother, Aron; and between Cal and his father. Biblical parallels with Adam, Eve, Cain, and Abel, reinforced by the setting, are made explicit in the second part of the novel, in which Samuel Hamilton reads aloud to a despondent Adam Trask the first sixteen verses of Genesis: 4. Steinbeck, himself, was born in Salinas and spent much of his life in nearby Monterey, which he used as a setting in other novels.

Trask ranch. Family ranch located in the richest part of the Salinas Valley, where the land is lush and fertile. The opposition of good and evil, light and dark—the overt theme of the novel—is further reflected in the contrast between the Trask ranch and the Hamilton farm, which is located in an arid, barren section of the valley.

The Trask ranch parallels the biblical **Garden of Eden** in that all is not perfect within it. Adam Trask's wife, Cathy, who is born with a sinful nature, is restive. To get away, she shoots Adam, wounding him both physically and spiritually. A subsequent alteration of the setting represents a reversal of fortune as well. Samuel Hamilton's introduction of a windmill changes his wasteland into a productive farm. Adam, on the other hand, fails disastrously in his effort to ship lettuce packed in ice by rail to the East Coast. His ranch deteriorates, his house becomes derelict, and his fields, gardens, and orchards are left unattended. The Trasks are metaphorically expelled from the Garden of Eden.

*Salinas. Major urban center in the Salinas Valley. Steinbeck uses a wealth of naturalistic detail in describing this community during the late nineteenth and early twentieth centuries. Its original settlers, the Mexicans, are succeeded by Americans from the East and, still later, by Irish and Chinese immigrants. Exciting and sometimes troubling new inventions—the windmill, the motorcar, refrigeration—are introduced into the town and its environs. Steinbeck shows how the economy and the very character of the community are altered by the advent of World War I. Salinas also is the place where Cathy Trask, after abandoning her husband and infant sons and changing her name to Kate, eventually becomes rich as the proprietress of a notorious brothel.

Connecticut farm. Place where Adam and his half-brother Charles grow up before coming to California; its location is identified only as being on the outskirts of a small town that was near a big town. As a boy, Adam hates his father, who is passionately loved by Charles. Conflicts between father and son and between brother and brother that are treated more fully later in the novel are introduced here. Much of the first quarter of the narrative, up until Adam marries Cathy in the West takes place in this setting. Adam goes to California hoping to find the happiness that has eluded him in the East. Steinbeck traces the history of this deteriorating New England family along with that of Samuel Hamilton's Irish immigrant family, thereby revealing the diversity among those who came to California to make a new start.

Massachusetts town. Unnamed place in which Adam's future wife, Cathy Ames, grows up. She appears to be innocent but is actually a manipulative sociopath. After her parents thwart her first attempt to leave home, she burns down their house, killing them and faking her own death. Afterward she becomes the mistress of a Boston man who operates a string of brothels and later the wife of the unsuspecting Adam. In California she becomes a terrible corrupting Eve figure—or perhaps the serpent—in the Eden of the Salinas Valley.

— *Patrick Adcock*

EASTWARD HO!

Authors: George Chapman (c. 1559-1634) with Ben Jonson (1573-1637) and John Marston (1576-1634)
Type of work: Drama

Type of plot: Comedy
Time of plot: c. 1605
First performed: 1605; first published, 1605

George Chapman, Ben Jonson, and John Marston collaborated in using several London locations, including the Counter, a debtors' prison, and the muddy River Thames to create a rollicking farcical satire on gullible middle-class seekers after wealth and aristocratic social positions.

Touchstone's goldsmith shop. London shop that establishes the industrious middle-class nature of the goldsmith Touchstone. The shop helps to define the shrewd common sense that underlies Touchstone's skepticism about the foolish dreams of his daughter Gertrude, who hopes to become a lady by marrying the improvident Sir Petronel, and the pretensions of Quicksilver, his apprentice, who imagines that he can become a gentleman of leisure by following untrustworthy friends and romantic illusions fostered by unrealistic plays.

Sir Petronel Flash's castle. Nonexistent "castle in the air" in Essex that is the major reason for Gertrude's marriage to Sir Petronel. It is also the source of Gertrude's disillusionment when she makes a journey by coach into Essex only to find that the castle does not exist.

*****Virginia.** Proposed North American site of an English colony, which is advertised as the source of great wealth, an illusory fantasy for Sir Petronel and his fellow adventurers, Scapethrift and Spendall. Since Virginia had not been settled at the time of the play's first performance, the truth about its actual hardships was not known.

Cuckholds' Haven. Landing on the Isle of Dogs in the Thames where the adventurers are shipwrecked by a sudden squall as they are setting out to go "Eastward Ho" down the river to begin their voyage to Virginia. Their belief that they have found refuge on the coast of France provides one of the play's funniest moments, as Sir Petronel tries to communicate in French to the first gentleman they encounter, only to exasperate him when he learns they are actually English.

*****The Counter.** Debtors' prison in which Quicksilver, Sir Petronel, and their cronies are incarcerated, and where they all conveniently undergo religious "conversions." Although Touchstone initially is adamant in his refusal to pay their debts and secure their release, his compassion toward them is aroused when his virtuous former apprentice and current son-in-law Golding, who is sympathetic toward Quicksilver, has himself jailed there on a technicality. Forced to visit the prison, Touchstone relents, and in a Dickensian ending forgives his erring former apprentice, and his son-in-law, Sir Petronel, and pays their debts, thereby gaining their release.

— Edgar L. Chapman

EAT A BOWL OF TEA

Author: Louis Chu (1915-1970)
Type of work: Novel
Type of plot: Domestic realism

Time of plot: 1941-1949
First published: 1961

This novel's settings are not merely physical or geographical locations but are symbolic, representing customs, traditions, and assumptions that are integral to the characters in the story. Against the backdrop of Chinese communities in New York and San Francisco, author Louis Chu delineates the passage of Chinese immigrant bachelor societies to Chinese American family societies.

*New York Chinatown. New York City's Chinese quarter, which is the novel's primary setting. The author lived there and was an active and notable figure in the community. At the close of World War II, Chinatown is a close-knit, predominantly male society of aging bachelors. These old men, separated by racist immigration laws from their wives and families who remain in China, loyally cling to their inflexible, chauvinistic Cantonese sensibilities and customs, oblivious to the changes that China has undergone in their absence and isolated from mainstream American culture. A homogeneous society with a strong adherence to tradition, parental authority, and strict supervision, Chinatown represents the "old world" these men have left behind and functions as a prison, ensnaring its inhabitants in nostalgia and thus rendering them powerless.

To illustrate how New York's Chinatown is a closed community, the story's action occurs inside buildings such as barbershops, restaurants, apartments, and clubhouses. These establishments provide refuge for the Chinese exiles who live out their days gossiping with other bachelors, gambling and playing mah jong, and participating in Chinese social and political organizations, such as the Wang Association, the Chinese Masons, the Kuomintang, the Chinese Elks, and Ping On Tong. Chinatown's settings are often depicted as dingy, dimly lit basement dwellings that are dark and empty.

This symbolizes the stagnant, decaying state of Chinese immigrants who, during the period in which the story is set, are denied United States citizenship.

In New York's Chinatown, newly married protagonist, Ben Loy, like the Chinese bachelors separated from their wives and families, cannot reproduce. In Chinatown, Ben Loy is imprisoned by his dutiful sense of obedience to his father and his father's traditional ways and by guilt over his own youthful indiscretions. Consequently, Ben Loy is stripped of his masculinity and becomes impotent with his traditional Chinese wife.

Sunwei District (sewn-way). Region in southern China in which Wah Gay's and Lee Gong's home villages, Sun Lung Lay and New Peace Village, are located. In contrast to New York's Chinatown, these Chinese villages are depicted as rural and natural with roads of cobblestone and dirt. To Wah Gay and Lee Gong, who have spent more than half of their lives in the United States, the villages of Sunwei nostalgically represent the China of their youth—a China that no longer exists. To Ben Loy, however, the villages of Sunwei seem old, narrow, and staid and represent stifling traditions, set ways, and limited choices. With its gouged countryside and dismantled railway system, Sunwei District reflects the cultural and political upheavals China experienced during the early part of the twentieth century.

*San Francisco Chinatown. San Francisco's Chinese quarter, in which Ben Loy and Mei Oi eventually make their home and where Ben Loy establishes his independence from his father, regains his virility, and accepts Mei Oi as the wife of his choosing and not of his father's. For Ben Loy and Mei Oi, San Francisco's Chinatown symbolizes a hopeful future, new ideas, and new frontiers as they rediscover their love for each other in this place of new beginnings.

Stanton. Connecticut town to which Wah Gay sends seventeen-year-old Ben Loy to live when he first comes to America because Stanton is a small and safe town, in contrast to New York City—a big city filled with temptations. Stanton is also the town where Ben Loy and Mei Oi briefly move after Mei Oi's affair with Ah Song is discovered.

— *Tammy J. Bowles*

EDWARD II

Author: Christopher Marlowe (1564-1593)
Type of work: Drama
Type of plot: Historical
Time of plot: Fourteenth century

First performed: The Troublesome Reign and Lamentable Death of Edward the Second, c. 1592; first published, 1594

The central space of this play is that of England, with London's royal palace at its figurative center. The various actions and events, however, include scenes from a variety of locations in England, France, and Wales, and developments in the story of King Edward's fall are strongly influenced by events occurring outside England, particularly in France. Although the locations are varied, the action of the play moves with a crispness that unifies the work, and the rapid shifts of location seem coordinated with the shifts in Edward's mercurial personality and in the changes of his fortunes.

London. Center of English political power and of King Edward's monarchy. Several locations within London are settings for important scenes, including the royal palace, the new temple (a center of legal authority), and the Tower of London, the traditional place of detention for important political prisoners. The first scene of the play is set on a London street and the last at the royal palace.

Paris. Capital of the French monarchy and home of Edward II's queen Isabella, sister of the French king. It is in Paris that Isabella meets Kent and the younger Mortimer, with whom she plans to invade England and make war against her husband.

Neath Abbey. Church in Glamorganshire, Wales, where King Edward is arrested by his enemies after failing to escape to Ireland. Edward II was born in Carnarvon Castle in Wales and was England's first Prince of Wales.

Berkeley Castle (BAHRK-lee). Castle in Gloucestershire that is the place of Edward's final incarceration and murder.

— *Robert W. Haynes*

EFFI BRIEST

Author: Theodor Fontane (1819-1898)
Type of work: Novel
Type of plot: Domestic realism

Time of plot: Second half of the nineteenth century
First published: 1895 (English translation, 1914)

This novel begins and ends at Hohen-Cremmen, the ancestral manor of the Briest family, where they enjoy the privileged lifestyle of Germany's landed gentry, a lifestyle on the way out since the Industrial Revolution. The novel contrasts the stability of traditional life at Hohen-Cremmen with the more transitory lifestyle of an up-wardly mobile civil servant stationed temporarily in the small Baltic port of Kessin. Finally, his career move to the capital city of Berlin reveals the large metropolis as a center of anonymity and isolation.

Hohen-Cremmen (HOH-uhn KREHM-uhn). Large country estate in the Mark Brandenburg region of north-eastern Germany whose manor house has belonged to the Briest family since the early seventeenth century. The manor house is covered in ivy, has parklike grounds, a pond, a swing, and colorful flowerbeds. It borders on the churchyard wall, and its pastor is an important mentor to young Effi von Briest. The Briests live securely in the comfort of inherited wealth. Effi's father need only concern himself with grain prices and can otherwise take long walks through the fields and enjoy his magnificent surroundings.

An early sign that modern life is passing the Briests by is the sound of a modern through-train half a mile away. A change in the grounds at the end of the novel sends a similar message. When Effi dies, her parents remove the sundial from the circular flowerbed and replace it with her gravestone. Her time has run out, as has the time of the landed gentry with their large country estates.

Kessin. Small German port in Pomerania on the Baltic Sea. Elements of the fictional town of Kessin are modeled on Theodor Fontane's memories of Swine-münde, where he lived as a boy. The lodgings that Effi's new husband, Baron von Innstetten, rents are nothing more than two rooms on the main floor of an old-fashioned framework house formerly owned by a sea captain. In some ways, it seems as if the former inhabitants are still present. Hanging from the ceiling in the front hall are the captain's model ship in full sail, a stuffed shark, and a crocodile. However, the effect of these unusual objects is negligible in comparison with the apparent presence of restless spirits who make the upper floor uninhabitable for Effi, who hears sounds of gowns sweeping across the floor and learns that the captain's niece disappeared from there on her wedding night.

Kessin is a port of call that is busy with tourists in the summer season and all but deserted in the winter. In contrast to Hohen-Cremmen, Kessin does not have an influential and respected pastor. The provincial narrow-mindedness of the place is illustrated by its residents' treatment of their last pastor, who was harassed to an early death for suggesting that the sea captain's Chinese servant be granted a churchyard burial. Now it seems that the ghost of the Chinese man, who danced with the niece, remains in the house.

Natural and supernatural dangers abound in Effi's Kessin home. The upper floor of the house is haunted, and the lower floor houses a crazed coachman's wife with a black hen on her lap. There is a shipwreck off the coast, and carriages narrowly avert getting sucked into a type of quicksand. Effi feels so vulnerable and threatened in Kessin that she wishes she were hidden by a protective wall of snow. The place leaves its mark on her.

*Berlin.** Capital of Germany to which Baron von Innstetten takes Effi when he is promoted to section head of a ministry department. There, they choose to live in one of the tall new Keith Street houses that is divided into several apartments. The still-damp plaster they find when they move in seems to signify an auspicious new beginning. However, six years later the past resurfaces to ruin Effi's marriage. Fontane portrays Berlin as a fickle society in which friendships are superficial and contingent on a rigid moral code. After Effi is divorced, only her elderly physician and her maidservant attend to her, and her church is of no help. Furthermore, as Effi's husband discovers, the famous Berlin opera and other cultural diversions are inadequate substitutes for meaningful human contact. It is an interesting coincidence that Koniggratzer Street, where Effi lives in ignominy after her divorce, not only effectively allows her to disappear within the large metropolis, but also itself has disappeared from the map of Berlin.

Fontane himself lived in Berlin, and his descriptions of the central part of the city are still accurate, thanks to the Germans' restoration of the re-united Berlin as closely as possible to its pre-1945 configuration. Dorotheen Street, for example, which the East Germans renamed Clara Zetkin Street, is once again Dorotheen Street. It is easy to trace Effi's route from the Friedrichs Street train station to Dorotheen Street to Schadow Street, and to locate Keith Street just southwest of the Tiergarten. It remains one of the better areas of the city.

— *Jean M. Snook*

EGMONT

Author: Johann Wolfgang von Goethe (1749-1832)
Type of work: Drama
Type of plot: Tragedy

Time of plot: Sixteenth century
First published: 1788 (English translation, 1837); first
performed, 1789

Partly a historical drama and partly a character drama, this play is set in Brussels at a moment when the peoples of Europe's Lowland countries are on the verge of rising against their Spanish rulers. Brussels becomes a scene for iconoclastic attacks on churches that worry the country's Spanish rulers. Count Egmont, torn between his devotion to his people and his loyalty to the Spanish king, is imprisoned by the representative of the Spanish Inquisition. His execution represents the end of the Spanish and Dutch cooperation that he embodies and sets the stage for the later, historically successful, revolt of the Netherlands.

***Brussels.** Prosperous Flanders city (now part of Belgium), whose streets are gathering places for merchants, soldiers, and simple people to discuss politics freely. However, a revolt against Spanish rule fanned by Calvinist preachers has brought political turmoil. When the occupying army under the duke of Alba enters the city, the streets of Brussels are emptied and silenced by martial law. Gallows, built at night and shrouded in black on the town square, point up the treachery of Alba, the intolerance of the Spanish rule, and the end of the freedoms the citizens have enjoyed.

Alba's palace. Official Brussels residence of the duke of Alba, the emissary of the Spanish king, Philip II. The palace, in keeping with his harsh regime, is an armed camp. Stiff, motionless soldiers line its corridors; entrances are tightly guarded; ministers fear to speak. Lured to the palace under false pretenses, Count Egmont is arrested and chained in its subterranean dungeon. In his despair he dreams that the prison wall opens, and a female figure in the guise of his beloved Clara predicts that his death will bring his people freedom. When he awakes, surrounded by soldiers who will conduct him to the gallows, the victory symphony stimulates the audience to contemplate the eventual triumph of Dutch independence, as well as the tragedy of Egmont's unjust execution.

Clara's house. Home of Clara (Clärchen), a commoner who loves and is loved by Egmont. The house is clearly a domestic space, in which women sew together and talk of marriage. While Clara's suitor Brackenburg and her lover Egmont frequent the house, Clara sings of her longing to be a soldier rather than a bride. She and her mother are often drawn to the windows and doors of the house, leaning out to watch marching soldiers. In Clara's demeanor as well as in her house, private, domestic life is connected to public, political concerns. From her house Clara gives a rousing speech to the citizens, urging them to take up arms to rescue Egmont after he has been imprisoned. Unfortunately it falls on deaf ears, and Clara poisons herself.

— *Julie D. Prandi*

THE EGOIST: A Comedy in Narrative

Author: George Meredith (1828-1909)
Type of work: Novel
Type of plot: Psychological realism

Time of plot: Nineteenth century
First published: 1879

This novel draws on characteristics of its author's own egotistical personality to create Sir Willoughby Patterne, an English country squire whose self-absorption causes him to be unsuccessful in courting any woman to be his wife. Willoughby's insistence that a dutiful spouse should have no independence in either behavior or thought drives away two fiancés who value their personal liberty over the lures of money and prestige. Their fear of becoming prisoners in his estate plays a major part in their decisions to escape from Willoughby. Ostensibly a comedy, The Egoist *is also a stinging indictment of individuals whose penchant for ignoring others' feelings causes much emotional anguish among those for whom they ostensibly care.*

Patterne Hall. Home of Sir Willoughby Patterne, the "egoist" of the title. Using a technique more common to drama than to the Victorian novel, George Meredith sets virtually every scene of the novel somewhere on the grounds of Patterne Hall. Sir Willoughby's country estate is not merely his home; he considers it a kind of earthly paradise where he and others wise enough to follow his lead can escape the vexations of the modern world. After leaving the hall for a three-year tour of the Continent when he was jilted, Willoughby has returned to settle down, bringing friends and acquaintances to Patterne Hall to impress them with his wealth and wisdom.

Described at various places in the novel as both a fortress and an aerie, Patterne Hall serves as Willoughby's Garden of Eden, in which he can pursue idiosyncratic pleasures. The grounds of the estate are spacious and variegated, consisting of woods, farm lands, and several cottages in which tenants and other dependents live. Sir Willoughby's second fiancé, Clara Middleton, is at first taken with the magnificence of the hall but eventually finds it is a prison in which she is likely to become trapped if she marries Willoughby. Much of the novel is taken up with her struggle to be released from her engagement and leave Patterne Hall. Clara finds it difficult to escape, however; her friends and family believe her engagement to Willoughby is a coup for her, since her father has wealth but only minor social status. The notion that the hall is a kind of heaven on earth is reinforced when Willoughby punishes his cousin and ward, Crossjay Patterne, in a manner he finds most appropriate and harsh: he banishes him from the estate. Meredith makes the hall a symbol of its owner: As other figures feel trapped at Patterne Hall, Willoughby is likewise a man trapped in his own self-absorption.

Railway station. Railway stop to which Clara rushes in her attempt to free herself from Sir Willoughby. Frustrated in her attempts to get him to call off their engagement, Clara plans to escape to London to visit a friend. Willoughby's close friend Colonel De Craye finds her at the train station and persuades her to return to Patterne Hall; their conversation makes it clear that Clara feels trapped in her relationship with Willoughby.

Laboratory. Room in Patterne Halle that Willoughby uses as a retreat whenever he wishes to escape social pressures at Patterne Hall. He affects to be a man of science, but the laboratory seems more a refuge where he can tinker with experiments. His claim that women are incapable of understanding science is a convenient ruse to keep the many women who visit the hall from following him into this inner sanctum.

Dining hall. Center of much of the social activity at Patterne Hall. Meredith uses occasions such as luncheons and dinners not only to further the plot but also to bring together various characters for discussions of politics, social relationships, religion, science, and matters pertaining to culture and civilization. In the dining hall, Sir Willoughby is able to dominate conversations and thereby display his exceptional self-centeredness.

— *Laurence W. Mazzeno*

THE ELDER STATESMAN

Author: T. S. Eliot (1888-1965)
Type of work: Drama
Type of plot: Allegory

Time of plot: Mid-twentieth century
First performed: 1958; first published, 1959

The first act of this play takes place in the drawing room of Lord Claverton's house in London, and the second and third acts take place on the terrace of Badgley Court, a convalescent home not far from London. In the privacy of both his home and Badgley Court, Lord Claverton is haunted by memories from his past that are renewed by the unexpected appearance of two past friends.

Claverton town house. Stately London home with a generous library, drawing room, and at least one servant, Mr. Lambert. This house is strangely empty since Lord Claverton's wife has died some time ago and this retired elder statesman has few visitors. His daughter, Monica Claverton-Ferry, acts as his nurse and spends only a few hours at a time with her fiancé, Charles Hemington. For all of their care, they cannot keep away the ghosts of Lord Claverton's past, as Señor Gomez demonstrates when he pushes his way into this private home and reminds his host of his past failings and tendency to corrupt others at Oxford.

Badgley Court. Convalescent home near London that is designed to look like a hotel to give its patients a positive attitude about their treatment center. Only the rich can afford to stay here, and they must be curable. When Claverton is sent here, his doctors do not expect him to live long, so his promised privacy is quickly lost. Mrs. John Carghill, his first lover, confronts him with his moral lapses and insensitivity in the distant past. Then his son, Michael, shows up with numerous problems, followed closely by Gomez, who seizes the opportunity to corrupt Lord Claverton's son as Claverton had supposedly done to Fred Culverwell during their Oxford days together. These ghosts function like vultures preying on Lord Claverton's flagging sense of self worth. In the end, he confesses his sins to Monica and Charles and faces his accusers. In a sense, Claverton finally dies to his pretended self once he has learned not to fear life. Badgley Court thus serves as a place of trial where Lord Claverton pleads guilty, gives up his son, and finally moves beyond his past mistakes with the help of Monica and her fiancé, who is a lawyer.

— *Daven M. Kari*

ELECTIVE AFFINITIES

Author: Johann Wolfgang von Goethe (1749-1832)
Type of work: Novel
Type of plot: Love

Time of plot: Eighteenth century
First published: Die Wahlverwandtschaften, 1809
    (English translation, 1872)

The locales of this novel are restricted almost exclusively to the country home and surrounding landscape of two principal characters, Edward and Charlotte, who have married in middle age, only a few years following the deaths of their first spouses. Into this idyllic setting each invites another person to share their lives, with tragic consequences.

Edward and Charlotte's home. Extensive country estate in Germany—a home worthy of an aristocratic couple who have withdrawn from fashionable court life to share a cultivated though not reclusive retirement. Their large manor house with two wings is surrounded by domestic gardens and a nearby landscape of villages, fields, lakes, and hills. Johann Wolfgang von Goethe almost seems inclined to conceal the fact that the locale of his story is German, choosing instead to evoke a generic European landscape comparable to a landscape portrayed by noted seventeenth and eighteenth century painters.

By avoiding details of a specific locale, Goethe focuses attention on the psychological content of his narrative that permits him to suggest that his story's tragic events are underlain by social and philosophical issues that are continental in scope. His story's narrow topographical range also gives its setting—and the novel itself—a sense of being a laboratory of social relationships, a circumstance that agrees with the novel's title, which is borrowed from contemporary scientific speculation about the physical interaction of chemical substances.

Gardening and the alteration and management of the estate are essential themes in the novel from its opening; the fateful events that are to overwhelm Edward and Charlotte, along with their companions Ottilie and the unnamed "Captain," are set in motion in the first chapter by Edward's insistent question of Charlotte, "Are my gardening and your landscaping to be for hermits only?"

Moss hut. Small, rustic outbuilding that Charlotte is building at the beginning of the novel. A picturesque place overlooking part of the estate, the hut is an organic structure that Charlotte intends to visit with Edward. When Edward first sees it he pointedly observes that although the hut has a fine view, it seems a little small. However, he quickly adds that it has room for a third person because he hopes to secure Charlotte's consent to invite the Captain, his lifelong friend, to live with them for a time. Charlotte herself is soon to ask that her niece, Ottilie, also join their family circle, and she in turn concedes that the hut will even accommodate a fourth person. This brief, early, scene in the hut is the inception of the disturbance of Edward and Charlotte's marriage that is to be caused by the introduction of two elements from the outside.

The rustic hut decorated with evergreen boughs expresses the affection that Charlotte has for her marriage and her country estate, but the arrival of the Captain heralds the ends of both her tranquil relationship with Edward and her landscaping project. Charlotte's hut is soon overshadowed by an ambitious plan promoted by the Captain to build a summerhouse on a higher, more commanding location beyond the hut. Soon, both domestic harmony and a refined, intimate relation to nature are sacrificed to unpredictable currents of passion between Edward and Ottilie and between Charlotte and the Captain.

Lake and village. Edward and the Captain formulate plans to improve both the lake and the village that adjoin the estate, thus indulging in another round of technical and engineering activity which, in the context of the emotional turmoil brewing in their midst, is somewhat irrational and self-indulgent. Their penchant for improvements alarms Charlotte, who is sensibly concerned with the financial stability of the estate.

The lake is also the scene of the novel's most unsettling passage, in which Charlotte's infant child accidentally drowns while in Ottilie's care. The contrast of this tragedy with the men's preoccupation with civil and social engineering is a striking instance of the author's eighteenth century Enlightenment sensibility confronting newer currents of Romanticism.

Village church. In a subsequent passage of the novel concerning a talented young architect, Charlotte herself is the sponsor of a project to restore the village church and decorate its chapel. Here Goethe reveals the depth of his knowledge of contemporary and historical art by describing an interior space that recalls the work of the German painter Philip Otto Runge, a younger contemporary of Goethe's and a representative of the transition from Neoclassicism to Romanticism within their cultural milieu.

— *Clyde S. McConnell*

ELECTRA

Author: Euripides (c. 485-406 B.C.E.)
Type of work: Drama
Type of plot: Tragedy

Time of plot: After the fall of Troy
First performed: Ēlektra, 413 B.C.E. (English translation, 1782)

The setting of Euripides' play is the land around a farmhouse that on one side looks out at the road to Argos, the city of which Electra regards herself as princess, and on the other at the road to Sparta, home of fierce warriors.

An altar fronts the house, but the rural setting is unusual for action that delves into regal intrigue, betrayal, and vengeance. The farmhouse is one of Euripides' contributions to the story of Electra. It is a place that undercuts the presumptions of royalty and the high seriousness of earlier versions of the stories about them.

Farmhouse. Farm near the Greek city Argos. No farmhouse seems fitting for a princess to inhabit. In such locations one expects to encounter wholesome bucolic activities. Ironically, the place is used for royal machinations, including regicide and matricide. In Euripides' version of the story the queen and usurping king are slaughtered by the queen's children, not in a castle, but on a farm, where animals may be killed for food. The location challenges and reinforces other challenges in the play to conventional beliefs about the pitch of royalty.

The farm houses Princess Electra, in Euripides' version of the story married off beneath her class in order to delegitimate any offspring she might have. Once nubile, but now twisted in her desires, Electra has maintained her virginity during her time in rural exile, while per-

versely embracing what she regards as the demeaning chores of a farm wife. Averse to frequent baths, a privilege of the rich, she ironically insists on hauling water from the well, actively underscoring her outrage at the mean place to which she has been relegated.

Euripides' play suggests that the farm and its cultivator are morally superior to the palace, its scheming residents, and its exiles. The humble land of a decent farmer, is here a ground of virtue in relation to which the excesses, base motives, and seamy deeds of aristocrats can be evaluated. The farm, the farmer, and people like him are admirable. Tragically, the petty and untrustworthy nobility, who pursue their selfish ends in the guise of heroism, hold dominion over the good.

— *Albert Wachtel*

ELECTRA

Author: Sophocles (c. 496-406 B.C.E.)
Type of work: Drama
Type of plot: Tragedy

Time of plot: c. 1250-1200 B.C.E.
First published: 418-410 B.C.E. (English translation, 1649)

All the onstage action of Electra *takes place in front of the palace of Argos, whose royal family has been cursed since the time of their ancestor Tantalus, particularly for crimes connected to the sacrifice of children.*

*****Argos** (AR-gohs). Ancient city in southeastern Greece, adjoining the Gulf of Argolis. Its area was prominent in the Bronze Age; therefore, its very name summons an ambience of antiquity and myth for Sophocles' audience. In the play, the first speech (by Orestes' mentor Paidagogos) introduces Argos as the old and sacred homeland for which Orestes has yearned. Like a guidebook, Paidagogos enumerates its most famous sights: the river Inachus (believed to have been a god and the first king of Argos), the marketplace (consecrated to the god Apollo), the temple of the goddess Hera, and the palace. By providing so much geographical informa-

tion, Paidagogos reminds the audience that he is—as his name suggests—like a pedagogue, the tutor who led children to school in Ancient Greece. Therefore, Orestes' coming to Argos is likened implicitly to education for him (and, presumably also for the audience, brought into this fabled place of splendor and tragedy).

Appropriate to the function of Greek drama as both religious instruction and ritual, the play concerns the spiritual cleansing of Argos. Despite Paidagogos's acute awareness of the city's beauty and venerable tradition, his speech presents the kingdom as desecrated and thus in need of the purification Orestes and Electra will bring by avenging their royal father's death. According to a notion common among many ancient religions, only more blood can cleanse the earth from the impurity generated by the shedding of a king's blood, in this case that of Agamemnon, murdered by his wife. Consequently, through a divinely ordained execution of the murderers, Orestes expects to make the land flourish again.

— *James Whitlark*

THE ELEGY OF LADY FIAMMETTA

Author: Giovanni Boccaccio (1313-1375)
Type of work: Novel
Type of plot: Love

Time of plot: Fourteenth century
First published: Elegia di Madonna Fiammetta, 1343-1344 (English translation, 1587)

Although this realistically framed prose lament for a lover gained and lost is veiled in classical language and place names, its setting is certainly Naples and its exotic surroundings. More important to the progress of the elegy is the married Fiammetta's bedchamber, scene of her longings, trysts, and bitter reflections.

***Naples.** Seaport in southern Italy in which Giovanni Boccaccio spent several years before writing *The Elegy of Lady Fiammetta.* His book paints a glowing civic portrait of Naples, which he describes as "joyful, peaceful, rich, magnificent and under a single ruler." Beautiful people reside here, and life in the upper class is ornamented with luxuries and spectacles. The noblewoman Fiammetta's own beauty is displayed in the unidentified church in which she first meets the young Panfilo, in an echo of Petrarch's first glimpsing of his beloved (and also married) Laura. Ironically, in this place of divine worship the tinder of the adulterous affair is kindled. It is in a Neapolitan convent that Fiammetta first realizes that another woman—a young nun—has also fallen for Panfilo's charms.

Fiammetta's bedchamber. Room in Fiammetta's husband's house in which she dreams her dreams and watches her beauty blossom before ever meeting Panfilo. Here she suffers her nightmare about a field in which she is bitten by a venomous snake that presages her failed affair. After her initially flirtatious but innocent meetings with Panfilo become carnal, her bedchamber becomes the sexual playground that only they share, away from prying eyes or nosy servants. Even her nurse, apparently, does not know what her lover looks like. Here Fiammetta meets the Roman goddess Venus and the Fury Tisiphone, with whom she has imagined conversations about her love and eventual grief. Eventually despairing of her love, she decides—within her bedchamber—upon suicide, which drives her into a kind of madness from which she is saved by her nurse and servants.

***Baia.** Rugged seaside retreat on the Bay of Naples that Fiammetta and her husband visit in the hope that the local baths will help cure her of the depression into which she sinks after Panfilo leaves. However, since she and Panfilo have previously romped in this same resort, every rock and tree she sees there reminds her of him, and the effect of her visit is the opposite of what her cuckolded husband hopes for. Fiammetta's spoiled looks, neglected dress, and grieving contrast with the ruddy beauty and boisterous gaiety of other vacationing aristocrats, who engage in hunting and gather together for amorous festivities and wedding ceremonies.

***Florence.** Historic center of culture and political power in central Italy from which Panfilo comes and to which he returns to tend to his father's business. The virtues of Naples are depicted in sharp contrast to the rowdiness of Florence, the "noble city of Etruria." Florence is full of people who are cowards and big talkers, as well as haughty, jealous, and greedy men under not one ruler but as many as there are citizens.

In the early 1340's Florence was torn by civil strife related to the failure of two major banks and a change in regime. In Boccaccio's book, Neapolitan peacefulness is set against the turbulent Florentine society that conducts war both within and with others, perhaps suggesting that Panfilo's apparently flighty character is a reflection of the unstable city. That Panfilo would choose to leave noble Naples—and Fiammetta—for rowdy Florence shocks Fiammetta. She worries about what might be happening to her beloved in that distant city and madly resents the hold Florence has on him. Though the book's narrative never visits Florence itself, the city's presence is keenly felt.

Mediterranean Sea. Though Panfilo could travel from Naples to Florence and back by land, he makes the first leg of his journey by the sea, which symbolically and geographically separates him from Fiammetta. At first, Fiammetta worries about the dangers the sea holds for her love; after his return to Naples begins to appear unlikely, she wishes the sea's perils on him.

— *Joseph P. Byrne*

ELEGY WRITTEN IN A COUNTRY CHURCHYARD

Author: Thomas Gray (1716-1771)

Type of work: Poetry

First published: 1751

This famous elegy deserves a place in world literature because of its elegance of phrasing and balance of line and rhythm. The feelings the poem evokes come to almost every thoughtful person at one time or another. The images of the poem arise from its setting: a country churchyard cemetery. The churchyard itself prompts the poet's meditations.

Country churchyard. Cemetery adjoining an unnamed rural or village church. There is no way of knowing which particular country churchyard Thomas Gray was looking at or thinking about when he composed this poem. It is known, however, that he spent most of his life quietly as a professor at Cambridge University in Cambridge, England. He traveled in the summer to Scotland and the Lake District in northwest England, and as a youth he traveled to Europe. A churchyard scene such as he describes in the poem would be familiar to most Europeans.

Place is significant in Gray's elegy. The poem opens with a peaceful, evocative description of a country churchyard at close of day. The twilight scene is simple but unmistakable. The elm and yew trees shade the graves where the common people of the town have been laid for their final rest. The wealthy folk are buried in the walls and floors of the church; their graves have statuary or beautiful decorations.

The poet muses on the lives of the persons buried there. He pictures their lives as simple farmers and housewives. The chief poignancy of the poem lies in the poet's suggestions that some of the people buried in the churchyard may not have fulfilled the potential of their lives because of their poverty and rural isolation. Despite any talent they may have possessed, their lives were very much tied to the place in which they lived. Though they were unlearned, they had joy in their simple yet productive lives and did not look forward to death.

In the right environment some might have turned out to be great poets, like John Milton, or civic leaders, like John Hampden. He concludes the poem by considering what people may say of him when he joins those buried in the churchyard.

— *Toni J. Morris*

ELMER GANTRY

Author: Sinclair Lewis (1885-1951)

Type of work: Novel

Type of plot: Satire

Time of plot: 1915-1925

First published: 1927

By contrasting tiny rural towns with the great metropolitan city of Zenith, Sinclair Lewis uses the midwestern locations in which the novel unfolds to sharpen his satirical depiction of the hypocritical Fundamentalist preacher Elmer Gantry and his followers.

Paris. Kansas village in which Gantry grows up. With some nine hundred residents, it is smaller than the real town of Sauk Centre, Minnesota, in which Lewis grew up, and the fictional Gopher Prairie, which Lewis satirizes in *Main Street* (1920). Pretentiously named Paris, Gantry's hometown is even more culturally impoverished than either Sauk Centre or Gopher Prairie, and appears to have not even a pubic library or a social club. A small Baptist church and its Sunday school are the leading institutions of the village. Except for Fourth of July parades and circus bands, the only music Gantry hears is played during church services. Other than occasional political campaign speeches, weekly sermons provide his only exposure to oratory. Sunday school offers examples of painting and sculpture; Bible stories and the words of hymns provide Gantry's main experience of literature. Lewis concludes his description of Paris by asserting that the church and Sunday School taught Gantry everything he needed, "except, perhaps, any longing whatever for decency and kindness and reason." (There is a real town named Paris in north-central Kansas, but Lewis's Paris probably has no connection with it.)

Winnemac. Fictional midwestern state in which Gantry preaches before being advanced to a large city. Its villages include Schoenheim, Banjo Crossing, and others, all of which Lewis disparages as he does Paris. The narrow cultural climate of midwestern rural villages produces narrow, bigoted people, easily impressed by Gantry and readily manipulated by him.

Clontar. Fictional New Jersey coastal resort where Gantry and the itinerant revivalist Sharon Falconer try to start a permanent church. The two revivalists plan to transfer their increasingly mechanical operations to an enormous and deteriorating auditorium, in which an opera company earlier went bankrupt. To the cheaply built knotty-pine building, decorated in red and gold paint, they add a huge revolving cross covered with yellow and ruby electric lights. Freed from having to share the donations their revivals harvest with the community churches that sponsor them as they move from town to town, they

hope to reap great personal profits. However, their greed causes them to ignore fire safety, and their flimsy wooden church building goes up in flames, ending Falconer's life and Gantry's hope of wealth.

Zenith. Largest city in the state of Winnemac and the site of Gantry's greatest preaching success. He is promoted from a small town pastorate to a church in a run-down neighborhood mostly populated by Italians and other immigrants. However, he discovers that his own Methodist congregation consists primarily of transplanted rustics who grew up in the same cultural milieu as their pastor. One parishioner has become a wealthy manufacturer, yet chooses to remain in the denomination of his childhood, rather than join a more prestigious congregation. Another member, a successful, though not very pious lawyer, values religion's effectiveness in controlling workers—believing it focuses their thoughts on higher things than instigating strikes and increasing wages.

Gantry uses flamboyant feats of showmanship to censure the people of Zenith. Although he himself indulges in drinking and womanizing, he leads raids into the city's red light district, excoriating the immoral gambling, bootleg liquor, and prostitution he finds in an area heavily populated by poor immigrants. He inveighs against such vices, blaming the godless materialism of the urban population for being their source. Gantry condemns the city as a cesspool of decadence, an evil Sodom that contrasts sharply with the virtuous countryside where his own boyhood congregation grew up.

Gantry's theatrics attract favorable media attention and increasing membership for his congregation, turning his rundown church into a financial success, and gaining him invitations to join the Rotary and Tonawanda Country Clubs, where he can mingle with the bankers and industrialists who rule Zenith. When Gantry tours Europe, Lewis savagely satirizes Gantry's inability to understand its culture, the background from which much of Zenith's population originally came.

— *Milton Berman*

THE EMIGRANTS OF AHADARRA: A Tale of Irish Life

Author: William Carleton (1794-1869)

Type of work: Novel

Type of plot: Social realism

Time of plot: 1840's

First published: 1848

This didactic novel protests against the system of land tenure prevailing in nineteenth century Ireland and particularly against the manner in which it obliged many Irish families to emigrate to America. The novel employs few real place names, emphasizing the fact that the problem was common throughout the island. Nevertheless, it cultivates a keen sense of place in order to emphasize the tragedy of forced departure from one's homeland.

***Ireland.** Second-largest of the British Isles, a dependency of Great Britain throughout the nineteenth century. Among the novel's several commentaries on the sorry state to which Ireland has been brought by its absentee landlords (even before Ireland's great mid-century famine, which Carleton describes in other novels) there is one in particular—in chapter 24—which waxes lyrical about the unique affection that the Irish people have for their native soil, and the affliction of "home sickness" that eats away at exiles and sometimes kills them. It is an affection that is still preserved by American celebrations of St. Patrick's Day.

Ahadarra. Hill farm in the Ballymacan district, one of two—the other being Carriglass—that have been in the M'Mahon family for generations. Ahadarra is now farmed by Bryan M'Mahon, whose father retains the other. Being in a mountainous region, the farm is necessarily extensive. Its fertile fields are widely spaced among barren slopes, but it has potential, including some three hundred acres of rough but cultivable land. Bryan has to invest heavily in order to develop this marginal terrain and thus stands in desperate need of the renewal of his family's tenancy, which is promised but never delivered by the agent representing his aristocratic landlord Chevydale (whose name proclaims his English descent, although Carleton does not emphasize his alien origin).

Jemmy Burke's farm. The first setting introduced by the novel is characterized by the cheerful neglect to which the long slate-roofed farmhouse and its surrounding terrain has been abandoned. Its iron gate is so difficult to shift that even the Burkes prefer to use an informal side-path. Although the ill-kept farmyard stinks and the house is both cluttered and dirty, the majority of its multitudinous residents are generous and hospitable—the exception being Jem's sly son, Hyacinth "Hycy"

Burke, whose defective character reflects the slovenliness in which he has been reared. The general state of chaos at the farm makes the theft of Jemmy's savings understandable as well as undetectable.

Gerald Cavanagh's farm. Although smaller than Jemmy Burke's holding, Cavanagh's far more orderly establishment is presented as a carefully contrasted model of what an Irish farm and home ought to be. The house is a thatched cottage built in the shape of a cross, located on a small rise overlooking a hundred acres of rich meadow. The adjacent green is carefully cut and the two thorn-trees close to the house are neatly clipped. It makes an appropriate setting for the local festival of rustic skills and dancing that Carleton calls a "spinsters' kemp."

Poteen still-house. Hycy's illicit still is initially located in the hills beyond the boundary of his father's land, three miles to the southwest. It is situated in a cave at the end of a covert approached by a narrow glen. The necessity of moving it—because it has been too well advertised by its regular patrons—offers Hycy a means of bringing down his rival for Kathleen Cavanagh's affections.

*United States.** Although no American setting is featured in the novel, reference is occasionally made to the United States as the place to which most emigrants from Ireland go. Although Carleton deeply regrets this necessity, he speaks of America in warmly favorable terms, as a place where honest and hard-working Irishmen can reap the rewards that are their just and natural due. By contrast, he disdains to mention, let alone to praise, England—to which many Irish emigrants went as itinerant laborers—and will not condescend to name the place (Australia) to which the plot's actual emigrants are eventually transported when justice is done and the M'Mahons are saved.

— *Brian Stableford*

ÉMILE: Or, Education

Author: Jean-Jacques Rousseau (1712-1778)
Type of work: Novel
Type of plot: Novel of ideas

Time of plot: Eighteenth century
First published: Émile: Ou, De l'éducation, 1762
   (English translation, 1762-1763)

A novel only in name, this book is a treatise about an idealized education, from childhood to adulthood, involving the five senses, inborn curiosity, and probing questions by a tutor. Émile's development takes him through the purity of nature, to simple rustic villages, semicorrupted towns, morally bankrupt Paris, and finally a two-year journey of growth on his own in Europe. The outer journey is an inner journey as well. Émile learns to be intellectually, morally, and practically self-sufficient in preparation for adulthood.

Nature. Place from which all education springs. It is in Nature that the French orphan boy Émile is to learn the most important lessons, with the help of a tutor. Sunrises and storms reveal the beauty and power of the Creator, ripples caused by stones cast into ponds reveal Newtonian physics, watching the Sun rise in one place and set in another introduces Émile to cosmology. Nature also provides ample stimulus for healthy physical development. For Jean-Jacques Rousseau the role of the tutor is merely to ensure that the path is not strewn with glass as the naked child runs freely down the path.

Civil society. In contrast to Nature, the world that humankind occupies. For Rousseau, civil society reflects varying degrees of perversity. For example, large cities represent the abyss of the human species. Towns and villages are closer to the "General Will." Rousseau finds that least-cultured people are generally those who are the wisest. When Émile tours Europe for nearly two years to achieve his final stage of growth, he travels to remote provinces instead of major cities.

*Paris.** France's leading city is to Rousseau a place of noise, smoke, and mud that lacks both honor and virtue. Anyone seeking the important things in life—happiness and love—can never be far enough away from Paris. Rousseau considers it a misfortune for any child to be born rich and Parisian. When Émile is of age and looking for a wife, he is finally taken to Paris. The effort is a waste of time, except that it shows Émile what he does not want in a wife. He eventually finds his future wife, Sophie, in a little house in a simple little hamlet.

*Ancient Rome.** Rousseau finds much that is good and virtuous about ancient republican Rome. The city's social and civic virtues, and willingness to speak in actions as well as words, provide positive models for the type of moral growth needed by Émile.

*Ancient Greece.** Rousseau claims that the purest thoughts originate from ancient Greece. He argues that being closest to Nature, the Greek city-states were more original in genius. When Émile is ready for books, his tutor steers him toward the ancients. Rousseau often uses the ancient Greek city-state of Sparta as an example of a practical, natural, sensible, and action-oriented society.

Farmer's garden. Place where the tutor arranges an important life lesson for the young Émile, who derives considerable joy from planting and caring for beans. However, the farmer who owns the land rips out Émile's beans to plant melons, thus traumatizing the boy. From this lesson, Émile learns about private property. He also learns about negotiation when an arrangement is made for him to plant beans in the garden in the future.

Robinson Crusoe's Island. Imaginary island in Daniel Defoe's novel *Robinson Crusoe* (1719), the only book the tutor allows young Émile to read because it teaches self-reliance, and learning from nature in order to survive. Émile's travels among the so-called talented people of Paris lead him to the conclusion that none of them would be of any use on the island. Unlike Defoe's Robinson Crusoe, none are intellectually, morally, and practically self-sufficient.

*Montmorency.** Suburb north of Paris in which Rousseau lived from 1756-1762. Although lost in a forest with his tutor, Émile uses spatial relation lessons learned over previous days to navigate out of a forest wilderness and into Montmorency. Tired, hungry, and thirsty, he and his tutor eat an elegant meal in town. However, another lesson is at hand: How lacking an elegant meal is compared to the simpler rustic fare.

— *Irwin Halfond*

EMMA

Author: Jane Austen (1775-1817)
Type of work: Novel
Type of plot: Domestic realism

Time of plot: Early nineteenth century
First published: 1816

This novel is set in and around Highbury, a fictional village near London, England. Highbury may be small and restricted, but it represents a model of moderate and conservative civilization, near enough to London to escape being provincial but far enough away to escape the city's bustle and vice.

Highbury. English village sixteen miles southwest of London. Although Jane Austen says it is a populous place, readers find it quite small indeed. A short walk away from the village center are Ford's, a clothing and fabric store; a bakery; the Bates apartment, over a place of business; a church and a vicarage; the Crown Inn; and Mrs. Goddard's school. Less than a mile from Emma's home is **Randalls**, a little estate belonging to the Westons. Adjoining Highbury is Donwell and its most important estate, Donwell Abbey, the old-fashioned home of Mr. George Knightley and the center of his large farming enterprise. Located on his land is Abbey Mill Farm.

The novel tells of Emma's growth into adulthood. The isolated and restricted village in which she lives reflects her own initial isolation. For the first twelve chapters, she never strays far from home, which she shares with her unmarried father. Besides Mr. Knightley, her most frequent visitor is a silly school girl named Harriet Smith. Soon Emma's horizons begin to expand, until, by the end of the novel, she has learned a great deal about many other people—and herself. This movement is expressed geographically. Sometimes Emma makes journeys from home. She socializes more with the people of Highbury, even attending a party given by her social inferiors. She goes to Randalls on Christmas Eve; she visits Donwell Abbey. More often, however, Emma's expanding horizons are suggested by people coming to Highbury from other parts of England.

*****London.** Capital and largest city in Great Britain. Emma's sister Isabella and her family live in Brunswick Square and travel often to Hartfield. Frank Churchill rides to London, ostensibly to get his hair cut.

*****Bath.** City in the southwest of England, about one hundred miles from Highbury. After he is spurned by Emma, Mr. Elton travels to Bath, where he meets and marries Augusta Hawkins, who lives with her sister Selina at Maple Grove near Bristol. These places suggest the less-than-admirable nature of Mr. Elton's mar-

riage: Bath was a fashionable and racy pleasure resort, not the place to contract a serious engagement. Maple Grove was situated in a part of England which did not have the social standing of Hartfield.

*****Weymouth.** English seaside resort slightly more than one hundred miles southwest of Highbury, a place suggesting youthful frivolity. Frank Churchill saved Jane Fairfax's life in a boating accident there. Both these characters complicate Emma's life.

Enscombe. Yorkshire estate located perhaps two hundred miles north of Highbury, belonging to the Churchill family. Like Bristol, any place in Yorkshire is a long way from this novel's favored locations. The Churchills, including Frank, show their restive nature by traveling. Near the end of the novel they live in Richmond, a town nine miles from Highbury.

Balycraig. Estate of Mr. Dixon somewhere in Ireland, far away from Highbury and the woman Emma suspects is the object of his passion.

*****Box Hill.** Famous high hill near Dorking in Surrey, about seven miles from Highbury. Near the end of the novel, Emma's widening perspective is shown when she makes two journeys. At Donwell Abbey she learns more about two of her friends and admires the expanse of the English countryside. The next day she and others take a picnic to Box Hill, where one of the climaxes of the novel occurs: Emma insults Miss Bates and is reprimanded by Mr. Knightley.

Hartfield. Emma Woodhouse's own residence, in which many indoor scenes are set. Hartfield combines civilization and nature: a comfortable large mansion is set amid pleasant walks and shrubbery—a good place for a proposal of marriage.

*****Southend-on-Sea.** English seaside resort thirty-six miles east of London on the bank of the Thames estuary. Mr. Woodhouse objects to the Knightley family's bathing there.

— George Soule

THE EMPEROR JONES

Author: Eugene O'Neill (1888-1953)
Type of work: Drama
Type of plot: Expressionism

Time of plot: Early twentieth century
First performed: 1920; first published, 1921

The last seven scenes of Eugene O'Neill's eight-scene play are set in the great forest of an unnamed island in the West Indies resembling black-ruled Haiti, which has been taken over by the American Brutus Jones. The first scene is set in the island's government palace. O'Neill used locale expressionistically to sharpen the contrast between the civilization over which Jones attempted to preside and the raw forest surrounding the small community of luxury and privilege he has created within the palace.

Island. The play unfolds on a small, unnamed island in the West Indies that provides O'Neill with an appropriate microcosm for his drama that depicts the primitive forces that close in on a domesticated, avaricious African American. The island bears a loose resemblance to the West Indian nation of Haiti, which had a long and chaotic political history after black slaves wrenched control of the western end of Hispaniola away from France in the early nineteenth century. Like O'Neill's Brutus Jones, Haiti's first rulers styled themselves "emperors."

Jones's palace. The play opens in the lavish palace building of the unnamed island nation, where Jones, an escaped convict and former Pullman porter from the United States, lives. With the help of his Cockney sidekick, Smithers, he rules the island as its "emperor." Jones and Smithers have tricked the superstitious islanders into thinking that Jones has magical powers and cannot be hurt, except by a silver bullet. Jones keeps one to use on himself if suicide becomes necessary. Having extorted money and services from the impoverished islanders, Jones lives opulently.

Great forest. The last six scenes of the play occur at night in the great forest that surrounds the palace. Within this forest, Jones—who is running around in circles—is visited by the apparitions of people whom he has killed or cheated. His past returns to haunt him. Meanwhile, the beating of tom-toms is pervasive, beginning at seventy-two beats a minute, the rate of the human heart, and accelerating as Jones's terror increases.

The play's dark and forbidding jungle scenes contrast with the palace scene. O'Neill uses the forest locale and the darkness to highlight Jones's isolation and desperation. In the final scene, dawn breaks. As angry islanders advance on the deposed emperor, a shot rings out and Jones falls. Lem, the local ruler whom Jones overthrew, explains that the islanders spent the entire night fashioning a silver bullet.

Slave ship. Imaginary vessel that appears in Jones's hallucination in scene five. To demonstrate his mental deterioration, Jones imagines that he is a slave being auctioned off at a slave sale. In the following scene, wearing only a breech cloth, Jones huddles in the hold of a crowded ship surrounded by shadowy figures, presumably slaves who have been snatched from their homes and are being transported to a market. His groans and cries fill the theater as the light fades. As the hallucination ends, Jones scrambles off into the underbrush of the great consuming forest.

Altar. Structure before which the exhausted, disoriented Jones sinks in scene seven and experiences another hallucination. He imagines that a witch doctor from the Congo appears and does a macabre ritualistic dance, making Jones realize that he is to be sacrificed upon the altar, the symbol of an authority greater than his.

— *R. Baird Shuman*

THE END OF THE ROAD

Author: John Barth (1930-   )
Type of work: Novel
Type of plot: Existentialism

Time of plot: 1951-1955
First published: 1958

The small college town of Wicomico on the Eastern Shore of Maryland, is the setting that demonstrates that even the most prosaic of environments can be the location for marital infidelity and existentialist angst.

Wicomico. Small town on the Eastern Shore of Maryland (most likely patterned on the actual town of Salisbury) where the novel's plot unfolds amid a commonplace backdrop. John Barth gives slight description of the town itself, merely noting that it has little character. A typical mid-Atlantic town of the mid 1950's, Wicomico's main importance is that it provides an appropriately bland external setting for the highly charged internal and interpersonal dramas which occur in the book.

Jacob Horner's room. Boardinghouse room rented by Jacob Horner, the novel's main character, in a house near the college where he teaches. There Joe and Rennie Morgan confront Horner after the first time he and Rennie have sex and where the couple continue to commit adultery on a regular basis at Joe Morgan's insistence. Symbolically, despite the fact that the room is the site of many of the novel's dramatic scenes, it is a bare, almost barren setting. The room is large, with high ceilings, big windows and a large bed high off the floor, all of which fit Horner's hard-to-please requirements. It houses Horner's few possessions, including his records, all Mozart except for a single Russian dance, a combination that matches his psychological mood. The most notable features are a rocking chair on which Horner sometimes sits for hours, hardly moving or thinking, and a small statue of the Greek mythological character Laocoön which sits on the mantelpiece. This statue becomes a symbolic representation of Jacob's existential plight in the novel: He is caught in the snares of life and unable to extricate himself. At the end of the novel, Horner simply leaves the room, abandoning everything, including his statue of Laocoön on the mantelpiece.

Remobilization Farm. Unorthodox psychiatric and medical facility in a large old farmhouse located somewhere in the Maryland-Pennsylvania area. This is where the doctor treats patients such as Jacob Horner with approaches of his own such as mythotherapy. A key part of the facility is the **Progress and Advice Room**, which is completely white and has only two straight-backed chairs. The setting of this room is designed to force the patient to confront the choices posed to him by the doctor. Its decor is echoed in that of the Morgan house in Wicomico. The Remobilization Farm is where Jacob Horner takes Rennie Morgan for the abortion which results in her death.

Morgan apartment. Half of a duplex rented by Joe and Rennie Morgan, located near the edge of Wicomico and near fields and forests, which in some ways is an almost idyllic setting. The apartment is large, with almost bare rooms and sparse but very functional furniture. There are no rugs on the hardwood floors, and no drapes or curtains, only white venetian blinds which match the white walls and ceilings, an echo of the Progress and Advice Room at the Remobilization Farm. Jacob Horner and Rennie Morgan first commit adultery here while her husband, Joe, is away on academic business.

Wicomico State Teachers College. Institution housed in a single large and rather ugly pseudo-Georgian brick building in which Jacob Horner teaches grammar. There he meets Joe Morgan, who teaches history there. Horner's classroom is most notable as the site for his series of highly charged, sexual daydreams and fantasies about his female students.

MacMahon farm. Farm owned by Rennie's parents, located near Wicomico, Maryland. Jacob Horner and Rennie ride horses through the woods here and stop to talk. It is during these conversations that the affair between them first begins to emerge without conscious thought from either.

*Ocean City. Coastal resort on the Maryland shore where Jacob Horner picks up Peggy Rankin, a forty-year-old English teacher from Wicomico with whom he has an affair.

— *Michael Witkoski*

ENDGAME: A Play in One Act

Author: Samuel Beckett (1906-1989)
Type of work: Drama
Type of plot: Absurdist

Time of plot: Indeterminate
First performed: 1957; first published, 1957 as *Fin de partie* (English translation, 1958)

The setting of this strange, ambiguous, and surrealistic play, which suggests a postnuclear world, is a shelter, apparently the last inhabited place on earth. Both the world within the shelter and the world without are dying.

Shelter. Unnamed place which is apparently the last refuge of humankind on Earth. In addition to providing the characters with protection from the outside world and sustaining them in the last moments of their lives, the shelter serves as both a prison and a tomb. High up on the left and right sides of the back wall are two small windows with curtains drawn. These windows look out on the other world, nature. All that is visible are an ashen gray sea, sky, and sun in the ever-fading light that represents the winding down of time and the extinction of life. Covered by a sheet in the center of the room is Hamm, the blind master of the house. Confined to a chair on castors because he cannot walk, Hamm must be awakened every morning with stimulants and painkillers, fed, and then "put to bed" in the evening. Clov, Hamm's servant, provides these functions, without which Hamm would die. The shelter contains two other characters, both legless, Nagg and Nell, the remnants of Hamm's parents, who are confined to ash cans located at the front of the stage. This confinement suggests their status as "garbage" to Hamm, who refers to them as "accursed progenitors." Periodically, they poke their heads out of their covered cans and speak to each other or ask for sustenance.

Outside world. Although dying, the world outside the shelter appears to be more desirable than the world within, which is a psychological hell and a prison almost devoid of provisions. Three of the four characters are physically unable to leave, and the fourth, Clov, who seems to be preparing to leave, is tied psychologically to Hamm. Hamm, a sadistic master, "father figure," and adult child enjoys tormenting his dependents. However, at the end of the play, Clov, suitcase in hand, waits at the door, apparently ready to leave.

— *Richard Damashek*

ENDYMION: A Poetic Romance

Author: John Keats (1795-1821)
Type of work: Poetry
Type of plot: Narrative

Time of plot: Ancient times
First published: 1818

An allegory told in four sections, this narrative is a poetic romance that unfolds in loose rhyming couplets, relating a version of the Greek myth about Endymion, a mortal shepherd who goes to sleep on Mount Latmos and so entrances the goddess Diana that she falls in love with him. Endymion yearns for the ideal love that Diana represents; however, as a mortal he is forbidden to love a god and must undergo some change to make his love possible. He meets his lover when he sleeps but loses her when awake; he goes on a quest to find his dream lover.

Mount Latmos (laht-MOHS). Pastoral location in Greece on which much of the poem takes place. At the beginning of the poem, John Keats tells readers that he needs to be outside the city and its noise in order to relate the story of Endymion and Diana. Many of his allusions are to Greek gods and goddesses whose powers help explain the wonders of natural creation. Keats also describes in great detail the forests, glens, and dales of

Latmos. Shepherds personify perhaps the most peaceful human occupation imaginable. The land on which Endymion watches his sheep is a magical place, where a lamb separated from the flock would never be harmed. Latmos represents the best of the pastoral tradition, where Pan's music can still be enjoyed.

A woodland altar on Latmos is a gathering place for the shepherd bands, damsels, and other youths who keep alive the pursuit of beauty under the guidance of the woodland god Pan, whom Latmos's denizens adore. Music is valued as the truest expression of contentment. Ebony-tipped flutes fill the air with Pan's music. Endymion's evident distress stands in direct contrast to the peaceful setting, thereby hinting at conflict.

Bowers. Shady leaf-covered recesses on Latmos that are the centers of many of the actions in *Endymion*. Places of repose, bowers are usually located in beautifully wooded areas. To Endymion, they are sources of healing and rest—sanctuaries in which he can sleep, dreaming of his beloved Diana, who reveals herself to him in dreams and visions. With Peona, his beloved sister, Endymion voyages to an island bower to which Peona used to take friends. Keats describes this bower as being located in quiet shade, with a couch of flower leaves. Here Endymion experiences the magic sleep that enables him to confide in Peona about his distress. At another point, the bower is referred to as a nest, a place of nurturing. When Endymion is at last united with his love, they are borne away to a crystal bower, at which time they vanish. Peona returns to Latmos, traveling through the dark forest unafraid.

Garden of Adonis. Endymion's first stop on his search for his dream lover. After meeting with a naiad who warns him that he must search in remote regions for the woman of his dreams if he hopes to find consummation, he descends to the Garden of Adonis, the mortal lover of the goddess Venus. Adonis awakens from his "winter-sleep" as Venus arrives and beseeches her to have pity on Endymion. When Venus and her minions vanish, Endymion wanders on until he sees a huge eagle, which he rides even farther down into the depths.

Cave of Quietude. Secret grotto to which Endymion goes after a beautiful Indian maiden he meets disappears. The cave is a gloomy den that may represent a kind of despair or perhaps an important stage in Endymion's spiritualization. After Endymion finally lands on Earth, he is still torn between his earthly and divine loves, and when the Indian woman tells him that his love for her is hopeless, Endymion decides to live as a hermit. The Indian Maiden then reveals that she is Cynthia, and, as Endymion's sister Peona watches in amazement, the lovers abruptly vanish together.

Book I ends as Peona and Endymion go aboard ship, setting out across the river to the hollow, a fearful place, albeit set in the pastoral landscape. Searching and finding within the context of a darker pastoral setting suggests that Endymion must undergo trial before he succeeds.

Sea. Place of mystery, of Sirens who lure the unwary to doom. At the end of book 2, Endymion awakens to see the sea above his head. It frightens him, reflecting the Moon (Diana) growing pale, as if his lover is dying at the hands of the sea god, Neptune.

Here Endymion exhibits fear, an emotion unknown in his ideal Latmos. Endymion's quest takes him to the bottom of the sea in book 3. There he encounters Glaucus, an ancient man who welcomes him as a savior, explaining that he has been condemned to sit at the bottom of the ocean for one thousand years by the witch Circe, who was once his lover. Endymion helps Glaucus escape. Afterward, Venus tells Endymion she has discovered the identity of his immortal dream lover.

— *Martha Modena Vertreace-Doody*

ENEMIES: A Love Story

Author: Isaac Bashevis Singer (1904-1991)
Type of work: Novel
Type of plot: Domestic realism

Time of plot: Mid-twentieth century
First published: Sonim, de Geshichte fun a Liebe, 1966 (English translation, 1972)

New York City's Brooklyn and Bronx boroughs provide the primary settings in this tragicomic tale. Only rarely do its principal characters venture beyond the confines of this city, in which they feel relatively safe, surrounded by associates who share their memories of the Old World and are psychologically imprisoned by its threats. The abundant American land that has embraced these hunted refugees does not beckon them into its interior.

***New York City.** Largest city in the United States and the first destination for most of its European immigrants during the early twentieth century. In perhaps no other city, even Israel's Tel Aviv, could Isaac Bashevis Singer have so keenly observed post-Holocaust Jewish psychology. As his fictional Polish immigrant Herman Broder moves about New York City, making his living ghostwriting books and lectures for a rich rabbi, he mingles with Jews of several economic strata and varying political opinions and religious practices. In this microcosm of world Jewishness, the effects of the Holocaust may be observed everywhere. Some survivors keep the religious law, while others despise it. Broder's mistress hates God because of her experiences in the German death camps. Others, like her own mother, love God all the more because of what she has suffered. Broder's own brain is still stocked with the lore of the Jewish Diaspora and Hebraic learning, now useful to him only because of the types of books he writes.

Perhaps it is only in post-Holocaust New York that a man such as Broder could so easily fall into the predicament he soon faces. After he marries the servant who saved his life in Poland, his first wife, Tamar, whom he had believed lost in the camps, reappears. As if two wives, after the secular law, were not enough, his mistress, Masha, then tricks him into marrying her according to Jewish law.

Singer wrote his novels initially in Yiddish, the language in which he felt most artistically comfortable, though his largest readership was always in English. Nevertheless, even in translation, the Yiddish-tinged New York speech of his characters remains essential to the total effect of his books. Alternately sad and awkwardly funny, these people, whose lives were scrambled in another world, question the efficacy of their Jewishness but cannot cast it off in American assimilation.

***Catskill Mountains.** Resort area in New York State that is a popular vacation spot for Jews; a place where the Jewish heritage and American affluence make an uneasy compromise, and where many Jewish entertainers enjoy their first successes. Broder, too, is able to experience here the few moments of respite from anxiety and alienation that are allowed him, before he returns to the city and its entanglements. Singer sets a brief romantic interlude in the Catskill Mountains, suggesting what might have been possible could more New York Jews have freed themselves from city restraints and their own fears and inhibitions and ventured deeper into the American interior.

***Poland.** Eastern European country from which many New York Jews emigrated—especially after the Holocaust. In *Enemies* Poland exists only in the memories of his characters. To many of its characters, the Poland of memory and imagination seems more real than either New York City or the Catskills. Nevertheless, these memories direct the lives of all the novel's characters. Broder, for example, constantly seeks places to hide, in the unlikely event that Nazis should appear on American streets. The hayloft in Poland where he eluded Nazi agents still haunts his dreams, even as he lies beside Yadwiga, the Polish Gentile servant who hid him there at risk to her own life and who is now his wife in the United States. Broder learned well the lesson of hiding in Poland; in New York, he finally evades his three wives by disappearing.

Masha, who always talks of the German death camps, even during lovemaking, commits suicide. Yadwiga embraces the Judaism for which she yearned even as a peasant girl in Poland. Even after Broder deserts her, she looks forward to the birth of his child. Tamar, who has always loved causes more than she loves people, alone has learned from her Holocaust experiences the uses of adversity. She aids Yadwiga and establishes for herself a new life and career in America.

— *Allene Phy-Olsen*

AN ENEMY OF THE PEOPLE

Author: Henrik Ibsen (1828-1906)
Type of work: Drama
Type of plot: Social criticism

Time of plot: Late nineteenth century
First published: En folkefiende, 1882 (English
   translation, 1890); first performed, 1883

Like many of Henrik Ibsen's dramas, this play focuses on conflicts between private and public values. The protagonist, Dr. Peter Stockman, discovers that water feeding the newly constructed Baths in his seaside Norwegian hometown is polluted. Ignoring the economic and psychological consequences, he attempts to shut them down so the intake mechanism can be re-engineered. In the course of crusading for this change, he learns that public opinion is fickle and many leaders are more concerned about their reputations and finances than about serving the common good.

Baths. Newly constructed public spa in a Norwegian seaside town. As he does in many of his plays, Ibsen uses key features in the landscape to symbolize the values of those who live in the region. Hence, although his play unfolds in a number of private homes and public gathering places, the Baths dominate the dramatic landscape and take on symbolic significance. In a Norwegian town deteriorating from lack of business, the construction of the Baths means an economic boost through tourism. Literally, the Baths will bring much-needed cash into the region. Symbolically, they will bring new life, serving as a kind of baptismal font for the area's citizens whose prestige and pocket books will grow from the industry they will generate. Unfortunately, the Baths are polluted and pose a threat to those who use them. Symbolically, they also stand as a symbol for the pollution that has invaded the citizens of the town. Many would rather ignore the danger to themselves and the tourists who might use the Baths than admit there is a problem. The town's leaders are especially corrupt, as they are willing to hide the truth in order to protect their investments and save their positions of power. Ironically, the water that should bring new life becomes a source of further pollution; as Stockman observes at one point in the drama that it is not merely a question of water supply, but the "whole of social life that we have got to purify and disinfect."

— *Laurence W. Mazzeno*

LES ENFANTS TERRIBLES

Author: Jean Cocteau (1889-1963)
Type of work: Novel
Type of plot: Psychological realism

Time of plot: Early twentieth century
First published: 1929, as *Les Enfants terribles*
   (English translation, 1930)

Superficially, this novel is set in the French capital, Paris—the early chapters of it, if not the latter, in specifically identified districts and streets. At a deeper level, however, the greater part of the novel is confined by the figurative space of "The Room": an imaginary realm imaginatively extended from the cluttered environment of Paul and Elisabeth's narrow bedroom that expands in the end to possess—and ultimately destroy—the entire scope of their existence.

*Cité Monthiers (sih-tay mon-tee-er). District in Paris situated between the rue de Clichy and the rue d'Amsterdam. It is the site of the Lycée Condorcet, whose pupils use its streets as a playground. It is there that Paul is laid low by Dargelos's stone-loaded snowball; the incident gives rise to his temporary confinement and his friendship with Gérard. The master's residence, in an oblong court—which is inaccessible from the rue de Clichy because the way is blocked by wrought iron gates and hidden from the rue d'Amsterdam by a block of tenements—provides an image of confinement complementary to that of the Room.

Rue Lafitte. Street on which Gérard's home stands. There he lives with his guardian before moving into the house that Elisabeth inherits from Michael. In spite of Gérard's apparent importance within the story, it never figures as a setting; when Gérard and Paul meet outside the house in the rue Montmartre they do so in cafés (their one brief long-range excursion to an unspecified seaside resort is a disaster whose risk they are not tempted to repeat).

The Room. Initially a fantasized enlargement of the children's bedroom in their house in the rue Montmartre, beheld and sustained by virtue of their ability to enter the "Game." The Game is a state of altered self-consciousness of which all children are capable, but a privilege that they are supposed to surrender as they grow up. Although the actual bedroom is hardly big enough to contain two small beds, a chest of drawers and three chairs, all Paul and Elisabeth's prized possessions are crowded into it. Its door exits to a kitchen-dressing-room, whose other entrance is from the hall. The sickroom in which Paul and Elisabeth's dying mother is lodged is initially an alien space, but when Agatha moves into it, the Room begins to expand its tacit boundaries to take it aboard.

The actual location of Michael's far more capacious and splendid Paris residence, into which Elisabeth moves when she marries him, is never specified. To begin with, Elisabeth only claims a single room, decorated in imitation of the style of King Louis XVI, for her own, leaving the reception rooms, music room, gymnasium, and swimming pool to her husband. However, there is one room that Michael's Americanizing renovations have never managed to tame: a huge gallery, parts of which are adapted as study, dining room, and billiard room. Although Paul initially takes over Michael's room when he moves into the house, it is the gallery that becomes the focal point of the Room when it moves in with him. There, still insistently playing the Game, Paul establishes his own space, so spiritually isolated from the rest of the house that he has to resort to sending a letter to confess his love to Agatha—a letter which Elisabeth, still the only real cotenant of the Room, intercepts. It is, therefore, the hypothetical space of the Room in which Paul and Elisabeth remain confined thereafter, unable to release themselves even when Agatha's attractive force seems safely neutralized by her marriage to Gérard. It is in the Room, rather than in any definable physical arena, that they both die, never having really left the Game-created refuge that turns into a prison when the moment that they should leave the Game behind passes.

— *Brian Stableford*

THE ENORMOUS ROOM

Author: E. E. Cummings (1894-1962)

Type of work: Novel

Type of plot: Autobiographical

Time of plot: 1917

First published: 1922

During World War I, a four-month detention in a dirty French detention camp among mostly illiterate rejects becomes the means for the narrator (E. E. Cummings himself) to move from the status of victim to victor: He discovers that his sense of true identity and being evolves by transcending the tyranny of "official" thought and action and exercising his creative imagination in the making of symbols.

*Western Front. World War I combat zone in which the narrator's Norton Harjes Ambulance Service is serving the Allied forces. As an idealistic American volunteer in this Ambulance Corps, the narrator ironically experiences "prolonged indignities and injuries"; feeling badly deceived, he longs for release, a main theme of the novel. That initial release comes, paradoxically, when he is arrested by the French, along with his Harvard friend, B., on suspicion of being spies.

*Noyon** (NOH-yohn). Small French city north of Paris where the narrator is interrogated by an investigative board. Kept in a cell overnight, the narrator is overcome by "an uncontrollable joy" that comes from his first sense of regaining something of his selfhood. Because he refuses to say that he hates Germany, the enemy, he is remanded for continued custody in a detention center.

Prison. Detention center and site of the enormous room, in which the novel's main action takes place; located in the town of La Ferté-Macé in northwestern France's Orne department, west of Paris. This most unlikely of places, filthy, smelly, and crowded with the imprisoned riff-raff from a dozen different countries, becomes for the narrator the "finest place on earth," the place of his salvation.

Within the prison, the narrator is thrown into a huge darkened room, given a straw mattress, and told to go to sleep. In the darkness, he counts at least thirty voices speaking eleven different languages. The room is lined with mattresses down each side, with a few windows to let in light at one end. It smells of stale tobacco and sweat. Some of the prisoners are insane, and most of the others are afraid they might become so.

The narrator's choice of John Bunyan's novel *Pilgrim's Progress* (1678) as his structural myth emphasizes the "enormous room" odyssey as a metaphorical journey through the darkness of losing his tradition-dictated identity, and into the light of a new vision of self, the meaning of community, and the function of his art. Along the way, his teachers of darkness include authority figures—such as Apollyon, the head of the prison—who represent the symbolic structure of a corrupt civilization.

The narrator's fellow inmates become his teachers of light, particularly the four he calls "Delectable Mountains" (a gypsy, a Pole, Surplice the vagrant, and a black man). These men are outcasts but genuine human beings. Among them, the narrator experiences the bonds of true brotherhood. Enlightened, he emerges as a person who has gained an authentic self-identity, and as an artist whose creative consciousness has awakened and is ready to recreate his world through the creation of new symbols and new relationships between language and experience.

— *Henry J. Baron*

EPICŒNE: Or, The Silent Woman

Author: Ben Jonson (1573-1637)
Type of work: Drama
Type of plot: Comedy

Time of plot: Early seventeenth century
First performed: 1609; first published, 1616

With this play, Ben Jonson began using English locations rather than exotic foreign settings, directing his satire at his own society, the everyday world of seventeenth century England, assuming that his audiences would not need to have the milieus of the plays' action explained to them. In this play, the main characters move in clusters among the homes of members of their social group until everyone arrives at Morose's wedding to the "Silent Woman" of the title.

*London.** Jonson provides limited references to location, setting the play only in "London," an abstraction rather than a detailed place. The play's scenes move from home to home, beginning with that of Ned Clerimont's house, where the key characters meet in the first four scenes. Another scene is set in Sir John Daw's house, and three scenes are set in Captain Tom Otter's house, and then the plays moves on to Morose's home.

Morose's house. Since Morose is the center of attention, the wedding is his, and the joke is played on him, it is appropriate that most of the action occurs in his home. The wedding takes place there, as guests, food, and entertainment pour in from other homes. Unable to stand any noise except that of his own voice, Morose locks himself in his attic to escape the shrill chiding of his new wife. Although he goes to the law courts to seek a divorce, viewers hear about what happens here in his home, and the final unveiling of the bride takes place here too.

— *Andrew Macdonald and Gina Macdonald*

EPITAPH OF A SMALL WINNER

Author: Joaquim Maria Machado de Assis (1839-1908)
Type of work: Novel
Type of plot: Philosophical realism

Time of plot: 1805-1869
First published: Memórias póstumas de Bras Cubas, 1881 (*The Posthumous Memories of Brás Cubas,* 1951; *Epitaph of a Small Winner,* 1952)

This novel is presented as the posthumous autobiography of Braz Cubas, a Brazilian man about town for whom wealth and social position have functioned only as occasional distractions from the tedium of daily life. His failure to take religion, morality, or other people seriously is based on his inability to imagine that anything outside himself really exists, and the result is a fitfully comic as well as essentially pessimistic portrait of a man who has literally lost his place in society.

***Rio de Janeiro.** Capital city of Brazil in which most of the novel is set. In keeping with Braz Cubas's general lack of interest in his surroundings, Rio is depicted only in the vaguest and most generic terms; readers will be unable to form any precise visual image of what the city looks like. Although the narrative does involve travel between various locations in the city, exteriors are almost completely ignored in favor of moderately detailed attention to those interiors within which important plot events take place.

Cubas's house. Secluded home of Cubas that serves as the love nest he shares with his childhood sweetheart Virgilia, who has made an unhappy marriage that propels her back into Cubas's embraces. Their initial meetings occur at her home, where the unpredictable whereabouts of the servants make discovery a constant danger. Thus the establishment of a separate trysting place is both prudent and an emotional necessity for Cubas. So far as he is concerned, their cozy retreat is a symbol of his possession of Virgilia, a place where his ownership of the furnishings signifies his control over what happens amid them. For a while he even envisions the house as a kind of Eden on earth, although the passage of time and the intrusion of the outside world will eventually reduce it—as everything else in the novel is similarly reduced—to merely another example of life's failure to live up to expectations.

Lobo Neves's house. Residence of Virgilia and her husband, Lobo Neves. Domestic normality and banality are the primary characteristics of this location, which is depicted as the conventional, and thoroughly unsatisfying, standard against which Braz and Virgilia rebel. The house is essentially a showplace in which Lobo Neves, a politician, can entertain his confidants and further his career, and the novel stresses that this is both a pathetic form of human aspiration and a hindrance to the love of Braz and Virgilia.

Sabina and Cotrim's house. Home of Cubas's sister Sabina and her husband, Cotrim. Their residence is represented as the site of another version of normalcy, the mutually faithful "happy marriage." Its humdrum character is summed up by an old oil lamp in the living room, which though curved like a question mark has no answer to Cubas's meditations as to how he should resolve his relationship with Virgilia. Although Braz respects his sister's choice of a conventional life, his experience of her household reinforces his determination to follow a different path.

São Pedro Theater. Site of an awkward confrontation between Cubas and his lover's husband. The theater is notable as one of the few locations in which a social gathering figures in the novel's plot. Though brief, the scene emphasizes the gap between the elegant dress of the audience and the vulgar concerns that dominate their lives. It also occasions one of Cubas's many cynical reflections on human nature, as he hypothesizes that it is only by covering up their naked bodies that people are able to interest others in what lies underneath.

Marcella's house. Residence of Cubas's first adult passion, a courtesan of great beauty and even greater love of money. Marcella's expensive furniture, art works, and jewelry strike the young Cubas as the perfect accompaniment to her charms, although he does not realize that it is only while he helps to pay for them that she will continue to see him. His subsequent understanding that Marcella's feelings for him are strictly mercenary becomes a major reason why Braz adopts a pessimistic worldview.

— *Paul Stuewe*

EQUUS

Author: Peter Shaffer (1926-   )
Type of work: Drama
Type of plot: Psychological realism

Time of plot: Late twentieth century
First performed: 1973; first published, 1973

Although the main action of this play is set in Rokeby Psychiatric Hospital in southern England, the play's set avoids any suggestion of such a clinical locale. With few props except benches, the functional stage set allows a flexible use of theatrical space for reenactments of crucial events that occurred in prior years.

Rokeby Psychiatric Hospital. British psychiatric hospital to which teenager Alan Strang has been remanded by a court, after he blinded six horses with a metal spike. In contrast to the realistic clinical setting of Sidney Lumet's 1977 film version of *Equus*, which included white-coated doctors tending clearly psychotic patients, the set of the original play carefully avoids realistic imagery, other than the occasional appearance of a nurse.

John Napier's design for the set calls for a wooden square atop a wooden circle. The square resembles a boxing ring, which makes Alan and Dysart resemble evenly matched prize-fighters in their relentless rhetorical counterpunching. Functioning as witnesses, much like a Greek chorus, all other characters sit on benches behind the square, where they remain always visible to the audience. Napier's stage directions include three tiers of audience seats placed around the circle, "in the fashion of a dissecting theater." Metal horse-masks, donned by actors, are mounted on wooden poles.

Dalton's stable. Scene of the blinding incident, which is bloodlessly, almost balletically, reenacted at the play's climax. To Alan, the stable is a temple for clandestine worship of his horse-god, Equus—and the site of his failed first attempt at sexual intercourse with Jill Mason.

***Mycenae** (my-SEE-nee). Ancient Greek site of pagan rituals of worship that are idealized by psychiatrist Martin Dysart, in contrast to the sterility that he believes characterizes the modern world.

Strang home. Working-class household in southern England that is the site of various family conflicts, primarily over religion. In his bedroom, Alan reenacts secret rituals of worship before a poster-sized photograph of a horse, which has replaced an image of Christ in chains that his atheist father removed.

Beach. Site of six-year-old Alan's first ride on a horse, Trojan, which was interrupted when his father pulled him off the horse. The psychologically traumatic scene is reenacted during the play.

Field of Ha-Ha. Alan's name for the site of his exultant clandestine night ride, which is reenacted at the end of the first act. He takes the name from a passage in the Old Testament: "He saith among the trumpets, Ha, ha; and he smelleth the battle afar off, the thunder of the captains, and the shouting" (Job 39:25).

— *William Hutchings*

EREC AND ENIDE

Author: Chrétien de Troyes (c. 1150-c. 1190)
Type of work: Poetry
Type of plot: Arthurian romance

Time of plot: Sixth century
First transcribed: Erec et Enide, c. 1164 (English translation, 1913)

As the inventor of courtly romance, Chrétien de Troyes draws upon material about King Arthur that had been validated by the contemporary historian Geoffrey of Monmouth. He added other elements, including localities that serve to place events at a time that resembles the historical past, but with an added dash of finery that was not likely a part of that world. These semimythic locales parallel those in the author's other works, and provide them with a quality that transcends time.

*Cardigan. King Arthur's castle, which not only represents the splendor and honor that is so much a part of his legendary reign and of Chrétien's romances, but also the actual setting in Wales that exists at the present time. It signifies tradition and celebration. In addition, it is where the tale opens and the legendary white stag hunt custom is to begin. Erec and Enide are married there as well.

*Edinburgh. Another real locale in Scotland that is the perfect blend of modern and medieval aspects; it is a place of rich diversity and culture, as well as the place where the tournament is held and Erec is declared the victor of all attending knights.

Wilderness. This location seems deep and unknowable, just like the experiences that Erec and Enide face here.

*Nantes (nant). Port in Brittany, across the English Channel from Great Britain. Erec and Enide are crowned king and queen there on Christmas Day.

— *Adriana C. Tomasino*

EREWHON: Or, Over the Range

Author: Samuel Butler (1835-1902)
Type of work: Novel
Type of plot: Utopian

Time of plot: 1870's
First published: 1872

Using the device of a stranger visiting a strange land, this famous utopian fantasy depicts a society in which machines are forbidden, crime is considered an illness, and illness is considered a crime.

Erewhon (ee-ree-whon). Utopian land set vaguely in the South Pacific region—possibly in New Zealand, but because of Erewhon's vastness, some scholars have argued that it is more likely located in Australia. Early chapters show the struggle of the narrator, Higgs, to cross the unnamed mountain range between a coastal sheep pasture and the interior. He is in the company of Chowbok, an elderly Erewhonian. They travel on horseback to begin with, following the course of a river. After they spot the main range of mountains, with glaciers on their summits, the route becomes rockier, so they release their horses and continue on foot. Many gorges are unscalable or dead ends. After Chowbok deserts him, Higgs continues on alone. The difficult river crossings, dangerous precipices, snowy saddles, and magnificent views (often obscured by clouds) are described in great detail.

As Higgs descends toward the interior of the country, he sees the first evidence of another society: ten huge statues of semihuman forms. However, the people he encounters there are of normal human stature, handsome, and Mediterranean in their coloring. Their villages resemble those of northern Italy, where Samuel Butler spent many pleasant holidays.

As Higgs is taken, without force but on foot, from village to town, it becomes obvious that the vegetation of this land is similar to that of both New Zealand and the Mediterranean. However, the inhabitants' language is different, and the society completely rejects machines. The first evidence of a difference in Erewhonian philosophy comes when Higgs's pocket-watch is confiscated and placed in a museum of old and broken machines that houses fragments of steam engines, clocks, and other things that appear to be hundreds of years old. Higgs calculates that the society's culture is technologically similar to that of Europe in the twelfth or thirteenth century.

Imprisoned for his possession of a watch, Higgs comes to realize that illness is regarded as a crime; even catching a cold can result in a prison sentence. However, over the years, the law has produced a healthy and athletic people. Here, Butler puts Darwin's principle of the survival of the fittest into operation. On the other hand, criminal activities, such as embezzlement, are considered to be illnesses that should be treated.

Capital. Higgs is transported to Erewhon's unnamed capital city in a small carriage drawn by a single horse. Butler avoids description of the countryside by having Higgs travel blindfolded. Higgs estimates that his journey covers no more than thirty or thirty-five miles a day for a period of a month—figures that suggest a total of one thousand miles, a distance equivalent to almost the entire length of New Zealand's major islands. As Higgs gets closer to the metropolis, his blindfold is removed, and he sees towers, fortifications, and palaces. All the buildings Higgs describes are attractive and luxurious.

Nosnibor's home. Palatial house of Senoj Nosnibor in which Higgs is lodged. The house is a mansion on raised ground on the outskirts of the city, with rooms set around a central courtyard in the Roman style and with ten acres of terraced gardens. Nosnibor's name, like many in Erewhon, is an anagram of a familiar British name (Jones Robinson). "Erewhon" itself is an anagram of "nowhere." Butler uses anagrams as a technique of satirizing contemporary society through inversion of conventions.

Musical Banks. Important Erewhonian institution to which Higgs is taken by Zulora, the daughter of his host. Situated on a large central piazza, the building is an example of classical architecture, with pillars, towers and sculptures. Only its stained glass and choral singing seem unusual for a bank, but although money does change hands it soon becomes evident, to Higgs and to the reader, that this is Butler's satire of the established church. The money obtained from the Musical Banks is acceptable socially but is of no use in commerce. In contrast, the commercial banks are vital but not talked about.

Colleges of Unreason. Educational institution in the countryside outside the capital, to which Higgs is taken by a friendly Musical Banks cashier named Thims. The college buildings—like all other buildings in Erewhon—are exquisitely beautiful. Higgs reports that it is impossible to see them without being attracted to them. However, the institution itself does not offer teaching about the nature of tangible things; they mainly teach "hypothetics," or what might be, as the best way of preparing their students for life.

After many months living in Erewhon and learning how its society works, Higgs plans his escape, taking with him Arowhena, a young woman whom he loves. He excites the king and queen by mentioning balloon travel, and the queen allows him to construct a balloon and fill it with a lighter-than-air gas. When Higgs flies out of Erewhon, he notes that the ranges of mountains that separate the country from the rest of the world are about 150 miles across. Higgs and Arowhena pass over a plain and eventually come down in the sea.

*Sheep station. Higgs is introduced when he is contentedly working as a shepherd. He enjoys the grand countryside of plain and mountain, accepting the monotony as a trade-off for the view and the healthy life. This is a direct account of Butler's own feelings when he left England and his Cambridge studies after a quarrel with his father and went to New Zealand to farm sheep.

— *Chris Morgan*

ESTHER WATERS

Author: George Moore (1852-1933)
Type of work: Novel
Type of plot: Naturalism

Time of plot: Late nineteenth century
First published: 1894

This novel presents a vivid and realistic picture of the life of a servant in nineteenth century England in large country houses and lower-middle-class homes.

Woodview. House in southern England's Sussex countryside, close to Shoreham, that is owned by the Barfields, for whom Esther Waters becomes a kitchen maid. Although she is from London, Esther loves the countryside and spends much of her spare time walking on the Downs. Woodview is not so much a country house as a working stables, where racehorses are trained. Nevertheless, in many ways the establishment is typical of a small country house and is managed in the usual fashion, with a distinct hierarchy below stairs as well as above.

The house has been much expanded and altered, reflecting Mr. Barfield's intermittent prosperity. The establishment is unusual in that it is entirely permeated by the racing culture, with many of its staff members having been involved in racing for many years. Others gamble habitually, and servants are likely to be sacked if they discuss racing business, for fear this might give information to other racehorse owners. Although much of the racing culture is unpleasant to the religious Esther Waters, who is a member of the Plymouth Brethren, she is nevertheless happier at Woodview than at any other time and in any other place, and it is to Woodview, much diminished, that she later returns, to work for Mrs. Barfield once again, after her husband dies.

*London. Esther's original home and the city to which she returns after she becomes pregnant. After first going to her mother's home, she spends time in a lying-in hospital in Marylebone, in a lodginghouse, in a workhouse, sleeping rough on the Embankment, and in a succession of situations as she attempts to find enough money to keep herself and her son—who lodges with an old woman in Dulwich. George Moore vividly portrays Esther's attempts to find work, describing her long journeys on foot across central London to see prospective employers, the life on the streets, the temptations represented by the public houses. This is also reflected in

walks she takes with her friend Katherine, who also once worked at Woodview. Through their eyes readers see the lower-class life of Soho and Covent Garden.

The novel never crosses the River Thames to Southwark, where Katherine lives. Southwark was where brothels were traditionally situated, and it is clearly implied that Katherine is a prostitute. Moore also vividly describes the often appalling conditions in which Esther is obliged to work, from lodginghouses to the homes of shopkeepers, suggesting that while Esther keeps herself out of the workhouse, she nevertheless comes down in the world.

*Avondale Road. Street in London's West Kensington district where the decline in Esther's fortunes is arrested when she is hired by the undemanding Miss Rice, a writer who is impressed by both her story and her integrity. Miss Rice gives Esther a safe home and enough money to support her child. Avondale Road is a quiet household, situated in a quiet neighborhood with local shops and a sense of community among the domestic workers. The novel provides little description of Miss Rice's house other than the fact that it is in a redbrick suburb and has a garden.

*East Dulwich. Home of Mrs. Lewis, who cares for Esther's son, Jackie, and who has befriended and supported Esther. At the time the novel was written, Dulwich was on the outskirts of London, close to the open area known as Peckham Rye—a region considered healthy for children.

King's Head. Public tavern on Dean Street in London's Soho district. After becoming reunited with William Latch, the natural father of her child, Esther becomes the landlady of the public house. Although she and her husband run the place competently, it is financially successful only because William is also running an illegal betting house. When this fact is discovered, he is fined and obliged to return to work as a bookmaker on the racecourses, where he contracts tuberculosis. Unable to work, he once again runs an illegal betting house in the pub and eventually loses his license. William and others believe the public house to be unlucky (a man cuts

his throat there). It is in the tavern that William's tuberculosis finally overcomes him; he is taken to a hospital but eventually returns home to die.

— *Maureen Speller*

ETHAN FROME

Author: Edith Wharton (1862-1937)
Type of work: Novel
Type of plot: Psychological realism

Time of plot: Late nineteenth century
First published: 1911

In her introduction to this novel, Edith Wharton explains her belief that the fiction of New England missed the "outcropping granite" of the landscape and that the characters of this novel were her "granite outcroppings"— people living lives as stark and harsh as the New England region and its climate. Ethan Frome's life is as hard and bleak as the landscape until the arrival of Mattie Silver, but she, too, eventually succumbs to the local gloom. The novel, like the New England winter, is dark and bitter, and its characters are as severe and cold as their environment.

Starkfield. Fictional village in the hills of western Massachusetts's Berkshire County, where Wharton herself lived for many years. Small and rural, Starkfield lives up to its harsh name. Though connected by trolley to the larger town of Bettsbridge—which has libraries and theaters—Starkfield is isolated and lonely during the long New England winters. The village has a post office and a Congregational church. It also has one mansion, Lawyer Varnum's house, in which the narrator boards during his enforced residency in the community. The narrator refers to the "deadness" of the community only two pages after describing Ethan Frome as looking dead.

Ethan lives outside Starkfield on his own infertile farm, where he ekes out a meager living by the force of his labor in the fields and in the sawmill that he has inherited from his father. Ethan is the embodiment of the landscape, an "incarnation" of its frozen woes. Even as Wharton describes the loneliness and the accumulated cold of the hard, lean winters in the Berkshire Hills, she is also describing her protagonist. His life is as harsh as the climate, and his world as desolate as the village in winter.

Frome farm. Ethan's farm outside Starkfield, with a lonely New England farmhouse that seems to make the landscape even lonelier. Its starving apple trees grow out

of a hillside on which slate is more visible than cleared fields. The ugly house is made of thin wooden walls in need of paint. It is smaller than it was in Ethan's father's time because Ethan has removed the "L," which the narrator describes as the center or "hearthstone" of the New England farm. This suggests to readers how Ethan's life has narrowed, while the narrator sees in the "diminished dwelling" an image of Ethan's "shrunken body." The barren land reflects Ethan and his wife Zeena's childless marriage, and his unsuccessful sawmill serves as a reminder of Ethan's inability to get ahead.

The farmhouse is homelike only on the night that Zeena is absent. When Mattie decorates the table with Zeena's treasured red glass pickle dish, a wedding gift that Zeena herself refuses to use even for guests, Mattie transforms the drab house with that single little bit of color. When she and Ethan share their evening meal free of the misery caused by the whining Zeena, they briefly experience warmth and conversation that contrasts tragically with their normally cold, silent meals.

Ethan's property also includes a graveyard, which serves as a focal point for all the novel's images of death. A dead cucumber-vine dangles from the porch like a crepe streamer tied to a door for mourning. Other farmhouses dot the landscape like gravestones; the graves of

Ethan's ancestors mock any momentary desire for happiness. Indeed, there is even one headstone with the name Ethan Frome—the ancestor for whom the protagonist was named—that serves as a silent reminder of the death in life that pervades the novel.

School House Hill. Hill overlooking Starkfield that is the location of the climactic scene of the novel. The hill is also the site of sledding parties and moonlight kisses, but its hint of happiness and romance is always tempered by a dangerous curve at its base, where one mistake can mean serious injury or death. Here in the black and silent shadow of tall spruce trees that give Ethan and Mattie the feeling of being in "coffins underground," the two make the suicide pact that leads to the bleak and bitter ending in which there is little difference between the Fromes on the farm and the Fromes in the graveyard.

Bettsbridge. Sounding like a combination of the names "Berkshire," "Pittsfield," and "Stockbridge"—all actual names from the western Massachusetts region, Bettsbridge is the fictional city that Zeena goes to when she feels the need to see another medical specialist. She also refers to visiting Springfield, a real city in central Massachusetts, where she consults doctors whose recommendations invariably require expenditures that further stretch the Fromes' insufficient income.

*

Worcester (WEW-ster). City in the east-central portion of Massachusetts where Ethan attends college (perhaps Worcester Polytechnic Institute) and studies engineering. This site represents Ethan's lost opportunity. Now only a reminder of what Ethan wants out of life—intellectual stimulation and freedom to see the world—the memory of his life in the city provides a bitter contrast to his impoverished existence on the hardscrabble farm.

— *Paula L. Cardinal*

EUGÉNIE GRANDET

Author: Honoré de Balzac (1799-1850)
Type of work: Novel
Type of plot: Realism

Time of plot: 1819-1833
First published: 1833 (English translation, 1859)

This novel is set in the French provinces, where monomanias are concentrated, self-interest is both accepted and condoned, natural human feelings and emotions are often crushed, and conformity is strictly enforced.

Grandet house (gran-day). Home of Monsieur Grandet, his wife, his daughter, Eugénie, and his servant, Nanon. Located in Saumur, it is a typical provincial house of western France. Through highly detailed descriptions of both the exterior and the interior of the house, Honoré de Balzac reveals protagonists' social status and character. Bleak and cold in appearance, the house defines the monotonous and melancholy existence of its three female residents, an existence that is completely controlled by the tyrannical and miserly Grandet. Life is in fact so stifling that only when Grandet is away on business can the women breathe and be themselves. It is not surprising, therefore, that the parents never leave and will die there and that Eugénie views this dismal house as her entire universe. Only her cousin Charles

Grandet can free her, and when he chooses to marry another woman—despite making a promise to Eugénie of eternal love given in the Grandets' ill-kept and overgrown garden—Eugénie ultimately lives out her years in her father's home, unconsciously re-creating every detail of his own extreme frugality.

Large and in disrepair, the house has three rooms that have special significance. The poorly lit and heated gray parlor serves as the setting for family gatherings and penny-ante card games, always with the same six guests. Monsieur Grandet's doubly impenetrable study, whose access is forbidden to all, is compared to an alchemist's laboratory, since he "creates" real gold there out of shrewd economic sense and perfect market timing. Finally, Eugénie's bedroom is the scene of her virtual imprisonment, following her single act of rebellious independence directed at her father.

*Saumur (soh-MUR). Small town in the Anjou province on the Loire River in western France, best known for its wines and fruit crops. In this closed—and close—setting, everybody knows everything about everybody else, which is then thoroughly discussed and analyzed as gossip runs from house to house and shop to shop.

*India. South Asian subcontinent, which—like America, the West Indies, and Africa—represents a land of opportunity for adventurers, such as Charles Grandet, who are willing to work hard and who are not afraid to engage in unsavory practices in order to build their fortunes.

Marie-Caroline. Passenger brig sailing between America and Europe. Returning on the ship to France are newly rich Charles and the impoverished but noble and well-connected d'Aubrions, whose daughter he courts and eventually marries.

Hôtel d'Aubrion (oh-brih-YOHN). Mansion in the rue Hillerin-Bertin (now rue de Bellechasse) in the aristocratic Faubourg Saint-Germain district of Paris. Because young Grandet pays off the mortgages and liens on this property, he is able to marry Mademoiselle d'Aubrion and move into her parents' home.

*Angers (an-JEH). City in western France and capital of Anjou. Monsieur de Bonfons, Eugénie's husband, and Eugénie often commute between Angers and Saumur after he receives several promotions and appointments in the judicial and legislative branches.

*Paris. The capital of France, though hardly mentioned in the novel, acts not only as the moral inferior to Saumur by showing worse forms of corruption evident in the behavior of Guillaume Grandet and his son, but also as its defeated rival in the financial operations of Old Grandet and his daughter.

— *Pierre L. Horn*

THE EUSTACE DIAMONDS

Author: Anthony Trollope (1815-1882)
Type of work: Novel
Type of plot: Social realism

Time of plot: Late nineteenth century
First published: serial, 1871-1873; book, 1873

The settings of this novel are varied and geographically wide-ranging. Its protagonist, Lizzie Eustace, travels restlessly from one place to another, as she tries to keep possession of a disputed inheritance of diamonds. Much of the story's interest derives from the large cast of characters, who are in varying conditions of life and who inhabit these different settings.

Matching Priory. Ancestral home of the Palliser family, in the county of Yorkshire. Its owner, Plantagent Palliser, is devoted to politics. Matching Priory is the scene of political and social gatherings, and its description is sparse, save for a mention of one room, which is "small warm [and] luxurious."

Portray Castle. Castle in Scotland owned by Lizzie Eustace, who has inherited it from her husband. It is a large stone building, "really a castle," with battlements, tower, and gateway. The public rooms are magnificent but uncomfortable, and the bedrooms are "small and dark." The grounds are "sombre, exposed, and in winter, very cold." The castle is formal, showy, and stiff. This impressive but comfortless place is an apt setting for Lizzie, whose outward beauty masks inward selfishness, and who is herself disastrously influenced by people who are glib, rich, or titled but whose morals and manners are debased. A superbly funny moment at Portray occurs when Lizzie gazes out of a window at the sea and gushes to Miss Macnulty that the shining water reminds her of her dear, deceased husband. Miss Macnulty utterly fails to respond to Lizzie's affected romanticism, muttering that the "light is too much for my poor old eyes." The castle's name suggests a "portrayal," in particular one that is all surface show with little true substance or genuine worth.

*London. Characters in *The Eustace Diamonds* ricochet between their own or their friends' country homes and London houses. In contrast to the country, where entertaining, riding, and lovemaking are the focal activities, London is a center of business, law, and politics. Many scenes of conflict are set in London. The lawyers who are employed to recover the diamonds from Lizzie are located in London, and it is from London that Lizzie flees in order to try to keep the jewels. Furthermore, it is to London that the steward of Portray Castle, Andy Gowran, travels in order to denounce Lizzie for her loose behavior at the castle. Anthony Trollope says nothing about the appearance of London; it is, rather, a blank canvas upon which he paints the story's action.

Fawn Court. Country home of the Lady Fawn, her son Lord Fawn, and Lady Fawn's unmarried daughters.

Lizzie Eustace visits Fawn Court after becoming engaged to Lord Fawn. Some important moments in Frank Greystock's courtship of Lucy Morris also take place at Fawn Court.

*Naples. Italian port city to which Lizzie and her first husband, Sir Florian, travel and where he dies of consumption. Lizzie states that it is in Italy that he gives her the valuable diamond necklace, which his family wishes to have returned after his death. In several of Trollope's novels, Italy is portrayed as a place where shady dealings take place. Lizzie speaks with great sentimentality about her Italian sojourn: "I always think of those few glorious days which I passed with my darling Florian at Naples." However, it was in Italy that Florian realized that his wife was "utterly devoid of true tenderness."

— *Constance Vidor*

EVANGELINE

Author: Henry Wadsworth Longfellow (1807-1882)
Type of work: Poetry
Type of plot: Pastoral

Time of plot: Mid-eighteenth century
First published: 1847

This poem about seventeenth century French colonists expelled from what is now Nova Scotia uses geographical and historical facts to lend authenticity to its love story. Beyond its sentimental tale of star-crossed lovers, however, the poem recalls the biblical Eve ordered from Paradise. In her unending search for her lover Gabriel, Evangeline becomes a symbol of faithful womanhood as well as an icon of the French Acadians.

*Acadia. French colony in eastern Canada that overlapped the regions that became Nova Scotia, New Brunswick, Prince Edward Island, and other areas. Henry Wadsworth Longfellow's poem opens during the time of the French and Indian War (1754-1763), when many French-speaking Acadians fled or were driven out of the region by the British.

*Grand Pré. Largest Acadian village in Minas Basin, an inlet on the western shore of Nova Scotia, was the real home of the greatest number of French immigrants to Canada. The poem begins with a description of the lush, fertile valley surrounding Grand Pré, which it depicts as the home of peaceful shepherds and gentle farmers who live in thatched-roofed houses.

*Mississippi River. When Longfellow wrote his poem, this great river was the major highway of the United States, transporting goods and people from north to south. As Longfellow's characters row down the Mississippi, a panorama of America unfolds. Many Acadian families actually traveled down the river searching for places to live. Many settled in southern Louisiana, where their descendants became known as Cajuns.

— *Ginger Jones*

EVELINA: Or, The History of a Young Lady's Entrance into the World

Author: Fanny Burney (Madame d'Arblay, 1752-1840)
Type of work: Novel
Type of plot: Sentimental

Time of plot: Eighteenth century
First published: 1778

Setting in this epistolary novel plays on the popular eighteenth century city-country dichotomy. The heroine, lacking a guardian to help her enter London society, proceeds on her own but learns from her mistakes, as her instinctive responses to the people and public spaces of the city are astute. Nonetheless, her reactions to the places she visits depend upon the company she keeps—an idea the novel emphasizes by subjecting her to multiple visits to important locales. This pattern changes after she returns to her pastoral home and finds that being surrounded by old friends cannot overcome her disappointment in love.

Berry Hill. Country home of Mr. Villars, Evelina's guardian, located seven miles from Dorchester in southern England. Berry Hill's rural location signifies Evelina's innocent and unsophisticated upbringing. However, her natural grace and understanding hint at her having a noble lineage that transcends the limitations of her rustic education.

*****London.** Great Britain's capital city is the site of Evelina's entrance into the world and of her education in the world's ways. Her initial immersion in London's customs allows author Fanny Burney to satirize the fashions of the times, as seen through the eyes of an ingenue. As Evelina writes home, first from respectable Queen Ann Street and later from a hosier's in working-class Holborn, she records her own and others' impressions of city life.

Evelina's party visits a number of theatrical and musical performances during her first sojourn in London, and these episodes contribute to a debate over the value of art and its relationship to good taste. At a performance of William Congreve's *Love for Love* (1695) at Drury Lane Theatre, discussion of the play turns into an argument over how men should respond to beauty, either with passionate enthusiasm or with philosophic detachment. A later concert at the Pantheon returns to this idea, as a nobleman ogles Evelina and betrays an indelicacy unsuitable to his social position. The ultimate test of the characters' taste comes at the Haymarket Opera House. As Evelina strives to listen to the performance, her crude cousins, the Branghtons, talk incessantly, complaining about the very features of opera that distinguish the musical form as high art.

The reactions of *Evelina*'s characters to London's other tourist attractions help polarize English and French national tastes as well as the upper- and tradesman classes. Captain Mirvan refuses to be pleased by a performance of the Fantoccini puppet show merely because the comedy is performed in French and Italian. His stubbornness is contrasted with the superficiality of Madame Duval, who exclaims over the bejeweled mechanical objects at Cox's Museum. A similar tension occurs among the distinguished sites where the impeccable Lord Orville appears, such as the auction house in Pall Mall, Ranelagh, and Kensington Gardens, and the plebeian haunts of the Snow Hill set—the Branghtons.

In the company of her cousins, Evelina visits the Vauxhall and Marylebone Gardens, with each episode expressing the dangerous condition of Evelina's ambiguous place in society. At Vauxhall, the Branghton girls lead Evelina down the dark alleys, in which men ensnare and insult Evelina in a nightmarish scenario. Similarly, at Marylebone, Evelina loses her company and desperately calls out for help, only to find herself arm-in-arm with two prostitutes who refuse to part company with her.

*****Paris.** France's capital city is a place where the English are inevitably debauched or ruined. Evelina's grandfather once sought exile there in disgrace; her mother made an ill-advised marriage there; and Mr. Macartney fought his own father in a duel while there.

*****Scotland.** Homeland of the impoverished poet Macartney, whose differences from other characters are thus given geographical emphasis. Macartney contrasts the crass middle-class materialism of his landlords, the Branghtons, with a delicate sensibility that cannot bear the series of disappointments he experiences. His financial distress subjects him to stereotyping as a threadbare, impoverished Scot, but that is an unaccustomed state for him, and sympathetic observers know it.

Howard Grove. English home of Lady Howard, a friend of Mr. Villars who counteracts the clergyman's over-protectiveness of Evelina with gentle remonstrances. Her influence in her own home is overrun by that of her son-in-law, Captain Mirvan, when he returns from sea and begins a new campaign of tormenting Madame Duval.

*****Bristol Hotwells.** Spa in southwestern England that is a destination for wealthy travelers. Evelina goes there by chance after being ill, and a neighbor, Mrs. Selwyn, is headed there. Ironically, the cure offered by the Hotwells waters cannot heal the larger, national illness of the members of the corrupt aristocratic class who frequent such places.

*****Bath.** Resort town in southwestern England famous for its hot mineral springs and its Georgian buildings. Once Evelina's identity is known, the nobility who scorned her seek out her favor by accompanying her on a sightseeing trip to this famous destination.

— *Jennifer Preston Wilson*

EVERY MAN IN HIS HUMOUR

Author: Ben Jonson (1573-1637)
Type of work: Drama
Type of plot: Comedy

Time of plot: Late sixteenth century
First performed: 1598; first published, 1601; revised, 1605, 1616

Revisions that Ben Jonson made in this play in 1616 make clear his concern for setting. In the play's original form, its characters and setting were Italian. By contrast, Jonson set his revised version in and around London, England, taking great pains to emphasize the English nature of his characters and theme. The play's principal characters are clearly types whom one might meet in the city, and their behavior—often suggested by or contrasted with their names, such as Brainworm, Deepdown, Knowell, and Wellbred—marks the work as a precursor to the comedy of manners that arose later in the seventeenth century.

*****London.** England's capital and largest city. While most of the play's scenes are set at the various London homes of its characters, Jonson does little to give symbolic significance to most settings. The actions that take place in such settings are conventional: For example, Knowell's home is a refuge from the dangers (both physical and moral) of London society, while the Windmill Tavern is a place of lusty intrigue and low-life braggadocio. Scenes set outdoors suggest that the London streets were places where people of every walk of life might pass and even exchange pleasantries without violating social norms associated with the class structure prevalent at the time.

Clement house. London home of the ebullient, jovial eccentric Justice Clement, and the one place that has special thematic significance in the play. Like many of his contemporaries, Jonson ends his comedy by suggesting some restoration of the social order, setting aright the machinations and plots of his characters. It is not surprising that the final act takes place at the house of Justice Clement. As his name suggests, this official is a man who passes judgment with both justice and mercy. Hence, it is fitting that his home becomes a visible symbol of the well-ordered society.

— *Laurence W. Mazzeno*

EVERY MAN OUT OF HIS HUMOUR

Author: Ben Jonson (1573-1637)
Type of work: Drama
Type of plot: Comedy

Time of plot: Turn of the seventeenth century
First performed: 1599; first published, 1600

Among Ben Jonson's comedies, this play may be the work in which the setting has the least important role. Although its characters have Italian names, there is no attempt to locate the play in any specific Italian city. Rather, Jonson suggests through his contrast of country gentry with the upper classes in the city the folly of believing that dressing and behaving like nobility will give social pretenders access and status among the higher classes.

Italian countryside. The play's opening scene and several others throughout the drama are set in the country. Many of the major characters are country folk, and they exhibit behaviors often associated with less sophisticated men and women who wish to ape the fashion and behavior of city dwellers. The appearance in the country of figures who have lived in the city and been to court is enough to cause people with a propensity for pretentious behavior to pay close attention to those who claim to be able to help them improve their social status and fortune by transforming their dress and manners.

Italian city. Several scenes take place in an unnamed city, where the country bumpkins become objects of ridicule. Jonson points out the hypocrisy and affectation of several of his major characters by contrasting their behavior with that of the more sophisticated citizens of the city.

Unidentified royal court. Two key scenes are set at court, which in this play represents both the legitimate center of culture and power and the place where the pretensions of country folks are most apparent. The Lady Saviolina, who rules at court, quickly sees through the shallow behavior of would-be courtiers, and rebukes them for their attempts to masquerade as nobility.

— *Laurence W. Mazzeno*

EVERYMAN

Author: Unknown
Type of work: Drama
Type of plot: Morality

Time of plot: Indeterminate
First published: Uncertain; earliest extant version: 1508

Although place may not be of obvious importance at first glance in this work, which is considered one of the greatest of the morality plays, the play's transcendence of time makes it relevant. Essentially, this allegory deals with death and the path to saving one's soul. The lesson to be learned is that no matter what one has in a lifetime, only those things that have been given can weather the journey between life and death. Therefore, salvation can only be achieved if the soul is in a "state of grace." This is a message that pertains to all people. As a result, the localities of special interest in this work are abstract rather than real, and include Everyman's journey and the House of Salvation.

Journey to Paradise. Long journey from life to death that Death orders Everyman to make. Everyman is to take with him his full book of accounts; he must be careful, as he has done many bad deeds and only a few good ones. When he reaches Paradise, he will be required to account for his life. Death permits Everyman to take with him on his journey any companions he wishes, but only Good-Deeds goes with him the entire way.

With several stops along the way, Everyman's journey takes on a dual purpose. On one hand, the image of his traveling from place to place to find a suitable companion is similar to a realistic trip; on the other, and on a more spiritual plane, Everyman's peregrination characterizes his quest for salvation. On this path, Everyman is damned until he realizes that he must free himself of his sins before he is permitted to enter the heavenly sphere. He can accomplish that task only with the help of the sacraments and his own good deeds.

House of Salvation. Place where Everyman receives the sacrament of penance from Confession. On a certain level, the House of Salvation represents Heaven and is where the play begins—with God speaking about humankind's forgetfulness of his son's sacrifice—and ends with the angel taking Everyman's soul, as does human life.

— Adriana C. Tomasino

EXILES

Author: James Joyce (1882-1941)
Type of work: Drama
Type of plot: Naturalism

Time of plot: 1912
First published: 1918; first performed in German in 1919; first performed in English in 1925

This play's two settings are rooms in the Dublin, Ireland, residences of Richard Rowan and Robert Hand, who contest the love of Richard's wife, Bertha. The contrasting locations highlight both the conflict between the two men and also their spiritual and psychological differences.

Rowan drawing room. Well-furnished house in Merrion, a Dublin suburb. It is a warm, late afternoon in June, 1912, with the sunlight just beginning to fade. (June, the month in which James Joyce first met his own wife, Nora, is always a significant time in his writings.) The room and its contents indicate that the family that lives here is moderately well-to-do, educated, and cultured. This is clearly a place of some refinement, which reflects the lives of its residents, and this is a room for quiet conversation and discussions. Joyce's stage descriptions are extremely detailed, not only specifying the arrangement of doors and furniture but requiring chairs upholstered in "faded green plush" and a floor of "stained planking." Joyce notes only one piece of art, a framed crayon drawing of a young man that hangs above a sideboard against a back wall.

The detail in Joyce's requirements for the play's setting is matched by his careful descriptions of the characters, their clothing and their actions. Richard Rowan, for example, is described as "a tall athletic young man of a rather lazy carriage" who has "lightbrown hair and a moustache and wears glasses." Later Richard's wife, Bertha, is described as wearing a lavender dress and carrying her cream gloves "knotted round the handle of her sunshade." The physical settings of *Exiles* have an essential role in presenting its artistic meaning.

Hand cottage. Home of Robert Hand, to which the scene shifts for the play's second act. It is now evening of the same June day. Hand, Richard's rival for Bertha Rowan, lives in a smaller, less expensive house in Ranelagh, another Dublin suburb. Again, Joyce provides extensive description of the scene, and the differences between the two settings distinguish fundamental divisions between the two male characters. Where the Rowan house is well and tastefully decorated, Robert Hand's cottage is self-consciously artistic. It has a piano with open music on it; there is a standing Turkish pipe next to a rocking chair; and on the walls, instead of the single, simple drawing in the Rowan house there are many framed black and white designs. The amount of furniture which Joyce crams into what must be a relatively small space should make the stage seem full, even cluttered—perhaps an accurate reflection of its owner's state of mind.

If Robert Hand's cottage is self-consciously artistic, so are his actions while waiting for the arrival of the Rowans. As the act opens Robert is discovered sitting at the piano, where he plays the appropriately moody and romantic opening of Wolfram's song in the last act of Richard Wagner's opera "Tannhauser." Breaking off, he meditates for a moment, then rises to pull out a pump from behind the piano and "walks here and there in the room ejecting from it into the air sprays of perfume." Done, he hides away the pump and sits, awaiting the arrival of his guests. In such a fashion, Robert's house as well as his actions and words reflect his elaborate and highly self-conscious "love" of Bertha and contrast dramatically with Richard's understated and much more sincere devotion and respect for his wife.

Rowan study. The third and final act of the play is set back in the Rowans' drawing room, and during part of the action Bertha opens a door to reveal Richard's study, a small, untidy room filled with books, papers, a writing desk and lamp. It is clearly the haunt of an intellectual, perhaps even a true artist. Although glimpsed for only a moment, it presents the audience with a fleeting insight into Richard Rowan's underlying character and again uses the physical setting to make a telling contrast between the two men.

— *Michael Witkoski*

THE EXPEDITION OF HUMPHRY CLINKER

Author: Tobias Smollett (1721-1771)
Type of work: Novel
Type of plot: Satire

Time of plot: Mid-eighteenth century
First published: 1771

This last and best of Tobias Smollett's novels chronicles a family's eight-month journey from their country home in Wales to England and Scotland and back to England, following a route popularized by contemporary travel literature. The journey is undertaken for various reasons—health for Squire Matthew Bramble, matrimony for his sister, and education for their niece and nephew. Symbolically, however, the journey represents the search for personal happiness through coming to terms with the world's and one's own limitations. In addition, the journey allows for numerous encounters with people and places along the way—subject matter for Smollett's biting commentaries on a range of political and social issues.

Brambleton Hall. Matthew Squire's country residence, an imaginary estate near the real town of Abergavenny, Wales. Throughout the novel, it serves as the basis of comparison for the new places the family experiences and comments on in their letters to friends at home. Smollett, himself a Scotsman, liked Wales and used Welsh characters in other novels. Choosing a Welsh protagonist like Matt provided Smollett with a not-quite-foreign outsider from a simple, rustic background to serve as witness and commentator on city life versus country life, tradition versus change, and England versus Scotland, while not alienating his English audience, who generally felt an affection for the Welsh that they did not feel for the Scots.

The family's journey ultimately ends where it begins, at Brambleton Hall, leaving the family content with their lives in the country, far from the city's squalor and squander. Coming full circle, their journey thus represents a symbolic joining of estranged countries into a unified, peaceful whole while rejecting rapidly evolving urban social values in favor of traditional rural virtues.

*****Bath.** Elegant English resort town and site of a natural mineral hot spring renowned for its reputed curative waters and fashionable clientele. Bath is the family's first major stop. The socially conservative Smollett practiced medicine in Bath and uses Matt's letters to excoriate the unhygienic bathing practices and the mingling of social classes at Bath Spa. He decries the high cost of living and unrestrained growth in Bath as well, lecturing against the luxury and extravagance caused by Britain's rapidly expanding global trade networks.

*London.** Capital of Great Britain and largest city in the British Isles. Smollett wrote extensively for London journals but never liked living in the city. Matt gives voice to his loathing of the sprawling metropolis with its hustle and bustle, adulterated food and drink, and corrupt politics.

*Scotland.** After leaving London, the family makes several stops before crossing the Tweed River into Scotland. Matt notes that the countryside on the English side of the river is not as well tended as that on the Scottish side, a comment echoing his generally critical view of the English towns and estates they see after departing the capital. The family's itinerary in Scotland corresponds to that of Smollett's travels through his homeland in 1766. Smollett spent most of his life forced to make his living in England during a period rife with anti-Scottish sentiment. Not surprisingly, the family's letters from Scotland reflect Smollett's enthusiasm for his beloved country. Matt admires the well-managed estates of the Scottish countryside and the fine university and hospitals of Edinburgh, even proclaiming that Edinburgh would be his city of choice if he were a city dweller.

*Glasgow.** Thriving Scottish industrial center. Matt favorably compares Glasgow to a beehive of industry. Unlike the unplanned, uncontrolled cities of England, Glasgow is depicted as the epitome of utility and order. Smollett's birthplace is perhaps not coincidentally just northeast of Glasgow. The family's remaining travels through Scotland are described in similarly complimentary terms. After they cross back into England, however, the letters concentrate on the machinations of the plot rather than the particulars of place.

Dennison estate. English estate owned by niece Liddy Melford's future father-in-law, who has brought it back from the brink of ruin after his dissolute brother allowed it to deteriorate. Throughout the novel, one of Smollett's themes is the superiority of the agrarian way of life, exemplified by the Dennison estate with its perfectly realized model community. Here the plot is resolved with the intermarriages of the Welsh, Scottish, and English characters, symbolizing the harmonious reconciliation and unification of three historically contentious countries fated to share one small island.

— *Sue Tarjan*

EXPLOSION IN A CATHEDRAL

Author: Alejo Carpentier (1904-1980)
Type of work: Novel
Type of plot: Social realism

Time of plot: 1789-1809
First published: El siglo de las luces, 1962 (English translation, 1963)

Several colorful Caribbean and European settings form the backdrops against which this novel of the French Revolution's impact upon a Havana family unfolds. The book's title is an allusion to a painting that depicts the destruction of a massive cathedral; the narrative connects this image with plot developments portraying the period's violent overthrow of political regimes, social institutions, and personal value systems alike.

Home of Carlos, Esteban, and Sofia. Havana residence of the three orphaned young-adult members of a prominent, although never named, merchant family. Both the dwelling and the offspring have been neglected by the late father, and in her new role as female head of the household, Sofia decides to refurnish the home completely. The result is a material avalanche of furniture, crockery, books, and musical instruments that turns their

living quarters into a labyrinth of stacked packing cases and narrow passageways. Carlos, Esteban, and Sofia move among these as if gingerly exploring a strange new world, while delighting in their random encounters with this profusion of worldly goods.

The bizarre manner in which these mostly European objects are treated, and in particular the many descriptions of how Havana's heat and humidity lead to the rapid deterioration of the new furnishings, exemplifies the novel's related theme of the breakdown of meaningful communication between Europe and its New World colonies. Although Carlos, Esteban, and Maria are initially delighted with the imported luxuries that their colonial wealth enables them to buy, they soon tire of this essentially meaningless pastime, and welcome the help of the Haitian merchant Victor Hugues in restoring their family's place in the world. Subsequent plot developments will provide many additional examples of colonial frustration with an inappropriate imperial heritage, and the novel's graphic portrayal of Old World materials literally destroyed by New World conditions makes this point with telling immediacy.

*Havana.** Capital of colonial Cuba and bustling commercial center where the novel begins. Business activity, and particularly the exchange of raw materials for manufactured objects, is a major component of the novel's colonial settings. The novel's characteristic delight in material profusion is here demonstrated by an exhaustive inventory of the family firm's warehouse that seems to revel in its mounds of salted fish, spices, grains, and many other articles of commerce.

*Paris.** Capital of France and center of the French Revolution. Here Esteban and his political mentor Victor, a Haitian businessman turned revolutionary activist, participate in a tumultuous world that sees one day's dictator become the next day's victim of the guillotine. The novel stresses the apparent randomness of these events, while visualizing them on a cinematic screen across which surging crowds and impassioned public meetings struggle for dominance.

*Guadeloupe.** French-ruled Caribbean island to which Victor is sent as governor, taking Esteban as his chief clerk. Protracted warfare between the incoming revolutionary officials and the old colonial regime, during which Guadeloupe's capital city is largely destroyed, leads Victor to introduce the guillotine and other aspects of the Parisian terror as a means of defeating his opponents. Although Victor eventually succeeds in establishing his control, the death and destruction that have resulted suggest that European revolutionary methods may not be the best solution to colonial problems.

*Cayenne** (ki-EN). Capital of French Guiana on the northeastern coast of the South American mainland. Esteban stops there on his return journey to Havana and is shocked by an authoritarian government that has established its own reign of terror on the Parisian model. Victor is subsequently appointed the colony's new governor and is forced to implement reactionary French laws that reinstitute slavery and negate the positive accomplishments of the Revolution. When many of the local subjects revolt and flee into the jungle regions inland, their defeat of the military expeditions sent against them again indicates that European practices are not necessarily effective outside their place of origin.

*Madrid.** Spanish capital where Esteban and Sofia spend their final days. Initially depicted as a haven from the instability of Caribbean and French societies, the murder of Sofia and Esteban in a riot makes the ironic point that there are no safe havens in a world where change is both inevitable and unpredictable.

— *Paul Stuewe*

F

A FABLE

Author: William Faulkner (1897-1962)
Type of work: Novel
Type of plot: Allegory

Time of plot: 1918
First published: 1954

This novel, which William Faulkner originally conceived as a screenplay, is one of his few novels not set in his mythical Yoknapatawpha County. It does, however, include a character from Yoknapatawpha and thus connects with Faulkner's Mississippi saga. Based on an actual peace movement that occurred during World War I, the story is an allegory that parallels the events of the last week in the life of Christ.

Chaulnesmont (SHON-mon). French town that is a site of Allied headquarters during World War I. Scenes in the novel are set in the town square of Chaulnesmont and in the surrounding countryside, including a country estate serving as the headquarters of General Gragnon. In Chaulnesmont the corporal and his men are executed after their court martial. There are also scenes set in the front-line trenches described as being "below the Bethune slagheap." These locales as well as others in *A Fable* have a somewhat detached and surreal quality, as if they were occurring in an unearthly setting. Some locales, such as the foxhole in which the soldiers live, are described in considerable detail, and the time element of each section is usually clearly specified, since the author wants his readers to associate the events and characters with the war. Nevertheless a sense of unreality prevails throughout the book, for Faulkner does not delineate the sights, sounds, and smells of specific places as in most of his novels and stories. The narrative approach he uses in *A Fable* befits a work that is closer to being a fable than a realistic novel.

Mississippi. A set piece told as a background story concerning the theft of a race horse in 1912 contains scenes in Louisiana and Mississippi. The Mississippi scenes might be read as being set in Yoknapatawpha County.

Paris. Several scenes are set in the French capital, including one in which a former British army officer identified only as the Runner goes to Paris to seek out the characters involved in the theft of the race horse. In one of the major coincidences of the novel the corporal who instigates the peace movement among Allied and German soldiers and has been executed for treason is buried in the city's Tomb of the Unknown Soldier.

St. Mihiel (sah[n] mih-heel). French town to which the body of the executed corporal is taken by his sisters. St. Mihiel parallels Nazareth in the life of Christ.

— *W. Kenneth Holditch*

THE FAERIE QUEENE

Author: Edmund Spenser (c. 1552-1599)
Type of work: Poetry
Type of plot: Allegory

Time of plot: Arthurian Age
First published: books 1-3, 1590; books 4-6, 1596

Although the Faery Land of Edmund Spenser's poem is at one level a generalized landscape for romance and at another a nonrepresentational version of England, it is primarily a canvas on which Spenser allegorically depicts the struggle for moral perfection.

Faery Land. Mythical country that serves as a setting for the romantic adventures of idealized knights, whose charge is to perfect themselves in their calling and rescue or protect innocent victims from their enemies. An array of forests, caves, and dungeons gives each knight (a different hero in each of the poem's six books) an opportunity to exhibit his skill and inspire gratitude and love in the person—usually a fair maiden—whom the dragon or monster of the moment is afflicting.

In a sense, Faery Land is also England, but not one visibly recognizable. While Spenser makes many references to English place names, as well as many more pertaining to other parts of the world, he makes no attempt to relate any part of his landscape in any realistic way to actual English sites. One effect of these allusions is to remind readers of England's historical culture and values.

Spenser's prefatory letter to Sir Walter Raleigh explains the "Faerie Queene" as signifying the woman who reigned in England through most of Spenser's life: Queen Elizabeth I. The Prince Arthur of the poem is not precisely the legendary King Arthur but an Arthur who, if Spenser had succeeded in bringing his poem to a conclusion (for he projected twelve, and possibly even twenty-four books), would have sought out Gloriana, the Faerie Queene, then wooed and married her. This union would have underscored the desirability of a marriage for Elizabeth which would presumably stabilize the royal succession and thus foster the integrity of the real English kingdom.

In its basic structure, however, the poem is a complex allegory with a stated purpose: "To fashion a gentleman or noble person in virtuous and gentle discipline." In the largest sense, then, its Faerie Land is the human soul.

Spenser believed strongly that it was the writer's goal to paint virtue in an attractive, active, even heroic manner capable of inspiring readers to perfect themselves morally and thus qualify as "gentle" or "noble" persons, whatever their social class. Faery Land might be called the landscape of the soul, and the movement from place to place symbolizes the soul's labors throughout life. Each book of the poem celebrates a particular virtue. The Red Cross Knight of book 1 seeks to perfect himself in holiness, Sir Guyon of book 2 represents temperance, and so on.

Typically in the course of each book, its hero comes to places that help or challenge him (or her, for Britomart of book 3 is a female knight devoted to chastity) in the quest for moral perfection. Thus the Red Cross Knight is challenged by the **House of Pride**, Guyon by the **Cave of Mammon**. Eventually the knight reaches a countering place that fosters virtue: the Red Cross Knight, the **House of Holiness**; Guyon, the **Bower of Bliss** (a good place because the Bliss depicted is natural and moderate). Spenser's descriptions of these places are often graphic. For example, Sir Scudamour of book 4 spends a night at the house of a blacksmith named Care, who along with six assistants wields "huge great hammers that did never rest," hammers which "like bells in greatness orderly succeed." The combination of this crew working all night and a pack of howling dogs permits the knight no sleep, but the purpose of the episode is not to represent the blacksmith's trade but to convey the anxiety of Sir Scudamour at this point in the narrative. What is most "real" for Spenser throughout is not the material, sensible world but the life of the human spirit.

— Robert P. Ellis

FAHRENHEIT 451

Author: Ray Bradbury (1920-   )
Type of work: Novel
Type of plot: Science fiction

Time of plot: The future
First published: 1953

This dystopian novel about the future creates a primary dichotomy between city and country. A complex juxtaposition of natural and mechanical images dominates the novel and reflects its central tensions between the country and the city, or culture and technology.

City. Unnamed urban center in which the protagonist, Guy Montag, lives and works. In this future world, culture is reduced to the lowest common denominator. Montag's wife, for example, is completely dependent on her wall-sized television screens. Books are banned because they contain contradictory ideas and can confront the comfortable prejudices and ignorance that abounds. Montag himself works as a "fireman"; his job is to burn books as they are discovered hidden in people's homes. In this world of state-sponsored book-burning, books are not simply carriers of potentially subversive messages—their very physical existence evokes a rich cultural tradition antithetical to the leveling tendencies of the mass media. When Montag discovers the joy of reading, he begins hiding books in his own house. Eventually, his wife reports him to the police, and he is sent to burn out his own house. He flees the city for his life.

Meanwhile, a constant threat of war overhangs the city, and most of its people view with suspicion anyone who lives outside carefully proscribed social boundaries. The book ends with the destruction of the cities by atomic bombs and the hope that civilization, like the mythical Phoenix, will rise again from its ashes. At the end of the story, the classical allusion to the phoenix is explained by Granger, the leader of the book people. The symbol is appropriate to their mission, he says, because like humankind, "every few hundred years he built a pyre and burnt himself up . . . But every time he burnt himself up he sprang out of the ashes, he got himself born all over again."

Countryside. The world outside the city contrasts sharply with the urban environment. Ray Bradbury is a romantic writer who often yearns for the simpler, rural life he knew as a child. When Montag is forced to run for his life from the city, the source of all the evils he has come to hate and fear, he escapes to the countryside. His journey ends when he comes upon an old railroad track, a symbol of the long-lost American past. There, he joins a new social group, made up of people who share his beliefs. Its outcast members, who have rejected society's standards, keep literature alive by memorizing books.

River. Wide stream down which Montag floats until he reaches the community of book people. This river operates as a dividing line between past life and new, signifying a kind of baptism: After he began "floating in the river he knew why he must never burn again in his life."

— *Gary Zacharias*

THE FAIR MAID OF PERTH

Author: Sir Walter Scott (1771-1832)
Type of work: Novel
Type of plot: Historical

Time of plot: 1396
First published: 1828

This novel is Sir Walter Scott's account of a legendary battle between the champions of two rival clans, a historical event that took place on the North Inch of Perth in 1392, although the reasons for the battle and the identities of the combatants are unclear. The novel absorbs into this event others that actually happened over the following ten years in the same region.

*****Perth.** County in the center of Scotland that embraces both highland and lowland regions. It is described by Scott's notional narrator, Chrystal Croftangry, as the most varied, picturesque, and beautiful of all Scottish counties; in the novel it becomes a microcosm of medieval Scotland. The early chapters of the novel are set within the town of Perth, which is two miles south of the ancient Scottish capital of Scone, and was itself regarded as the capital at the time in which the novel is set.

The most important settings within the town of Perth are Simon Glover's house in Couvrefew, or Curfew Street, and the Dominican monastery—which had been founded in 1231—at the junction of Blackfriars Wynd and Couvrefew. The architecture of the monastery is Gothic, including secret passages and a council-room, where the political conspiracies underlying the plot are hatched. Glover's daughter Catherine, the novel's claimant to the eponymous title, becomes caught up in these convoluted machinations after attending the monastery's church on Saint Valentine's Eve, where the rivalry between her two lovers—the armorer Henry Gow, whose smithy is in Mill Wynd on the western side of the town, and Conachar, heir to the chieftainship of Clan Quhele—first flares up. A sharp contrast is drawn between the gloomy monastery and the hill of Kinnoul outside the town, where Catherine takes instruction from a Carthusian white friar. There she observes an oak tree whose precarious situation—in the cleft of a rock split by lightning—symbolizes her own perilous situation.

Other featured locations within the town include the council house on the High Street, where Sir Patrick Charteris of Kinfauns presides—which is as gloomy as its equivalent in the monastery—and the High Church of Saint John's. The latter location is a natural selection as the meeting place for the trial by ordeal, by virtue of the fact that Saint John is the town's patron saint. The arena for the fight in which Henry defeats the assassin Bonthron is marked out in the nearby Skinners' Yards.

*River Tay. Scottish river on which the town of Perth stands. It follows a winding course eastward, then southward, from Loch Tay and then proceeds eastward from the town to the Firth of Tay. The novel's major settings outside the town are all distributed along the river. The river's eastward reach features in a significant expedition from Sir John Ramorny's bankside house in the town, which proceeds under the town's old bridge—whose Gothic arches were washed away in 1621—to the gibbet where Bonthron is hung and then to the fishing village of Newburgh on the edge of the firth, from which the party subsequently strikes south through the forest to Falkland Tower, a hunting lodge in Fifeshire (the present-day Falkland Palace is a much later construction). The northern reach is featured in Simon Glover's expedition to the mansion of the Booshaloch, below Tom-an-Lonach (which Scott translates as Knoll of the Yew Trees, although it actually means "meadowy hill"), from which Loch Tay can be seen; the hut where Simon confers with the recently elevated Conachar is nearby.

The Inch, where the crucial conflict takes place—in Scott's version between the branch of Clan Chattan occupying Perthshire and South Invernessshire and the ill-fated Clan Quhele—is on the bank of the Tay, not far from Falkland. The Abbey of Scone and the Castle of Kinfauns play host to the representatives of the two rival clans before the contest.

*Canongate. District of Edinburgh described in the novel as the "Court end of town." The series to which *The Fair Maid of Perth* belongs is titled "Chronicles of the Canongate" after it.

— *Brian Stableford*

THE FALL

Author: Albert Camus (1913-1960)
Type of work: Novel
Type of plot: Psychological realism

Time of plot: 1950's
First published: La Chute, 1956 (English translation, 1957)

The forward action of this novel takes place in Amsterdam during the early 1950's. During a series of meetings within a period of five days, the main character, Jean-Baptiste Clamence, relates to an unnamed listener his experiences during the 1930's and 1940's in Paris and in a World War II prisoner-of-war camp.

Amsterdam. Capital city of the Netherlands; at thirteen feet below sea level, it has the lowest elevation of any capital in the world. Its concentric canals are likened by Jean-Baptiste Clamence to the circles of Hell in Dante's *Inferno* (c. 1320; English translation, 1802). Its Zuider Zee is called by him almost a dead sea. He lives in the Jewish section and preaches in a bar, which he calls his church. Amsterdam, in this way, lends itself to various Judeo-Christian references, which include his own name, a pseudonym meaning "John the Baptist, crying out." The references are ironic: Clamence does not believe in the Judeo-Christian deity, by whom he would, as a believer, be judged. Needing to be judged, he must, lacking a judgmental deity, judge himself for having lived inauthentically. His self-judgment includes his self-imposed exile from Paris to the equivalent of Hell (Amsterdam), where his penance consists of confessing his inauthenticity to anyone who will listen. He calls himself a "judge-penitent": one who judges himself and carries out the penitential sentence imposed upon himself by himself. Furthering his secularization of the Judeo-Christian religious tradition is his recollection that, in the prison camp, he was given the role of "pope." In the camp he contracted a disease, possibly malaria, and the climate of Amsterdam has aggravated that disease.

Mexico City Bar. Saloon in Amsterdam. An actual "Mexico City" bar was located in Amsterdam by at least one diligent scholar, but its historicity is of less importance than its thematic suggestiveness. The name of the bar intones a contrast to the city of Amsterdam: Mexico City, the capital of Mexico, has, at seventy-two hundred feet above sea level, the highest elevation of any capital in the world. The bar is the "church" from which

Clamence "preaches." The ecclesiastical aspiration to spiritual ascension is secularized, adding to the theme that, in a world where there has ceased to be a God to effect judgment and salvation, the person in need of both must achieve them in and of herself or himself. This is the gospel which the secular John the Baptist is preaching, with gin as the baptismal liquid proffered in the bar. Amsterdam and Mexico City maintain the intimations of the low and the high (both spatially and morally) and are consistent with Clamence's inclination to identify himself in those terms.

Paris. The capital of France is the scene of the activities recalled by Clamence: his success as a lawyer, his ostentatious conference of kindnesses and benefits upon his fellow citizens, and his realization that his life has been a sham, an existence marked by hollow affectation. The realization is wrought by his experiences at each of two bridges. At the first, the Pont Royal, in 1936 or 1937, his prolonged hesitation resulted in his failure to attempt to rescue a woman who had leaped to her death from the bridge. At the second, the Pont des Arts, in 1939, he twice hears laughter, which, as it seems to go downstream, causes his heart to pound and his breath to shorten. Later, he hears some young people laugh on the sidewalk under his windows and assumes that they are laughing at him. When he looks in the mirror, his smile seems to be double: He has realized his duplicity. The two bridges, the two cities (Paris and Amsterdam), along with his double role as judge-penitent and numerous other instances of doubling, inform the major theme of the novel, the inherent duplicity of human nature, that is, every human being is both good and evil, spiritual as well as materialistic, and both honest and dishonest.

— *Roy Arthur Swanson*

THE FALL OF THE HOUSE OF USHER

Author: Edgar Allan Poe (1809-1849)
Type of work: Short fiction
Type of plot: Gothic

Time of plot: Nineteenth century
First published: 1839

This story is a remarkable alloy of the literal and the metaphorical. The house of its title is the symbolic embodiment of the exhausted fortunes of the Usher family. The symptoms of moral and psychological decline exhibited in the character of Roderick Usher are faithfully reflected in the fabric of the building, to the extent that the house becomes a model of his mind, literally cracking up as it suffers the nervous breakdown that eventually dissipates his sanity in the dark well of the unconscious.

House of Usher. Home of the madman Roderick Usher and his twin sister Madeline. Located in an unspecified place, the house and its bleak surroundings are primarily described in terms of the impressions they create in the narrator's mind. He is unnerved by the building itself, with its "vacant eye-like windows," but he takes worse fright from its image reflected in the "black and lurid tarn" which lurks around and beneath it. The house is connected to the surrounding land by a narrow causeway, but the link is tenuous and precarious. The atmosphere above and around the house has been poisoned by the exudations of the tarn, becoming eerie and pestilential.

The house is ancient, its whole exterior being infested by fungal growths. Although it retains its form when the narrator first sees it, he is aware that every individual stone comprising its walls is on the point of crumbling. He also observes an almost imperceptible crack extending in a zigzag fashion from the roof to the foundations.

The storm which precipitates the final destruction of the edifice is manifestly unnatural, originating within rather than without. The vaporous clouds which gather about the turrets of the house are lit from below by luminous exhalations of the tarn. These clouds part just once, as the narrator flees from the house, to display a blood-red moon. It is by the ominous light of that celestial lantern that he sees the narrow crack widen, tearing the house apart from top to bottom so that its debris might collapse entirely into the tarn.

Hallway. Entered through a Gothic archway, the hallway has black floors. Its walls are covered with somber tapestries and its corridors decked with creaky relics of ancient arms and armor.

Roderick's studio. Large but the narrow windows, set high above the floor, let in so little light that it is exceedingly gloomy; it is abundantly, if rather shabbily, furnished and chaotically cluttered with books, musical instruments and Roderick's phantasmagorical paintings.

Vaults. Numerous chambers contained within the walls of the building, in which Roderick's ancestors are entombed. It is in one of the deepest of these—a cramped, damp and lightless covert used in olden times as a dungeon—that Roderick and the narrator place the body of the seemingly dead Madeline Usher. Following her interment the house becomes noisier than before, even from the viewpoint of the narrator. The hypersensitive Roderick hears the miscellaneous knocks, creaks, and rumbles even more keenly, and the transformations imposed upon them by his vivid imagination are fed back into the fabric of the house.

The frequent use of the castles and mansions that are the centerpieces of most gothic novels to model the troubled minds of their owners was not always as deliberate, but Edgar Allan Poe understood exactly what was going on when such edifices were afflicted by supernatural visitations and battered by storms. No one else had drawn such parallels so minutely, nor mapped the course of a symbolic tempest so accurately.

— *Brian Stableford*

THE FAMILY OF PASCUAL DUARTE

Author: Camilo José Cela (1916-2002)
Type of work: Novel
Type of plot: Social realism

Time of plot: Early twentieth century
First published: La familia de Pascual Duarte, 1942
  (English translation, 1946)

The impoverished villages and bleak natural landscapes of western Spain provide an appropriately harsh setting for this story of a compulsive murderer's crimes. The mostly autobiographical narrative accepts that there must be some connection between Duarte's downfall and the wretched circumstances of his life. Differing and often contradictory assessments of his background by prison administrators and medical authorities, however, interestingly complicate a narrative that ultimately sees the human condition as a constrained and inexplicable one.

Duarte home. Modest house in the village of western Spain's Torremejía region, where Duarte grows up and twice marries. His home receives a more extensive description than any other location in the novel. His account is both apologetic and nostalgic. Although Duarte portrays his home as generally cramped, unclean, and poorly constructed, he also conveys many positive memories of the warmth and comfort of its kitchen. These conflicting images effectively represent his uncertainty as to whether or not his upbringing is primarily responsible for his subsequent crimes.

The environs of the house are unwholesome. The well is polluted, the stench from the adjacent stable is noxious, and ravines in the vicinity are full of dead animals. The creek that flows past the house is downstream from the estate of a wealthy landowner, and its filthy, odorous water symbolizes the relative social position of the Duartes, as well as the extent to which they see society as caring about their well-being.

*Torremejía (toh-RAY-may-hee-zha). Spanish village located in the province of Badajoz near the border with Portugal. Whereas the Duarte's water is polluted, the village's fountain has been dry for years, and communal life is correspondingly desolate. The clock in the town hall's tower has stopped, the road through the village is barren of traffic, and one of the town's few social amenities is a raucous tavern in which drunken arguments lead to deadly knife fights. The village's cemetery is, ironically, one of its liveliest locations. Death is a frequent occurrence in the village, and the funerals of five of Pascual's family members, as well as his first murder victim, all take place here. The cemetery is also the site of his seduction of his first wife, in a scene that graphically links the physical consummation of desire with the survivors' need to affirm life in the midst of death.

*Almendralejo (ahl-mehn-drah-LAY-hoh). Town about six miles from Torremejía. Although its lights are visible from the Duarte home, they are to Pascual a symbol of the indifference with which the rest of the world regards him and his kind. As he sees it, the residents of Almendralejo—and by implication Spain as a whole—have turned their backs on the likes of the Duartes, with the latter remaining outsiders looking on enviously at the places where more fulfilling lives can be pursued.

*Merida (meh-REE-dah). City where Pascual and his first wife spend their honeymoon. This is the only joyous episode in the novel, and it is a short but compelling one. The young couple glimpse the possibility of a better life in the spacious atmosphere and pleasant furnishings of their hotel room, which Pascual states has subsequently remained with him like the memory of a faithful friend. This idyll is unfortunately cut short by a misunderstanding with the local police, as society once again makes it clear to the Duartes that fate has something other than happiness in store for them.

*Chinchilla prison (chihn-CHEE-yah). Institution in which Duarte serves the sentences for his crimes. Although the penitentiary is represented as a gloomy and depressing place, after he is released Pascual finds the outside world just as repressive and prisonlike.

*Madrid. Spanish capital. After receiving an early release from his first term of imprisonment, Pascual spends a year and a half in Madrid attempting to make enough money to pay for his passage overseas. His inability to obtain anything better than menial jobs, and thus barely earn enough to support himself, serves as further evidence of society's prisonlike character.

— *Paul Stuewe*

THE FAMILY REUNION

Author: T. S. Eliot (1888-1965)
Type of work: Drama
Type of plot: Symbolic realism

Time of plot: Twentieth century
First performed: 1939; first published, 1939

Set in the drawing room of Wishwood, a country house somewhere in northern England, this play has a realistic-looking set, but it is made supernaturally symbolic by the Furies (Eumenides) who appear in the window to haunt Harry, Lord Monchensey, and by the use of a Greek chorus and the clock pattern at the end of the play to reveal the deeper truths about all of these characters.

Wishwood. English home of Amy, Dowager Lady Monchensey, and the location for the planned meeting for a family reunion. The name implies that Amy has tried hard to make the wishes of her children and herself come true, even though she has faced significant opposition. Even her effort to organize the family reunion is doomed to disaster. The play is set in late March, so no flowers are in bloom to adorn the tables. Amy's son John overdrinks and has an automobile accident that prevents his attendance at the reunion. Harry, Amy's oldest son and the heir apparent of the estate, arrives in a troubled state and abandons his mother for a spiritual quest. Harry, or Lord Monchensey, is driven by the appearance of Eumenides, who haunts him concerning his wife's recent death when she was swept overboard while sailing on a passenger ship with Harry. His various aunts and uncles quarrel with each other and, especially during the choral passages, reveal the superficial and deeply disturbing lifestyle they have been living. In the last scene, a lighted birthday cake is brought out, and Agatha and Mary walk clockwise around the cake as they gradually blow out the candles a few at a time. By this time Amy has died and the birth of some new era is symbolized in this party that declares the undoing of a family curse. With Agatha's help, Harry has been freed from the family curse and now sees the once frightening Eumenides as bright angels whom he must pursue beyond the artificial hopes of Wishwood.

— *Daven M. Kari*

THE FAR FIELD

Author: Theodore Roethke (1908-1963) *First published:* 1964
Type of work: Poetry

In this posthumously published volume, Theodore Roethke locates his poem within the context of a personal meditation, a dream of moving throughout his life. Written in four sections, the poem refers to places that illustrate various stages of understanding and acceptance that Roethke experiences. Each section speaks of the journey that the poet undertakes, a journey of self-discovery and definition within the context of natural revelation.

*****Cape May.** Peninsula located on the southern tip of New Jersey well known as a beach resort, Cape May has a lighthouse at the entrance to Delaware Bay. Although Roethke refers to bird shapes when he uses this word, many of his particular images echo the peninsular landscape. The poet travels throughout the peninsula to the field's end, where he discovers evidence of death and detritus. The shallows of the river, the sea, and the mountain all reveal to the poet that death is not the final step, but a period of renewal. Even in a mossy quagmire, the poet believes that the end of life is not the final experience—rather, that life goes on.

A peninsula juts out like a finger into a body of water; thus it experiences water on three sides. As Roethke experienced great despair during his life, the peninsula as a symbol reaches out as the poet catalogs the many forms of life that occupy the peninsula. Symbolized by this peninsula, the waters of the world are as much the poet's landscape as is the land itself. Memory itself houses the encyclopedic well from which each person draws. The peninsula is ultimately life-embracing; although living things die within its borders, this death is not permanent.

— *Martha Modena Vertreace-Doody*

FAR FROM THE MADDING CROWD

Author: Thomas Hardy (1840-1928)
Type of work: Novel
Type of plot: Psychological realism

Time of plot: 1869-1873
First published: 1874

The story and setting of this novel are pastoral. In contrast to Thomas Hardy's later novels, the novel's geography is not symbolic but represents literally a way of farm life that belonged to his boyhood. Hardy's birthplace, in fact, lies in the area described in the novel, and the many scenes of rural activity are accurate recollections of that period. The main pastoral episodes vividly portray the various seasons and the typical catastrophes and festivities of farm life.

Wessex. Imaginary English county in which this and other novels by Hardy are set. Wessex corresponds with the real county of Dorset in southwest England. More specifically, the story centers round the village of Weatherbury, events extending to the nearby town of Casterbridge, seven miles away.

Weatherbury. Typical English farming village in Wessex (modeled on Dorset's Puddletown or Lower Longpuddle). The town's parish church, in the graveyard of which Fanny and Troy are buried, dates from the fourteenth century. It has a tower in which are fixed the village clock and a number of grotesque gargoyle waterspouts. In front of it, a primitive form of baseball is played by the villagers. **Buck's Head Inn** is the main village inn, but the "chorus of yokels" prefer to gather at Warren's Malt-house, where malt is made for brewing, and which becomes a sort of social club. The village has several small stores. It lies in a valley that stretches eastward toward Shottover.

Weatherbury Upper Farm. Farm that Bathsheba Everdene inherits from her uncle. It is, as is typical of the area, a mixed farm, raising sheep, cattle, wheat, and barley. Its farmhouse was once the manor of a small estate, so it is spacious, with a stone front, columnar chimneys, and spiral staircases of oak. It has a number of outbuildings, many quite old, such as the Shearing Barn, and farm cottages. However, the house and farm are now leased from an aristocratic landowner who lives at some distance.

Hardy's description highlights the social change from gentrified farming to middle-class leaseholder with close ties to the laboring community by mentioning the about-turn of the house from its front gravel drive, to its rear with the functional buildings there. The local farm economy is prosperous when all the members of the community pull their own weight. However, outsiders such as Troy threaten the balance, and it is only the man-of-all-seasons, Gabriel Oak, who can re-establish the equilibrium.

Little Weatherbury. Community in which Weatherbury Lower Farm, which neighbors Bathsheba's farm, is leased by Bathsheba's suitor William Boldwood. The two farms together cover two thousand acres, a substantial area by the standards of the day. The farms are so similar that Gabriel can manage both by himself. Bathsheba's and Gabriel's marriage at the end of the novel formally cements the farms' union. Boldwood himself is a gentleman farmer, with a good stable of horses, and his farm's furnishings seem somewhat richer than Bathsheba's. However, at the end, his stable is left empty, a further sign of social change.

Casterbridge. Wessex town seven miles west of Weatherbury that is modeled on Dorchester. Casterbridge is the primary county town and features centrally in Hardy's *The Mayor of Casterbridge* (1886). The agricultural nature of the town's commerce is stressed in both that novel and *Far from the Madding Crowd*, with Hardy describing typical market activities, such as Oak's hiring and Bathsheba's selling her wheat in the Cornmarket. However, *Far from the Madding Crowd* also mentions other features: the barracks in which Troy's regiment is quartered briefly, the county jail, and South Street Almshouse, the Union House in which the homeless are sheltered.

The road between Casterbridge and Weatherbury is frequently described in the novel. Two hills border the road: Mellstock, about one mile outside Casterbridge, and Yallbury, about halfway between the two towns. On the east side of the latter lies Yallbury Wood and the village pub, where Poorgrass gets drunk while transporting Fanny Robin's coffin.

Budmouth. Fashionable town and port, modeled on Weymouth, where horse races at which Troy gambles are held regularly. Along the coast a few miles to the east lies Lulwind (Lulworth) Cove, where Troy's clothes are found after he is swept by the current toward Budmouth harbor.

*Bath. Another fashionable town a day's journey north of Casterbridge, where Troy and Bathsheba marry. The artificiality and lack of connection to the rural geography symbolize the uprooting of Troy and the destructive intrusiveness of his adventurism.

Norcombe. Town that is the site of Gabriel's first meeting with Bathsheba and the first dashing of his hopes, some twenty miles north of Weatherbury.

— *David Barratt*

A FAREWELL TO ARMS

Author: Ernest Hemingway (1899-1961)
Type of work: Novel
Type of plot: Impressionistic realism

Time of plot: World War I
First published: 1929

This novel is set primarily in Italy—with a brief excursion to Switzerland at the novel's end—where Frederic Henry has gone to serve in the Italian Army as an ambulance driver prior to America's entry into World War I.

*Italy. Country in which Ernest Hemingway's American protagonist, Frederic Henry, serves as a volunteer ambulance driver during World War I—just as Hemingway himself had served during that war. Moreover, Henry is also like Hemingway in being severely wounded and invalided to recuperate in an American hospital in Milan. There Henry experiences the first serious love of his life, The foreign location makes it easier for Henry to examine the meaning of his young life and allow him to mature as he confronts danger, death, and love. Throughout the novel, Henry struggles to grapple with the foreign language, Italian customs, and unfamiliar geography. All these struggles heighten his perceptions in ways that help bring about his maturation.

*Gorizia. Small town in northeast Italy near which several major engagements between Italian and Austrian forces were fought during the spring and summer of 1916. Frederic Henry is stationed in a town near Gorizia with the Italian ambulance corps. It is in this location and through his interaction with the other troops stationed there that he begins his maturation.

*Plava. Town in northeast Italy on the Isonzo River, north of which Frederic Henry is wounded. Henry's world is first truly shattered in Plava when he is suddenly forced to face death for the first time. The event, being hit by an Austrian trench mortar, introduces the theme of death's randomness and its unexpected appearance as well as the need always to be prepared to expect it. This presence of death haunts the rest of this novel as it did most of Hemingway's prose throughout his career.

*Milan. Large northern Italian city to which Henry is sent to recuperate from his wounds. The American hospital there with its American nurses offers a small bit of home amid the foreign environment. Henry experiences a reprieve from the war and has the time to reflect on his mortality in congenial and familiar surroundings. Here, too, he falls in love, which connects the themes of love and war. The love theme proves another experience in Henry's maturation. It also gives him a reason to reconsider his participation in the conflict and heightens the sweetness of life. Later in the novel, his love for Catherine, the American nurse, hastens his decision to leave the scene of death and destruction for the peace and safety of Switzerland.

*Caporetto. Battle site in Italy where the Italian forces experienced one of their most devastating defeats during the war. Henry joins the retreating troops there in one of the most memorable sections of the book. It is during the retreat that Henry makes his "separate peace" with the war, which later results in his desertion and flight with Catherine.

***Taglamento River.** River that the Italian forces cross during their retreat from Caporetto. During the crossing, Henry dives into the river to avoid being shot by the military police. This action can be seen as his "baptism" into a new life after he has made his "separate peace."

***Stresa.** Italian town northwest of Milan where Henry meets Catherine after his desertion. In a small boat they row some twenty miles up Lake Maggiore to Switzerland. Their escape over water reintroduces the baptism theme of Henry's immersion in the Taglamento River and suggests another rebirth.

***Switzerland.** Country to which Catherine and Frederic escape from Italy. They spend the winter at Montreux at the east end of Lake Geneva. When Catherine dies in childbirth, Henry again confronts the inexplicable presence of death. This event provides the final, if unresolved, event in his initiation into manhood.

— *Charles L. P. Silet*

THE FATHER

Author: August Strindberg (1849-1912)
Type of work: Drama
Type of plot: Psychological realism

Time of plot: Mid-nineteenth century
First performed: 1887; first published, 1887 as *Fadren* (English translation, 1899)

Although this is a play in three acts, it is confined to a single setting, which is described in some detail at the beginning of the first act. August Strindberg uses this confined area in a spacious two-story house to create a claustrophobic impression suggesting that the four women, along with other women the captain describes as "servant girls" have taken over the rest of the house, and that the captain is lord and master in name only. The room is not a private study but accessible to everyone, including officious intruders like Dr. Ostermark and the Pastor.

Captain's house. Home of a Swedish cavalry officer and amateur scientist. The stage directions at the beginning of act 1 indicate that the captain tries to use the sitting room as his office or private study. He has his guns and gamebags hanging on the wall and uniform coats hanging on clothes-pegs by the door. However, the fact that the room is not his private domain is immediately suggested by the presence of a large round table strewn with newspapers and magazines and, more especially, by the fact that three doors give access to other parts of the ground floor. The stage directions call for a door in the background to the right, a private door in the right-hand corner, and a door to the inner rooms to the left.

The women obviously do not regard the captain's sitting room as a private inner sanctum. The captain's wife, his daughter Bertha, and the nurse all enter without knocking. The captain is also within earshot of female squabbling, including the screams of his deranged mother-in-law, through the door leading to the inner rooms. As the curtain rises on act 2, and then again on act 3, the viewer sees exactly the same setting, and this reinforces the impressions of the monotony of the captain's domestic life and the fact that he is a helpless prisoner in his own home. As the pastor says in act 1, "There are too many women here governing the house," to which the captain replies, "Yes, aren't there? It is like going into a cage full of tigers." Strindberg's choice of the place for his drama helps to emphasize his misogynistic message that the captain, like many other married men, is a victim. He is like a prisoner or like a soldier desperately holding out in a last crumbling redoubt. He has no privacy or peace of mind even in his own home.

— *Bill Delaney*

THE FATHERS

Author: Allen Tate (1899-1979)
Type of work: Novel
Type of plot: Historical realism

Time of plot: 1860-1861
First published: 1938

Set in the early years of the U.S. Civil War, this novel dramatizes Allen Tate's agrarian philosophy, contrasting the traditional organic community of a fictional Virginia plantation with the modern political and commercial center of the Georgetown district of Washington, D.C.

Pleasant Hill. Buchan family plantation in Virginia's Fairfax County. Because author Allen Tate sees people and place as interconnected, his narrator, Lacy Buchan, explains how his father identifies his family as the "Buchans of Fairfax County" to underscore their roots and generational connection to the land. In contrast to magnificent opulence of many antebellum romances, the Buchan family home is depicted more as genteel farmhouse than mansion. From its peeling paint to its tobacco-depleted soil, Pleasant Hill's elegant shabbiness reflects the Buchan family's gradual decline in the face of modern mercantile society, which is represented by Lacy Buchan's brother-in-law George Posey. Tate locates the plantation near the first Battle of Manassas (also known as the Battle of Bull Run)—which is dramatized at the novel's end—to make it a microcosm of the causes of the Civil War and its long-lasting political, social, and moral effects.

To Tate, slavery is a symptom rather than root of the conflict. Lacy's father owns some twenty slaves but refuses to sell them, even though his failing fortunes can no longer maintain them. In contrast to this ideal of the Southern paterfamilias, the merchant George Posey sells his own half-brother, Yellow Jim, in order to buy a fancy horse. However, Tate is no simple apologist for slavery. He lays bare the Old South's delusions of grandeur by juxtaposing a neighboring plantation's "Tournament of Chivalry" with a pathetic scene of slaves who have been "sold down the river." He also critiques the casual brutality attendant upon the Southern code of honor. The Tournament of Chivalry ends with a fist-fight that foreshadows the thoughtless violence the Buchan clan perpetuates in the final section of the novel, in which Lacy's brother summarily executes Yellow Jim—who may or may not have raped young Jane Posey. Similarly, the Buchan household is redolent with family secrets and

sexual tensions that the adolescent narrator Lacy hints at but cannot openly address.

*****Georgetown.** Famous Washington, D.C., neighborhood that lies across the Potomac River from Alexandria, Virginia. Georgetown's proximity to both the Union capital and Confederate Virginia graphically illustrates the novel's central conflict between federal and states' rights. Georgetown is the symbolic antithesis to Pleasant Hill. After turning over their estate to George Posey, the Buchans move first to Alexandria, Virginia, then to Georgetown, residing in houses that lack both sense of place and tradition. Stripped of his duties in maintaining Pleasant Hill, Lacy's father idles away the hours with his devoted slave Coriolanus.

After the outbreak of the Civil War, Lacy moves to the Posey house in Georgetown. Half stone and half brick in construction, the Posey house symbolizes the transition between an older landed gentry still connected to the land and the modern capitalist class divorced from its traditional values.

*****Washington, D.C.** Federal capital. Tate uses Civil War Washington as a symbolic backdrop of his antifederalist philosophy. He notes, with historical accuracy, that both the dome of the Capitol Building and the Washington Monument are only half-finished—symbols that the national government has not yet consolidated its power over the states. He also satirizes the self-perpetuating, artificial aristocracy made up of Washington's political and social elite. Even the Northern writer Henry Adams makes a cameo in the novel—not as the future author of *Democracy: An American Novel* (1880) but as a intellectual blowhard who affects the grace and camaraderie of his Southern counterparts. However, the axiom that bad places give rise to bad literature is best illustrated by the fictional character Jarman Posey. George's Uncle Jarman is a kind of antebellum

Marcel Proust, a neurotic aesthete who never leaves his room and wastes his life writing an unreadable history of the Ice Age. He symbolizes both the modern dissociation from life-giving connection with the land and a new barbarism of the modern world built upon the forces of laissez faire capitalism as practiced by his nephew George.

— *Luke A. Powers*

FATHERS AND SONS

Author: Ivan Turgenev (1818-1883)
Type of work: Novel
Type of plot: Social realism

Time of plot: 1859
First published: Ottsy i deti, 1862 (English translation, 1867)

Set in Russia in the aftermath of its lost war in the Crimea during the ascension of Czar Alexander II, this novel is concerned with the conflict of generations in the years leading up to the czar's emancipation of the serfs. Scenic in structure, the plot is cast as a series of visits to four provincial locales that realistically depict Russian life during a time of important social, political, and industrial reform.

Marino. Family estate of the Russian gentleman Nikolai Kirsanov that is the first of four main settings in which the novel unfolds. Modeled upon Spasskoe, Ivan Turgenev's family estate in Orel, it is the place where Arkady Kirsanov grows up, returns after earning a university degree, and finally chooses to settle in order to raise a family and to assist his father in transforming their five thousand acres into a profitable "farm" that will benefit the peasants who work their property.

The novel begins in May of 1859, when the recently graduated Arkady and his "uncivil" nihilist friend, Yevgeny Bazarov, arrive at Marino, which to Arkady's discomfort, is in disarray. As such, it epitomizes so many estates throughout Russia that are owned by ineffectual nobles whose time has passed. Bazarov represents a defiant new force with which the Kirsanovs must contend, given that he rejects all that Marino symbolizes in the way of antiquated aristocracy and romantic idealism.

During his second visit to Marino, weeks later, Bazarov becomes involved in a farcical duel with Pavel Kirsanov, Arkady's aristocratic uncle. Bazarov shoots Pavel in the leg, tends his wound, and then leaves the estate. Metaphorically, the inconclusive rifts that are played out at Marino suggest that neither the liberal generation of the 1830's and 1840's (the fathers) nor the radical generation of the 1850's and 1860's (the sons) has achieved an ideological victory that will benefit Russia in its immediate future.

Provincial capital. Unnamed city to which Arkady and Bazarov journey after spending two weeks at Marino. There, they stay for a period of six days, during which time they encounter an assortment of vain government bureaucrats, revolutionary poseurs, and emancipated women intellectualizing about human rights while puffing on cigars. Scenes such as those at the governor's ball testify to centuries of uncompromising patriarchal conventions. The provincial capital embodies the political life of the province, dominated at the time by the intellectual split between Westerners and Slavophiles—between those who look to Western Europe for models of progress and those who look to Russia to carve its own unique national identity. Literally and figuratively, Arkady and Bazarov remain strangers to city life.

Nikolskoe (ni-KOHL-ska). Estate belonging to the twenty-nine-year-old widow Anna Odintzov, whom Turgenev describes as representative of idle, dreaming, cold, gentry ladies. She resides in an elegantly furnished Alexandrine-style manor house (a style then popular in Moscow) that showcases her penchant for luxury and order. While at Nikolskoe, Arkady becomes drawn to Katya, Anna's younger sister, and Bazarov unexpectedly falls in love with Anna. After enticing Bazarov to fall in love with her, Madame Odintzov retreats into her fashionable but listless surroundings, preferring her life of organized precision to any challenges posed by a loving a man who rejects social conventions. After his duel with Pavel Kirsanov, Bazarov revisits Nikolskoe, wanting to take a last look at the place where he has been pulled under by an emotion that he cannot explain to himself.

Bazarov estate (ba-ZAR-rof). Small estate belonging to Bazarov's doting mother. Bazarov's father, a retired army doctor turned agronomist, has decorated their plain six-room wooden house with an assortment of military weapons and anatomical drawings; his material belongings reflect his life. After being infected by love, Bazarov first ventures home, with Arkady in tow, to lose

himself in his work. However, parental sentimentality and ennui soon overwhelm him. One afternoon, while he is watching an ant labor in the shadow of a towering haystack, he feels deeply nature's indifference to human struggle. He later deliberately courts death after cutting his finger while performing an autopsy on a corpse and neglecting to cauterize the wound. Infected with typhus, he dies.

Village cemetery. Remote corner of the Russian countryside in which Bazarov is buried. It is described as a "sorry sight" of overgrown ditches and rotting wooden crosses. Bazarov's aggressive challenges to conventional thinking seemingly are buried with him in his grave.

— *Joe Nordgren*

FAULTLINE

Author: Sheila Ortiz Taylor (1939-   )
Type of work: Novel
Type of plot: Social realism

Time of plot: 1980's
First published: 1982

Although the Los Angeles and Mexican settings are treated as mere backdrop by most of this novel's zany characters, these places are integral to Arden Benbow's personality, and thus to her story. Southern California in particular regularly invents new lifestyle and cultural trends, which later diffuse across American society. While Arden's nonconformist traits are not necessarily unique to the Los Angeles region, it is hard to imagine the improbable events of her life happening during the early 1970's in a less tolerant locale.

Benbow's home. Arden Benbow's house located in Topanga Canyon, a rustic community in the Santa Monica Mountains west of Los Angeles. Arden's large, run-down house sits on a half-acre lot. Its lawn is worn down from constant use by her resident children and dogs. Behind the house is a small barn in which three hundred rabbits live when they are not in their tunnels. Behind the barn is scrubby land marked by meandering paths and evergreen trees—a play area in which children's imaginations can expand.

Even with a busy metropolitan freeway only a few minutes' drive from the house, the whole spread is a world away emotionally from both the area's suburbia of "ticky tacky" houses and the faux estates of the newly rich. Its ramshackle condition shows and symbolizes Arden's lifestyle. As a poet and lesbian, and in other

ways, she does not fit society's image of an ideal mother.

The house and surrounding area are where Arden can feel most herself. In her scale of values, it is an excellent place for children to grow up. Others feel differently. When Arden's ex-husband challenges her for custody of their six children, he cites the barnful of rabbits as proof of her instability. A social worker sent to observe the children is won over by the lively and welcoming atmosphere and the children's obvious well-being and gives Arden a glowing recommendation as a parent.

Ruby's Campground and Trailer Park. Small community in the northern Mexican state of Sonoma that shelters retirees and American travelers; owned by a former "showgirl" from the San Francisco dock district. In 1959, when Arden helps her frustrated Aunt Vi escape from a nursing home to tour Mexico, they and

Maurio, an orderly and magician's helper, stay at the campground for several weeks.

Ruby takes pride in running a clean and homey campground, where the electricity and sewage systems work reliably, unlike those in many parts of Mexico. The beach with its gazebo, and the homegrown mangoes and bananas, turns a stay at the campground into an almost idyllic low-budget vacation. It is Ruby's warm and eccentric presence that makes the camp most memorable, however. Ruby and Aunt Vi spend long quiet afternoons there talking about gothic romances. Maurio and Vi practice weightlifting, and Arden assembles a working motorcycle out of discarded parts left at the campground by Youth for Christ bikers. When the private detective sent by Aunt Vi's husband shows up, the laid-back atmosphere and Ruby's force of personality start to transform him from an adversary into an ally of the group. Arden learns a "life lesson" from this in how to win over troublesome agents of the powers that be. Ruby's Camp-

ground functions as a place for alternative lifestyles in an era when these were rare.

*San Andreas fault.** Geological faultline that runs nearly the entire length of California, near the state's coastline, and is the cause of geological instability and major earthquakes. Arden attributes her offbeat interests and life course to her having been born on the San Andreas fault. As a child she feared the earth might open up anytime and swallow the Los Angeles area.

One chapter of *Faultline*, titled "A Geological Aside," explains the role of the San Andreas fault in the big Southern California earthquake of February 9, 1971. The faultline, along with this earthquake, directly affects the story; Arden and her lover Alice huddle together during the earthquake's aftershocks and first become intimate then. The faultline also serves as a diffuse metaphor for the strangeness of southern California life during the 1970's.

— *Emily Alward*

FAUST

Author: Johann Wolfgang von Goethe (1749-1832)
Type of work: Poetry
Type of plot: Philosophical
Time of plot: Indeterminate
First published: Faust: Ein Fragment, 1790 (English translation, *Faust: A Fragment,* 1980); *Faust: Eine Tragödie,* 1808 (English translation, *The Tragedy of Faust,* 1823); *Faust: Eine Tragödie, zweiter Teil,* 1833 (English translation, *The Tragedy of Faust, Part Two,* 1838)

The metaphysical spaces in this play, stretching from Heaven to Hell, signify the grand possibilities and grave pitfalls inherent in human nature. In between these two places is the medieval city, whose confinement Faust and Gretchen seek to escape, and the great world of politics, the theater for Faust's ambition. Panoramic outdoor settings represent liberation and symbolic rebirth. The scenes in late medieval Germany contrast with those from classical Greek mythology.

Faust's study. Vaulted room with stained glass windows that shows the limitations of the world of the historical magician Faust, who lived in the sixteenth century. The clutter of scientific instruments shows Faust's past interest in science as a method of unlocking nature's secrets, and rows of dusty books point to the sterility of medieval learning. Faust looks for ways to escape by conjuring spirits and finally by signing a pact with the devil in this room.

*Auerbach's tavern.** Tavern in Leipzig, Germany, that was frequented by Johann Wolfgang von Goethe as a student. A scene set here features loud communal singing, comic drunkenness, and a barroom brawl. Mephisto is seen riding a wine keg out the door, an allusion to a wall decoration at the historical Auerbach's.

Gretchen's room. Simply furnished room containing a canapé bed, a leather armchair, a clothes cabinet, a mirror, and a spinning wheel. In his clandestine visit

Faust contemplates Gretchen's innocence and the domesticity reflected in the cleanliness and order of her room. The cabinet, where Gretchen finds the jewel box, and the mirror, where she admires herself, reflect her self-awareness as a woman. Her rhythmical spinning in a later scene emphasizes the driving force of her longing for Faust.

*Harz Mountains.** Steep, forested, rocky terrain in Germany that is the setting in which Halloween-like ghosts cavort. While vapors hiss and owls screech, witches dance and make love in an amusement park atmosphere lit by a reddish moon and little fires. Set on Broken, the tallest mountain in the Harz, Walpurgis Night is the witches' Sabbath of medieval German folklore. Although the devil presides here, Walpurgis is a positive occasion for Goethe, as it is a pagan festival which has survived the onslaught of medieval Christianity. One feels close to the powers of nature here, and frank sensual pleasure provides escape from the medieval world.

Hall of Chivalry. A stage is set up in this stately palace hall for a court audience to watch as Faust conjures a Greek temple with the silent, ghostly figures of Paris and Helen, illustrating Faust's desire to link his German heritage to this older tradition. Like his legendary counterpart, Goethe's Faust also spends time at the emperor's palace, where he is put in charge of spectacles for the court. Faust's attempt to rescue Helen from Paris, a chivalrous, medieval act impinging on a classical scene, triggers a dramatic explosion on stage, which symbolically heightens the contrast of the two worlds.

*Aegean Sea.** Arm of the eastern Mediterranean Sea between Greece and Turkey. Under moonlight, where a foaming sea rushes against the rocky shore, sirens sing from the cliffs as sea nymphs ride the waves. Galatea presides, enthroned in the shell of Venus, over the scene crowded with joyful sprites. This is the culmination of Walpurgis Night, which began with a trip through Greek nature mythology and followed the Peneios River to a spot on the seacoast. The focus on water reflects Goethe's belief that life originated in the sea, and Galatea represents fecund erotic beauty. This scene inspires reverence for the dynamic forces of nature, which appear as historical or mythological figures.

Castle courtyard. The imaginary Gothic castle over which Faust reigns in this scene is surrounded by elaborate medieval buildings. Courtiers and servants, lavishly dressed, demonstrate his power and wealth. Dressed in knightly attire here, Faust represents courtly medieval culture with its armor ready for war, and its troubadours, who pay homage to love and feminine beauty. Faust courts Helen, who with her retinue in Greek dress, is suddenly wafted forward into this time and space she never could have known. The scene symbolizes a marriage of the best aspects of the European Middle Ages with the cultural heritage of Greece.

Mountain gorges. In this final scene the natural landscape—a vertical cliff, a waterfall, and ascending crevices for three male anchorites—is complemented by a spiritual one, which includes angels vertically stratified and the Mater Gloriosa floating at the apex of the scene. It is a mysterious and sublime setting for the ascent of Faust's immortal part. Although Catholic iconography is employed (Virgin Mary), the meaning transcends it. The masculine principle, representing Faust's spirit, strives to be united with a feminine principle and advances not just by its own effort but also by the love Gretchen has for him and by an implied destiny that has characteristics of divine grace.

— *Julie D. Prandi*

FELIX HOLT, THE RADICAL

Author: George Eliot (Mary Ann Evans, 1819-1880)
Type of work: Novel
Type of plot: Social realism

Time of plot: 1831-1833
First published: 1866

Set in a period of English history that was obsessed with political reforms, this novel presents scenes and episodes that reflect the stages of the social history of England, as it has developed organically. Contrasted with the nation's political revolution is the internal revolution of values experienced by the novel's heroine, Esther Lyon. A sense of place reinforces the theme of reform throughout the novel, whose various places represent the phases of English social history and reflect the conflicting moral values that drive the plot.

Transome Court. Vintage Queen Anne mansion that is home to the life-defeated Mrs. Transome, who married thirty years earlier to meet social expectations about money and position. The unscrupulous lawyer who is the unacknowledged father of her son and mismanager of her estate has drained her both of energy for daily living and of funds necessary to keep up Transome Court. Mrs. Transome's enfeebled husband also lives here, occupying himself with relics and specimens of minerals and insects he once studied meaningfully.

From a distance, with her romantic dreams, Esther Lyon thinks of Transome Court as a joyful center of luxury. However, after she discovers that she is the estate's legal heir and visits it for several weeks, she becomes aware of the pain and despair within, of the uselessness and purposelessness as well as the dead but still agonizing souls there. The court thus represents the past feudal mansion that nineteenth century England is outgrowing.

Malthouse Yard. Name of the chapel of the independent church in Treby Magna presided over by the Dissenting minister Rufus Lyon, whom Esther grows up believing is her father. Lyon is actually her stepfather. It is these early ties, Eliot's insistence on one's true roots, that define radicalism as presented in Esther and in Felix Holt, opposed to the more common political radicalism that argued for sudden changes in Great Britain's parliamentary system. When Esther renounces her legal inheritance of Transome Court and her earlier yearning to be a lady, thereby returning to Malthouse Yard, formerly a place that represented privation to her, she is affirming her own roots as well as her love for Felix.

Outdoors. Fresh, unconstraining open places in nature represent for both Felix and Esther a freedom of emotional and moral feelings and ideas that seems unattainable in close places. For example, Esther feels that Transome Court signals the "oppressive urgency of walls and upholstery." Felix and Esther first develop feelings of love for each other when they walk together in an open place.

Sproxton. Mining village in which political campaign managers take local coal miners to the pubs to buy their votes. Felix proves to be right in his fear that too much ale may lead to rioting. The episode represents Eliot's view that some members of English society may not be ready for the franchise and that some election conductors take unscrupulous advantage of the laborers' susceptibility to free ale.

Treby Magna. Former market town for an agricultural area that is now an election center. As such, it is vulnerable to violent actions by workers who have been filled up with ale by campaign workers. The novel's scenes of civil disorder show the frightening possibilities of premature extension of the franchise, especially when the mob will no longer follow Felix and moves instead in the direction of Treby Manor.

Loamford. Town in the fictional county of **Loamshire** that is the scene of Felix's trial for appearing to have killed a man he meant only to bring down in his attempts to control the rioters. The trial affords Esther the opportunity to speak publicly in defense of Felix's sterling character, making both of them aware of her love for him. The court scene provides some of Eliot's best satire on the ways of lawyers, just as the election practices she depicts show the evils that political reforming intentions can lead to.

— Carolyn Dickinson

THE FELLOWSHIP OF THE RING

Author: J. R. R. Tolkien (1892-1973)
Type of work: Novel
Type of plot: Epic

Time of plot: Third Age in a remote legendary past
First published: 1954

This novel opens the epic trilogy of The Lord of the Rings. *As in* The Hobbit *(1937), which serves as a prologue to the trilogy's larger quest, the characters in this novel assume responsibilities that take them to exotic and often dangerous places before bringing them "back again," changed and enriched by their journeying. The settings go beyond offering colorful backdrops to dramatize themes of growth through experience, becoming part of a larger community, and the fragile beauty and value of nature.*

Shire. Homeland of the hobbits, J. R. R. Tolkien's "little people," whose environment and culture are provincial and innocent. The journey motif anchors the story in the Shire, which is an idealized adaptation of Tolkien's boyhood haunts in an English Midlands village. Free of industrial pollution, the well farmed countryside is pocked with underground housing, from the luxurious homes of the gentry to mere burrows, a correlative to the hobbits' preference for a snug way of life that demands little awareness of a larger world outside.

Rivendell. Northern haven where the representatives of the "free peoples" (elves, dwarves, men, and hobbits) meet to discuss the fate of the Ring. When Frodo accepts the burden of the Ring. He, his servant, and two kinsmen set out on the Great East Road to this distant stronghold. A detour leads them through the Old Forest, where hostile trees menace them, but Tom Bombadil, a benign nature spirit, befriends them. Quickly they discover that the natural world beyond the Shire can be either dangerous or welcoming.

The travelers ford a wild river to reach Rivendell, the palace of Elrond Half-elven, who maintains this enchanted retreat by the power of one of three Elvish rings. Concealed in a deep and narrow valley, Rivendell is called the Last Homely House East of the Sea, "a perfect house," as Bilbo once reports, "whether you like food or sleep or storytelling or singing, or just sitting and thinking best, or a pleasant mixture of them all." At present it is also a key political site at which men, Elf lords, dwarves (Tolkien's spelling), a wizard, and now hobbits confer about the rising dark power in Moria and his One Ring.

Reaching Bree. Village held jointly by hobbits and men. Frodo's servant Sam is daunted by the inn, his first sight of the tall houses of men. There the hobbits are joined by Aragorn, a ranger of the North, who leads them on secret paths through marshes and woods, paralleling the dangerous road.

Moria. Ancient dwarf kingdom. The Nine Walkers (Gandalf, four hobbits, two men, an Elf, and a Dwarf) set out with the goal of destroying the One Ring. They travel south, hoping to cross the Misty Mountains by the Redhorn Pass; however, blinding blizzards force them to take a terrifying underground passage through the ruinous Mines of Moria. Moria's decaying splendors, now dark except for light thrown by Gandalf's wand, house Orcs, coarse goblinlike creatures, and also, on a deeper level, a Balrog, a fierce fire spirit. Galdalf leads the party through eerie winding tunnels to safety. Confronted by the Balrog on a narrow stone bridge, Galdalf falls into an abyss. Aragorn leads the surviving Walkers out into **Dimrill Dale**, a sacred dwarvish place, and beyond it to the outskirts of the **Golden Wood**.

Lothlorien. Even more than Rivendell, Lothlorien epitomizes the Elvish (Tolkien's spelling) ideal in **Middle Earth**, but it, too, is vulnerable. Like Elrond, its Queen Galadriel wields an Elven ring, without which this demi-eden and its folk would "dwindle to a rustic folk of dell and cave, slowly to forget and to be forgotten." The necessary destruction of the One Ring may also negate the potency of the Three, ending the "stainless" beauty of a land that seems to Sam to be "*inside* a song." After receiving aid and resting under the golden flowered mallorn trees of Caras Galadon, the remaining travelers turn south on the great **Anduin River** toward **Minas Tirith**, the principal city of Gondor.

Gondor. Declining but still powerful South Kingdom of Men. The journey to Gondor affects two of the Walkers in an enlarging way. Gimli the dwarf and Legolas the Elf, two individuals whose cultural history is one of enmity and racial antagonism, become friends as they explore the Golden Wood, and they share one of the little boats. The companions, sensing the presence of Orcs on the east bank, and fearing that Gollum, a small, corrupt, sort of ur-hobbit who once held the Ring, is now stalking them, become careless in their calculations and are nearly undone by the rapids of Sam Gebir. Eventually they reach outlying relics of an older, stronger Gondor: first, the Argonath, immense stone pillars of "kings" who guard the river's gorge into a placid lake.

On the lake's west bank is Amon Hen, the "Hill of Sight," where in the days of the great kings a stone seat was placed for the rulers' contemplation. The Fellowship rests while Frodo, who carries the One Ring, slips off alone to Amon Hen in hope of guidance. Boromir, mad with desire for the Ring, follows and tries to take it by force. Frodo eludes him, and with Sam, escapes to the eastern shore, where they set off on foot for Mordor, the Dark Lord's realm. The other companions, searching for Frodo, are attacked by Orcs and scattered. The Fellowship is broken.

— *Nan C. L. Scott*

FENCES

Author: August Wilson (1945-   )
Type of work: Drama
Type of plot: Domestic realism

Time of plot: 1957-1965
First performed: 1985; first published, 1985

The entire play is set in the small dirt yard of the Maxsons' home in an unnamed industrial city of the late 1950's and early 1960's. The setting reveals metaphorically the psychological lives of the people who live there, particularly Troy Maxson, with his longings, his frustrations, and his defeated aspirations in a white-dominated world, a world which causes Troy to be divided from himself and to be angry, frightened, and increasingly alone.

Maxson home. African American home in an unspecified city, possibly Pittsburgh, Pennsylvania. The Maxsons' yard, which is an extension of their house, represents Troy Maxson's ambivalent feelings: his spirit, large like his body, desires the rootedness of home but resists its limitations. The responsibilities of his family bind him even more closely than did the prison in which he has spent fifteen years. The yard keeps Troy close to home, yet is not as confining as the house itself. The unfenced yard also signifies the era of the play, a time when African Americans were soon to loosen the bonds of some legal and social restraints, with the turbulent Civil Rights movement of the 1960's.

As Troy's friend Bono comments, "some people build fences to keep people out . . . and other people build fences to keep people in." The partially built fence surrounding the Maxsons' yard represents the conflicts of the play. Rose, Troy's wife, wants a fence to keep her world safe, to keep the family close, but to Troy, the fence represents confinement, so he has delayed its completion. The bond between Rose and Troy, like the incomplete fence, fails to prevent Troy's straying with another woman. Troy's inner fences and the fences that the white world has built around him trap him in his meager-paying job. The literal fence, that Troy and Cory were to have built together, could have strengthened their relationship, but Troy's procrastination and Cory's dreams of winning a football scholarship prevent this outcome. However, Troy, too, desires to keep things out; he wants to keep out Death, with whom he had once wrestled and won. Ironically, Troy completes the literal fence after his complete alienation from his wife and son, and his fence finally fails to keep out Death.

— *Jo N. Farrar*

FERDYDURKE

Author: Witold Gombrowicz (1904-1969)
Type of work: Novel
Type of plot: Farce

Time of plot: 1930's
First published: 1937 (English translation, 1961)

Ferdydurke is a thirty-year-old Pole whom society suddenly decides to treat as an adolescent. His bewildered attempts to escape this fate energize Witold Gombrowicz's social satire, as the protagonist is put through a repetition of his familial and educational experiences that demonstrates the essential absurdity of humanity's efforts to control its destiny. Although the novel's interest in place is generic rather than specific and treats the particular as a manifestation of the general, its locations are significant in that they represent the essential failure of all social institutions.

Piorkowski's school. Institution in which Ferdydurke is forced to enroll when mistakenly believed to be only half his actual age. Much of the humor of this section of the novel stems from Ferdydurke's realization that there is a sense in which he *does* in fact belong in school. Because he learned little during his earlier years as a student, a further round of education is in theory a reasonable prescription for his self-confessed ignorance. The education provided at Mr. Piorkowski's school, however, is not likely to prepare anyone for a successful future. This establishment is depicted as an anarchic wasteland whose staff members are incompetent, and whose students are clever only at avoiding the need to learn anything. Its classrooms are portrayed as war zones in which students oppressed by mindless rules strike back with stubborn silence. Ferdydurke eventually concludes that he must escape this madhouse if he wants to avoid being warped by its insane methods of operation.

Youthful home. Residence of the Youthful family, whose name symbolizes their commitment to the radical reform of society. Ferdydurke goes to live with them in hopes of discovering a more nurturing environment but soon finds out that the Youthfuls are, if anything, more oblivious to his real needs than are the people at Mr. Piorkowski's school: Where the school tries to stamp out student curiosity by force, the Youthfuls' efforts to abolish discipline and encourage liberal thinking produce only chaotic confusion.

The failure of the Youthfuls to guide their children's development is most tangibly illustrated by the place in which their own daughter sleeps. Although the family is fairly well off, Zutka does not have a room of her own but instead occupies a bed in a corner of the house's main hallway. Rejecting her parent's assumption that this arrangement symbolizes the relaxed, open character of their family's relationships, Zutka leads a totally self-centered existence and has acquired a legion of lovers with whom she carries on clandestine sexual relations. Ferdydurke observes that Zutka's circumstances reflect the topsy-turvy nature of contemporary existence, with the public hustle and bustle of her family life masking the ingenious private arrangements she has contrived as a means of expressing her inmost desires.

Aunt Hurlecka's estate. Affluent country property to which Ferdydurke is taken when his aunt realizes that he has been associating with people beneath him on the social scale. Intending to put their nephew back on the proper track of accumulating wealth and improving social status, his aunt and uncle introduce him to a way of life characterized by the meaningless repetition of rituals whose only purpose is to kill time and provide an illusion of activity. Scenes set in the Hurleckas' dining and living rooms have the quality of still-life paintings, as any thought of independent expression is quashed by the force of dark, massive furnishings and rigid social convention.

Life on the estate is portrayed as a microcosm of the human condition, with the oppression of its servant masses by an aristocratic elite symbolizing the general condition of society. When the servants eventually revolt in protest against the oppressive regime, Ferdydurke realizes that just as he has been entrapped by his school's attempt to return him to infancy, so have the estate's employees been treated like children who do not understand what is good for them.

Hotel Bristol. Site of a lunch at which two of Ferdydurke's college professors engage in ridiculous, pedantic arguments that mock their pretensions to intellectual superiority. This brief but memorably satiric scene extends the novel's attack on educational institutions to the university level.

— *Paul Stuewe*

FINAL PAYMENTS

Author: Mary Gordon (1949-   )
Type of work: Novel
Type of plot: Domestic realism

Time of plot: Early 1970's
First published: 1977

The narrator in this novel is a thirty-year-old woman who, after eleven years of caring for her incapacitated father, finds freedom at his death and struggles to create a new life for herself by leaving her conservative Roman Catholic environment and becoming involved with two married men, thereby striking out against the confines of home, father, and church.

*Queens. Borough of New York City that provides the novel's backdrop as the place in which the narrator, Isabel Moore, has spent her first thirty years living with her father in a one-family house on Dover Road. Nineteen of those years she has spent nursing her invalid father. To Isabel, Queens offers only sameness, dullness, predictability—not the cultural enrichments of opera, ballet, theater, concerts that nearby Manhattan offers. In Queens, domesticity is Isabel's role, one of duty and devotion. She leaves her Queens home only to go to stores or church. Filled with ordinary and dim days, Queens reflects Isabel's life itself, triggering tiredness and predictability in its sureness, until her father dies and she finds herself free.

Roman Catholic Church. Though not a specific place in the novel, the Church occupies a consuming place in Isabel's home and in her mind. Matters of spirituality and faith dominate all conversations between her father and the priests who visit her home. Indeed, the very first line of the novel mentions that Isabel's father's funeral is full of priests. The Church represents authority, devotion, liturgy, guidelines, rules, and holiness. The Church occupies a central place in the life of Isabel's father, and its characteristics engulf her life, too. Patriarchal and authoritative, the Church is sheltering, loving, demanding, and contemplative. It is the place and space in which Isabel is formed and the place that she must ultimately leave to avoid suffocation.

Ringkill. New York town, up the Hudson River from New York City, to which Isabel moves after her father dies. While visiting the home of her friend Liz Ryan, she finds Ringkill a place where there are mountains and water and a freshness that is not only in the air but in the newness of a different place. Liz also offers her something new—a relationship with a woman who is confident, independent, and individualistic. The prospect of these changes makes Ringkill a suitable setting for Isabel to change her life. There she takes a job with a social services agency surveying the arrangements of people who care for the elderly in their homes, a position that makes her look into a variety of homes, both loveless and loving. Simultaneously eager to experience life and made uncertain by her inexperience, she has an affair with Liz's husband, John Ryan, and confronts her own needs and sexuality. She also has a second affair with another married man, Hugh Slade. While John represents power, Hugh represents authority, both of which defined Isabel's life in her father's house in Queens. Finally, in revulsion, she leaves both lovers to care for Margaret Casey in Ramona to do penance for her earlier behavior.

Ramona. Town five hours by bus from Ringkill that is home to Margaret Casey, the now elderly woman who kept house for Isabel and her father for eleven years after Isabel's mother's death, until Isabel fired her when she realized that the woman wanted to marry her father. Now anxious to atone, Isabel goes to Ramona to take care of Margaret. There, however, she experiences loss, change, and feelings of servitude. She is demeaned and debilitated by a self-centered, old, and angry Margaret. Only time and introspection and acceptance of herself as a worthy person allow Isabel to leave the coldness of Ramona and return to the life she wants, devoid of guilt, trusting in love, valuing her friendships, and finally valuing herself.

— *Doris O'Donnell Jellig*

THE FINANCIER

Author: Theodore Dreiser (1871-1945)
Type of work: Novel
Type of plot: Naturalism

Time of plot: c. 1850-1874
First published: 1912; revised, 1927

Theodore Dreiser's third novel charts the rise, fall, and rise again of an archetypal American finance capitalist in nineteenth century Philadelphia by depicting in great detail the protagonist's houses as he ascends into the plutocracy at the end of the Civil War, only to end in prison after being convicted of larceny and embezzlement.

*Philadelphia. Principal city of Pennsylvania between 1837—the year of protagonist Frank Algernon Cowperwood's birth—and 1873—the year of a great stock panic that Cowperwood exploited to his advantage. Philadelphia was by implication a relatively crude major city compared to Boston and New York, without telegraphs, phones, stamps, city mail, ocean steamers, or streetcars as the novel begins. Its 250,000 inhabitants are dominated by a Republican hierarchy, many of whose leaders are uncouth. Although Cowperwood is under no illusions as to the quality of men he is dealing with, he aspires to join this establishment for what it can do for him. However, he ultimately fails when he is convicted of shady financial dealings and imprisoned.

The arts and amenities of Philadelphia hardly exist in a public sense; for example, one would never guess from the novel that the city was soon to boast a world-class orchestra. Dreiser does speak of "handsome parks" and "notable buildings" on the first page but almost never thereafter. Cowperwood demonstrates an increasing awareness of art and decor as he accumulates wealth, and the more sophisticated establishment figures furnish their grand houses handsomely; however, overall the lack of graciousness of the city—Dreiser never really depicts its public places—is a fit backdrop for the ruthless and cunning grasping after power and wealth by an immensely intelligent and amoral figure, an American Nietzschean who believes only in himself.

Cowperwood's homes. Between 1847, when Cowperwood is ten, until 1873, when he leaves for the Midwest, he changes homes around seven or eight times.

The moves are progressively upward until the end, when he is imprisoned. Each new home is precisely established in a financial, as well as a social, context. Indeed, Dreiser's mastery of complicated financial dealings is a feature of the novel: he is sometimes even wearying in the bulldog tenacity with which he pursues financial details.

Cowperwood's first move takes place when his father is promoted from bank clerk to teller, and the family moves from a two-story house to a three-story house with a piano in a "much better neighborhood." When the father is promoted to cashier, the family moves to a four-story house on the river. Here Frank meets a Mrs. Lillian Semple, an attractive woman five years his senior, whose husband dies a year later. Frank pursues and wins the semireluctant and deeply conventional widow and moves into her pretty house, also on the river, improving it with a garden, remodeling, and art objects. Some seven or eight years later Cowperwood, still in his twenties, has moved so far that, together with his father, he commissions the building of two large side-by-side granite domiciles and a new office. Dreiser use three full pages to describe the new house and observes that the "effect of a house of this character on its owner is unmistakable."

A multimillionaire at the end of the Civil War, Cowperwood acquires a mistress and installs her in an elegant love nest. He is riding high and seems at thirty-four to have it all. However, his fall begins with the Chicago Fire of 1871 and the subsequent failure of his bank.

— *Stanley Poss*

FINNEGANS WAKE

Author: James Joyce (1882-1941)
Type of work: Novel
Type of plot: Fantasy

Time of plot: Early twentieth century
First published: 1939

The history of humanity as enacted in a dream, this complex novel uses mythological characters who are found in fantastic settings which continually shift and change with the logic of sleep.

Dublin. Capital of Ireland in which the events of the novel that take place in the "real" world are set. Major city landmarks, such as Howth Castle, the Liffey River, and Phoenix Park are used symbolically as points of departure into the fantastic dreamworld that parallels the narrative.

Bedroom. Upstairs, above a public house in Chapelizod, a suburb of Dublin, Mr. and Mrs. Porter, their waking names, are asleep in their bed. In the novel's dreamworld they are known as Humphrey Chimpden Earwicker and Anna Livia Plurabelle, usually as HCE and ALP respectively. Down the hall are the bedrooms of their children, twin boys Kevin and Jerry and daughter Isabel, or Issy. These characters also take different names during the dream narrative. The "real" setting of *Finnegans Wake*—that is, the location in the waking world—is one of complete normality, even banality, and so stands in deliberate contrast to the fantastic settings of the dream actions of the novel. Almost all of these scenes and many of the characters are drawn from the domestic setting of the middle-class Irish bedroom. For example, the four posts of the bed become in the dream the four authors of the gospels, Matthew, Mark, Luke, and John, who sometimes merge into a single figure, Mamalujo. Throughout the novel fantasy retains firm, if slight, connections with reality.

*Howth Castle. Hill and medieval fortification overlooking Dublin harbor. In the novel this area becomes the setting of many of HCE's early, mythic adventures; later, it is where the giant HCE is buried, awaiting eventual resurrection. As the initials suggest, Howth Castle and Environs are also associated with HCE himself, and so represents the male principle or life force in the development of human history and society. A prominent feature of Howth Hill is Adam and Eve's Church, which reinforces the fact that the overall narrative is about the course of human history traced back to its primal sources.

*Liffey River. River that runs through Dublin and plays an important role in the history and life of the city. In one of the novel's most famous sections, the Liffey is the site of a dialogue between two washerwomen who recount the story of HCE and ALP. Through its association and identification with Anna Livia Plurabelle, the Liffey becomes the female counterpart to Howth Castle.

*Phoenix Park. Dublin park, famous for a nineteenth century terrorist attack by Irish revolutionaries. Phoenix Park, in various guises, is a repeated setting for actions in the novel, including an unnamed but apparently sexually related crime which may or may not have been committed by HCE. The three British soldiers who may have witnessed this possible crime help James Joyce shift the setting to the Crimean War. This setting's ties to Dublin's history help Joyce establish the relationship between the mythical phoenix, the bird that springs anew from its own ashes, and the theme of death and rebirth that runs through the novel.

*Crimea (KRI-mee-ah). Peninsula in the south of Russia (now the Ukraine) on the Black Sea, site of the Crimean War during the mid-nineteenth century. In the novel the Crimean War (which at times merges with the battle of Waterloo) serves as a representative setting for all the conflicts and wars in human history.

Haunted Inkbottle. House of Shem the Penman, the novel's figure of the artist, especially the artist-as-writer. Throughout the novel a constant rivalry runs between the twins Kevin and Jerry, most often known in the dream world as Shem and Shaun. The first is the figure of the artist and is his mother's favorite; the second is a more practical individual preferred by his father. Other aspects of this warring duo in the book are the Mookse and the Gripes and the Ondt and the Gracehoper. The settings of these struggles are generally less identifiable than Shem's Haunted Inkbottle.

— *Michael Witkoski*

THE FIREBUGS: A Learning-Play Without a Lesson

Author: Max Frisch (1911-1991)
Type of work: Drama
Type of plot: Absurdist
Time of plot: Post-World War II

First performed: Biedermann und die Brandstifter,
1953, as a radio play; first published, 1958 (English
translation, 1959)

This long one-act drama is a kind of morality play. Although its setting is modern, its action is not localized to any specific time or place. As with many absurdist plays, there is only a metaphysical present, a now, as opposed to a past or future. The details about things mentioned or used in the play are all generic, found everywhere, and, therefore, nowhere in particular. The play's leading character, Biedermann, is himself a kind of Everyman.

Biedermann house. Home of Gottfried Biedermann, a hair tonic manufacturer obsessed with the fear of arsonists. He lives in an unnamed large city; it could be any city, anywhere. The house itself is a gracious, somewhat ostentatious and pretentious, upper-middle-class dwelling. The whole effect is that of the nouveau riche, cushioned from the events in the real world by wealth. Money and financial reward constitute the major emphasis of the home and its residents. The staging of the play calls for a nonrealistic, simultaneous setting, showing the living room and attic.

The dangers of a life without principles are clearly illustrated by the fact that the attic is filled with cans of gasoline and other incendiary devices. Over everything hovers a sense of foreboding and impending doom represented by the attic, which is a sort of Hell. The setting for Hell is exactly the same as for the rest of the play: the Biedermann home. This device makes the point that a heaven can be a kind of Hades at the same time. Also, human beings must face the consequences of their acts, or the lack of them, at some time.

— *H. Alan Pickrell*

THE FIXER

Author: Bernard Malamud (1914-1986)
Type of work: Novel
Type of plot: Historical realism

Time of plot: Shortly before World War I
First published: 1966

Because this novel is based on an actual historical event, its pre-World War I Russian setting is essential to the parallels between the actual event and the story Bernard Malamud portrays. The novel demonstrates the anti-Semitism that existed during this specific time and place.

Shtetl. Small Jewish village near Kiev, Russia. Before leaving for Kiev, Yakov lives his entire life here. He leaves the village because he considers it a prison, in which he is unable to survive economically. He believes that if he leaves the shtetl his luck will change. Yakov's sentiments about the shtetl become ironic: He leaves what he thinks is a prison only to be confined to a real

prison, and instead of prospering when he leaves his community, he becomes the victim of anti-Semitism.

Yakov's cell. Faded stucco prison building in a commercial section of Kiev, near the brickyard where Yakov works. Most of the novel takes place in Yakov's prison cell. He spends almost three years here, where he is placed in solitary confinement and tortured. Although imprisoned and tortured, Yakov refuses to confess to a crime he did not commit. He willingly continues to be the scapegoat for the Jewish people, as he comes to understand that if he had not been accused, another Jew would have been. Despite horrendous suffering while imprisoned, he learns to appreciate his culture and fight for his people.

*Kiev (KEE-ev). Russian city (now part of Ukraine) situated on the Dnipro River in what was the Ukrainian province of Russia during the earliest period in which the novel is set; Kiev is now a city in independent Ukraine. Yakov journeys to Kiev from the shtetl. Although little of the action of the novel occurs in Kiev, this broader setting is important because it provides historical accuracy to events that occur to Yakov, a fictional character based on Mendel Beilis, who was arrested in Kiev in 1911 for a crime similar to the one Yakov is accused of committing. The novel portrays a specific historical time in which Russia attempted to extinguish its Jewish population. The setting also accurately demonstrates some of the unscrupulous tactics Russian czars used for political gain prior to the Russian Revolution in 1917.

*Lukianovsky. District of Kiev that Jews are not allowed to enter. The brickyard where Yakov works for Nikolai Maximovitch Lebedev is located in Lukianovsky. Yakov at first declines the offer to work but Nikolai persuades him to accept and offers him a place to stay in the brickyard. Yakov is unable to decline Nikolai's offer without admitting that he is a Jew, a fact he has hidden from Nikolai, who is an admitted anti-Semitic. Living and working in Lukianovsky plagues Yakov with fear, worry, and guilt. Although Yakov feels like a traitor, he soothes his conscience by determining to make some money and leave. The body of the boy Yakov is accused of murdering is found in a cave near the brickyard in Lukianovsky.

— *Laurie Champion*

THE FLIES

Author: Mariano Azuela (1873-1952)
Type of work: Novel
Type of plot: Historical realism

Time of plot: Early twentieth century
First published: Las moscas, 1918 (English translation, 1956)

Thus satirical novel about the early twentieth century Mexican Revolution is set in south-central Mexico as the armies of Venustino Carranza and rebel leader Pancho Villa chase each other around the region. The novel's city and train car settings embody the confusion and social disruption the years of civil war brought to ordinary Mexicans.

Train. Railroad train traveling from Mexico City to Irapuato whose hospital car is the principal setting for the first half of the novel. The Reyes Téllez family, fleeing with their portable belongings, is first to find this relatively empty space on a crowded train. Soon others join them, revealing a cross-section of humanity under stress as the train chugs forward through the night. Because there are no sick or wounded in the car the doctor in charge cannot turn the able-bodied away. The Reyes Téllez women set up a makeshift cooking area and offer him eggs and toast, ensuring his goodwill. People sprawl out on the floor or discuss rumors, which are as plentiful as the sparks flying off the train's wheels.

The furnishings within the hospital car are rudimentary but not primitive, reflecting both the era and place and the middle-class status of the riders. Riding atop the roof and in the dangerous spaces between train cars are other people, presumably poorer and more desperate, of whom readers catch brief glimpses. The division is more significant than it first appears. People inside the hospital car are trying to hang on to what they have, be it General Malacara's big gray motorcar or Matilde Reyes Téllez's caged canary. The peasants and migrant workers, lacking land, have nothing to hang on to. The author, as a supporter of Pancho Villa, is sympathetic toward the latter, but his focus during the train journey and in the novel is on how the minor functionaries are not certain where their own best interests lie.

The train's jerky motions and belches of smoke form a metaphor for the Mexican Revolution, whose turmoil lasted many years, with noise and action obscuring the hoped-for social reform. Outside, the train, as it travels all night and early morning, is a landscape of distant gray hills, mesquite-dotted valleys, and bright yellow-painted houses. If the train symbolizes the wars wracking Mexico, the scenery may stand for the land's eternal value, serene and impervious to history. One passenger—the attorney Donaciano Rios—sees it differently. Unable to sleep, Rios looks out the window and imagines telegraph pole shadows becoming attacking soldiers. With daybreak, he finally sleeps, but when the passengers leave Irapuato, he is still so shaken he forgets his expensive leather travel bag.

*Irapuato.** Provincial market city in west central Mexico where the train makes an unexpected stop, and its passengers disembark. Most decide to go into the city's center, as the train's stop promises to be lengthy. Carranzista troops are rumored to be closing on Villa's rear guard outside the city, and the rebels are preparing to abandon the city. The train's passengers know this only by seeing the panicked Irapuato residents loading their belongings into carriages and carts, preparing to flee their homes, just as the train's passengers themselves did the day before. Nevertheless most of the passengers go to the market—an enclosed square full of soldiers and peasants, overripe fruit and farm produce, and useless toys. While the Reyes Téllez women buy supplies, the merchandise rapidly disappears. Soon the crowd disappears as well. The rapid changes that war, and even rumors of war, bring occur before the characters'—and the readers'—eyes. Nevertheless, the women stay focused enough on the main chance to persuade the doctor to buy the daughters some fine footwear at a boot shop.

Irapuato resembles most cities in the path of war. Mishaps—such as a tire blowout on the general's car with no tools left to fix it—occur several times. However, Rubén Reyes Téllez is able to find a former schoolmate who claims to know General Alvaro Obregón, who is rumored to be advancing on the city. Nobody in town knows what is really going on, and few tell the truth about where their loyalties lie. Meanwhile, trains full of troops leave the local station, puffing black smoke. The book's last scene shows Pancho Villa in his own Pullman car, pulled by a shiny locomotive with an eagle decoration, leaving Irapuato. On this day, he may be the only character who knows where he is going to be the next day.

— *Emily Alward*

THE FLIES

Author: Jean-Paul Sartre (1905-1980)
Type of work: Drama
Type of plot: Existentialism

Time of plot: Antiquity
First performed: 1943; first published, 1943 as *Les Mouches* (English translation, 1946)

At the time Jean-Paul Sartre wrote this play, ancient Greece was a fashionable setting for French plays—a fact that enabled him to count on his audiences' unquestioning acceptance of the Greek setting of this play. This was an ingenious subterfuge, for his play appeared while France was occupied by German troops during World War II, and overt discussion of the Occupation was prohibited. Sartre wanted to reject the cult of communal guilt that the regime encouraged and to justify acts of resistance, however horrendous, provided that individuals acted in good faith and accepted the consequences.

*Argos.** Ancient Greek city in which the play is set. The square is dominated by a statue of Zeus, god of flies and death, and it has two purposes within the drama.

First, Sartre emphasizes visually the overbearing influence of Zeus. Second, by assuming that his audiences are aware that public squares in ancient Greece were places through which everyone had reason to pass, he avoided having to contrive pretexts for the meetings that set in motion the action of his play. In the square, Orestes and his tutor come into contact with assorted citizens, none of whom welcome them. There, they are also accosted by Zeus (disguised as a human traveler) and meet Electra as she goes about her business. Later, Orestes meets Clytemnestra there. This sequence of meetings contrasts with the absence of Aegisthus from this public place, creating a sinister aura which in turn is reinforced by references to his spies and to his palace, showing how he dominates the minds of the inhabitants even when not present.

Mountain cavern. Ostensible resting place of the souls of the dead, who emerge on this day each year. This artificial device, invented by Aegisthus and Zeus, justifies the permanent state of remorse in which the inhabitants of Argos are kept by their ruler, the better to control them. (Parallels with Occupied France cannot be missed here.) Here, too, Zeus can play his magician's tricks with the rock that normally blocks the entrance—a childish display that impresses the inhabitants of Argos but leaves Orestes unmoved.

Palace. Home of Aegisthus and Clytemnestra; place in which Orestes spent his earliest years. His memories provide a flavor of innocence that contrasts with and emphasizes the horrendous nature of his act when he kills his mother in the very palace in which she gave birth to him.

The throne room of the palace, like the public square, is dominated by a statue of Zeus. Aegisthus's death at the foot of the statue hints that Orestes's blow is aimed as much at Zeus as at his henchman, and the curse Aegisthus lays upon Electra and Orestes, reinforced by his warning to beware of the flies, is more menacing because it is Zeus who will give effect to the curse and unleash the flies.

Sartre locates Clytemnestra's death offstage, though still within the palace. As Electra listens to the commotion on stage beneath the statue of Zeus, her self-confidence wanes, and later Zeus regains control over her.

*Temple of Apollo. Place in Argos. In the late 1930's, French archaeologists unearthed ruins in Argos that they declared to be a temple dedicated to Apollo. The discovery became known in France as a French achievement. The outbreak of World War II prevented further digging, but when Sartre needed a place in his play in which Electra and Orestes could seek sanctuary, he remembered the temple of Apollo and realized it lent plausibility to the location. The fact that the temple is dedicated to the god Apollo is irrelevant to the drama. What matters is that Electra and Orestes should be safe from the baying crowd while Zeus tempts them with his offer of protection if only they will show remorse.

— *William Brooks*

THE FLOATING OPERA

Author: John Barth (1930-   )
Type of work: Novel
Type of plot: Psychological realism

Time of plot: 1930's
First published: 1956; revised, 1967

While the primary setting of this novel is the small Maryland town of Cambridge, the specific locale is enlarged by the philosophical musings of the narrative and the arrival of the traveling showboat called the Floating Opera.

*Cambridge. Largest town and seat of Dorchester County, Maryland. It sits along the Choptank River on the DelMarVa peninsula, an area best known as the Eastern Shore. The economy is sustained mainly by natural resources: the crabs, oysters, and seafood of the Chesapeake Bay and the tomatoes and other crops of the rich, flat farms of the area. Cambridge is where the novel's narrator, Todd Andrews, was born and raised;

except for his service in the U.S. Army during World War I and his college and law school days, he has never lived anywhere else.

Founded during colonial times, with its first house dating to 1706, Cambridge embodies much of the history of the Tidewater region of Maryland and thus is richly evocative of the personal background of the novel's characters, especially Todd Andrews, a multigenerational Marylander. As described in the novel, Cambridge is a sleepy, southern town, in many ways outside of time and largely unaffected by modern life. In such a setting, characters such as Todd and his friends, the Macks, are free to concentrate upon their inner lives and more abstract, philosophical concerns.

Dorset Hotel. Residential hotel located in the heart of Cambridge, just across the street from the courthouse where Todd practices as an attorney and only one block from his offices on "Lawyers Row" on Court Lane. After his father lost all of his money in the Great Depression in 1930 and hanged himself, Todd was forced to sell the family property, including the home, to settle the remaining debts. He then moved into the Dorsetwhere he has lived in a single room ever since. Because of his heart condition, which, while it does not limit him physically, literally could kill him at any moment, Todd makes a habit of paying his bill and reregistering on a daily basis at the hotel. The Dorset is also the residence of a group of elderly characters who comment upon the persons and actions of the novel, much in the fashion of a Greek chorus. Todd has formed this set of elderly gossips into a loosely organized group which he has named The Dorset Explorers Club.

Cottage on Todd Point. Summer place on the Chesapeake Bay belonging to Harrison Mack, a friend of Todd's. It is at this cottage that Todd and Jane Mack first make love (with her husband Harrison's knowledge and approval) and thus begin the three-person relationship which is the center of the novel.

****Argonne Forest.** Site of a battle in France during World War I between the Allied forces, primarily Americans, and the Germans. During this engagement Todd stumbles into a shell hole where he unexpectedly confronts a German soldier. After a tense night spent watching one another, the two men collapse into an impulsive embrace of friendship. However, after the German falls asleep, Todd begins to leave and the other awakes; they struggle and Todd kills the German with his bayonet.

Floating Opera. Fabulous floating showboat that plies the Chesapeake Bay and the waters of upper North Carolina. The extravagant vessel is described in a fashion that signals that it is clearly impossible in reality: Not only does the ship's theater seat seven hundred but it boasts a full kitchen and restaurant as well as ward rooms and state rooms—and yet draws only fourteen inches of water. As Todd explicitly states in his description of the vessel, the widely varied acts its carries and its travels along the coast make it a symbol both of the art of storytelling and of human life itself. At the climax of the novel Todd attempts to blow up the vessel during its gala performance; characteristically, he fails.

— *Michael Witkoski*

THE FOLKS

Author: Ruth Suckow (1892-1960)
Type of work: Novel
Type of plot: Domestic realism

Time of plot: Early twentieth century
First published: 1934

This novel is set amid the upper-middle-class circle of Belmond, Iowa, in which the Ferguson family lives. Fred and Annie Ferguson are members of a generation that is leaving family farms for towns so their children can have "something better." To realize their parents' dream, the Ferguson children flee the security of Belmond for destinations offering better opportunities. When Fred and Annie retire, they, too, are tempted by promises of an easier life elsewhere. However, none of the characters finds the illusive "something better" they all seek. For Ruth Suckow, it is the constant desiring that brings discontent, not the actual places in which her characters live.

Ferguson farm. Family farm located outside Belmond, Iowa, that the novel idealizes as a source of goodness. It is the source of the family's heritage and wholesome food, and the family's therapeutic retreat. Suckow idealizes the American pioneering family farm but recognizes that it cannot continue to be the foundation of American society.

*Belmond. Small town in north-central Iowa whose name is derived from the French words *belle monde* for "beautiful world." Suckow uses the name ironically, for though the town is a beautiful world, since people accept their lot in life and their interdependence, Belmond embraces small-town narrow-mindedness, conventionality, and interference in others' affairs. The town functions as a character commenting on and evaluating the characters as they grow into adults, search for work, create families, and start their lives.

Belmond affirms the Ferguson family's two "all-American" children, Carl and Dorothy. Carl, Belmond's high school football hero, basks in the town's admiration. However, he also acquiesces to its emphasis on security in marriage and career and abandons his dreams. Dorothy is the town's darling, and its residents envy her when she marries the charismatic Jesse Woodward, who whisks her away to California with visions of wealth, prosperity, and marital bliss.

Belmond also censures the two Ferguson children who do not conform. Its residents are mystified when the outgoing Bunny overlooks the nearby church college and instead attends the state university. There he meets and marries the most "un-American" woman, according to the town's perception, since she is an older, working-class, communist immigrant. In a conformist town, the rebel Margaret finds support in books. Social pressure stifles Margaret into silence until she flees to New York City.

*Greenwich Village (GREH-nich). Section of New York City's Lower Manhattan that Margaret idealizes as a place of freedom because of its bohemian lifestyle. There she lives in a basement apartment, enduring physical poverty while enjoying mental liberty. However, she quickly becomes disillusioned with bohemian poverty and begins an affair with a medical doctor because of his loving adoration of her.

*Geneva. Small Iowa town thirty-six miles east of Belmond where Carl attends the church college and later settles. Named Geneva after the capital of Switzerland, the peace-making nation, the town is used symbolically. There, Carl, unwilling to break with conformity, resigns himself to replicating the security of his father by not following his own dream for self-fulfillment. He resigns himself to his marriage with a passive-aggressive wife and a job that he merely tolerates.

*California. Pacific coast state which, since its mid-nineteenth century gold rush, has occupied a place in the American psyche as a land of golden opportunity. Jesse and Dorothy are drawn to California, where they live extravagantly. People in Belmond are agog when they hear the reports of the four servants who run Jesse and Dorothy's household. Jesse and Dorothy's dreams are dashed, however, when the stock market crashes in 1929, and they are forced to rent out their magnificent home.

*Pasadena. Southern California bedroom community near Los Angeles to which Fred and Annie go to retire. Pasadena is a place offering a luxuriant retirement but no sense of belonging. Retirees are not needed but are kept busy. Repelled by this, Fred and Annie return to live out their lives in Belmond, where they feel needed. Of the novel's main characters, only these two are willing to forego the gilded promises of places that are not home and accept the idiosyncrasies of small-town America. In accepting themselves and their place, they find greater contentment than do their children.

— *Douglas W. Werden*

FOMA GORDEYEV

Author: Maxim Gorky (Aleksey Maksimovich Peshkov, 1868-1936)

Type of work: Novel

Type of plot: Psychological realism

Time of plot: Late nineteenth century

First published: 1899 (English translation, 1901)

In a straight, realistic fashion, this novel depicts life in a town on Russia's Volga River in the late nineteenth century, while tracing the rise and fall of the merchant class in the river shipping business, seen through fortunes and misfortunes of the two generations of the Gordeyevs.

Gordeyevs' town. Unnamed Russian town in which the novel's protagonists, the Gordeyevs, live and work. Situated on the Volga River, the town is probably Nizhny Novgorod, Maxim Gorky's birthplace (later renamed Gorky). As a native of that area, Gorky manifested everlasting love for it and allegiance to it.

Foma Gordeyev offers a vivid picture of Russian life at the turn of the twentieth century and of the merchant class, the backbone of the Russian society before the Russian Revolution. The novel traces the rise and fall of the merchant class, embodied in the fortunes of Ignat Gordeyev and his son Foma. An owner of boats and barges on the Volga, Ignat is a powerful and ruthless businessman who brutally mistreats the people under him; however, his harsh methods bring him great wealth. He explains to his young son that life is not a loving mother but a stern taskmaster. The father and son eventually find themselves at opposing ends. Although Foma admires his father's success, he also feels sorry for him because success has not brought him happiness. Foma becomes a reserved, taciturn young man, self-confident, upright, with a strong sense of justice. After his father's death, he gradually brings the family fortunes to ruin. What prevents him from preserving his father's fortune is his idealization of the working class and his desire to look for a heart in a man. He becomes a displaced, superfluous man, who is declared insane and who spends the rest of his life roaming the streets in rags.

Gorky uses this plot to point out the injustice and the inhumane character of Russia's social order at the time. He also uses the beautiful and bountiful nature of the region, the heart of Russia, to contrast the gifts of nature with the insensitivity of human beings. Although tendentious, as many of Gorky's works are, *Foma Gordeyev* depicts an important aspect of nineteenth century Russia.

*Volga River. Longest river in Europe and the most important commercial waterway in Russia; the river rises northwest of Moscow and flows generally southeast to the Caspian Sea. The river is dotted with towns and villages in which most of the business of central Russia takes place. Boats and barges loaded with various merchandise float up and down the river. Southward, they go all the way to Astrakhan on the Caspian Sea, and northward, to the large towns of Kazan and Perm. The Gordeyevs' fortunes rise and fall with their ability to run business on the river.

Business is only one part of the importance of the Volga in the novel. The river provides a special way of life for the inhabitants along its banks. The Volga is so much like a human creature that the people living around it call it "Mother Volga." Gorky waxes poetic describing its charms. The river's left bank is flat, stretching all the way to the horizon, covered with a thick green carpet drenched with sunlight. Its right bank is stiff and craggy, with wooded cliffs reaching high into the sky and couched in stern tranquility. The broad-breasted Volga flows between them, in a majestic sweep, silently, solemnly, unhurriedly, decorated on the right by the dark shadows of the cliffs and, on the left, by the green and golden velvet of water-meadows and sandy shores. Occasionally, villages come into sight, on the cliffs or in the meadows. Ever-present sunlight glistens on the glass windows of huts, on the gold and velvet of thatched roofs, and on the gold crosses of churches half hidden among the trees. There are also the gray arms of the windmills revolving slowly in the breeze and factory chimneys emitting smoke into the sky.

The pastorale river scenes are enlivened by shouts of children along the river's banks as they greet passing steamboats and occasionally jump into the river to swim in the boats' wakes. The river is also energized by the workers along its banks pulling barges in the rhythm of the famous Russian chant "eeey ukhnyem." The lyrical depiction of the river scene complements the rough, dog-eat-dog atmosphere of the novel, making it tolerable and worth living.

— *Vasa D. Mihailovich*

FONTAMARA

Author: Ignazio Silone (Secondo Tranquilli, 1900-1978)

Type of work: Novel

Type of plot: Social realism

Time of plot: Early 1930's

First published: German edition, 1930; Italian edition, 1933; revised, 1958 (English translation, 1934, 1960)

This first volume in Ignazio Silone's Abruzzi Trilogy focuses on the plight of the cafoni, *peasants living in the isolated Italian village of Fontamara, as they experience increasing deprivation under the growing bureaucratic restrictions of Benito Mussolini's Fascist regime. It is also a novel, as are the other Abruzzi stories, about the growing sense of political and social consciousness, and eventually of action, of a people downtrodden for centuries.*

*Abruzzi (ah-BREWT-see). South-central region of Italy near the eastern coast of the country, along the Adriatic Sea. An area of plains, hills, and mountains, it is the setting for all the volumes in Silone's Abruzzi Trilogy. It is a poor area of marginal farming and small villages and embraces a traditional way of life. Since Silone's intention was to write about Italy's poor during the period before World War II, the Abruzzi proved an appropriate place in which to set his stories of *cafoni*, or peasant life, since largely it had remained socially, economically, religiously, and politically traditional, a land of estates on which the people eked out a meager living from the unforgiving soil. Most of the peasant tenants lived in one-room hovels with their livestock, who provided a source of warmth during the winters. The Abruzzi was also rather isolated, and since one of the main themes of *Fontamara* is about the disruption of the local traditions caused by a remote Fascist government in Rome, it proved a congenial setting for Silone's social realism.

Fontamara. Typical Abruzzi village, containing some fifty dilapidated dwellings grouped around a central piazza with a church, nestled in the hills between the mountains and the Fucino plain. Its people are traditional peasants: poor, superstitious, and isolated. As in the other Abruzzi novels, the locals are depicted as grotesques, although not without compassion for the bleakness of their lives. When the novel opens the community is living much as it has for generations, enduring an endless round of seasonal deprivations brought about by a succession of rulers: Bourbons, Spaniards, Piedmontese, and the Vatican. Because Silone intended his novel to depict the gradual political awakening of the *cafoni*, it is necessary that he portray his subjects as already impoverished, but accepting their lot. However, by the narrative's end they are driven by the further extremes of poverty and violence into a recognition of the need to act against their oppressors.

*Lake Fucino (few-CHEE-noh). Having been drained in order to reclaim more arable land for cultivation, the now-dry lake bed provides practically the only work available to the peasants and offers a contrast between the spare agricultural opportunities of Fontamara and the more prosperous life down on the plain. It is this contrast which Silone uses to highlight the distance between the villagers and the wider, outside world from which comes change and finally a liberation of sorts.

*United States. Because so many southern Italian peasants emigrate to the United States, Silone uses the idea of "America" to indicate a state of economic opportunity, as well as social and political freedom. A favorite phrase used in the novel when one of the locals comes into some money is to describe that person as having "discovered America" in the person's own part of the world.

*Rome. As the capital of Italy and the location of the legal and military power of Mussolini's Fascist regime, Rome represents the intrusive influence of modern life as experienced by the Fontamaresi, as the Black Shirts bring a new and more violent oppression to the lives of the peasants. Rome also is the place where one of the central characters, Bernardo, has his social consciousness awakened by the communists, who are in opposition to the Fascist state. There he is eventually martyred at the hands of the Fascists, an act that ultimately provides the spark that ignites the resistance of the people of Fontamara.

— Charles L. P. Silet

FOOL FOR LOVE

Author: Sam Shepard (Samuel Shepard Rogers, 1943-   )
Type of work: Drama

Type of plot: Hyperrealism
Time of plot: Late twentieth century
First performed: 1983; first published, 1983

The play is set in a motel room in the Mojave Desert that reflects themes of wandering, emptiness, and transience. The room's shabby interior conveys a sense of fatigue and desolation.

*Mojave Desert (moh-HAHV-ee). Southern California desert that is a defining image of the American West. It is a vast and dangerous place that one must travel through, just as May and her half-brother Eddie navigate through their troubled relationship. The desert creates a forbidding atmosphere as it imposes its vastness around the shabby motel.

Motel. Located on the edge of the Mojave Desert, this dingy, unnamed motel is the home of May. For playwright Sam Shepard, the motel room symbolizes the loneliness and romance of the American Highway. It is a place to rest and replenish as one travels through the vast wilderness of relationships. May originally comes to the motel to escape Eddie and their incestuous love affair. However, the motel offers little comfort. Although Eddie has driven more than two thousand miles to find May, the transient nature of the motel room setting and the open road that lies outside foreshadows his inevitable abandonment of May. It also parallels their father's constant traveling from household to household, woman to woman, eventually abandoning Eddie's mother, who commits suicide. Not a destination in and of itself, the motel room reflects the idea that the real action in May and Eddie's lives occurs in their *traveling* from place to place.

*Wyoming. Rocky Mountain state in which Eddie promises to make a home for May. He has plans to move their trailer to a ranch there. The theme of the American West is displayed as May rejects Eddie's offer just as she rejects his "Marlboro" man lifestyle as a rodeo cowboy and stuntman. Nevertheless, Eddie dreams of the cowboy life as he cleans his gun, dons metal spurs, and coils his lassos performing rope tricks to entice May.

— Rhona Justice-Malloy

FOOLS CROW

Author: James Welch (1940-   )
Type of work: Novel
Type of plot: Historical realism

Time of plot: 1868-1870
First published: 1986

This historical novel, set early in the period of the late nineteenth century Indian Wars, depicts a Blackfeet Indian's struggle to live a traditional life and serve as a tribal leader during a period of Anglo-American western movement and settlement in what became Montana, and the U.S. government's war against the Plains Indians. Because the Lone Eaters, Fools Crow's band of Blackfeet, live directly in the path of westward migration of American settlers, their dilemma is either to fight a futile war or to vacate their ancestral lands.

*Bozeman Trail. Anglo-American migration route that begins in the northwestern corner of Colorado and extends northwestward, through the panhandle of Nebraska and across Wyoming, bisecting both Crow and Blackfeet settlements on its way toward the town of Bozeman, located at the southern end of Montana's Gallatin Valley. Although the trail is not mentioned by name in the novel, it is the unstated cause of the increasing numbers of westward settlers during the time period of the novel, traversing Crow and Blackfeet encampments, and is thus central to the white-Indian conflict that builds toward the novel's conclusion.

*Bighorn River. Largest tributary of the Yellowstone River; rises in west-central Wyoming and joins the Yellowstone in southern Montana. The Little Bighorn River—near which the 1876 battle between the U.S. Cavalry and the Oglala Lakota was fought—separates from the Bighorn River in southeastern Montana in what was historically Crow country, west of Cheyenne settlements and generally south of the various bands of the Blackfeet.

*Fort Benton. Seat of Chouteau County in north-central Montana on the Big Missouri River, which allowed the town to develop into a regional steamboat port. The town experienced boom times due to gold-seekers and cattlemen who used the town as a supply port.

*Milk River. River in northwestern Montana, both of whose branches flow northeastward into Alberta then back into Montana. Fools Crow fears the movement of the Napikwans (white men) from Many Houses (Fort Benton) to the Four Horns Agency on the Teton River, since it put his people into closer proximity and contact with culturally different outsiders.

*Montana Territory. Setting for the entire novel. The territory was originally populated by a variety of Indian tribes, including the Cheyenne, Nez Perce, Blackfeet, Crow, Assiniboine, Cree, Gros Ventre, and Flathead. The Lewis and Clark Expedition of 1804-1806 opened the area to American penetration—first to trappers and traders, later to Roman Catholic missionaries and settlers. The immense geography of Montana can perhaps best be appreciated by the fact that among the states of the United States, only Montana has rivers that drain into three different watersheds: the Pacific Ocean, the Gulf of Mexico, and Hudson Bay.

The novel is filled with references to Indian place-names in Montana whose locations cannot be identified with any certainty: Woman Don't Walk Butte, Heavy Shield Mountain, Jealous Woman Lake, Old Man Dog Mountain, Sweet Grass Hills, Bear Paws Hills. These names are either James Welch's fictional creations or are sufficiently localized not to appear in any territorial or state map of Montana.

— *Richard Sax*

FOR COLORED GIRLS WHO HAVE CONSIDERED SUICIDE/ WHEN THE RAINBOW IS ENUF: A Choreopoem

Author: Ntozake Shange (Paulette Williams, 1948-   )
Type of work: Drama

Type of plot: Social realism
Time of plot: Twentieth century
First performed: 1976; first published, 1977

This play, which Ntozake Shange calls a "choreopoem," is a collection of seven set pieces: On a dimly lit stage, seven unnamed black women, each dressed in a different color of the rainbow, perform twenty poems. Each woman announces she is outside a city—Chicago, Detroit, Houston, Baltimore, San Francisco, Manhattan, or St. Louis—which has a large inner-city minority population.

***Camden.** City in lower east-central New Jersey, about an hour's drive south of Mount Holly; both towns are in southern Mercer County. Named in the second poem of the series, this area is home to working-class people, the majority of whom might attend trade and technical schools.

***Southern Boulevard.** Thoroughfare in New York City's south Bronx area that formerly had a large Hispanic population but still has several Hispanic dance studios. Real places, such as this, encourage audiences to believe the experiences expressed in the poems.

***Lower East Side.** Neighborhood in New York City's Manhattan that has historically been home to streams of immigrants who have found cheap housing in the neigh-borhood's tenement buildings. The neighborhoods have traditionally been ethnically mixed, as are other neighborhoods mentioned in the poems in South Central Los Angeles and Upper Manhattan's Harlem. By mentioning these well-known neighborhoods, the playwright shows that despite the minimal and abstract stage setting, the women discussed in the poems are true to life.

***Port au Prince.** Capital city of Haiti, the black-ruled Caribbean island nation. It, like West Africa's Accra and North Africa's Tunis, is depicted in the poems as a stop along the historical routes that carried slaves from Africa to the New World. These places remind audiences of the historical events relevant to the lives of the characters.

— *Ginger Jones*

FOR WHOM THE BELL TOLLS

Author: Ernest Hemingway (1899-1961)
Type of work: Novel
Type of plot: Impressionistic realism

Time of plot: 1937
First published: 1940

In this novel of the Spanish Civil War, the savage conflict within Spain reflects the diverse potential of the human personality, and the young American Robert Jordan fights his own internal struggle as he interacts with people in whom the war has brought out the best and worst aspects of human nature. Jordan's love of Spain often contrasts with the attitudes of the partisans he encounters. The presence of troops and volunteers from other countries brings Spain into focus as a microcosm of twentieth century conflict.

Bridge. Strategic target of the Republican offensive and the objective of Jordan's mission. Pablo opposes the attack on the bridge because he knows that it will provoke retaliation by the fascists, but the other guerrillas eventually agree to support Jordan. Once the Republican bombardment begins, Jordan, with help from the guerrillas, destroys the bridge with explosives.

Comandancia. Headquarters of Commissar André Marty, a paranoid and demented old fanatic who delays the delivery to General Golz of Robert Jordan's warning that the Republican attack is expected by the fascists.

Escorial. Site of the headquarters of Republican general Golz, who orders Jordan to blow up a bridge behind enemy lines.

La Granja. Village near Pablo's camp where the guerrillas obtain supplies and news.

Hilltop. Location where El Sordo and his men are trapped and finally killed by the fascists. The desperate courage of the guerrillas is futile in the face of the advanced weaponry brought against them in the form of the fascist airplanes.

Hotel Gaylord. Madrid building used as a headquarters by the Soviet agents who effectively control many aspects of the Republican struggle against the fascists. Jordan finds the Gaylord to be not only a place that provides comforts difficult to find elsewhere but also a place where he can discover the truth about what is happening behind the scenes in the ongoing struggle.

Maria's village. Place where the Falangists savagely execute the local Republicans and their sympathizers, including Maria's parents. The brutality displayed here balances that described earlier in which Republicans led by Pablo engage in mindless cruelty.

Montana. Jordan's home state in the United States. References to Jordan's boyhood and family past become increasingly conspicuous as the narrative develops, and his preoccupation with his grandfather's heroic career as a soldier and his father's suicide finally are revealed to be shaping influences on him. Allusions to the massacre of George Armstrong Custer and his men at the Little Big Horn in Montana, also foreshadow Jordan's own final confrontation of overwhelming forces, while echoing the earlier annihilation of El Sordo and his men.

*Segovia. Town in central Spain to the north-northwest of Madrid that is the military objective of the attack by the Republicans upon the fascist forces.

*Valencia. City on Spain's Mediterranean coast. Pilar reminisces about a delightful visit there in the days before the war, when she was the mistress of the bullfighter Finito.

— Robert W. Haynes

THE FORSYTE SAGA

Author: John Galsworthy (1867-1933)
Type of work: Novel
Type of plot: Family

Time of plot: 1886-1920
First published: 1922: *The Man of Property*, 1906; *In Chancery*, 1920; *To Let*, 1921

This trilogy traces the stories of the children, grandchildren, and great-grandchildren of Jolyon "Superior Dorset" Forsyte, a stonemason who becomes a master-builder and moves his family from Dorset to London, where he builds ugly, inexpensive houses.

*England. Country in which virtually all the action in the novels takes place. Although John Galsworthy was not comfortable with the characterization, many of his contemporaries considered him the era's leading chronicler of England's upper-middle class. He himself was the son of a lawyer who owned considerable real estate, so he knew that class intimately. His portrayals of the British aristocracy and of working-class people are considered less successful. In *The Forsyte Saga* Galsworthy sets many scenes and chapters in locations he personally knew. For instance, a chapter in *To Let* is set at the annual cricket match between the great public schools Harrow and Eton in London. A graduate of Harrow, Galsworthy regularly attended the event. Part of *In Chancery* is set at Oxford University, where Galsworthy studied law.

*London. Capital and largest city of Great Britain, in and around which much of the action takes place in scenes at various houses, clubs, streets, restaurants, art galleries, opera houses, parks, courtrooms, train stations, cemeteries, and theaters.

Robin Hill. Small village near which Soames Forsyte—the title character of *The Man of Property*—decides to build a country house and engages Philip Bosinney to build, furnish, and decorate the house for him. He wants a large house within commuting distance of London in which to keep his collection of paintings and his wife, Irene. He regards Irene as his most precious possession and thinks he can control her better by keeping her out of London. When she and Philip fall in love, Soames seeks his revenge by suing Philip for going over budget on his house.

Soames never lives in the house, a two-story rectangular structure with a courtyard covered by a glass roof. Jolyon Forsyte buys the house and lives in it with his son, young Jolyon Forsyte, and his son's family until his death a few years later. Later, Irene marries young Jolyon and lives with him in the Robin Hill house. At the opening of *To Let*, set twenty years later, Irene and Jolyon are still living at Robin Hill

Galsworthy based the grounds of Robin Hill, but not the building itself, on his boyhood home of Coombe Warren. The house is more than a plot device, however. Soames's problems with the house parallel his problems with Irene and with life in general. Galsworthy believed that it was futile to try to control everything in a person's life, especially the people in it. The more Soames tries to control his world and to plan other people's lives, the worse his own life becomes.

Timothy's house. Home of the aging bachelor Timothy on London's Bayswater Road, in which, at the beginning of *The Man of Property*, Timothy lives with three sisters. The redbrick house overlooks a park and is a regular gathering place of the Forsyte clan. Timothy himself, a hypochondriac who lives to the age of one hundred, rarely leaves his bedroom. His funeral at London's Highgate Cemetery takes place in the last chapter of the last novel, signifying that the saga has ended.

— *Thomas R. Feller*

THE FORTUNES OF NIGEL

Author: Sir Walter Scott (1771-1832)
Type of work: Novel
Type of plot: Historical

Time of plot: Early seventeenth century
First published: 1822

This novel offers a Scotsman's view of London: that the English capital is a wicked and decadent city where an honest Scot will do well to keep a careful hand on his purse and keep his wits about him, lest he be robbed or cheated. Such cautions apply not merely to an innocent like Nigel Olifaunt but even to a king; the tacit opinion of the novel's narrative voice is that when Scotland's King James VI became King James I of the United Kingdom, he fell into bad company.

*London. Traditional capital of England and capital of all of Great Britain after the union of England and Scotland in 1707. At the time in which Sir Walter Scott's story is set, much of what is now "Greater London" lay outside London's city gates. Thus, the Greenwich described here is a park where the king goes hunting, and Enfield Chase is a heath. The River Thames is the story's principal thoroughfare; most of its settings are distributed along the river's banks and can be reached by boat. The protagonist, Nigel Olifaunt, goes by river to visit King James's court at Whitehall Palace, and returns by the same route when the treacherous Lords Huntinglen and Dalgarno try to inveigle him into heavy losses in Beaujeu's gambling den. On the other hand, George Heriot goes to Whitehall by passing through Temple Bar (here a mere wooden barrier rather than the stone monstrosity it later became), then riding along the Strand and through Charing Cross, both of which are being built up at the time of the novel. Scott observes that Covent Garden is, at this time, still a garden rather than a cultural center.

Other famous London landmarks featured in the novel include St. James's Park, where Nigel is accosted by Sir Mungo Malagrowther and encounters the diminutive Prince of Wales (the future Charles I) before quarrelling with Dalgarno; the Tower, where Nigel is imprisoned along with the disguised Margaret Ramsay; and Saint Paul's Cathedral, on the crown of Ludgate Hill, where the climactic wedding takes place. Hyde Park and the Fortune Theatre are briefly encountered as Nigel passes through.

*Lombard Street. Place where the Scottish goldsmith George Heriot lives, in the east of London proper, on the far side of Ludgate Hill from the areas in which most of the novel's action takes place. It is not surprising that his fine house should have belonged to a baronial Roman Catholic family in the time of Henry VIII, or that it has been divided up in more recent times—although it still retains the so-called Foljambe apartments, where Lady Hermione and Monna Paula take up residence. Had it survived to the present day Heriot's house would undoubtedly be a business premise. Although Heriot,

like David Ramsay, was a real historical figure, the house described as his in Scott's novel is fictitious.

*Whitefriars. District of London lying between Fleet Street and the River Thames, adjacent to the Temple, so-called because a Carmelite monastery was established there in 1241. It inherited from this monastery certain privileges of sanctuary, which gave it a dubious marginal status—hence the nickname of "Alsatia," after the Continental region of Alsace, which has been contested by France and Germany since the Middle Ages. It is in Whitefriars, in the house of the ill-fated usurer Trapbois and his daughter Martha, not far from "Duke" Hildebrod's tavern, that Nigel is forced to take refuge after his rash confrontation with Dalgarno, having been guided there by Lowestoffe (who is imprisoned in the Marshalsea for his pains).

Several other significant settings lie just outside the boundaries of Whitefriars. David Ramsay's shop is close to Temple Bar, near St Dunstan's Church. The house of the ship-chandler John Christie, where Nigel originally lodges, is near Paul's Wharf, in a tortuous maze of narrow lanes destined to be destroyed by the Great Fire of 1666. Fleet Street is the site of Benjamin Suddle-chop's barber shop (Scott was writing before the first appearance of the legend of Sweeney Todd, the "demon barber of Fleet Street," so he intended no slur on Suddle-chop's reputation) and the establishment of the apothecary Raredrench.

*Edinburgh (EDH-en-behr-oh). Capital of Scotland, a city infinitely preferable to London in the opinion of every true Scotsman. Here, in the dark vaults of a book-shop, the notional introducer of the text, Cuthbert Clutter-buck, engages in sardonic discussion with the anonymous notional author.

— *Brian Stableford*

THE FORTY DAYS OF MUSA DAGH

Author: Franz Werfel (1890-1945)
Type of work: Novel
Type of plot: Historical

Time of plot: 1915
First published: Die vierzig Tage des Musa Dagh,
1933 (English translation, 1934)

Musa Dagh, "the Mountain of Moses," which rises from Turkey's Antioch plane at the Mediterranean cross-roads between West and East, is the dominant image and, in a sense, the essential protagonist of this historical novel. Like other featured locations in this narrative, it is a real place, one whose deeper symbolic significance stretches back to the beginnings of Near Eastern and world religion. It was a region where prophets spoke from mountaintops and where Noah's Ark is said to have rested on nearby Mount Ararat. In recent Armenian history, Musa Dagh is commemorated as the site of a heroic resistance to the Armenian genocide perpetrated by Turkey during World War I. Musa Dagh is the Armenian Masada—a mountain, as both natural object and symbol, that links a realistic narrative to the deeper philosophical and religious threads of the novel.

*Antioch. Ancient Turkish city near the northeast corner of the Mediterranean Sea. Although little action unfolds here, a detailed account of a visit there near the beginning of the book is essential to highlighting the life of Levantine Armenian merchants before the Armenian genocide. Antioch's people lived and prospered in a rich, multiethnic society. In the city's bustling bazaar Armenians, Greeks, and Syrians surge past one another, wearing European dress but readily identifiable by their different headgear. Kurds, Circassians, and Bedouins stand out in their vibrant tribal wear, their women in veils and capes. Fragrant herbs blend with the aroma of simmering mutton fricassees, while the sounds of Muslim prayers mingle with the cries of street vendors. Prosperous Armenian traders tend their shops and stalls. They are the bankers, carpet merchants, and makers of the exotic jewelry that adorns all the women.

*Musa Dagh (mew-sah dag). Mountain in eastern

Turkey to which Armenian villagers retreat to resist the government's deportation order; the mountain becomes their ark of salvation. The view from the mountain peak is dramatic, with the Mediterranean Sea to one side and the ancient city of Antioch, dear to Armenian Christian tradition, lying to the other. On this holy mountain, Armenians make their stand for life, freedom, and the survival of their apostolic Christian church. Before their eventual rescue by Allied ships, they must endure trench warfare against the vastly more numerous Turks, along with disease and near starvation. Although the historical siege of Musa Dagh lasted fifty-three days, the novel reduces it to a more symmetrical forty days, thus linking the resistance thematically with the many biblical events that transpired over the same mystical length of time.

Despite his occasional use of artistic license, Franz Werfel based his narrative on authenticated documentation of the siege, and his book has been recognized as a tribute to the Armenians who suffered in the calamity, as well as a celebration of the survival of the Armenian nation itself. When the novel became a best seller, its success alerted millions of readers to what has been called the "forgotten genocide."

***Armenian villages.** Seven villages around the base of Musa Dagh figuring into the novel have exotic names: Yoghonoluk, Wakef, Kheder, Begt, Azir, Bitias, and Kebussiye. In contrast to the cosmopolitan ambiance of Antioch's bazaar, life in the villages faithfully adheres to Armenian custom and style. On Sunday evenings, after religious observance, the streets are filled with people happy to be alive, old women gossiping, young mothers exchanging advice, and girls teasing their suitors. The Turkish peril seems vague and far away, while the orchards and vineyards flourish and the sound of the tar, the Armenian guitar, fills the streets. The skilled crafts of the villagers demonstrate Armenian energy and creativity: silks, woodwork, religious carvings from ivory. These villages provide glimpses of what Paradise must have been like, Werfel seems to suggest. For here, along this very Syrian coast, are found the four rivers near which tradition locates the Garden of Eden.

— *Allene Phy-Olsen*

THE FOUNTAINHEAD

Author: Ayn Rand (Alice Rosenbaum, 1905-1982)
Type of work: Novel
Type of plot: Parable

Time of plot: 1922-1930's
First published: 1943

The New York City of the 1920's presented in this novel is a larger-than-life place. Architect Howard Roark, the central character, is based on real-life architect Frank Lloyd Wright. Many of Roark's designs and attitudes parallel Wright's.

New York City. In the 1920's and 1930's, New York City was an exciting place for architecture. Skyscrapers were new to the city and the world at large; the first one had been built in Chicago in 1883. Soon, however, New York was the leader in skyscraper building. Ayn Rand was fascinated by skyscrapers, towering toward the sky, and felt they were among humankind's greatest achievements. She endowed Roark with this fascination but coupled it with her ideas of Objectivism—an egoist view in which all human actions are self-serving. Throughout the book, Roark thinks only of the things that matter to him—his architecture being paramount—and the only place he can do this is in New York City.

Rand chose New York because real-life skyscrapers were being constructed there, and the chance for conflict would therefore be high. The conflict between Peter Keating and his old-fashioned style and Roark and his modern design methods drives the story. The buildings they design together reveal this conflict.

Cortlandt homes. Low-income housing project that Roark designs with Keating's support. Even though Keating claims credit for the project, Roark sees it as a way to design something of which he can be proud.

Throughout the book Roark finds himself at odds with the established style of design. When Ellsworth Toohey alters Roark's design while Roark is on vacation, Roark decides to dynamite the structure and is arrested. This event is the prelude to the final courtroom battle and Roark's (and Rand's) grand statement about Objectivism.

Aquitania Hotel. Establishment that Kent Lansing hires Roark to build. The Aquitania represents Roark and his attempt to develop a new type of architecture, while fighting Ellsworth Toohey and others who want nothing to do with it. Eventually building is halted for legal reasons, but Lansing promises to complete it. Roark finally finishes it himself.

Stoddard Temple. Nonsectarian building that Roark agrees to build, not knowing that Toohey wanted Roark to build it. When Roark is finished, Toohey criticizes it in a New York *Banner* article. Instead of being a triumph, the temple becomes a disgrace, and Roark finds himself trying desperately to land new architecture projects. Even so, Roark continues to believe in his design and develop his style. Rand has given her protagonist a larger-than-life philosophy, but she had an even larger goal in mind—bringing Objectivist philosophy to the people.

*Connecticut. When Roark learns that the design for the Manhattan Bank Building project is his, with minor modifications, he quits architecture and moves to a quarry in Connecticut. The mansion where Dominique Francon lives is in sharp contrast to the busy life of New York City: fast-living versus slow-living.

— *Kelly Rothenberg*

THE FOUR HORSEMEN OF THE APOCALYPSE

Author: Vicente Blasco Ibáñez (1867-1928)
Type of work: Novel
Type of plot: Historical

Time of plot: Early twentieth century
First published: Los cuatro jinetes del Apocalipsis, 1916 (English translation, 1918)

This novel traces the history of a French family that has returned to France after making its fortune in Argentina. After the family patriarch originally left France out of protest against his country's involvement in the Franco-Prussian War, the next generation find themselves in Paris as World War I is about to erupt.

*Paris. Capital of France in which the members of the Desnoyers family settle after vacating their inherited fortune from the late gaucho grandfather. Don Marcelo and his family establish their residence in avenue Victor Hugo, a posh section for the well to do. Their son, Julio, lives in a studio in rue de la Pompe, apparently to get away from his millionaire father's scrutiny and his mother's constant worries about his extravagant ways while claiming that he needs quiet so he can paint. However, free from parental supervision, he carouses well into the night and sleeps well into the day. His Parisian lifestyle reinforces the novel's depiction of the city's decadence on the eve of World War I, to whose approach the Desnoyers are oblivious. Meanwhile, rumors of a coming war reach a fever pitch in Paris. Julio's Russian neighbor equates the coming war with the biblical story of the four horsemen of the apocalypse: Plague, War, Famine, Death.

*Berlin. Germany's capital city is depicted differently. Its residents welcome the prospect of war and celebrate German militarism.

*Lourdes (lewrd). Town in southwestern France near which the Desnoyers own a castle and a cattle farm. After Germany invades France, Don Marcelo travels mostly on foot to the town to check on his property. He finds that the Germans have pillaged the town and his castle, which they make their temporary headquarters. At Lourdes, he finally grasps the reality of war when he sees the full horrors of the German invasion.

— *Hanh N. Nguyen*

FOUR QUARTETS

Author: T. S. Eliot (1888-1965)   *First published:* 1943
Type of work: Poetry

Each of the four parts of this long poem is named for an actual place. However, rather than providing anything resembling specific historical or geographical references, the poems' settings suggest broad thematic associations such as the conjunction of time and eternity, the quest for identity and redemption.

*Burnt Norton.** English country house in Ebrington, that T. S. Eliot once visited. His 178-line philosophical poem about the nature of reality and time begins and ends with references to the house's gardens. The speaker suggests an edenic world of innocence and timelessness when he imagines walking through the door that opens into the rose garden, following the elusive voices of the hiding/playing children echoing in memory there, and following tentatively those sounds. But this "first world" is hardly a lush verdant place teeming with life and simple beauty; rather, the speaker takes readers into an empty alley, to look down into a "drained pool." The dry concrete pool, stands for the illusiveness of time and meaning. In fact, the lack of extensive specific description of place in the poem is a deliberate teasing about the tangible boundaries of the physical world, underscored by the haunting suggestion that humans cannot bear much reality.

*East Coker.** English village in Somersetshire where Eliot's ancestors originated and where Eliot himself is buried. Again, the specific place is valued only because it stands for a general, universal process of dying and regeneration. This poem is about the idea of origin and destination and ironic redemption. A key to understanding Eliot's detachment from actual place is seeing the essentially paradoxical nature of place: "where you are is where you are not." For Eliot, setting is essentially metaphysical, a part of a moral endeavor. That moral process values the dissociation from place; he favors union not with place but with state of being. Eliot's inclination is to escape the world's increasing strangeness through love. Time and place decline in importance so love can increase.

*Dry Salvages.** Group of rocks, with a beacon, off the coast of Cape Anne, Massachusetts. This third part of *Four Quartets* relies on water symbolism and the play between relative stability of rock or earth and changeability of sea as they relate to the themes of variation and timelessness. The only American place in the "Quartets," the Dry Salvages is paradoxically both a place symbolic of guidance and a place of wreckage, a place of concealment and of revelation. As with the other places mentioned in *Four Quartets*, the Dry Salvages is important as a metaphoric backdrop for a philosophical or moral process: the ways time and experience wash over human beings, the ways moments or occurrences guide people by being monuments or beacons. The refrain of the poem, "fare forward voyagers," suggests the sea as the place for travel; however, the course covered by travel is not as important to Eliot as the process itself of faring. Similarly, the experience of place is valuable only as a prompt toward meaning.

*Little Gidding.** Religious community established in England's Huntingdonshire by Nicholas Ferrar in 1625. This culminating quartet implies the value of creating a religious community in times of political and religious upheaval. Like the other quartets, it is essentially a call for exploration: Besides exploring time and place, this poem suggests that the power of immediate love for one's own fields develops into the extended love of country. Despite this attachment to field and land, for Eliot all spirits are "unappeased and peregrin"; human beings are all between oppositional worlds, worlds that can be variously conceived as time and place, immediacy and generality, or earth and heaven.

— *Scott Samuelson*

FRANKENSTEIN: Or, The Modern Prometheus

Author: Mary Wollstonecraft Godwin Shelley (1797-1851)

Type of work: Novel

Type of plot: Gothic

Time of plot: Eighteenth century

First published: 1818

This novel tells the story of a brilliant scientist, Victor Frankenstein, who blends alchemy with modern science to bring to life a creature made from dead body parts. Repelled by what he has done, he rejects his creation and then commences a long journey to escape its angry revenge.

*Arctic Circle. *Frankenstein* is told at a great distance, both physically and psychologically. The epistolary novel opens with letters from Robert Walton to his sister in England. Walton is on an exploring expedition to the far north, and his letters are dated from locations farther and farther north, starting with St. Petersburg, Russia, then Archangel, then unspecified locations, as Walton passes into unexplored territory. When his ship is surrounded by fog and ice floes, his crew sees Victor Frankenstein crossing the ice with a dog sled. They rescue him; Frankenstein tells his story. Before he does so, however, Frankenstein indicates that the desire to find the North Pole is as dangerous as his inquiry into unknown scientific regions, asking Walton, "Unhappy man! Do you share my madness?" When Frankenstein's story is complete, he dies. His monstrous creation, after finally forgiving him, flees across the polar sea and out of human knowledge.

*Geneva. City in western Switzerland that is home to Victor Frankenstein, who describes it lovingly, speaking of its "majestic and wondrous scenes" and the "sublime shapes of the mountains." The countryside is described more fully than the city, but enough details are given to indicate that Shelley knew Geneva well. While Shelley was staying near Lake Geneva with her husband, Percy Bysshe Shelley, and Lord Byron, and other friends, they had a competition for the best ghost story. Shelley said the core idea for *Frankenstein* came to her then, in a dream. Visiting or leaving Geneva has powerful consequences for the characters in the novel. After they met, Frankenstein's father and mother moved to Geneva. When Victor was five, his father went to Milan, and returned with Elizabeth, the lifetime friend and nearly sister to Victor whom he marries.

When Victor returns to Geneva, everything seems to be different. His creation's presence transforms his home, which earlier seemed to be a paradise, into a place of pain and chaos. Victor's brother William is killed, and a life-long family servant is sentenced to death. Late in the novel, Victor returns to Geneva for the last time to marry Elizabeth. When his creation kills Elizabeth on their wedding night, the transformation of Geneva into a hell on earth is complete.

*Ingolstadt. City in Bavaria, Germany, where Victor Frankenstein entered the University of Ingolstadt when he was seventeen and to which he returns in later years. The university had a great deal of autonomy during the seventeenth century, and was known for its support of Enlightenment rationality. Few specifics are given about Ingolstadt itself. Frankenstein studies there and escapes the stabilizing influence of his family but connects only with his professors, not with a community or place. There he learns modern chemistry from his professor Monsieur Waldman, which he blends with his earlier knowledge of alchemy to create life. Once he does, Ingolstadt becomes essentially haunted; Victor wanders its streets, afraid of his creature. Only the arrival of Henry Clerval, his old friend from Geneva, calms him.

*Mont Blanc. Highest mountain in the Alps, to which Victor retreats when he is upset by the thought that his creation has caused the deaths of William and Justine. While gazing upon the awful beauty of Mont Blanc, he speaks aloud to the spirit of the place, which seems so pure. His creation answers, indicating that no place is free of the taint Frankenstein his created. The mountain's glacier becomes a courtroom of natural philosophy as the creature accuses Victor of defaulting on his responsibilities as creator.

Cottage. Home of a poor family in which the creature observes human interaction. When the creature tells the story of his life since his creation, the cottage where he observes a family, is central to it. He learns to speak by listening to the cottage's inhabitants, and from them he learns about the possibility of love. Before this time, he is ignorant as an animal, but now, he becomes a tortured soul. Observing the small society in the cottage brings him close enough to humanity to realize what he is denied.

***London.** Capital of Great Britain to which Victor Frankenstein goes to investigate another scientist's discoveries before he can meet the creature's demand that he make him a woman to be his companion. In London, Victor establishes a lab, and begins work, but he and Clerval also travel throughout England and Scotland. Their travels are idyllic, but everywhere they go, Victor is sure the creature follows him.

***Scotland.** Country to which Victor goes to continue his work because it is farther from civilization. There he works on a mate for the creature then reconsiders and destroys it. The creature appears at that moment, confirming Victor's fears that he has been followed. When Victor tries to sail home, he gets lost at sea and almost dies, symbolizing the danger inherent in his unchecked scientific explorations.

***Ireland.** Country in which Victor is arrested for the murder of his friend Clerval, whom the monster has killed, after he lands there and goes ashore to ask for directions. While he is jailed in Ireland, he falls into a guilty fever for months. His imprisonment in this remote land confirms his growing fear that there is no place to which he can go to escape responsibility for his actions.

— *Greg Beatty*

FRANNY AND ZOOEY

Author: J. D. Salinger (1919-   )
Type of work: Novel
Type of plot: Domestic realism

Time of plot: November, 1955
First published: "Franny," 1955; "Zooey," 1957; novel, 1961

This novel is actually two shorter stories involving Franny and Zooey Glass, two members of a family still dealing with the death of their sibling, Seymour Glass, seven years earlier.

***Manhattan.** Borough of New York City that seems to be a place where much is offered. In reality, however, this is not the case. Wintertime has traditionally reflected death, and in the Glass house it has been winter for seven years; Seymour's death haunts the other characters, who have not yet recovered from his passing. J. D. Salinger knows Manhattan well, having lived there through most of his early publishing life. The fact that he does not go into detail about the city the way he does in *Catcher in the Rye* (1951) reflects his assertion in this novel that people are more important than places. *Franny and Zooey*, for the most part, could take place anywhere.

Glass living room. At once homey and forbidding, the Glass living room is a reflection of the Glasses themselves. The house sits a story higher than the school across from it, suggesting the Glasses' superiority in things intellectual (all the Glass children have been on the quiz show "It's a Wise Child"). All the furniture is marred in one way or another and does not match, just as Zooey and Franny do not match. Even though it is bright and sunny, the light brings out the worst in the living room (stains from pets, for example). As wonderful as it is outside, Franny and Zooey stay inside as if trying to keep the outside world from crashing in on them.

Glass bathroom. Zooey Glass spends most of his time in the family bathroom, which also serves as a meetinghouse between Zooey and his mother. It is also where Zooey reads a letter from his older brother, Buddy, about bringing Seymour's corpse home after Seymour has committed suicide. The room itself is not symbolic, but it serves as the template for the entire family's feelings about Franny and the overall theme of Seymour's death.

Seymour Glass's bedroom. After seven years, Zooey Glass finally goes into Seymour's bedroom for the first time. Going into this room serves as closure for Zooey and Franny, who have all put their thoughts and feelings on hold since Seymour's death. The bedroom, which Seymour shared with his brother Buddy, is decorated with many religious sayings and thoughts, some of which Buddy writes about in his letter to Zooey. Here Zooey finds the knowledge that he has been looking for—comparing Jesus and the Fat Lady—which he shares with Franny.

Sickler's. Manhattan restaurant frequented by the intellectual students of Princeton. Everything about the restaurant, from the table to the women's bathroom, suggests an atmosphere in which everything is in its place, except Franny. Franny looks like she belongs to this group of people who frequent this restaurant, but her feelings are in conflict. As she sits in the bathroom, she clings to the belief that all this—the restaurant, the theater, her boyfriend Lane—is not as important as the simpler things in the book itself. She wants to give everything up and live simply, the exact opposite of how she is living now.

— Kelly Rothenberg

FREE FALL

Author: William Golding (1911-1993)
Type of work: Novel
Type of plot: Bildungsroman

Time of plot: 1917-c. 1950
First published: 1959

Artist Samuel Mountjoy looks back over his life from his childhood in England's Kent County to his maturity in London and his experiences in a prison camp during World War II, trying to determine at what point he had his "free fall" from grace.

Rotten Row. Alleyway of slum housing in an unnamed Kent town, where Mountjoy was born and where his earliest memories are located. The name is probably merely colloquial; the only two parts of the town that William Golding names in the novel are Rotten Row, where Mountjoy was a child, and **Paradise Hill**, where he lives as a successful adult. The symbolism of these names is clearly intentional. Seen through the eyes of an innocent child who generally does not comprehend what he sees, Rotten Row is described at greater length and in far more detail than any other location in the novel. Readers see its dirty terraced houses with outdoor lavatories and the mud and puddles that litter the alley, as well as the petty feuds and rough society that allow people to survive in these grimy circumstances. They also see the pub at the end of the row, which, despite its poverty, aspires to a slightly higher social standing. The small focus of the residents' lives is shown when the lodger dies, and the upstairs rooms where he lived remain unoccupied, Mountjoy and his prostitute mother continuing to live in their cramped ground-floor rooms.

Town. Unidentified town in southeast England. Despite the stunningly visual passage that opens the book—"I have walked by stalls in the market-place where books, dog-eared and faded from their purple, have burst with a white hosanna"—Mountjoy the artist provides remarkably little in the way of visual detail. Once he leaves the somber colors of Rotten Row for school, the town in which he lives ceases to be a coherent whole and becomes rather a sequence of unconnected sites in which significant incidents in his fall from grace occur. Never named, these sites are given only general appellations: the airfield, the school, the church, the hospital. At the airfield, Mountjoy is timidly following his more daring and admirable pal, Johnny, as he trespasses; at school he becomes a bully under the sly prompting of another friend, Peter, who also urges the desecration of the church where Mountjoy will be caught and hurt by the sexton, which lands him in the clean, white hospital where he learns his mother has died and the priest has become his guardian. None of these locations, not even the church, is a solid presence, the whole story of Mountjoy's moral decline is told in his relationship with people not his environment.

***London.** Great Britain's capital city, located in southeastern England, not far from Kent. Mountjoy leaves his hometown only twice. He attends an art college (never seen) in south London, where he seduces, then abandons, Beatrice Ifor in a small, featureless flat. He also attends Communist Party meetings and marries another woman.

Prison cell. Punishment cell in which Mountjoy is confined in a German prison camp during World War II. During the war Mountjoy becomes a war artist and is captured by the Germans; however, the circumstance of his capture are never explained. In the camp to which he is taken, he is questioned by SS officers about his fellow prisoners' escape plans. Since he has nothing to tell, he is locked in a tiny, pitch-black cell—the only place in the novel other than Rotten Row that is vividly described. Like the rocky island of Golding's *Pincher Martin* (1956), the cell is a reflection of the inside of the main character's head. As the claustrophobic Mountjoy gropes around in the dark, he discovers a damp patch in the middle of the floor and touches a wet soft mass that feels unspeakably horrible; he imagines it to be human organs. The empty shell becomes the setting for all his terrors and doubts, but the soft mass turns out to be merely wet rags and his cell a broom closet. It is only here, confronted with his own emptiness, that he can come to recognize who he is and begin the process of revisiting and understanding his life.

— *Paul Kincaid*

FREEDOM OR DEATH

Author: Nikos Kazantzakis (1883-1957)
Type of work: Novel
Type of plot: Historical

Time of plot: 1889
First published: Ho Kapetan Michales, 1953 (English translation, 1956)

Kazantzakis's novel about the 1889 uprising in his native Crete uses historical events as a backdrop for exploring the nature of humankind and the struggle of human beings to create meaning in their lives. It also dramatically presents the indomitable spirit of the Cretans who, through numerous foreign occupations, continuously fought to regain independence. The setting plays a crucial role in the novel, in which Crete becomes a microcosm for the world itself—the place in which people struggle against all forms of oppression to achieve independence and dignity.

*****Crete** (kreet). Island south of Greece and Turkey in the eastern Mediterranean Sea. Although Kazantzakis is careful to create detailed settings for the action, *Freedom or Death* is really about the struggle of Crete to become free from outside oppressors. The novel is filled with descriptions of the countryside and its people. Throughout, Kazantzakis uses personification to create the impression that Crete is a living being. At one point, the island is compared to a woman being ravished. At another, the sufferings of Crete are compared to the sufferings of Christ. Like many nautical novelists, Kazantzakis uses the isolation of the island to create a sense that life-and-death issues must be resolved without resort to outside help. In this way, he manages to suggest that the island stands for the world itself—a place where men and women must struggle alone to establish their identity and define their self-worth against forces that would suppress them and strip them of their humanity and dignity.

The final scenes of the novel are set in Cretan mountains where Michales and other rebels take refuge from the invading Turkish forces. Amid the rugged terrain, a small band resists a much larger force, demonstrating their willingness to die for a cause in which they believe. The rugged landscape is an apt backdrop for such action, suggesting the rugged character of Michales and his band of patriots.

*Megalokastro** (meh-gah-loh-KAS-troh). Cretan village under the rule of the Turks. The village is a microcosm of the island, as the island is a microcosm of the world. In Megalokastro, Cretans and Turks live in tenuous co-existence; the slightest insult by a member of one group against the other sets off skirmishes that eventually lead to armed conflict. In this primitive village the Cretans struggle to make a living, but also enjoy the elemental pleasures of family life and friendship. Despite not having any of the modern conveniences available in the late nineteenth century, the Cretans display a lust for living and a deep commitment to their country.

Captain Michales's house (meh-KAH-lehs). Modest home in Megalokastro that is the Cretan patriot's refuge from the political turmoil that runs through his village. Scenes at this home dramatize Cretan domestic life in a patriarchal society dominated by concerns for both immediate and extended family. Michales's house is also the location where a small group of dissatisfied Cretans plot a rebellion against the Turks.

Nuri Bey's estate. Home of Michales' blood brother, the Turkish political ruler in the region. Nuri Bey retires there to escape the pressures of government as Crete's people become increasingly discontented with Turkish rule. The estate is like an oasis amid the tumultuous political landscape created by the arbitrary and oppressive rule of the Muslims over the Orthodox Christian Cretans. The sanctity of this retreat is violated, however, when Nuri Bey's wife Eminé entertains her lover, Captain Polyxigis, when her husband is away.

Monastery of Christ the Lord. Centuries-old monastery that stands as a symbol for Greek Orthodoxy and for the independent spirit of the Cretans. Captain Michales leads a band of defenders against the Turks, who launch a day-long attack on the monastery. In the evening, he learns that the Turks have captured Eminé, now wife of Captain Polyxigis. Inflamed with passion for her himself, he leaves his men to rescue her. In his absence, the monastery is taken. Through the episode, Kazantzakis makes clear the duty of the freedom fighters to remain committed to their task, and symbolically the duty of men to pursue the ideal rather than the temptations of the flesh.

— *Laurence W. Mazzeno*

THE FRENCH LIEUTENANT'S WOMAN

Author: John Fowles (1926-   )
Type of work: Novel
Type of plot: Symbolic realism

Time of plot: 1867-1869
First published: 1969

This novel's actions are set in southern England in places ranging from a seaside town to the nation's capital. Its hero's physical journey mirrors his mental journey as he learns how traditional attitudes toward sex, religion, class, and human fulfillment are beginning to crumble.

*Lyme Regis.** Old Dorset town on the English Channel. Its manners are old-fashioned, just the place for a conventional and traditional courtship. The novel opens on the Cobb, an ancient breakwater along the shoreline. There Charles Smithson and his intended bride, Ernestina Freeman, see the French lieutenant's woman, Sarah Woodruff, staring longingly out to sea, evidently trying to find something more than Lyme can provide. Charles lives at the White Lion Hotel (now the Royal Lion Hotel) on Broad Street. Ernestina stays with her aunt a few yards to the north on the west side of that same street. Sarah is a servant in a house located on higher ground not far away. In 1867, at the base of Broad Street on the sea's edge stand the Assembly Rooms where Charles and Ernestina attend a concert. Dr. Grogan's rooms are also close to the sea, but farther west near the Cobb.

*Ware Cliffs.** Also known as the Undercliff, a mile-long slope caused by the erosion of the ancient vertical cliff face, located at Lyme's boundary, stretching west from where the Cobb juts out into the sea. Because the slope tilts toward the Sun, its vegetation is lush and exotic, appropriate to the values that challenge Lyme's (and Charles's) conservatism. Here, in stone outcrops, Charles hunts for fossils. Here, too, Sarah walks. In this romantic and erotic place, several miles from conservative Lyme, they meet. Walking back from their first encounter, Charles stops at a farm. That farm, which still exists, is where John Fowles himself lived when he began writing this novel.

***Wiltshire.** County in England between Dorset and London where Charles's uncle has his estate, Wynsyatt, located near Chippenham. At the beginning of the novel, Charles is heir to his uncle's land and aristocratic title. In the past, Charles shot one of the last great bustards on the nearby Salisbury Plain.

***Exeter.** Inland city in Devon located about forty miles west of Lyme Regis, a place where Charles experiences both sexual and religious awakenings. Sarah takes a room in Endicott's Hotel in a gloomy lower-class part of the city as it slopes westward down to the river Exe. When Charles comes to Exeter, he stays on higher ground at the Ship, an old-fashioned inn probably not far from the cathedral. After Charles's climactic visit to Sarah, he enters a small nearby church, which is unnamed but still exists.

***London.** Great Britain's capital city and the place of both the new (commerce and art) and the old (sin)—all challenges to the values of Lyme. Charles and Ernestina are both Londoners. Charles owns a big house in Belgravia, an elegant district, but he lives, appropriately to his scientific interests, in a smaller establishment in Kensington, a more intellectual part of the city housing several newly opened museums. When she is not in Lyme, Ernestina lives with her parents on Bayswater Road, a middle-class street running along the north edge of Hyde Park. After he has been disinherited, Charles goes here to see Ernestina's father, Mr. Freeman. Charles then walks eastward into Mayfair and wanders north until he is horrified to see Mr. Freeman's great store on Oxford Street.

Charles's lessons have just begun. He repairs (probably a short distance south) to his club and then to Ma Terpsichore's brothel, which can be located to the east of Mayfair in Soho. After leaving there, he meets a prostitute who leads him northeastward to her lodgings off Tottenham Court Road, near Warren Street. Later, after he breaks his engagement, he faces Mr. Freeman's lawyers in chambers at the Inns of Court, located off the Strand.

Several years later when he is told that Sarah has been found, Charles returns to London and goes to her address, 16 Cheyne Walk, home of the poet and painter Dante Gabriel Rossetti. Cheyne Walk is a newly fashionable street on the banks of the River Thames in Chelsea, southwest of the Houses of Parliament. Sarah has been taken up by the most vital and forward-looking artists of that time. At the very end of the novel, Charles, now bereft of all his illusions and old-fashioned assumptions, stands alone on the banks of the Thames, the river of life.

— *George Soule*

FRIAR BACON AND FRIAR BUNGAY

Author: Robert Greene (1558-1592)
Type of work: Drama
Type of plot: Historical

Time of plot: Thirteenth century
First performed: c. 1589; first published, 1594

This loosely structured comedic chronicle play turns on travel—across the English countryside, from rural fields and forests and country fair to court and university, and across social boundaries—as Friar Bacon attempts and fails to put a brass wall around the "little world" of England. Greene's fantasy England is a tribute to wonders wrought by Queen Elizabeth in securing and uniting England as a nation.

*England. Greene's idealistic portrait of a benevolently democratic English aristocracy may reflect the outburst of patriotism in England following the 1588 defeat of the Spanish Armada. Also indicative of this nationalistic theme are Friar Bacon's plan to build a protective brass wall around England and his humiliation of the German emperor's necromancer Jaques Vandermast. A noteworthy aspect of *Friar Bacon and Friar Bungay* is how it brings together royalty, nobility, and commoners, preserving some traditional class barriers but breaking through others.

Fressingfield Park. Royal hunting preserve in Suffolk, where the play opens as the Prince of Wales and his entourage have been hunting deer before stopping for refreshment at the keeper's lodge. There the prince falls in love with the keeper's daughter, Margaret.

*Oxford. English town that is the seat of one of the country's great universities. The play's action moves between Fressingfield, a local fair, the Court of England, and Oxford, with Oxford clearly the showplace of the nation's superior accomplishments and intellectual pursuits. While the Prince of Wales travels to Oxford—disguised as a gentleman in waiting—to seek the advice of Friar Bacon, and the friar himself conjures wonders and contemplates exotic feats, Margaret and friends go to Harleston Fair. As the king and his guests set out for Oxford, Friar Bacon sees through the prince's disguise as he strolls the streets of Oxford, shows him Margaret being courted and won by a go-between, and magically stops their wedding by transporting Friar Bungay to Oxford.

— *Gina Macdonald*

THE FROGS

Author: Aristophanes (c. 450-c. 385 B.C.E.)
Type of work: Drama
Type of plot: Satire

Time of plot: Fifth century B.C.E.
First performed: Batrachoi, 405 B.C.E. (English translation, 1780)

The primary location for this play is the Greek underworld, Hades. Some action also occurs on a boat circling a large lake that divides Earth from the underworld. Both locations are in public and open spaces, which is crucial to the ancient Greek concept of communication. For them communication, even among the gods, was conducted in open and public places so democratic rule of the people could be protected from private manipulation.

Underworld lake. The god Dionysus, in whose honor all the Greek plays were performed, is sad that two of the great tragic writers—Aeschylus and Euripides—have died. He does not like the work of their survivors and descends to Hades to bring one of them back to earth to write plays for him. To reach Hades, he must row the ferryboat of Charon across a large lake. (This body of water is known as the **River Styx** in other Greek stories.) Throughout his journey across the lake, he is tormented by the croaking of a swarm of frogs, played by the members of the play's chorus.

Hades (hay-deez). To the Greeks, Hades was an underworld to which all mortals went after they died. Not a place of punishment, it is an open area, except for the palace of Pluto, the god of the underworld. Dionysus goes to **Pluto's palace**, but does not enter. After a number of farcical episodes in front of the palace, Euripides is finally allowed to hold a contest between Aeschylus and Euripides to determine which of them will accompany him back to earth. Each poet recites lines, which Dionysus judges using a huge scale. Aeschylus wins and as the play ends everyone enters the palace for a banquet.

— *August W. Staub*

THE FRUIT OF THE TREE

Author: Edith Wharton (1862-1937)
Type of work: Novel
Type of plot: Social realism

Time of plot: Late nineteenth century
First published: 1907

The two major New England locations in this novel, both owned by Bessy Westmore Amherst, demonstrate the contrast between the lives of the upper and lower classes. The first is Westmore, the factory community where John Amherst is determined to improve conditions by implementing his plans for social reform. The second is Lynbrook, the society home where his wife Bessy lives a life of easy opulence. While Westmore reveals the effect of industrialization on the workers, Lynbrook shows the effect of that wealth on the lives of those who enjoy but do not earn it.

Hanaford. Fictional New England community supported by Westmore, its industrial suburb. Home to the Westmore cotton mill, Hanaford is the home of the mill owners and managers. Factory money provides them with country houses, gardens, servants, and entertainments.

Westmore. Mill village containing shabby row houses for its workers and a company store. The Eldorado roadhouse, the one building which is actually kept up, is an additional source of income for the factory manager, who receives payment from the landlord. Readers see the sordidness through a reformer's eyes when Amherst describes the run-down houses and poor inhabitants of Westmore. He calls attention to the isolation and deadness of this place.

Overshadowing the smaller buildings, the Westmore cotton mill looms over workers' lives and landscape, its very size emblematic of its oppressiveness. The factory itself comprises noisy workrooms filled with oversized machinery. The rooms are crowded, dirty, and poorly ventilated. The brutal cacophony of the enclosed rooms contrasts vividly with the stillness of luxury.

Lynbrook house. Located in fictional Lynbrook, Bessy Westmore's New York mansion is everything that Westmore is not. Descending gardens, terraces, tennis courts, and stables surround the grand house, all of which represent the factory owner's luxurious life and provide a striking contrast to the impoverished landscape of the workers whose labor supports her upper-class lifestyle.

The big house has all the accoutrements associated with money: drawing rooms, windows with views of the countryside, objects d'art, soft rugs and oak paneling, gracious staircases, long dinner tables with candles and flowers, and servants to maintain the house and grounds. Edith Wharton focuses on more than the amenities of the house, however. She characterizes Lynbrook as indolent and narcissistic, filled with inhabitants whose only interest is the pursuit of their own pleasure. They have no energy for work but seek only diversions. Despite the beauty of the surroundings and the "finer graces of luxurious living," the reader is left with no doubt about the contempt in which the author holds the residents and guests at Lynbrook.

*****Adirondack Mountains.** Upstate New York mountain range in which Bessy vacations when Amherst's mill improvements force a reduction in her expenditures. Using the real mountains to provide verisimilitude, Wharton invents a "woodland cure" for members of the upper class who wish to escape the city in summer but who, like Bessy, cannot afford a European tour.

Hopewood. Recreation center at Westmore that serves as an ironic finale to the novel. The center is built from blueprints drawn up for Bessy before her death. Whether or not he knows in his heart that the building was designed for Bessy's own pleasure, Amherst declares that her final thoughts were for the factory operatives. The lavish gymnasium, bowling alley, pool, squash court, and marble fountains of Bessy's original plans are redesigned on a smaller scale, with modest materials, and built for the entertainment of the mill workers.

— *Paula L. Cardinal*

GABRIELA, CLOVE AND CINNAMON

Author: Jorge Amado (1912-2001)
Type of work: Novel
Type of plot: Social realism

Time of plot: 1925-1926
First published: Gabriela, cravo e canela, 1958
  (English translation, 1962)

The setting of this novel is a real place, Ilhéus, a port in the cacao-growing region of southern Bahia in northeastern Brazil, where Jorge Amado spent his childhood. Although the characters are fictional, they reflect the rich and unique culture of this particular place.

*Ilhéus** (ihl-YAY-us). Hot and humid port on the seacoast of tropical northeastern Brazil's Bahia state, where most of the action takes place. After years of violent land disputes among the powerful cacao barons, Ilhéus is enjoying an economic boom. Amado chronicles the folkways and growing prosperity of the town, depicting with subtle irony and humor the elite cacao planters, who enjoy houses in Ilhéus, where they keep their mistresses and control local politics. His other characters include members of the intelligentsia, titled aristocracy, urban-class professionals, prostitutes, gunmen, and migrants escaping the drought of the backlands.

*Sandbar.** Natural obstacle in Ilhéus's harbor that is the principal problem preventing large ships from entering the harbor, thereby threatening the prosperity of Ilhéus. Mundinho Falcão, a bachelor and wealthy, politically ambitious exporter recently arrived from Rio de Janeiro, wants to improve the harbor. Through his family and political contacts, he eventually succeeds in bringing an engineer, skilled workmen, and equipment to dredge the harbor. This ensures his political success, especially when his rival, Ramiro Bastos, dies.

*Town square.** Center of life in Ilhéus. Located here is the church, where prayers are offered up for relief from drought or floods threatening to ruin the cacao crop. The women gather here to gossip. The Model Stationery Store, where the intelligentsia gather to discuss politics, is located here. Also here are the houses of the wealthy: Colonel Ramiro Bastos, the aging town boss who opposes progress and hates Falcão for his port project; Colonel Melk Tavares, whose daughter Malvina ignores the lovesick Professor Josué pacing outside her gate; and Colonel Coriolano Ribeiro, whose lonely, voluptuous mistress Glória sits in the window, trying to seduce the men of Ilhéus who pass below.

Vesuvius Bar. On St. Sebastian Street near the square, the most popular bar in Ilhéus, where the elite male population gathers to drink and gossip. It is owned by Nacib Saad, whose popularity and success depend on the delicious snacks served in his bar. When he loses his cook, the desperate Nacib hires a dirty migrant, Gabriela, who is transformed after a bath into a cinnamon-brown *mulata* smelling of clove. She soon gains a reputation as the best cook in Ilhéus and loves working in the bar, where she is sought after as a cook and mistress by many of the rich men in town.

Nacib's house. House in which Gabriela is content to sleep with Nacib and work for him, but he fears losing his cook and mistress and decides to make her his wife.

*Cacao region.** Region served by the port of Ilhéus. Although Rio de Janeiro is the capital of Brazil at the time the novel is set, there is little national political unity, and each region enjoys great autonomy. Cacao has made this the richest region in the state, following the violent land struggles of the cacao barons during Amado's childhood. The barons control the votes in their districts and hold the real power.

***Bahia.** Northeastern Brazilian state where Ilhéus is located. The region is at the mercy of severe droughts, which cause mass migrations of peasants from the backlands seeking work in Ilhéus and the cacao region.

***Salvador.** Former capital of Brazil, in Bahia, to which landowners send their children to be educated. Located north of Ilhéus, Salvador is the principal port of the state of Bahia. Because of the sandbar in Ilhéus, cacao must be shipped abroad through this city, causing an immense loss in exportation taxes to Ilhéus.

***Itabuna.** Metropolis of the vast interior of Bahia west of Ilhéus. Falcão gains the support of the mayor there, who is then attacked on a visit to Ilhéus and left for dead by a hired killer of the Bastos supporters. The people of Itabuna rally behind Falcão.

— *Edna B. Quinn*

GALILEO

Author: Bertolt Brecht (1898-1956)
Type of work: Drama
Type of plot: Historical
Time of plot: 1609-1637

First performed: Leben des Galilei, first version, 1943; second version (in English), 1947; third version (in German), 1955; first published, 1952; third version, 1955; revised, 1957 (English translation, 1960)

Although the settings of the three versions of this play about the great Italian scientist Galileo proceed chronologically through the cities in which Galileo spent most of his life as a scientist, the interpretation changes from the scientist as the duplicitous hero of free inquiry to the social criminal who pursues scientific knowledge to the neglect of the well-being of humanity. The principal reason for Bertolt Brecht's revisions was the creation by scientists of the atomic bomb during World War II.

***Padua.** Northern Italian city at whose university Galileo is a forty-six-year-old professor of mathematics when the play opens. Both the place and person are in tension because the mercantile republic of Venice desires power, wealth, and prestige, and Galileo wants to advance scientific knowledge, boost his career, and make his life comfortable. Although he knows that the telescope is a Dutch invention, he presents himself to the Venetian senators as its creator, assuring them "on the most scientific and Christian principles" that it has been "the product of seventeen years patient research at your University of Padua."

***Florence.** Powerful city-state in central Italy that is the site of the play's middle scenes. The play depicts Florence as a more totalitarian state than the Venetian republic. Although Galileo despises the despotism of the Medici rulers of Florence, he nevertheless writes a groveling letter to ask for their patronage for his work. Besides Medicean control, Florence is also subject to powerful papal influence. Thus Galileo, having compromised his freedom for security, runs the risk of having his research frustrated by both state and church.

***Rome.** Center of the Papal States at the time the play is set. Several pivotal scenes occur in the Vatican, which, for Brecht, represents not only spiritual but also intellectual and worldly authority. Galileo's Copernicanism so troubles church officials that he is eventually put on trial, which leads to him to recant his belief that because the earth rotates around the Sun, the earth cannot be the center of the universe. In the earliest version of the play a cunning Galileo recants to preserve his chances for completing his scientific work. The versions that Brecht wrote after World War II treat Galileo less sympathetically because the postwar Brecht questioned the alliance between scientists and the state. In this interpretation Galileo capitulates out of cowardice and his dedication to science becomes a vice since he practices it without concern for humanity.

— *Robert J. Paradowski*

THE GAMBLER

Author: Fyodor Dostoevski (1821-1881)
Type of work: Novel
Type of plot: Psychological realism

Time of plot: Mid-nineteenth century
First published: Igrok, 1866 (English translation, 1949)

In setting his novel in the fictional German town of Roulettenburg, Fyodor Dostoevski creates a unique world in which customary rules of conduct are suspended and fixed values lose their meaning. The pursuit of money is the highest concern, and people who come to Roulettenburg find themselves under the sway of forces they cannot control.

Roulettenburg. Dostoevski modeled his invented town of Roulettenburg on the German spa town of Baden-Baden, where he himself used to gamble in the famous casino. By calling the town Roulettenburg, Dostoevski underscores the central importance of gambling (and specifically, the game of roulette) to those who visit the town. Dostoevski does not show many different aspects of the location but focuses on those places where visitors and tourists congregate: the elegant hotels, the casino, the park. One of the distinctive features of the Roulettenburg setting is its international or cosmopolitan character. People of various nationalities—Russian, French, German, Italian, and Polish—congregate there, and this international flavor evokes an atmosphere of rootlessness. Winnings and losses are calculated in a variety of different currencies, from French to Russian. Even the hotel names point to the international aura; one hotel is called "Hôtel d'Angleterre" ("Hotel England"). What is more, townspeople place tremendous emphasis on appearance and external form. It is of paramount importance to appear to have great wealth and rank in society. Yet it often turns out that people are not what they seem. Identities are deceptive and fluid, and personal fortunes may fluctuate dramatically depending on a simple turn of the roulette wheel. Dostoevski's treatment of the town and its visitors exposes the danger and the folly of placing one's dreams of joy and fulfillment on mere games of chance. Indeed, the novel's central character, the narrator Aleksei Ivanovich, loses the opportunity to find true love because he becomes obsessed with playing the game of roulette.

Casino. Much of the novel's most intense action occurs in the casino, which Dostoevski depicts as a kind of hell on earth. Among the crowds thronging the gambling tables, one finds lost souls, desperate to change their luck, as well as vicious swindlers, demons of a sort, who prey on the unwary. In one important episode, an elderly Russian woman, whose death is eagerly anticipated by family members who stand to inherit her fortune, unexpectedly arrives in Roulettenburg, and soon proceeds to lose a colossal amount of money at the roulette table. This is money she had originally planned to use for the construction of a church. Chastened by her losses, she returns to Moscow with a new sense of humility. The example she sets is lost on Aleksei Ivanovich, who goes to the casino and wins a large sum of money, thereby setting him on the path to a ruinous gambling addiction.

*****Paris.** Capital of France to which Aleksei Ivanovich travels with the French adventuress Mademoiselle Blanche after winning his fortune at the Roulettenburg casino. The Paris that Aleksei Ivanovich experiences is one of frivolity and light entertainment. Mademoiselle Blanche cheerfully spends his winnings on clothes, horses, and furniture, yet he remains indifferent to this, for his underlying ambition is to return to the gambling tables.

*****Moscow.** In contrast to the tainted foreign cities of Roulettenburg and Paris, the old Russian city of Moscow symbolically represents traditional values and spiritual firmness.

Schlangenberg. Mountain peak near the town of Roulettenburg. The name of the peak in German means "Snake Mountain." In a desperate attempt to convince the woman he loves that he is devoted to her, Aleksei Ivanovich tells the woman that he would jump off the Schlangenberg if she so commanded. This episode recalls the story of the temptation of Jesus by the devil in the New Testament.

— Julian W. Connolly

GARGANTUA AND PANTAGRUEL

Author: François Rabelais (c. 1494-1553)
Type of work: Fiction
Type of plot: Mock-heroic
Time of plot: Renaissance
First published: Gargantua et Pantagruel, first

complete edition, 1567; *Gargantua,* 1534 (English translation, 1653); *Pantagruel,* 1532 (English translation, 1653); *Tiers livre,* 1546 (*Third Book,* 1693); *Le Quart Livre,* 1552 (*Fourth Book,* 1694); *Le Cinquiesme Livre,* 1564 (*Fifth Book,* 1694)

Just as Gargantua and Pantagruel *is a mixture of folk tale and classical learning, its setting is a mixture of fantastic kingdoms and historical France, a mixture of the past and the author's present.*

***Paris.** French city to which the affable giant prince Gargantua is sent to be educated. In the City of Light, he is exposed to the light of humanist learning. The Paris portrayed in this book is that of Rabelais's own day. Gargantua travels there on a brood mare the size of six elephants. After his arrival, he undergoes a rigorous regimen of classical studies and physical exercise, directed by his tutor, Powerbrain, and some of Paris's truly learned scholars. This learning is contrasted with that of Paris's Sorbonne, the college of powerful and conservative theologians at the University of Paris. Combining mental and physical exertion, Gargantua swims across the Seine River while reading a book which he holds high above the water with one hand.

Later, Gargantua's own son, Pantagruel, also goes to Paris to study. He falls into company with Panurge, a brilliant but almost criminal trickster, who explores the seamier side of Parisian life. Although the people of Paris, who are represented realistically in the text, marvel at the giants, they easily accept their presence in their midst.

***Touraine.** Region containing the Loire valley in west-central France, the so-called "garden of France," where Panurge was born and reared. Touraine was also the birthplace of Rabelais himself.

Thélème Abbey. Church along the Loire River, two leagues from the forest of Port-Huault, that Gargantua builds to reward Friar John for his help in winning the mock-heroic war against Picrochole. The abbey is the thematic center of the work, with its credo that instinct forms the only valid basis for morality and social structure. Befitting his gigantic nature, Gargantua's construction expenses are enormous: millions of gold pieces and English pounds to build and maintain the abbey. The building is hexagonal in shape with a round tower sixty

feet in diameter located at each angle of the hexagon. It has six floors, counting its subterranean cellars. The abbey is immense, containing 9,332 suites, each furnished with an antechamber, a private reading room, a dressing room, and a small personal chapel. Beautiful libraries are well stocked with books in Greek, Latin, Hebrew, and the Romance languages. Large, open galleries are painted with scenes of ancient heroism, episodes from history, and fascinating plants and animals. In the inner court is a magnificent alabaster fountain featuring statues of the three Graces. Both men and women live at Thélème. In front of the women's quarters is a playing field (for some game like lawn tennis), a horse-riding circle, a theater, and swimming pools with attached baths. Next to the river is a beautiful pleasure garden with a handsome labyrinth at its center.

Thélème is the exact opposite of the monasteries from which Rabelais was fleeing during most of his adult life. The men and women of Thélème are physically attractive, well born, intelligent, and educated (in contrast to the ugly and socially inept who, Rabelais strongly suggests, usually enter the cloistered life). They dress grandly in bright colors and are constantly attended by perfumers and hairdressers. Men and women mingle freely, ruled only by their own virtue. Should they fall in love, they are encouraged to marry. The constitution of the abbey contains but one clause—"Do what you will." Within all Rabelais's writings, Thélème most clearly illustrates his concept of ideal Renaissance society.

***Holy Bottle.** Fountain oracle in upper India to which Panurge, Pantagruel, and Friar John go. From Saint Malo, they sail in twelve ships, making the trip in only one month by sailing across the Frozen Sea north of Canada. They have many adventures along their way. On the **Island of the Ennasins**, they find a race of people with noses shaped like the ace of clubs. People on the **Island of Ruach** eat and drink nothing but wind. The **Ringing Islands** contain a strange race of Siticines who long ago turned into birds. On **Condemnation Island**, they fall into the power of Gripe-men-all, archduke of the Furred Law-cats, and Panurge must solve a riddle before the travelers are freed. When they finally reach the island of the Holy Bottle, they come upon a large vineyard planted by Bacchus himself. They then go down into a deep underground vault to the Holy Bottle.

— *Patrick Adcock*

THE "GENIUS"

Author: Theodore Dreiser (1871-1945)
Type of work: Novel
Type of plot: Naturalism

Time of plot: 1889-1914
First published: 1915

Place functions in a variety of important ways in this novel. First, the small towns and big cities of America shape the character of its hero Eugene Witla, in both positive and negative ways. Second, they provide inspirations and subject matter for Eugene's paintings. Further, the opulent, fast-paced, materialistic and ruthlessly competitive big cities inspire him to achieve fame, fortune, self-confidence, and social polish, while at the same time undermining his moral character, so that his life ends in ruin for both him and his wife.

Alexandria. Illinois hometown of Eugene Witla; a typical midwestern town of about ten thousand people. Although Eugene feels too ambitious to remain there, his character is irrevocably influenced by the tranquil beauty of the region and the conservative values of his God-fearing parents, friends, and neighbors. In Alexandria, as in every other place used in this novel, Theodore Dreiser describes Eugene's surroundings in lavish detail to emphasize his hero's impressionable nature and artistic sensitivity, which set him apart from ordinary people and make him feel an outsider everywhere.

Blackwood. Wisconsin hometown of Angela Blue, who becomes Eugene's wife and remains the most important person in his life despite his womanizing. Angela, too, has been stamped by the traditional conservative values of small-town middle America, but in contrast to Eugene she never questions or revolts against them. The powerful moral influence of Blackwood and Alexandria forces Eugene to marry Angela, although he has strong misgivings about doing so from the beginning. Blackwood serves as an unchanging standard by which to measure the changes that take place in Eugene's character as he and Angela return to visit her family. The townspeople remain the same, while Eugene realizes he has become both sophisticated and corrupted by exposure to the opportunities and hedonistic values of the big cities.

*Chicago. At first Eugene is most impressed by the raw ugliness of the mushrooming city, but he also admires it because it is vigorous, aggressive, and forward-looking, like himself. He achieves a measure of artistic fame by painting—not beautiful scenes to adorn the walls of bourgeois homes—but realistic scenes that emphasize the brutality and ugliness of a coldly commercial city indifferent to aesthetic values and the plight of its downtrodden underclass, yet possessing a barbaric beauty he can capture on canvas.

*Speonk. Long Island town about seventy-five miles from New York City. At about the midpoint in this autobiographical novel Eugene suffers a nervous breakdown, not unlike the one that Dreiser himself experienced. Eugene not only experiences poverty and failure but loses confidence in himself as an artist. In order to recover from his "neurasthenia" he decides to work at manual labor and ends up in a Speonk railroad shop. Hard labor and Eugene's respect for the humble, honest men who do the world's dirty work have a therapeutic influence that enables him to return to the struggle in New York City, where he loses himself in herculean toil for many years and achieves growing financial success and social recognition.

*New York City. America's biggest city was and remains the mecca for ambitious young Americans because it offers more opportunity for talent than any other city in the world. Because the city attracts so much talent and ambition, as well as greed, lust, chicanery, and criminality, it is also intensely cruel and competitive. Eugene is fatally attracted here like a moth to a flame. New York City gives him everything he thinks he wants. Eventually, however, it destroys him because his one fatal weakness—his foolish infatuation with beautiful young women—undermines his competitive drive and his instinct for self-preservation in a dog-eat-dog social and business environment.

While-a-Way. Luxurious mountain lodge in Quebec, Canada. Dreiser uses this place to symbolize the wealth, power, influence, and social connections of Mrs. Dale, who belongs to a social class to which Eugene hopelessly aspires to belong. Mrs. Dale spirits Suzanne to this remote lodge in a private railway car in order to get the headstrong girl away from Eugene's influence. With great risk to his career, Eugene pursues Suzanne to this

cold, remote mountainside only to realize that she is beyond his reach. Just as Angela's character has been irrevocably shaped by her small-town upbringing, so the character of Suzanne, the beautiful New York debutante who causes Eugene's ruin, has been shaped by her privileged upper-class eastern environment.

As always, Dreiser was writing in elaborate detail about what he knew from painful personal experience. New York turns Eugene the artist into Eugene the big businessman. He is always conscious, however, of living a lie. He remains an artist at heart and can never change his true identity. New York gives him fortune but destroys his motivation to produce great art. In a very real sense, Eugene's pilgrimage from his humble roots in Alexandria to success and failure in glamorous New York illustrates the truth of the ancient question: "For what will it profit a man if he gains the whole world, and loses his own soul?"

— *Bill Delaney*

GERMINAL

Author: Émile Zola (1840-1902)
Type of work: Novel
Type of plot: Naturalism

Time of plot: Nineteenth century
First published: 1885 (English translation, 1885)

This novel is Émile Zola's attempt to explain the lives of coal miners in northern France. By setting this novel in coal camps and coal mines, Zola presents real situations faced by workers and the ever-tightening grasp of mine owners upon their workers' lives.

Montsou (mon-sew). Company-owned coal mining town in northeastern France, Montsou is the center of all the novel's actions. The town is actually a congested ghetto of buildings into which the miners and their families are crowded. Montsou becomes a microcosmic symbol for a world into which all workers have been forced. This setting permits Zola to confine his realistic portrayal of workers' lives to a recognizable location instead of being obliged to depend upon mere rhetoric. Zola's dividing the world of Montsou into its various components—especially the homes, the company store, and the mine pit itself—shows the complex society in which the miners and their families must live.

Maheu home (mah-HEW). Instead of the loving, domestic picture often presented in literature, the homes in

Germinal, most clearly represented by that of the Maheu family, show how the most positive of symbols can be altered. The life presented depicts the economic deprivation and moral depravity created by the totalitarian world in which the miners live. In contrast, the Grégoire home shows the luxury in which the mine owners live, marking the sharp contrast between the owners and the workers, a situation which eventually results in the climactic labor strike to which all earlier actions lead. The reader sees this contrast most clearly when Maheude Maheu takes her small children to beg sustenance from a rich family, a clear indication of the economic determinism controlling the workers' lives.

Company stores. Similar to the homes, the company stores are also physical manifestations of the economic sway the companies have over their workers. The scenes occurring in the store allow the reader to witness the control the store owner holds over the workers, from drawing the customers into further debt to demanding sexual favors from the female customers in exchange for food. Here Zola has found another symbolic means of condemning the treatment of the workers.

Mines. The mines themselves prove to be the central metaphor for the lifestyle which Zola intends to address. Because of the economic ramifications of mining coal as cheaply as possible, this setting more than adequately depicts the wider scope of workers' lives. From the mo-

ment miners enter the "cage" to be lowered into the earth's interior, their lives, whether they be young or old, male or female, are revealed as hellish. At every turn, the workers are tested. By visualizing this situation, the reader gains more perspective on these workers' lives than mere verbal arguments could provide.

Through his choice of settings, Zola permits his readers to witness the types of lives the workers of this period lived. This witnessing creates reader empathy, resulting in acceptance of the workers' eventual violent strike.

— *Tom Frazier*

GERMINIE LACERTEUX

Authors: Edmond de Goncourt (1822-1896) and
   Jules de Goncourt (1830-1870)
Type of work: Novel

Type of plot: Naturalism
Time of plot: Nineteenth century
First published: 1865 (English translation, 1887)

This novel is about imprisonment—the ways in which people are shackled by their own passions and instincts and the circumstances of their births. The novel's protagonist is confined in these ways, but her fundamental imprisonment is expressed also by her entrapment in Paris—indeed, in a well circumscribed section of the great metropolis.

*****Paris.** City in which the entire novel is set, with a particular focus on the dregs of nineteenth century Parisian society. The plot spans a number of years, a chronology that would include, historically, a series of political and social upheavals—the rise and fall of Napoleon Bonaparte's empire, the restoration of the French monarchy, and several revolutions of various kinds. *Germinie Lacerteux* shows the extent to which the French working classes and poor suffered because of political and social instability; in particular, the novel presents characters whose lives are without hope or a future.

At the time of the novel's action, the Paris city limits are still clearly marked by its medieval walls. This kind of enclosure is echoed as well in the "exterior boulevards," main roads inside the walls but which encircle the city. The Goncourts make frequent reference to the city walls, the boulevards, and many other sorts of walls—literal and figurative—in order firmly to establish their key notion—that Paris's poor and sick have no escape.

*****Montmartre** (mon-MAR-treh). Hill situated on the

northeast outskirts of Paris that is one of the city's highest points. Montmartre is the scene of most of what takes place in *Germinie Lacerteux;* it is where Germinie goes to work for Mademoiselle Varandeuil, in the rue de Laval, and it is where she dies. Germinie is buried—without an identifying marker—in the Montmartre Cemetery, halfway down the Montmartre butte.

In the novel, and well into the twentieth century, Montmartre was a transitional area. In some senses, Montmartre was still part of the countryside, but Paris was encroaching, in the form of industry, homes, businesses, taverns, and prostitution. Ironically, the section in which Germinie lives and dies represents the city streets, which to some extent kill her, and the country, where she longs to be and where, on at least two occasions, she is happy. The city, with its numerous concentric circles of walls, is a prison for Germinie and others of her kind; the countryside beyond the walls is everything the city is not—open, free, and fresh—a symbol of hope for the future.

The steep streets of Montmartre are, in the novel, as many of them remain in the twenty-first century, lined by high stone walls. The streets thus become narrow, sometimes dark tunnels that lead to the top of the butte. The final chapters of the novel contain several images of asphyxiation and choking and eventually tell how the walls in Germinie's tiny apartment, which she never leaves in the last months of her life, weigh in and on her. In tragic logic, Germinie dies of consumption— unable to breathe. Ultimately, for Germinie Lacerteux, the streets of Montmartre lead not up to the open spaces of Clignancourt and beyond but only down the hill to the Montmartre Cemetery—where her unmarked grave lies next to a wall that borders a slope. One final cruel stroke in a sad story.

Rue de Laval. Nineteenth century Paris street that no longer exists, having been destroyed during urban renewal or absorbed into the city under another name. Mademoiselle Varandeuil moves here after all of her family members have died. She formerly lived at a much better address, in the rue Taitbout, closer to the Seine River and to the heart of Paris society. However, Mademoiselle wants to be nearer to her deceased relatives, who are buried in the Montmartre Cemetery.

For most of her life, the rue Laval is the center of Germinie's activity. She shops here, makes friends here, becomes entangled in a number of sordid affairs, loses herself in alcoholism and addiction, works the streets as a prostitute. As she falls lower and lower, she lies in the street's gutters, where the rain that falls is already muddy. Indeed, even before her death, Germinie becomes earth, is earth-colored, sinking as low as one can go.

*Clignancourt (kleen-ah-KEWR). Hamlet north of Montmartre. In the novel, this is where the countryside begins, where Germinie acquires a real sense for what lies beyond the streets, the slums, and Paris's walls. She has the same insight during a later trip to Vincennes, a forest on the eastern edge of Paris. Germinie's story is one of ups and downs, real and metaphorical, of attempts to climb out of the streets into daylight and open spaces. For one reason or another, including her own lusts and poor judgment, she repeatedly slips down and back into the abyss of poverty and self-ruin. She never gets beyond the city's old fortified walls, and the Goncourts make reference after reference to less spectacular but equally sinister walls that oppress Germinie throughout her life.

— *Gordon Walters*

GHOSTS

Author: Henrik Ibsen (1828-1906)
Type of work: Drama
Type of plot: Social realism

Time of plot: Nineteenth century
First published: Gengangere, 1881 (English translation, 1885); first performed, 1882

This play investigates the issue of heredity versus environment to see which is the more important. Its symbols— the rain that beats darkly on the large parlor window and represents the moral ghosts of the play, the sun that rises at the close to shine on Oswald's darkness—mesh closely with the action and with the themes of the play.

Alving home. Family estate located in Rosenvold on one of western Norway's fjords. The house's garden provides the play's primary setting. This room has a door on the left and two doors on the right. Also on the left wall is a window, in front of which is a small sofa with a worktable in front of it. In the center of the room is a round table covered with books, magazines, and newspapers. Chairs are positioned around the table. The back

of the room is a glass conservatory, and a glass door leads to the garden. All in all, it is a very prosaic, if expensively furnished room, in the style of the late nineteenth century.

The glass wall at the back of the garden room sets the atmosphere for the drama as it shows and reflects what is happening in and around the estate. Most of the time, the scene is a gloomy fjord shrouded in mist, which prepares the audience for the subject matter of the play. Later, a huge fire that destroys a new orphanage is visible through the glass. As the play ends, the new day's dawn sunlight comes through the window. The reading materials on the table also show something about the house and its owner. These items represent the publications of new findings in science at the time, and as the play is a debate over science, they reinforce the subject matter of the script: that a fine house and wealth do not guarantee personal happiness.

— *H. Alan Pickrell*

GIANTS IN THE EARTH: A Saga of the Prairie

Author: O. E. Rölvaag (1876-1931)
Type of work: Novel
Type of plot: Regional

Time of plot: Late nineteenth century
First published: I de dage, 1924 and *Riket grundlægges*, 1925 (English translation, 1927)

This novel portrays the experiences of Per Hansa and his wife Beret during the early years of Norwegian settlement in Dakota Territory, revealing the psychological impact of the vast open prairie and harsh winters upon settlers in the late nineteenth century. An overwhelming presence, as well as a mythic character in its own right, the prairie powerfully influences the lives of its new inhabitants.

*Great Plains. Also known as prairie land, the largely flat grassland region of central North America spanning the region between Oklahoma and central Canada that is used for extensive cattle ranching and grain crops. To Per Hansa—a former fisherman—the prairie appears a sea of grass. At sunset its glowing rim resembles the horizon of a vast ocean. His wagon leaves a track like the wake of a boat, closing in rather than widening out astern.

As the novel opens Per Hansa has temporarily lost his way. Calming his anxiety he dreams of opportunities the prairie offers—on this land he could build a kingdom of his own. His wife, Beret, finds the immensity of the prairie frightening. To her, the landscape appears cold, bleak, and full of terror. She is uneasy in a world so different from the beloved Norway she has left behind and fearful that trolls might lie in wait within this strange new environment.

In the second half of the novel, after Beret gives birth to Peder Victorious (whose story continues in *Peder Victorious*, 1928), the Great Plains environment becomes increasingly hostile. The problems afflicting the settlement convince Beret that trolls are at work; the prairie is attacking the intruders. Rölvaag makes use of disasters that actually struck Dakota's pioneers. The grasshopper plagues of the late 1870's devastated many settlers. All who lived through the powerful winter snows of 1880-1881 remembered that year with horror. The incredible snow winter is the inspiration for Rölvaag's final chapter, "The Great Plain Drinks the Blood of Christian Men and Is Satisfied." Per Hansa, seeking a minister to attend a dying friend, ventures into the snow and is not found until spring. He is sitting frozen against a haystack, facing west.

Spring Creek. Fictional settlement in what became South Dakota, located near the border with Minnesota, some twenty-six miles north of Sioux Falls. The site is close to where O. E. Rölvaag's father-in-law homesteaded in 1873, and Rölvaag consulted him frequently for details of life on the prairie during the 1870's and 1880's. The novel includes his descriptions of building sod huts as temporary homes, of disastrous grasshopper plagues, and of uneasy relations with Indians.

Per Hansa is proud of his accomplishments at Spring Creek: successfully planting crops; building a two-room sod hut, one room serving as a barn to protect his animals during the winter; and establishing friendly relations with local Indians. He glories in the successful establishment of a new society in the wilderness by Norwegian immigrants. In contrast, Beret becomes increasingly disenchanted, disgusted by life on the prairie. To her it appears that people are becoming beasts, living like animals as they burrow into the soil to build sod huts. Ignoring the customs of the home country, they no longer seem ashamed to sin.

***Norway.** Although none of the novel takes place in Norway, the culture and society from which its immigrants come provide essential background. Rölvaag implicitly structures the westward movement of Per Hansa and his friends as a parallel to the Viking conquest of Iceland and Greenland. Beret is particularly sensitive to the losses entailed in frontier living; she is driven insane by the lack of order and familiar customs. Beret cherishes a seventeenth century chest that belonged to her great-grandfather. The major physical piece of Norway she carries with her to America, the chest embodies the country and traditions she reveres. When she fears she will die in childbirth, she hopes to be buried in this chest; when the locust plague descends on Spring Creek, she hides within it. When a Norwegian Lutheran minister visits the settlement, Beret's chest becomes his altar and communion table.

— *Milton Berman*

THE GIFT OF THE MAGI

Author: O. Henry (William Sydney Porter, 1862-1910)
Type of work: Short fiction
Type of plot: Moral

Time of plot: Early twentieth century
First published: 1905

The setting of this short story is essential to its meaning. Jim and Della Young live in a furnished apartment best described as shabby. Their poverty plays a central role in this narrative, which describes their devotion to each other and the sacrifice each makes for a happy Christmas.

New York City. Crowded city in which the Youngs rent for eight dollars per month a second-story flat. It is furnished, but with obviously second-hand and outdated furniture. O. Henry skillfully evokes the shabbiness of the rented rooms and the building that contains them, calling attention to such details as the nonfunctional mailslot in the lobby and the broken doorbell. Within the flat itself, he points out the worn carpet and couch and the almost useless piece of mirror that Della has for making herself up.

It is essential that the narrator explain the poor circumstances in which the loving couple do live. The lack of any elegance or pride in their immediate surroundings must be emphasized so readers understand why it is so vital that each character present the other with a wonderful Christmas gift. Surroundings so dismal make both Jim and Della yearn for any possession of substantial beauty and worth as a gift. However, what each sacrifices to please the other makes the other's gift useless.

— *Patricia E. Sweeney*

THE GILDED AGE: A Tale of Today

Authors: Mark Twain (Samuel Langhorne Clemens, 1835-1910) and Charles Dudley Warner (1829-1900)
Type of work: Novel

Type of plot: Satire
Time of plot: Late 1840's to early 1870's
First published: 1873

Although this novel is a genuine collaboration of Mark Twain and his friend Charles Dudley Warner, it takes its primary sense of place from the history of Mark Twain's own family, whose migration west from Tennessee in search of wealth it recreates. To this narrative thread, it adds a complex story of government corruption in Washington, D.C., but ties both strands together in its central theme: the futility of searching for easy riches. The novel's very title gave a name to the late nineteenth century era of American greed.

Obedstown. Tiny village in eastern Tennessee whose few homes are so widely dispersed among trees that it is difficult for visitors to realize that they are in a "town." The novel opens with the village postmaster, Si Hawkins, receiving a letter from his friend Colonel Sellers urging him to bring his family to Missouri because that state offers easier riches. Hawkins's giving up on Obedstown is the first of the novel's many relocations in search of easier wealth.

Twain modeled Obedstown on Jamestown, Tennessee, where his own parents lived before following a kinsman to Missouri. The fictional Obedstown takes its name from the real Obed (or Obeds) River, a tributary of the Tennessee River.

"Tennessee Land." Large tract of commercially worthless land in eastern Tennessee that Hawkins buys before moving west. Throughout his life, he beguiles his children with the promise of the riches to come, admonishing them, "never lose sight of the Tennessee Land." However, the land brings his children nothing but disappointment. After the Civil War, it becomes the focus of a federal government scandal when Washington Hawkins, Colonel Sellers, and Senator Abner Dilworthy try to push a bill through Congress to get the government to buy the land for the proposed **Knobs Industrial University** for freed slaves. The scheme collapses when Dilworthy's corruption in buying votes is exposed.

Like Si Hawkins, Twain's own father, John Clemens, owned a huge parcel of land in eastern Tennessee on which his children counted for future prosperity. However, they, also like the Hawkinses, never reaped anything from their Tennessee Land but disappointment. Twain took a deep interest in the debilitating effect that land had on his family. Late in life, he was thinking of that land when he said that to begin life "poor and prospectively rich" is a "curse." *The Gilded Age* reaches its climax when Washington Hawkins finally lets the family's title to the Tennessee Land go by not paying its tax assessment, declaring, "The spell is broken, the life-long curse is ended!"

*Mississippi River. North America's great river plays a brief but important role in the novel as a stage in the Hawkins family's migration from Tennessee to Missouri. While the Hawkinses are riding the steamboat **Boreas** upriver, its pilot engages another steamboat, the **Amaranth**, in a race. The *Amaranth*'s boilers explode, killing many passengers, apparently including the parents of Laura Van Brunt, whom the Hawkinses then adopt—an action that changes all their lives. Scenes aboard the *Boreas* provide the fullest descriptions of a steamboat that Twain wrote in any of his novels.

*Missouri. Midwestern state that represented the threshold of the Western frontier during the period in which *The Gilded Age* opens. For the Hawkinses to migrate to Missouri in the late 1840's was almost as daring as later pioneers' migrations to points farther west. As a frontier region in the novel, Missouri represents a land of rich promise, but every get-rich scheme the novel's characters undertake in Missouri eventually comes to nothing—further proof of the illusory nature of easy wealth.

Hawkeye. Missouri town in which the Hawkins family settles after a brief residence in the much smaller **Murpheysburg**, whose limited commercial prospects disappoint Si Hawkins. Hawkeye is ten miles from Stone's Landing, which Sellers wants to develop into a major railway and river transportation hub, but his dream is dashed when the people of Hawkeye buy enough shares in the railway to ensure that it will pass through their town instead of Stone's Landing.

Stone's Landing. Missouri village that embodies all the false hopes, lies, and deceptions that the novel depicts. The village is nothing more than a handful of cabins along the muddy bend of Goose Run that Sellers hopes to develop into a vast metropolis to be renamed **Napoleon**. He wants the federal government to bring in a railway line and transform Goose Run into a navigable stream to be renamed the **Columbus River**. The whole project dies an ignominious death after the government decides to route the railroad through Hawkeye.

Sellers's grandiose plans are a satire of greed and government mismanagement that is summed up in his description of one of the villages to be developed along the proposed new railroad route: **Corruptionville**, the "gaudiest country for early carrots and cauliflowers . . . good missionary field, too. There ain't such another missionary field outside the jungles of Central Africa. And patriotic?—why, they named it after Congress itself."

*****Washington, D.C.** National capital of the United States that provides a second major target of satire as the primary setting for the second half of the novel, which depicts the city as a hotbed of intrigue and corruption in which every politician has a hand in someone else's pocket. The embodiment of all that the capital city represents is Missouri's corrupt senator Abner Dilworthy, who sniffs profits for himself, first in the scheme to develop Stone's Landing and later in the Knobs Industrial University scheme. Dilworthy lures beautiful Laura Hawkins to Washington, where he makes her a powerful lobbyist for a bill to get the federal government to buy the Hawkins family's Tennessee Land.

*****Washington Monument.** Giant obelisk in Washington, D.C., that was begun in 1850 and not finished until 1885. Twain regarded the unfinished landmark as a pathetic symbol of the capital city's false promises and used *The Gilded Age* to make fun of it, saying it has the "aspect of a factory chimney with the top broken off."

Ilium. Railroad stop in Pennsylvania near a tract of wild land in which Charles Dudley Warner's character Philip Sterling prospects for coal. In contrast to most of the novel's other characters, Sterling eventually succeeds in finding profitable coal deposits through careful and persistent work and personal sacrifice.

— *R. Kent Rasmussen*

GILES GOAT-BOY: Or, The Revised New Syllabus

Author: John Barth (1930-   )
Type of work: Novel
Type of plot: Fantasy

Time of plot: A time like the 1960's
First published: 1966

This novel is the tale of a new redeemer, whose destiny is to reconcile the historical, philosophical, and theological problems afflicting the faculty of a university. In order to accomplish this the redeemer must move through the entirety of the university's symbolic geography, from the most far-flung corner of its map to the very center— and then, in the end, to some mysterious region beyond the map (although he leaves behind a Visitation Room where his followers might be able to maintain contact).

University. The world.

New Tammany College. Institution whose West Campus is the cultural heart of the western part of the unnamed university, which George Giles enters as a naïve aspirant Grand Tutor. (The story told by the novel is, in essence, the spiritual autobiography of the Grand Tutor in question, whose teachings have been codified in a Revised New Syllabus which—somewhat belatedly, and by far-from-universal consent—has absorbed, modified and replaced the obsolete Enochist Curriculum.)

Tower Hall. Core of the West Campus, situated at the opposite end of the Great Mall from the Main Gate. The College Senate and various other committees meet there, and it is the location of the Main Stacks. The basement beneath it are the primary locations of the enormous computer WESCAC. The computer provides the ruling principle of the West Campus; its calculations determine the ultimate success or failure of all the students, and its system of examination defines the social order of the entire university, with the support of the technologically superior defensive program EAT. Within WESCAC's Belly, Giles—or, as it turns out, GILES— was conceived and gestated. It is also within the Belly of the computer that Giles and Anastasia Stoker finally consummate their sexual relationship, contriving a significant and potentially earth-shaking climax.

Amphitheater. Huge arena jointly managed by the Sub-Departments of Ancient Narrative and Theatrical

Science, where *The Tragedy of Taliped Decanus*—whose exemplary text is reproduced in its entirety in the novel—is performed.

Military Science Cube. Largest building on campus after the stadium, in terms of volume, although it is not as tall as the clock tower of Tower Hall.

Turnstile. Apparatus about seven meters tall, adjacent to the Left Gate, at which athletes are subjected to Trial-by-Turnstile. Its mechanism is jammed by Giles's wrapper and amulet before he proceeds through the Registration Room to the Assembly-Before-the-Grate, where he meets the chancellor.

Scapegoat Grate. Iron grid that dispenses assignments; it gives Giles a list of seven tasks "To Be Done at Once, in No Time," thus commencing the active and seemingly impossible phase of his studies.

Infirmary. Location where Giles must fulfill the third of his seven assigned tasks. It is unclear at first whether he requires access to the main building or the Psychiatric Annex, and readers are free to wonder whether that particular question is ever provided with a satisfactory answer.

Main Detention. Giles's place of confinement when his mission enters its most desperate phase, his Assignment having temporarily defeated him. Conveniently—and perhaps paradoxically, given that its occupants are serving time—there is no time there, so his sojourn encourages and eventually enables him to solve the remaining problems of his Assignment.

Hill. Location of the barn in the College Farms, an obscure rural backwater of New Tammany College, where Giles spent his childhood as Billy the Goat-Boy.

Siegfrieder College. Institution from which the Bonifacists launched the attacks on neighboring quads that eventually embroiled the whole university in the Second Campus Riot. Siegfrieder was allied in the later stages of the Second Campus Riot with Amaterasu College, but following their surrender both colleges acknowledged the educational hegemony of WESCAC.

Nikolay College. Principal institution promoting the ideals of Student-Unionism, systematized by WESCAC's rival EASCAC. Although the two computers share a single power source on Founder's Hill, their opposition, the Boundary Dispute, gives rise to the Quiet Riot. Settling the Boundary Dispute is the second of the seven key tasks contained in Giles's Assignment, but not the easiest.

— *Brian Stableford*

THE GILGAMESH EPIC

Author: Unknown
Type of work: Poetry
Type of plot: Adventure

Time of plot: Antiquity
First published: c. 2000 B.C.E. (English translation, 1917)

In all versions of this most ancient Sumerian tale, the demigod King Gilgamesh extends his power to new lands, each more menacing than the previous one and each embodied by a supernatural guardian. The significance of these lands varies somewhat among the various versions, and no single version contains the entire narrative.

*****Uruk** (EW-rewk). Ancient city in what is now Iraq (now called Tall al-Warka) over which the demigod Gilgamesh rules. During the period in which the epic is set (c. 2600 B.C.E.), Uruk was one of the largest cities in the world. Protected by brick walls, it preserved urban technology and order. In all versions of *The Gilgamesh Epic*, the city's king or "shepherd," Gilgamesh (also known as Bilgamesh), combines within himself civilization and fierce lawlessness, so that he can relate both to the city and to the barbarous rest of the world.

The split within Gilgamesh's character helps the urbanites, since it gives Gilgamesh the ferocity to defend them. Nonetheless, they resent his disorderliness, particularly his leading the young in revels throughout such sacred precincts as Egalmah, the temple complex governed by the goddess Ninsun, Gilgamesh's mother. Because of public resentment, Gilgamesh's Uruk appears to be a grim totalitarian state. However, the prostitute whom he employs to lure Engidu (also called Enkidu) there, extols Uruk as a joyous place in which people wear wide belts and attend festivals every day that are celebrated with beautiful music.

Nagbu (NAHG-bew). Chaotic abyss, believed to exist at the center of the earth. It is the source of all rivers and maintains the aboriginal condition before order (and mortality) came to the world. Its most characteristic figure is Utnapishtim, a Noah-like being who survived a world-wide flood, thus preparing him to dwell forever amid Nagbu's timeless waters. Appropriately, Gilgamesh finds within the abyss the plant of immortality. In the best-known and fullest version of *Gilgamesh*, that composed by the exorcist priest Sin-leqi-uninni (c. 1600-1000 B.C.E.), Nagbu is especially important, with Gilgamesh identified in the very first line of the poem as the one who saw this abyss. Knowledge of it is presumably why he is then described as the "lord of wisdom" who knows everything.

Edin (AY-din). Grassland surrounding Uruk. Embodying the almost total wildness and contradictoriness of that hinterland, Engidu, its heaven-appointed guardian eats grass with gazelles and releases animals from traps but also defends shepherds from wolves. A primordial savage, Engidu reflects the vitality of the region, thus threatening Gilgamesh, who therefore introduces Engidu to a human relationship with a woman in order to weaken him. After sleeping with the woman, Engidu sees his vitalizing link to the land weakened; animals desert him, and he loses in battle to Gilgamesh. However, Engidu retains sufficient rustic skills to help Gilgamesh during campaigns through Edin.

Although the epic does not dwell on the economic importance of Edin as Uruk's primary source of raw materials or its strategic importance as a buffer zone around the city, readers should be aware of these functions. They explain why Gilgamesh must subdue Engidu, thereby symbolically conquering Edin.

Cedar wood. Gloomy, dense forest area even farther from civilization than grassy Edin. Early versions of *The Gilgamesh Epic*—those in Babylonian and Hittite—locate this forest in the east (presumably in what is now

Iran). Because of gradual deforestation in that zone, late Akkadian versions of the epic, such as Sin-leqi-uninni's, place this forest in the west, probably in the Anti-Lebanon Mountains of Syria.

The guardian of the cedars is named Humbaba in Akkadian and Huwawa in Sumerian, Old Babylonian, and Hittite. Since the guardian breathes fire, some scholars have speculated that he personifies an eruption of lava, and thus the forest must be on a volcano. Equally, he might allegorize forest tribes conquered by Uruk; therefore, description of him as a monster who deserves death would explain how writers of *The Gilgamesh Epic* justified killing and robbing those tribes of their precious cedars. The earliest versions declare the guardian to be a danger to humanity, and Sin-leqi-unnini's version terms Humbaba an enemy of Shamesh, the god of light and law. As early as the Old Babylonian version, Huwawa's voice is likened to the flood (thus comparing him to Nagbu, a place of chaotic waters) and he is also described as a "siege-engine," a metaphor that treats him (and consequently the region he represents) as an enemy of cities such as Uruk.

Heaven. Realm of the gods above the earth. It can be reached via Mashu, which is also the route to Nagbu. Although Gilgamesh does not conquer Heaven itself, he does kill the Bull of Heaven—the guardian sent from Heaven to earth to destroy Gilgamesh. In a sense, Gilgamesh makes his power felt even in Heaven. Modern readers might assume that Heaven is the supreme power; however, in coercing the heavenly gods to attack Gilgamesh, Ishtar threatens to raise Nagbu, thereby implying that Nagbu is more fearsome than Heaven.

Mashu (MA-shew). Legendary mountain with twin peaks, connecting the three realms: the "above" (Heaven), the "land" (Earth), and the "below" (Nagbu). These realms guard the route of Shamash, the sun god. Mashu means "twins." A possible reason for the mountain's having twin peaks includes their symbolizing the principal divisions in the Sun's journey, its light, celestial path during the day and its dark, subterranean one during the night.

Embodying Mashu's role as guardian are a pair of scorpion people, so fearsome that at first they terrify Gilgamesh. They open Mashu's gates, allowing him to enter caverns through which the Sun passes by night. After traveling through these caverns for twenty-four hours, Gilgamesh reaches a Garden of Precious Stones. The garden's vine-covered cedar trees with carnelian fruit and lapis-lazuli leaves make it is an earthly paradise that may threaten Gilgamesh's journey by tempting him to stay.

Sea. "Waters of death" believed to surround land. At its "lip" (its shore), Siduri the Barmaid (presumably a manifestation of the goddess Ishtar) guards the sea. She embodies its inherently feminine qualities. No mortal has previously traversed it, but, with the aid of the supernatural boatman, Urshanabi, Gilgamesh crosses the sea to Nagbu.

— James Whitlark

THE GLASS KEY

Author: Dashiell Hammett (1894-1961)
Type of work: Novel
Type of plot: Detective and mystery

Time of plot: 1930's
First published: serial, 1930; book, 1931

Dashiell Hammett's detective story is set in a fictional, unnamed metropolis located in upstate New York. The city's anonymity allows it to function mythically and symbolically within the narrative.

City. Unlike Hammett's story *The Maltese Falcon* (1930), which carefully delineates the streets and buildings of San Francisco, *The Glass Key*'s primary locale is an unspecified eastern city of apparently modest size. The generic city locale allows Hammett to generalize about American society and the effect of political corruption and crime on the social structure of U.S. urban environments. Hammett was critical of the form of capitalism that he saw operating in the United States and used his criticism in his fiction to fashion a world of injustice and exploitation. The use of a mythical, unnamed city also provided him with a location lacking in familiar touchstones which might prove distracting to his readers and deflected the social and ethical impact of the narrative.

Log Cabin Club. Gambling club on China Street that is the scene for several key episodes. The image of gambling is important in the novel's narrative and reinforces Hammett's generally existential view of a world ruled by chance and of the loss of a uniform set of values.

***New York City.** An interlude set in New York City provides a concrete locale that neatly replicates the nasty world left unspecified by the anonymous one. The presence of New York suggests that in both the fictional world of the novel and the real world corruption and violence are in control.

Beaumont apartment. Residence of the amateur detective Ned Beaumont in the unnamed city. Hammett does not give this place an address or offer much in the way of description. The apartment functions as a place to which Ned retreats, in which he sleeps (but not all the time), and in general where he goes to recoup his strength. The lack of detail says something about the man who lives here. He is in many ways a cipher, undifferentiated, and undefined except by his actions: a man without a social context.

Matthew home. Home of the newspaper publisher Matthew, outside the city. Hammett moves the action of his novel outside the city several times, most prominently to Matthew's home. The location underscores the complicity of the media in distorting the truth and helping to perpetuate the lawlessness and evil of the city culture. The newspaper, as an instrument of economic and political exploitation, contributes to the novel's pervasive sense of corruption.

Senator Henry's house. The senator in the novel represents the most blatant symbol of political depravity, and this depravity is reflected in his dysfunctional family. The senator's house is also where the finale of the narrative takes place when Senator Henry confesses that he accidentally killed his son but was too afraid of losing the election to admit it, which, again, highlights the book's focus on hypocrisy at the highest levels. And all of the emptiness of the senator's social, economic, and political power is finally revealed when he commits suicide in his own house.

East State Construction and Contracting Company. Ostensibly honest business that is the source of money that the corrupt manipulator gets from construction projects he arranges through his political connections. Business and politics go hand in hand in promoting devaluation of the social order. Unlike the gambling club, which suggests something clearly unsavory if not criminal, the construction company is an ostensibly legitimate business and symbol of respectability, but it, too, is corrupt. Hammett undermines the old American myth of Horatio Alger by having his character rise from the streets only to be destroyed by overreaching himself when he desperately wants to escape his past through "marrying up" and courting the "better" political element by backing the senator.

Taylor Henry's apartment. Trysting place used by the senator's son. This apartment is used to illustrate Hammett's theme of the wages of sin; it reflects the generational effects of the father's nefarious political life. It becomes emblematic of the deceptive and seamy life that results from an upbringing in an underlying atmosphere of evil and deceit. Only this time these values are extended to sexual relations as well.

— *Charles L. P. Silet*

THE GLASS MENAGERIE

Author: Tennessee Williams (Thomas Lanier Williams, 1911-1983)
Type of work: Drama

Type of plot: Psychological realism
Time of plot: 1930's
First performed: 1944; first published, 1945

Tennessee Williams's play is based on his experience of having lived in St. Louis, from which he selectively draws the setting to create dramatic tension.

Wingfield apartment. St. Louis, Missouri, home of the narrator, Tom Wingfield, and his mother and sister. Along with its outside fire-escape landing, this apartment is the setting for the entire play. It is too small for the Wingfields' needs—Laura sleeps on a sofa bed in the living room—and its contents are worn and aging. The contrast between the dingy apartment and the world in which Tom's mother, Amanda, alludes to having grown up in is striking. During the play's first scene, Amanda relates a well-worn story of her youth in Blue Mountain in rural Mississippi. Her story contains a significant allusion to the front porch on which she received gentleman callers—some seventeen young men by her account. Williams contrasts the porch in Blue Mountain with the apartment's fire-escape landing, on which the family watches the moon rise over a delicatessen.

Alleyways. According to Williams's opening stage directions, the play's audiences should see alleyways running on either side of the apartment building and its rear wall before they see the apartment rooms in which the action will take place. The alleys are described as "murky canyons of tangled clotheslines, garbage cans, and the sinister latticework of neighboring fire escapes." This is significant, as the alleys remain visible throughout the play. Williams uses them to generate a constant visual comment on the action within the apartment. The alleys strike a strong contrast to the idyllic life Amanda describes from her youth and are in conflict with Tom's vision of a life of high adventure.

***Famous-Barr Department Store.** St. Louis's leading department store at the time in which the play is set, in whose lingerie department Amanda works. Williams uses the store to emphasize Amanda's frustration over the way her life has turned out. In the opening scene when she talks about her suitors, she blames her poor choice as the cause of her public humiliation of having to sell bras at Famous-Barr.

— *Glenn Patterson*